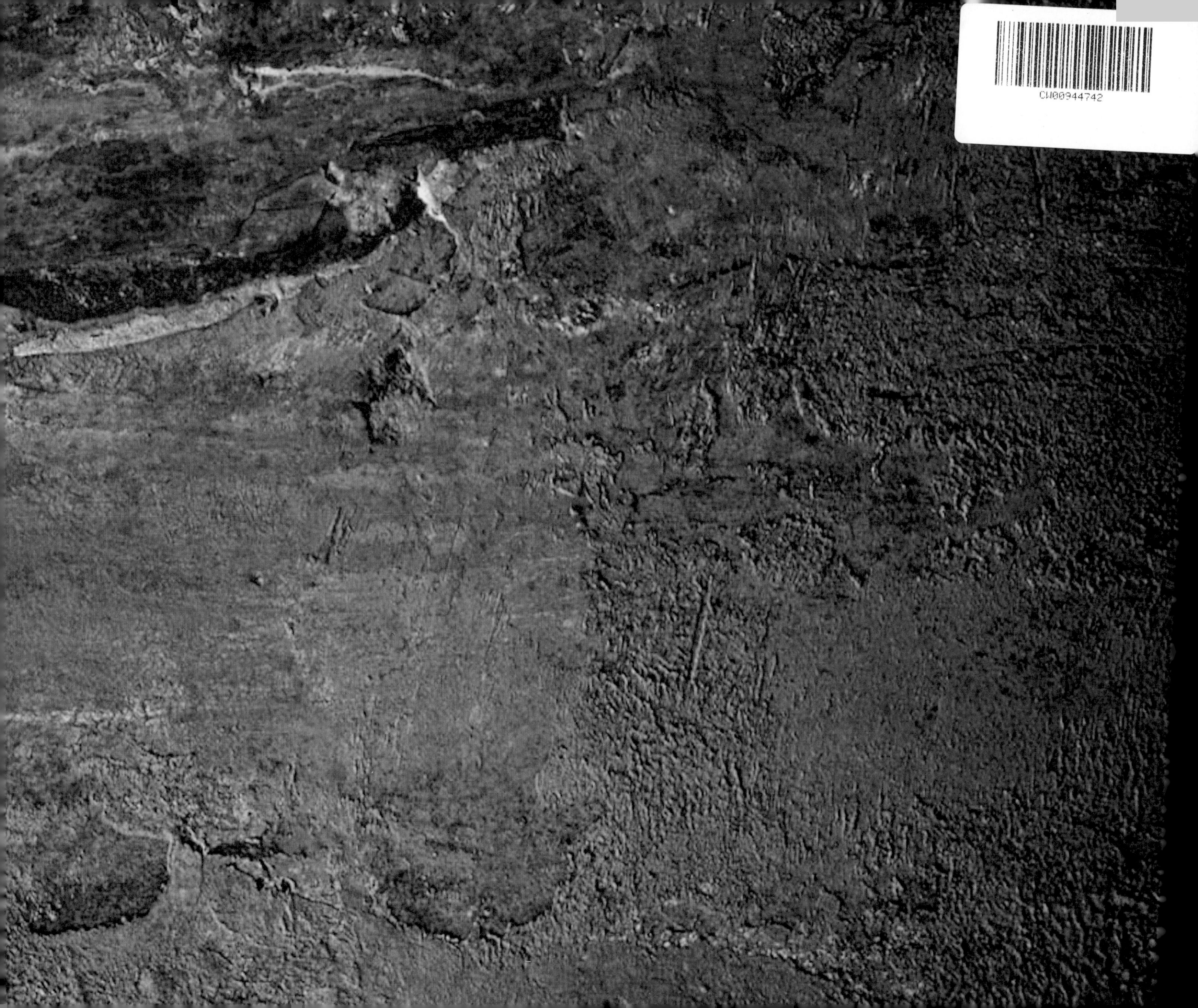

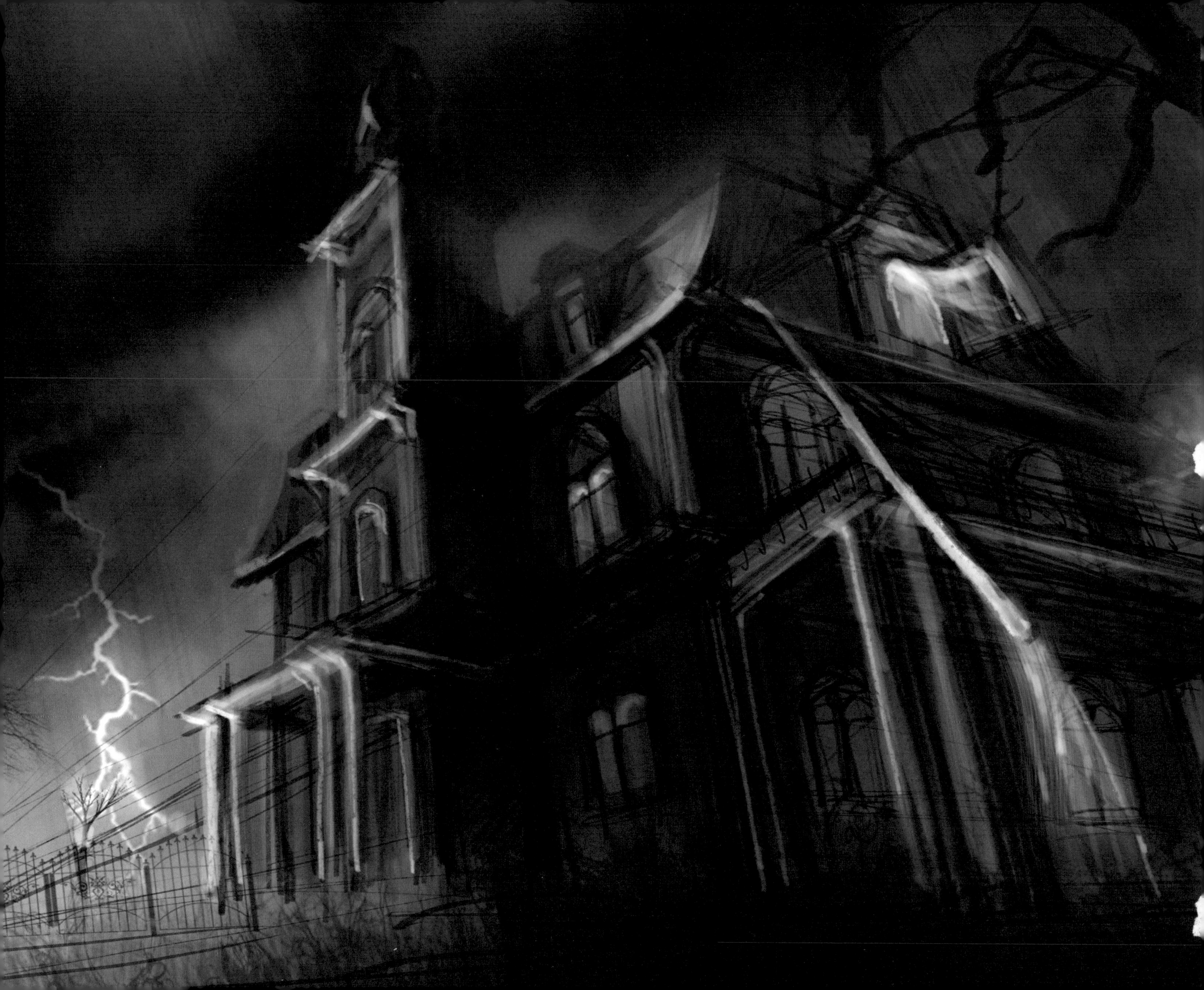

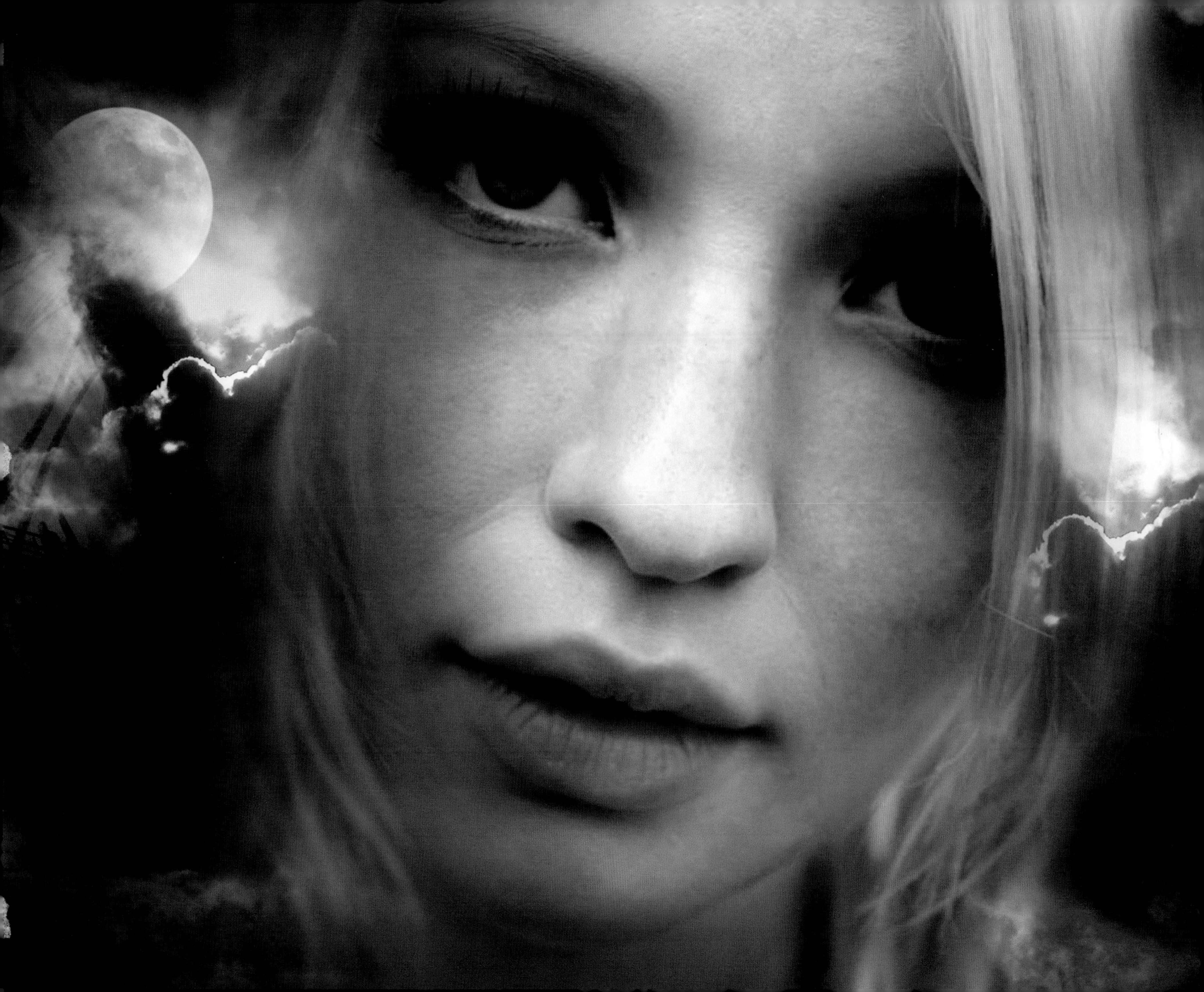

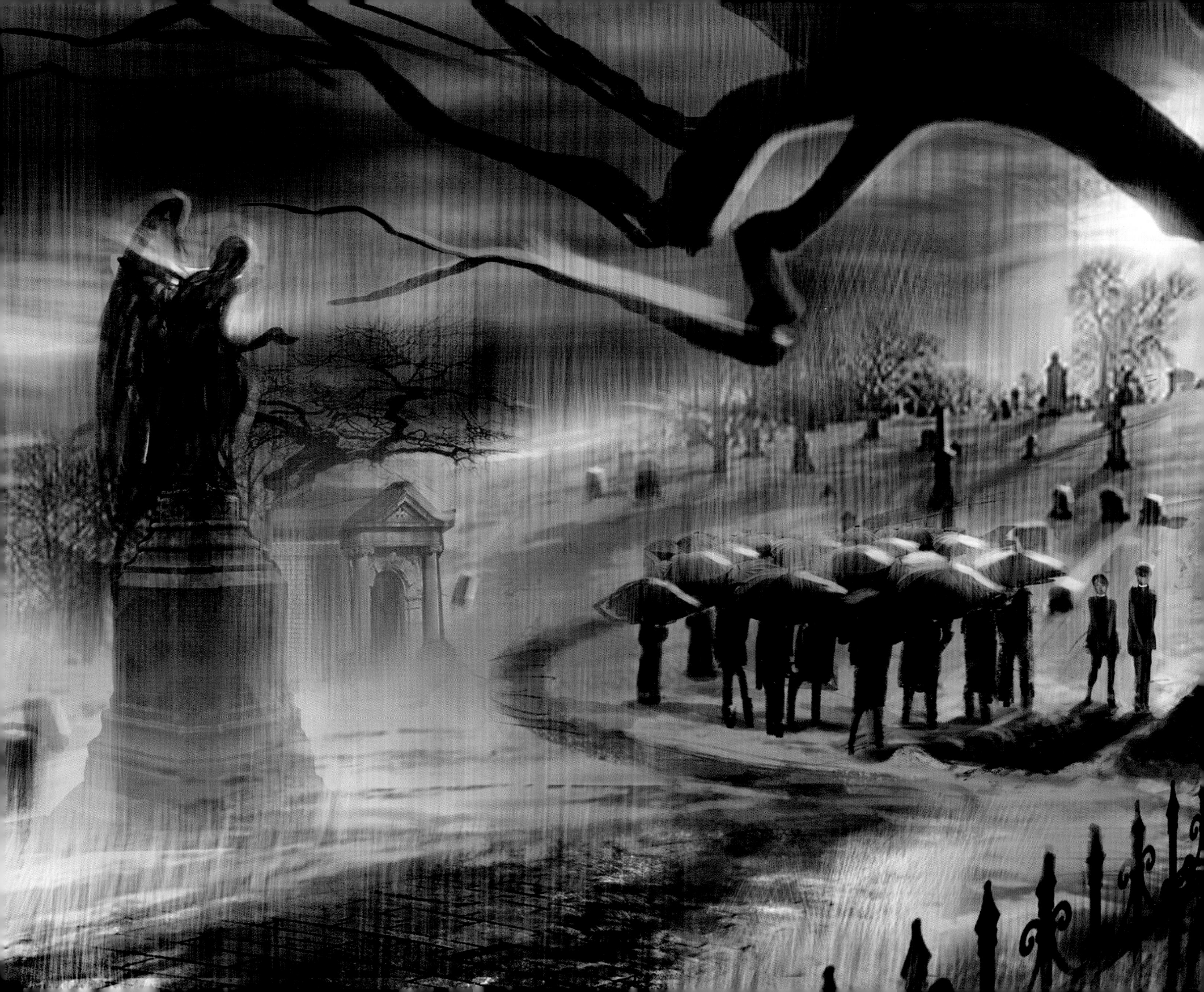

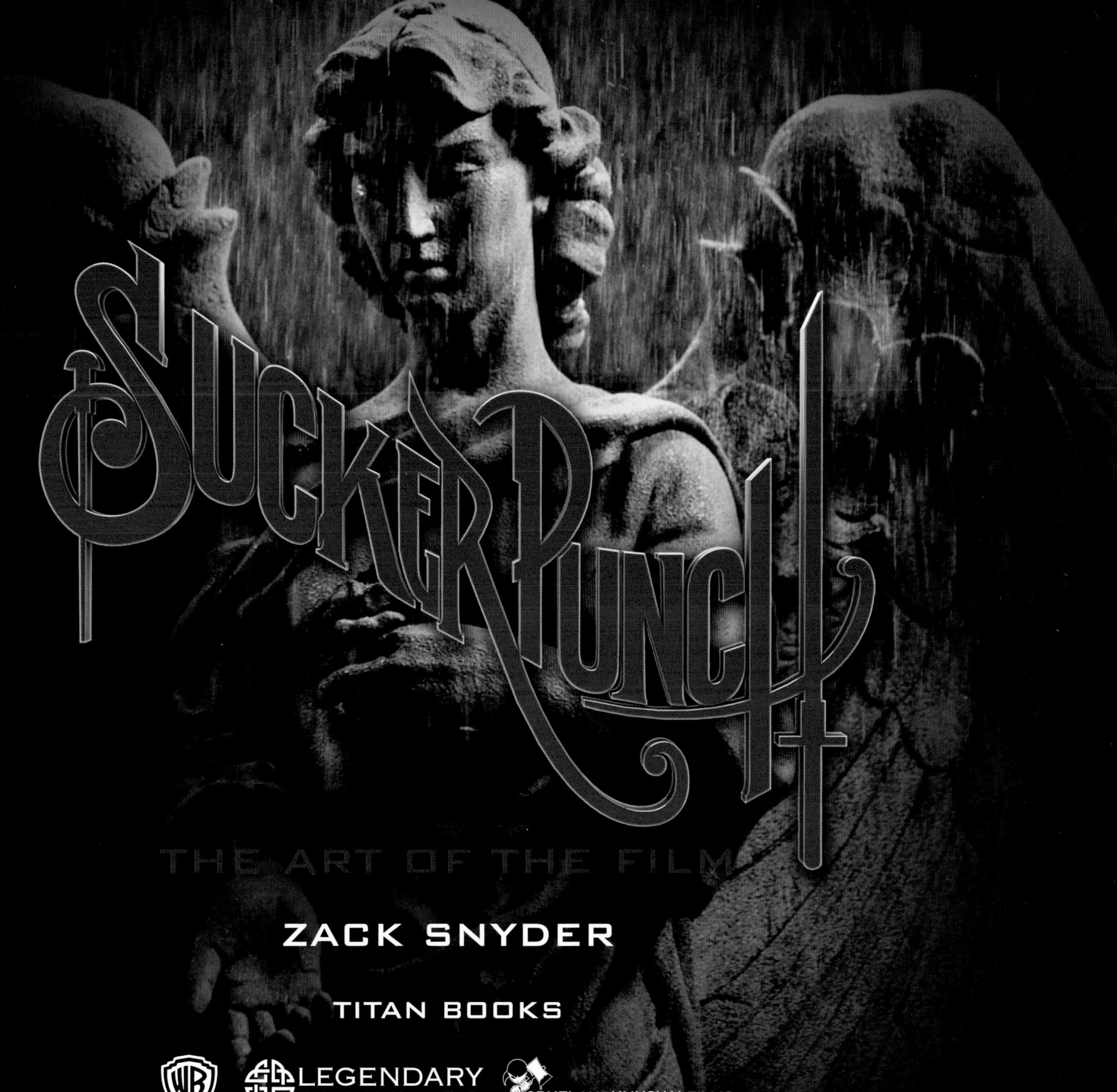

SUCKER PUNCH

THE ART OF THE FILM

ZACK SNYDER

TITAN BOOKS

WB LEGENDARY PICTURES CRUEL AND UNUSUAL FILMS

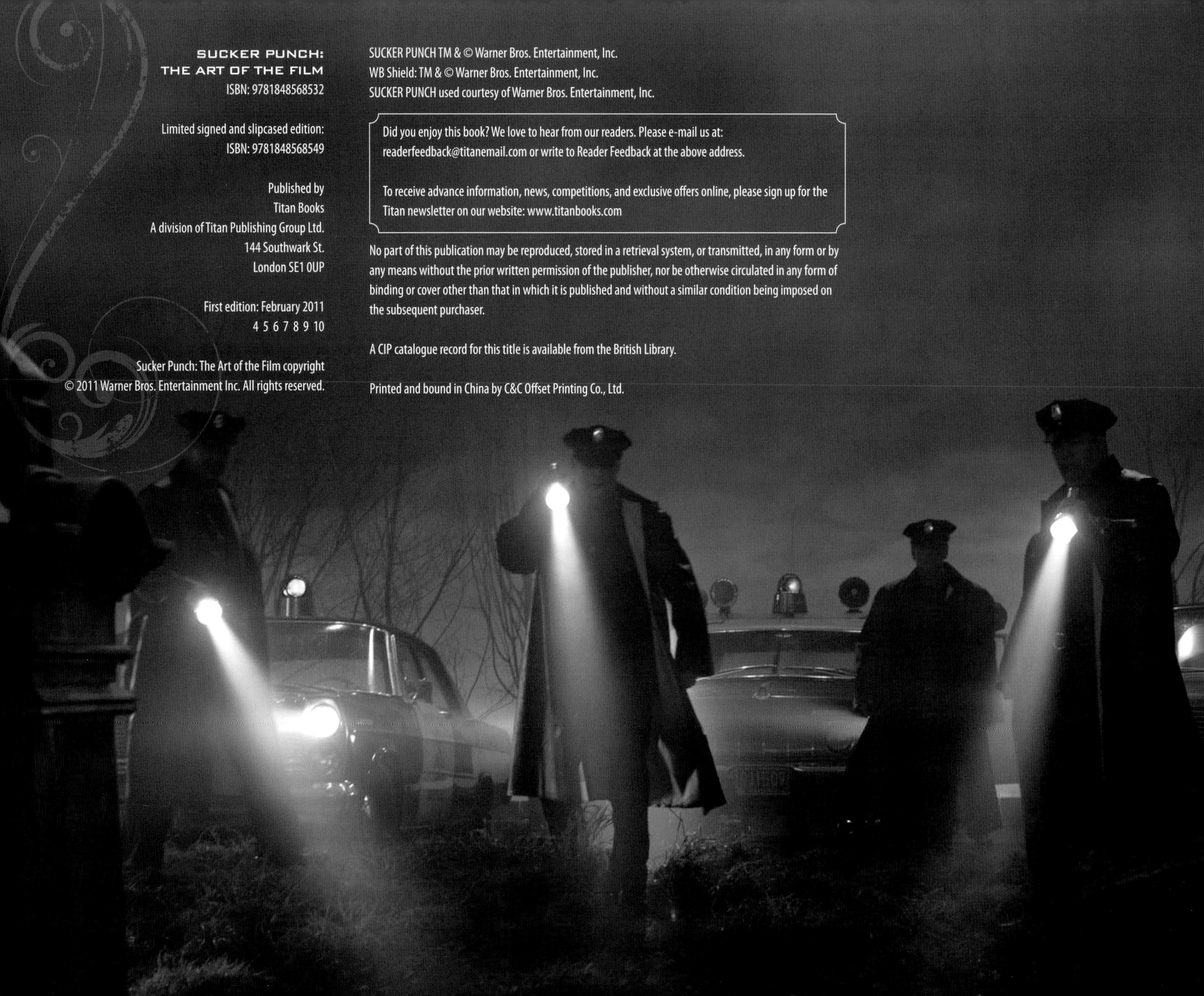

SUCKER PUNCH:
THE ART OF THE FILM
ISBN: 9781848568532

Limited signed and slipcased edition:
ISBN: 9781848568549

Published by
Titan Books
A division of Titan Publishing Group Ltd.
144 Southwark St.
London SE1 0UP

First edition: February 2011
4 5 6 7 8 9 10

Did you enjoy this book? We love to hear from our readers. Please e-mail us at: readerfeedback@titanemail.com or write to Reader Feedback at the above address.

To receive advance information, news, competitions, and exclusive offers online, please sign up for the Titan newsletter on our website: www.titanbooks.com

A CIP catalogue record for this title is available from the British Library.

Printed and bound in China by C&C Offset Printing Co., Ltd.

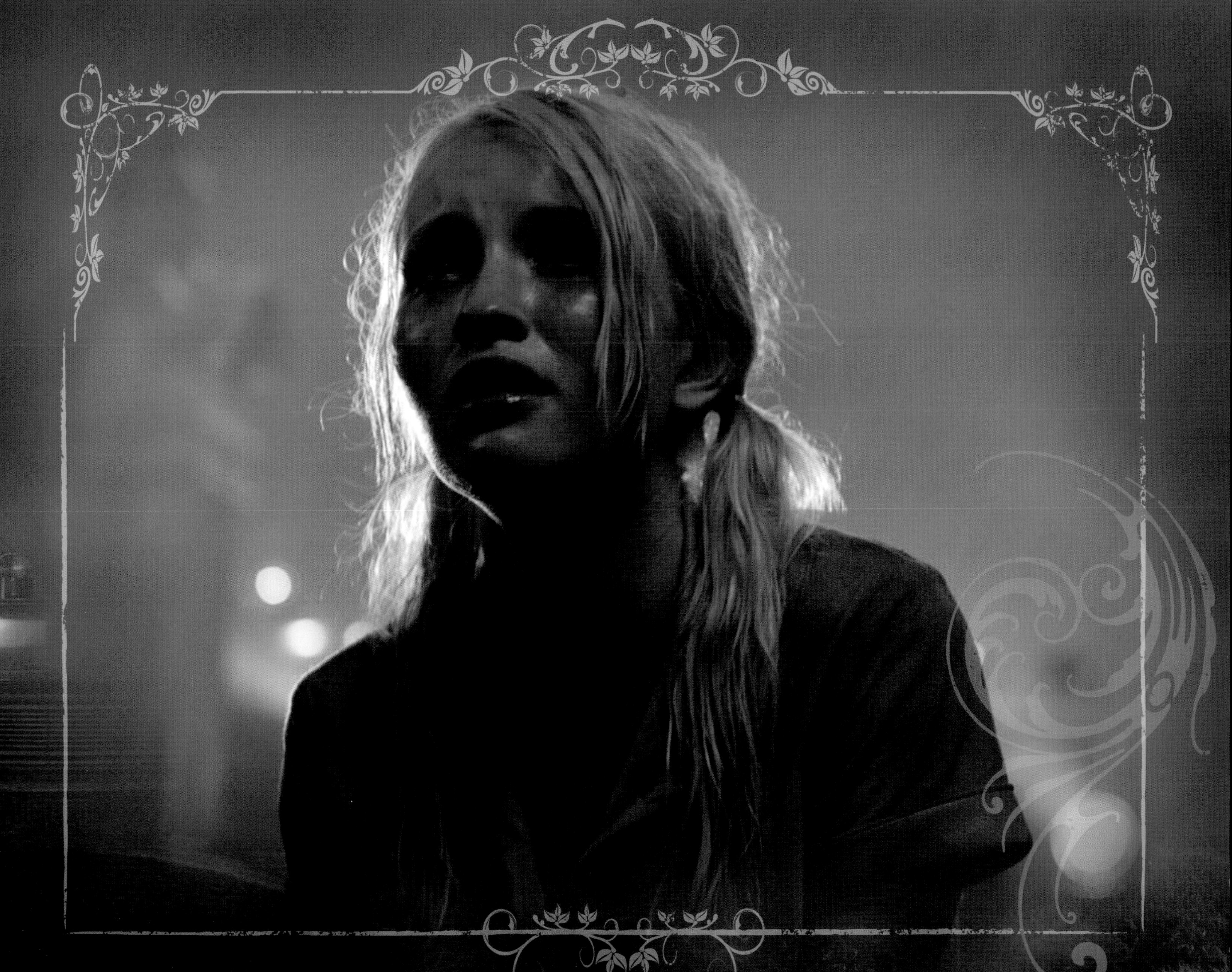

Contents

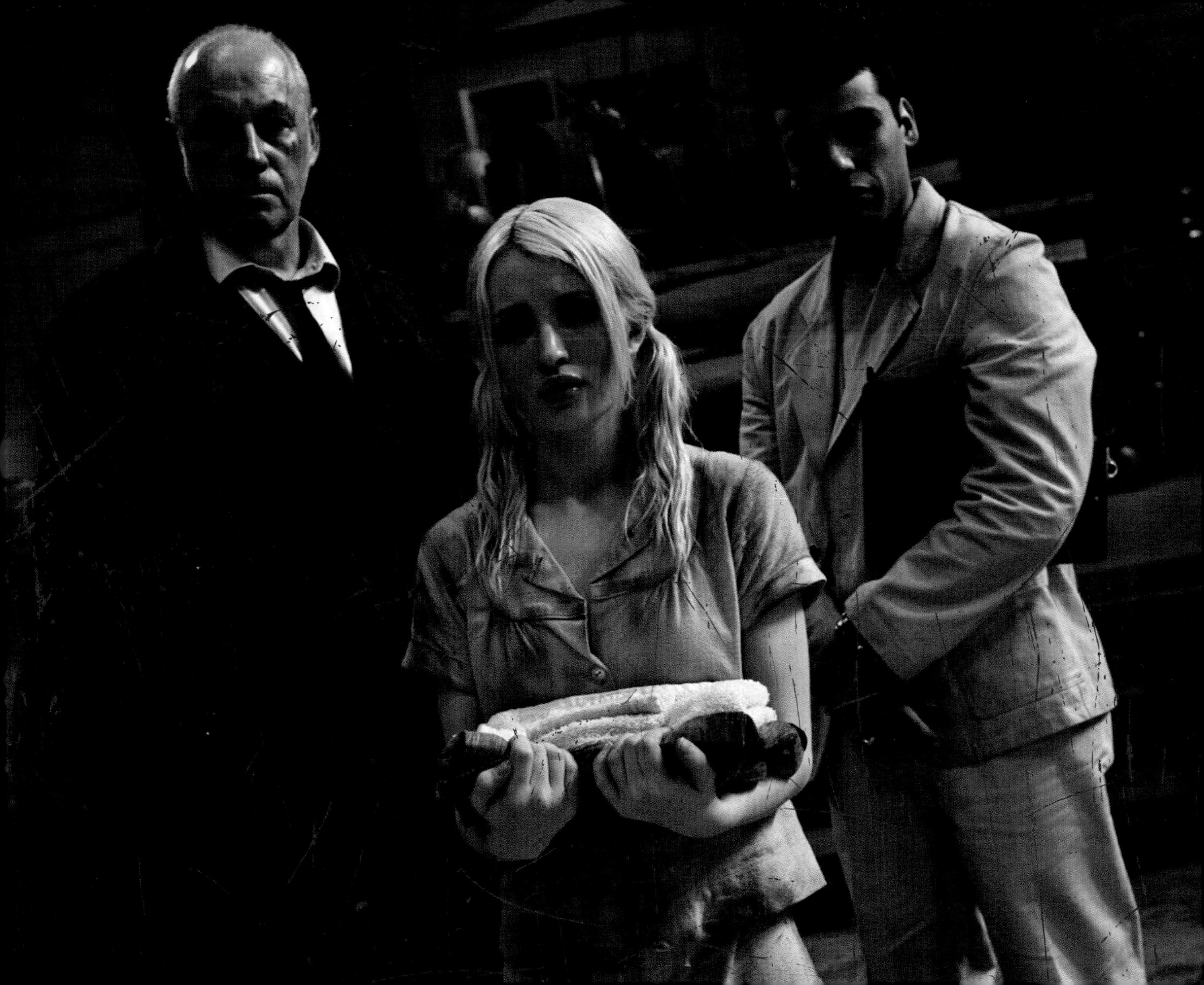

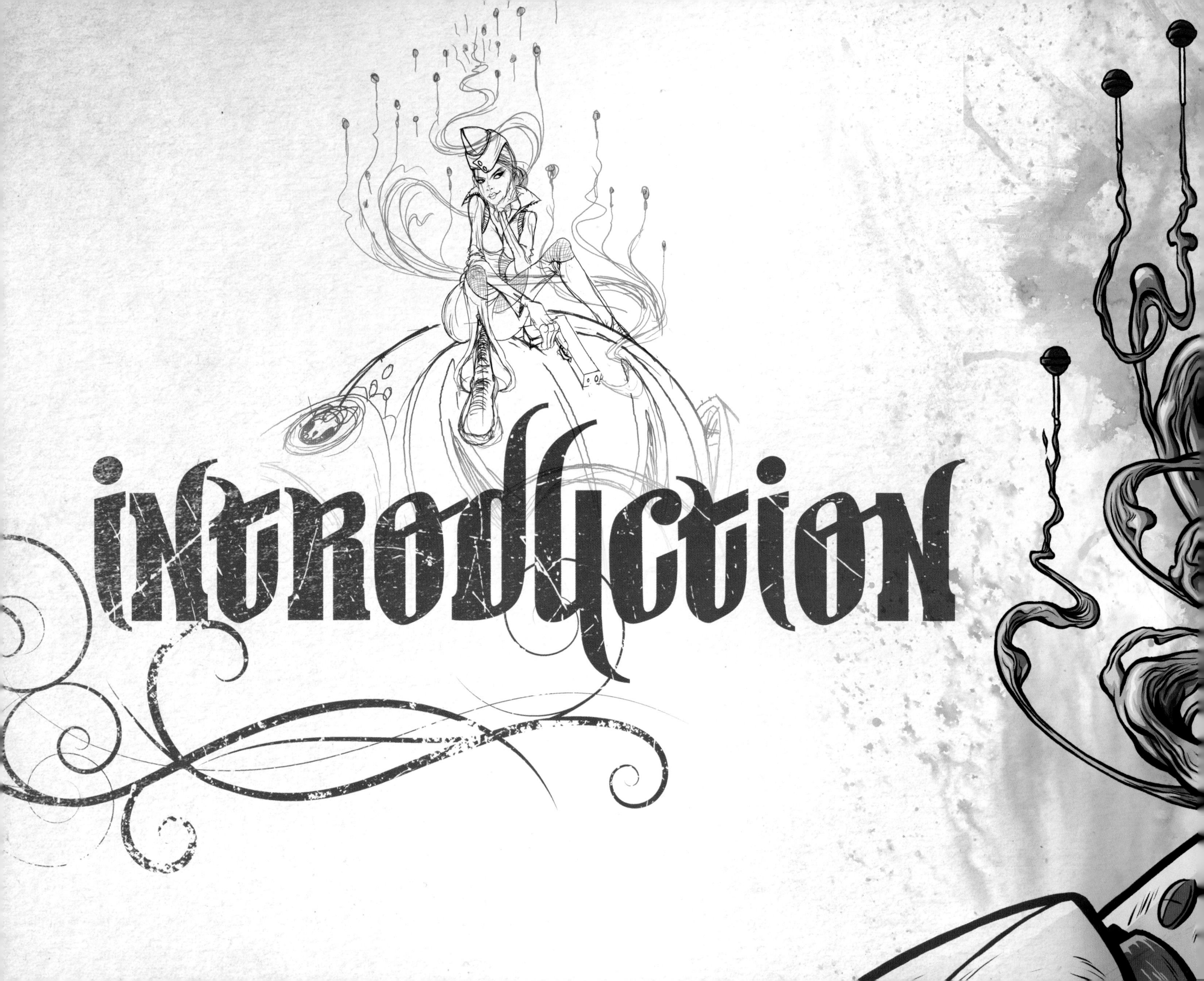
Introduction

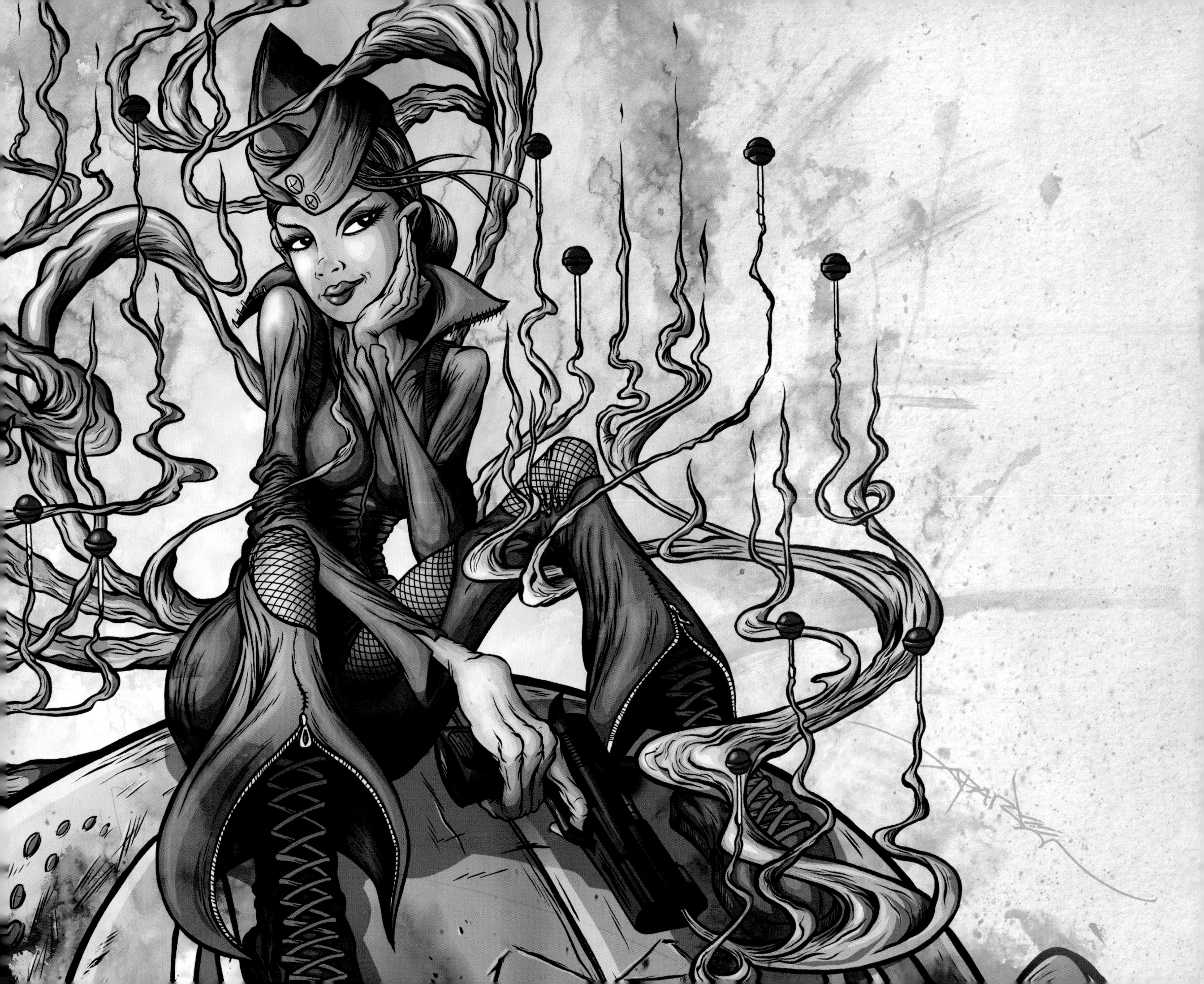

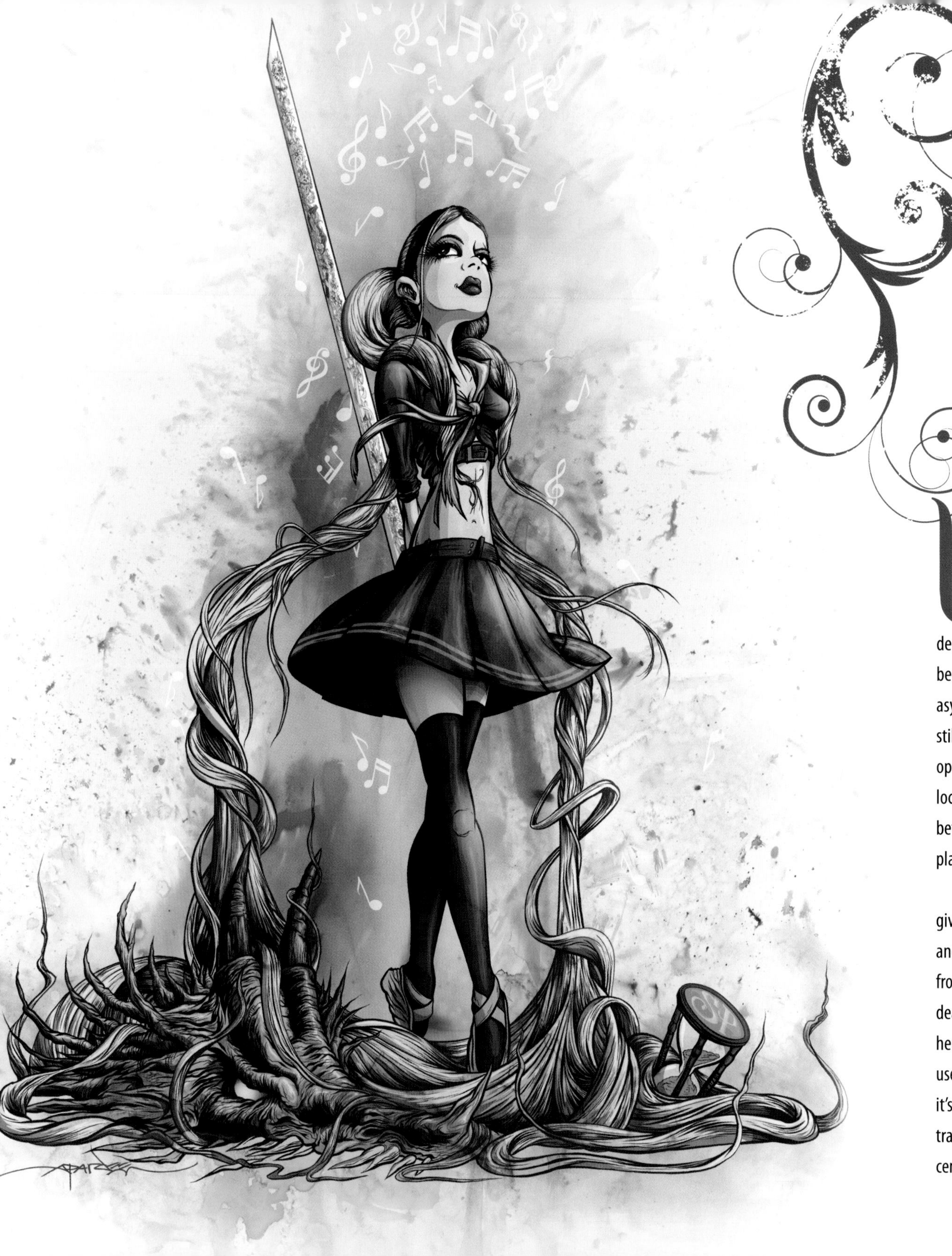

How much pain and sorrow can a fragile young mind take? Perhaps more importantly, to where does that mind escape when it can't take any more? Babydoll is a character I've been kicking around inside my head for almost a decade now. She's a girl on the verge of womanhood whose entire world has just been destroyed. Numbed by grief and guilt when she enters Lennox House insane asylum, Babydoll faces a grey existence devoid of love, devoid of hope. But her still-childlike imagination summons up new, fantastic worlds to inhabit: first an opulent brothel, and then a series of combat missions set in increasingly otherworldly locations in order to gain the means of her escape. These worlds are not necessarily better than her reality – in fact, they're quite a bit more dangerous – but these are places where she can take *action*.

What begins as a fearful retreat becomes an empowering coping mechanism that gives her incredible strength. Traversing the uncanny terrain of her mind, Babydoll and her sisters-in-arms face off against whole legions of her innermost demons – from tearing through battlefield horrors of an unreal past to dancing with high-tech death on a distant planet. In the process, she attempts to heal the psychic wounds of her past. She stops being a victim and learns to become a powerful woman who can use her body to mesmerize, her mind to plot, and her hands to deal death. Whether it's possible to survive this redemptive experience – filled as it is with such carnage, tragedy, and sacrifice – whole, free, and with one's innocence intact, is one of the central questions of the film.

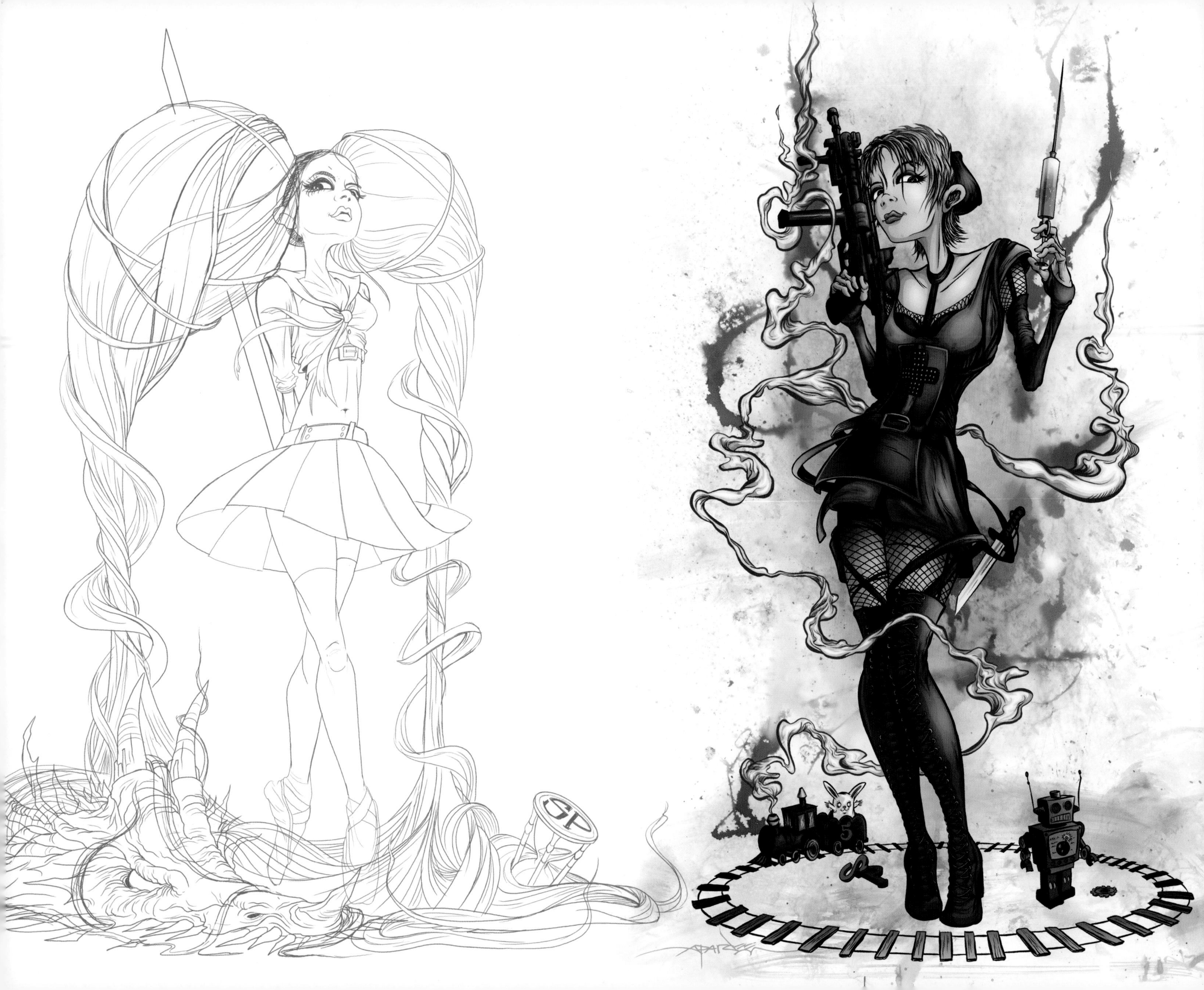

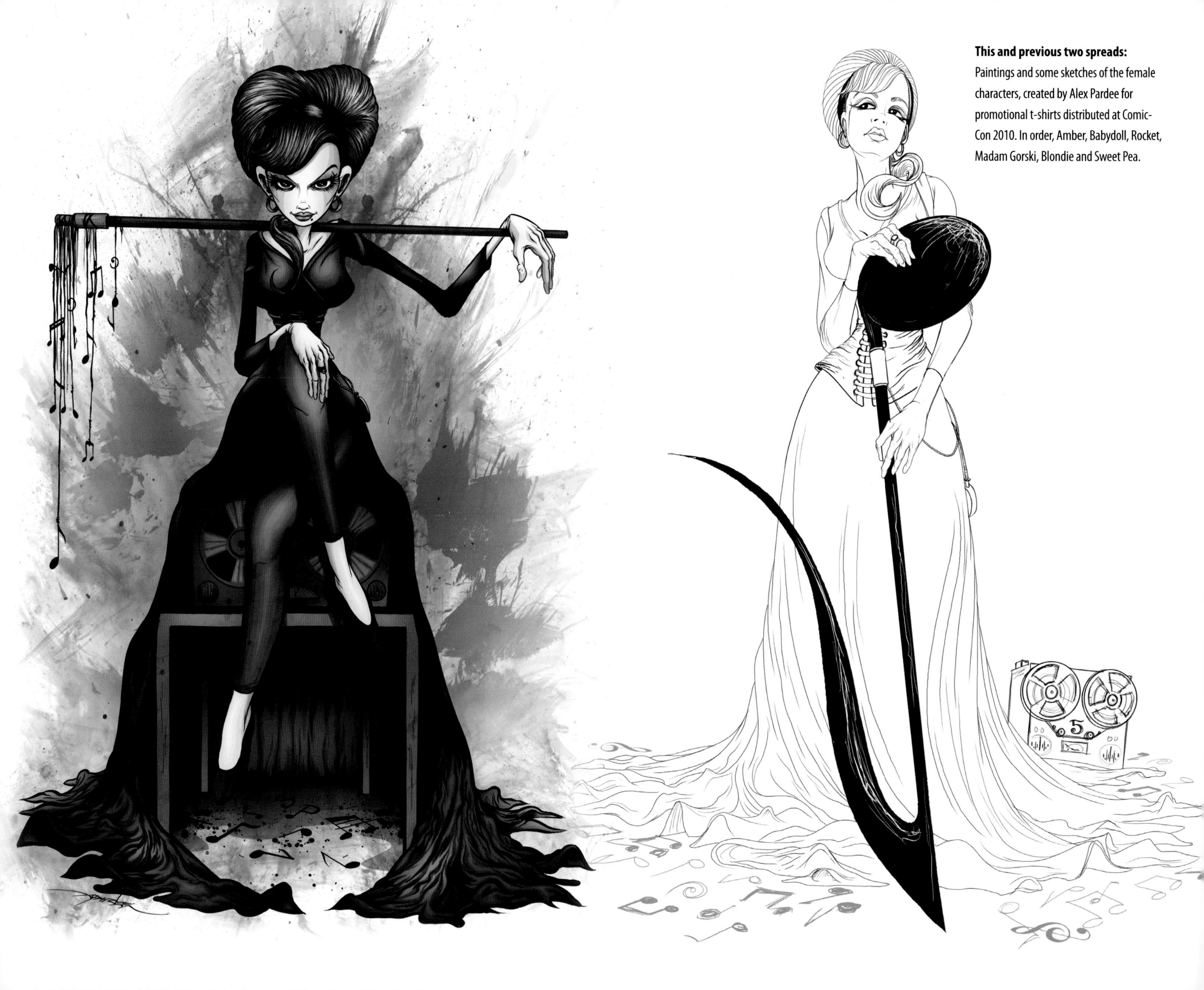

This and previous two spreads:
Paintings and some sketches of the female characters, created by Alex Pardee for promotional t-shirts distributed at Comic-Con 2010. In order, Amber, Babydoll, Rocket, Madam Gorski, Blondie and Sweet Pea.

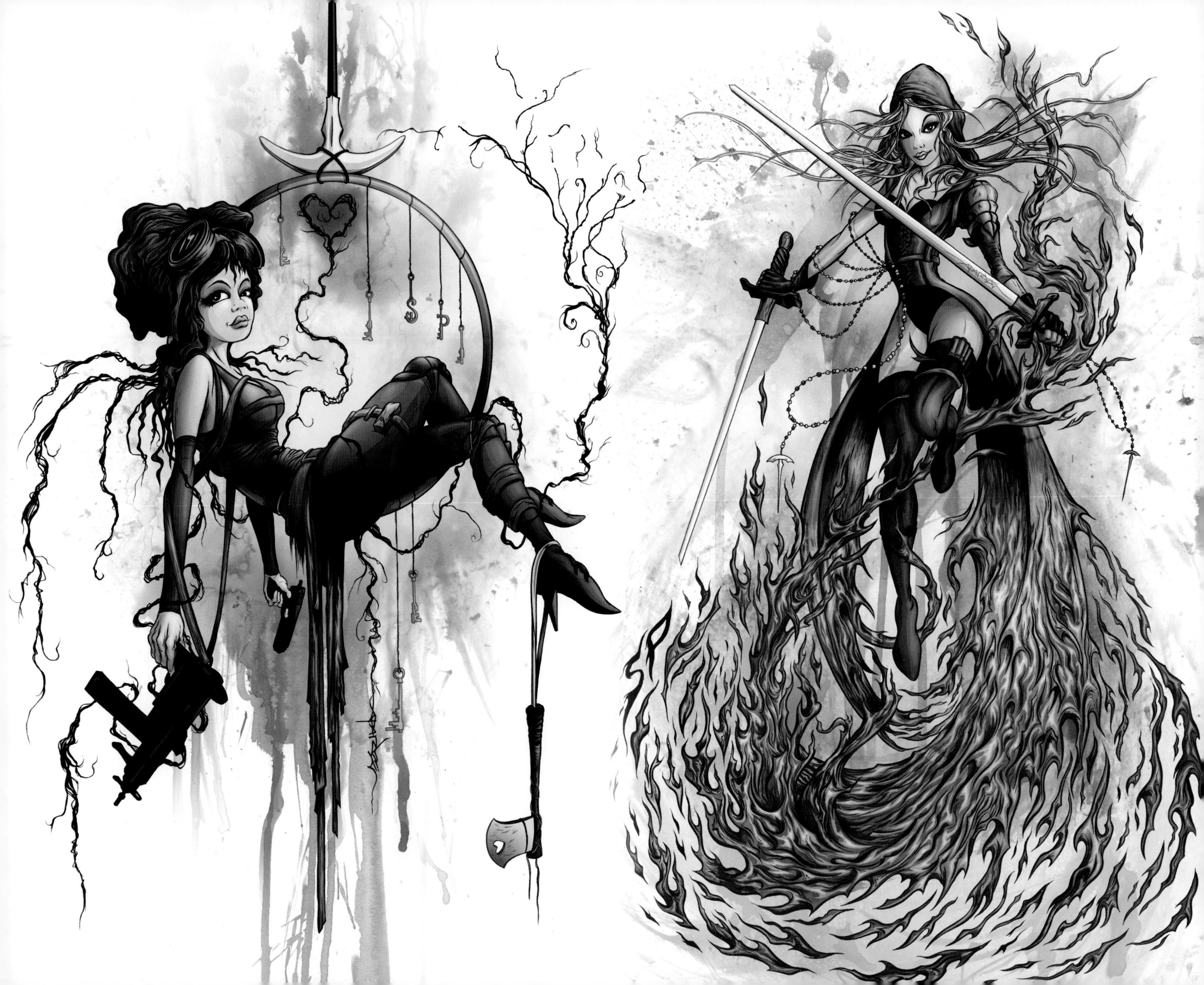

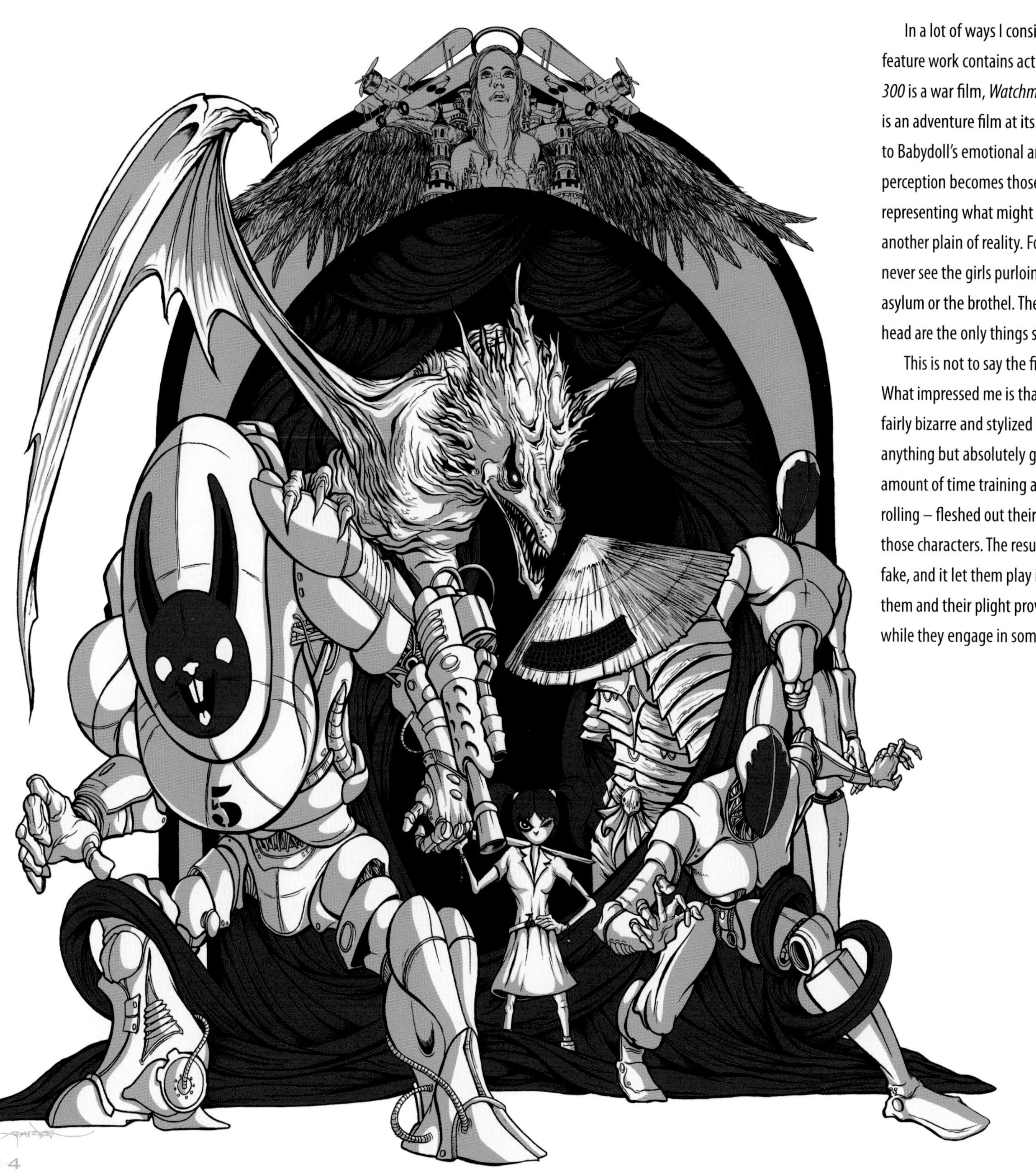

In a lot of ways I consider this my first real action film. While all my previous feature work contains action of one kind or another, *Dawn of the Dead* is a horror film, *300* is a war film, *Watchmen* is overwhelmingly a drama, and *Legend of the Guardians* is an adventure film at its core. But in *Sucker Punch*, the action sequences are integral to Babydoll's emotional and mental journey. They are a window into her mind and her perception becomes those action sequences completely enveloping and ultimately representing what might otherwise be considered important events happening on another plain of reality. For example, we never actually see Babydoll dance. We also never see the girls purloining the items they need for their escape – either in the asylum or the brothel. The fights for their lives that are taking place inside Babydoll's head are the only things she's focused on at those times, and therefore, so are we.

This is not to say the film is all action with no heart, which would be pointless. What impressed me is that while they had to bounce back and forth between some fairly bizarre and stylized worlds, the actors never portrayed their relationships as anything but absolutely genuine. The five girls especially – who spent an incredible amount of time training and bonding together before the cameras even started rolling – fleshed out their individual back stories and goals, and truly came to inhabit those characters. The result was an obvious chemistry on screen that you just couldn't fake, and it let them play it all so hard and convincingly real. The sincerity felt for them and their plight provides the necessary emotional core for us to hang on to while they engage in some pretty insane battles.

This spread: Alex Pardee's design for the VFX crew t-shirt (left), and his early designs for the *Sucker Punch* logo, the charms that hang from Babydoll's pistol grip, and her sister's stuffed toy rabbit.

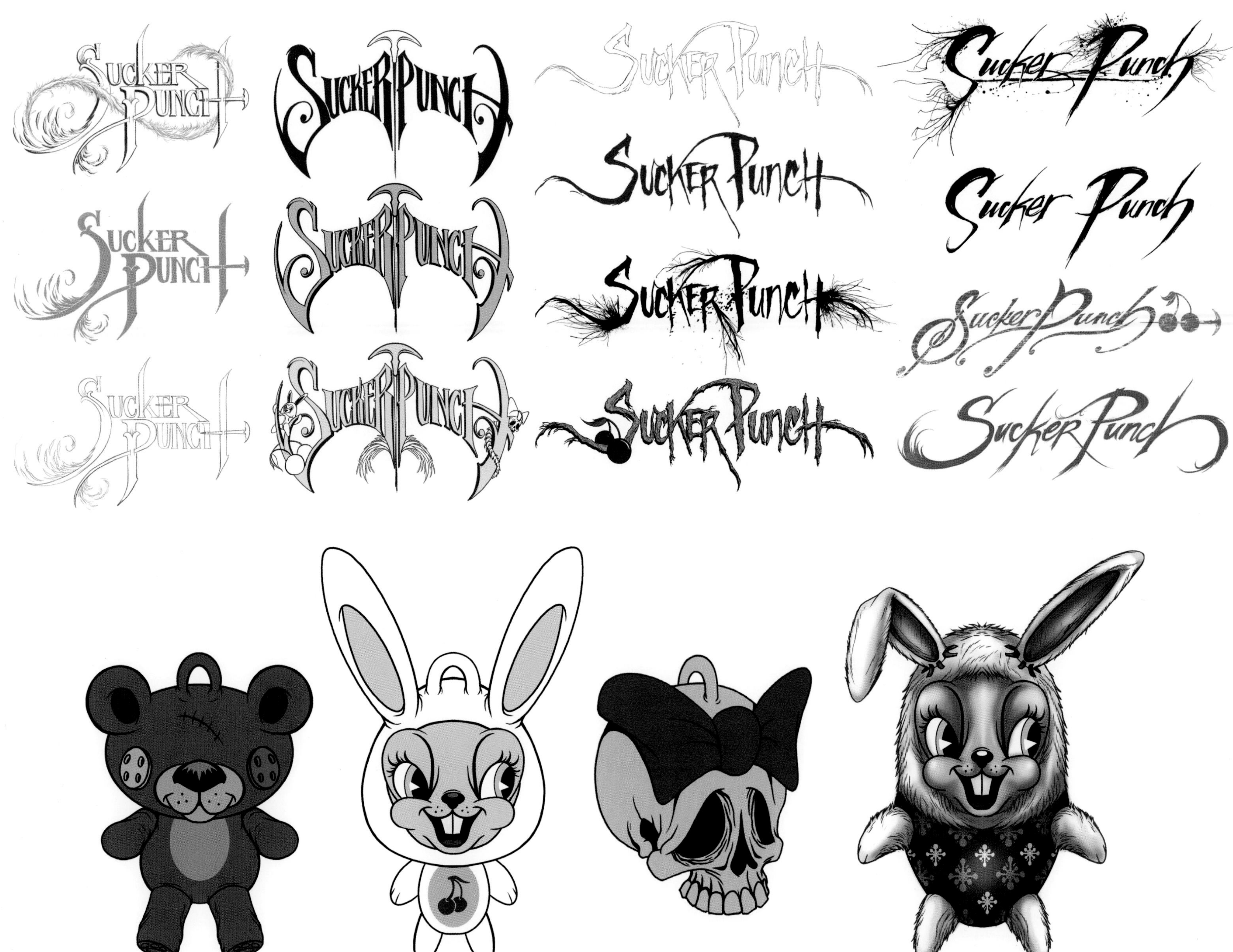

Sucker Punch

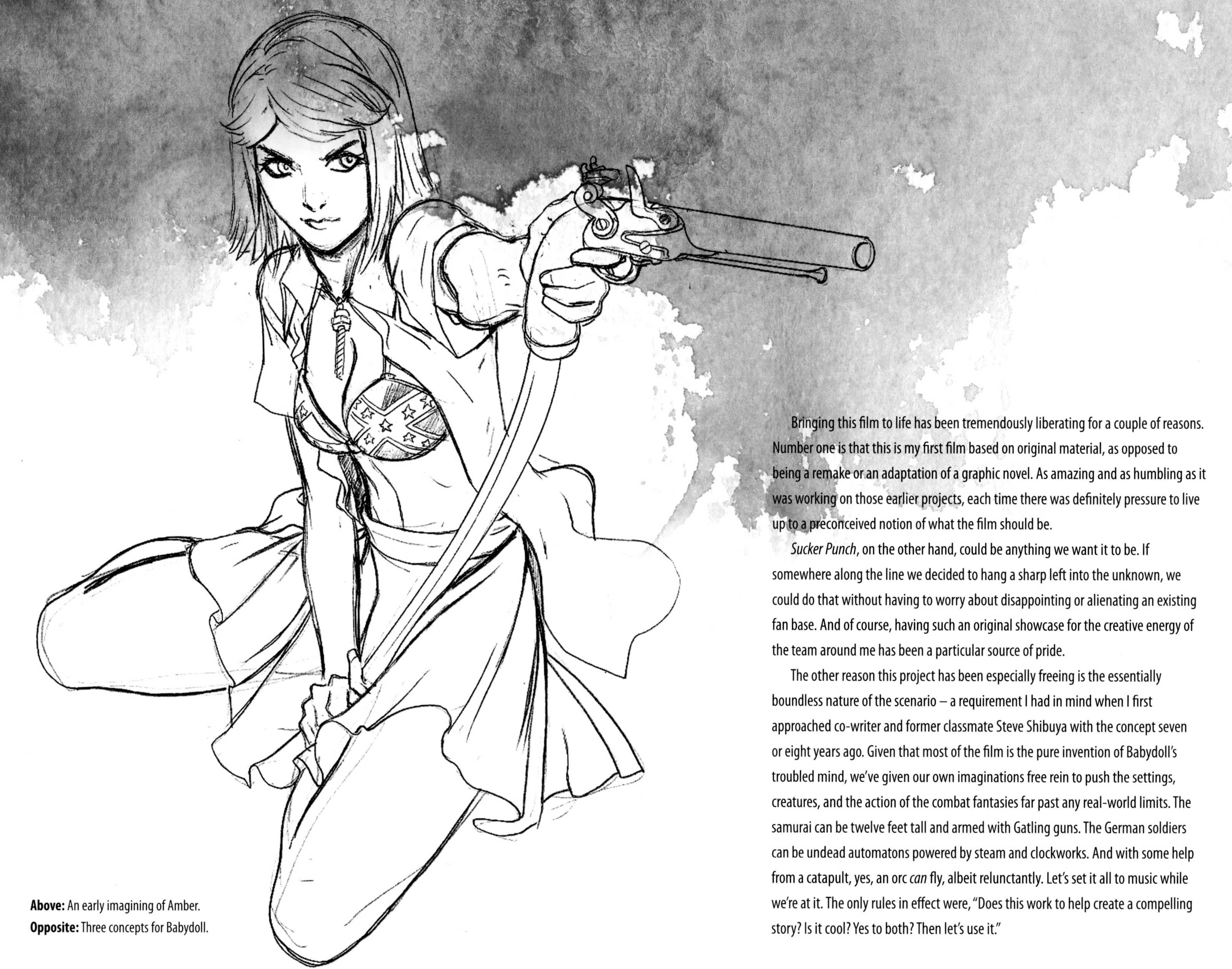

Above: An early imagining of Amber.
Opposite: Three concepts for Babydoll.

Bringing this film to life has been tremendously liberating for a couple of reasons. Number one is that this is my first film based on original material, as opposed to being a remake or an adaptation of a graphic novel. As amazing and as humbling as it was working on those earlier projects, each time there was definitely pressure to live up to a preconceived notion of what the film should be.

Sucker Punch, on the other hand, could be anything we want it to be. If somewhere along the line we decided to hang a sharp left into the unknown, we could do that without having to worry about disappointing or alienating an existing fan base. And of course, having such an original showcase for the creative energy of the team around me has been a particular source of pride.

The other reason this project has been especially freeing is the essentially boundless nature of the scenario – a requirement I had in mind when I first approached co-writer and former classmate Steve Shibuya with the concept seven or eight years ago. Given that most of the film is the pure invention of Babydoll's troubled mind, we've given our own imaginations free rein to push the settings, creatures, and the action of the combat fantasies far past any real-world limits. The samurai can be twelve feet tall and armed with Gatling guns. The German soldiers can be undead automatons powered by steam and clockworks. And with some help from a catapult, yes, an orc *can* fly, albeit reluctantly. Let's set it all to music while we're at it. The only rules in effect were, "Does this work to help create a compelling story? Is it cool? Yes to both? Then let's use it."

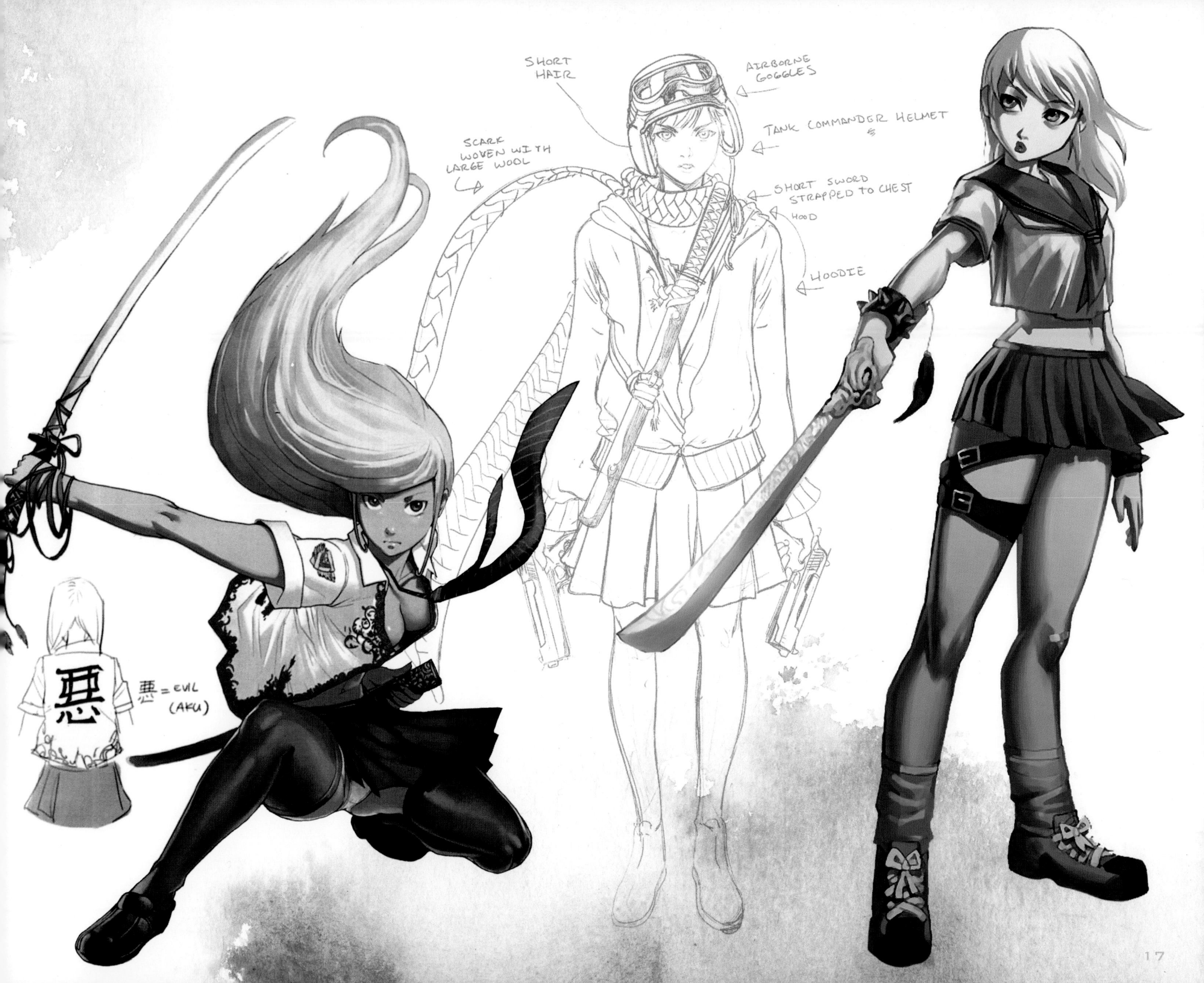
SHORT HAIR
AIRBORNE GOGGLES
TANK COMMANDER HELMET
SCARK WOVEN WITH LARGE WOOL
SHORT SWORD STRAPPED TO CHEST
HOOD
HOODIE
悪
悪 = EVIL (AKU)

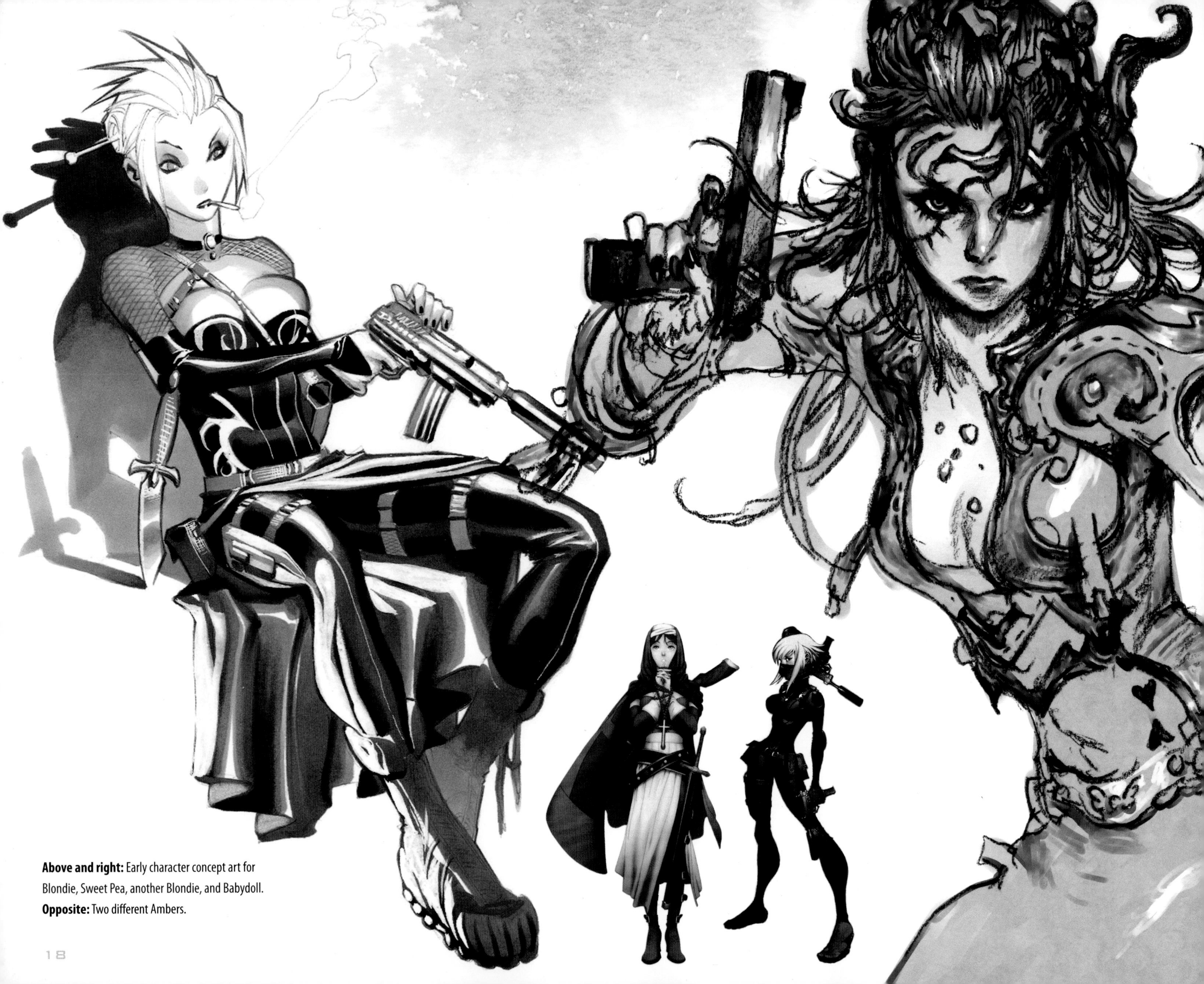

Above and right: Early character concept art for Blondie, Sweet Pea, another Blondie, and Babydoll.
Opposite: Two different Ambers.

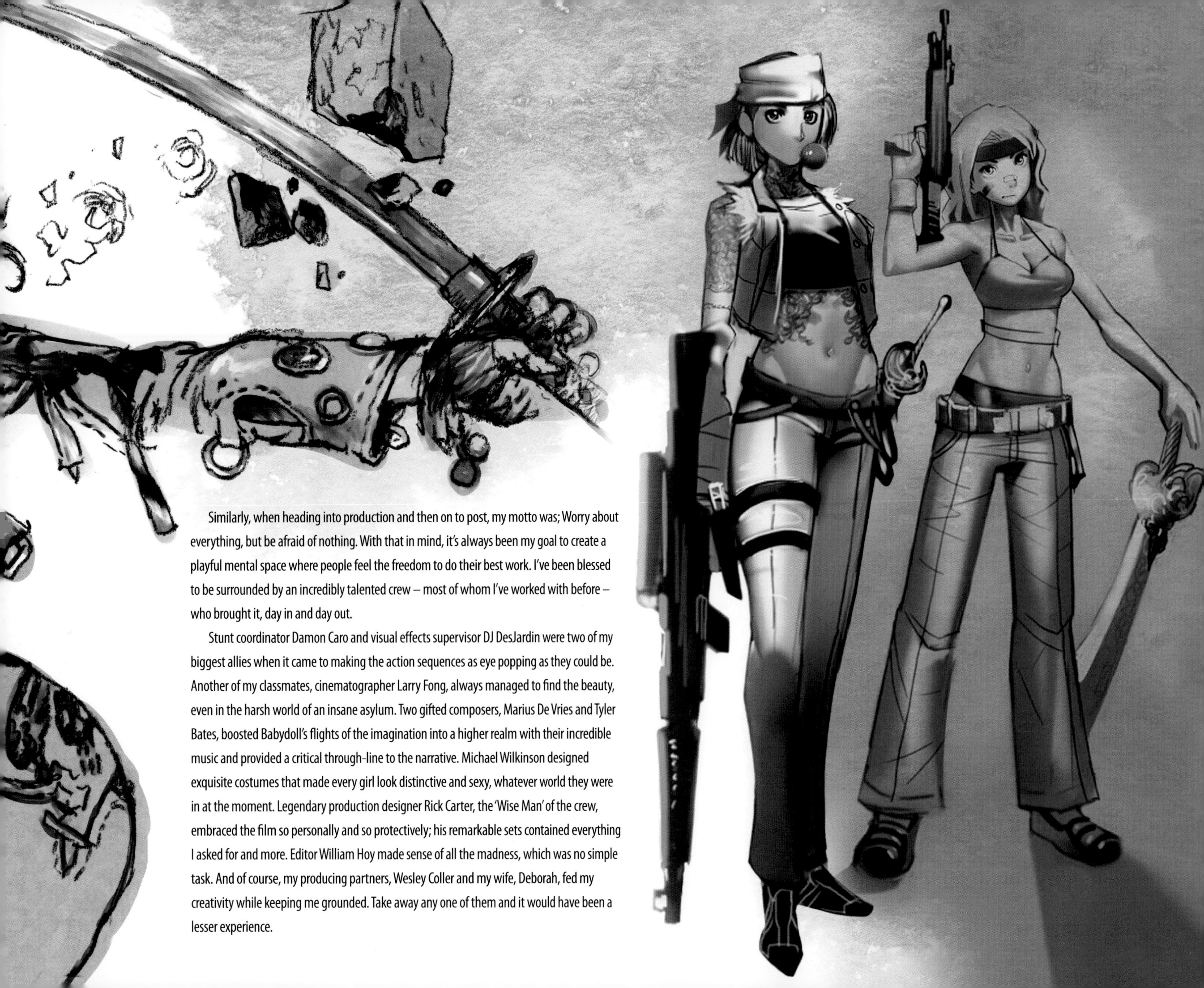

Similarly, when heading into production and then on to post, my motto was; Worry about everything, but be afraid of nothing. With that in mind, it's always been my goal to create a playful mental space where people feel the freedom to do their best work. I've been blessed to be surrounded by an incredibly talented crew – most of whom I've worked with before – who brought it, day in and day out.

Stunt coordinator Damon Caro and visual effects supervisor DJ DesJardin were two of my biggest allies when it came to making the action sequences as eye popping as they could be. Another of my classmates, cinematographer Larry Fong, always managed to find the beauty, even in the harsh world of an insane asylum. Two gifted composers, Marius De Vries and Tyler Bates, boosted Babydoll's flights of the imagination into a higher realm with their incredible music and provided a critical through-line to the narrative. Michael Wilkinson designed exquisite costumes that made every girl look distinctive and sexy, whatever world they were in at the moment. Legendary production designer Rick Carter, the 'Wise Man' of the crew, embraced the film so personally and so protectively; his remarkable sets contained everything I asked for and more. Editor William Hoy made sense of all the madness, which was no simple task. And of course, my producing partners, Wesley Coller and my wife, Deborah, fed my creativity while keeping me grounded. Take away any one of them and it would have been a lesser experience.

I've been asked quite a few times what the title means. Sure, the audience is apt to feel a surprise sock to the gut at certain points in the film, but calling it *Sucker Punch* was really our way of giving it almost no title at all. It can't be neatly pigeonholed into any one genre, and we didn't want a title that would even try to encapsulate what the film is, or even what it isn't. For me, *Sucker Punch* is a story of redemption, friendship, imagination, and freedom – and when the curtain goes up, that's true no matter which side of the looking glass you're on.

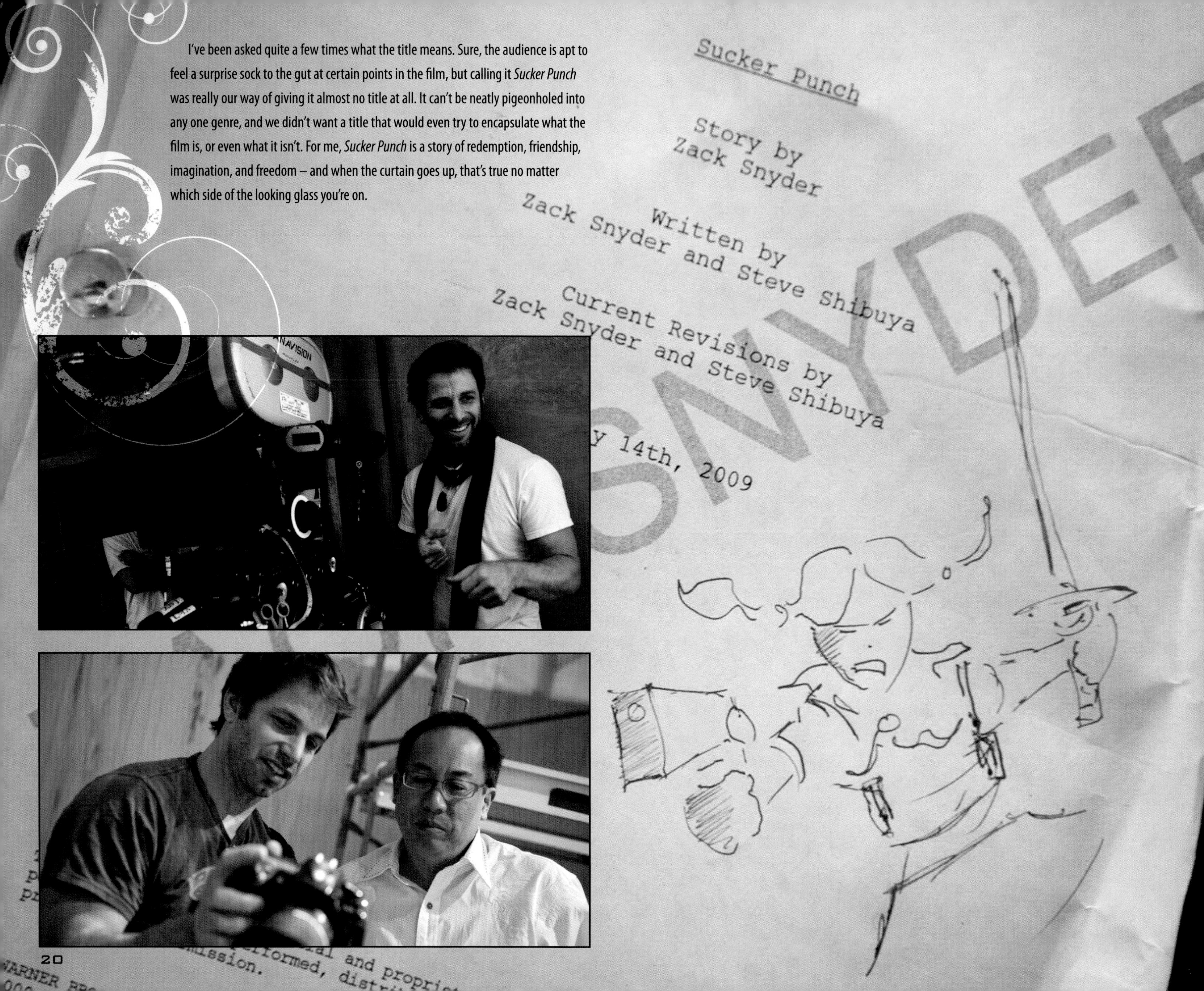

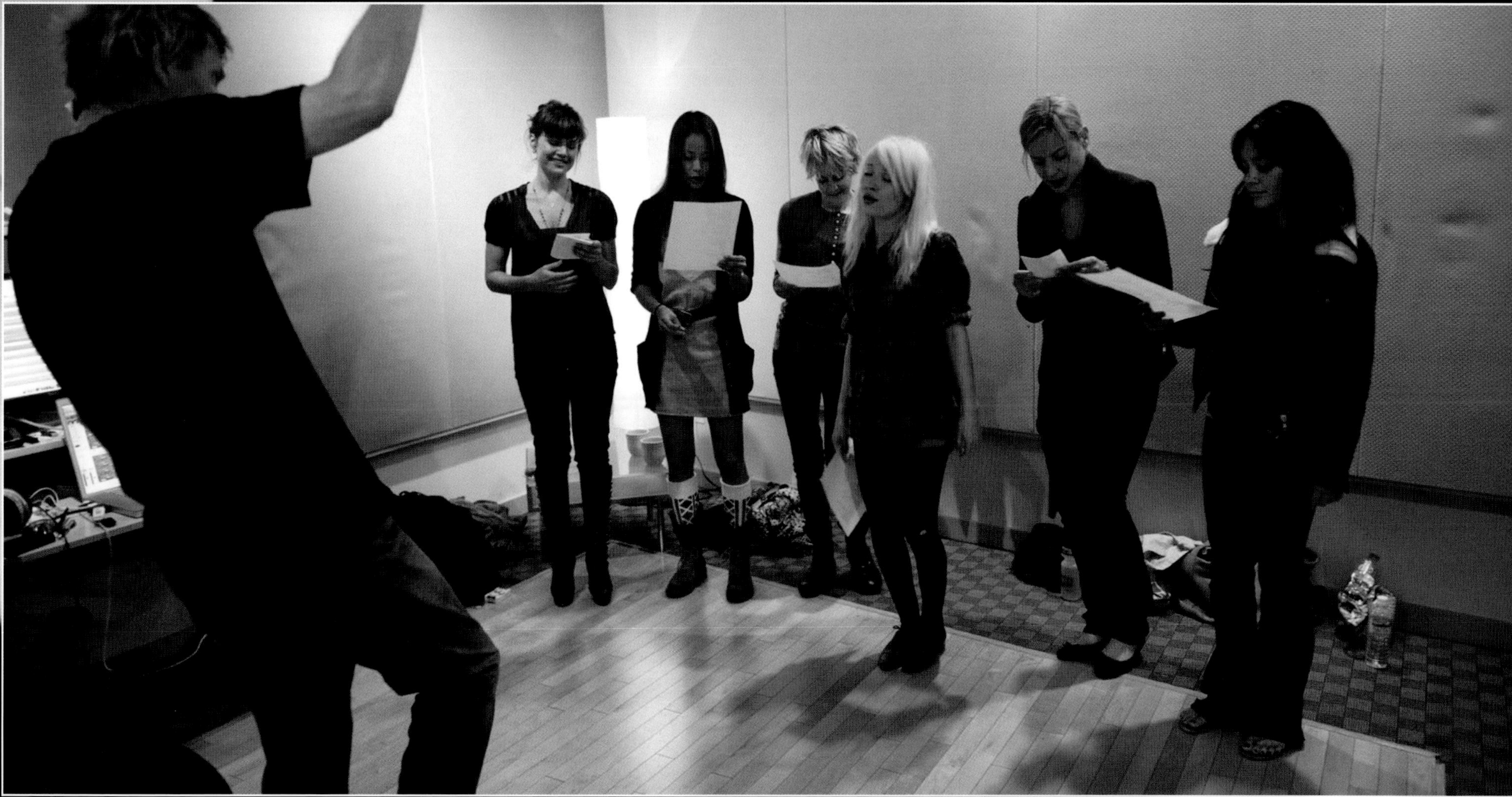

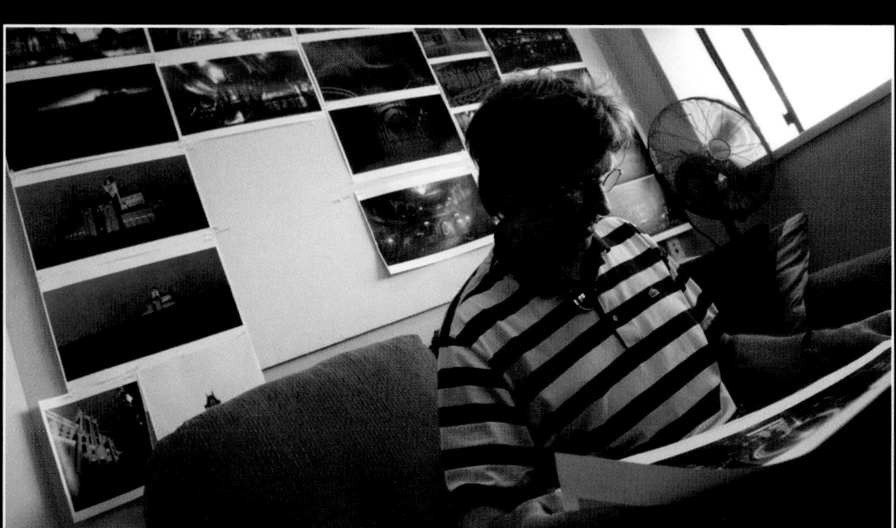

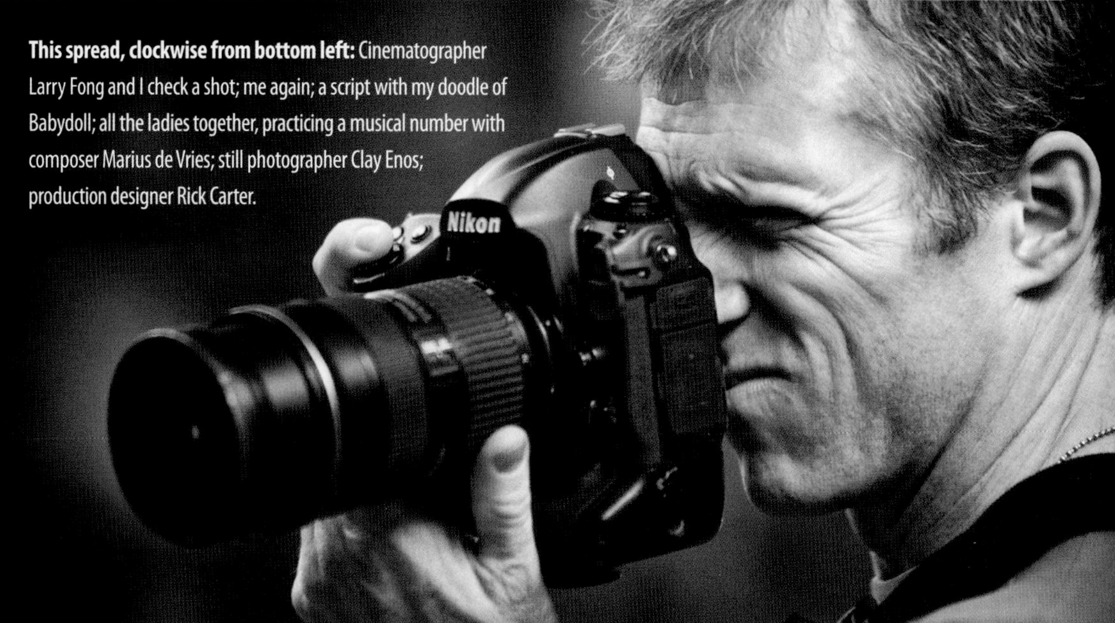

This spread, clockwise from bottom left: Cinematographer Larry Fong and I check a shot; me again; a script with my doodle of Babydoll; all the ladies together, practicing a musical number with composer Marius de Vries; still photographer Clay Enos; production designer Rick Carter.

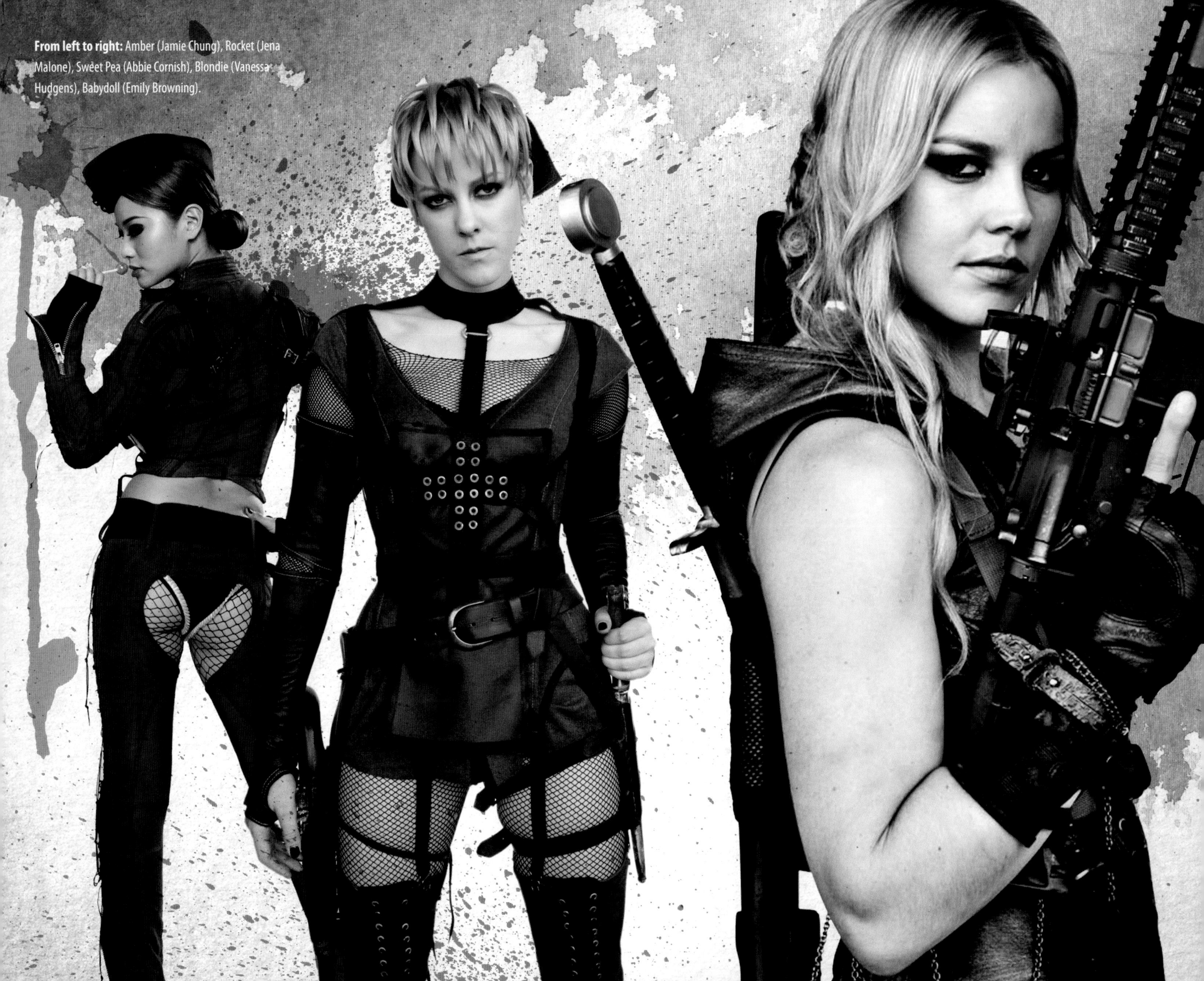

From left to right: Amber (Jamie Chung), Rocket (Jena Malone), Sweet Pea (Abbie Cornish), Blondie (Vanessa Hudgens), Babydoll (Emily Browning).

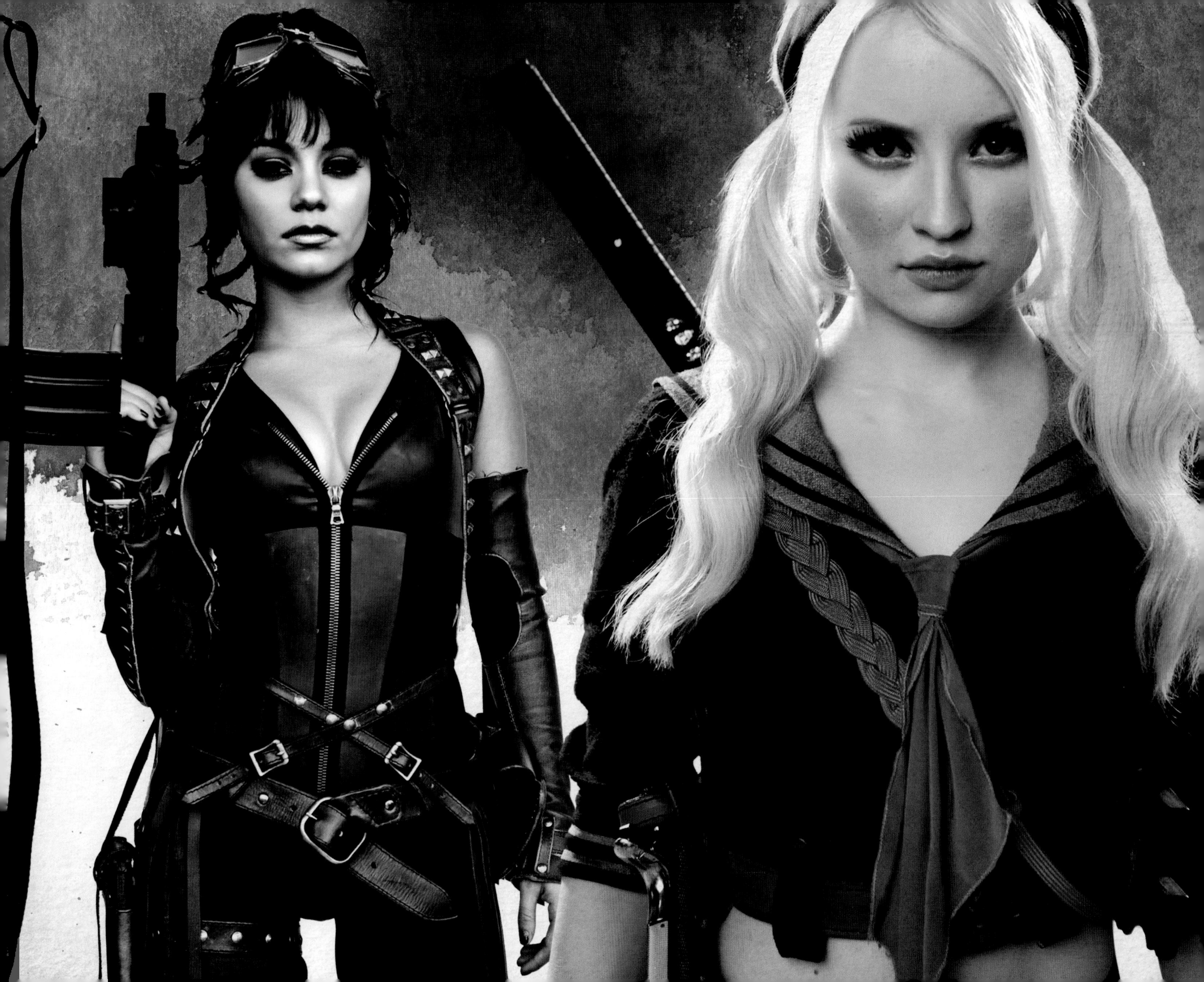

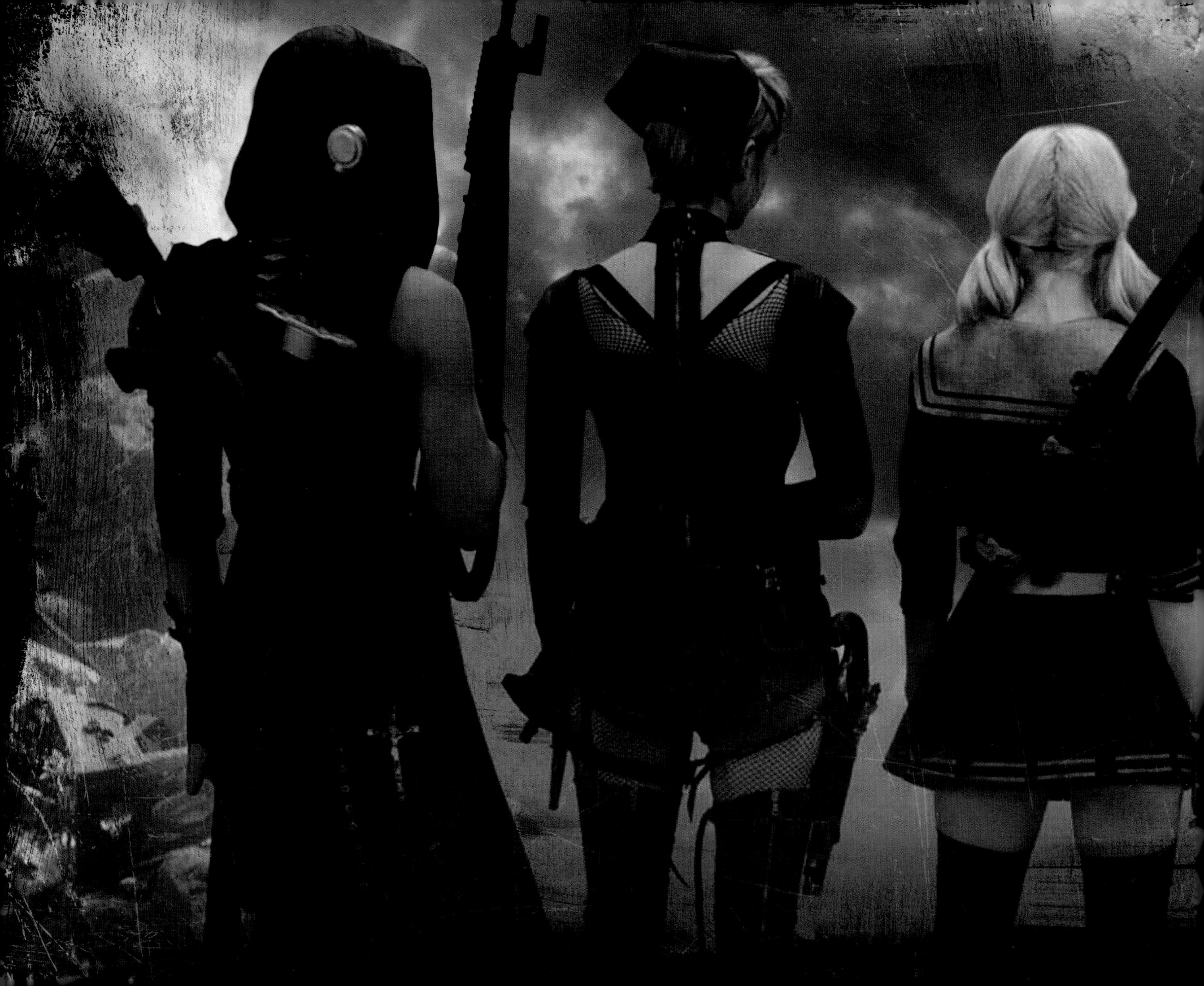

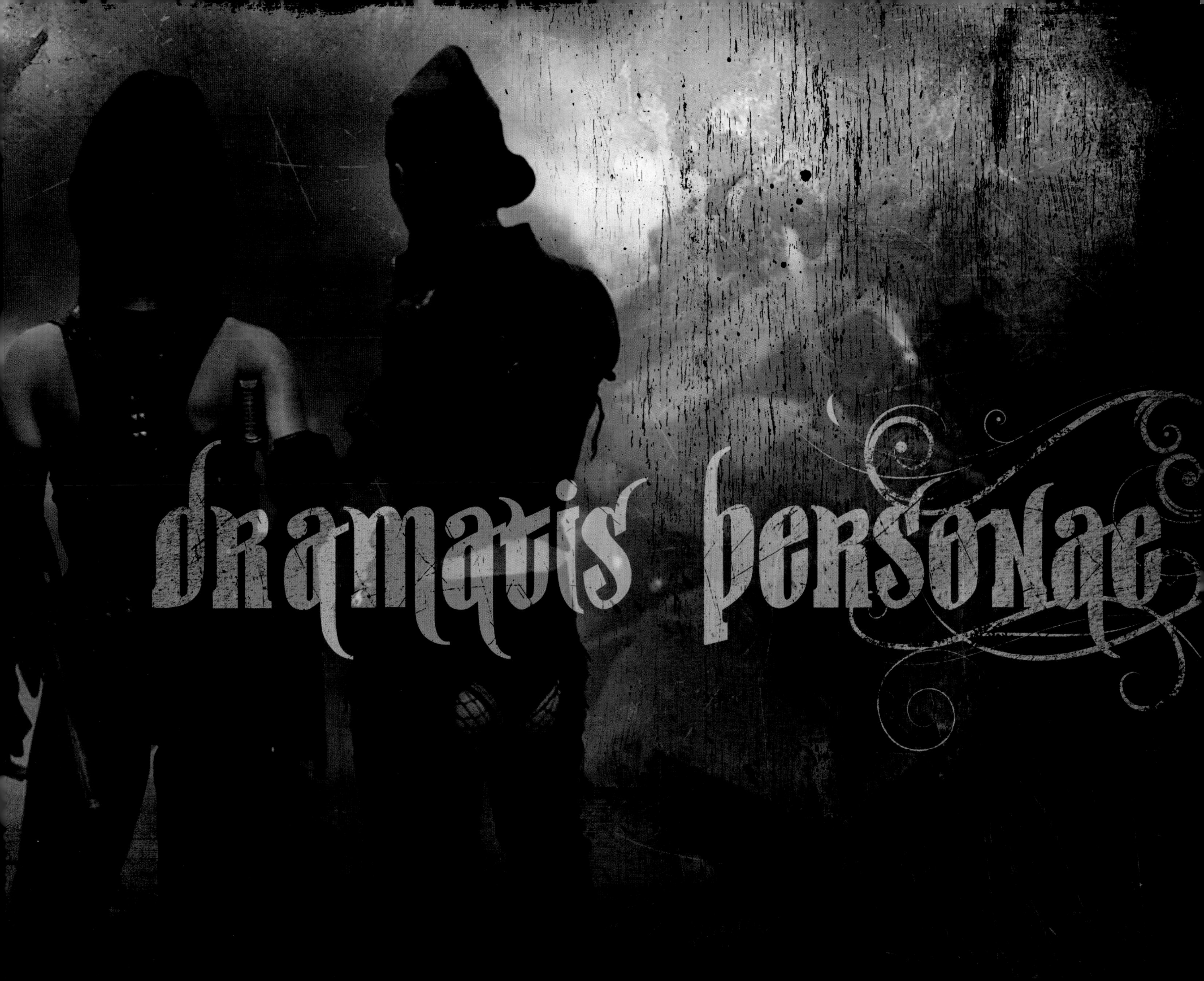

dramatis personae

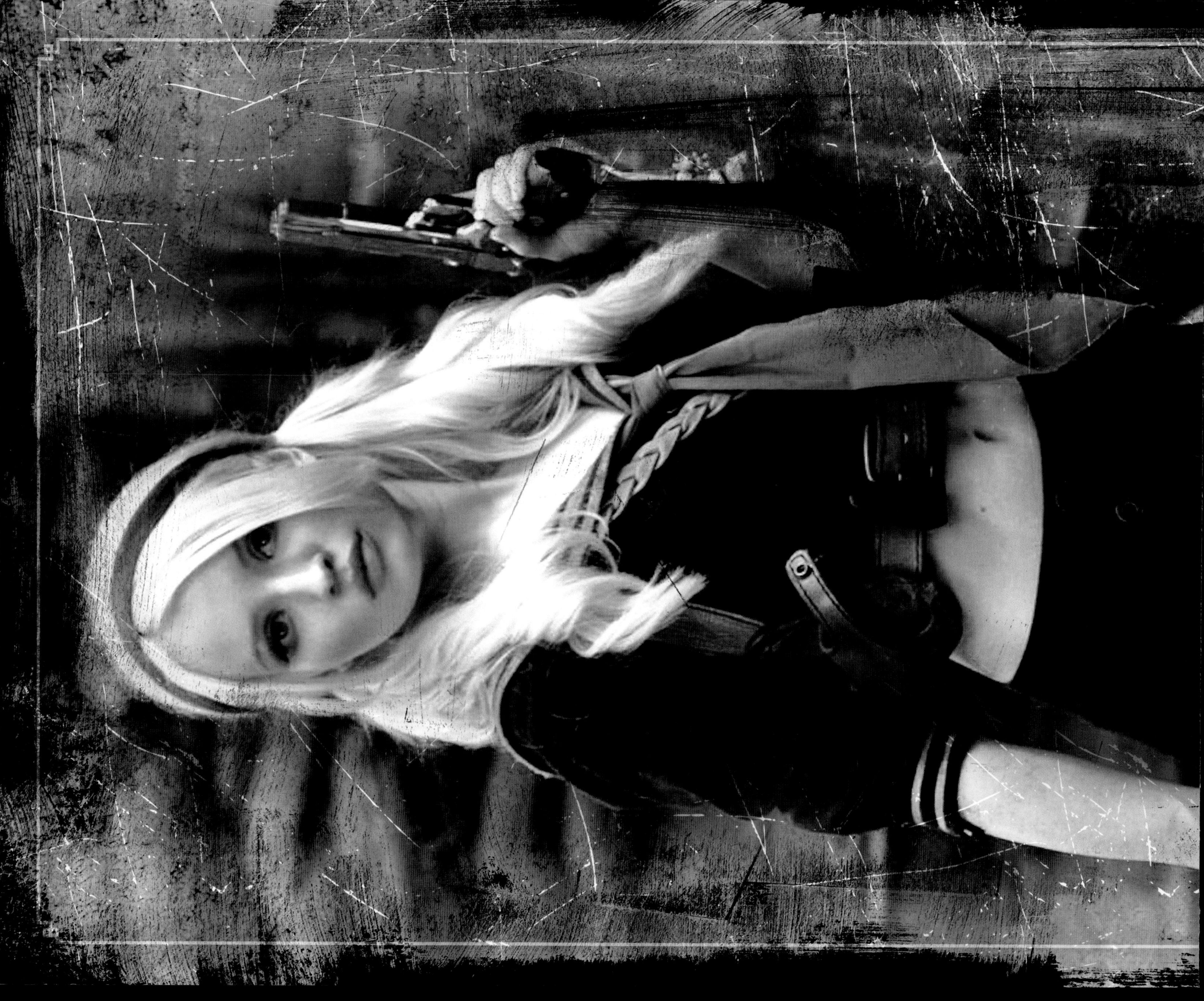

BABYDOLL

"IF YOU WANT ME TO SHUT
UP, YOU'RE GONNA HAVE
TO COME MAKE ME."

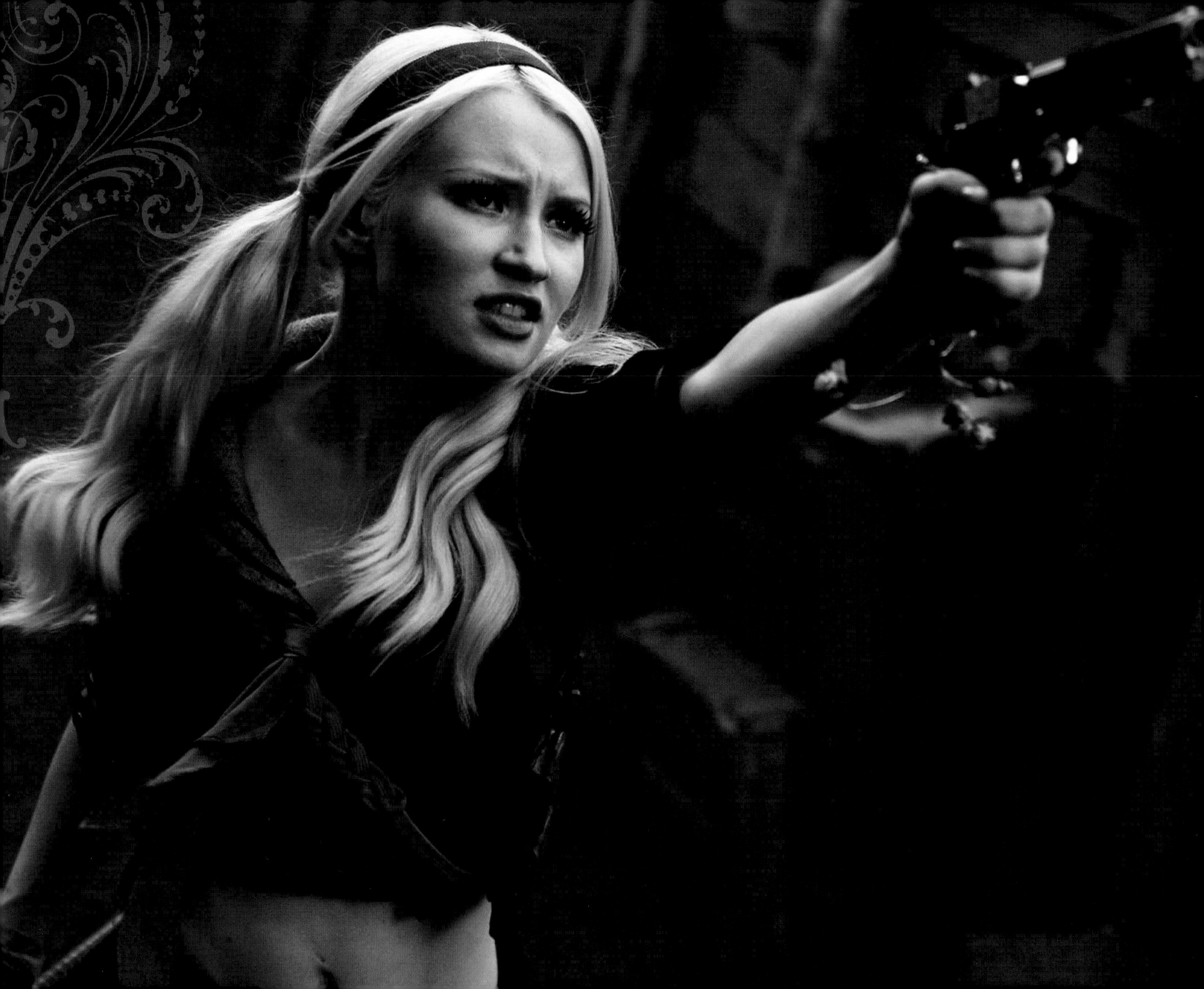

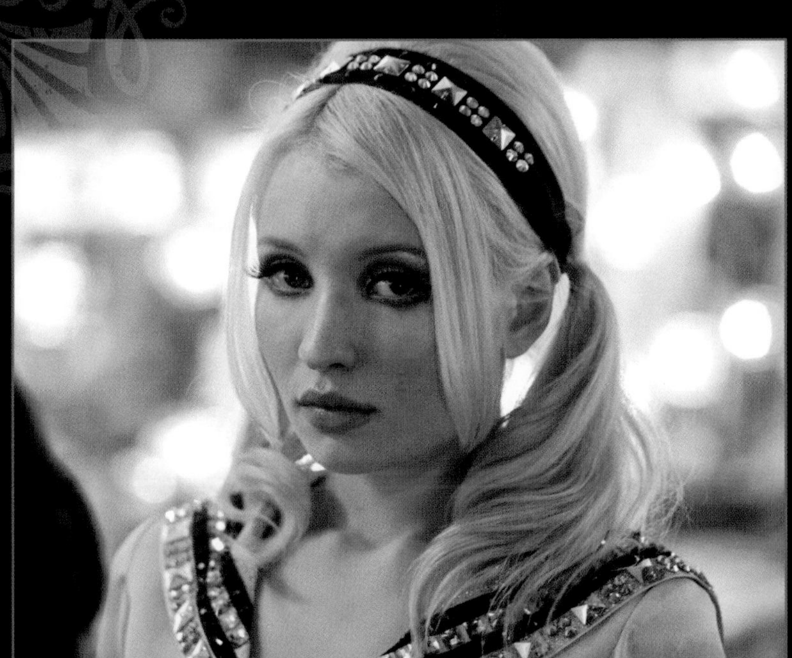

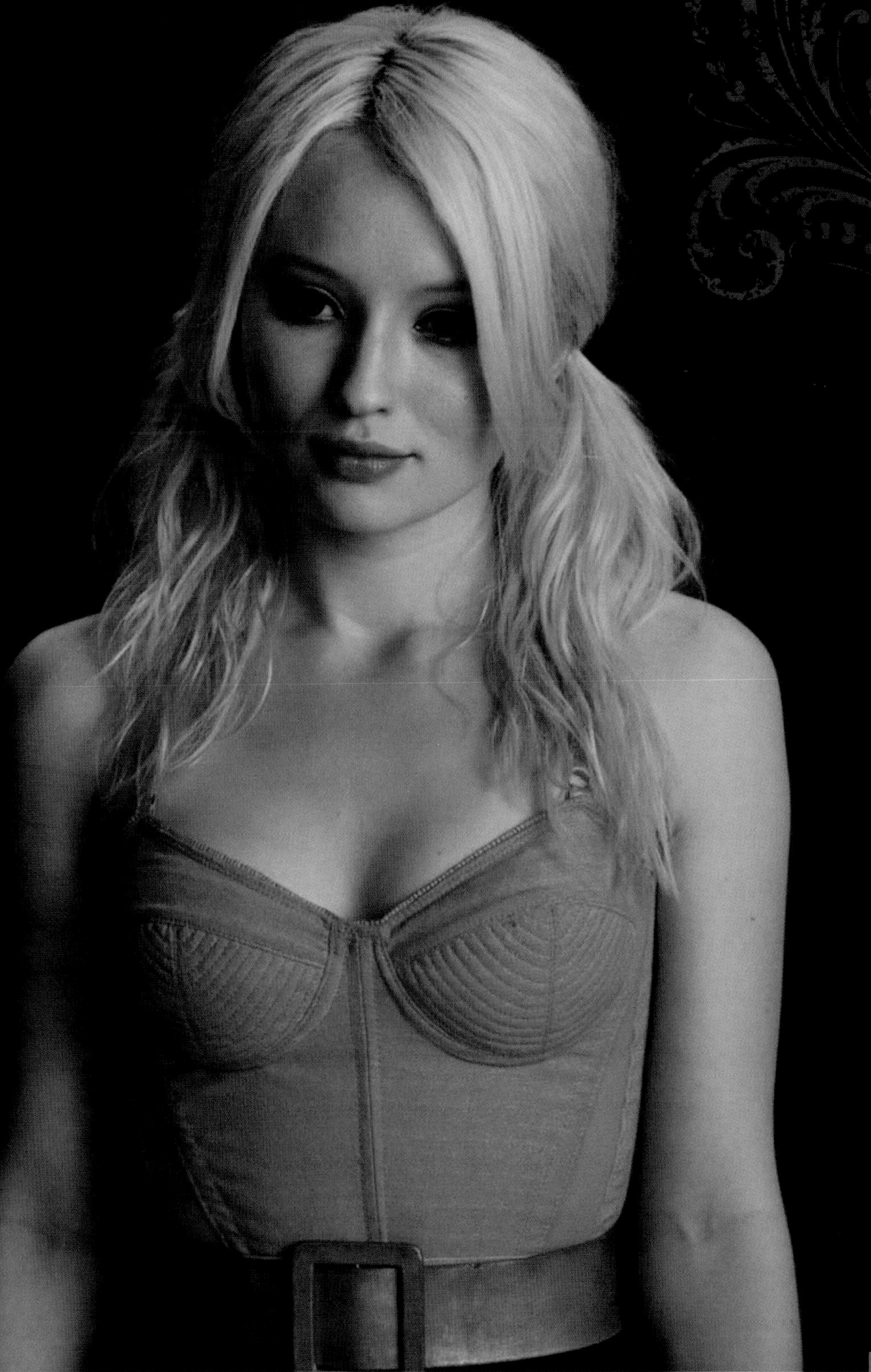

BABYDOLL

Even in her darkest moments of despair, the idealistic Babydoll never loses her perspective on right and wrong. She may seem like a fragile and naïve little schoolgirl, but her enemies underestimate her at their own peril. This prized pupil quickly masters her Japanese short sword and .45 automatic to become incredibly powerful – perhaps even invincible. Emily Browning has such a timeless, mystical, almost otherworldly quality about her. So many times, using just a look and a pose, she exudes just the right combination of quiet intensity and transcendent vulnerability. I couldn't have asked for a more perfect Babydoll.

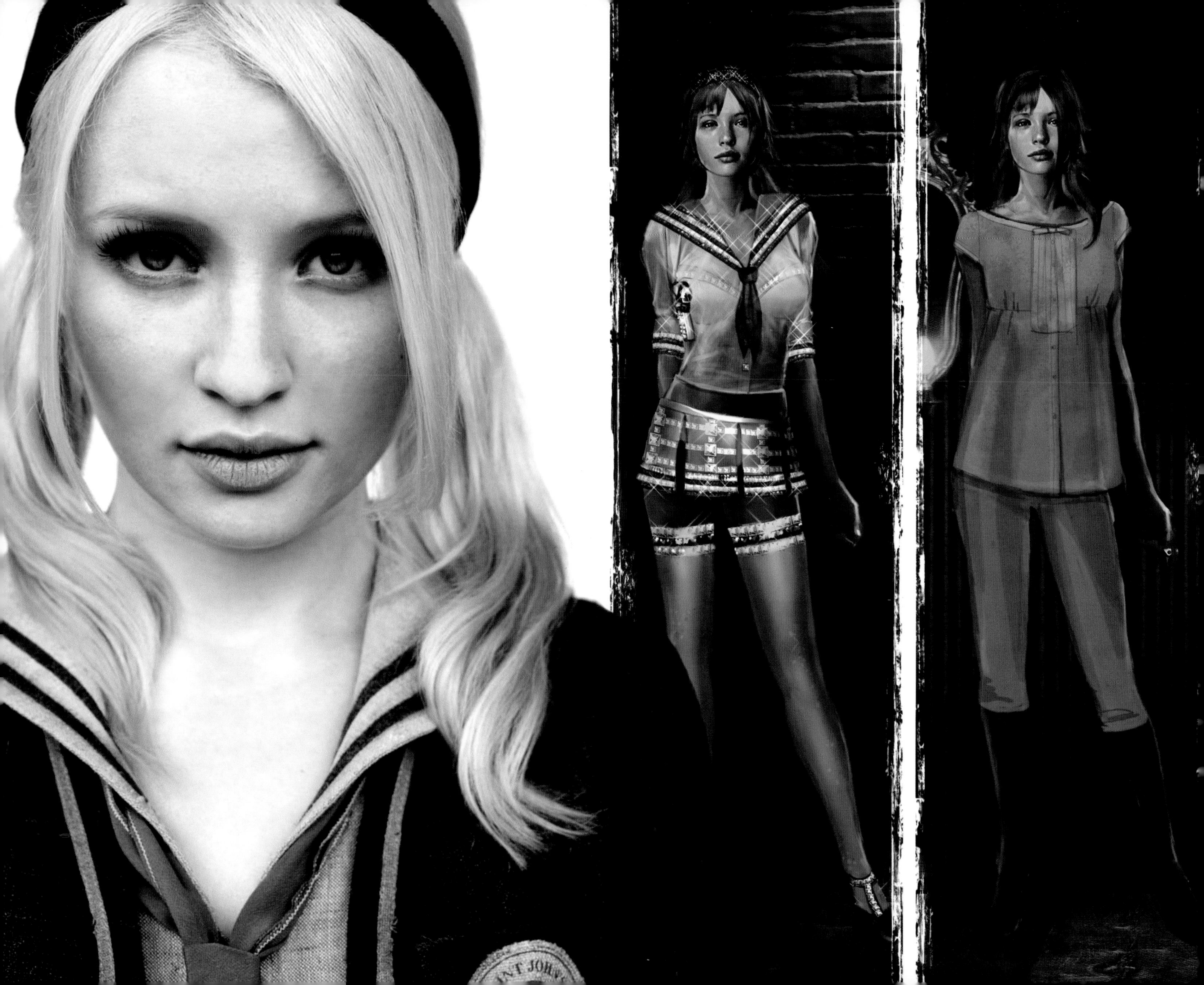

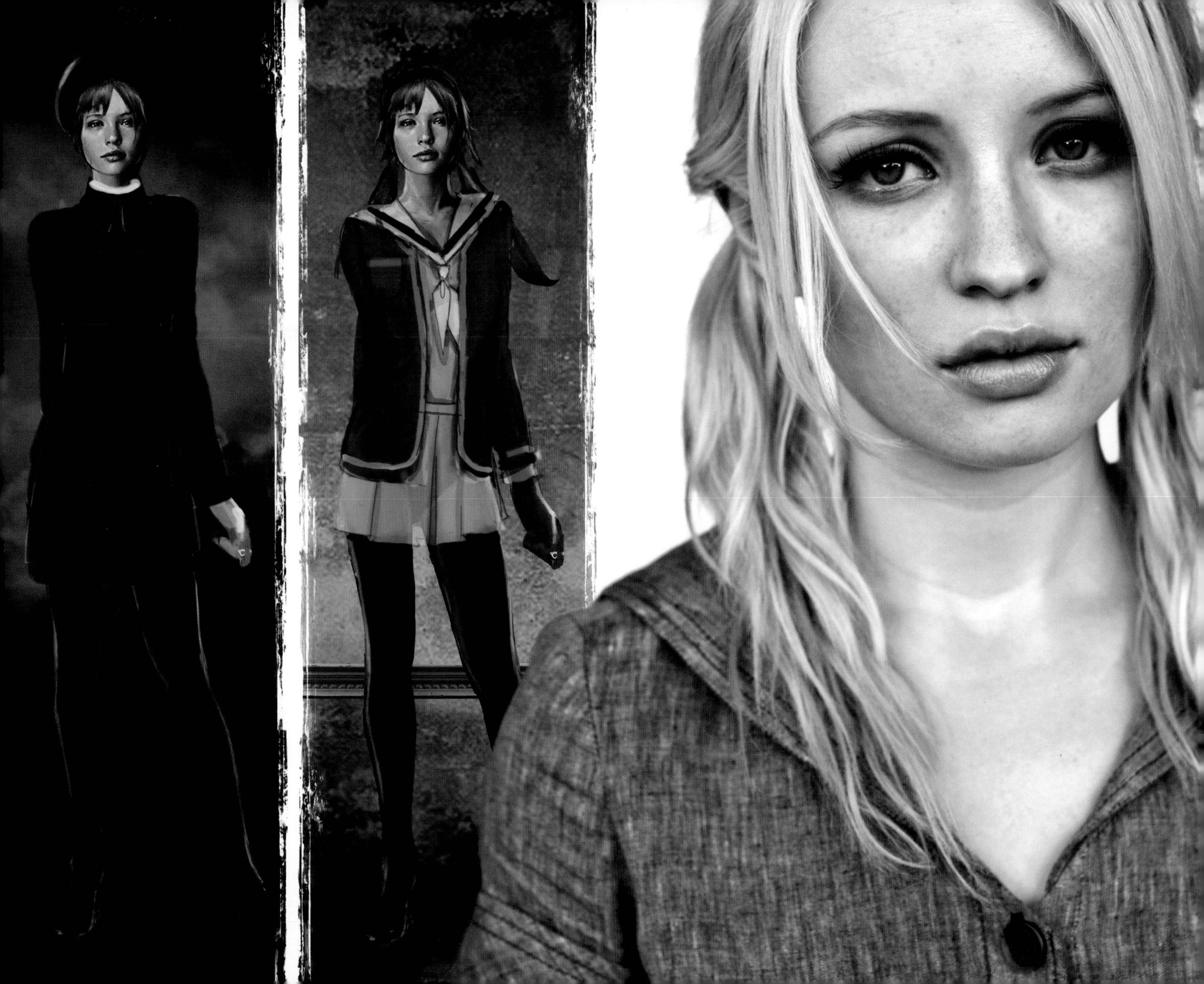

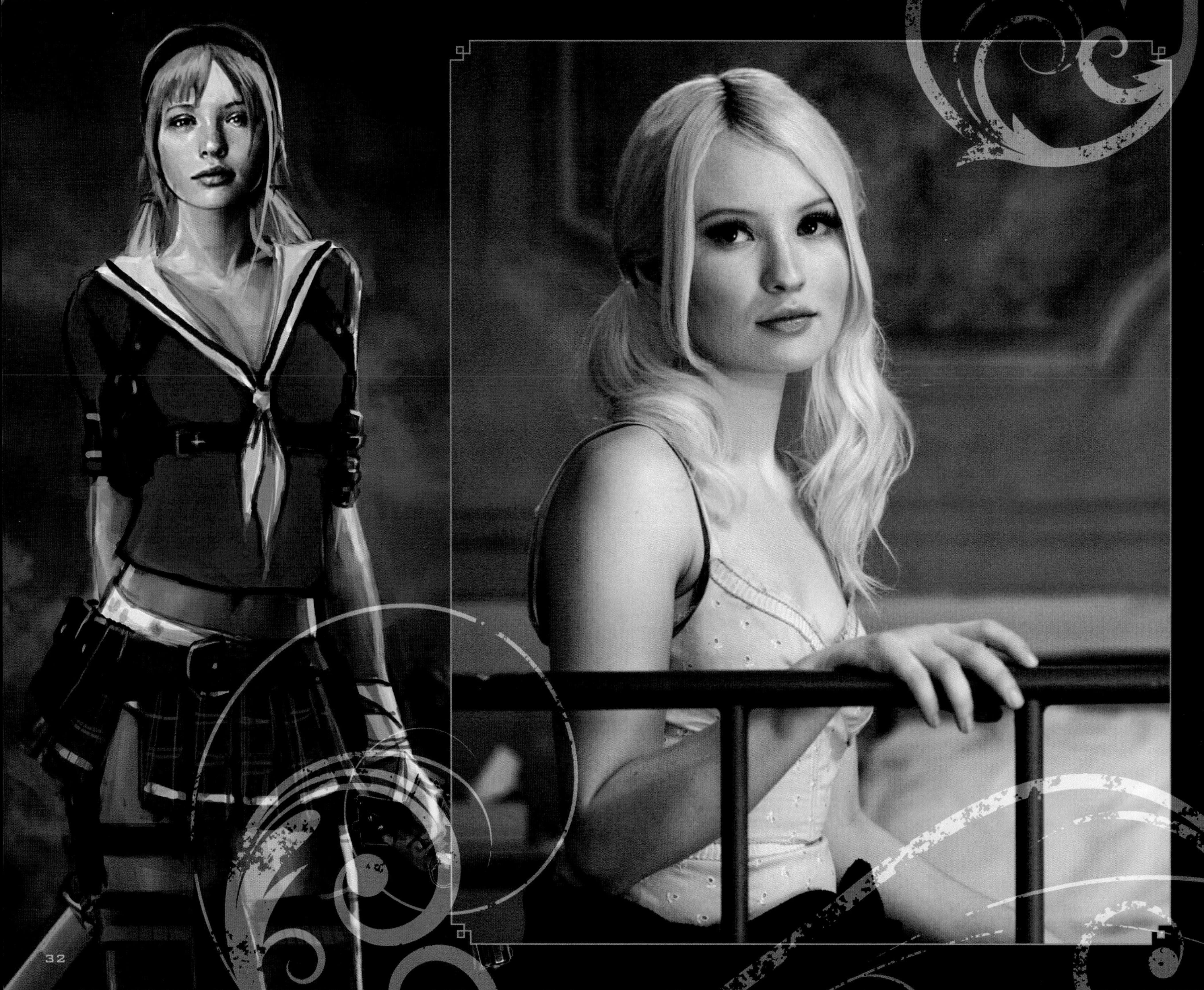

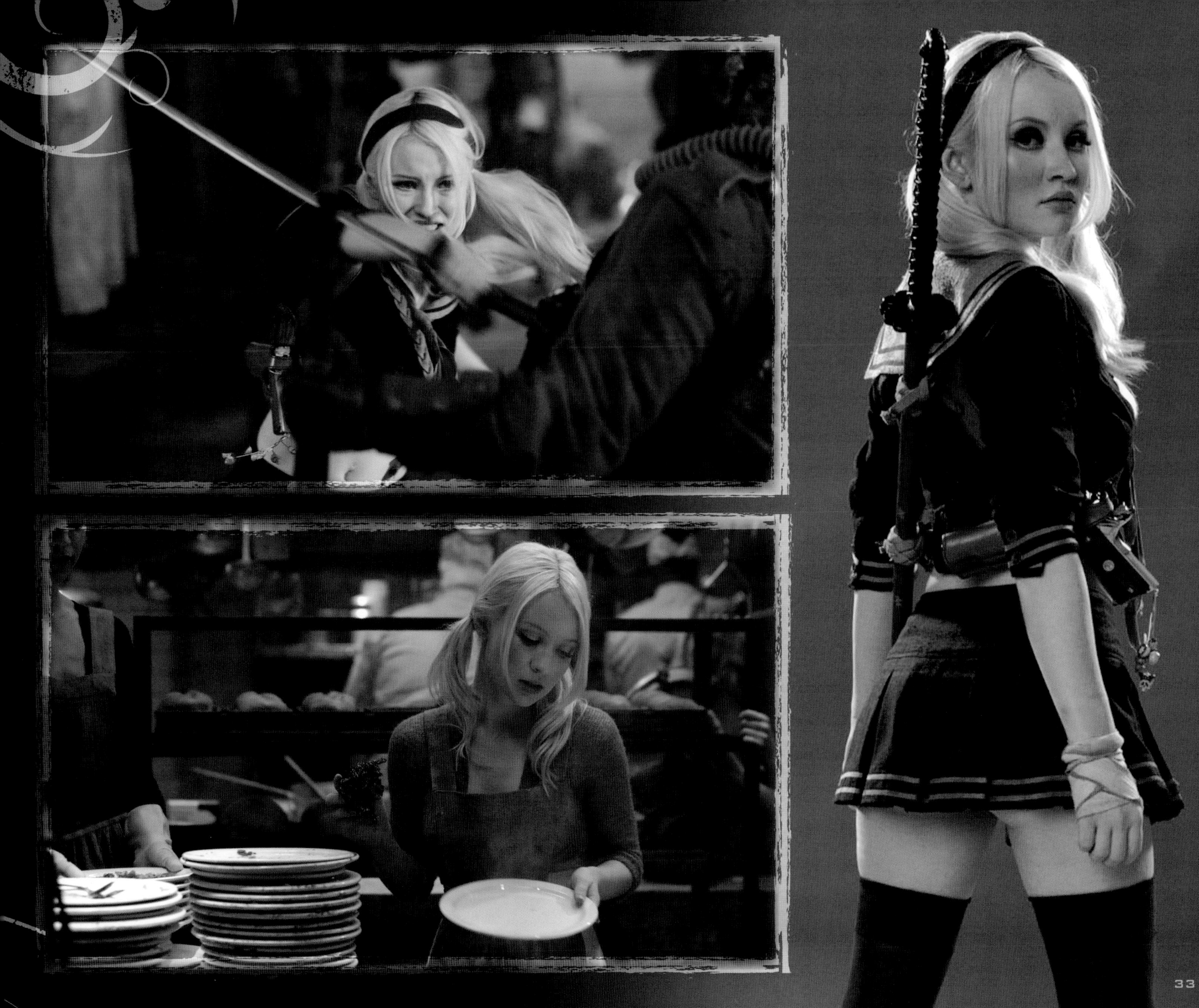

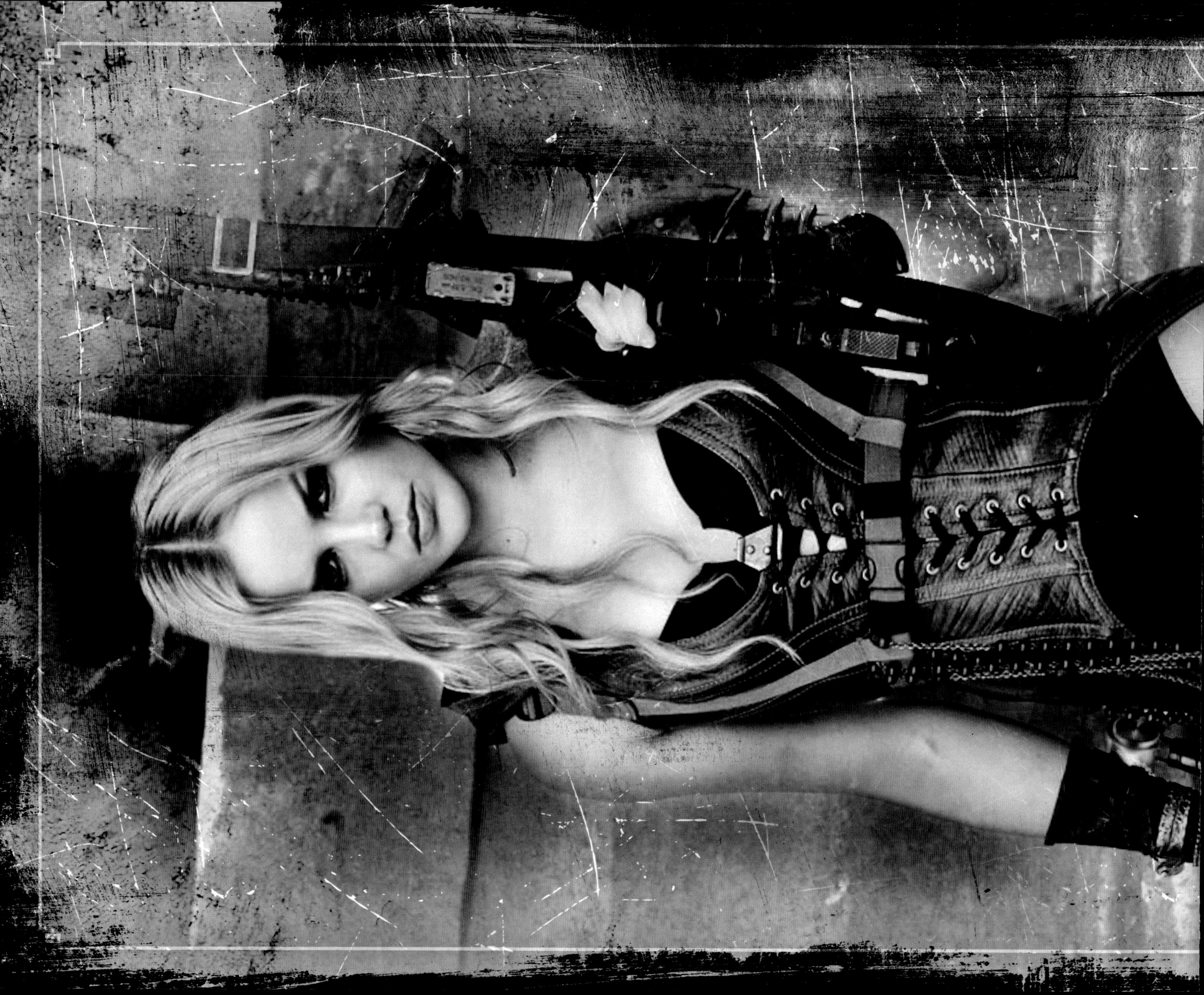

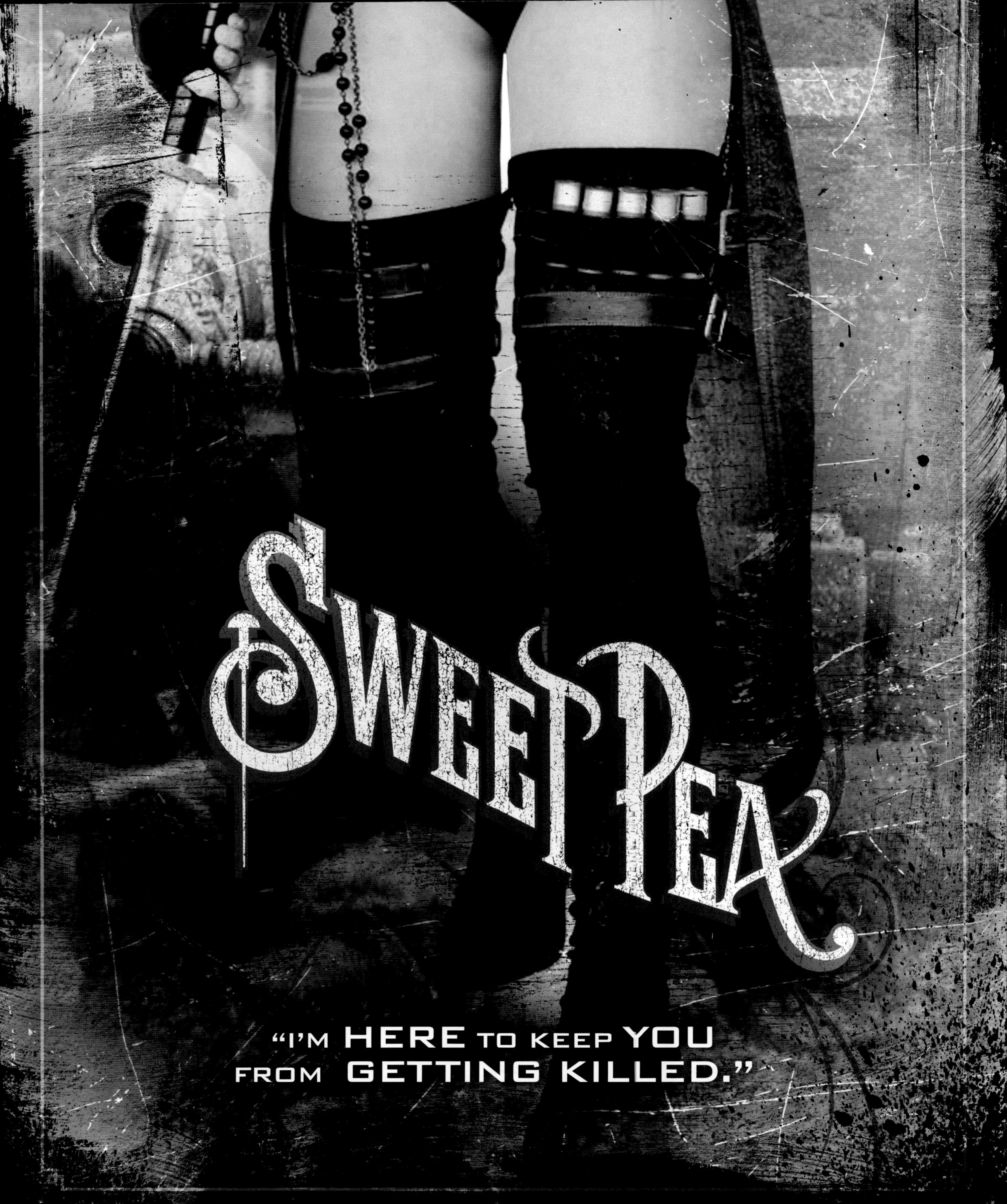
SWEET PEA
"I'M HERE TO KEEP YOU
FROM GETTING KILLED."

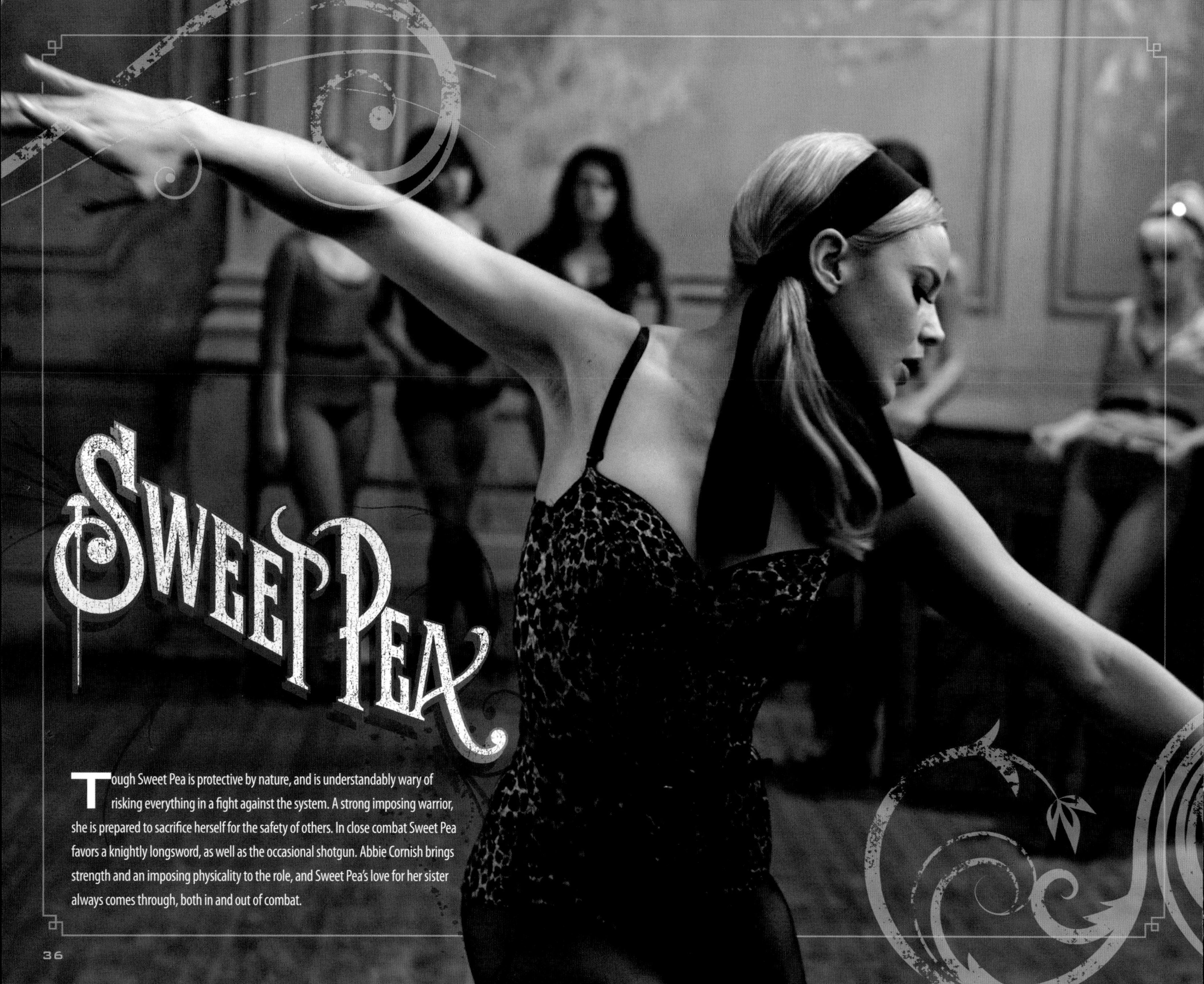

Sweet Pea

Tough Sweet Pea is protective by nature, and is understandably wary of risking everything in a fight against the system. A strong imposing warrior, she is prepared to sacrifice herself for the safety of others. In close combat Sweet Pea favors a knightly longsword, as well as the occasional shotgun. Abbie Cornish brings strength and an imposing physicality to the role, and Sweet Pea's love for her sister always comes through, both in and out of combat.

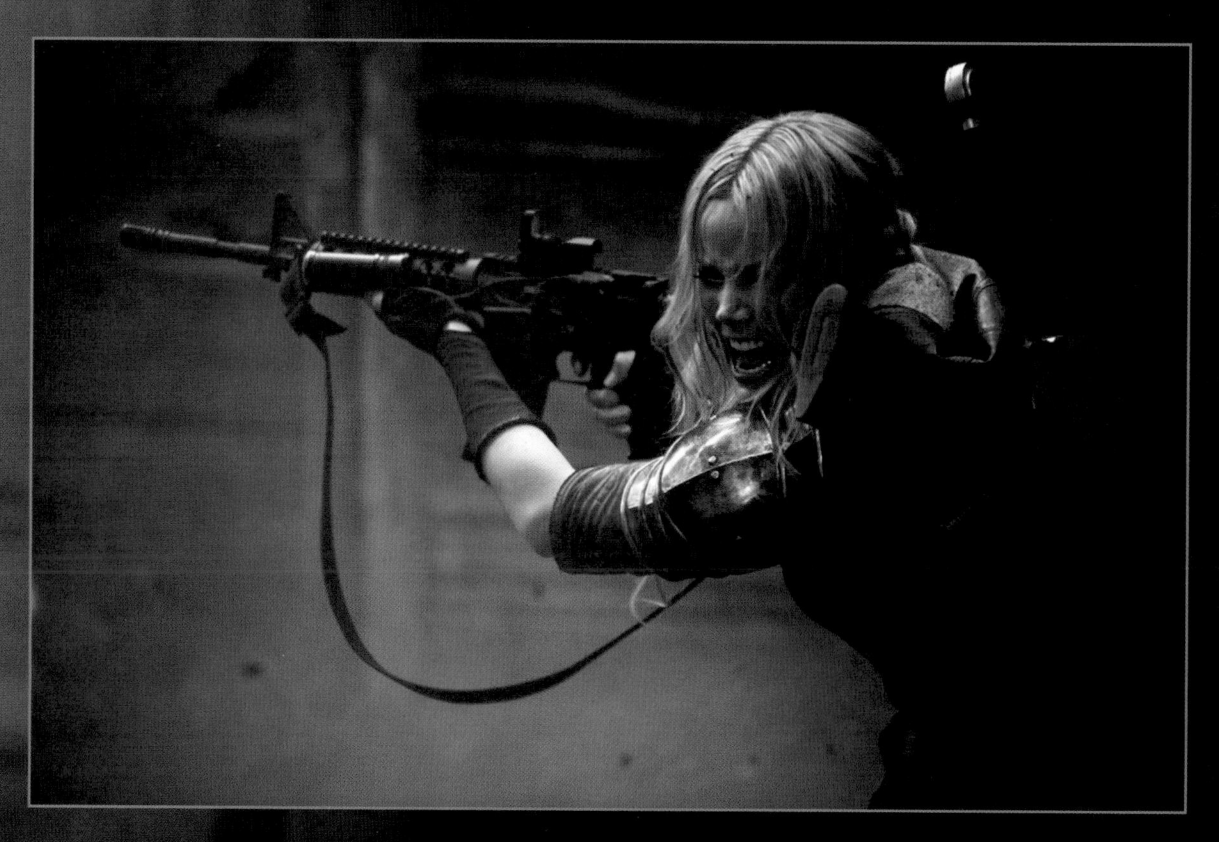

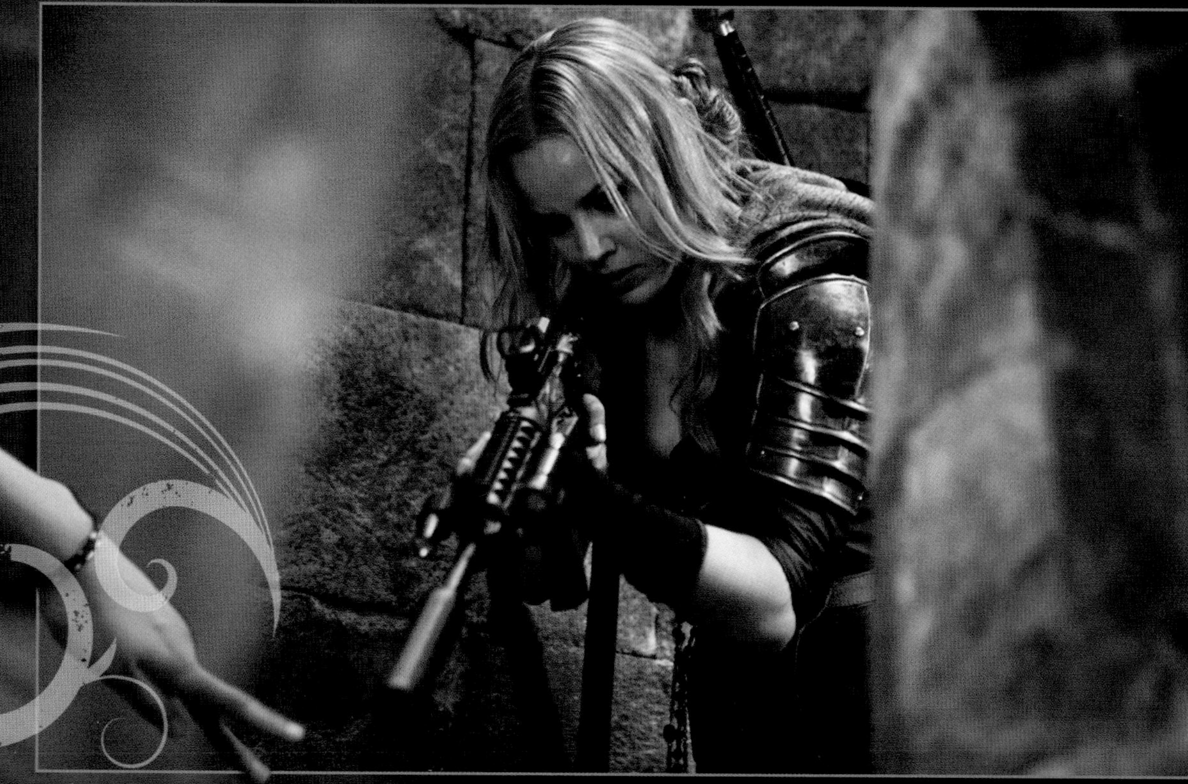

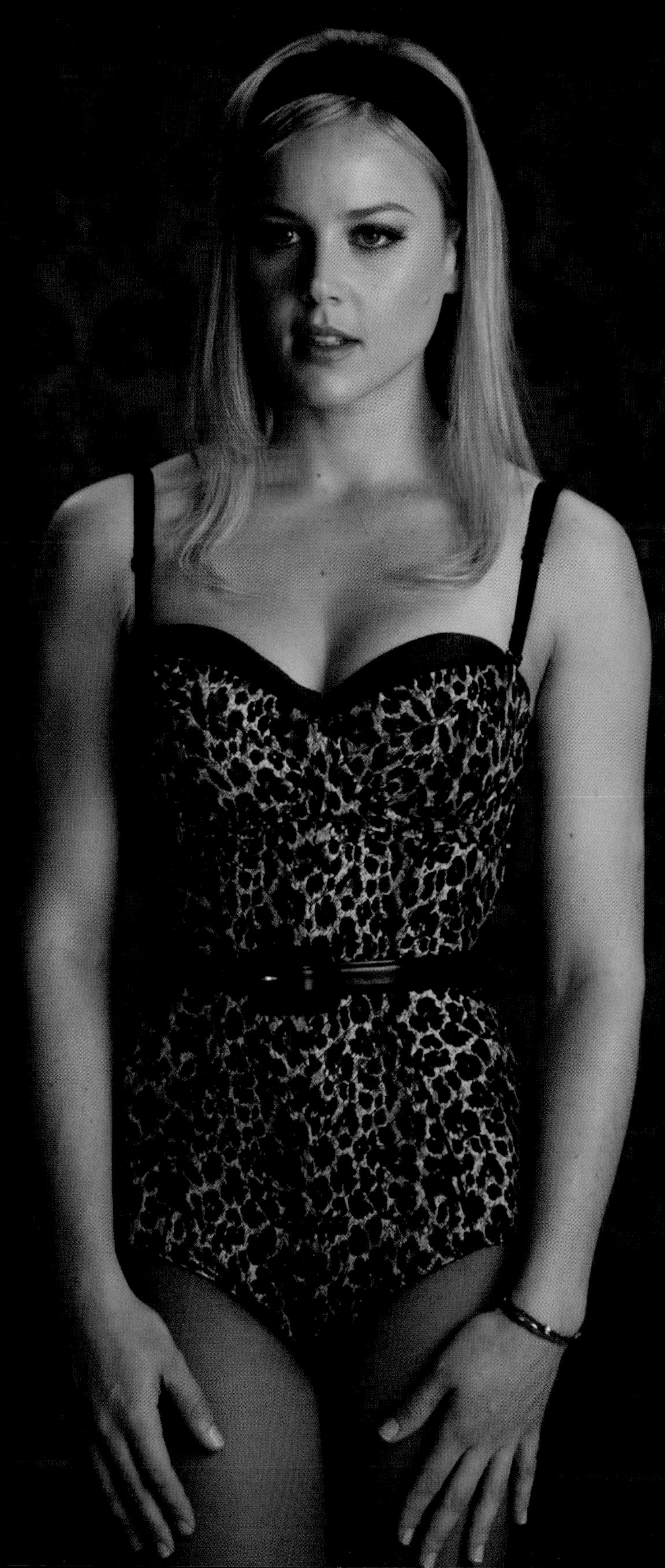

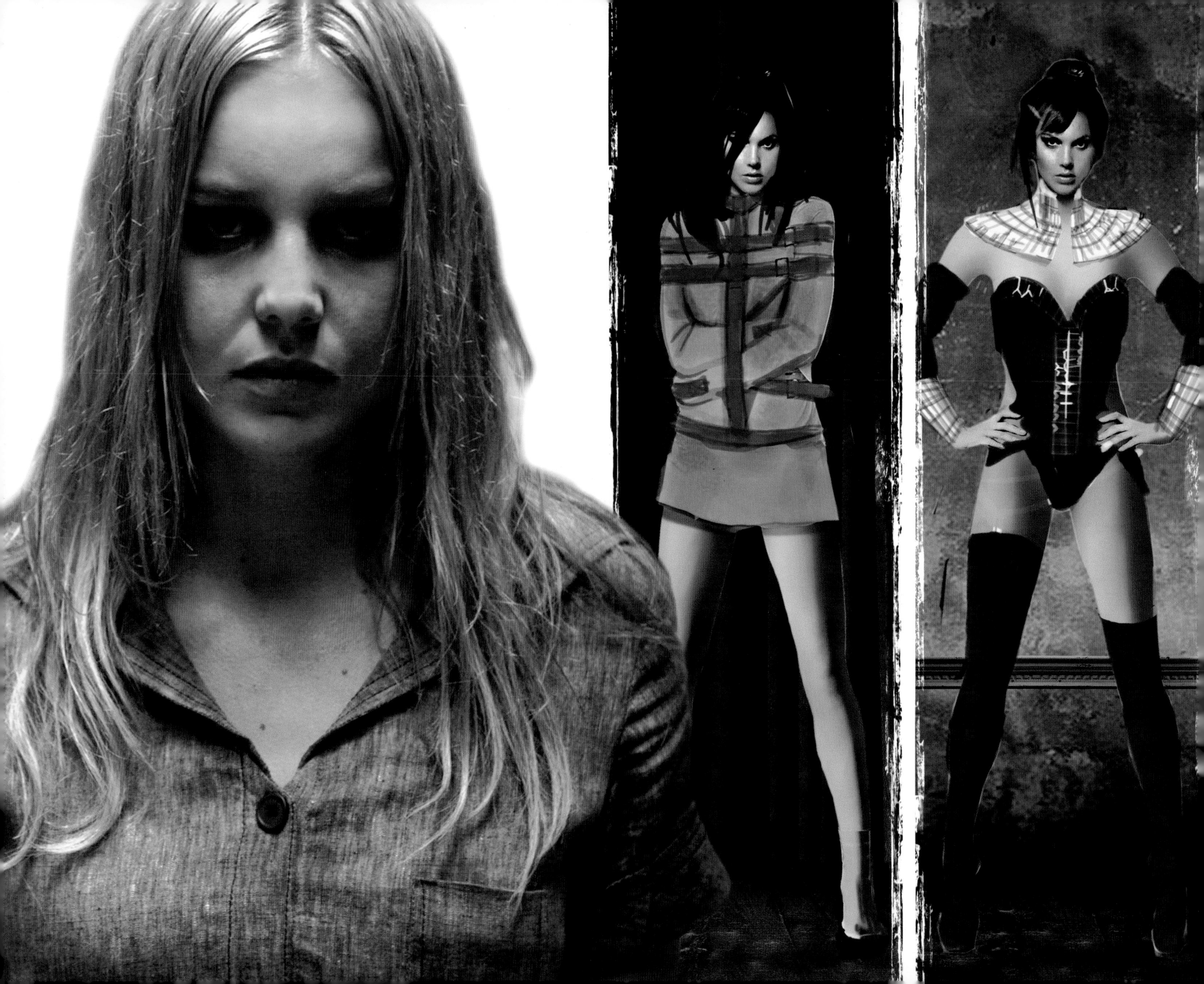

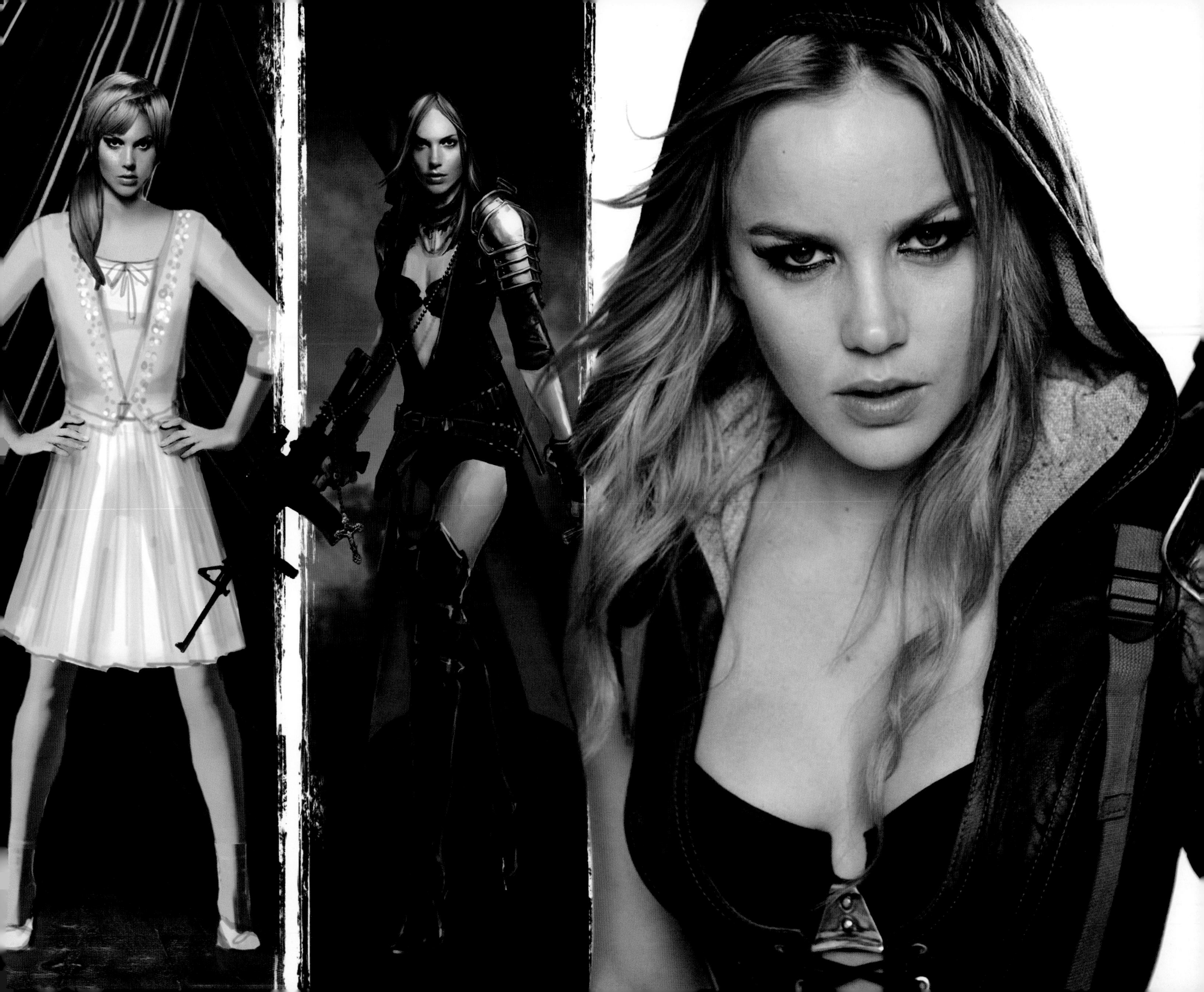

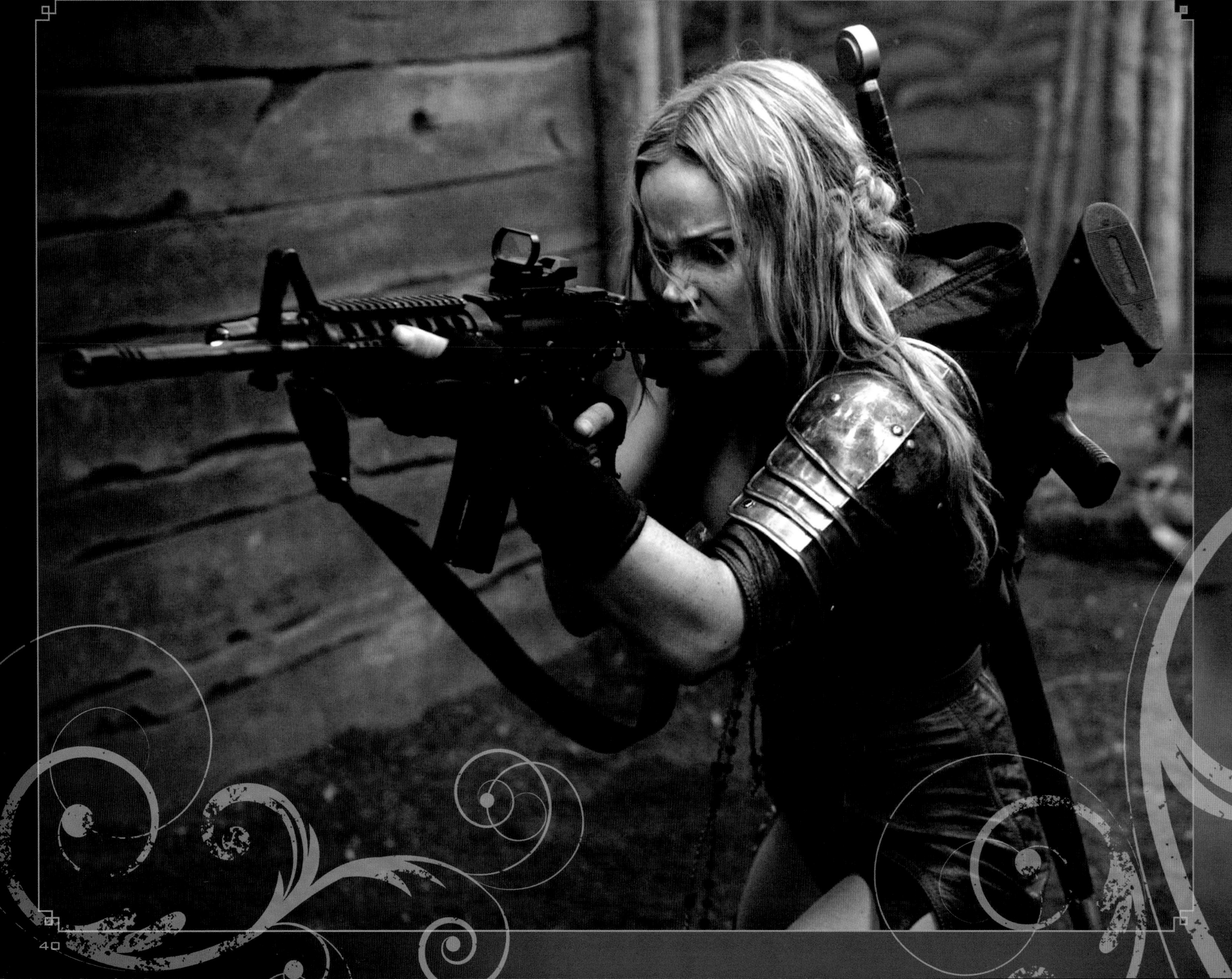

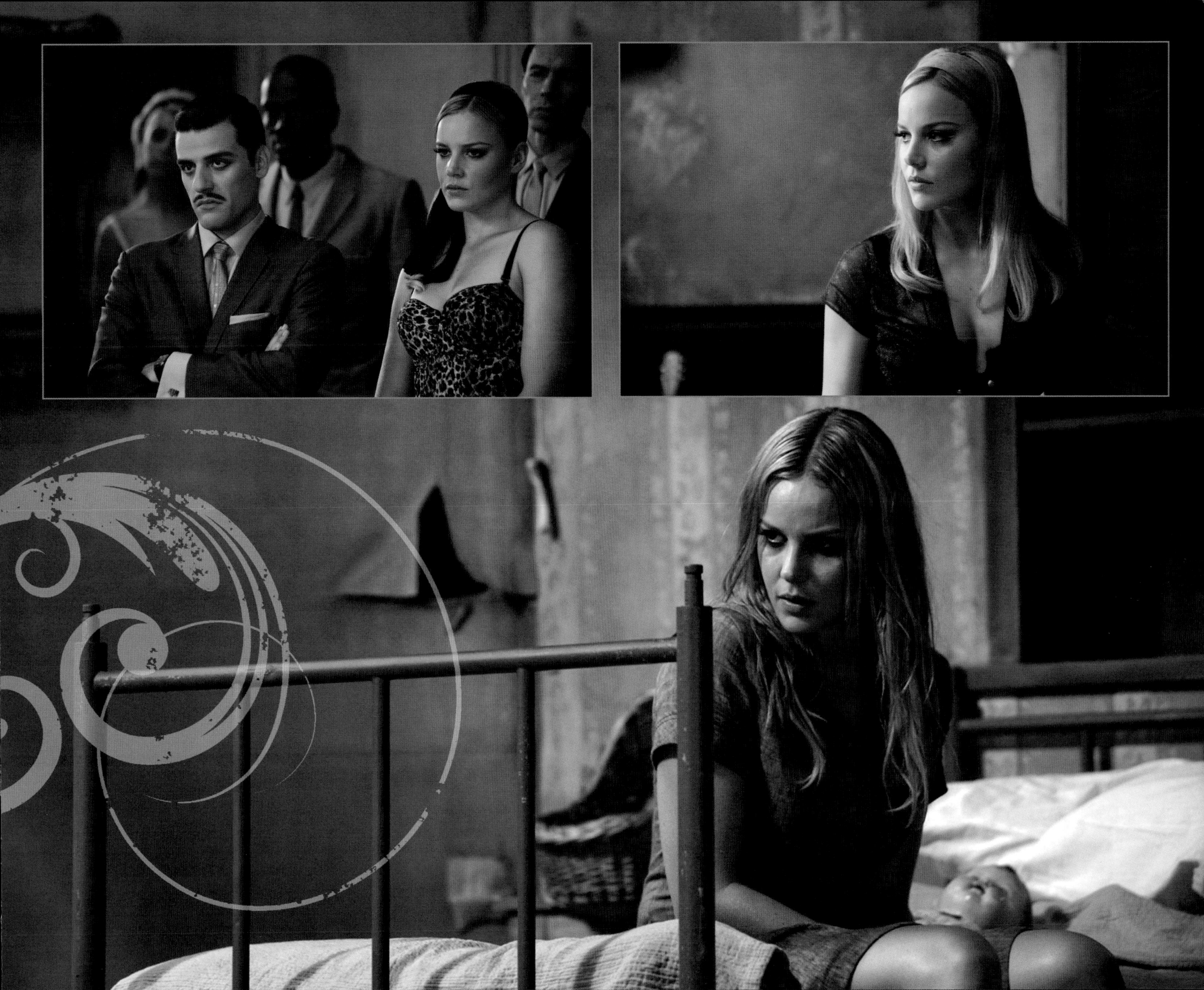

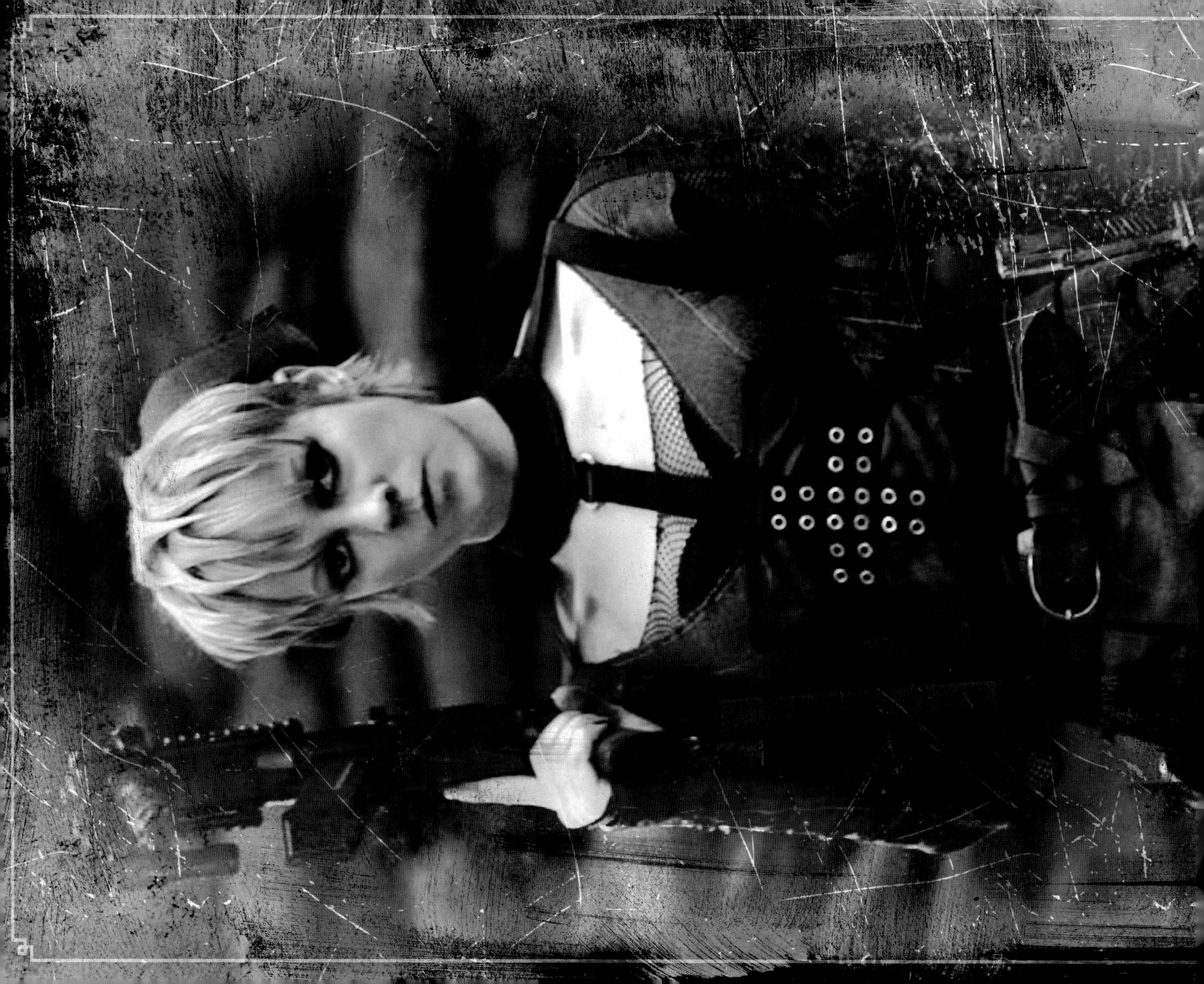

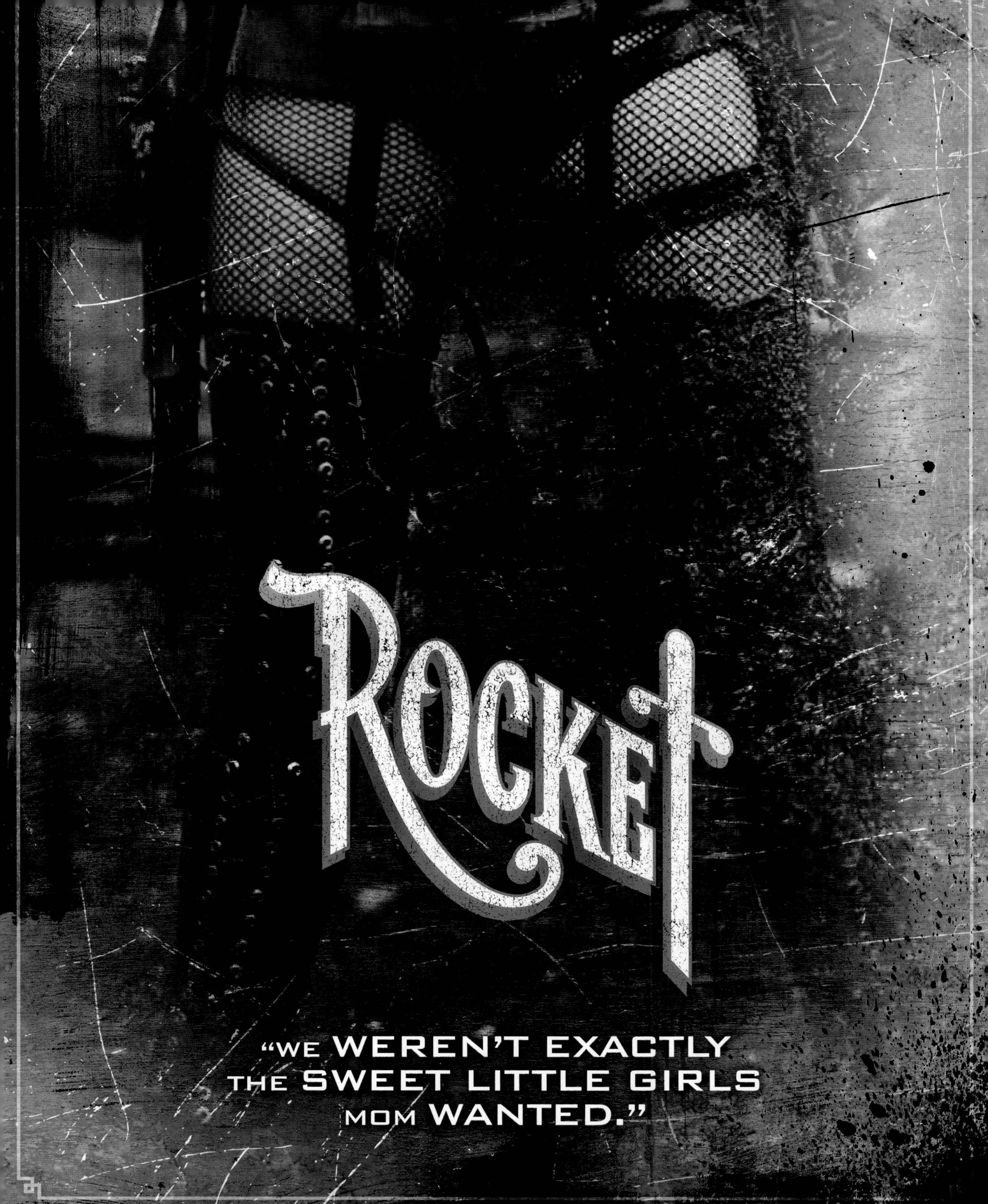
ROCKET
"WE WEREN'T EXACTLY
THE SWEET LITTLE GIRLS
MOM WANTED."

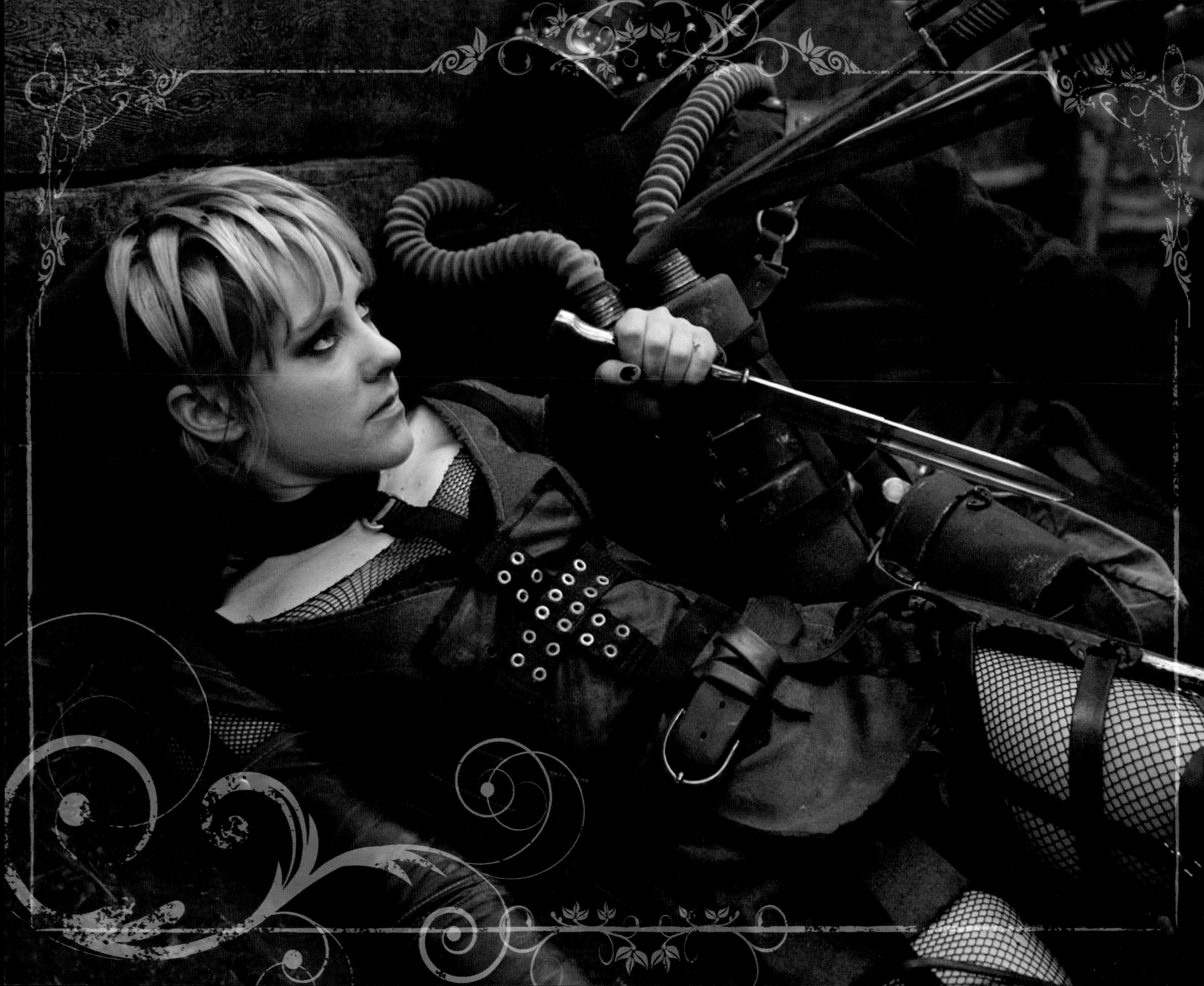

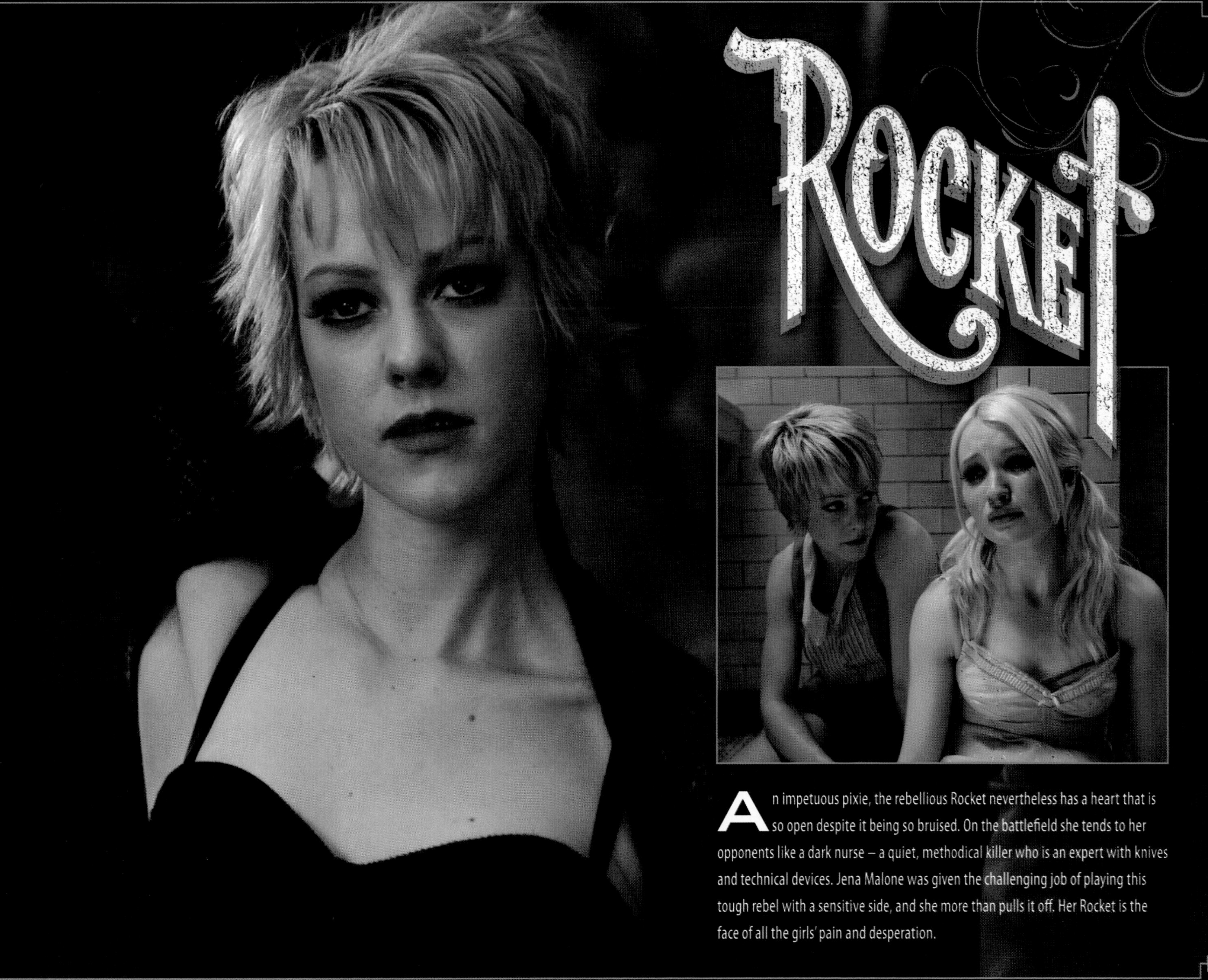

Rocket

An impetuous pixie, the rebellious Rocket nevertheless has a heart that is so open despite it being so bruised. On the battlefield she tends to her opponents like a dark nurse – a quiet, methodical killer who is an expert with knives and technical devices. Jena Malone was given the challenging job of playing this tough rebel with a sensitive side, and she more than pulls it off. Her Rocket is the face of all the girls' pain and desperation.

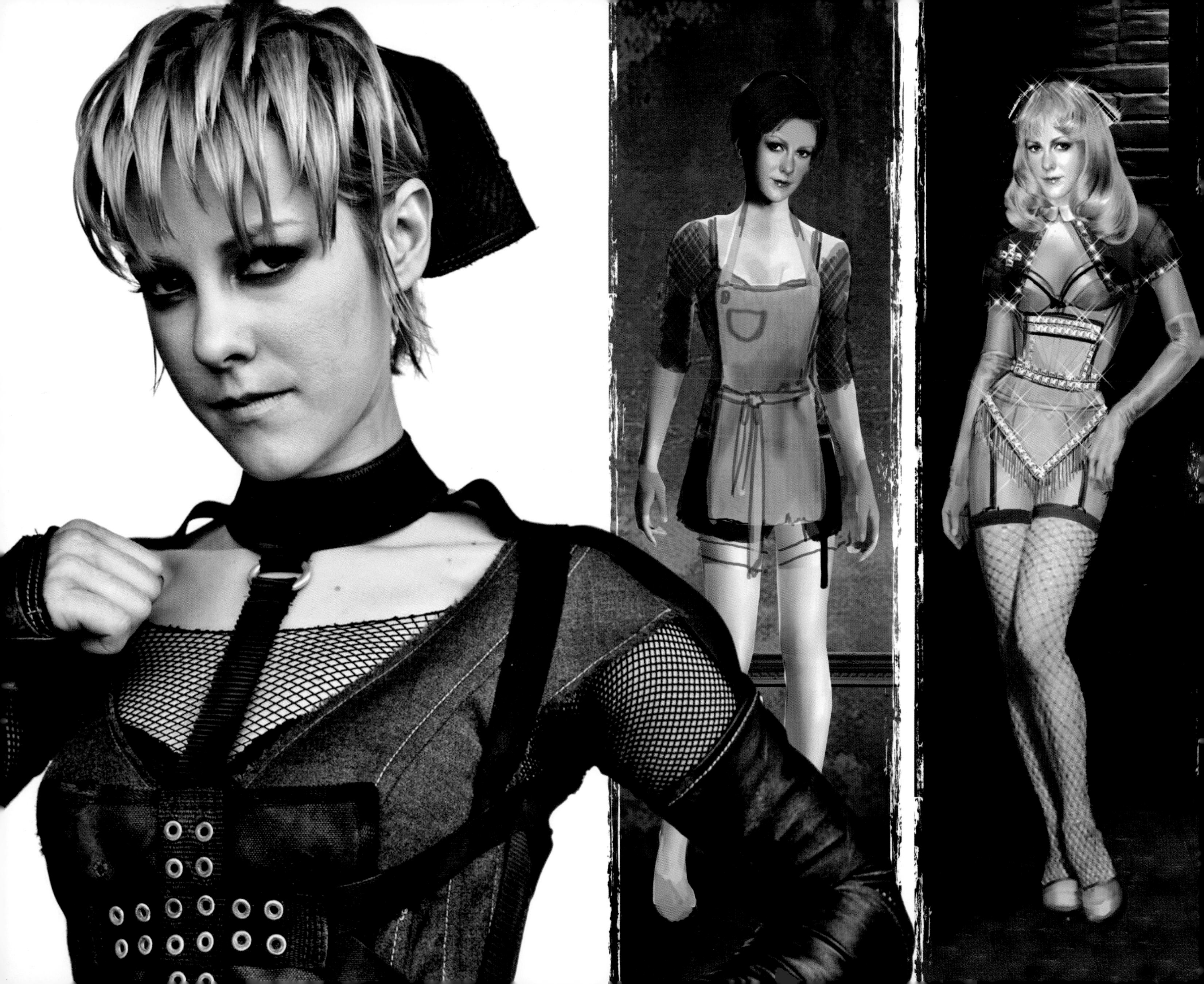

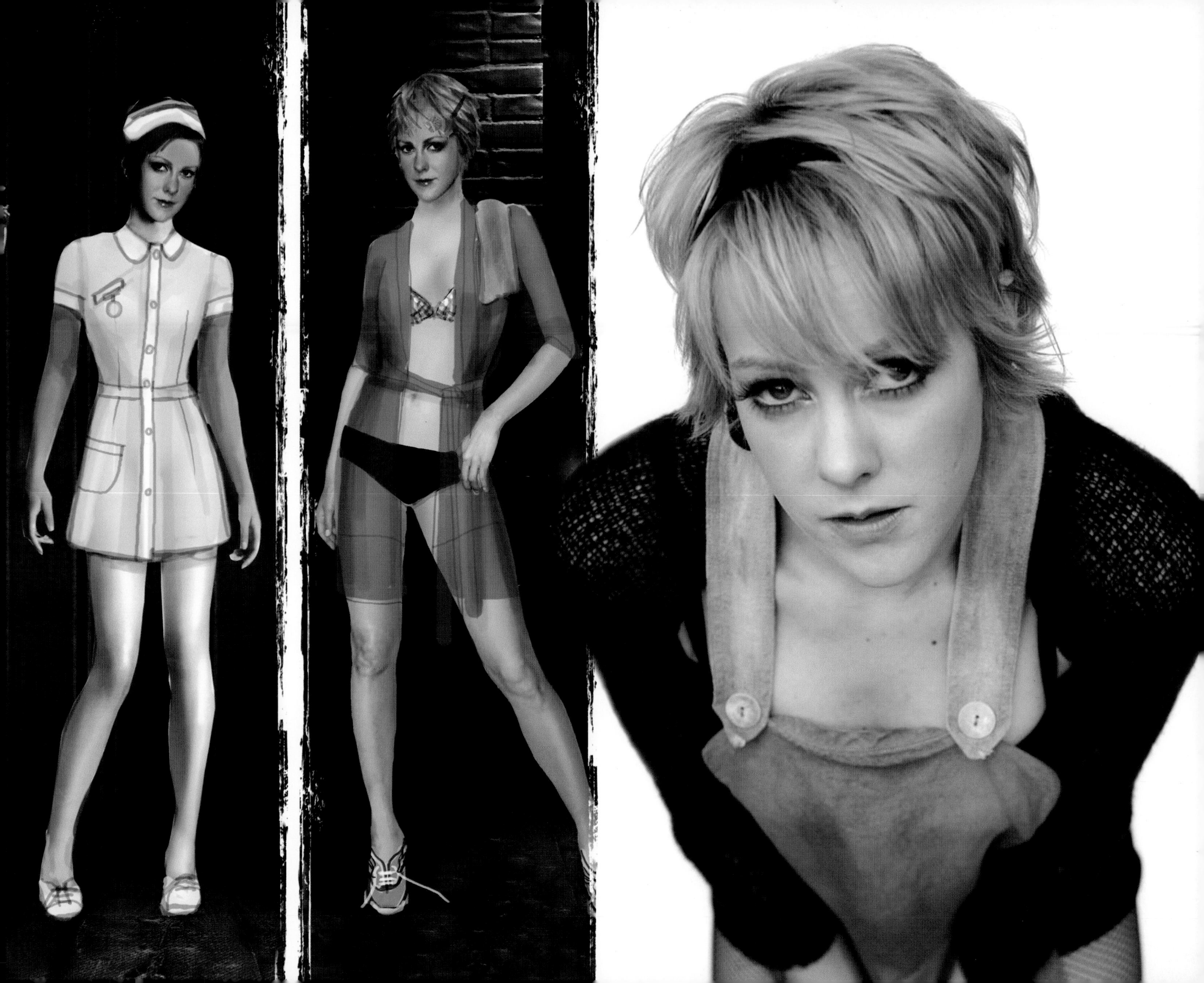

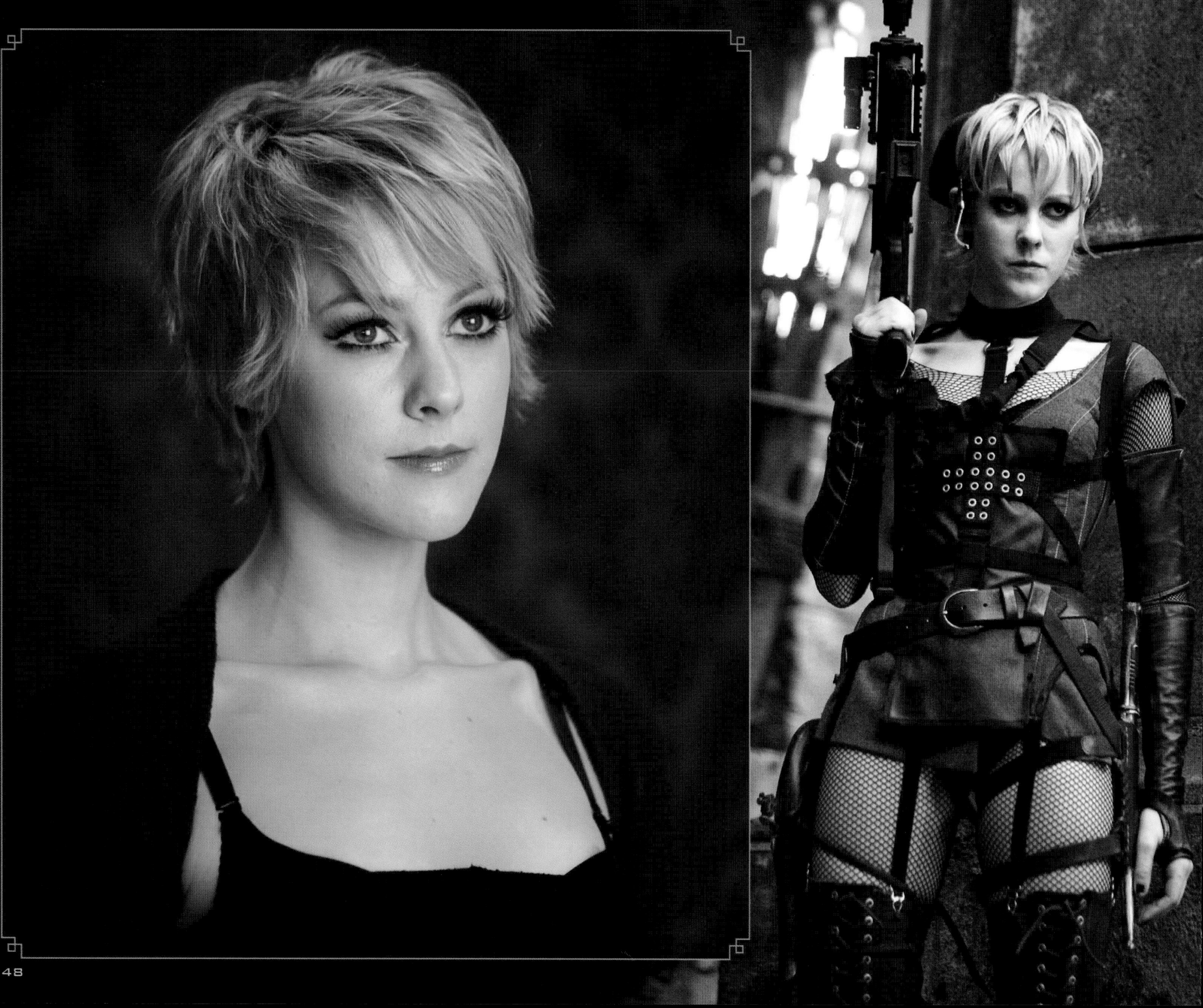

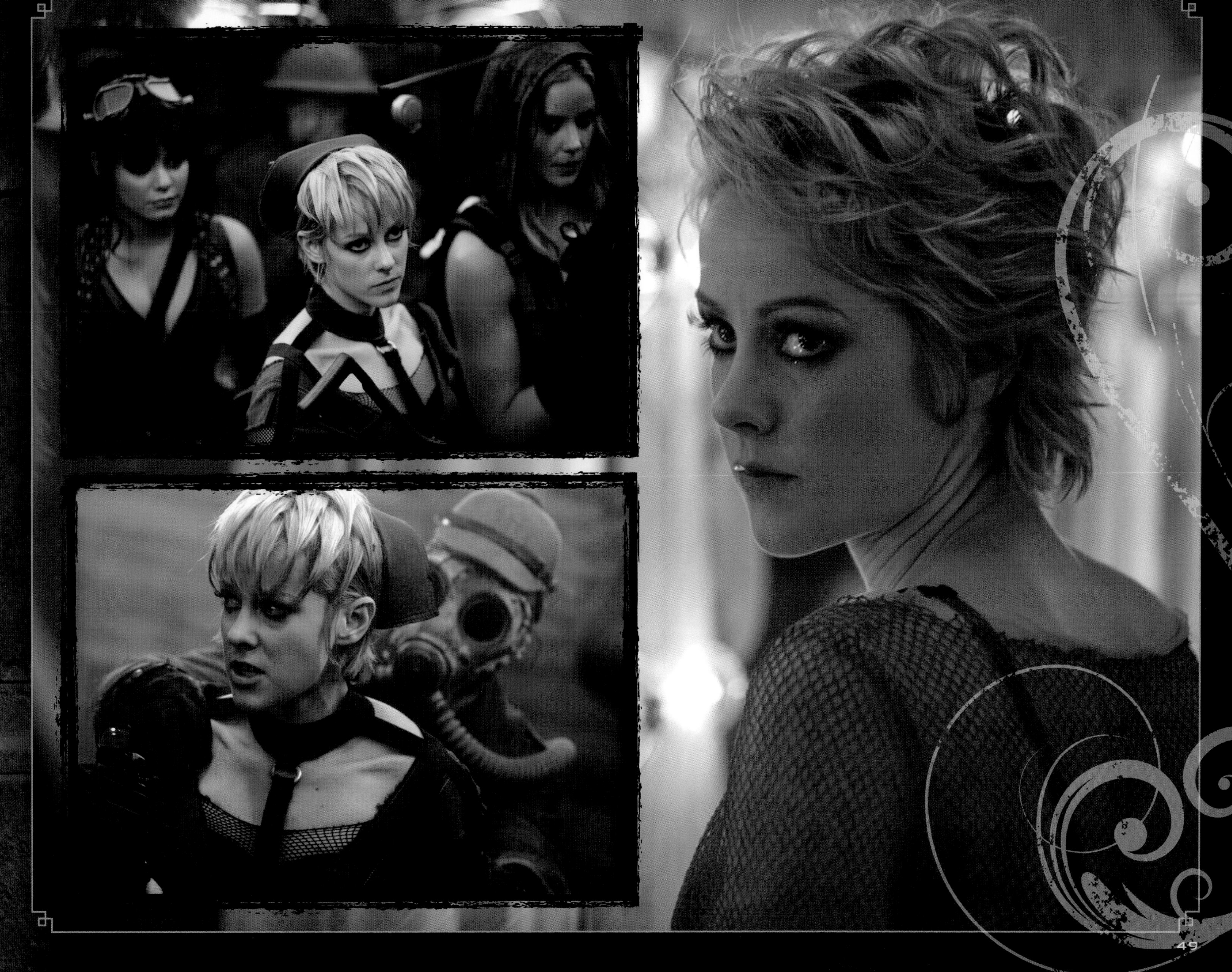

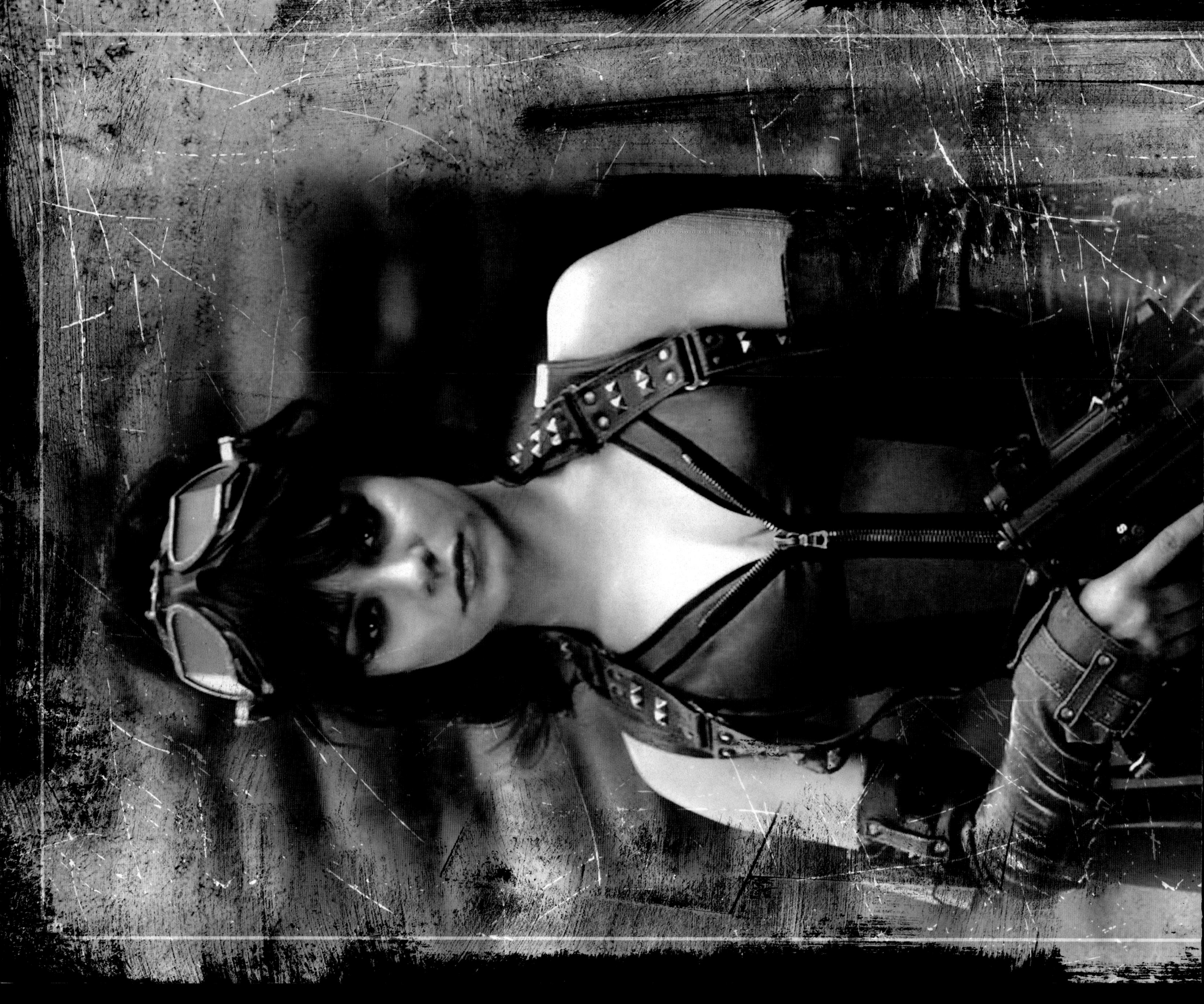

BLONDIE

"EAT LEAD YOU UGLY MOTHERF#*%KERS!"

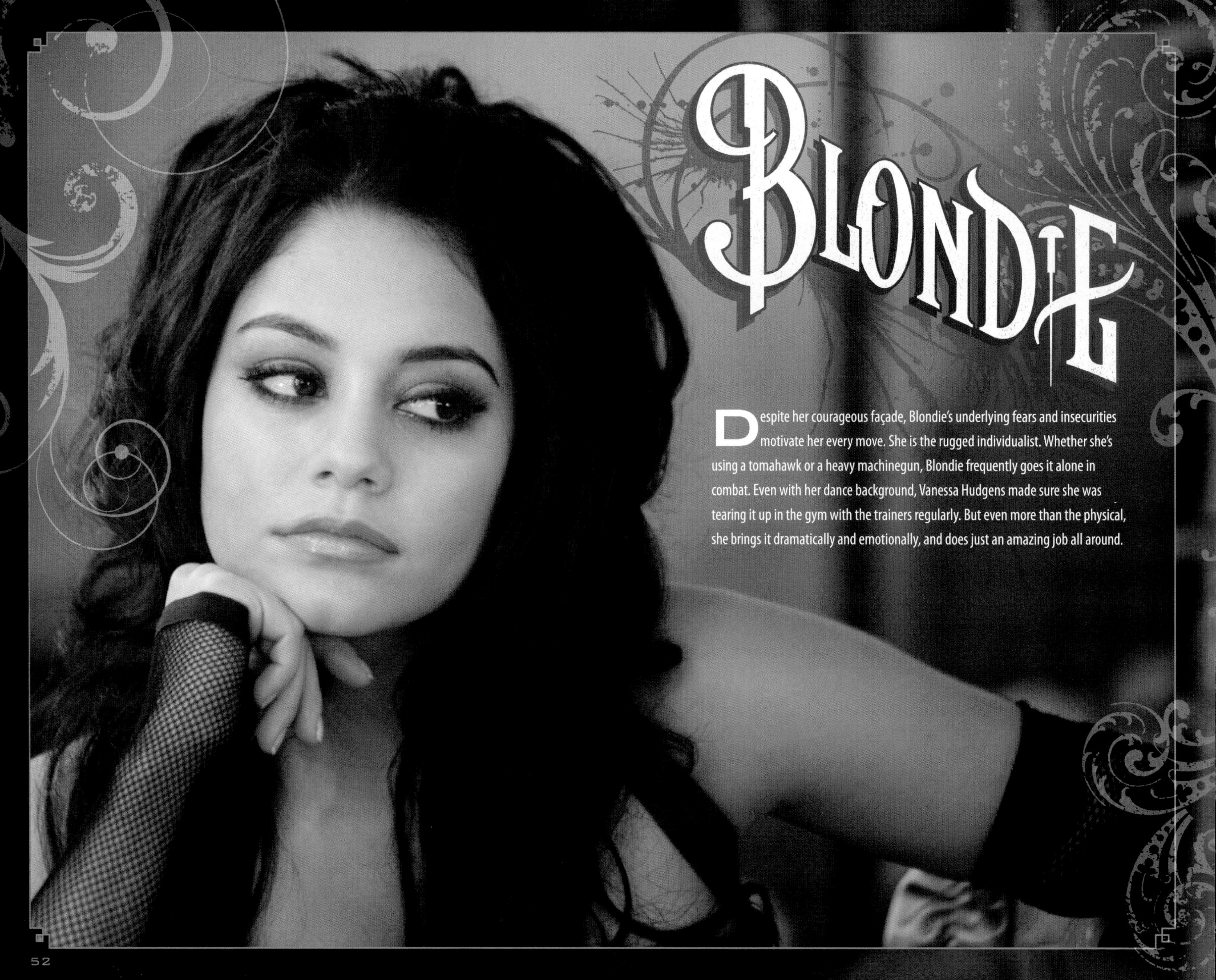

BLONDIE

Despite her courageous façade, Blondie's underlying fears and insecurities motivate her every move. She is the rugged individualist. Whether she's using a tomahawk or a heavy machinegun, Blondie frequently goes it alone in combat. Even with her dance background, Vanessa Hudgens made sure she was tearing it up in the gym with the trainers regularly. But even more than the physical, she brings it dramatically and emotionally, and does just an amazing job all around.

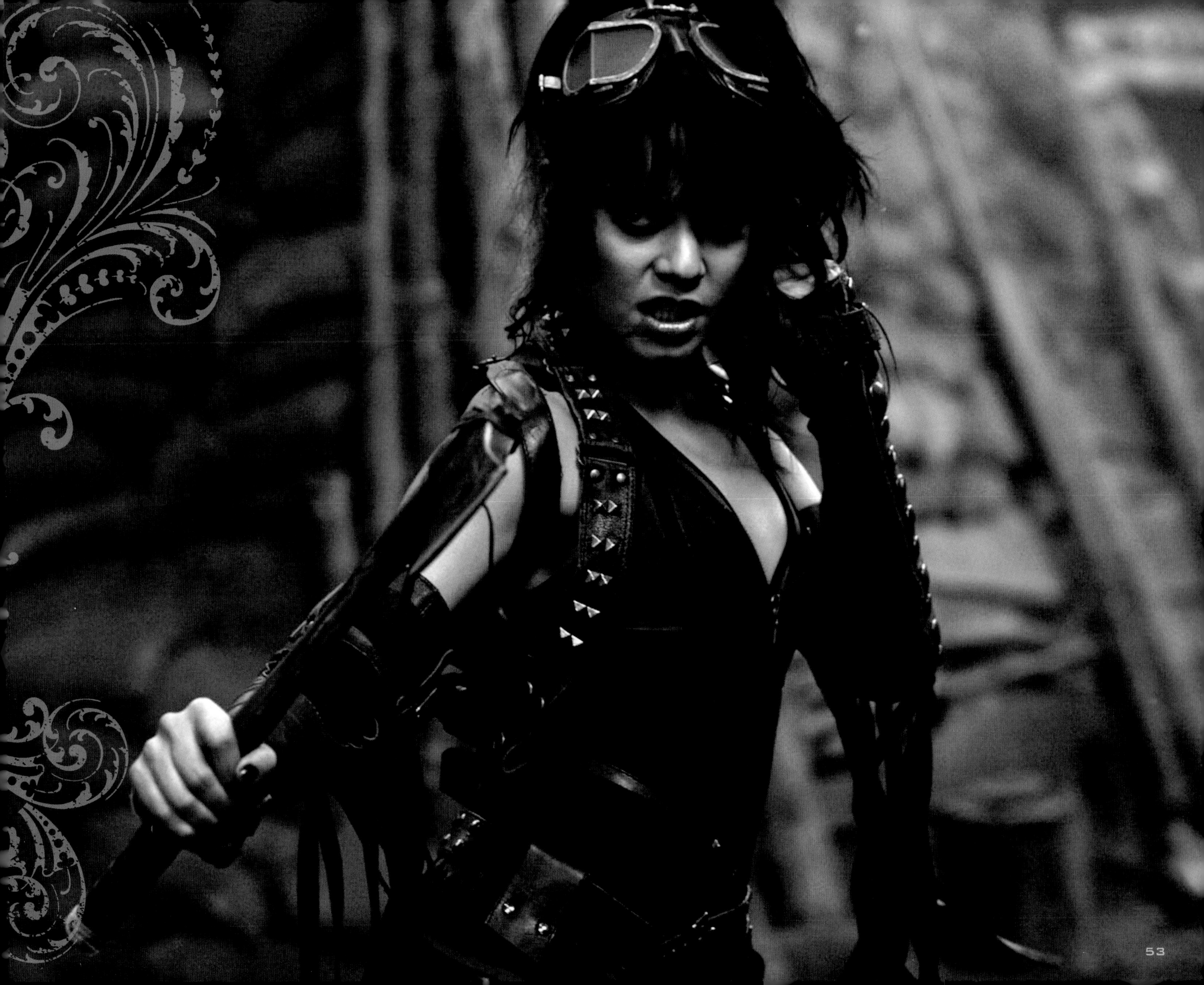

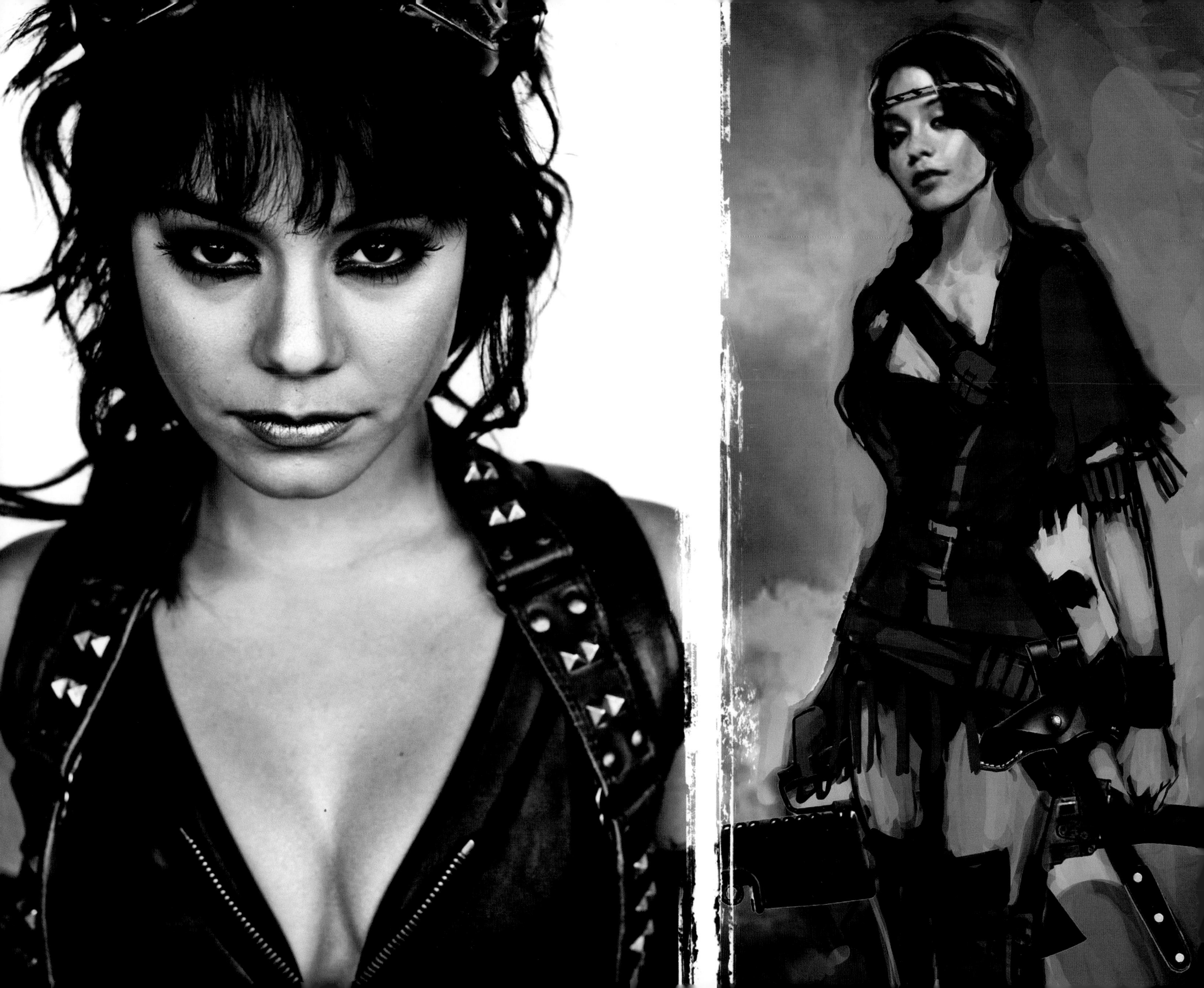

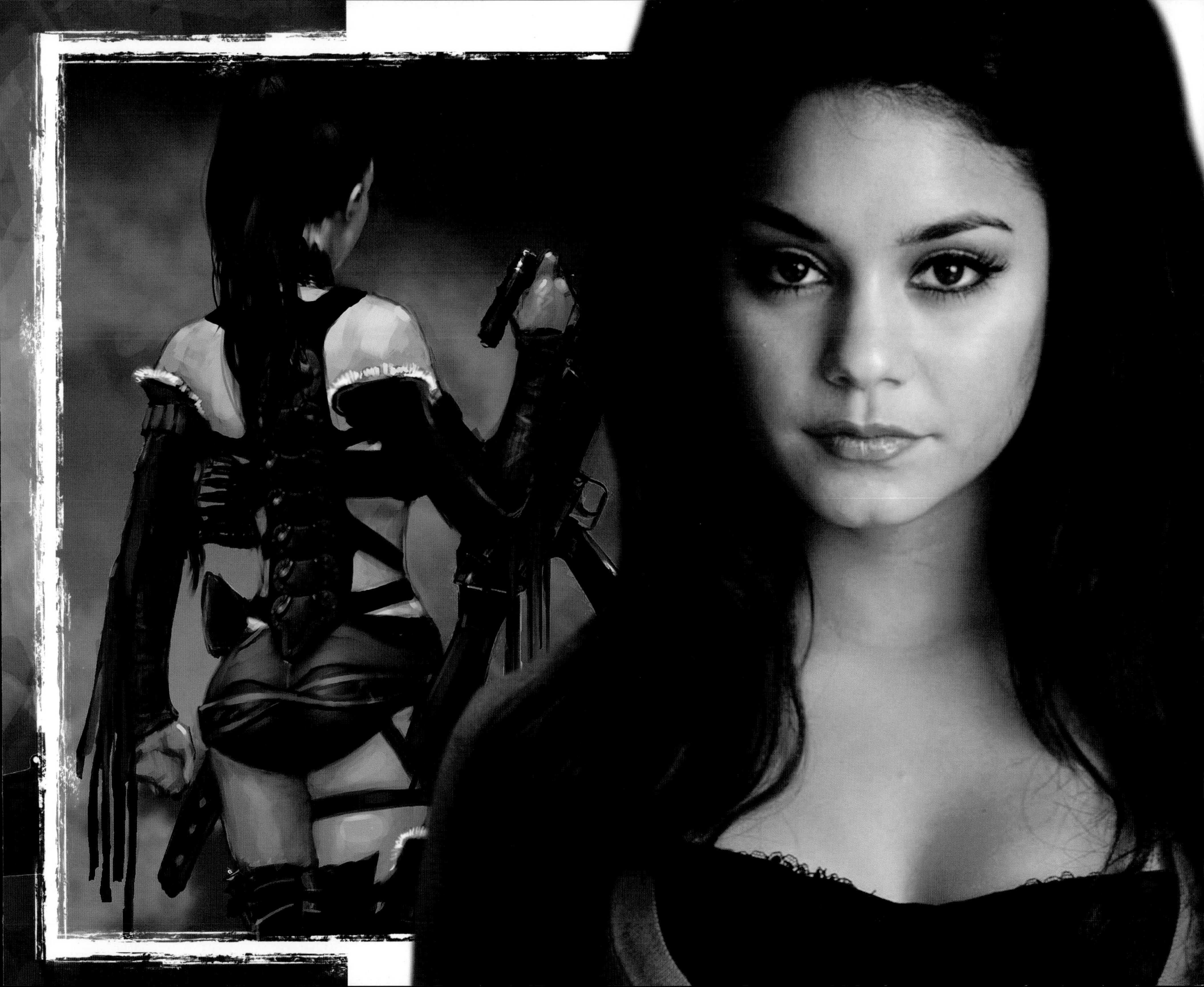

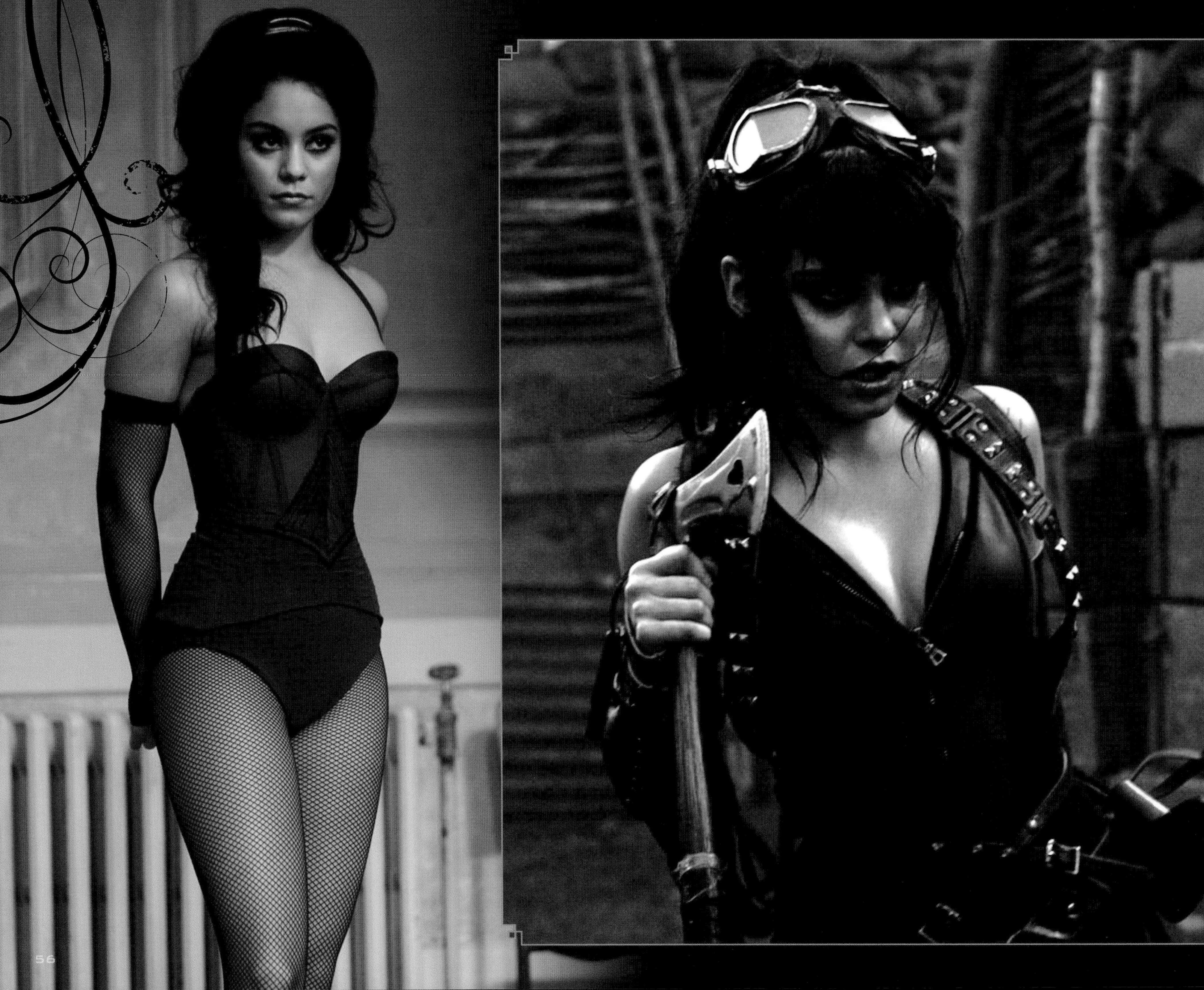

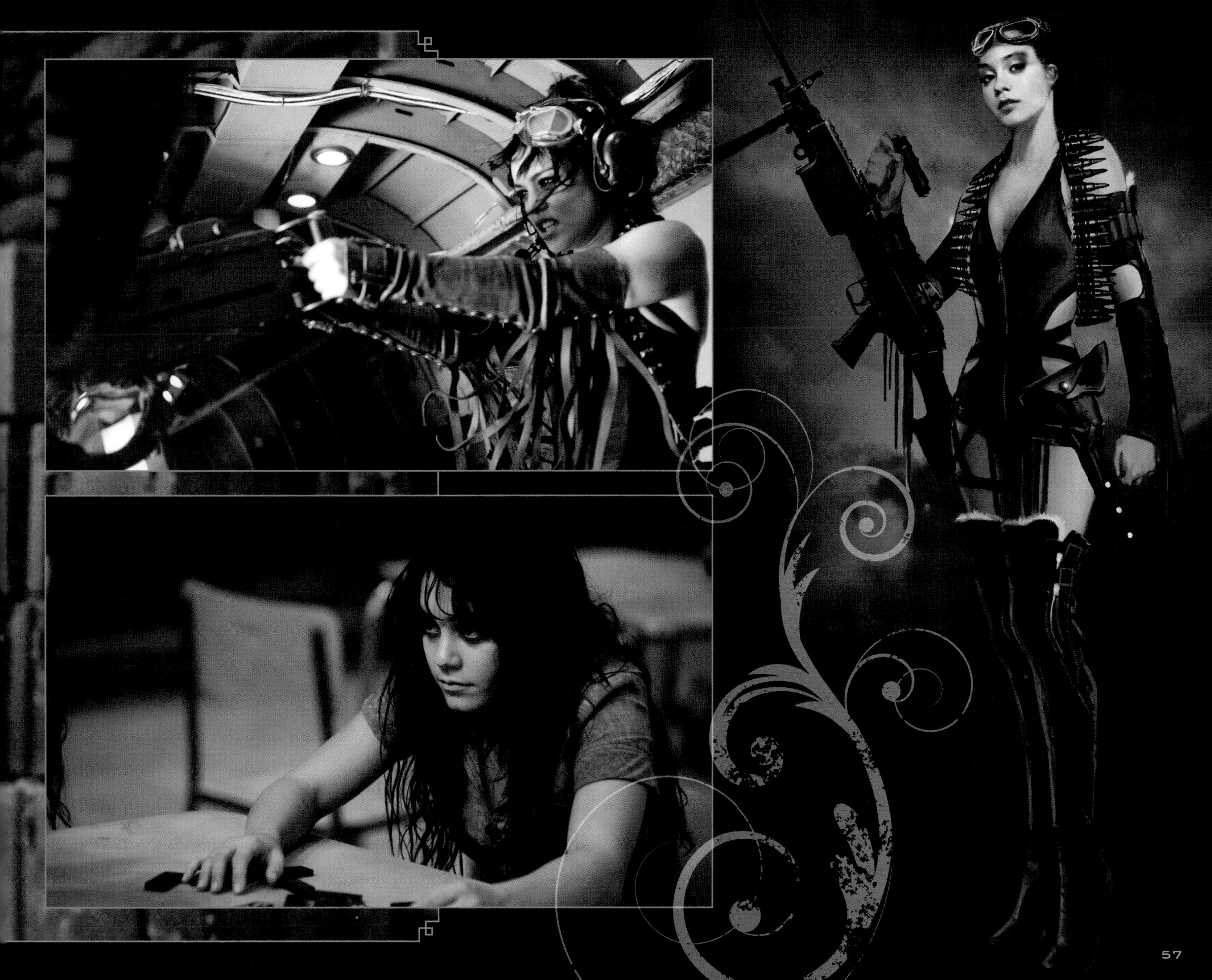

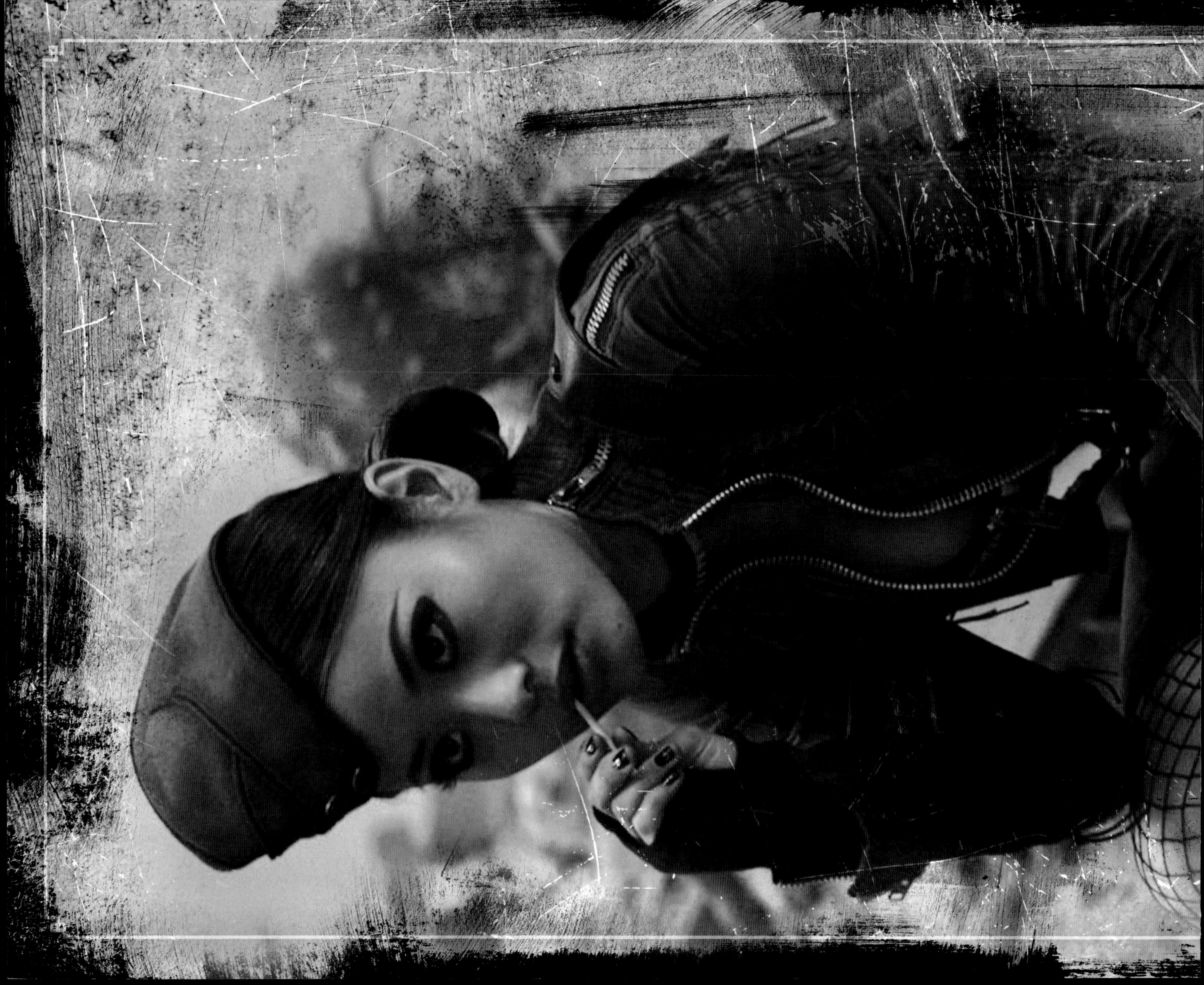

AMBER

"I LIKE IT."

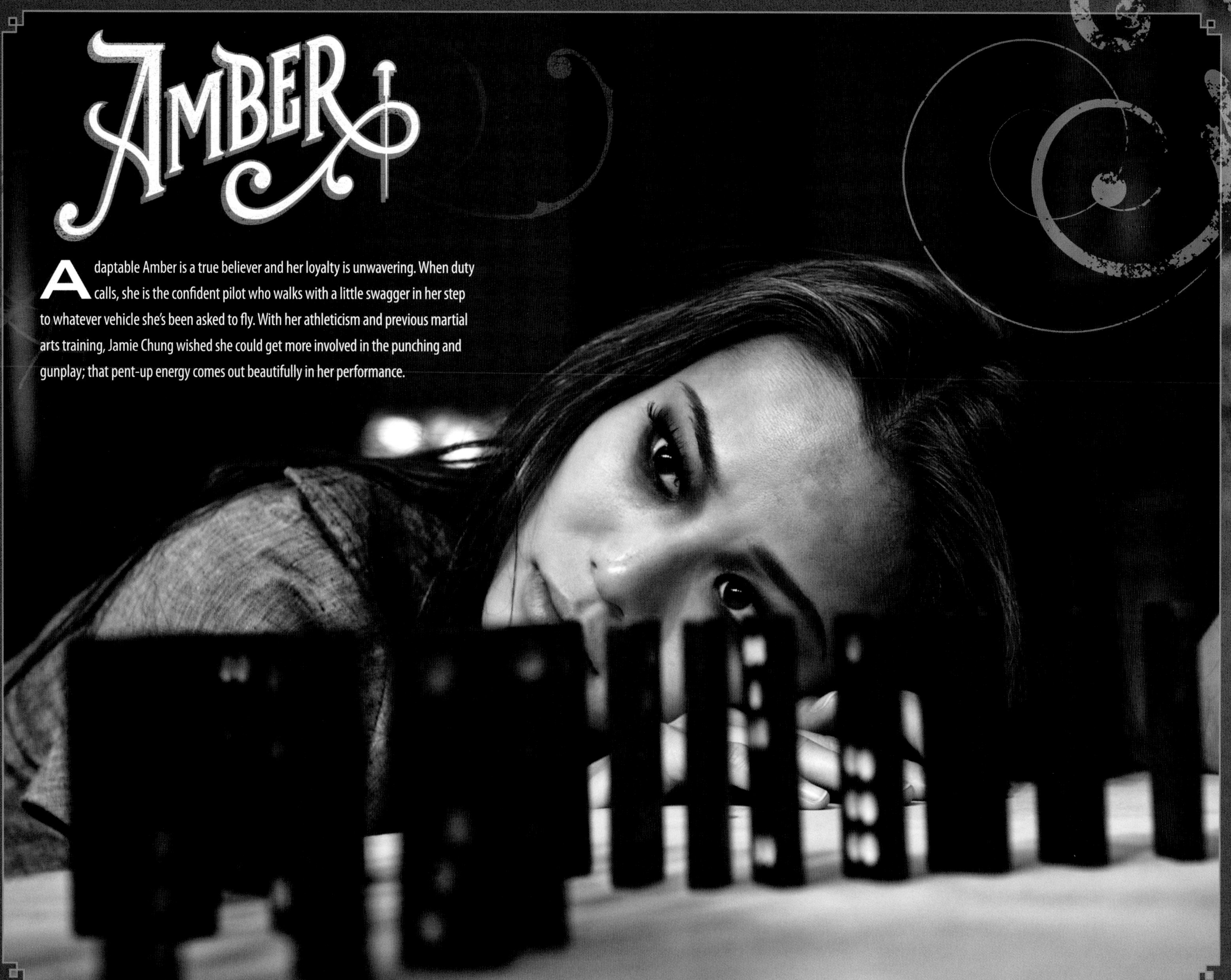

Amber

Adaptable Amber is a true believer and her loyalty is unwavering. When duty calls, she is the confident pilot who walks with a little swagger in her step to whatever vehicle she's been asked to fly. With her athleticism and previous martial arts training, Jamie Chung wished she could get more involved in the punching and gunplay; that pent-up energy comes out beautifully in her performance.

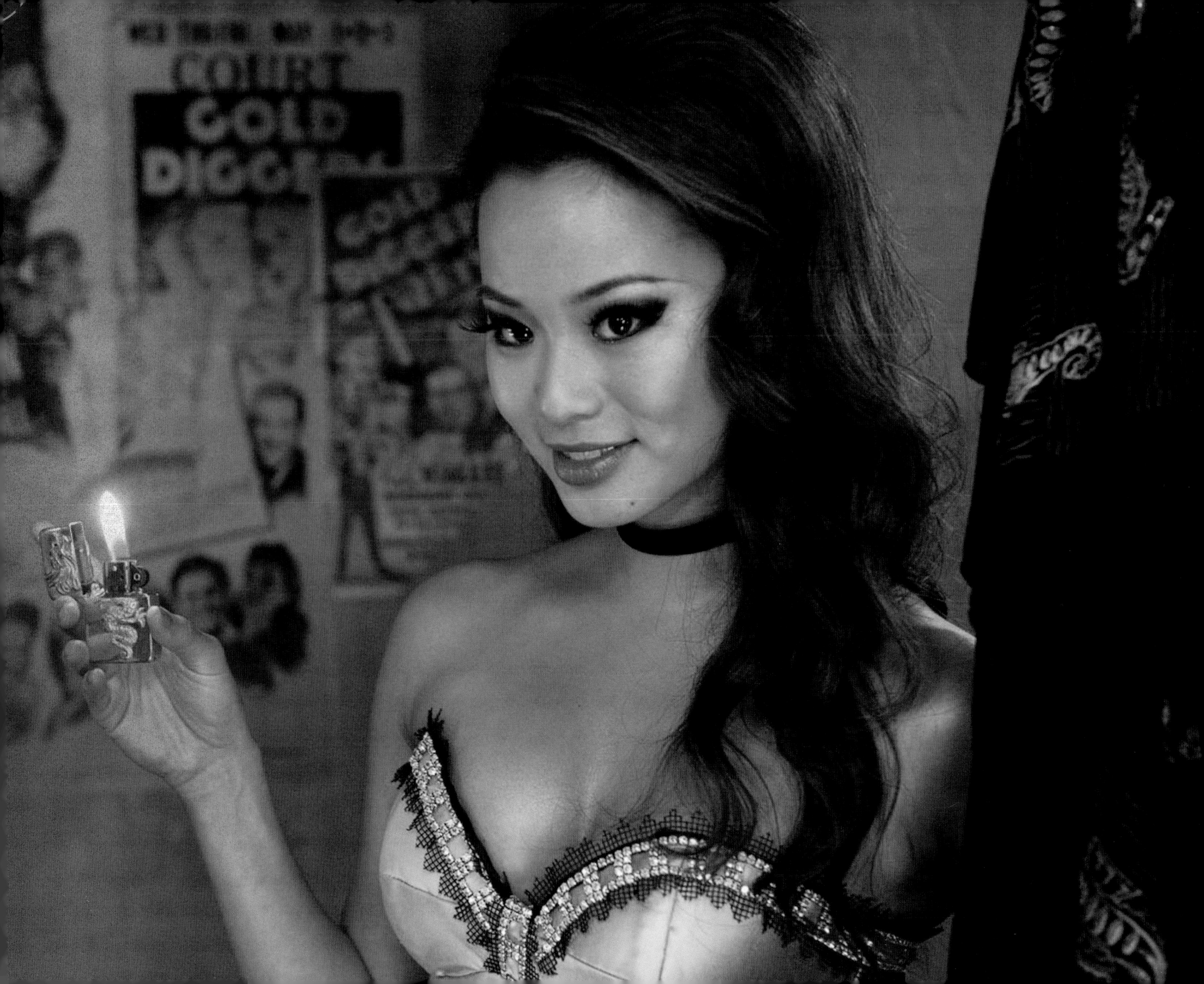
COURT
GOLD

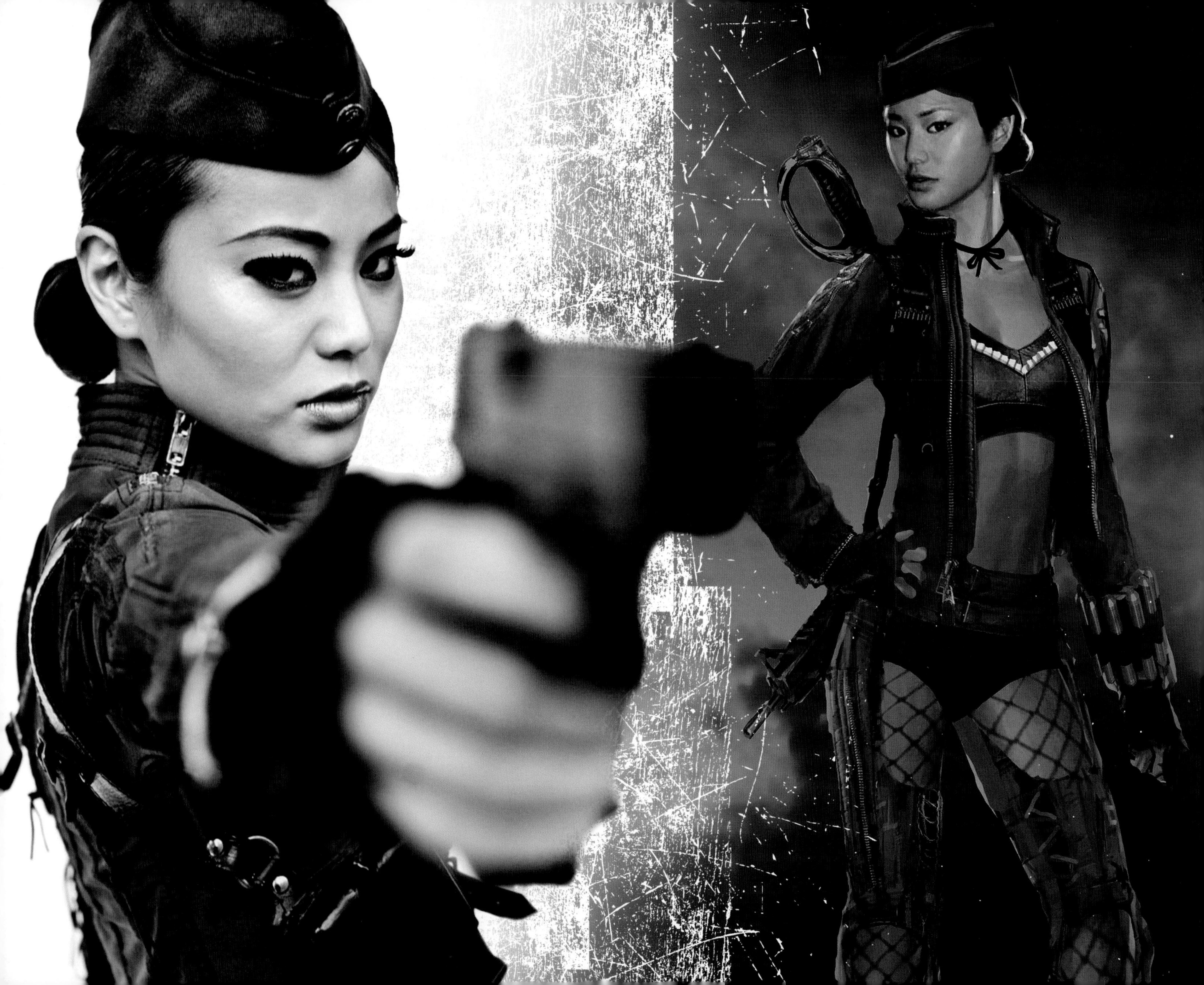

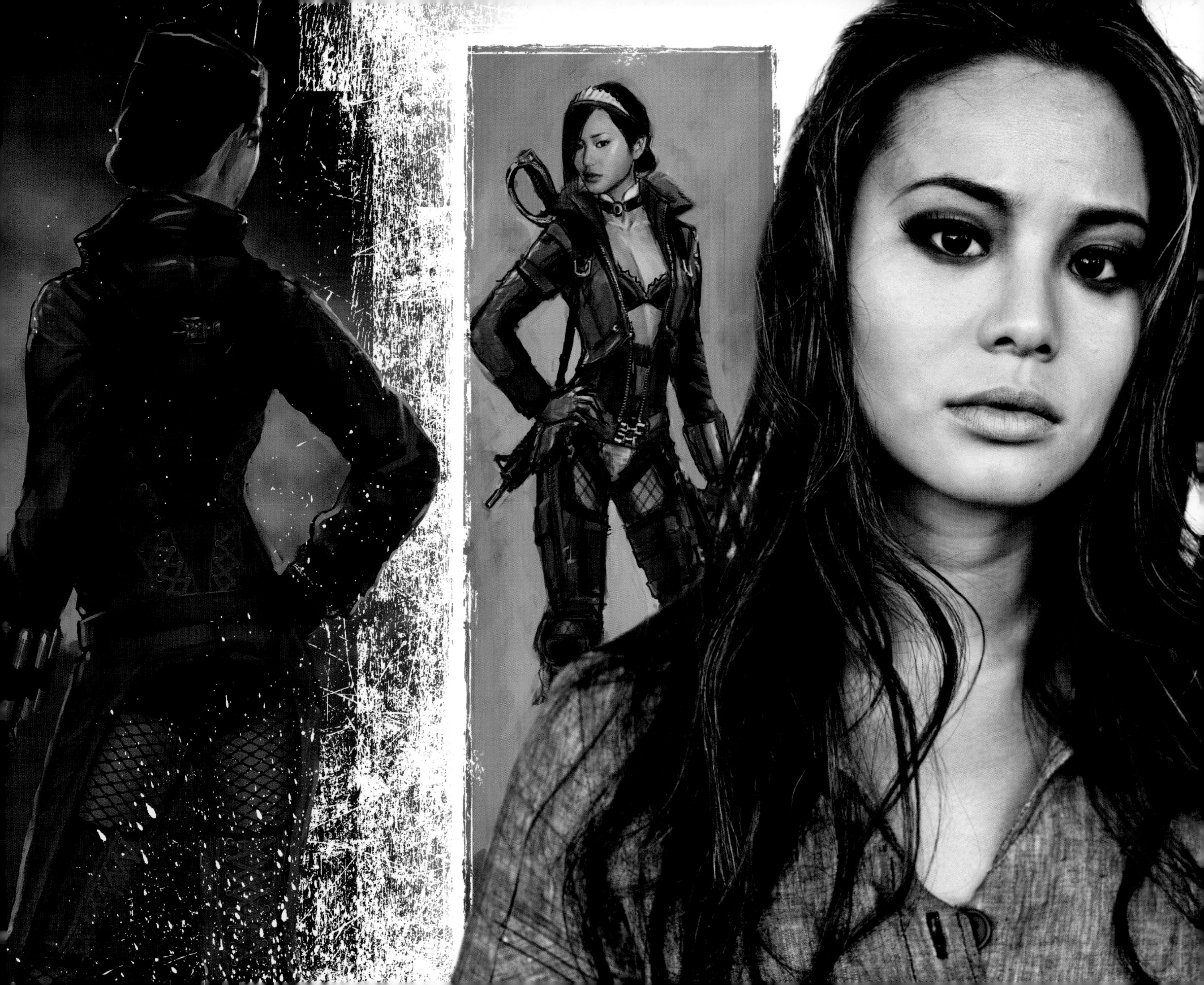

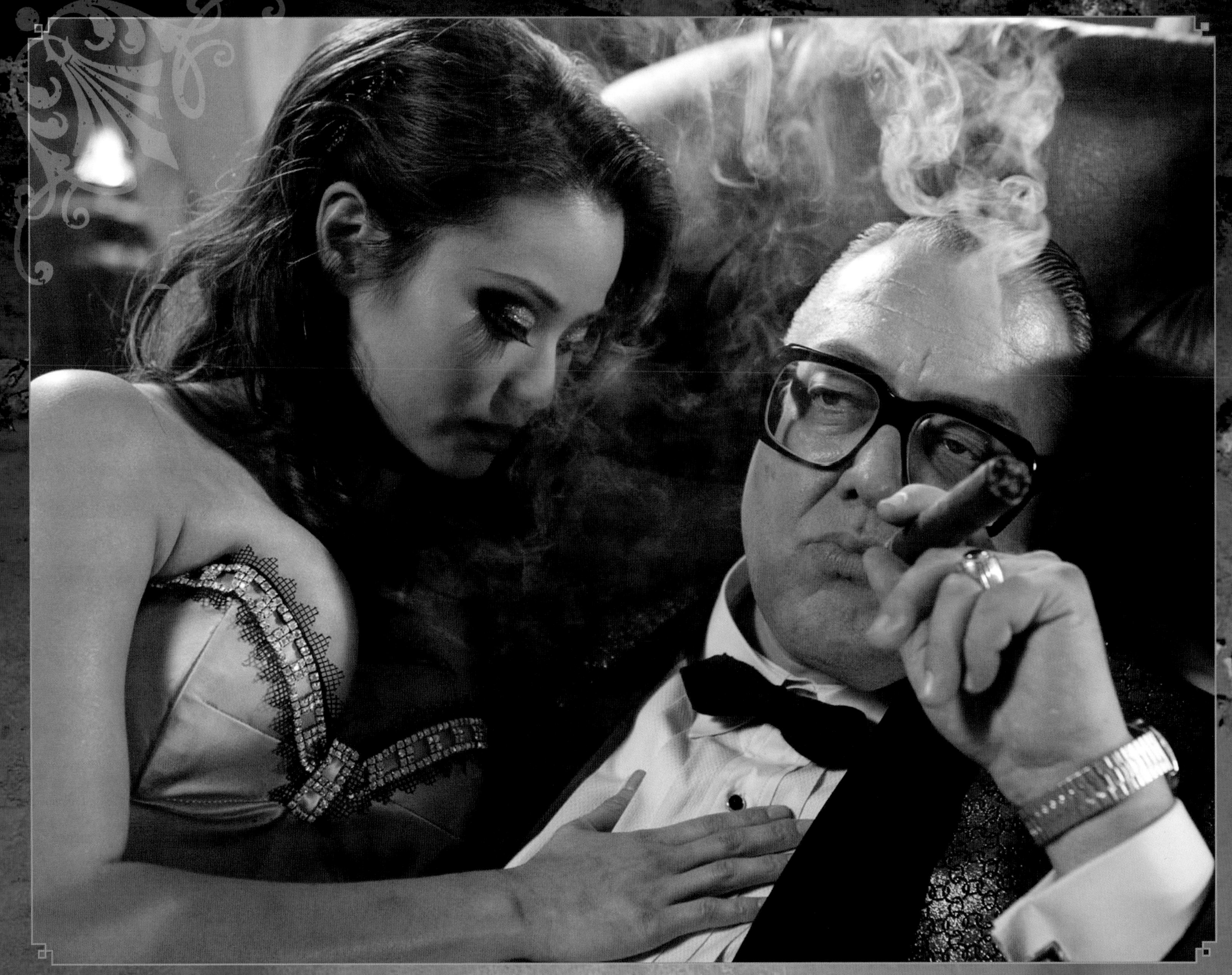

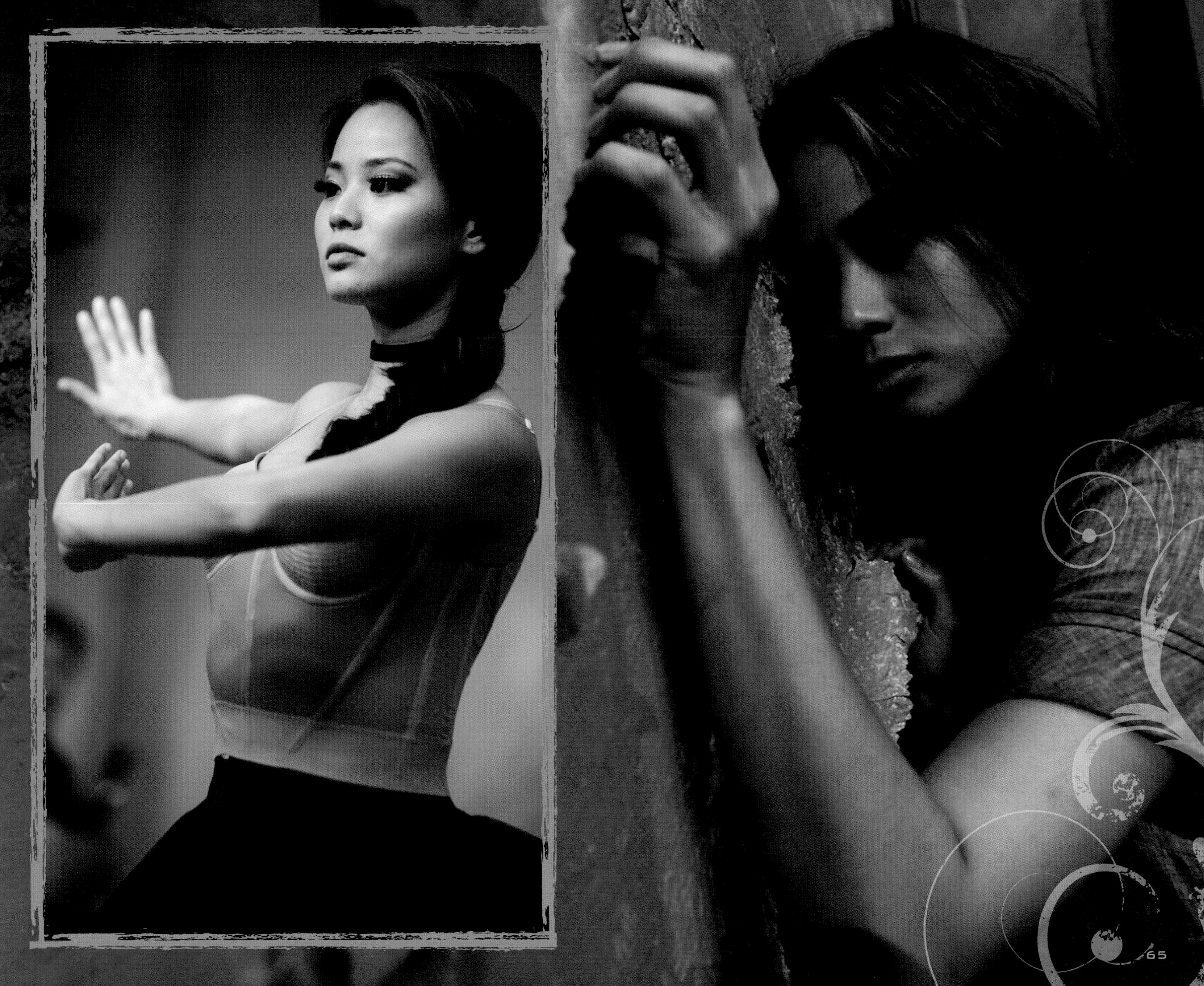

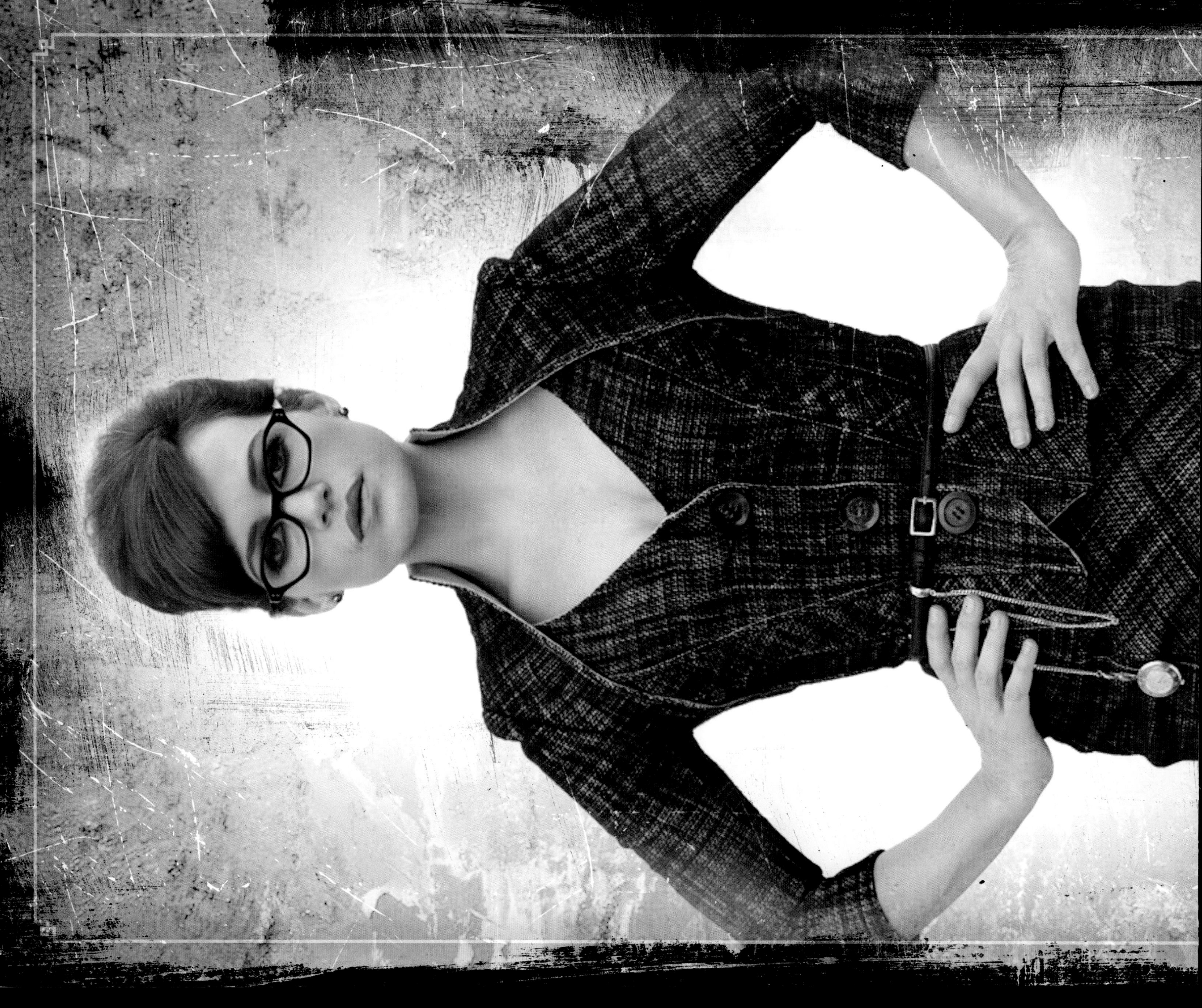

MADAM GORSKI

"YOUR FIGHT FOR SURVIVAL STARTS RIGHT NOW."

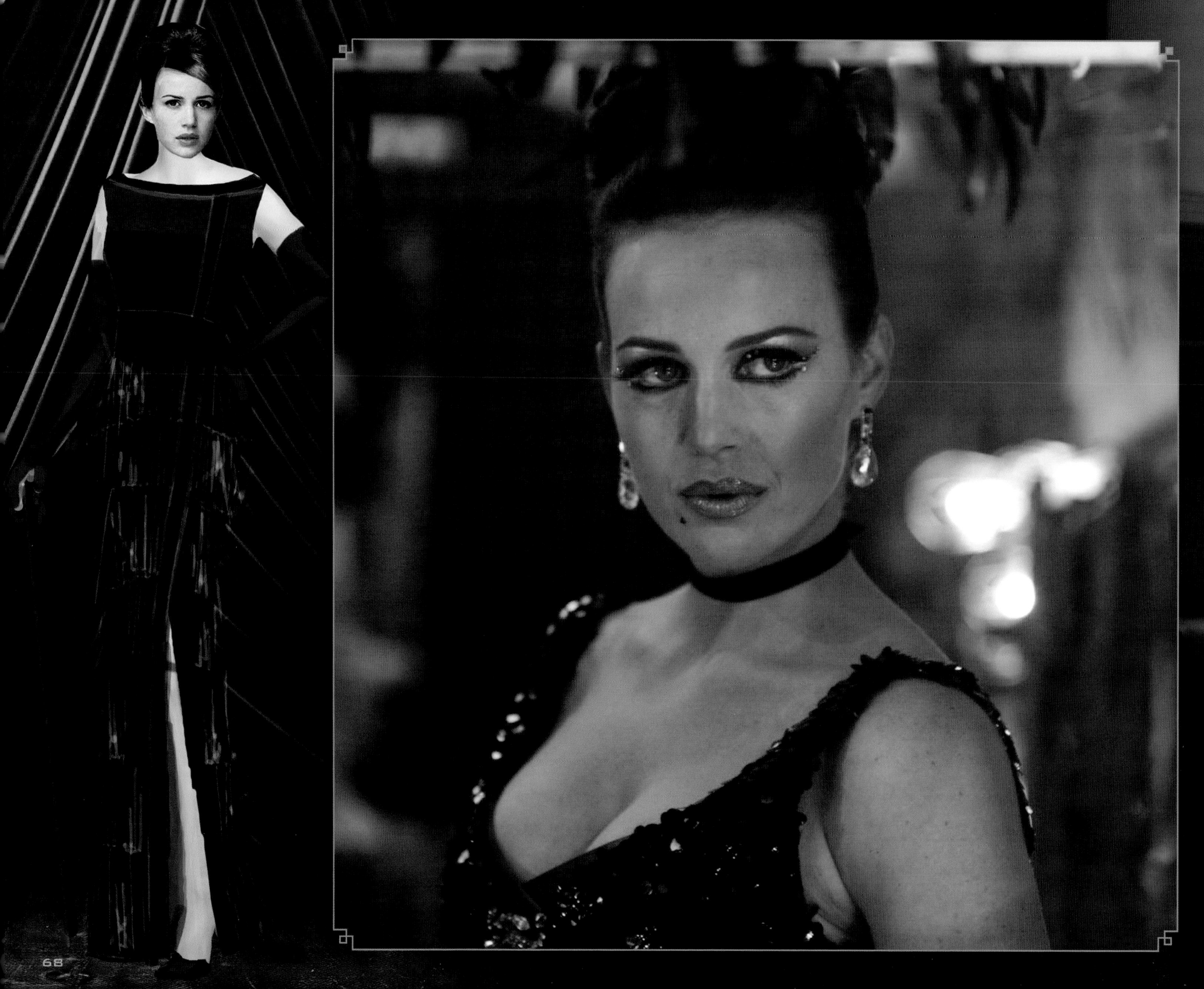

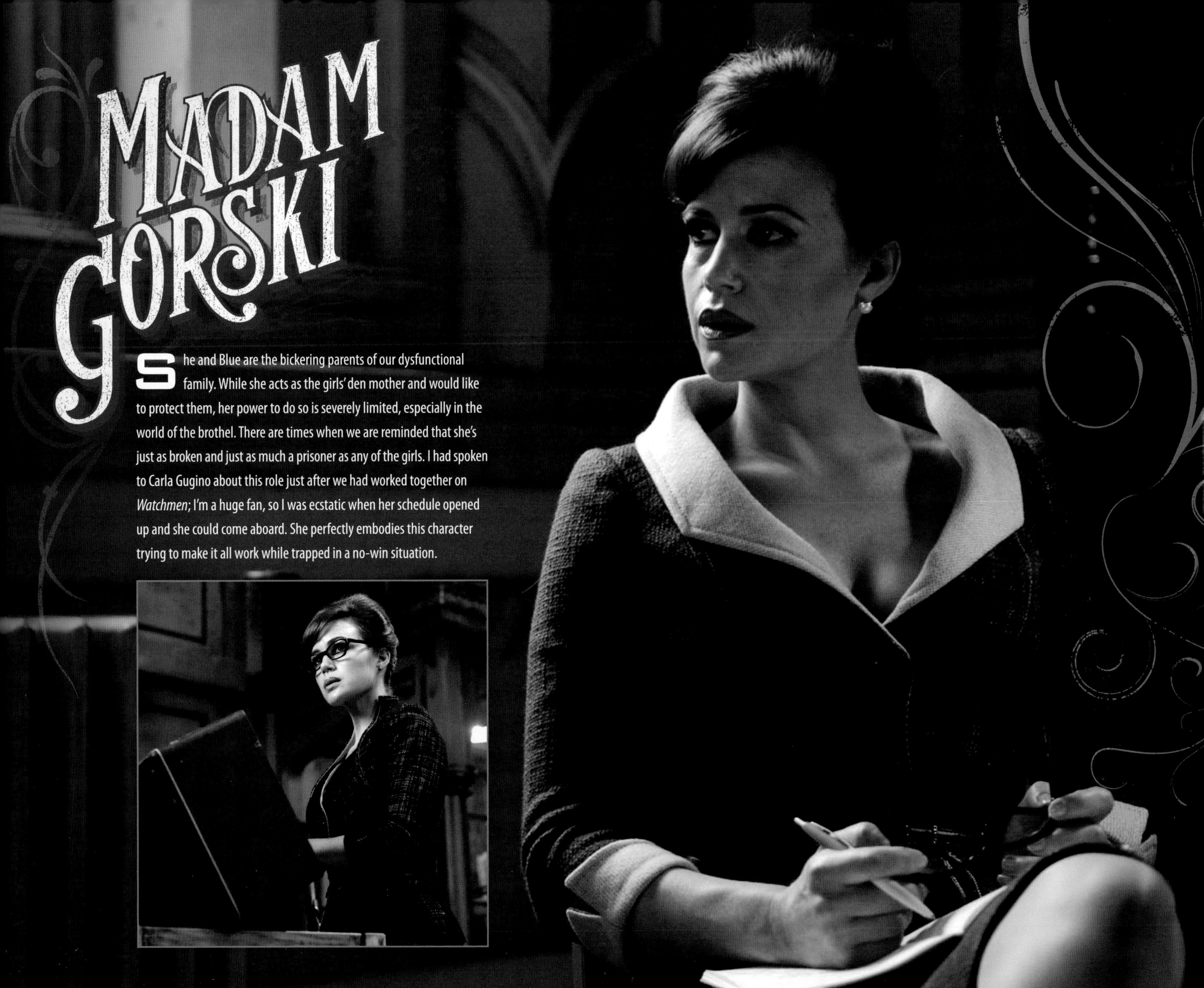

Madam Gorski

She and Blue are the bickering parents of our dysfunctional family. While she acts as the girls' den mother and would like to protect them, her power to do so is severely limited, especially in the world of the brothel. There are times when we are reminded that she's just as broken and just as much a prisoner as any of the girls. I had spoken to Carla Gugino about this role just after we had worked together on *Watchmen*; I'm a huge fan, so I was ecstatic when her schedule opened up and she could come aboard. She perfectly embodies this character trying to make it all work while trapped in a no-win situation.

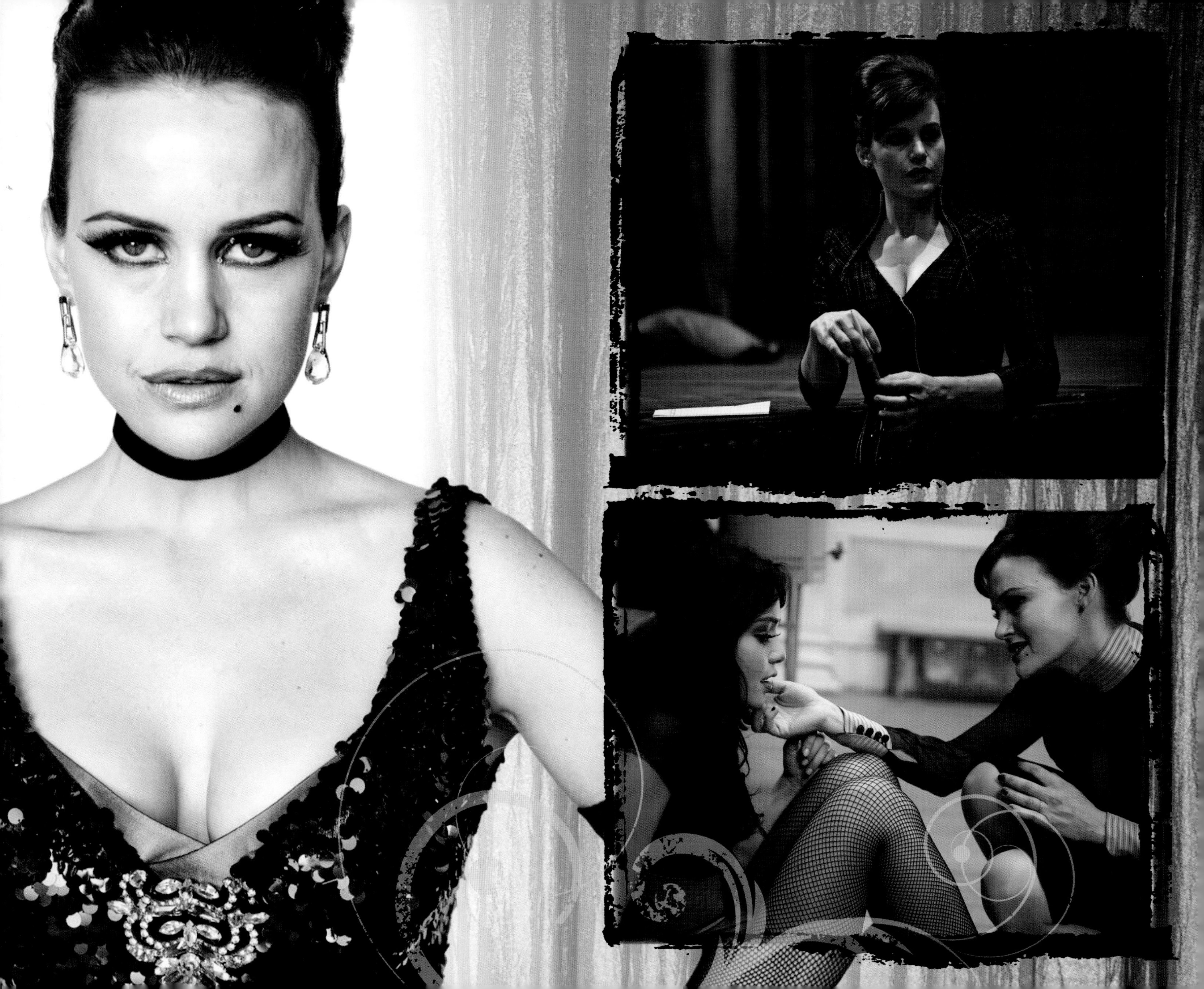

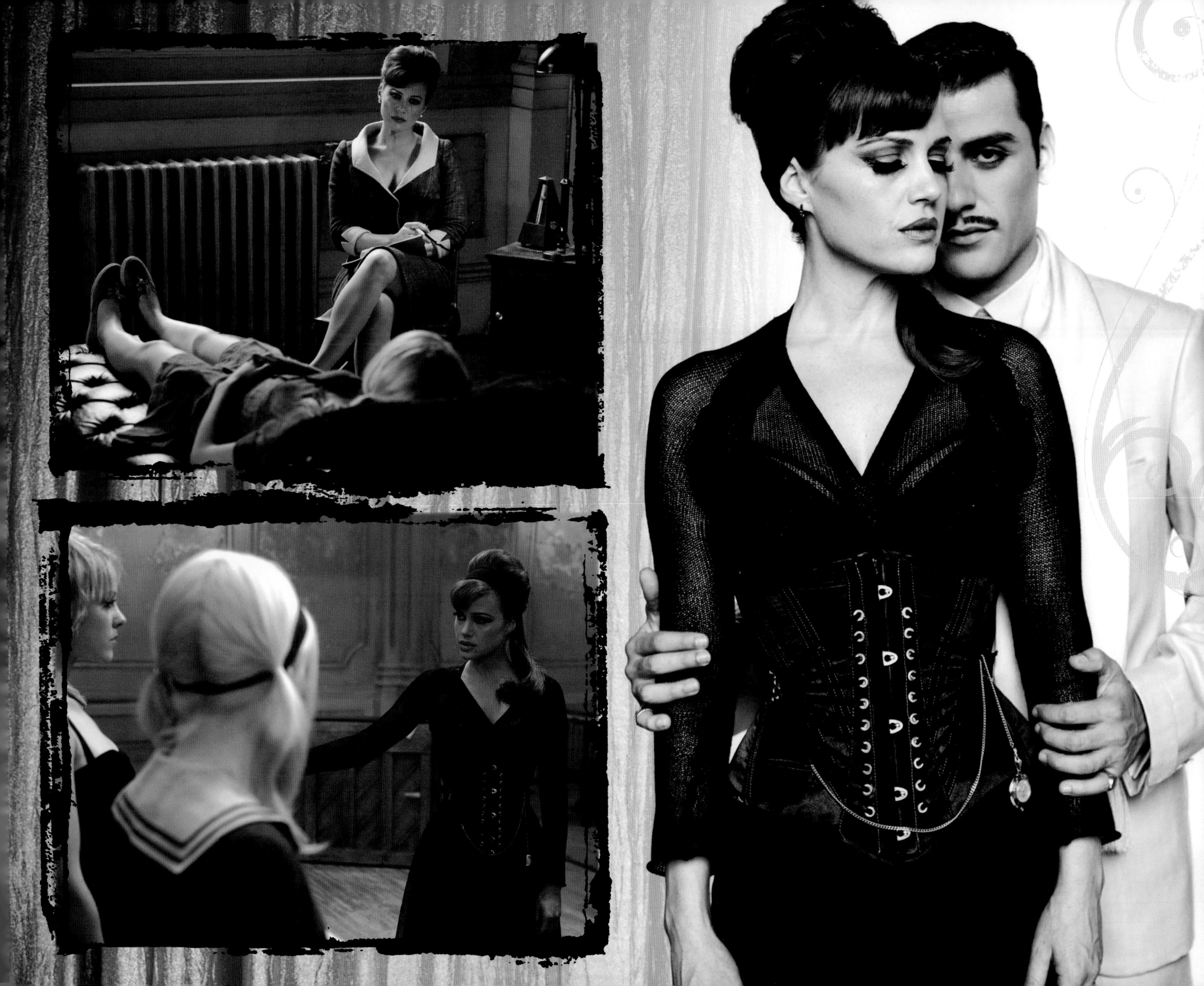

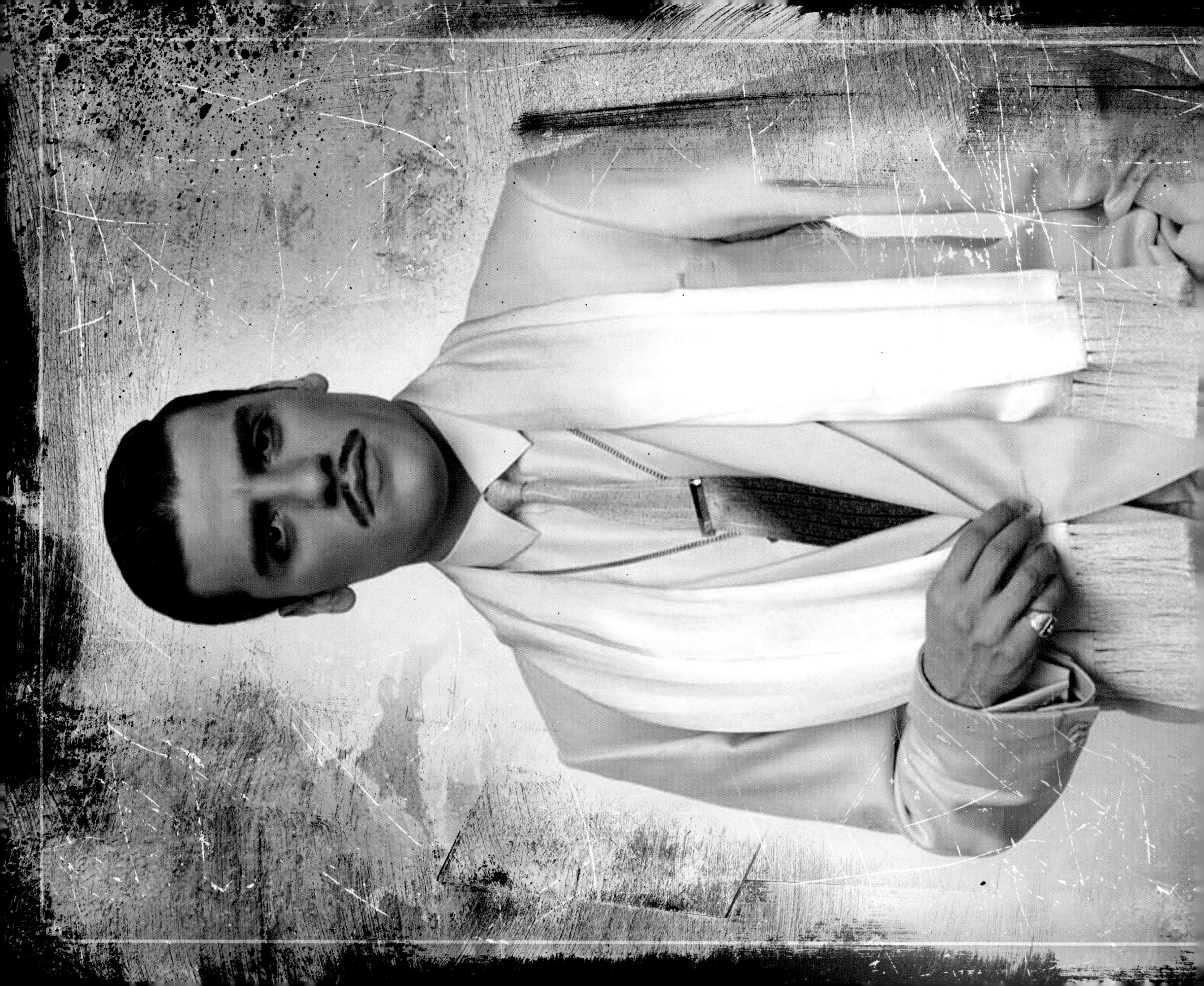

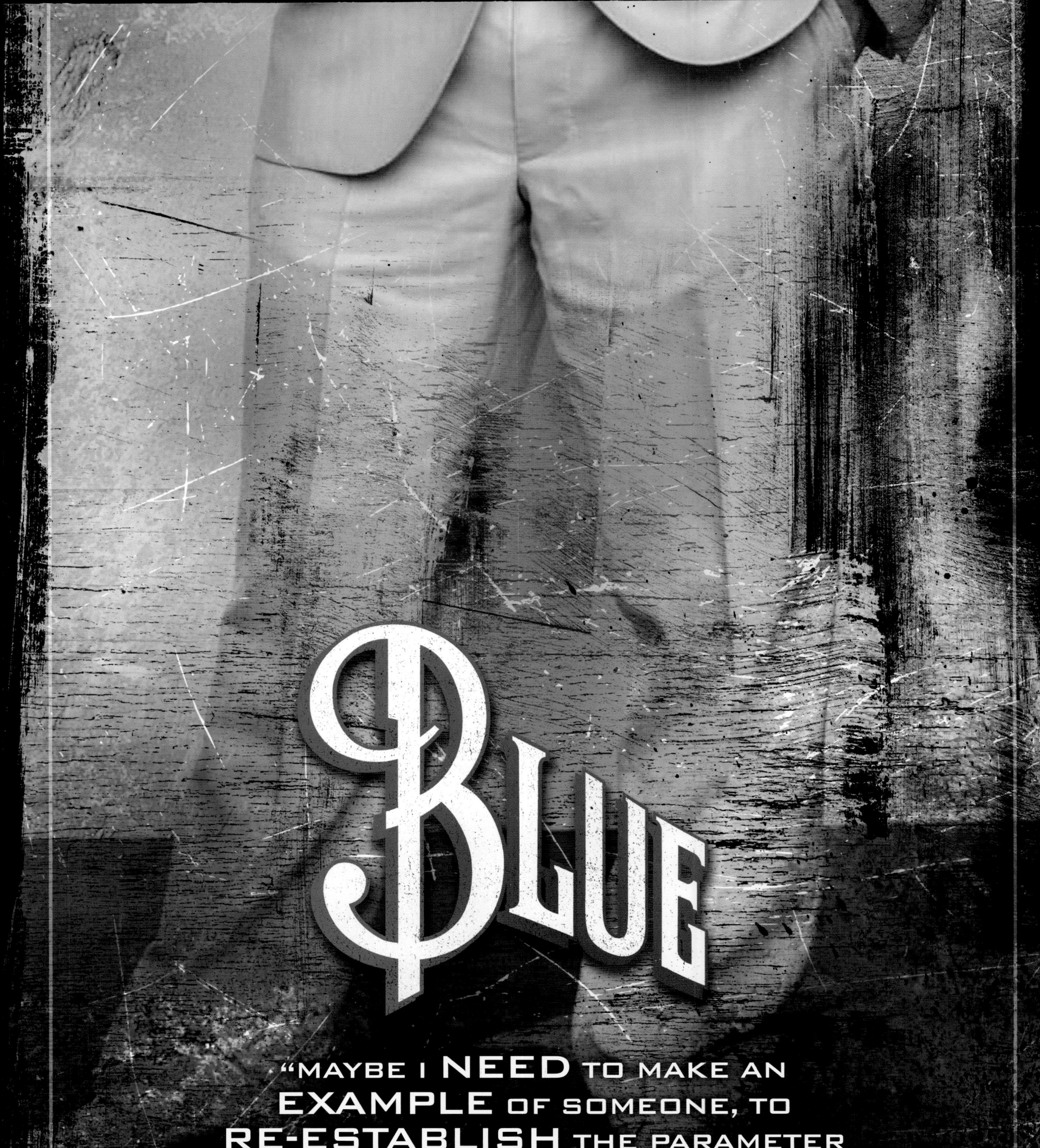
BLUE
"MAYBE I NEED TO MAKE AN
EXAMPLE OF SOMEONE, TO
RE-ESTABLISH THE PARAMETER
OF OUR RELATIONSHIP."

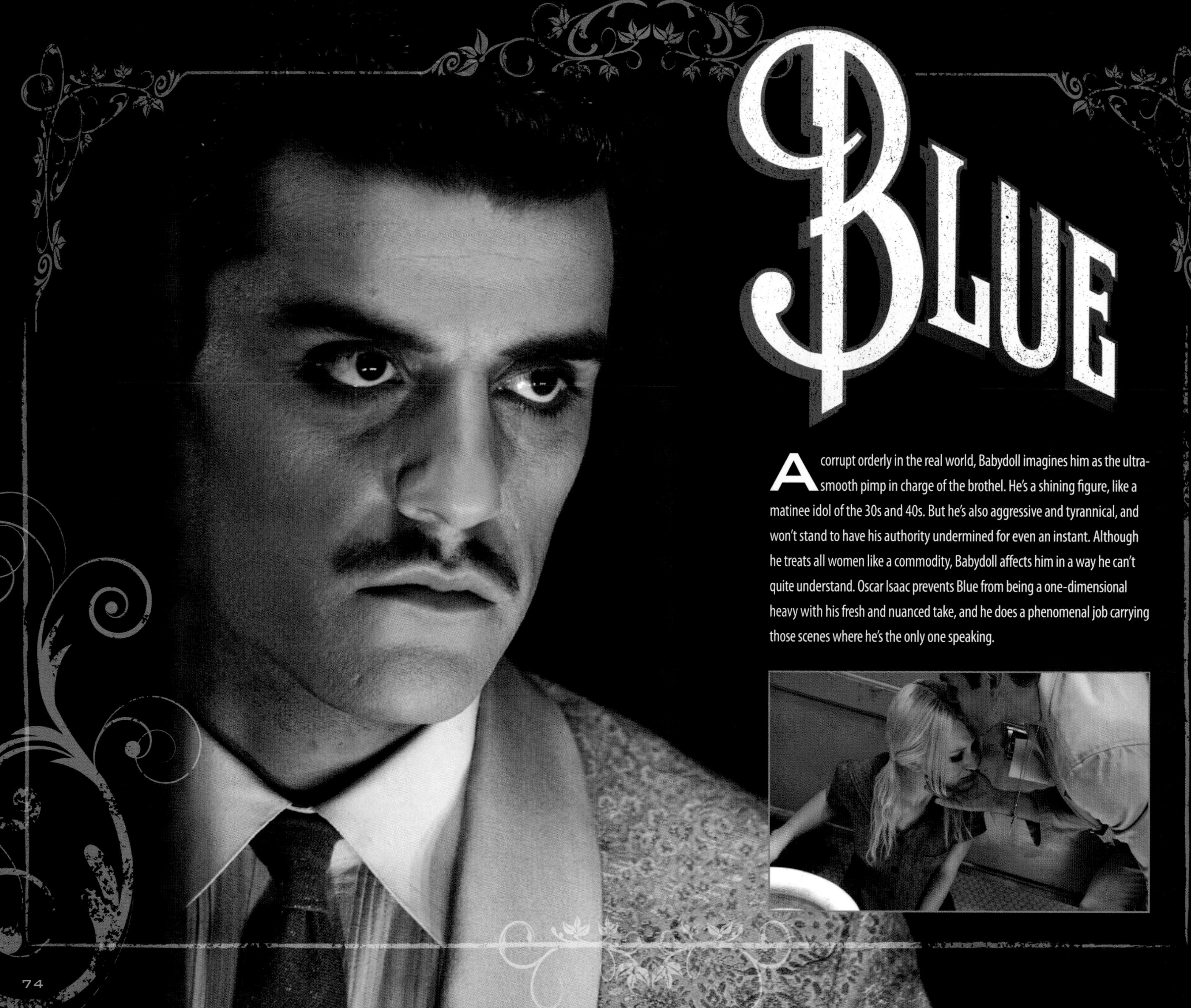

BLUE

A corrupt orderly in the real world, Babydoll imagines him as the ultra-smooth pimp in charge of the brothel. He's a shining figure, like a matinee idol of the 30s and 40s. But he's also aggressive and tyrannical, and won't stand to have his authority undermined for even an instant. Although he treats all women like a commodity, Babydoll affects him in a way he can't quite understand. Oscar Isaac prevents Blue from being a one-dimensional heavy with his fresh and nuanced take, and he does a phenomenal job carrying those scenes where he's the only one speaking.

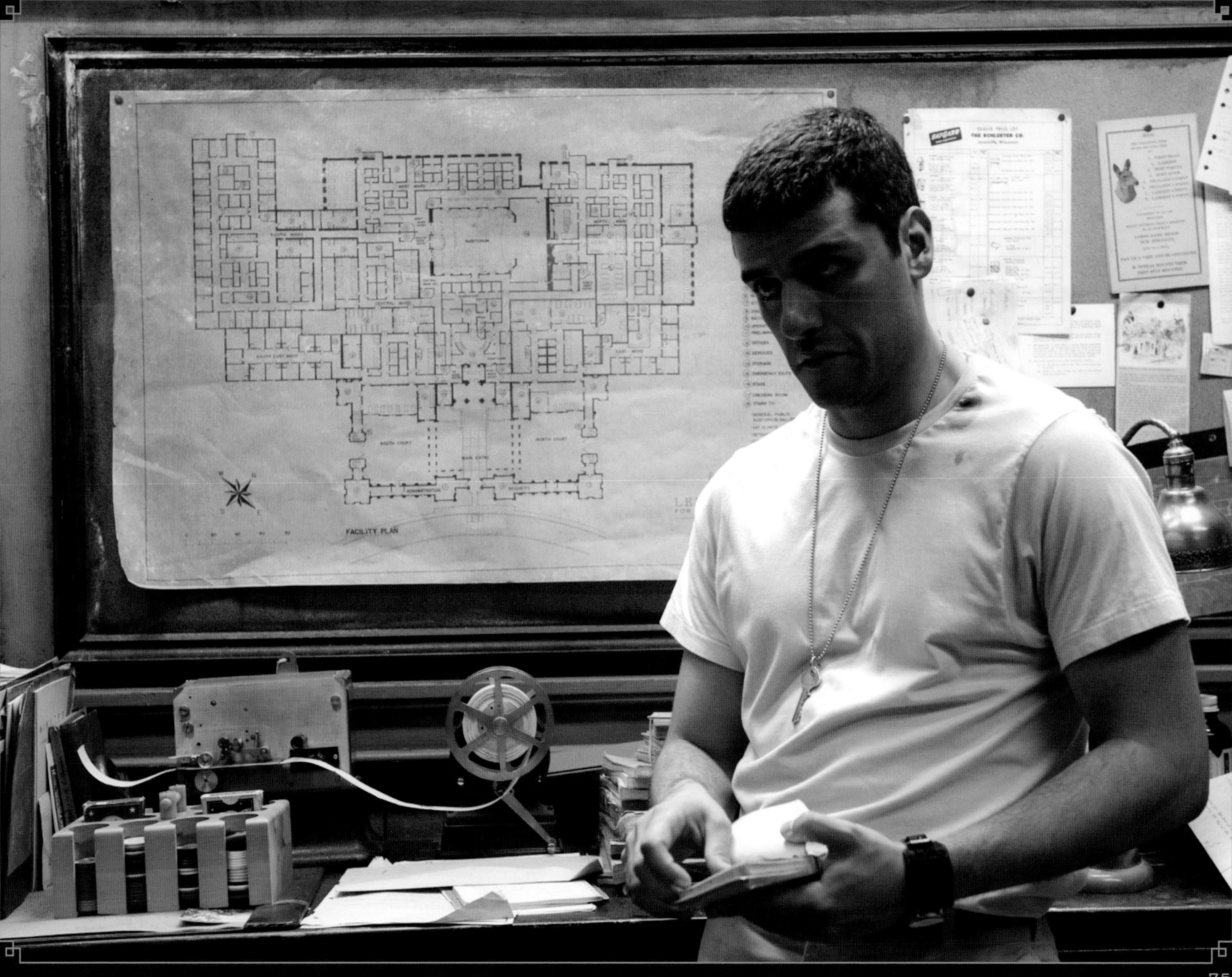
FACILITY PLAN

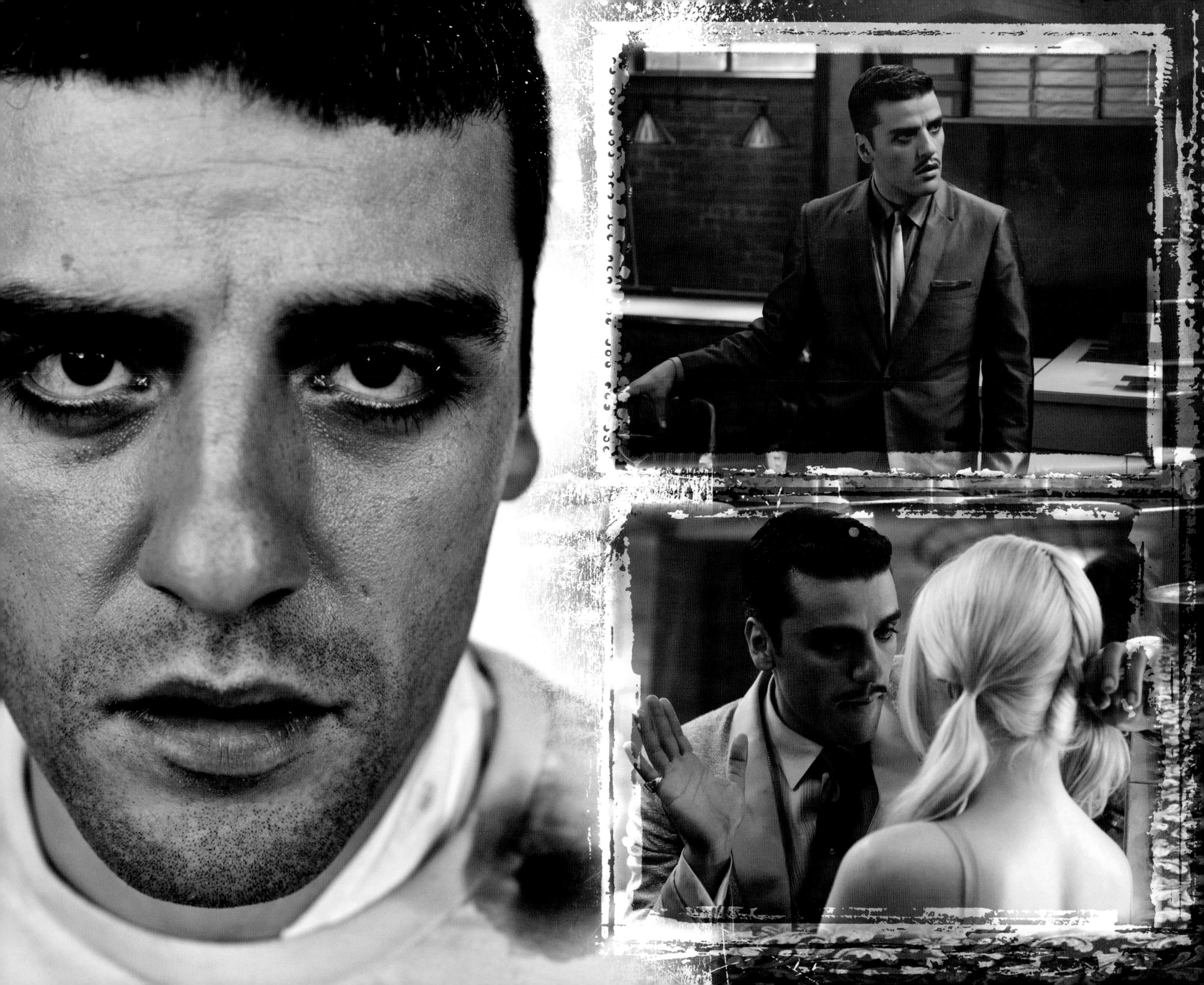

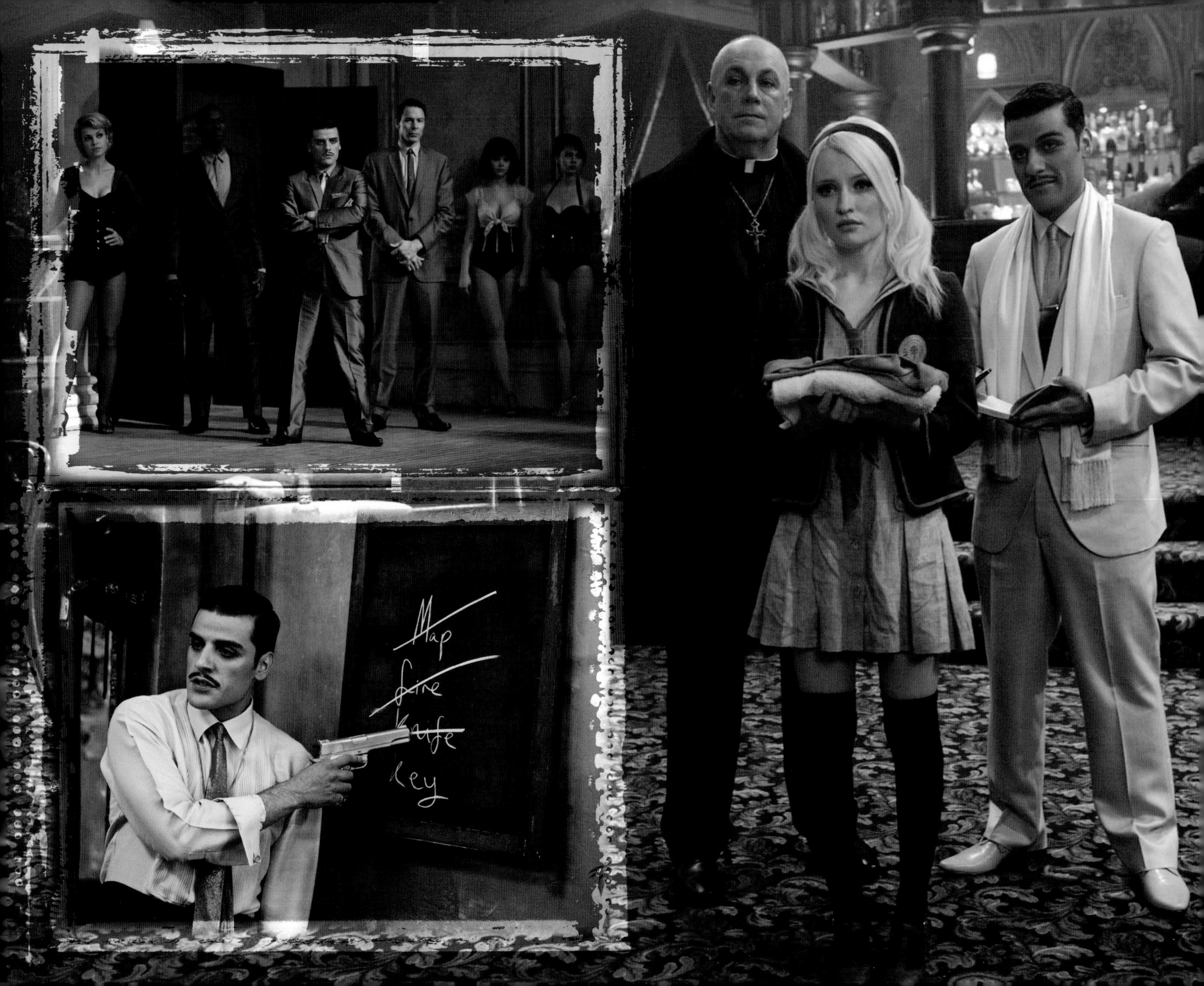
Map
fire
knife
key

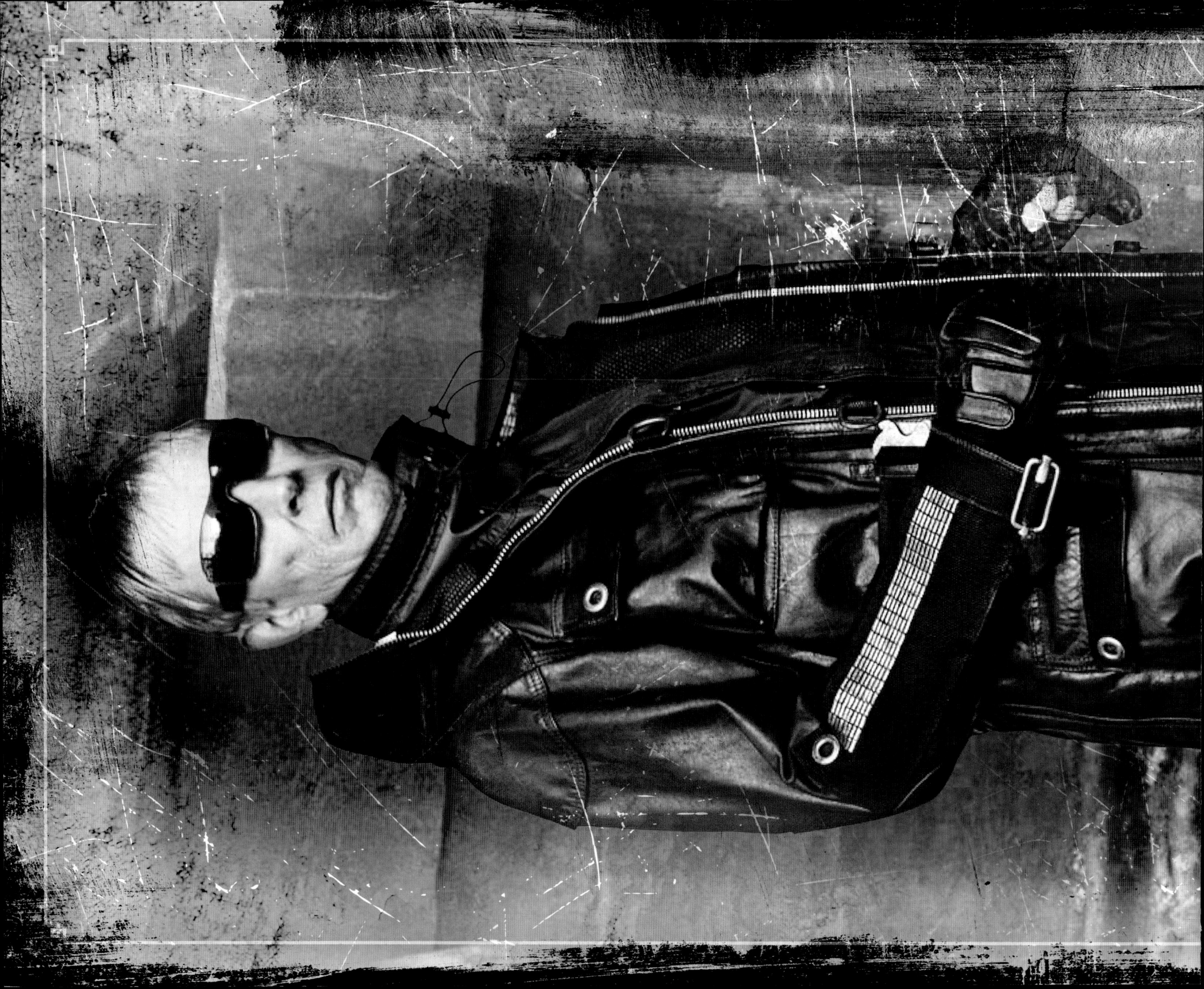

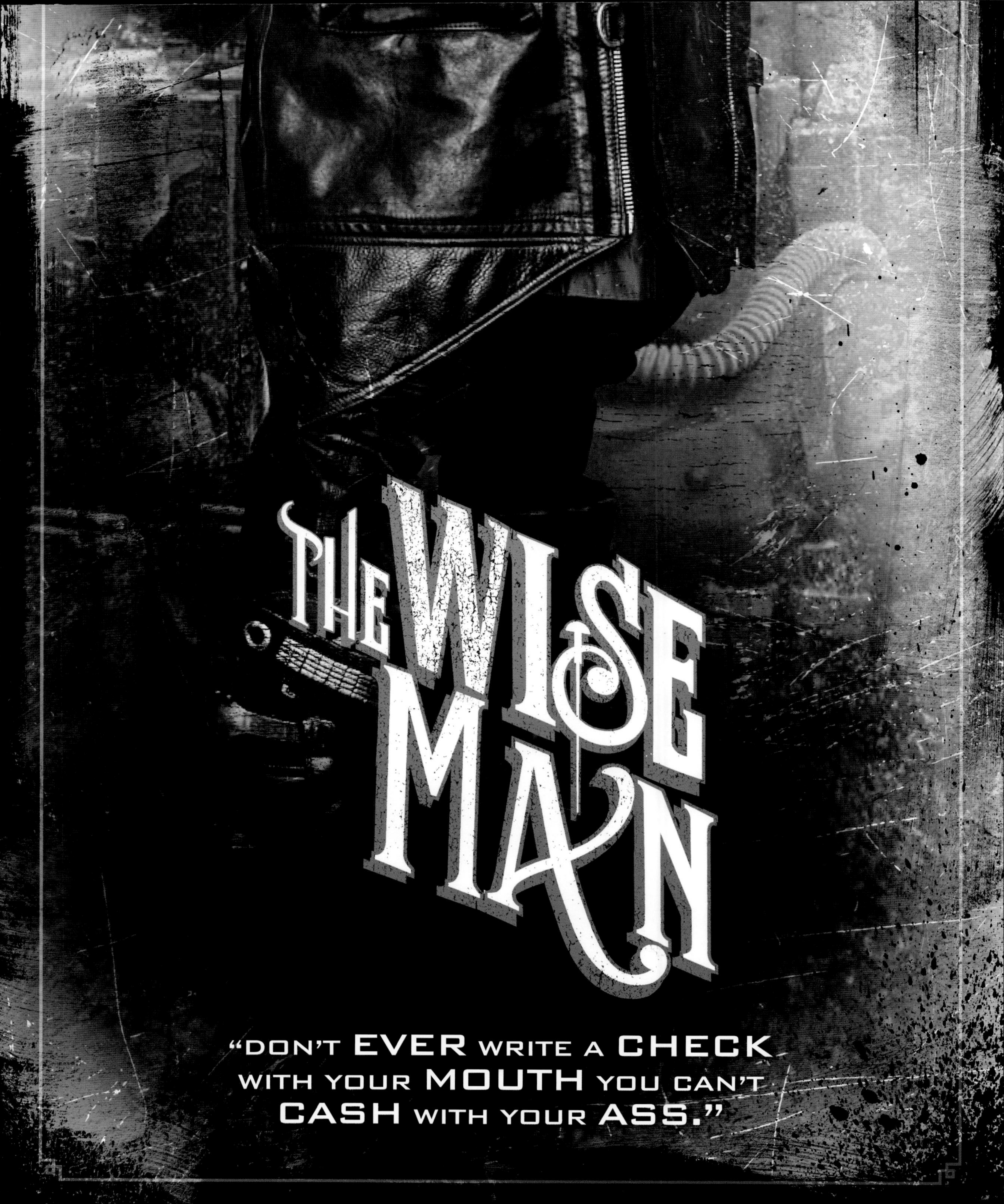
THE WISE MAN
"DON'T EVER WRITE A CHECK
WITH YOUR MOUTH YOU CAN'T
CASH WITH YOUR ASS."

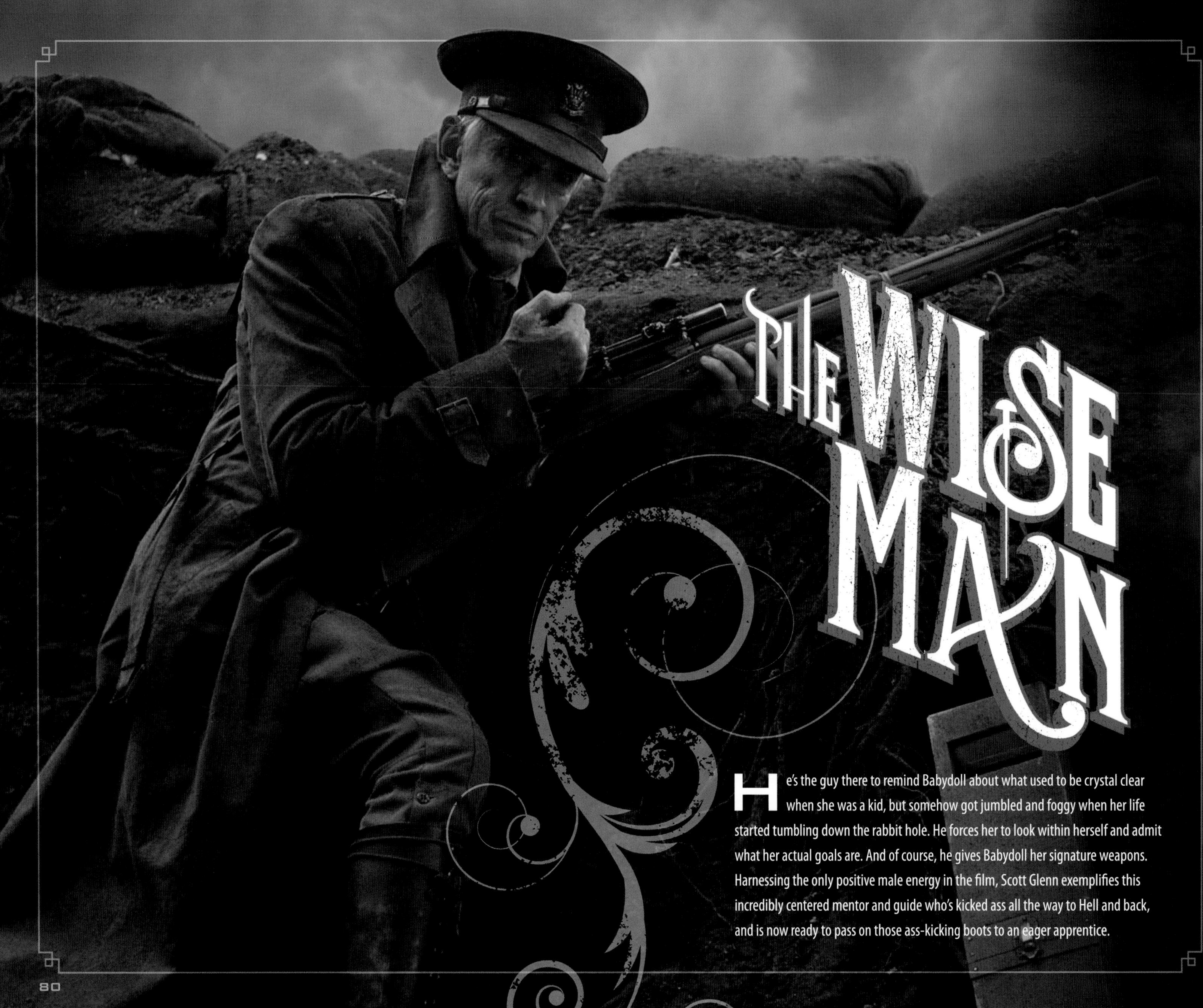

THE WISE MAN

He's the guy there to remind Babydoll about what used to be crystal clear when she was a kid, but somehow got jumbled and foggy when her life started tumbling down the rabbit hole. He forces her to look within herself and admit what her actual goals are. And of course, he gives Babydoll her signature weapons. Harnessing the only positive male energy in the film, Scott Glenn exemplifies this incredibly centered mentor and guide who's kicked ass all the way to Hell and back, and is now ready to pass on those ass-kicking boots to an eager apprentice.

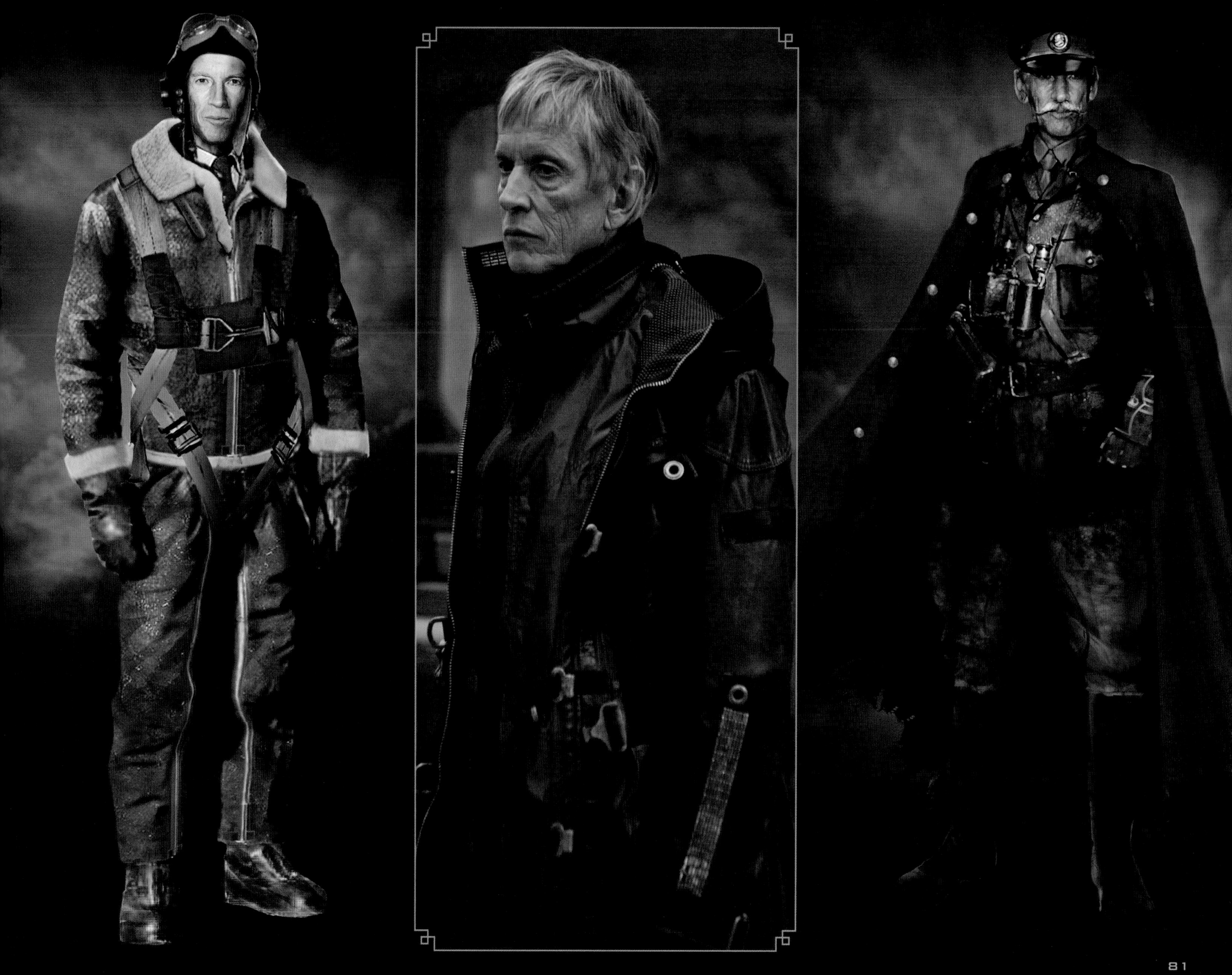

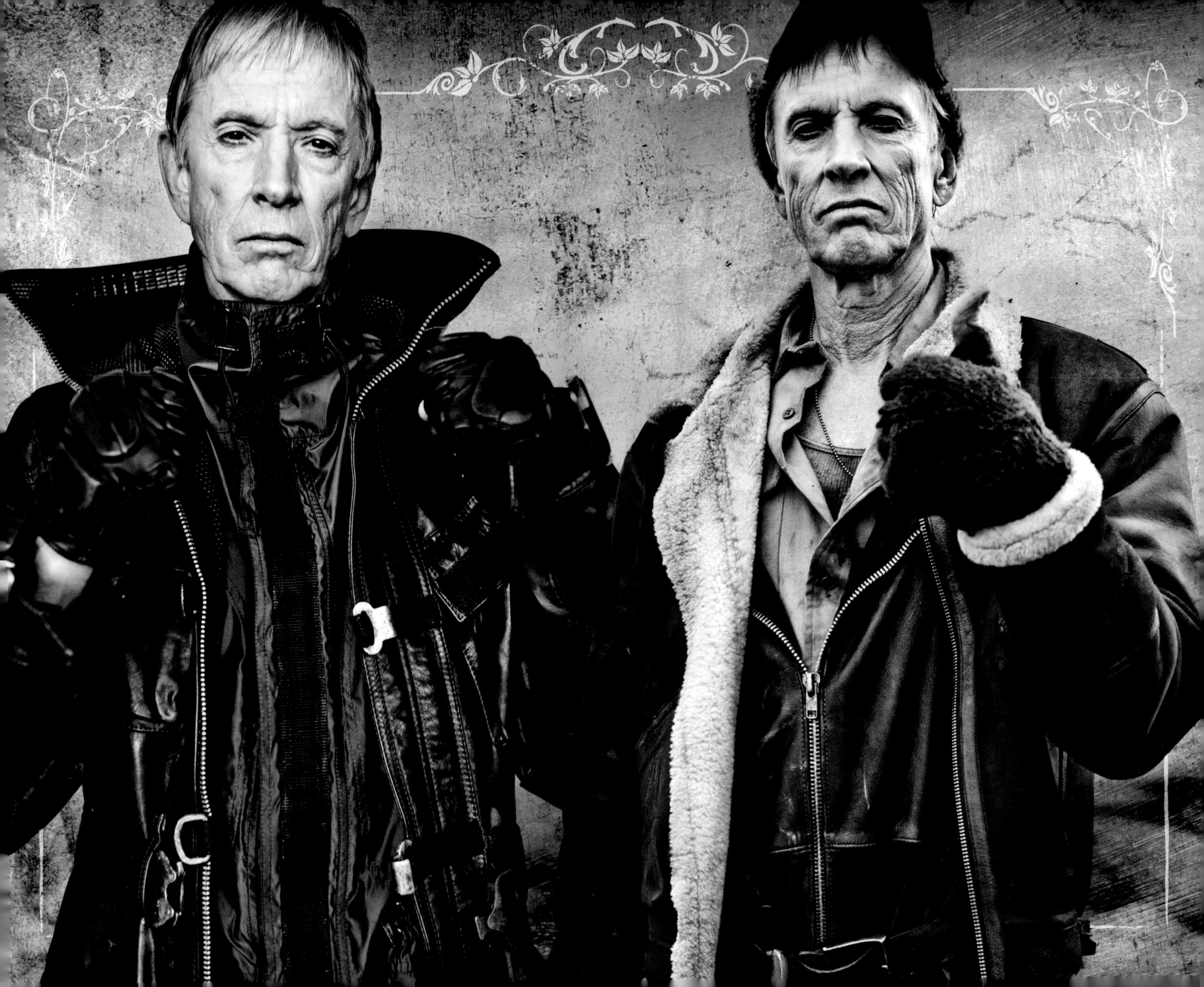

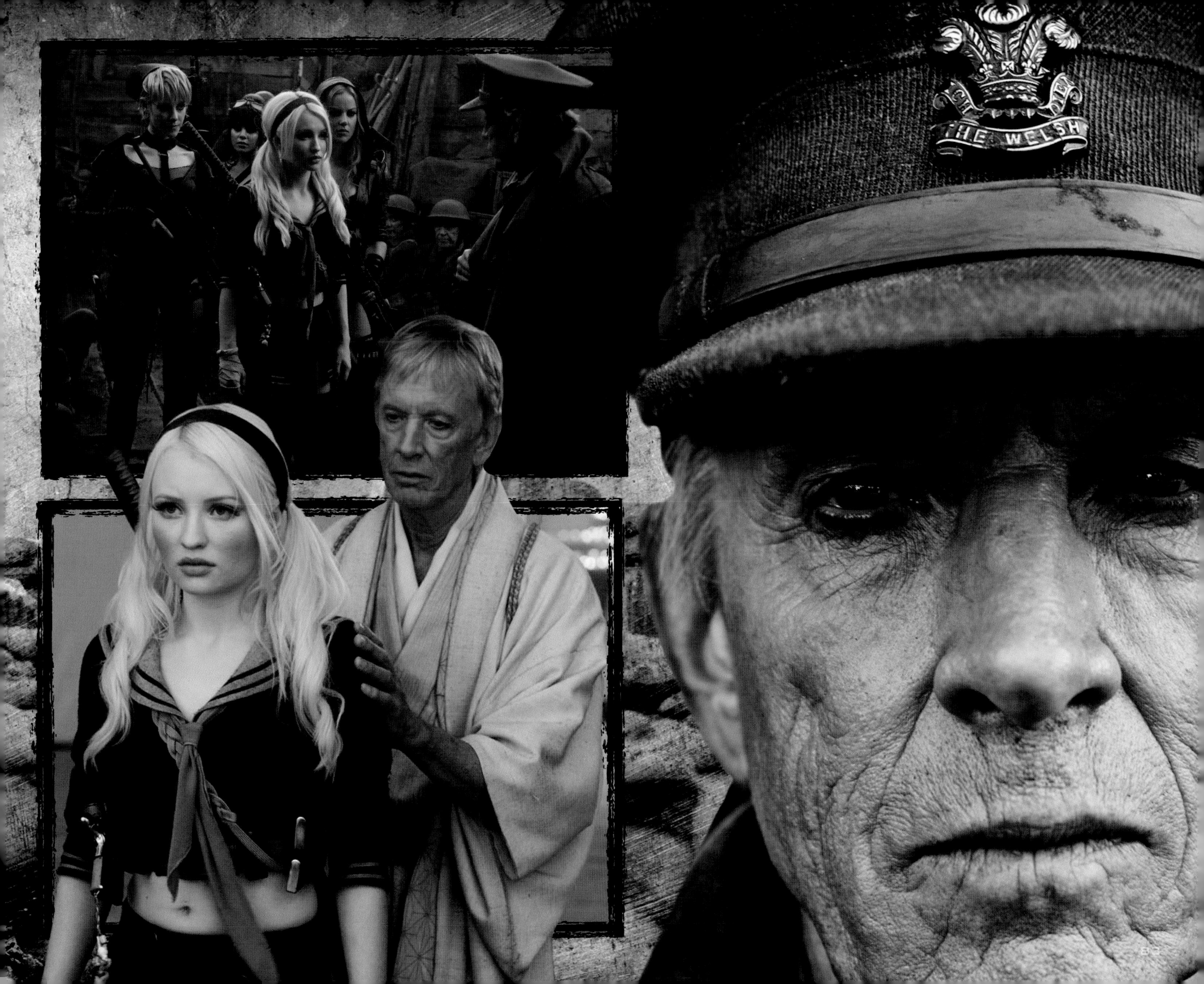
THE WELSH

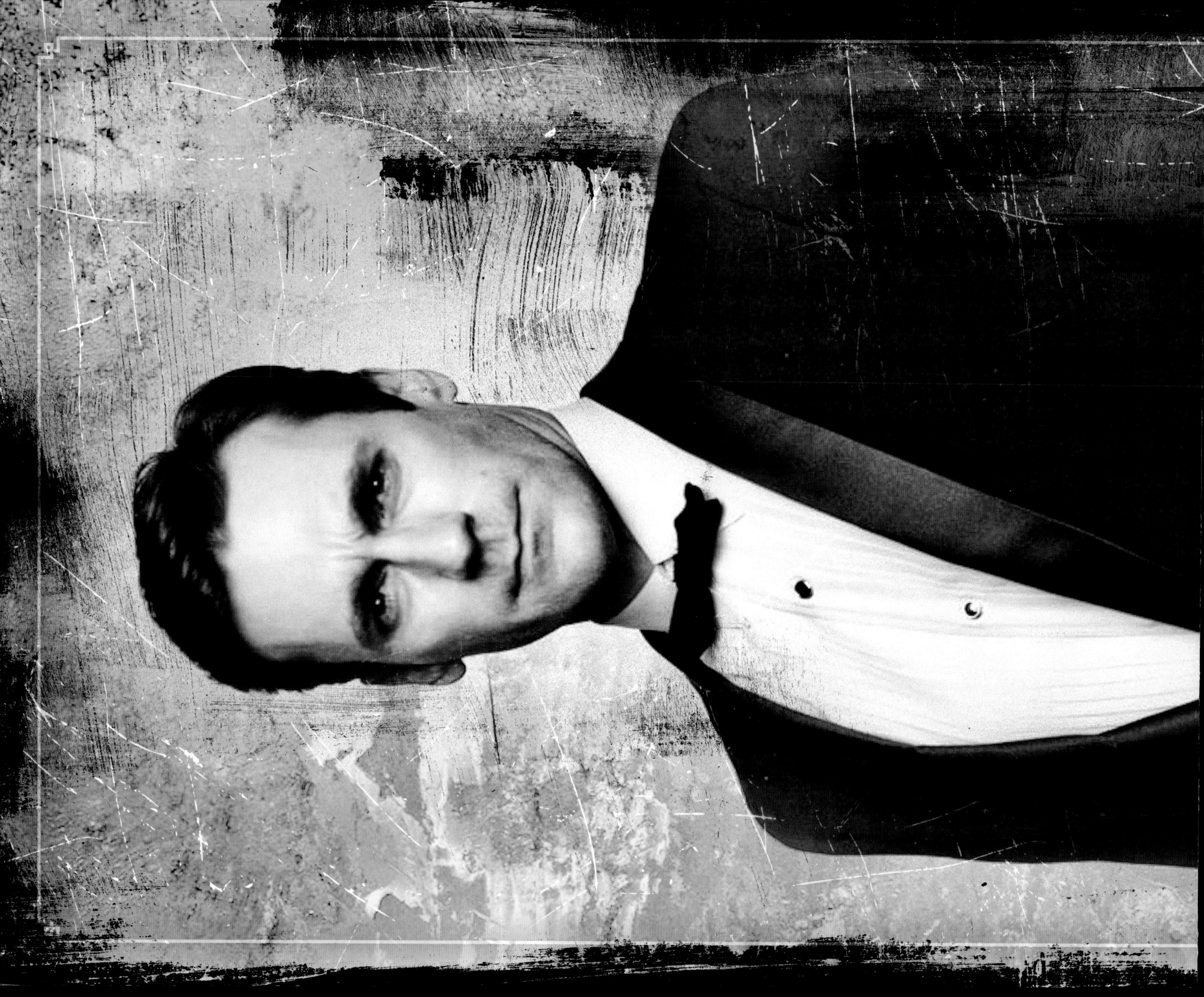

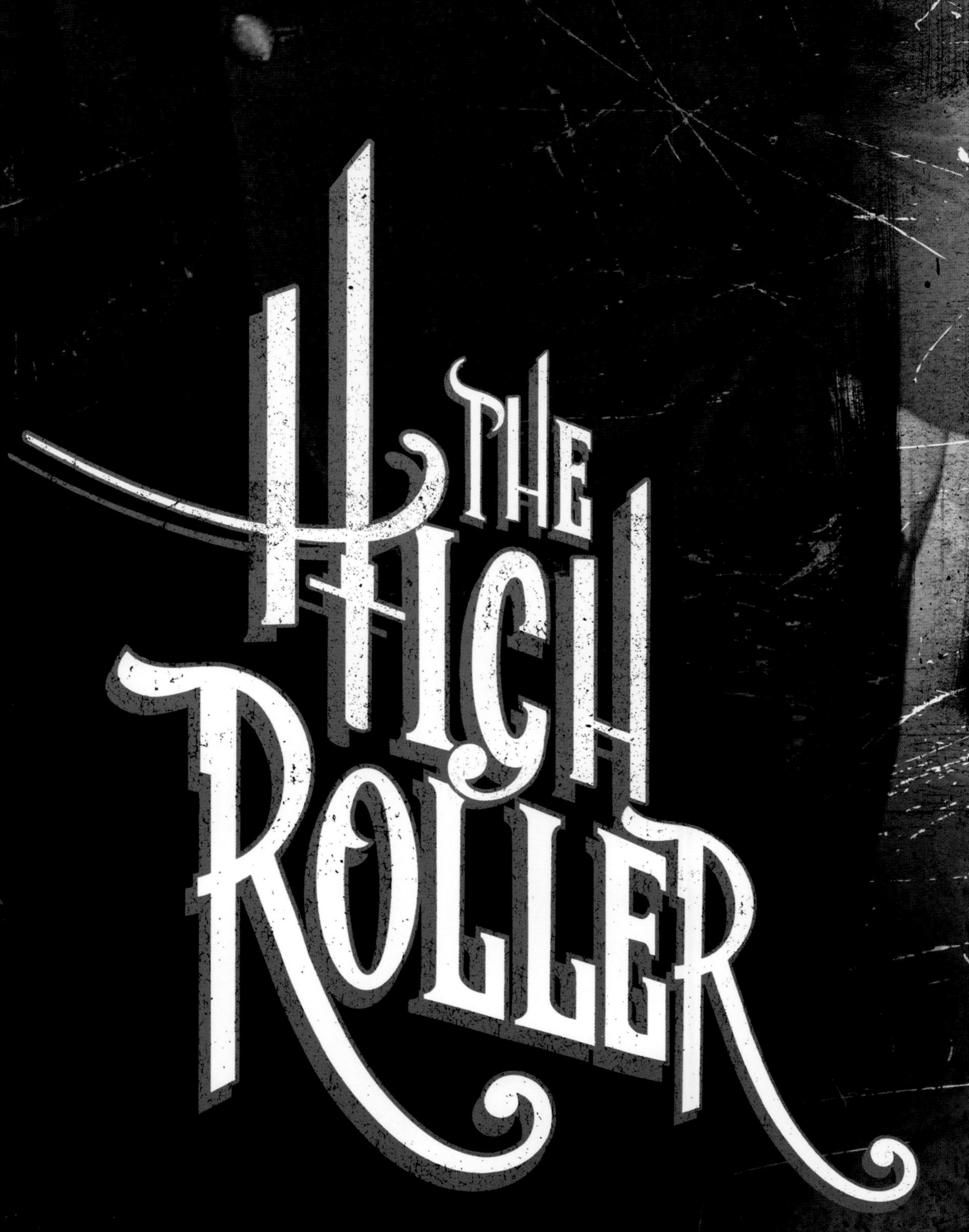
THE HIGH ROLLER
"I'VE SEEN A LOT OF
TORTURED SOULS IN HERE."

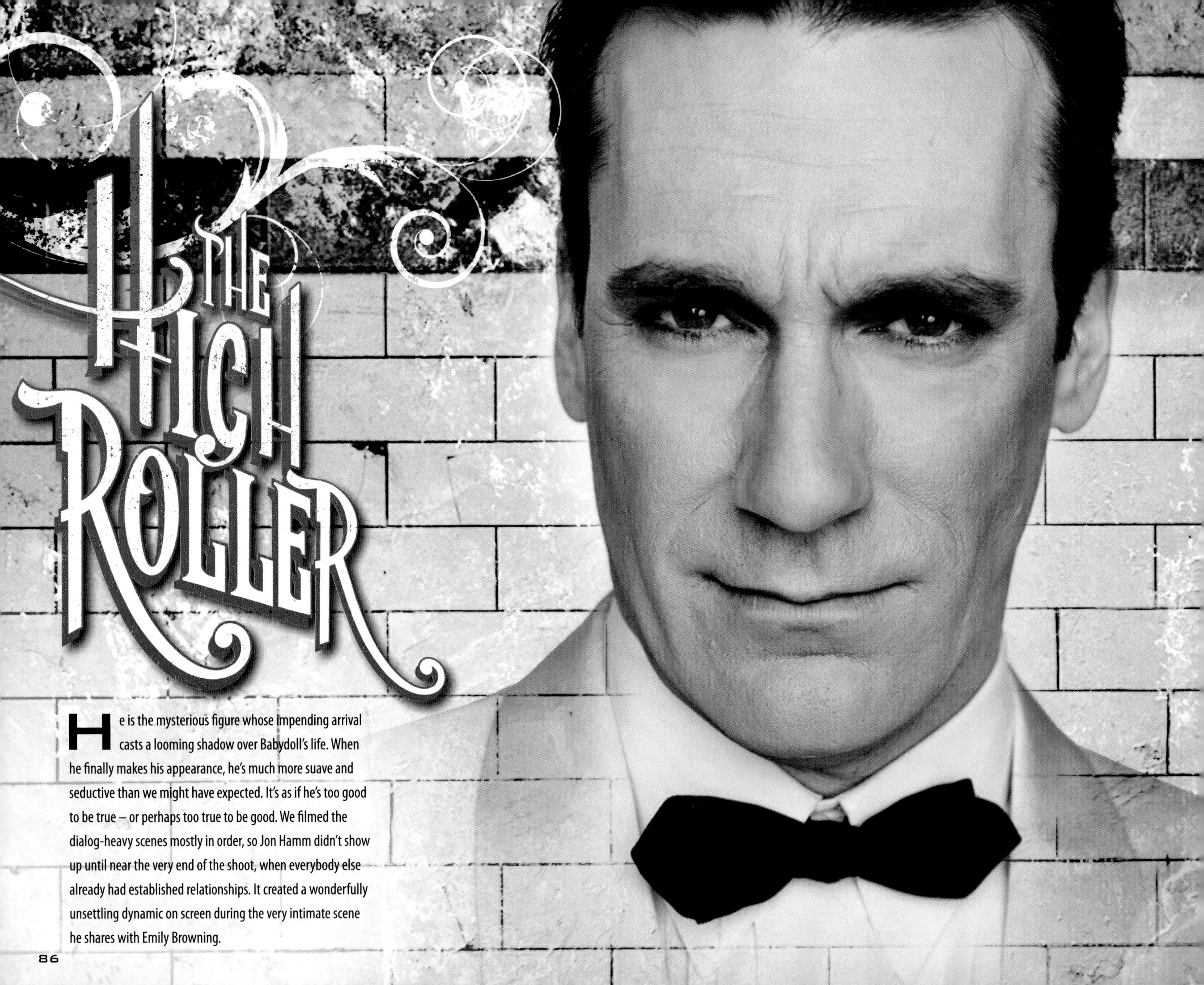

The High Roller

He is the mysterious figure whose impending arrival casts a looming shadow over Babydoll's life. When he finally makes his appearance, he's much more suave and seductive than we might have expected. It's as if he's too good to be true – or perhaps too true to be good. We filmed the dialog-heavy scenes mostly in order, so Jon Hamm didn't show up until near the very end of the shoot, when everybody else already had established relationships. It created a wonderfully unsettling dynamic on screen during the very intimate scene he shares with Emily Browning.

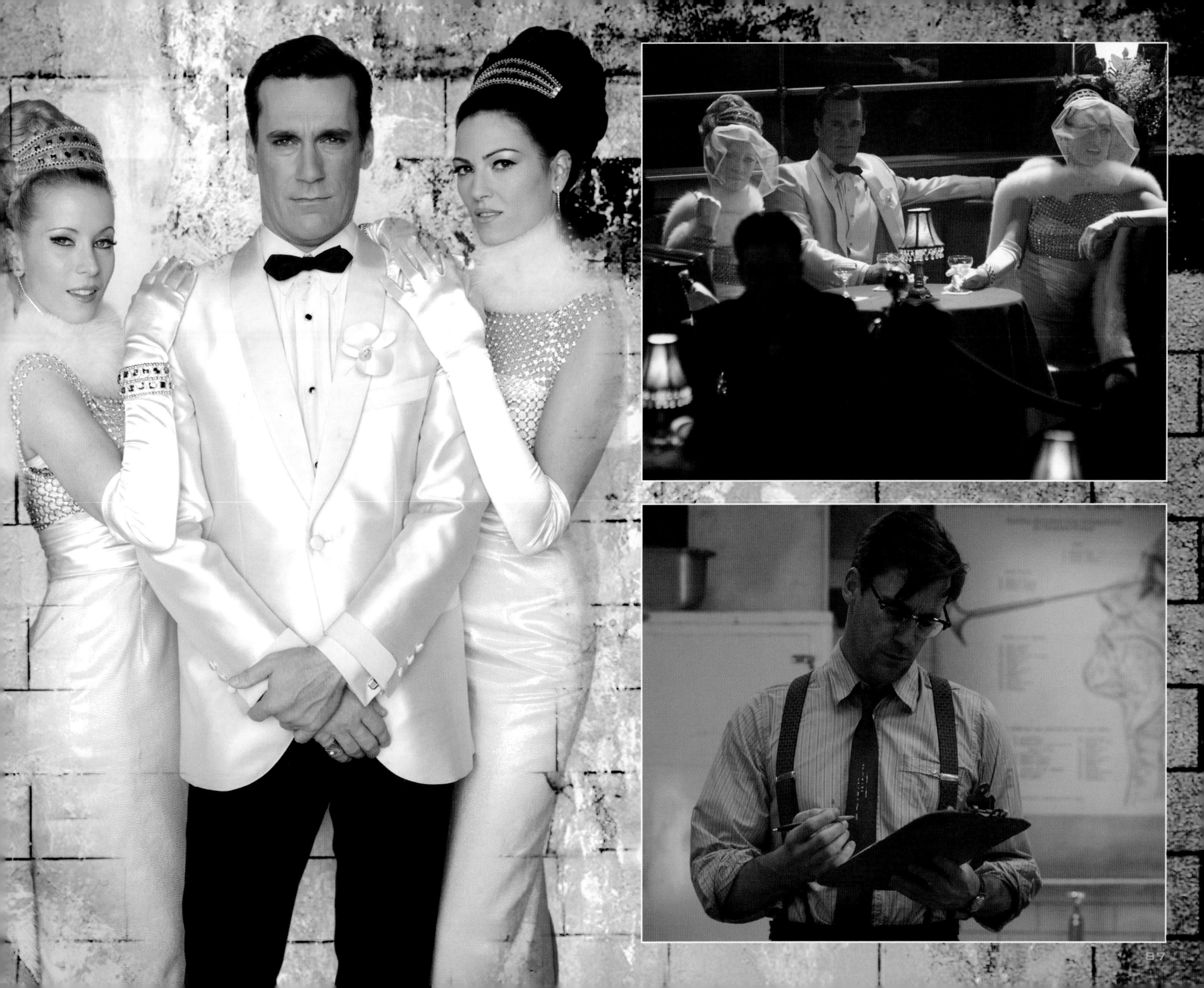

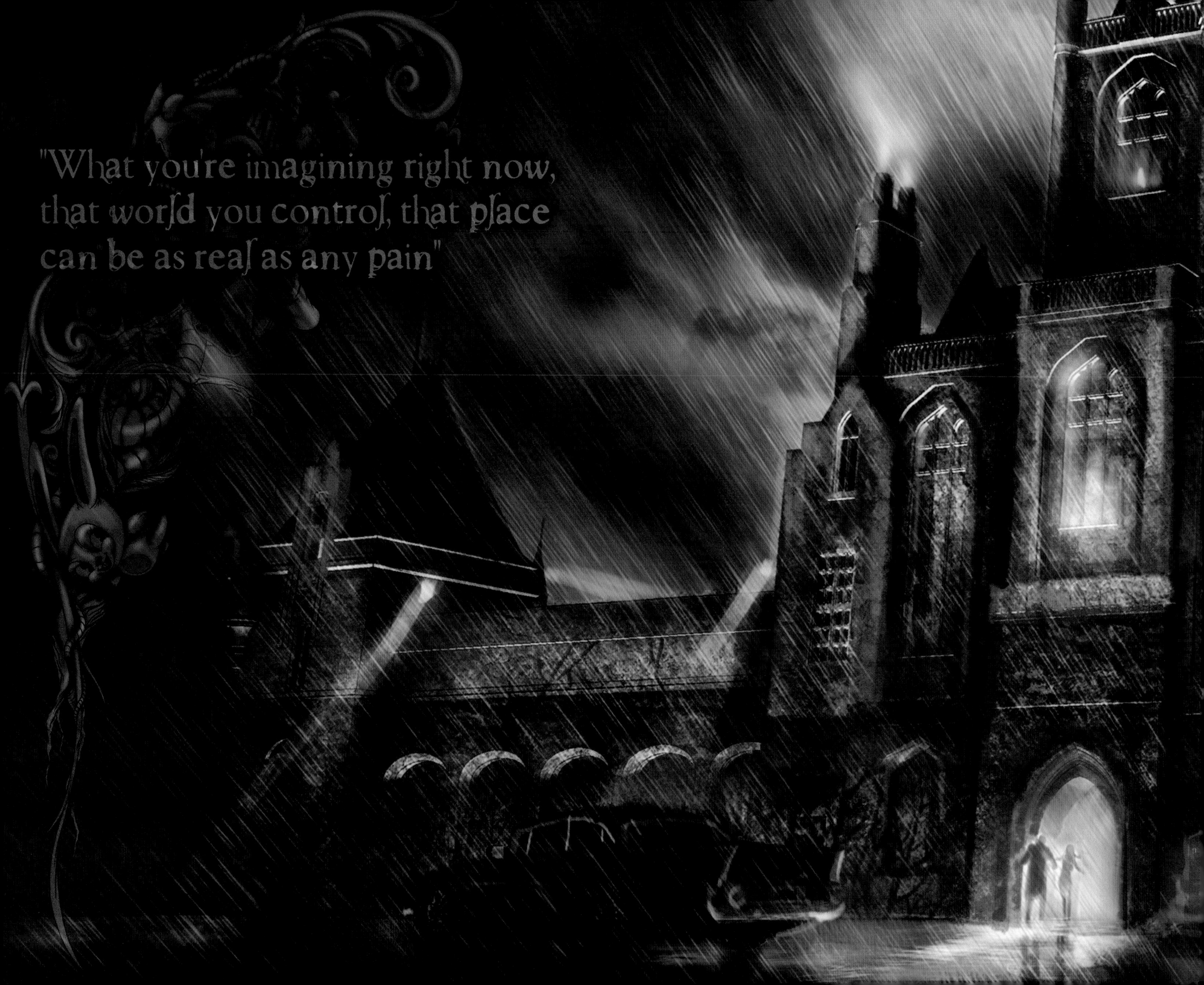
"What you're imagining right now,
that world you control, that place
can be as real as any pain"

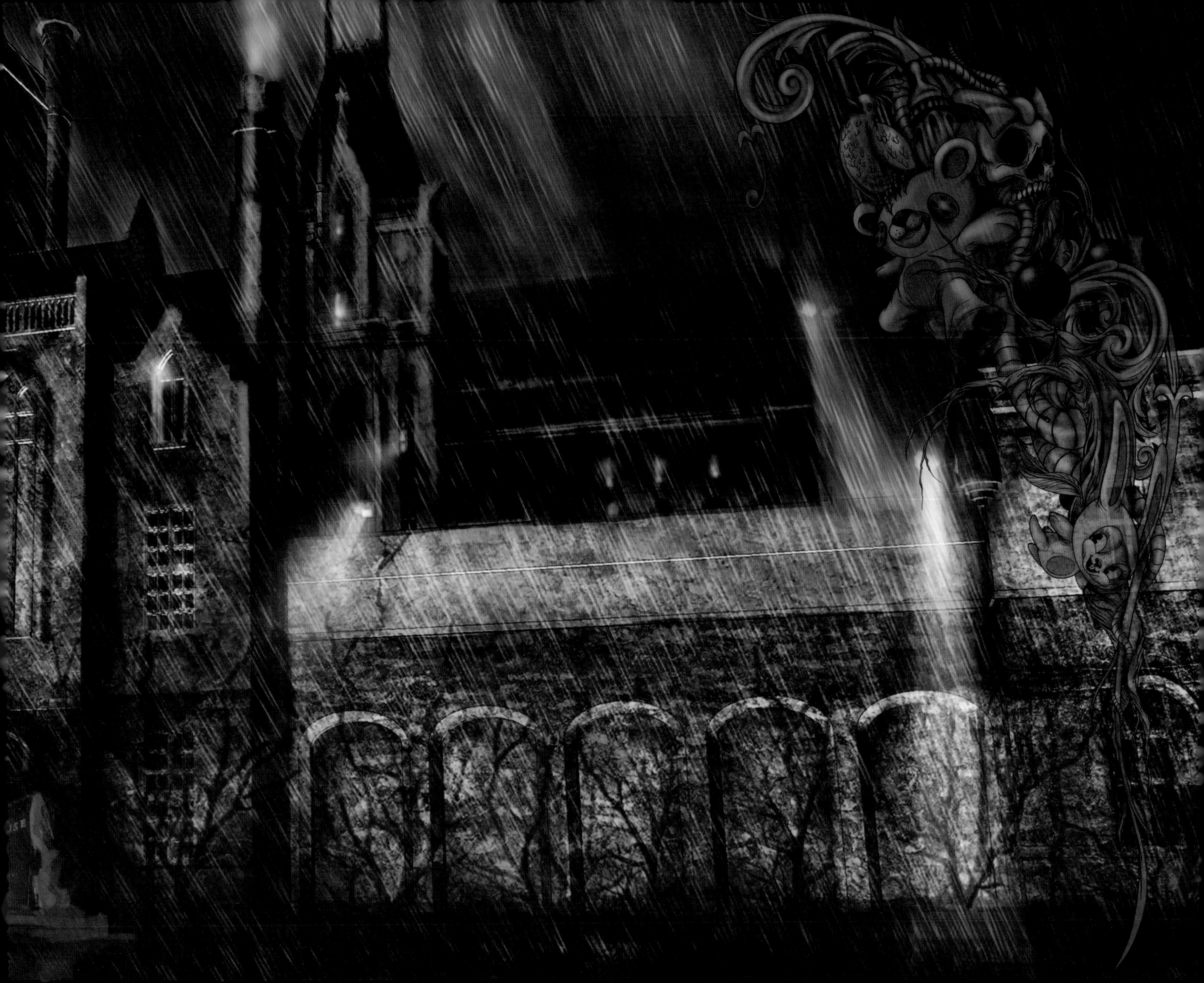

Arrival

The film is set in the 1960s, when places like Lennox House existed to shut away women who didn't conform to the expectations society had set for them. Many were truly mentally ill, but others were simply too outspoken, too promiscuous, or too uncontrollable. Any excuse was used to call them crazy and lock them up rather than deal with them. Lobotomies, which often had the effect of turning intractable patients into virtual zombies, were still being carried out in the institutions of the time; the majority of these were performed on women. Lennox House itself is a commentary on certain dark aspects of that era: it's a bleak, callous, and rundown place, and although some pioneers are attempting new, more humanitarian forms of therapy, male dominance and corruption seem to have the upper hand.

The most significant space in the asylum is a large hall we term the gymnasium, but which serves the girls as a social center, and more importantly, as a theater. There are many images and architectural elements here that will turn up again later in Babydoll's fantasies. With a proscenium surmounted by an angelic face resembling Babydoll's own and sunlight streaming down through grimy windows, it's easy to see why Rick Carter has called it, "a church to eternal innocence." It is a portal of the imagination where we literally peel back the wallpaper to increase the theatricality a hundredfold.

In Babydoll's mind the space is transformed into the Paradise Theater, where girls dance in public before clients select them for more private services. It is the colorful center of the gaudy brothel of which Blue is the undisputed overlord. The girls are still prisoners, but at least here they are the main attraction. At least here they have some worth. And just perhaps, here is where they might find the tools to fight back.

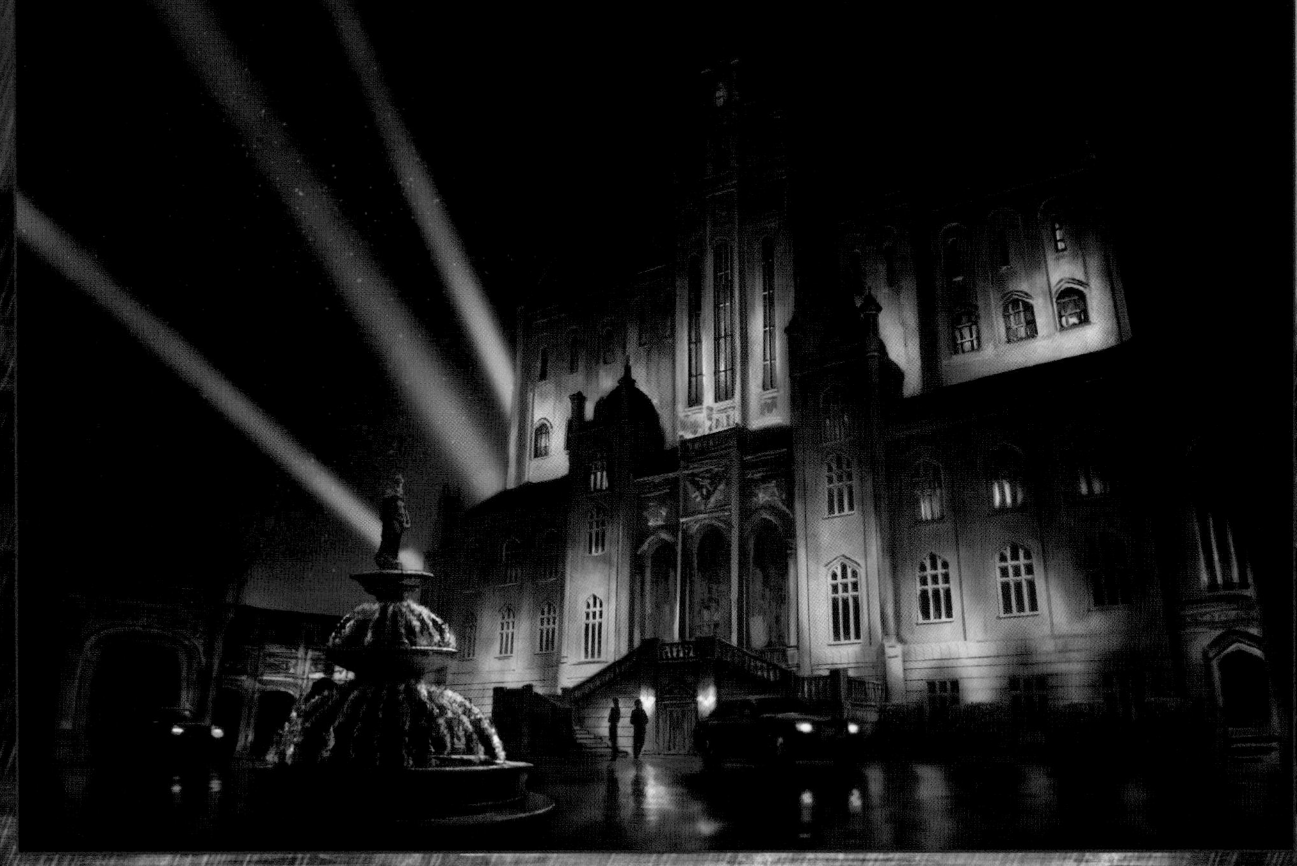

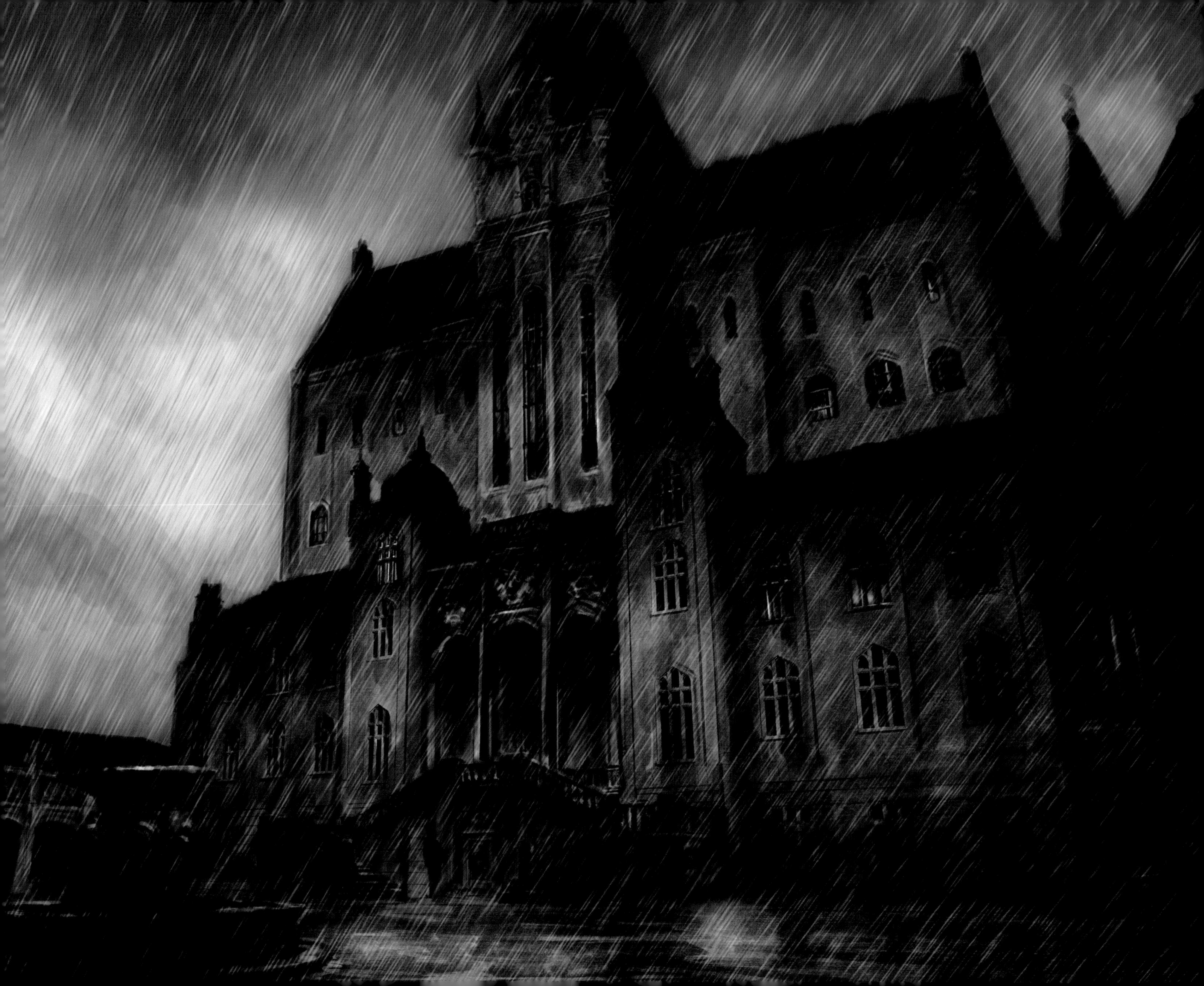

The Institution

Previous spreads: Concept art for the exterior of Lennox House, both as a forbidding institution and the brothel of Babydoll's imagination.
This page: Renderings of Blue's secluded hideaway, and a shot of the kitchen.
Opposite: Plans and the architectural model of the asylum.

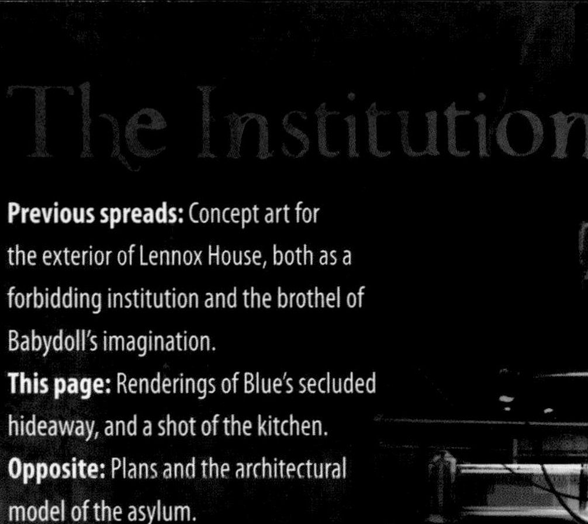

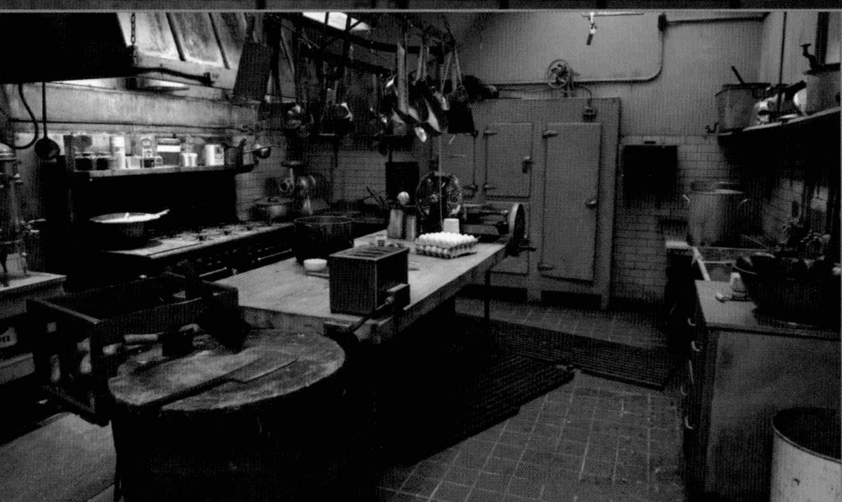

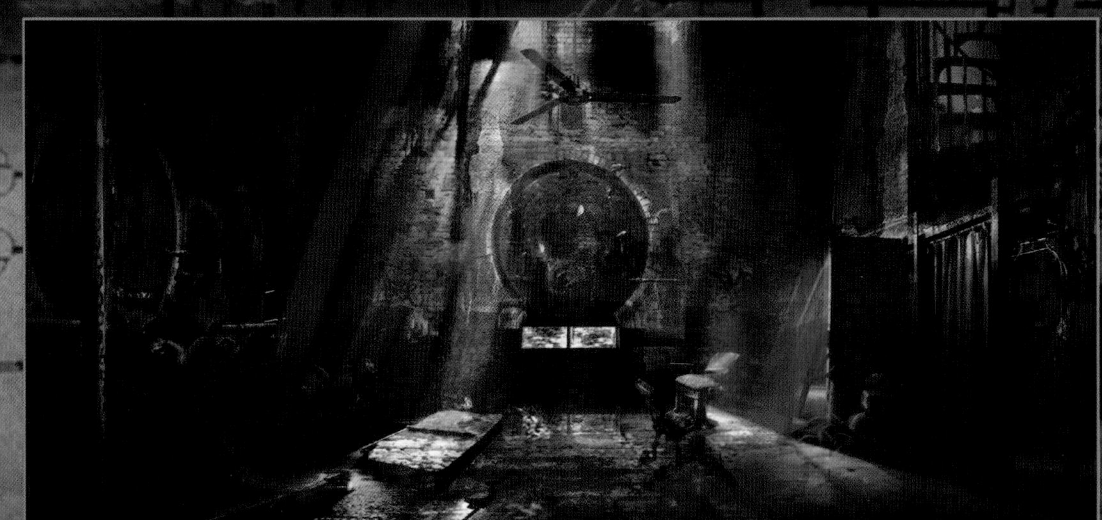

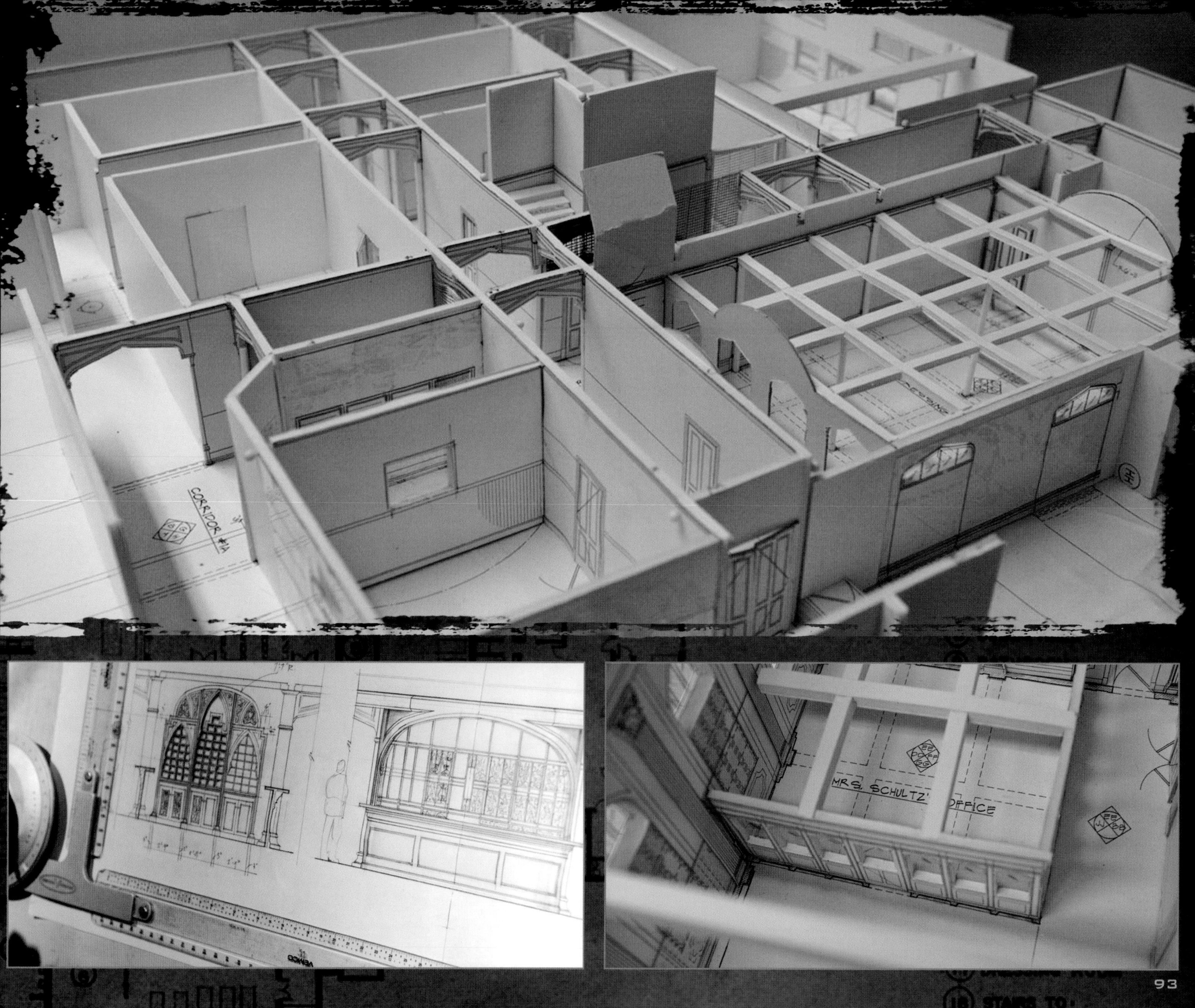
CORRIDOR #1A
MRS. SCHULTZ' OFFICE
STAIRS TO

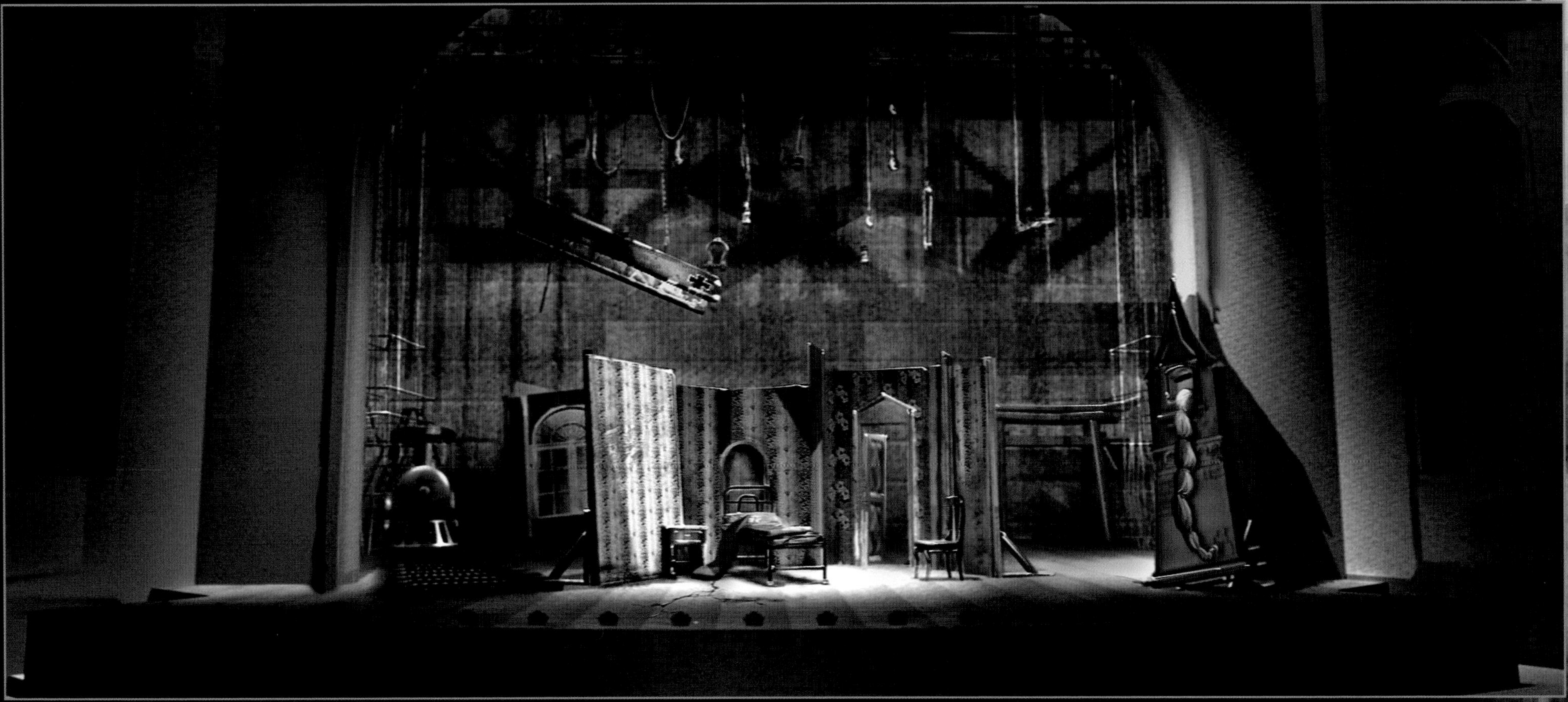

On Stage

This spread: Concepts for the stage used for therapeutic theater sessions.

Right: A shot of the stage constructed for the film.

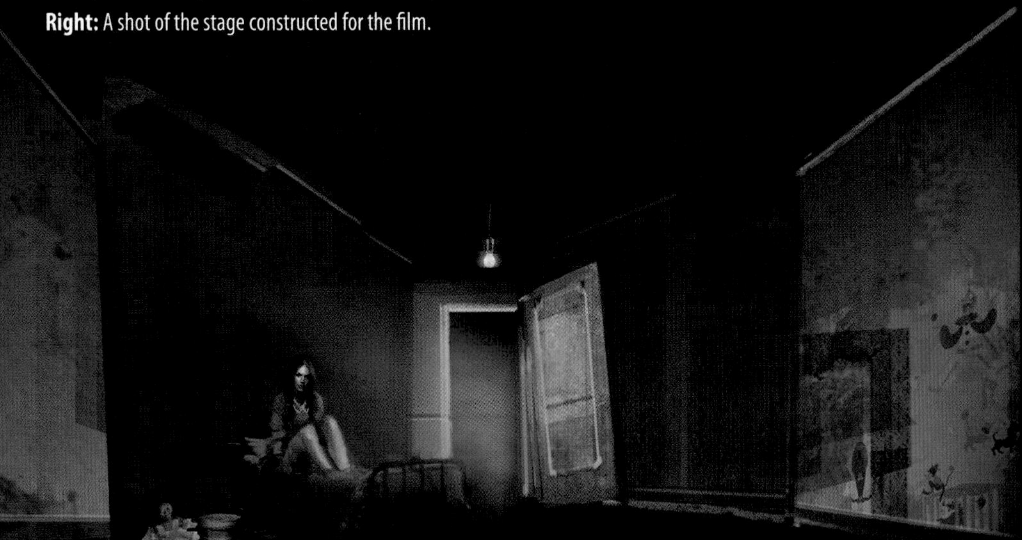

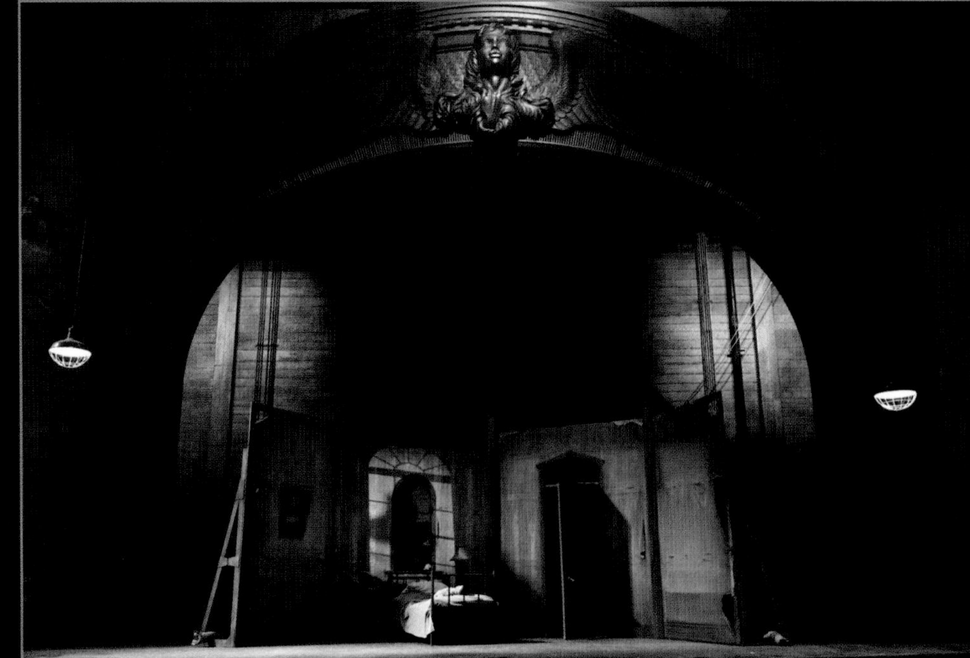

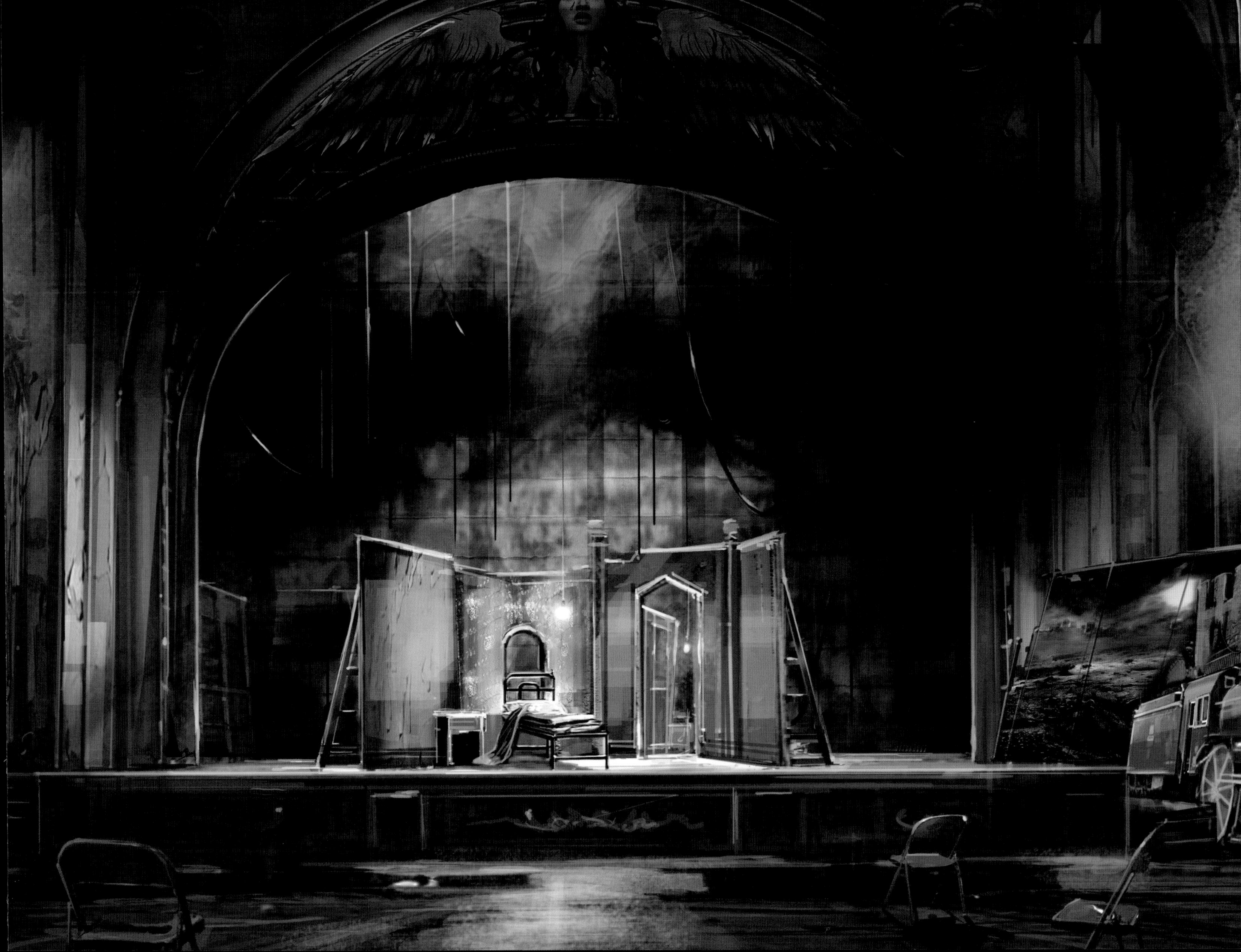

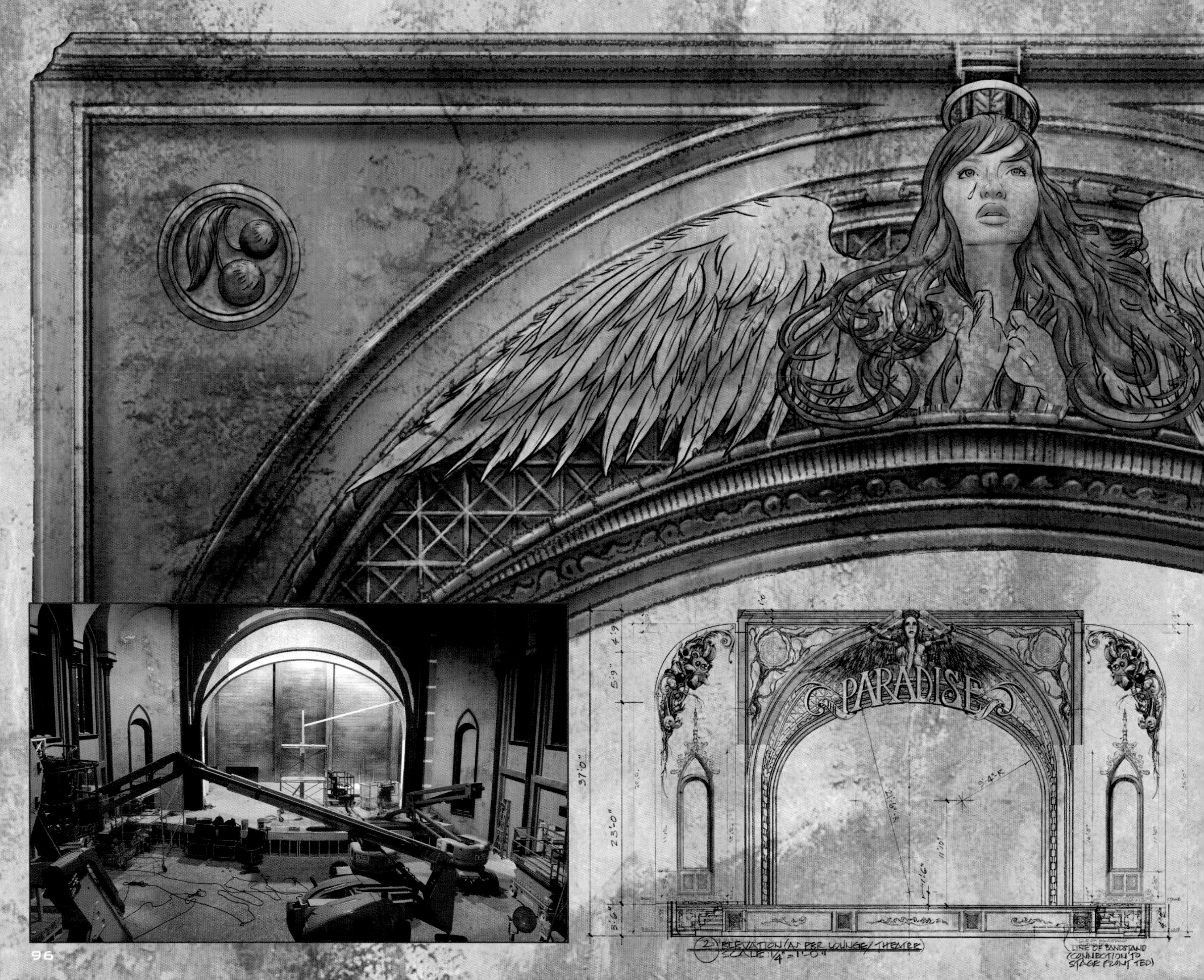

PARADISE
37'0"
23'-0"
5'9"
4'9"
3'6"
9'-4" R
2 ELEVATION (AS PER LOUNGE/ THEATER)
SCALE: 1/4" = 1'-0"
LINE OF BANDSTAND
(CONNECTION TO
STAGE FRONT TBD)

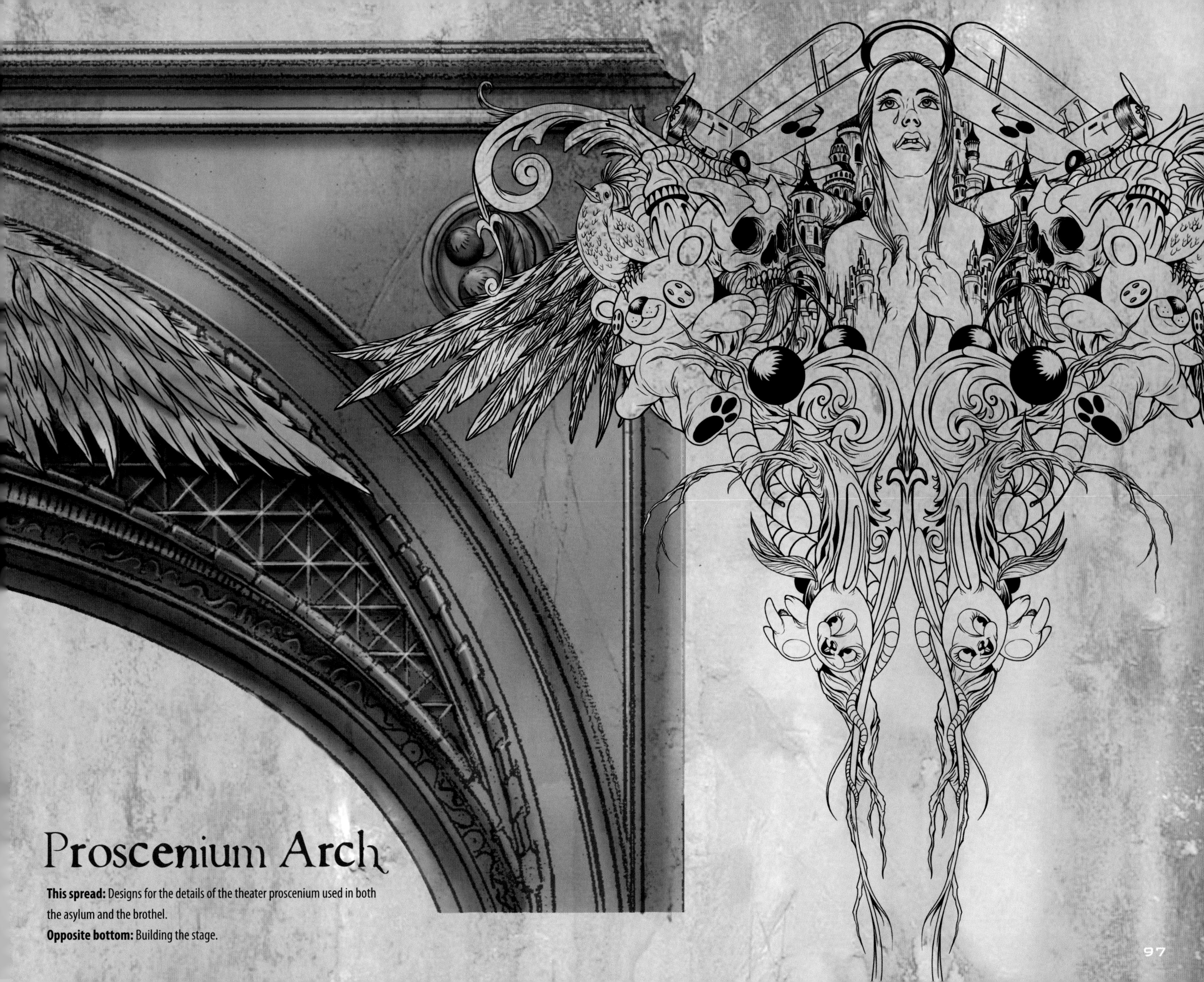

Proscenium Arch

This spread: Designs for the details of the theater proscenium used in both the asylum and the brothel.

Opposite bottom: Building the stage.

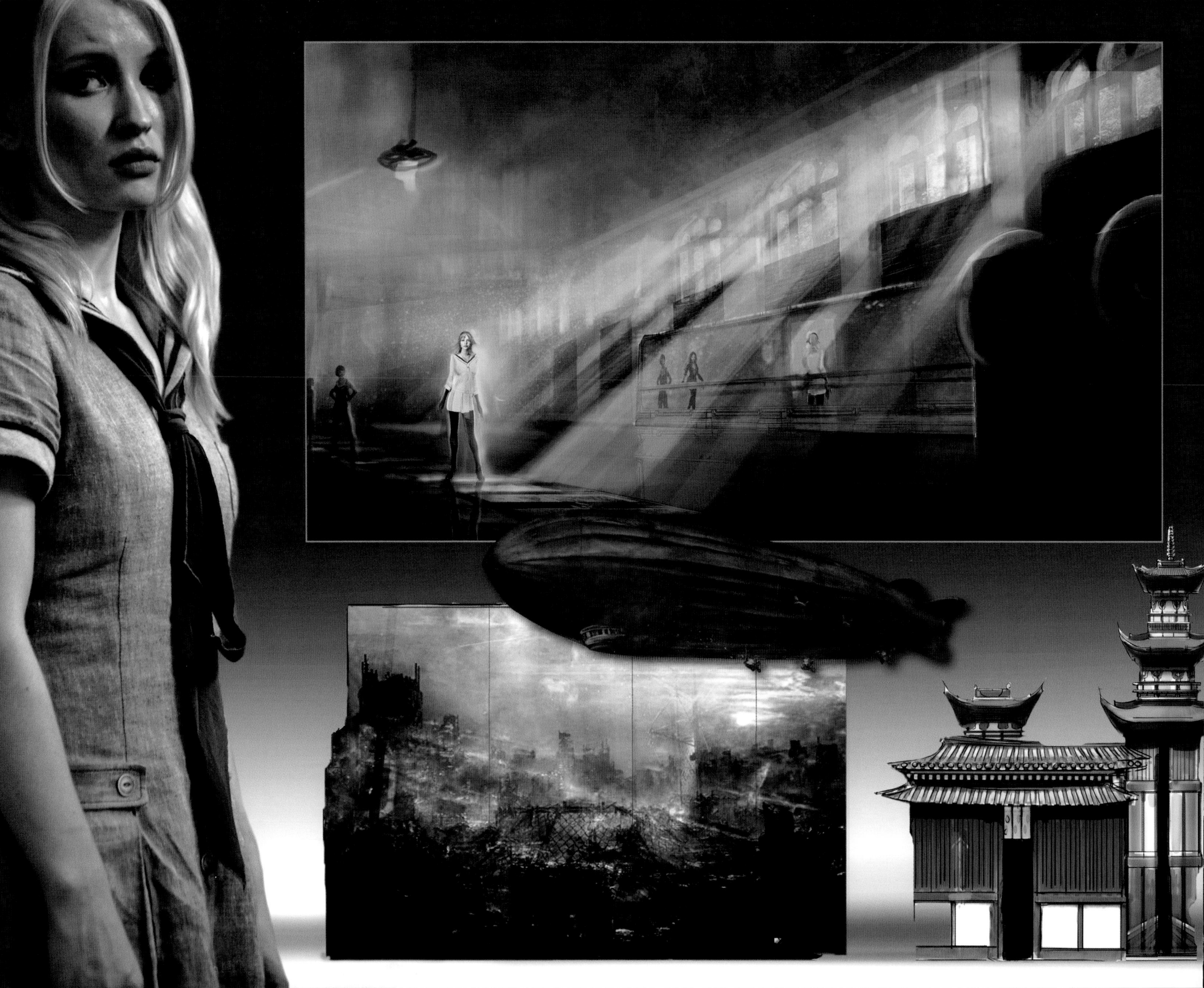

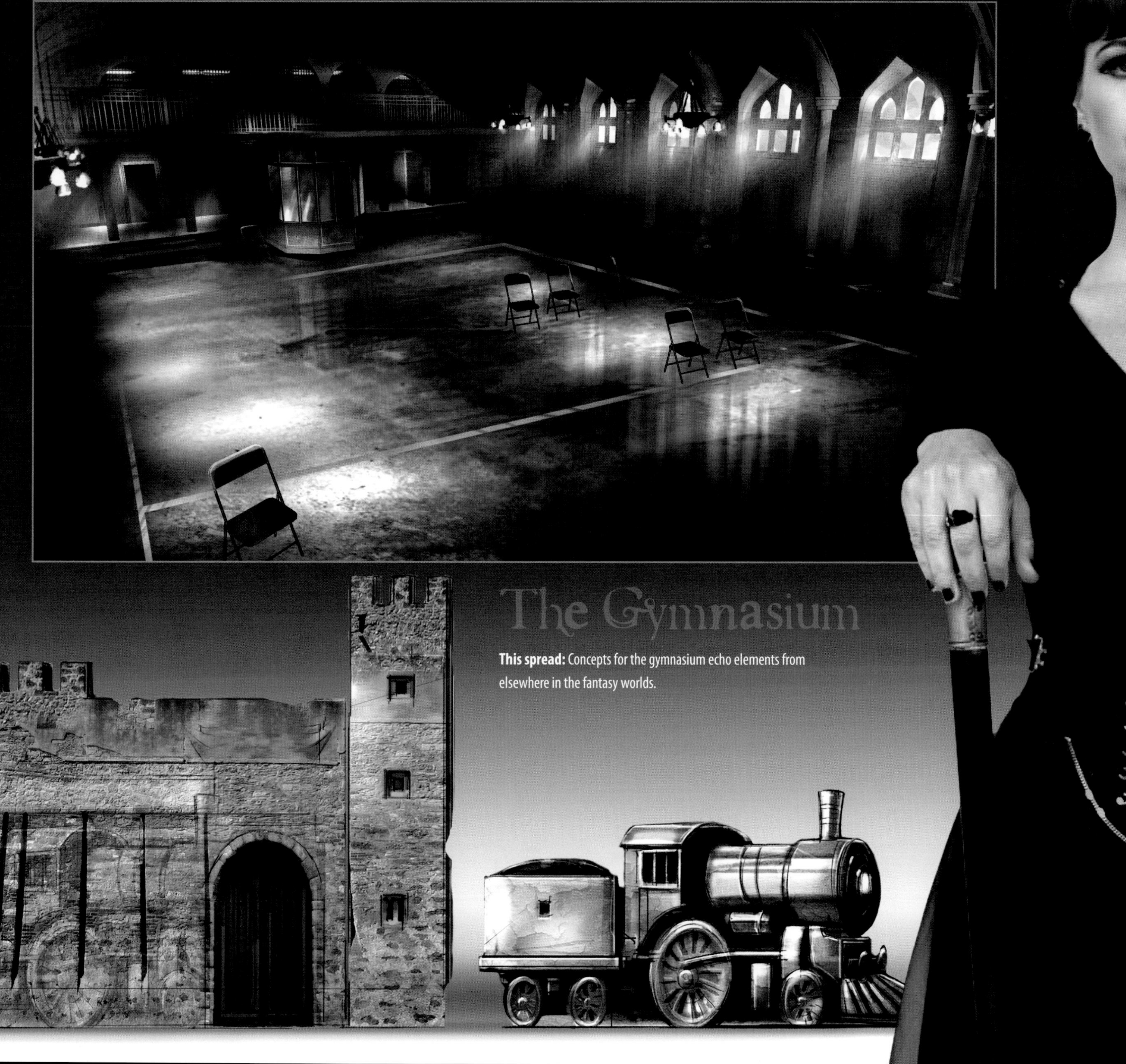

The Gymnasium

This spread: Concepts for the gymnasium echo elements from elsewhere in the fantasy worlds.

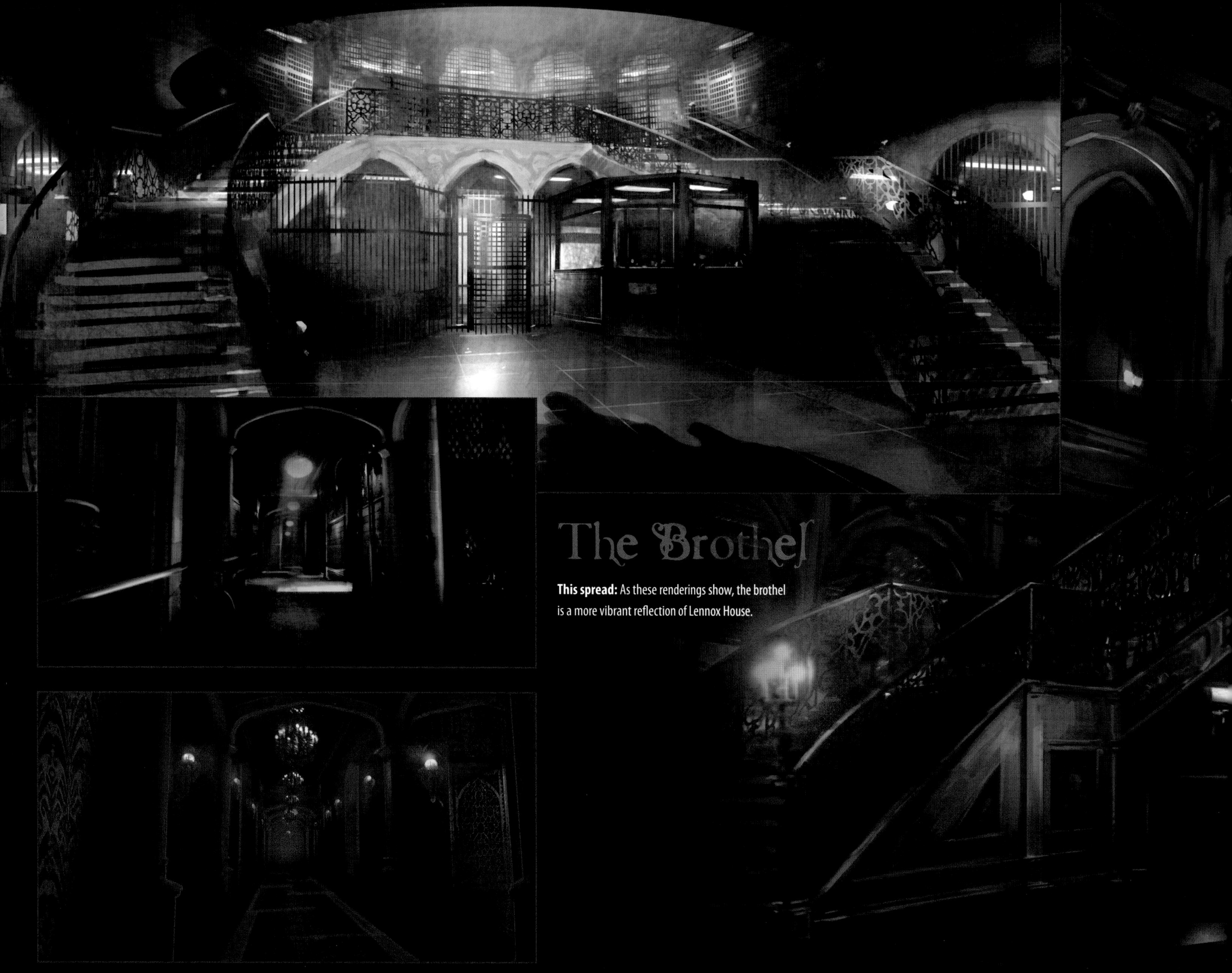

The Brothel

This spread: As these renderings show, the brothel is a more vibrant reflection of Lennox House.

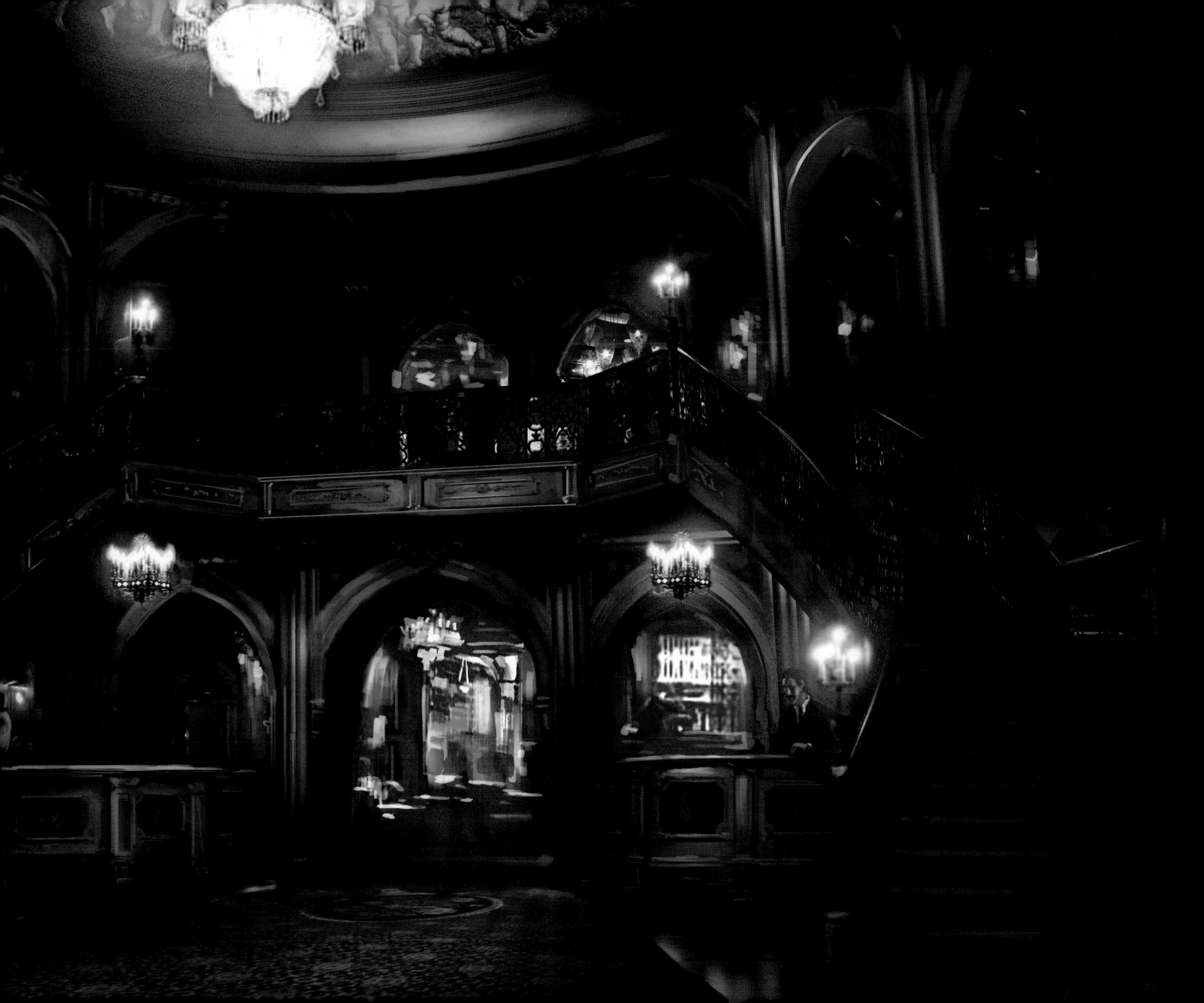

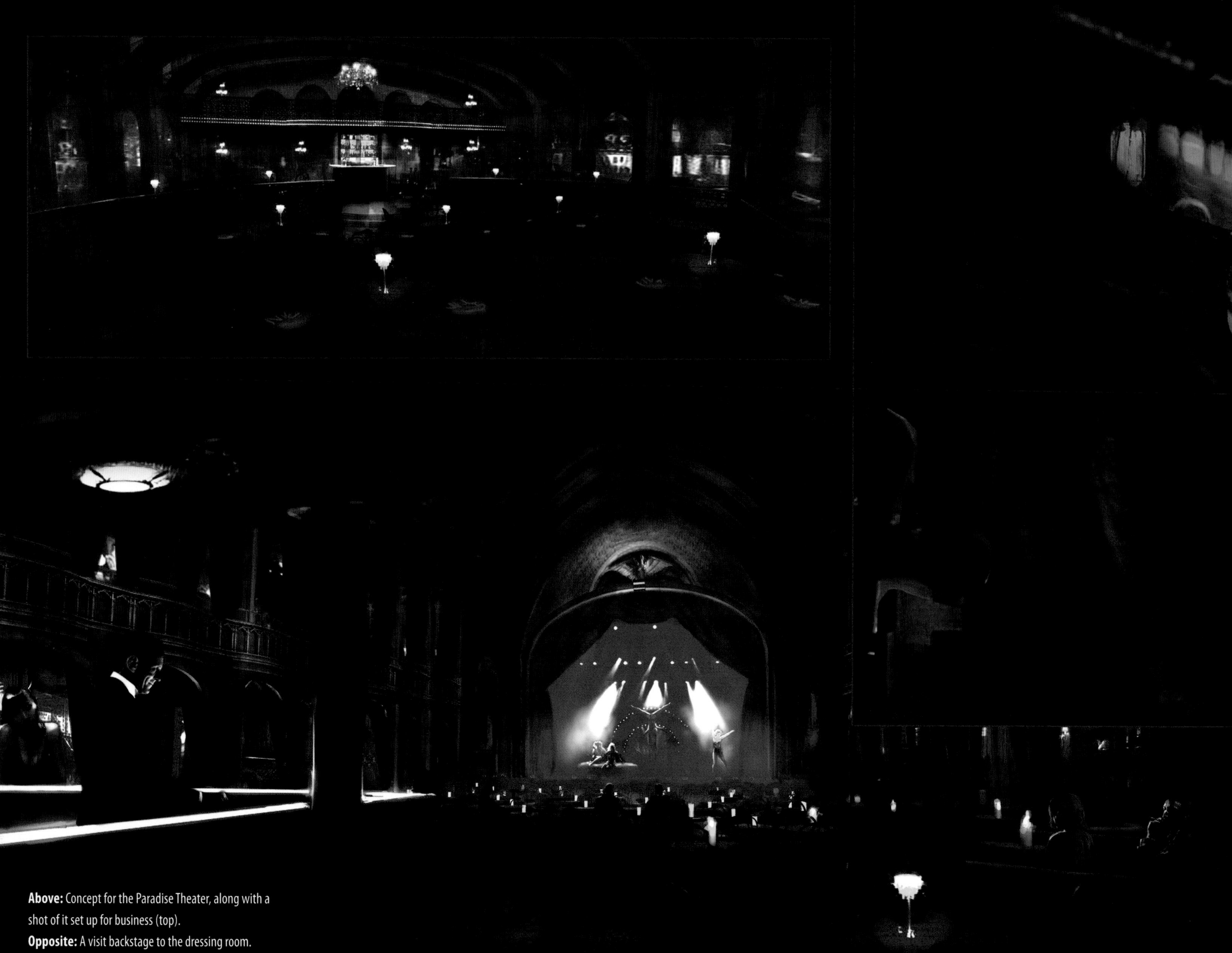

Above: Concept for the Paradise Theater, along with a shot of it set up for business (top).
Opposite: A visit backstage to the dressing room.

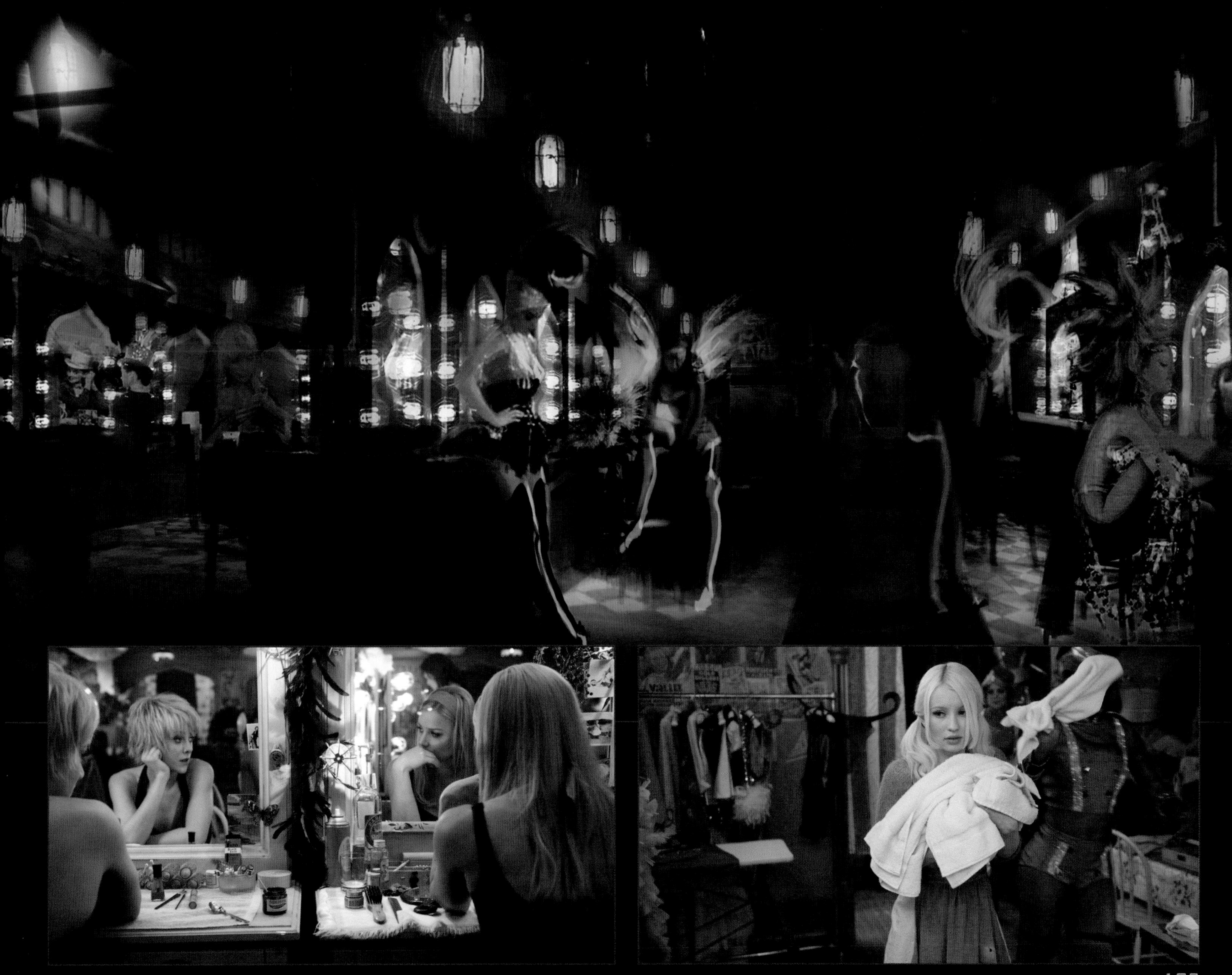

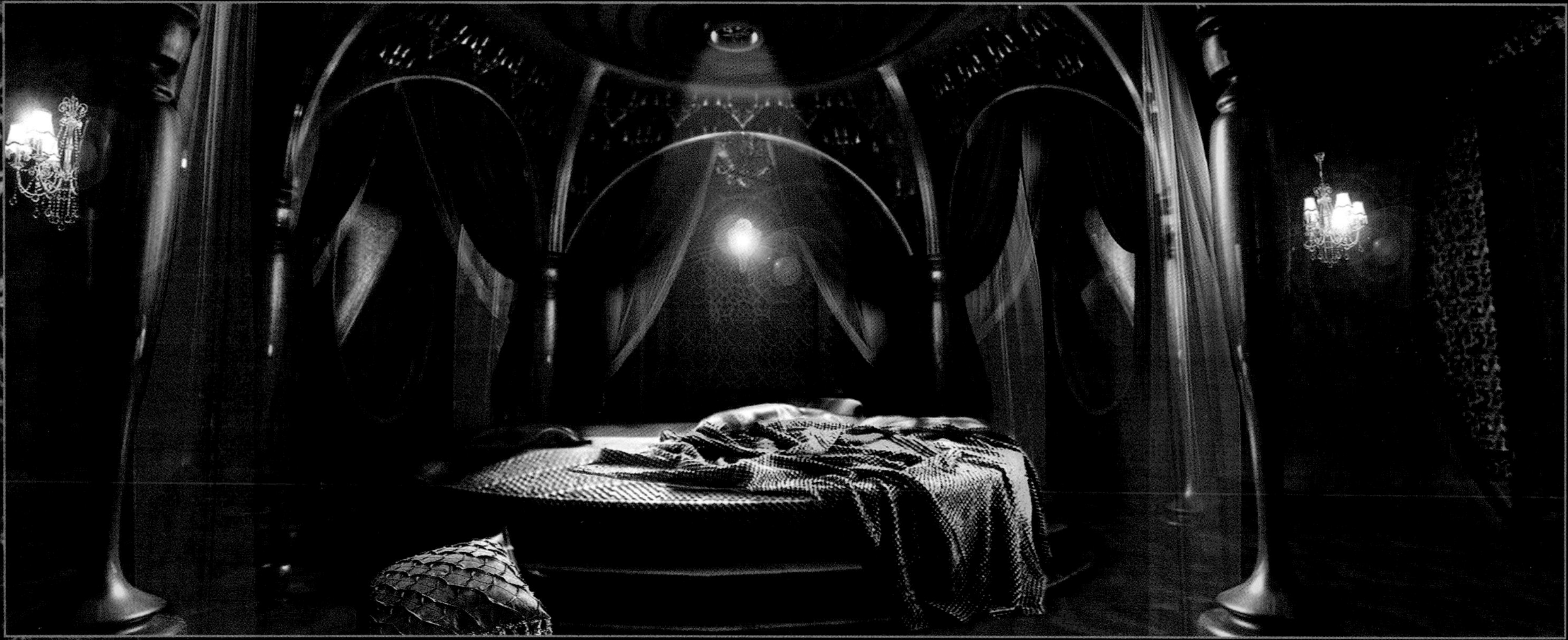

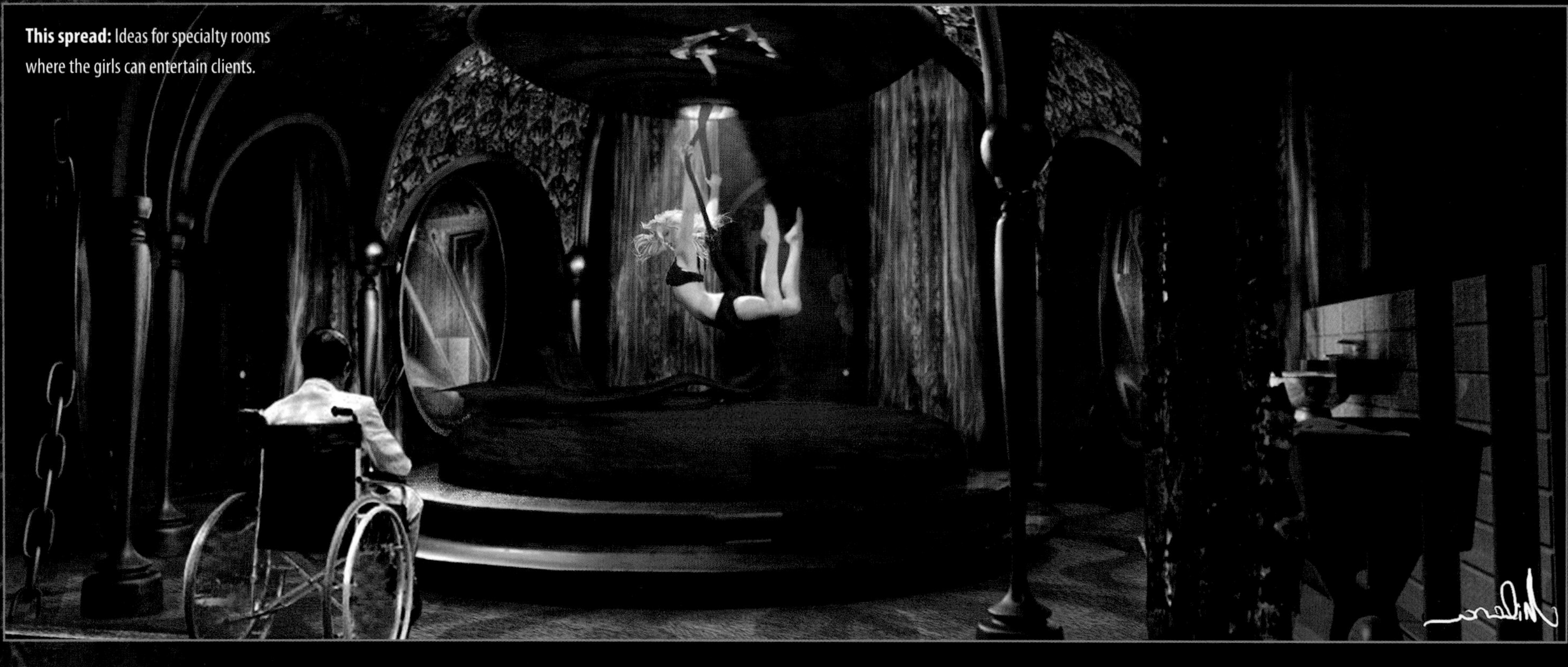

This spread: Ideas for specialty rooms where the girls can entertain clients.

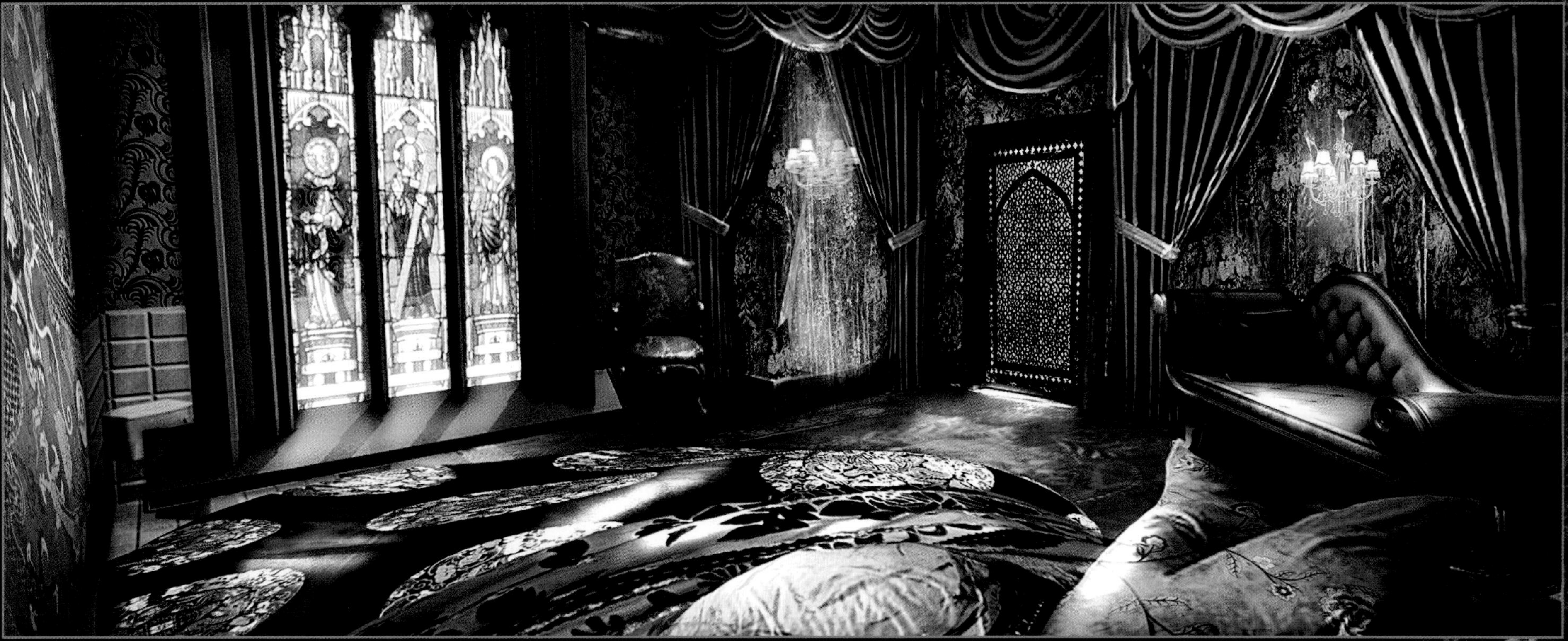

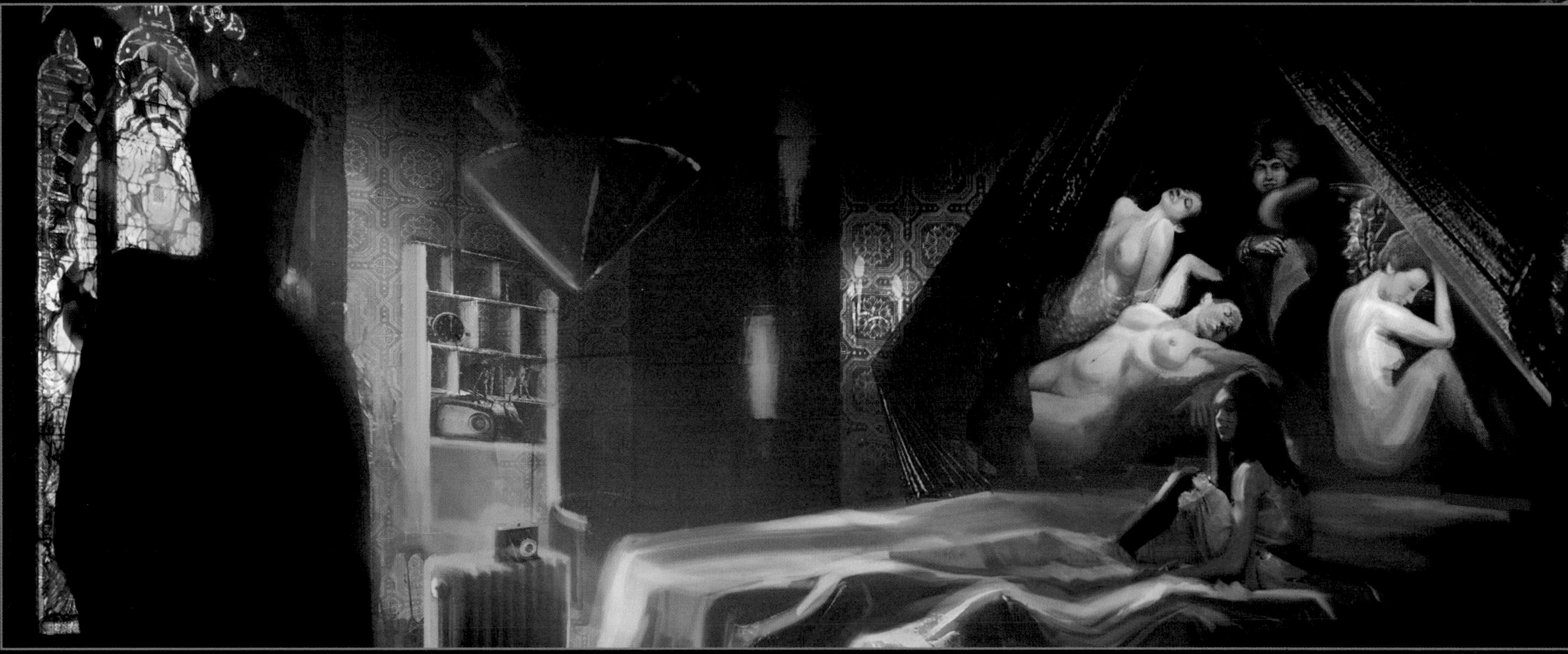

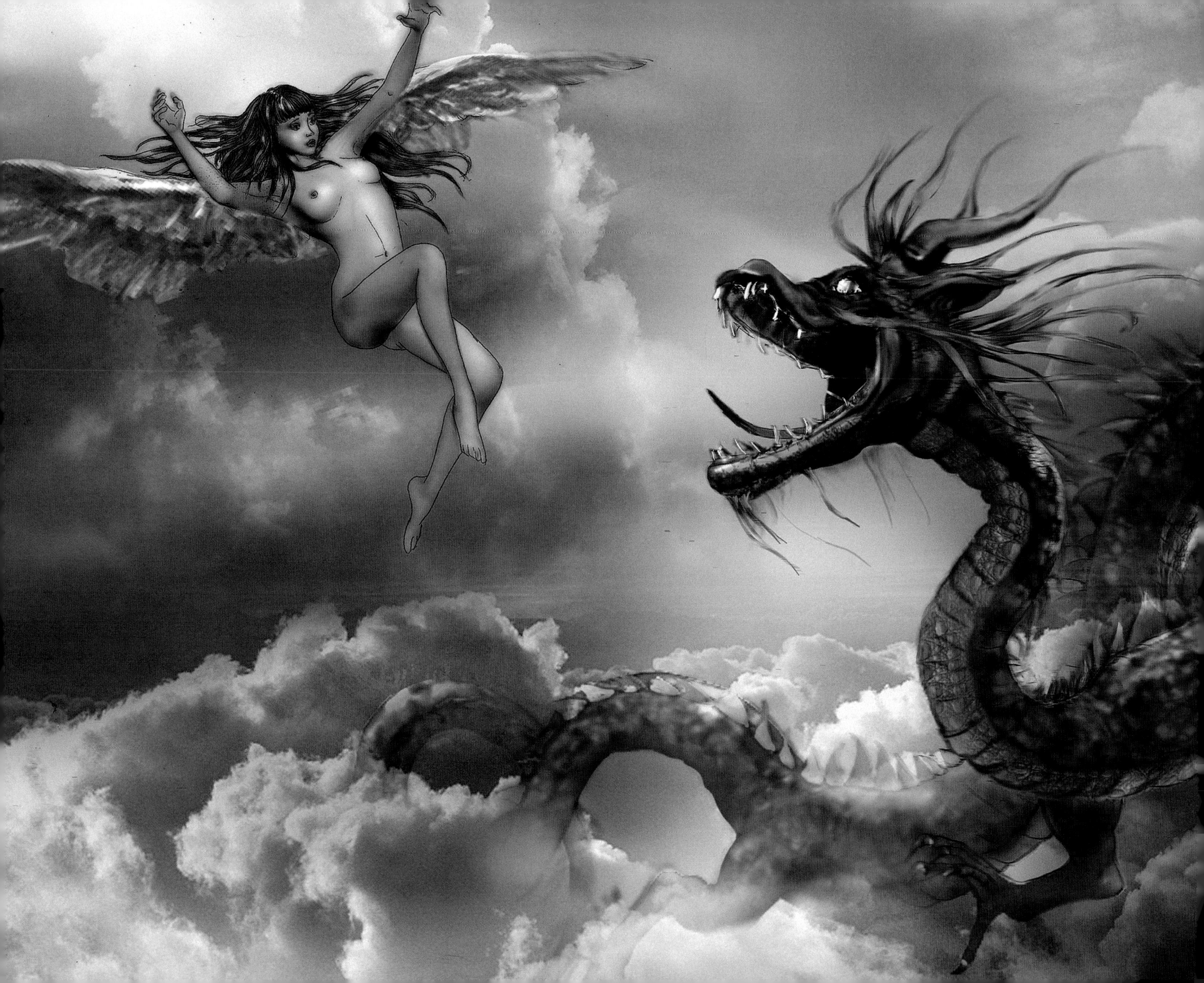

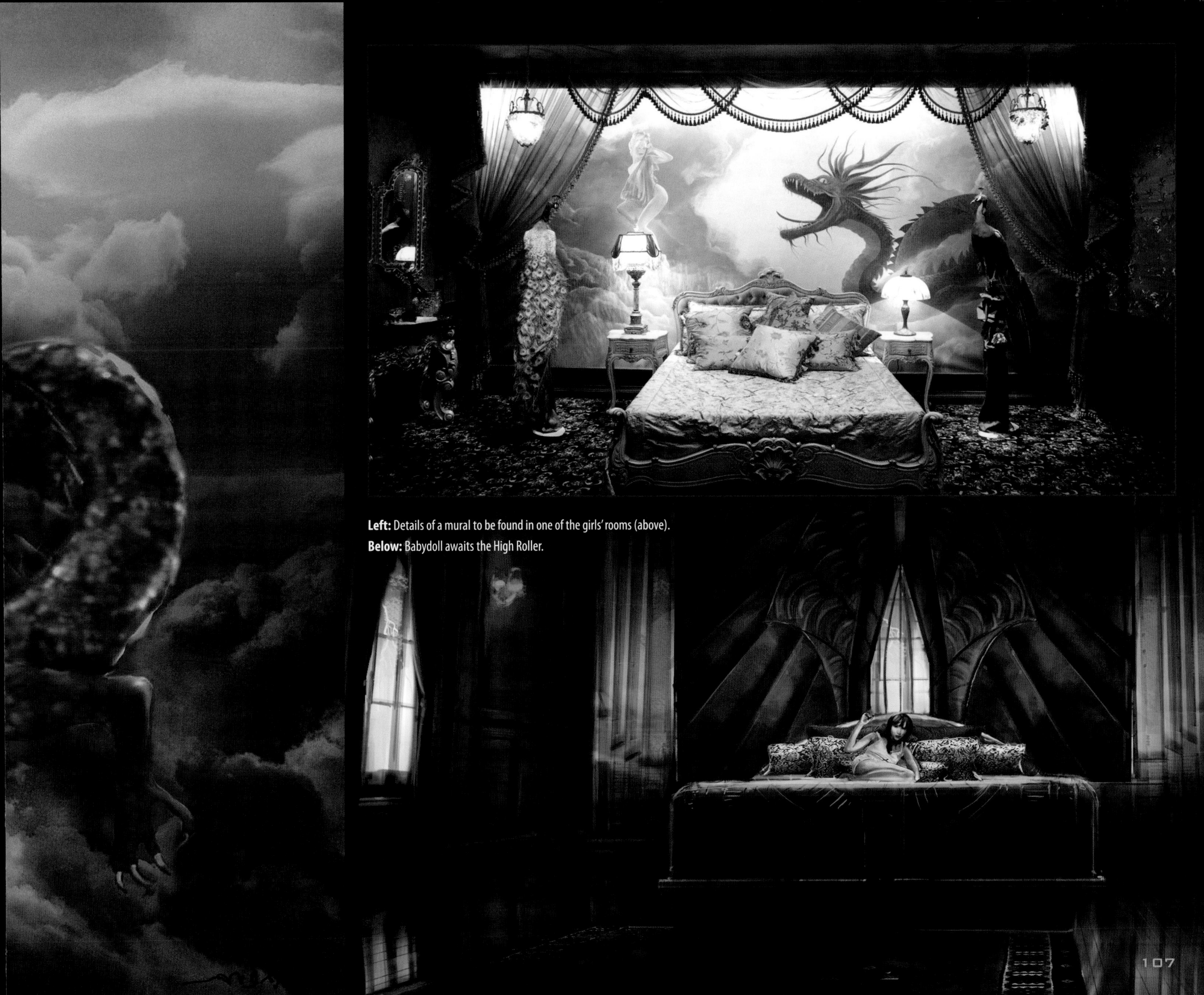

Left: Details of a mural to be found in one of the girls' rooms (above).

Below: Babydoll awaits the High Roller.

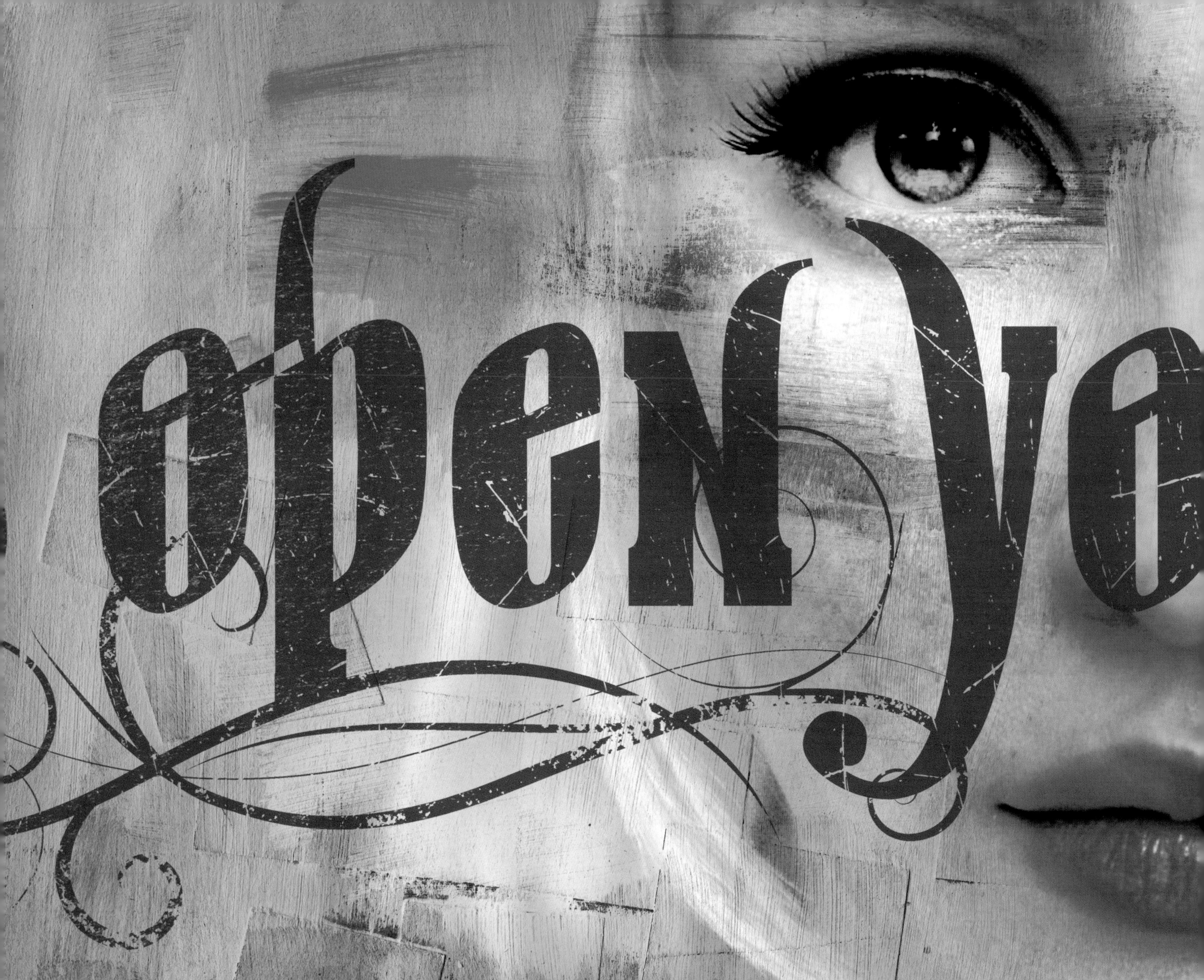
open ye

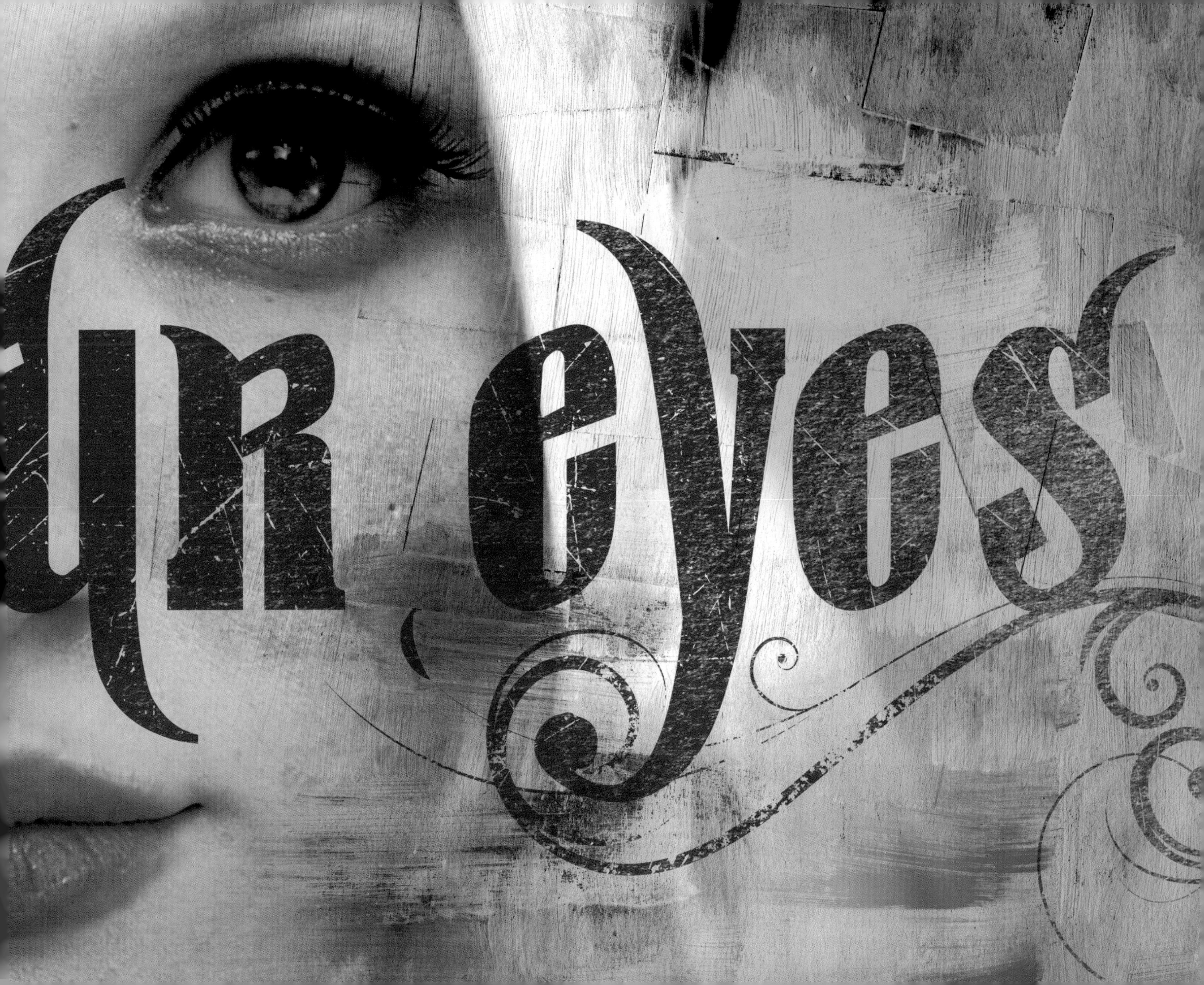
eyes

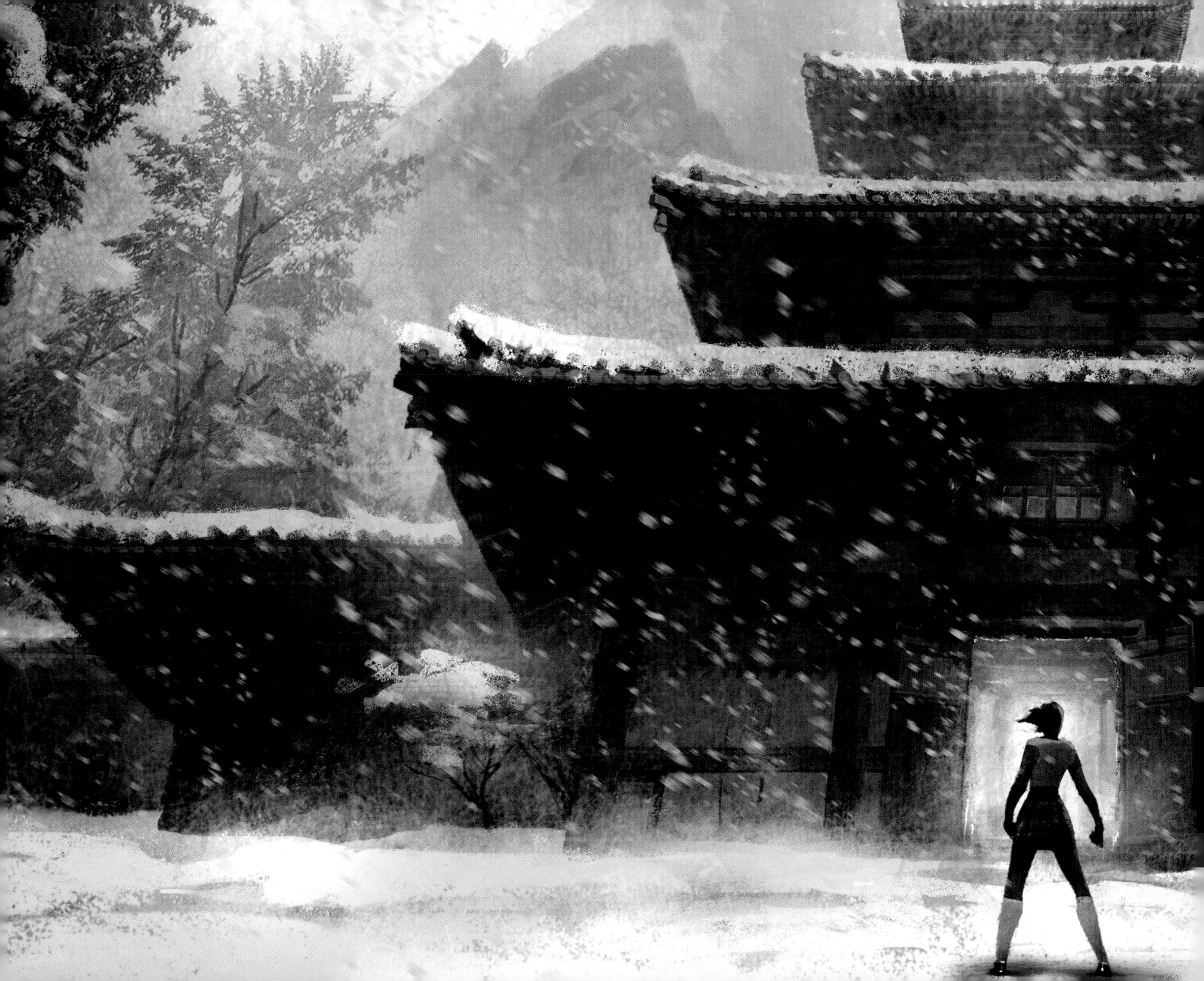

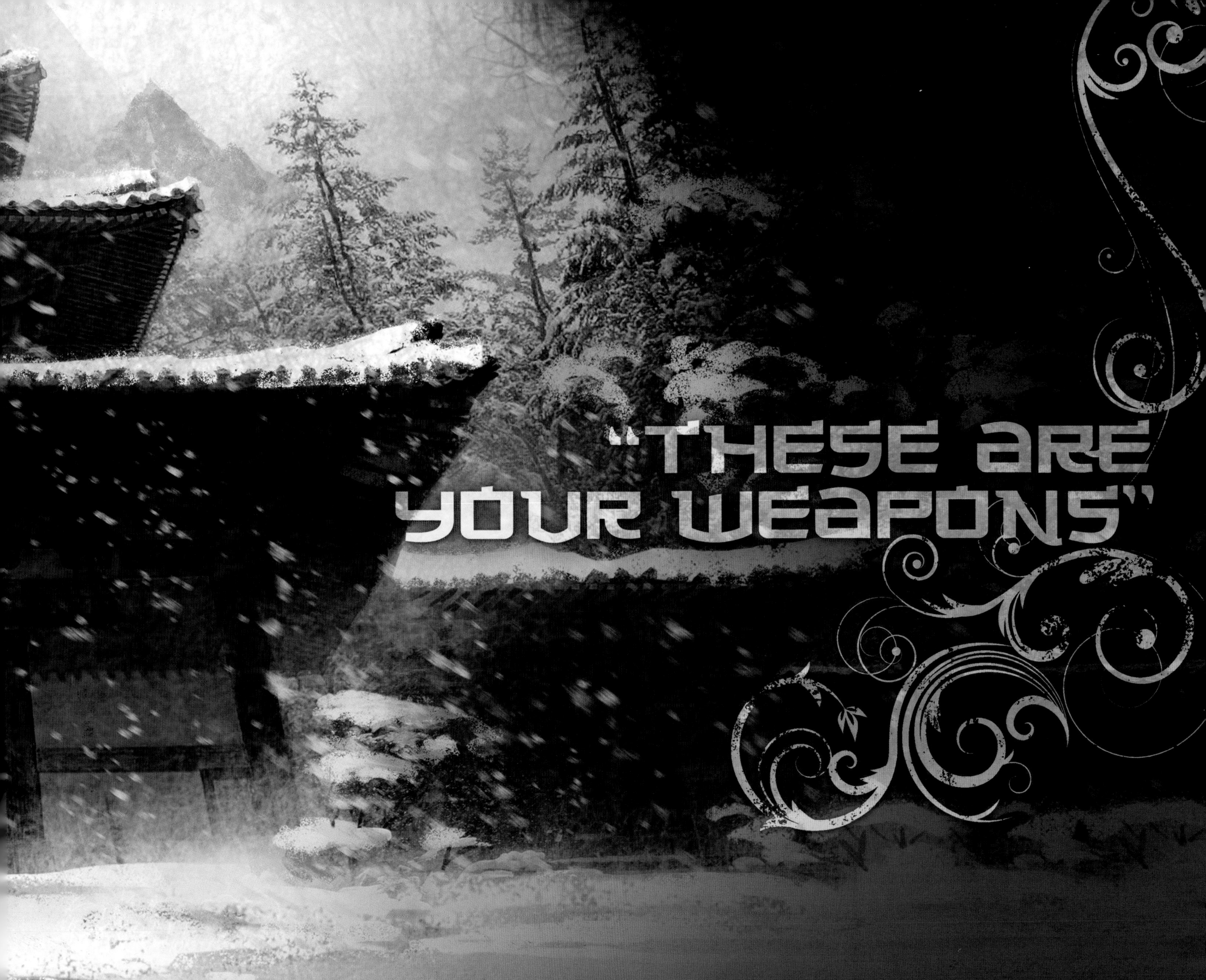
"THESE ARE
YOUR WEAPONS"

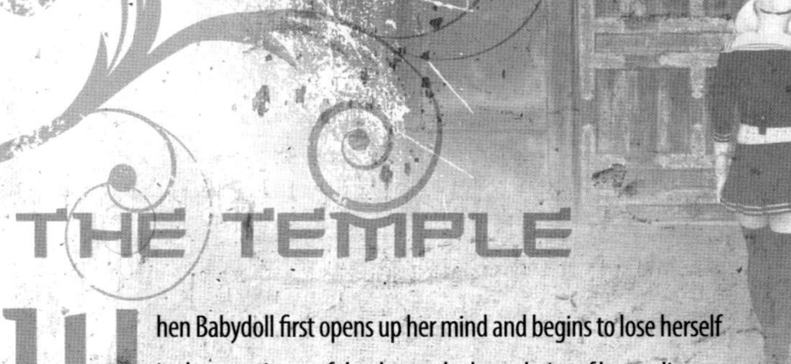

THE TEMPLE

When Babydoll first opens up her mind and begins to lose herself in the experience of the dance, the boundaries of her reality blur even more than they already have. She finds herself standing before an immense Japanese temple in the midst of gently swirling snow flurries. Inside she encounters a Wise Man, who gets her to realize that she wants to escape more than anything. Towards this end, he imparts to her two crucial things: a list of talismans she'll need to break out of her prison, and the weapons she'll need to acquire the talismans.

The five talismans are a Map, Fire, a Knife, a Key, and a fifth thing that is to remain a mystery until Babydoll (and only Babydoll) solves it. He offers no explanation of how they are supposed to be used, or how or when they are to be obtained; like the fifth item, it is assumed she will just know. Her weapons include a custom-made .45 automatic – eerily similar to the one involved in the recent tragedy back home – and a Japanese short sword of unusual make. Etched into its fine blade are symbols of Babydoll's journey, from the happier days of her childhood, through to the dark times ahead. If only she could decipher them. . .

But for now, the only things between her and continuing on that journey are three gargantuan samurai wielding a variety of high-powered weaponry. The Wise Man vanishes, and she is left to face them all alone. It is her first test.

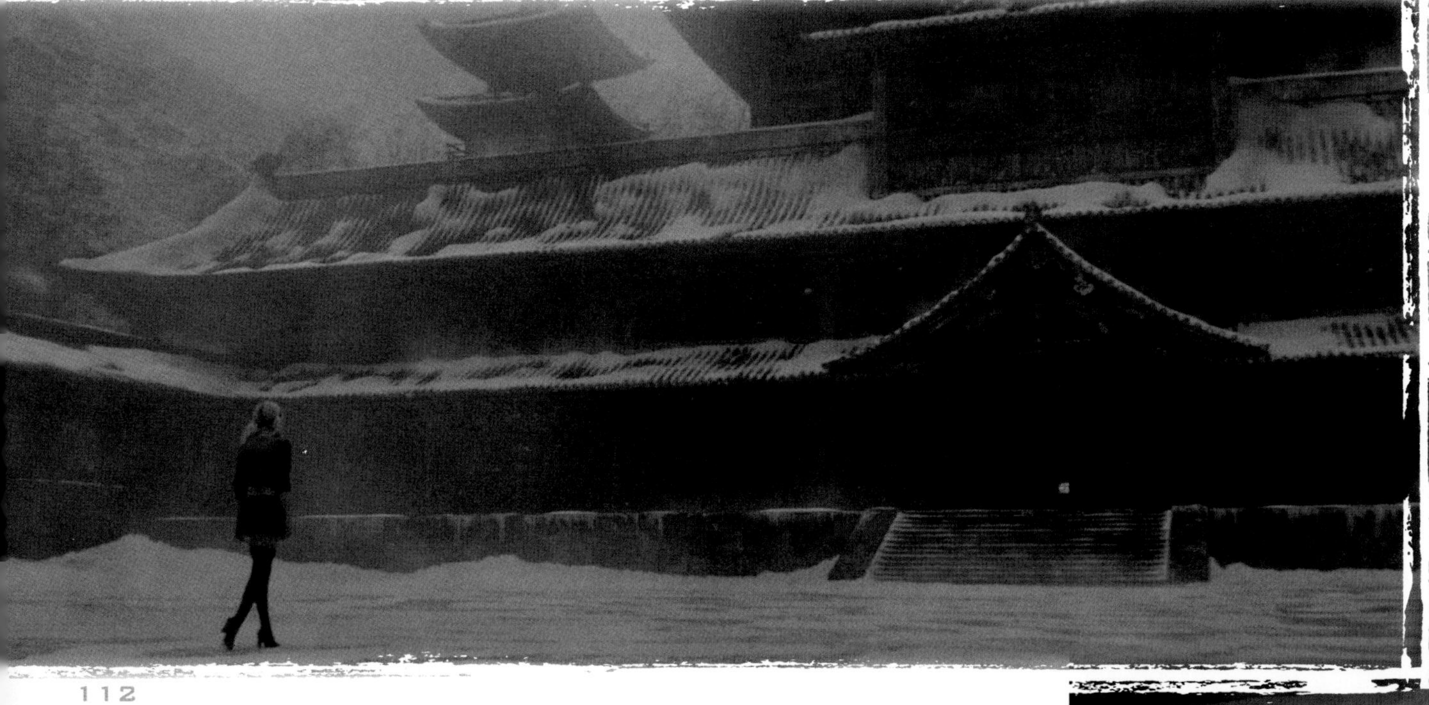

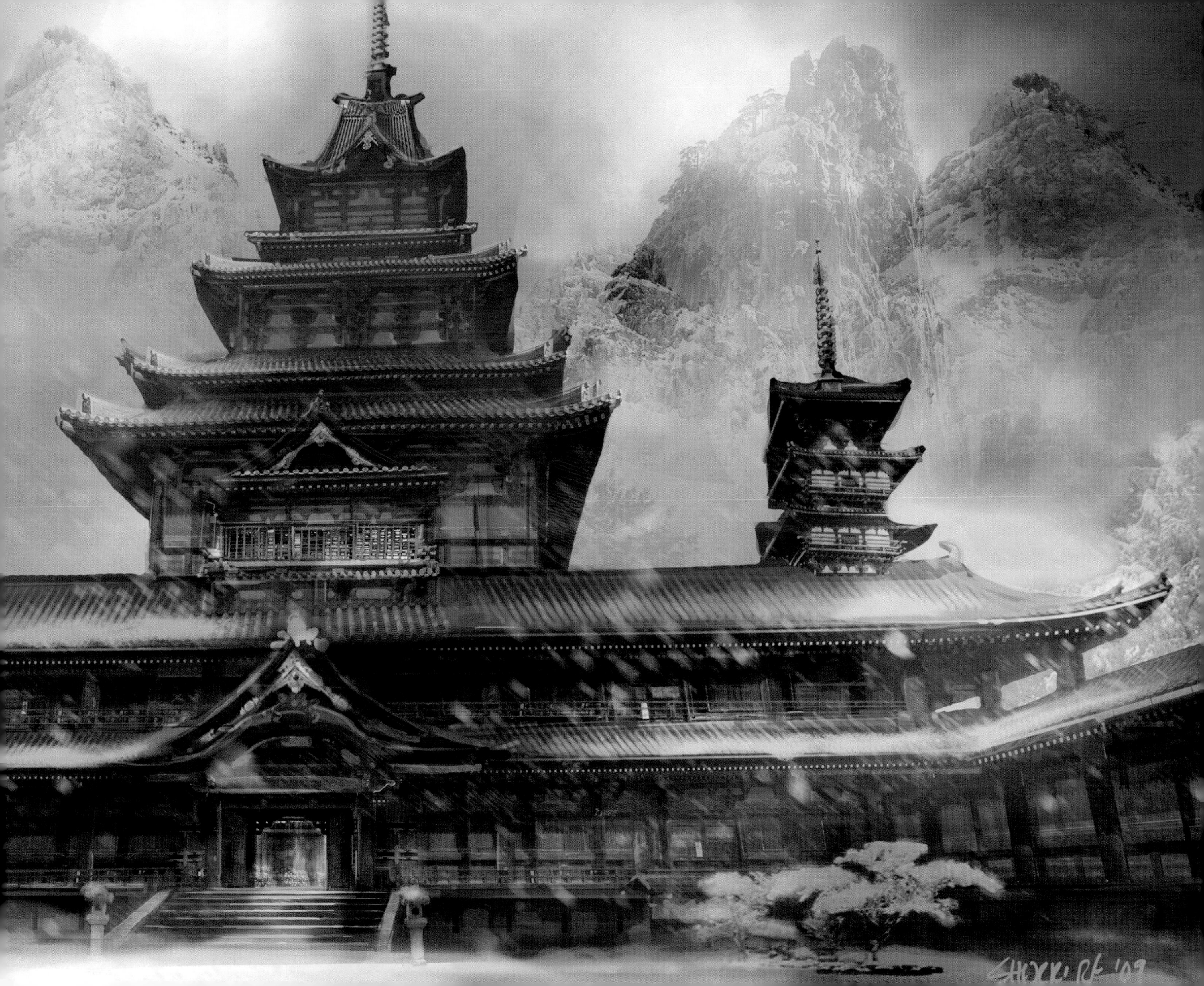

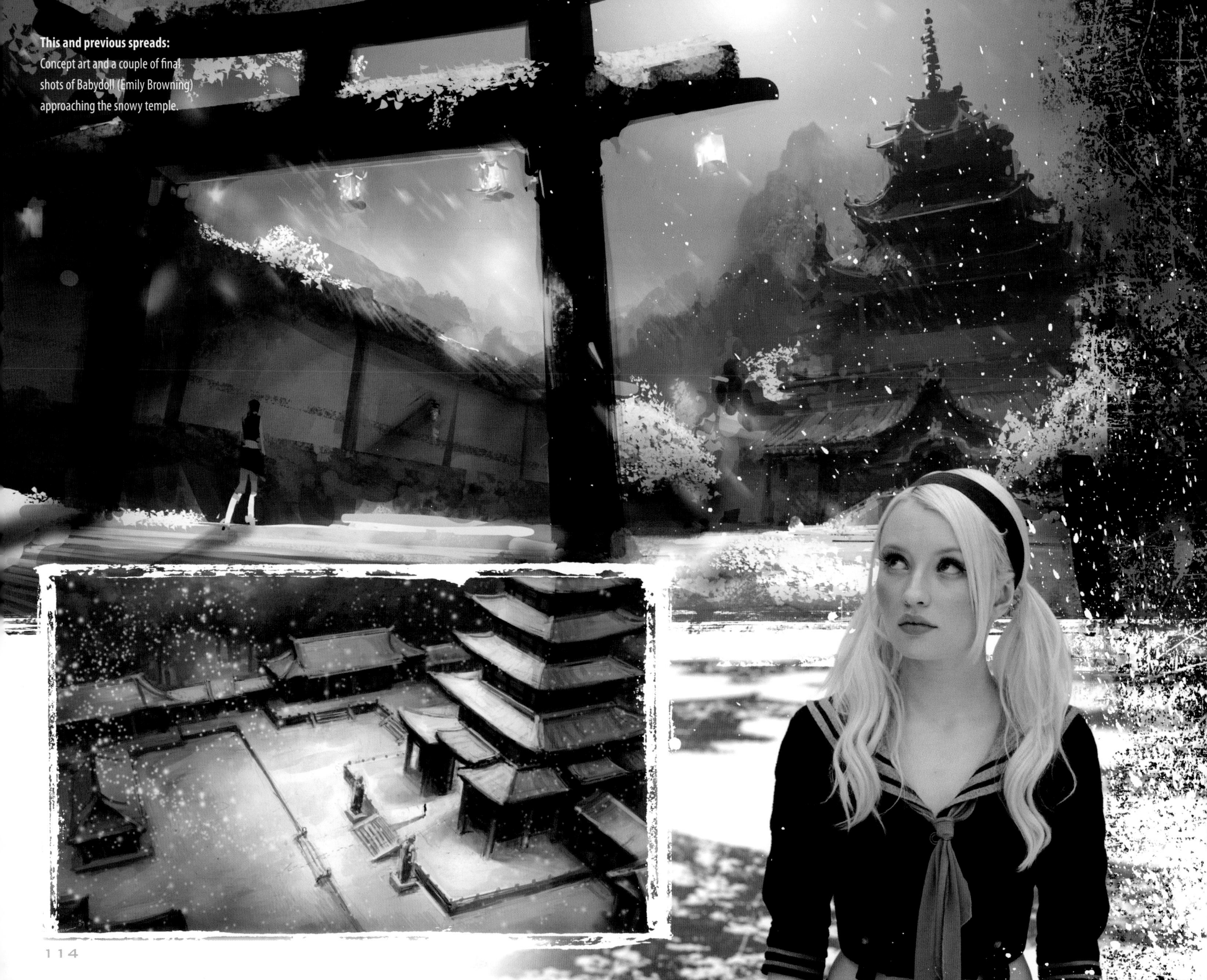

This and previous spreads:
Concept art and a couple of final shots of Babydoll (Emily Browning) approaching the snowy temple.

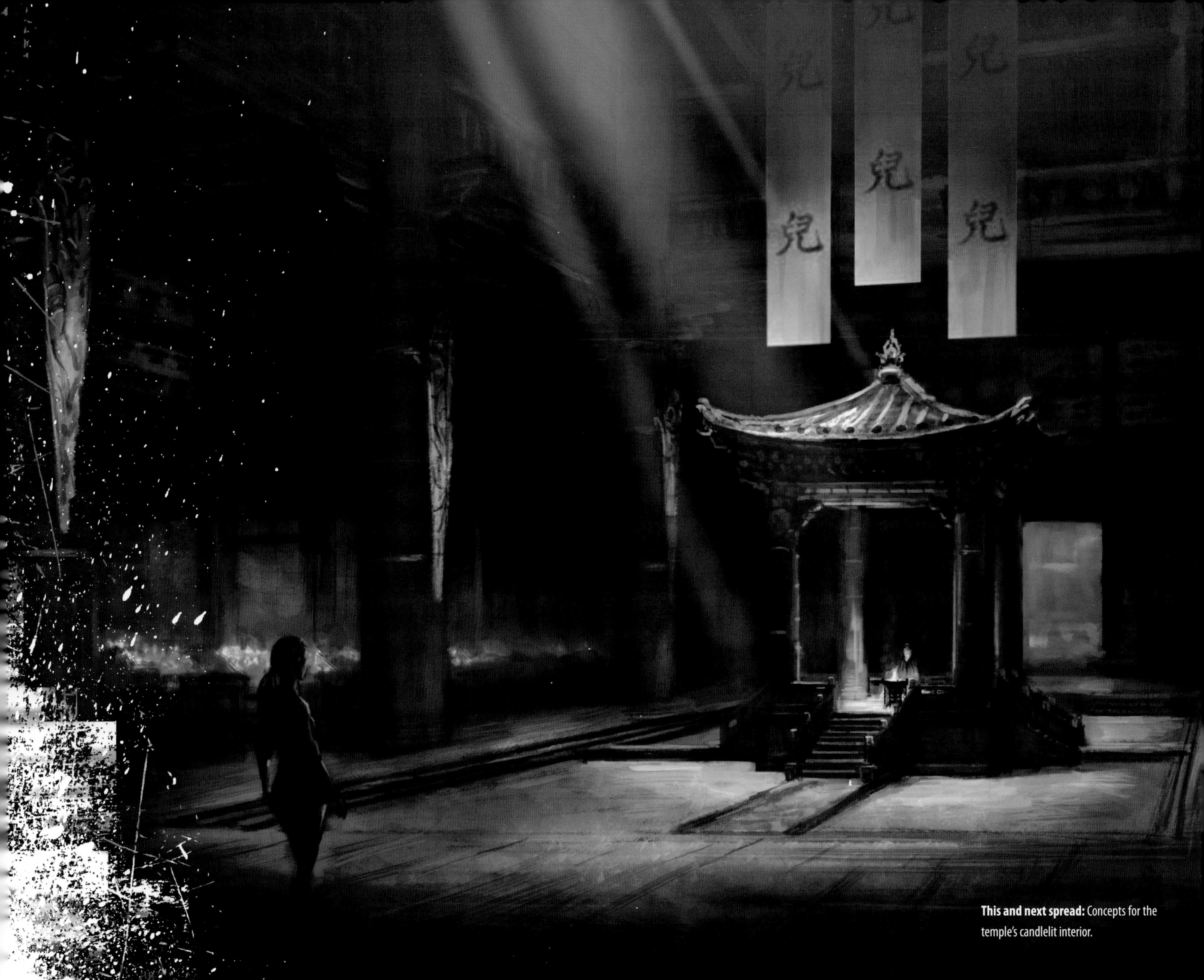

This and next spread: Concepts for the temple's candlelit interior.

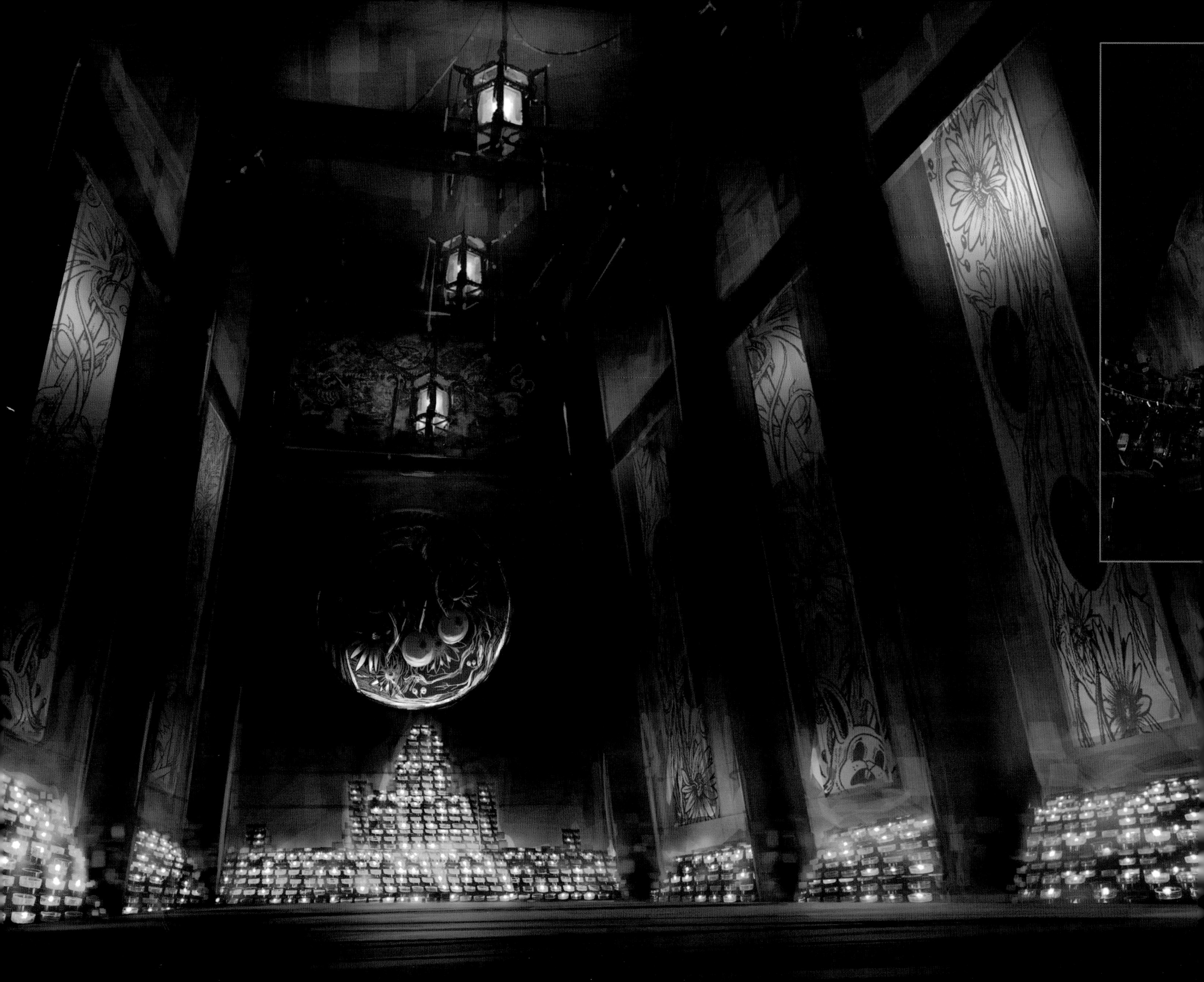

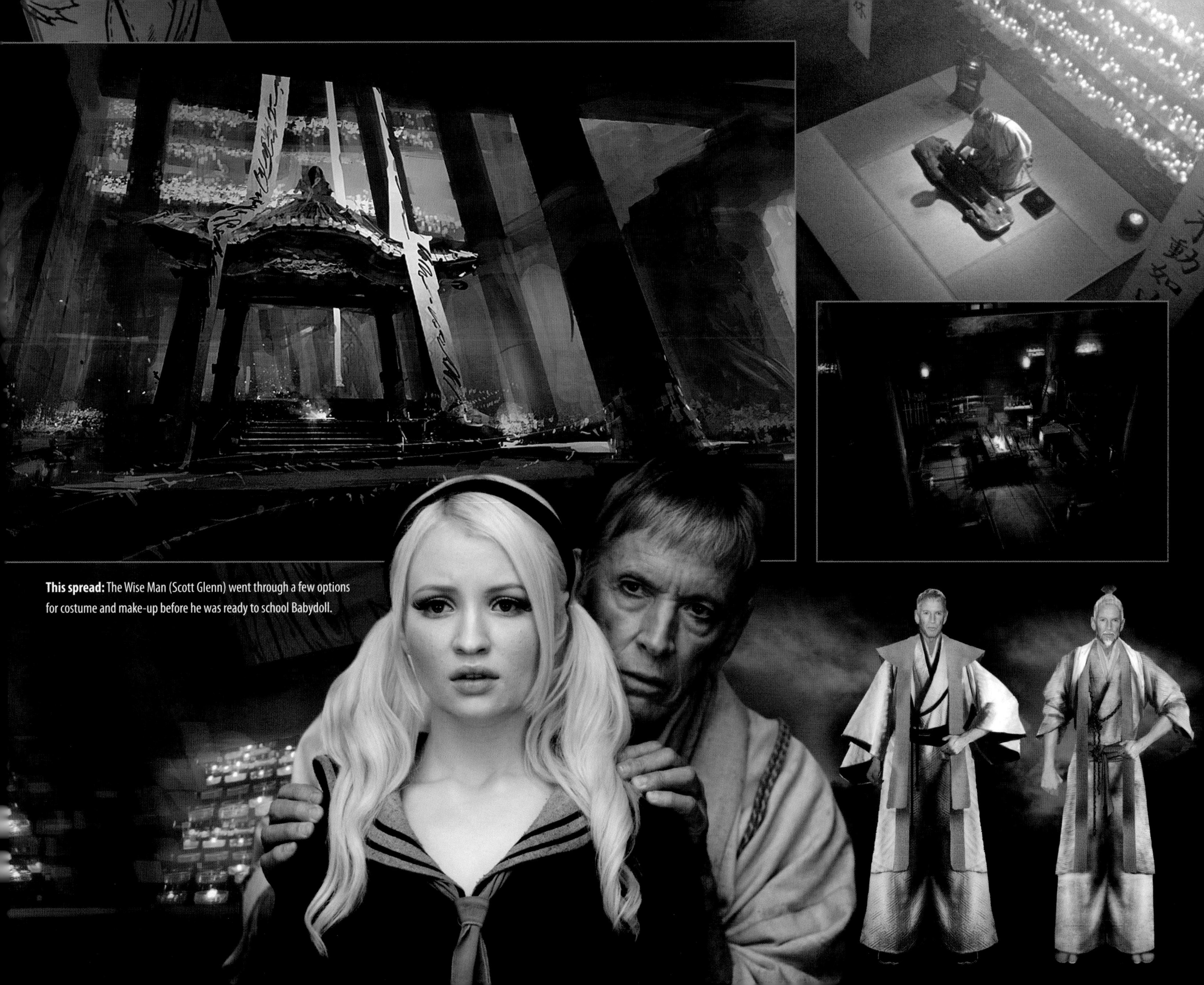

This spread: The Wise Man (Scott Glenn) went through a few options for costume and make-up before he was ready to school Babydoll.

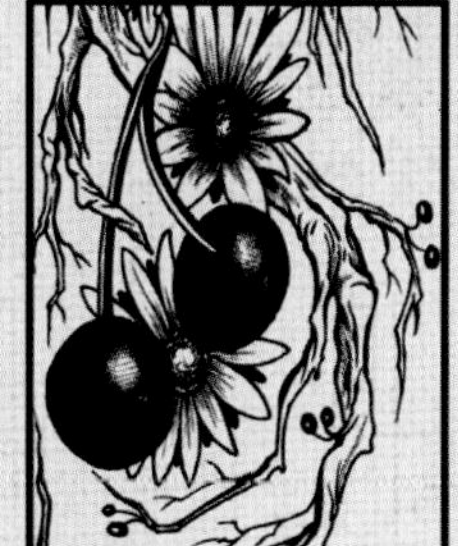

The beginning of the sword/story, showing the symbols of cherries and daisies (both representing innocence & purity), growing from a strong foundation (the tree)...

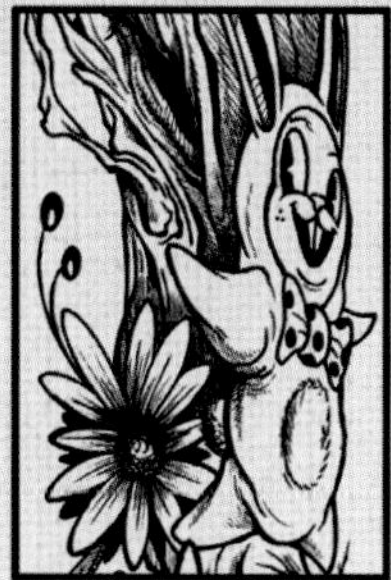

...also showing a doll/stuffed rabbit, symbolizing both childhood as well as "something close to her."

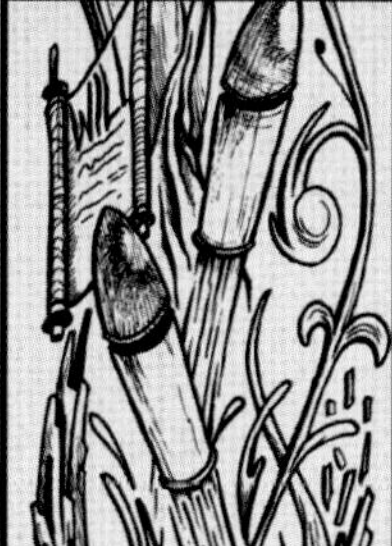

The foundation (tree) is destroyed by bullets (when her sister is shot, etc.) the will is revealed to be the catalyst of...

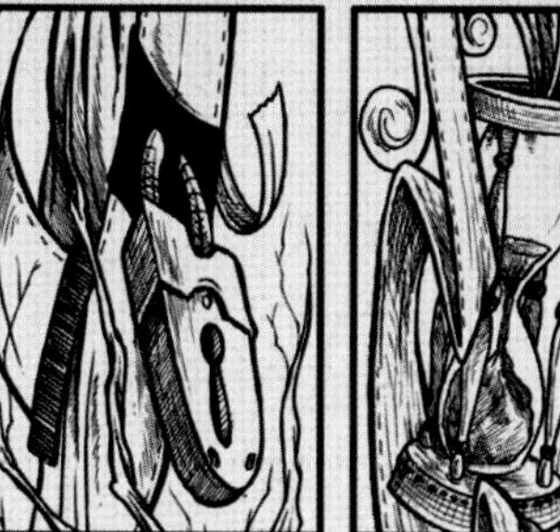

Babydoll's commitment to the hospital. This segment is intertwined with a strait-jacket taking the place of the tree as the foundation.

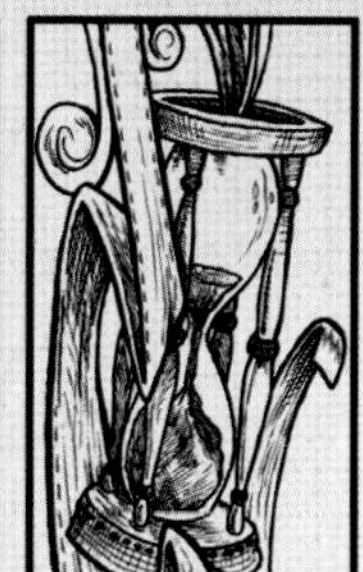

Once in the hospital, the countdown begins, forcing Babydoll to begin depending on her FANTASIES...

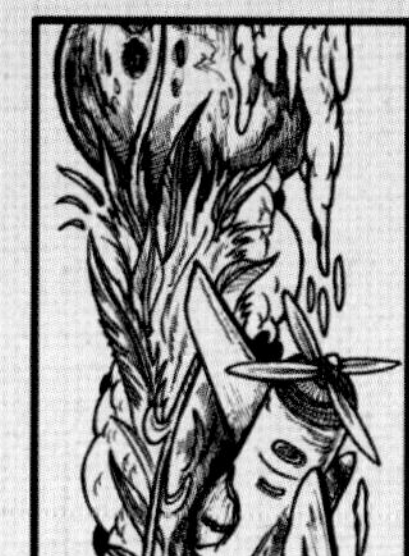

Her fantasies overtake her, dreams of WW2 planes fighting and flying by the moon....

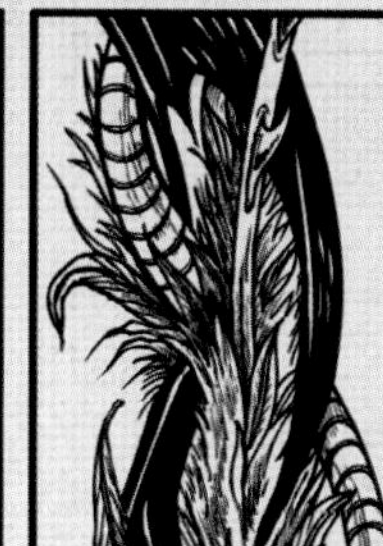

Dragon wings and steampunk-ish gas mask hoses intertwine with this stage's "foundation", which is Babydoll's dance, represented by the feathered boa.

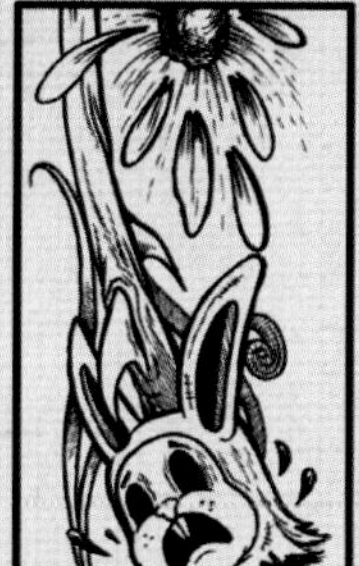

Though she has fought, her friends are dead and her innocence is taken from her, the pure daisies are destroyed, the object "close to her" is decapitated, and...

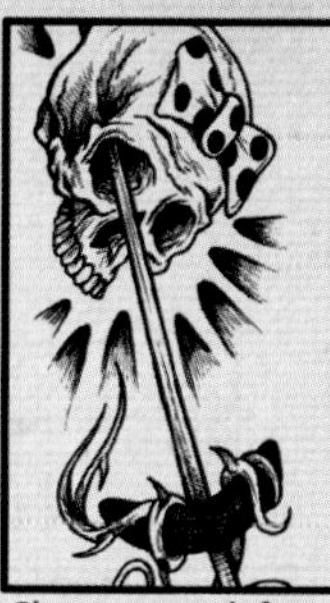

She accepts defeat as the lobotomy doctor proceeds, but Babydoll, having nothing left, becomes enlightened by her acceptance.

HABAKI (BRASS FERRULE)

SHINOGI (BLADE RIDGE)

ENGRAVING ON REAL JAPANESE KATANAS IS RARE, ANY ENGRAVING THAT I HAVE SEEN HAS BEEN ON CEREMONIAL SWORDS AND EXTENDS MAYBE ONE THIRD DOWN THE BLADE AT MOST. YOU CAN TALK TO ZACK ABOUT HOW FAR DOWN HE WANTS TO GO WITH IT.

HAMON (TEMPER LINE)

* ENGRAVING SHOULD NOT CROSS ONTO HAMON

- HAMON ON EACH SWORD WILL DIFFER BUT ALL WILL BE SIMILAR TO THIS ONE.

WEAPONS

Above: Beautiful etching designed by Alex Pardee for the blade of Babydoll's sword reveals milestones on her journey from innocence to enlightenment. **Opposite:** Babydoll's monogrammed .45, complete with symbols and trinkets from her past and future.

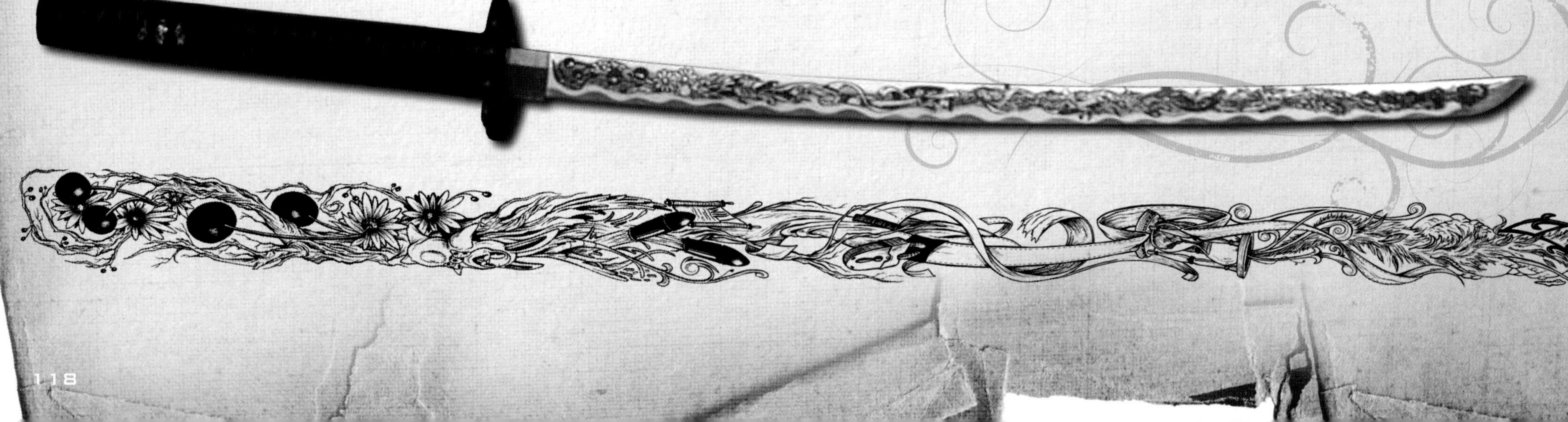

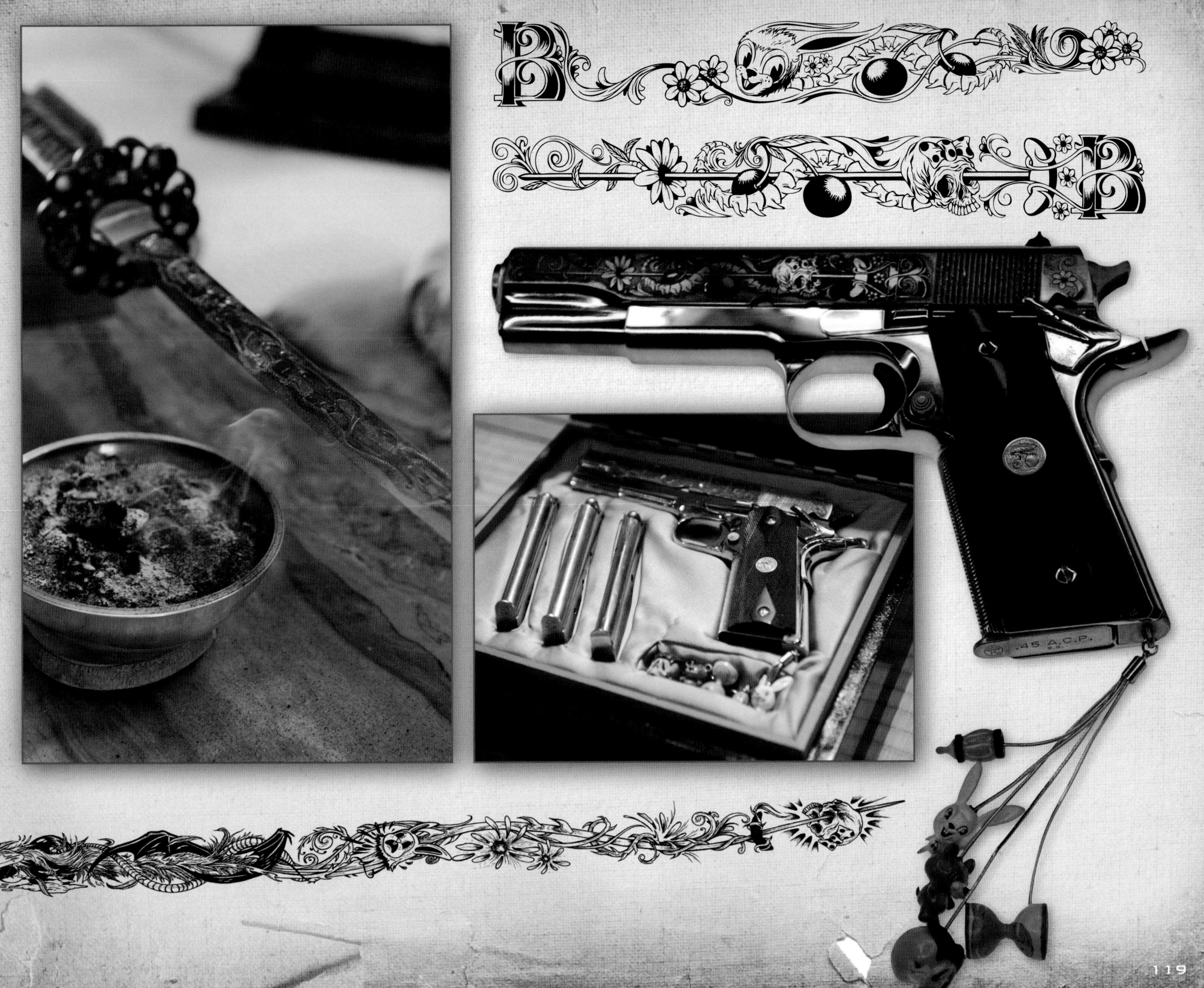
.45 A.C.P.

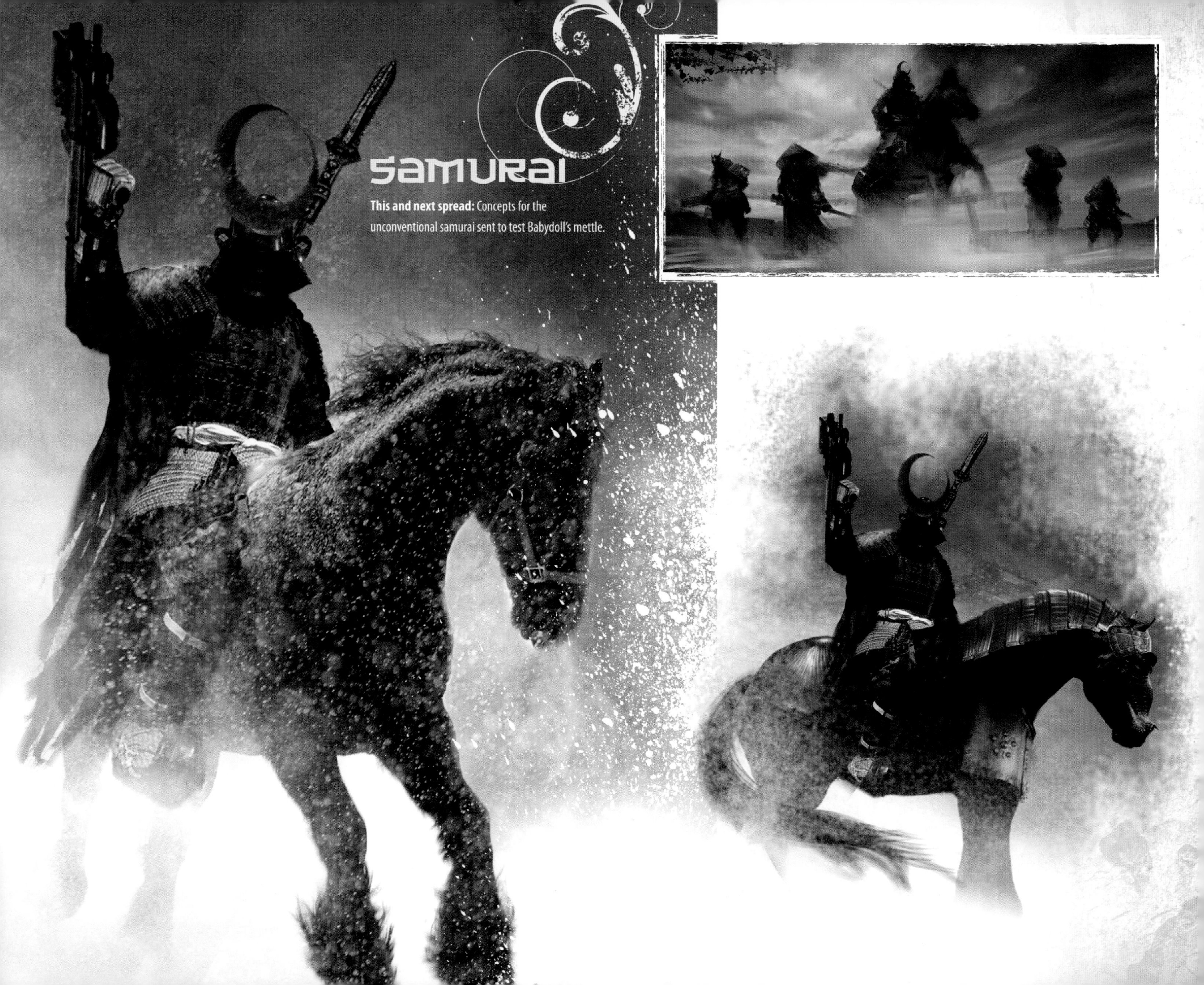

Samurai

This and next spread: Concepts for the unconventional samurai sent to test Babydoll's mettle.

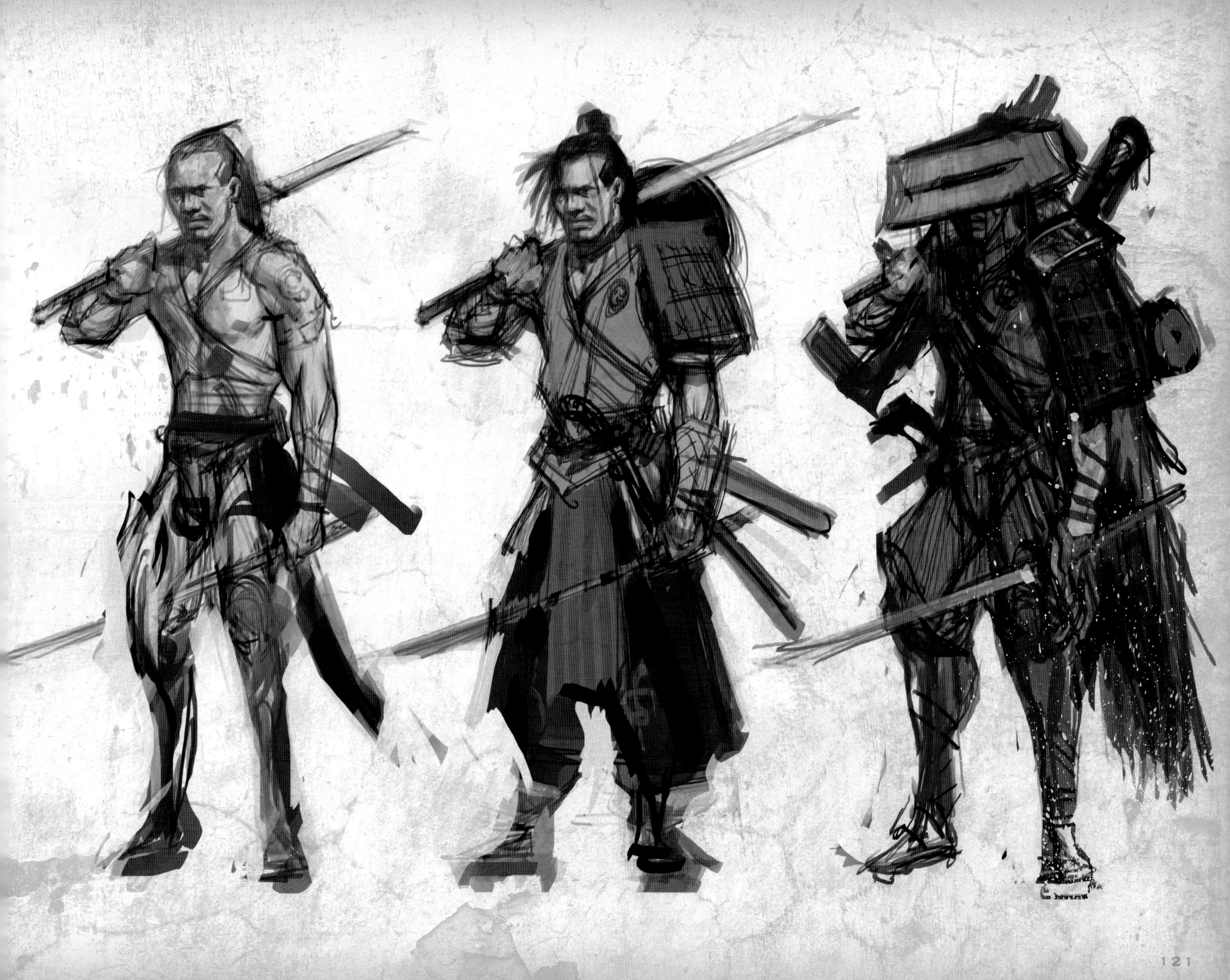

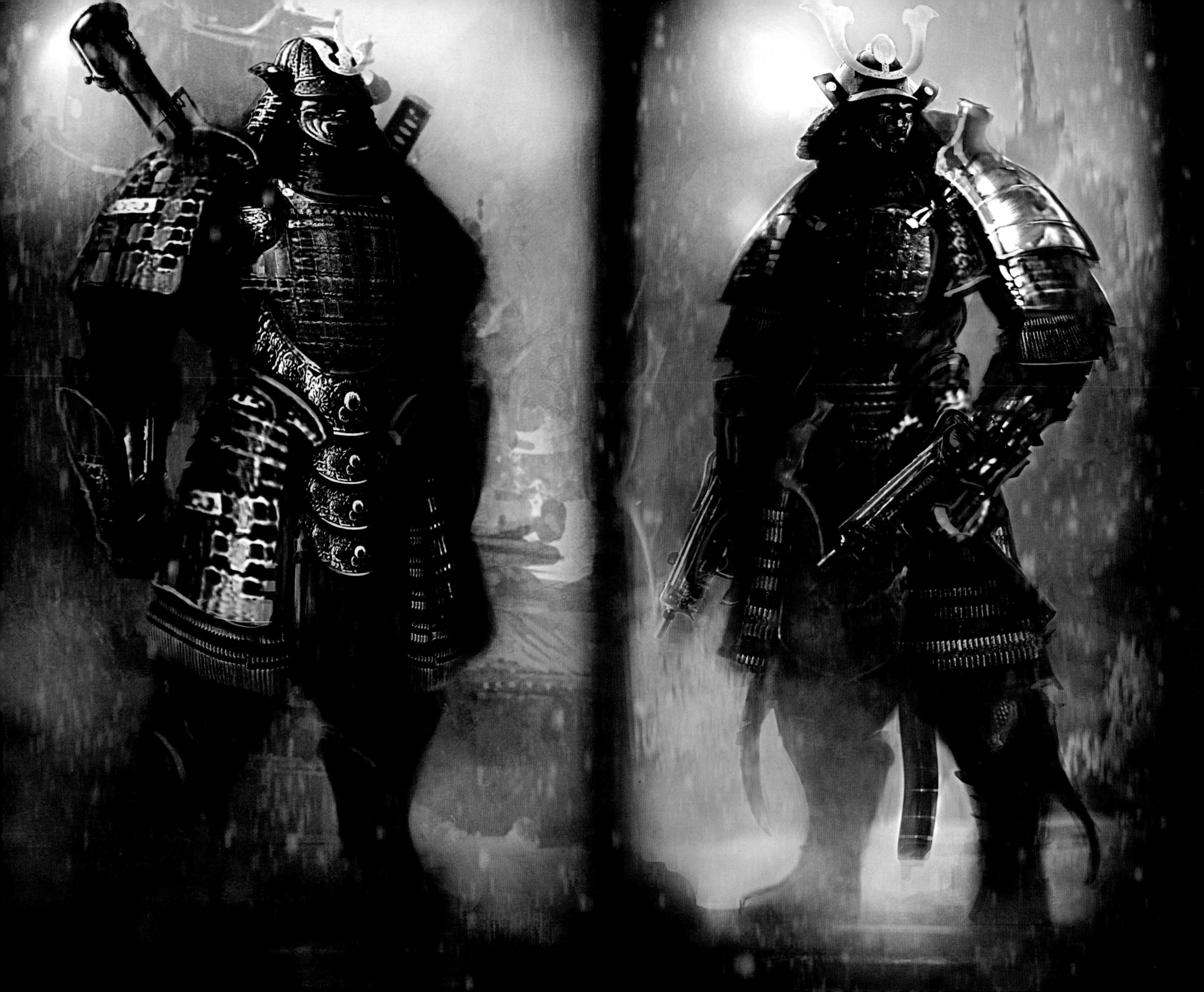

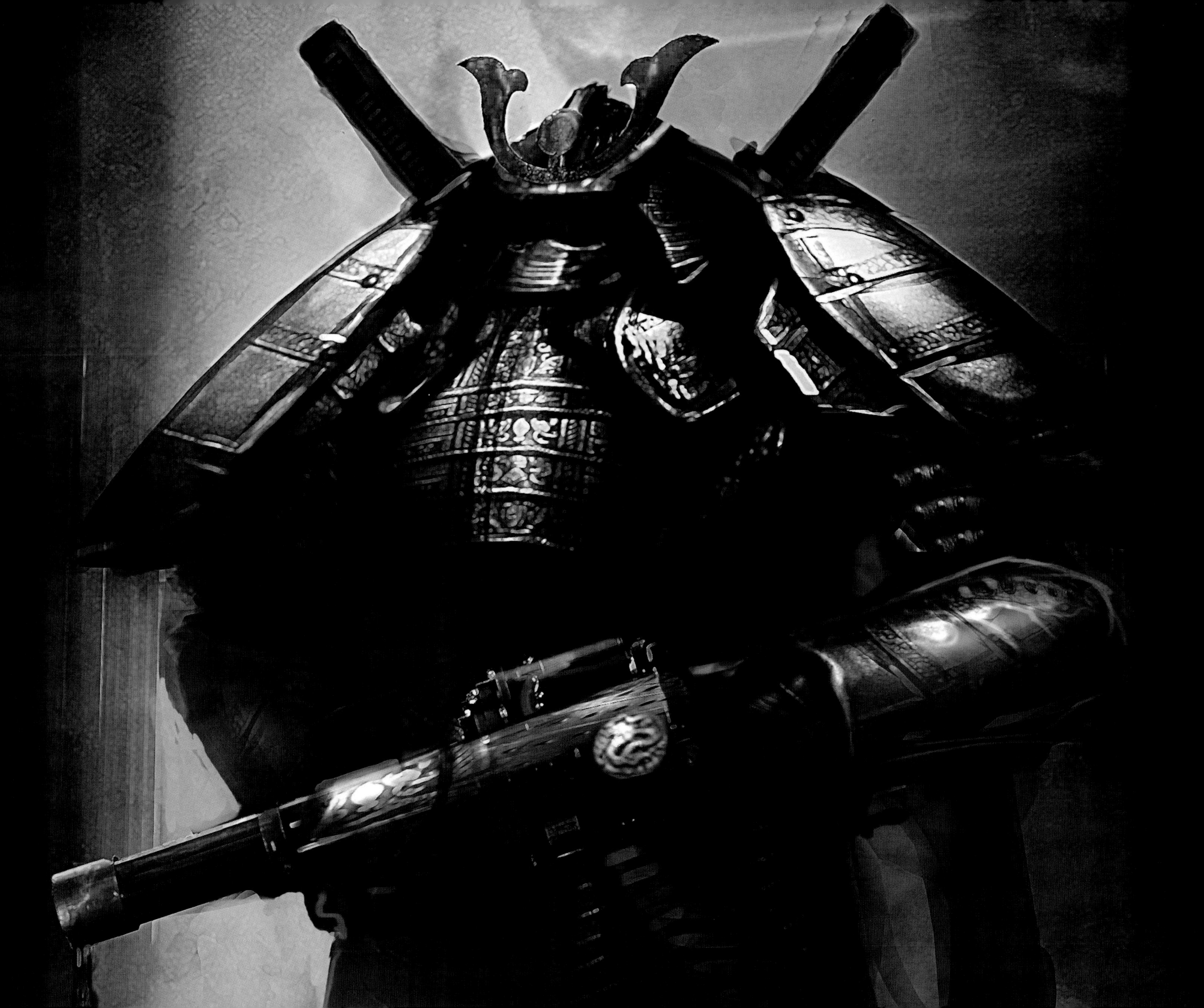

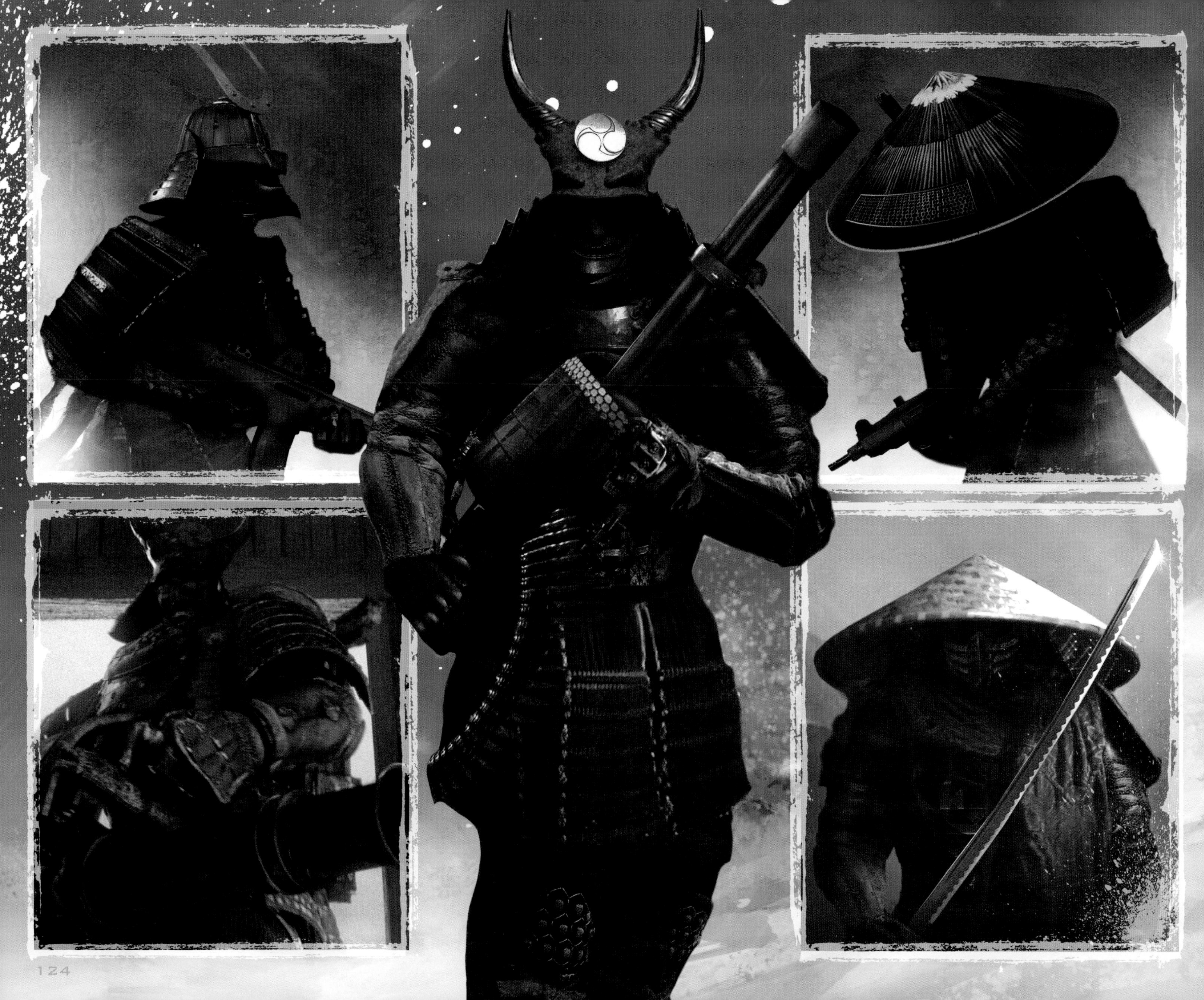

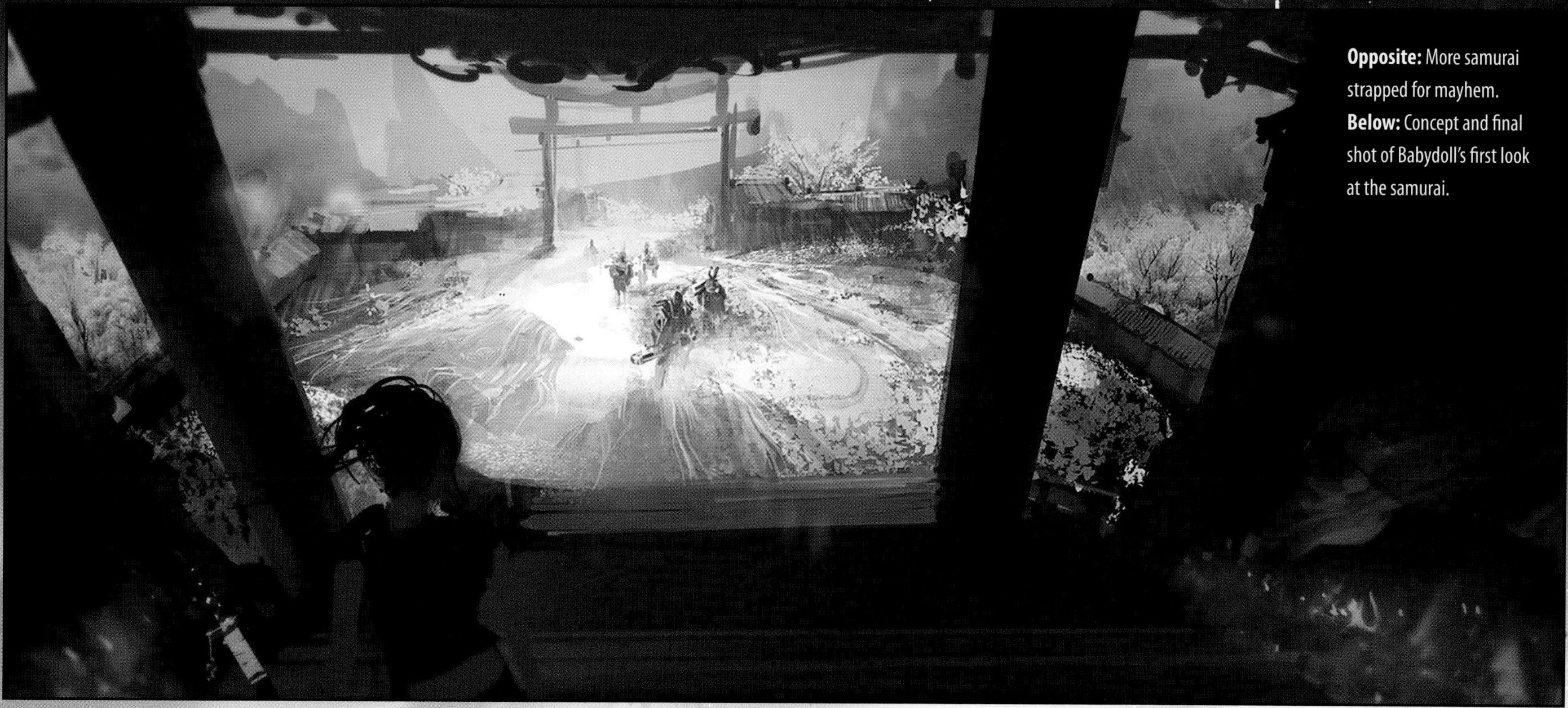

Opposite: More samurai strapped for mayhem.
Below: Concept and final shot of Babydoll's first look at the samurai.

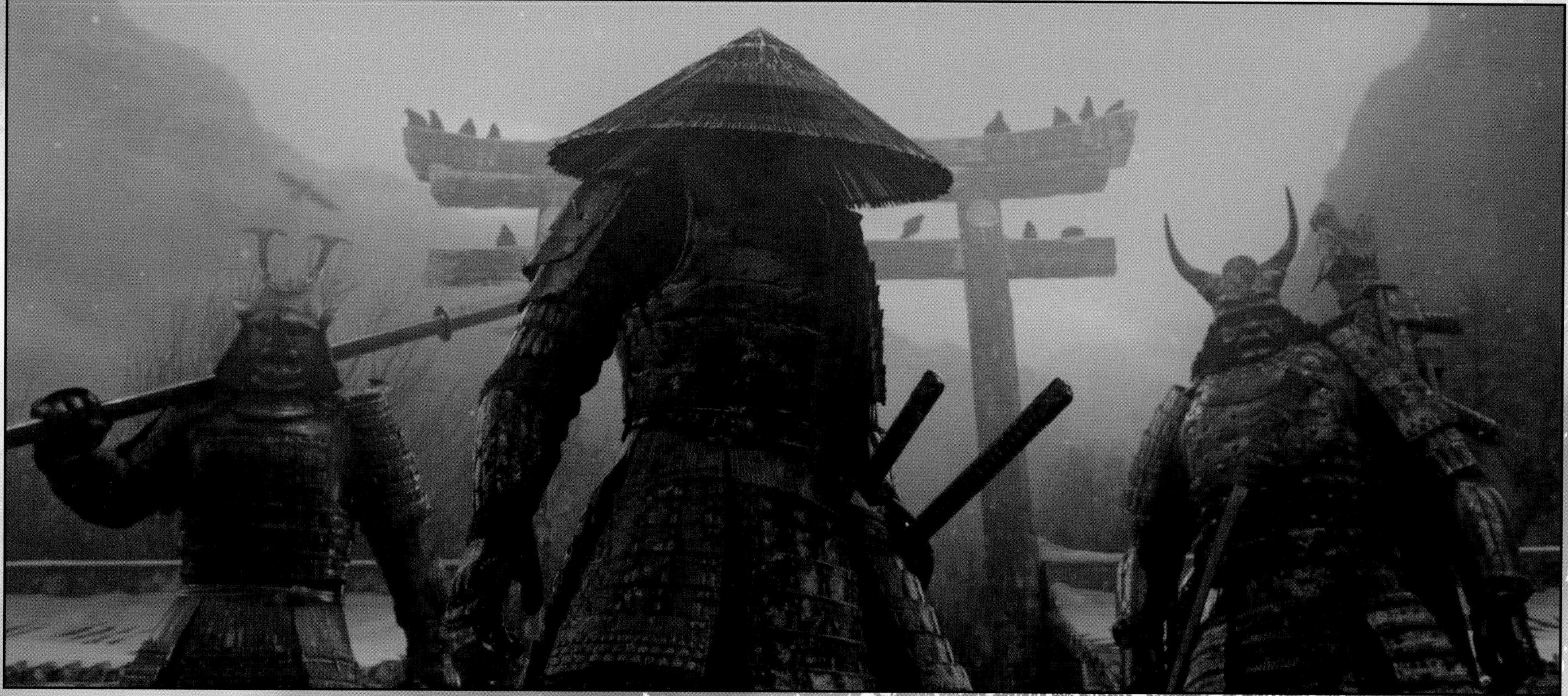

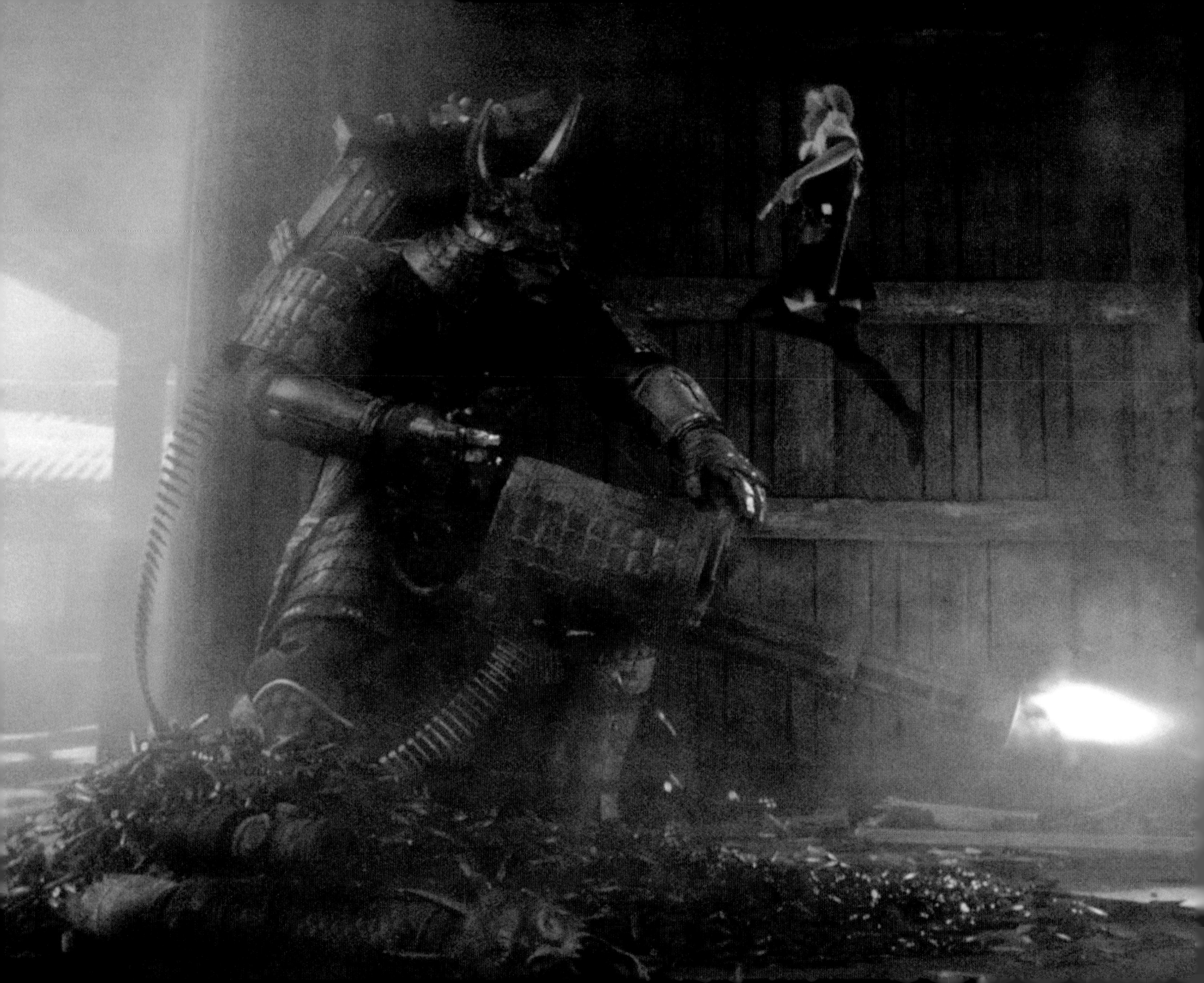

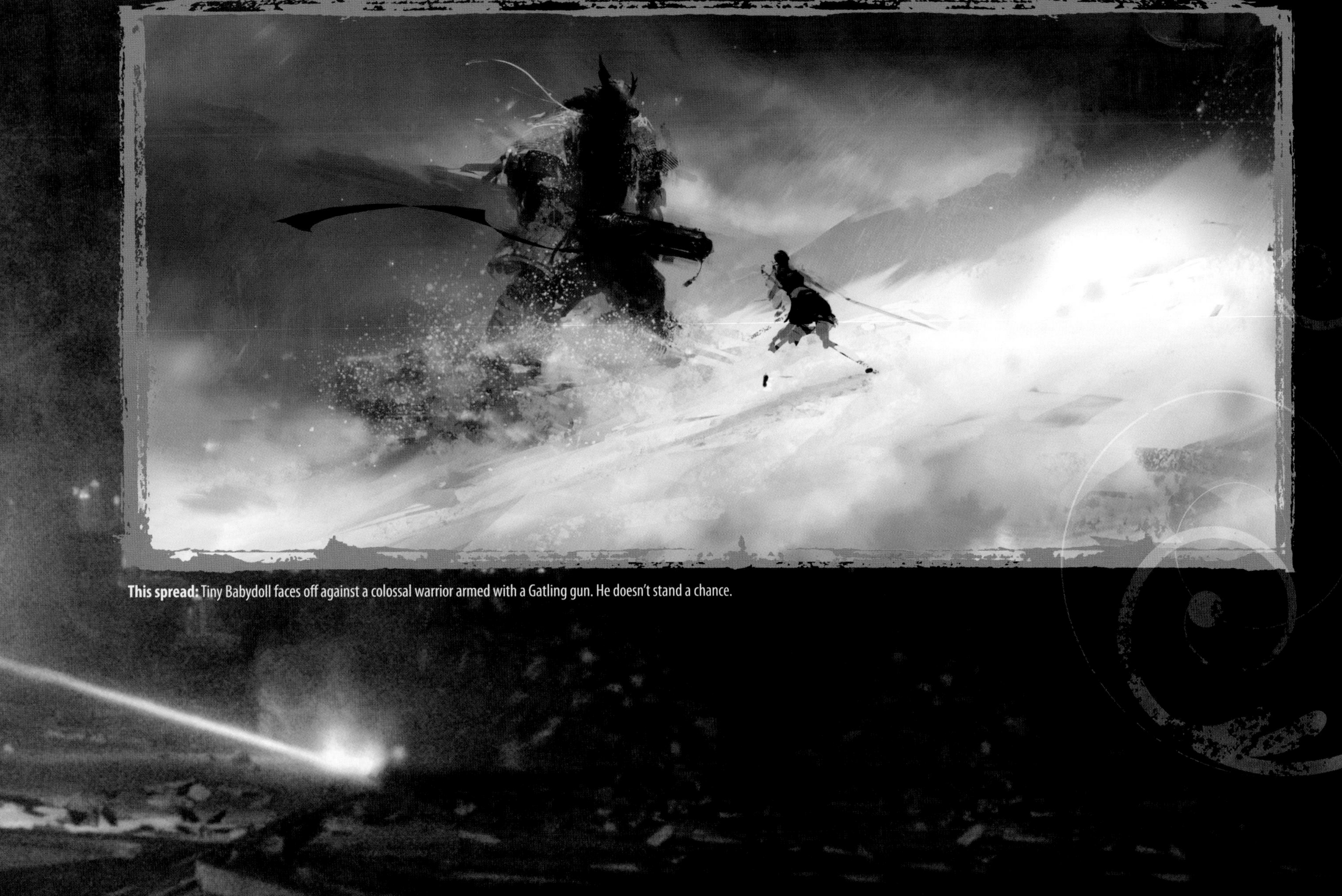

This spread: Tiny Babydoll faces off against a colossal warrior armed with a Gatling gun. He doesn't stand a chance.

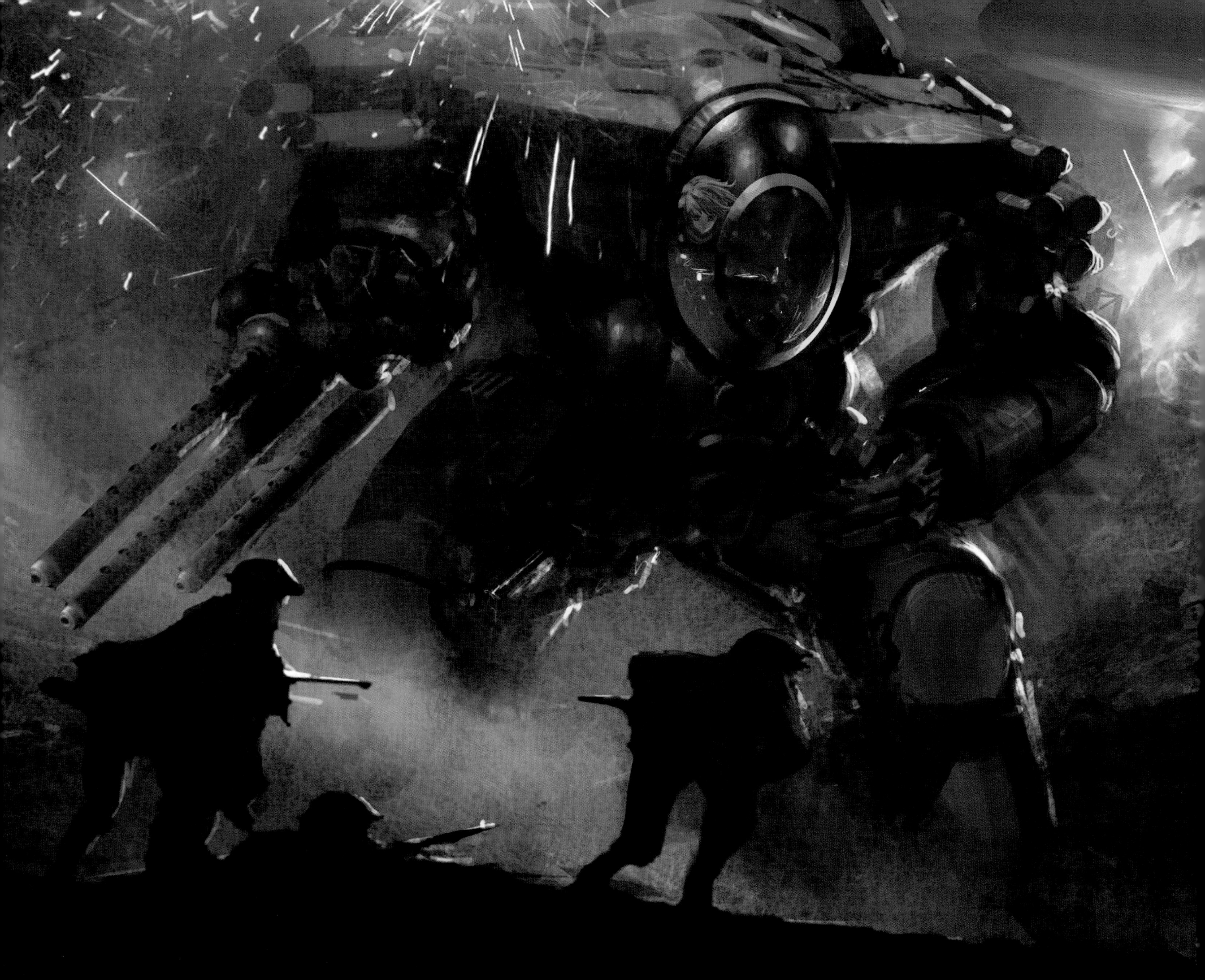

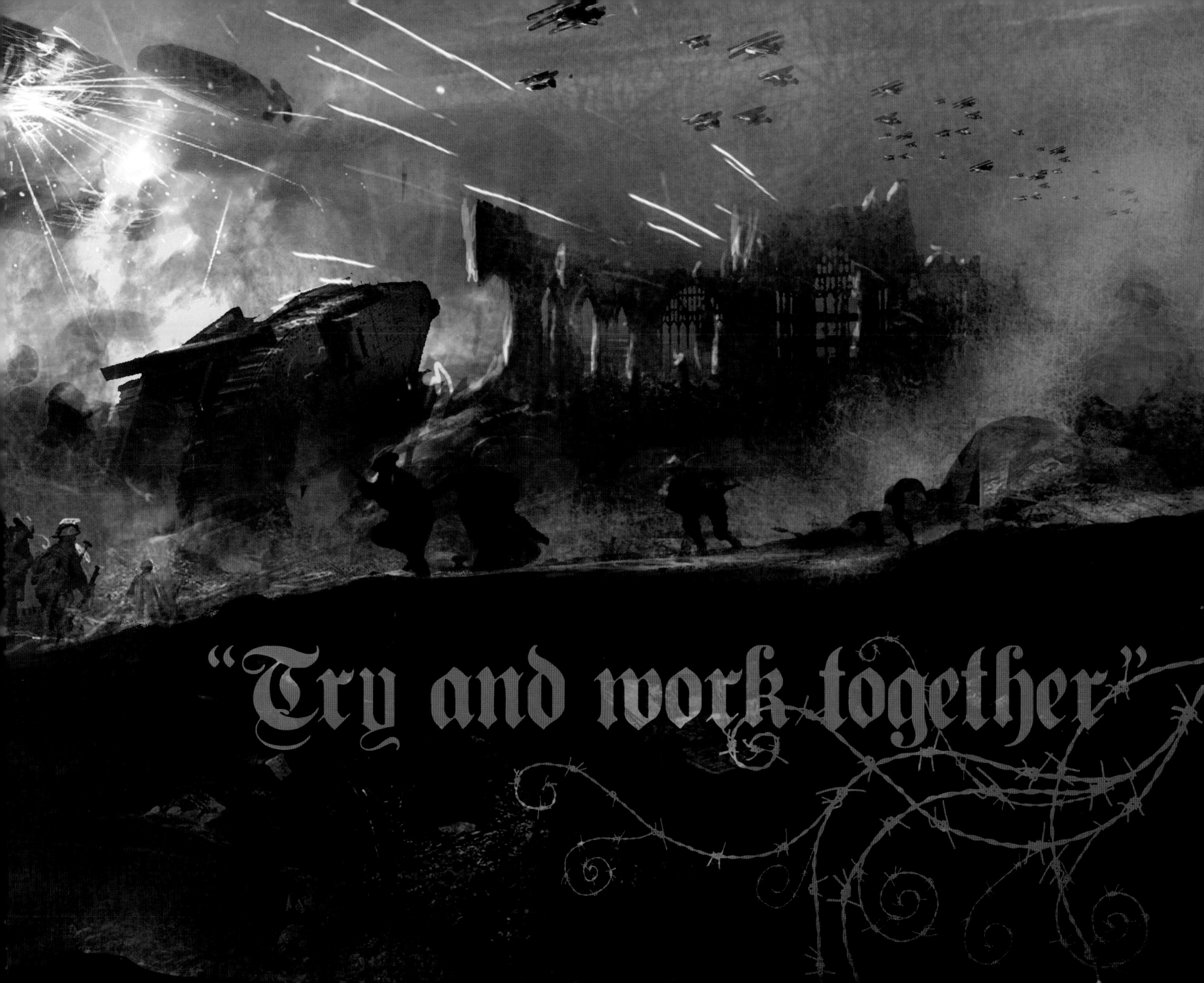
"Try and work together"

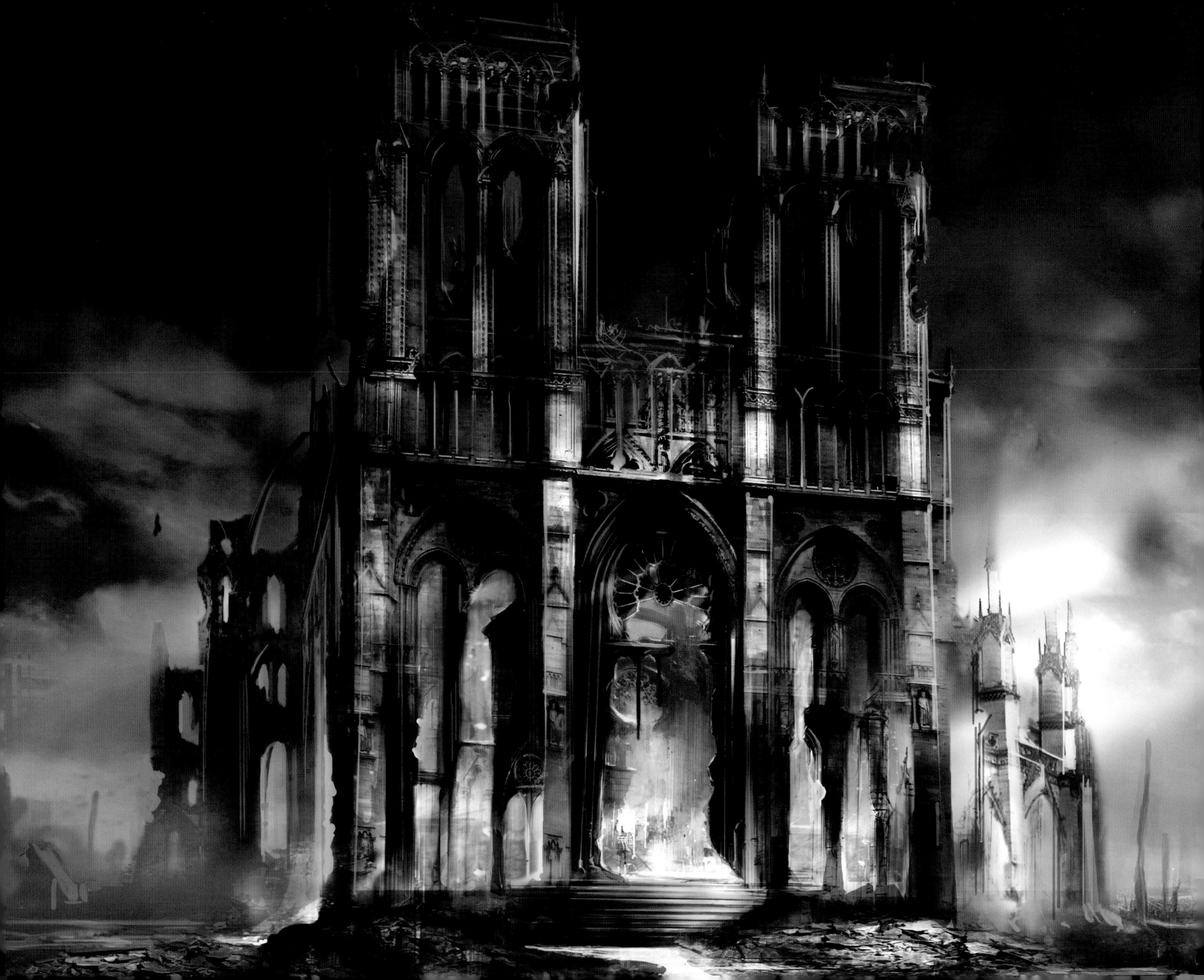

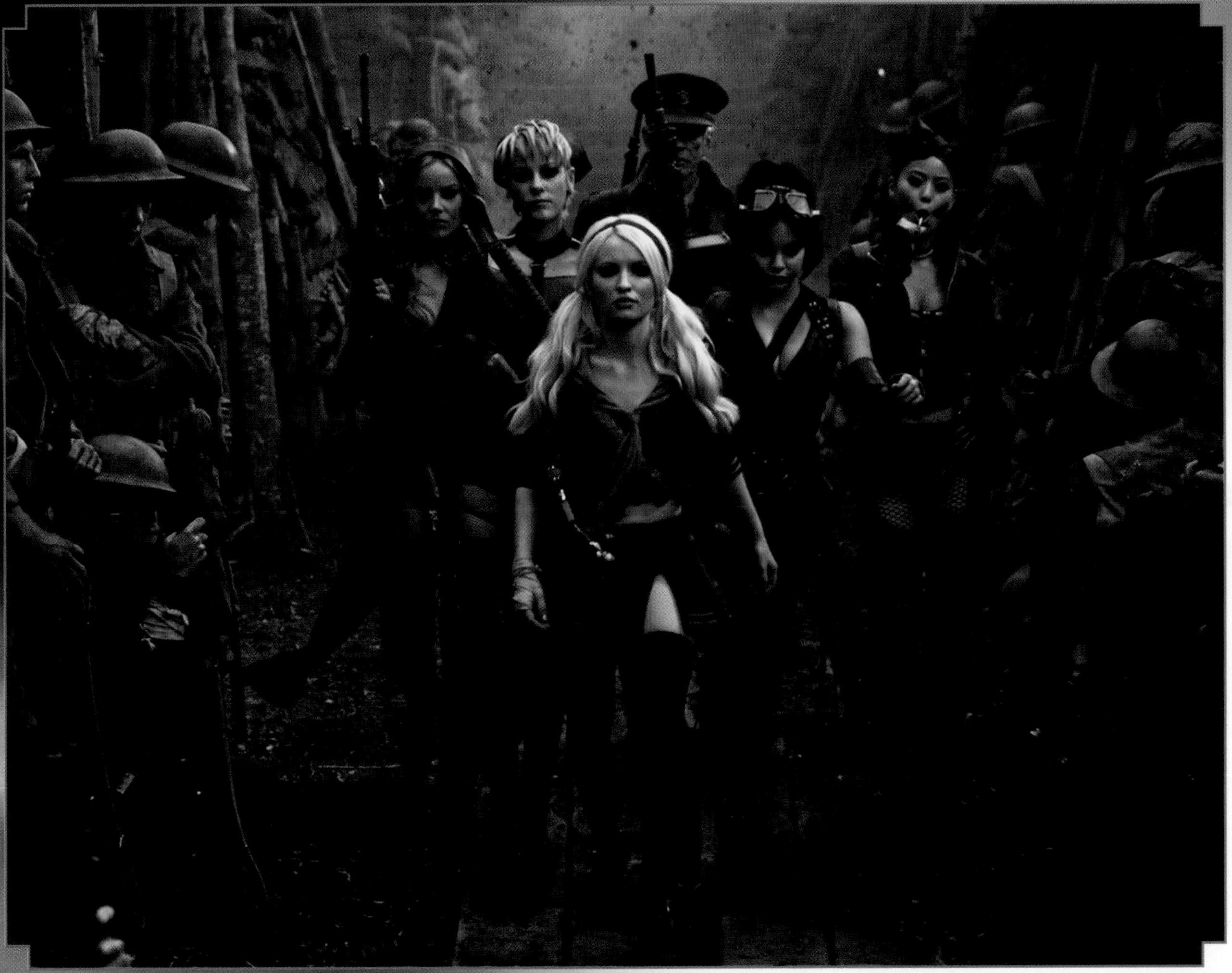

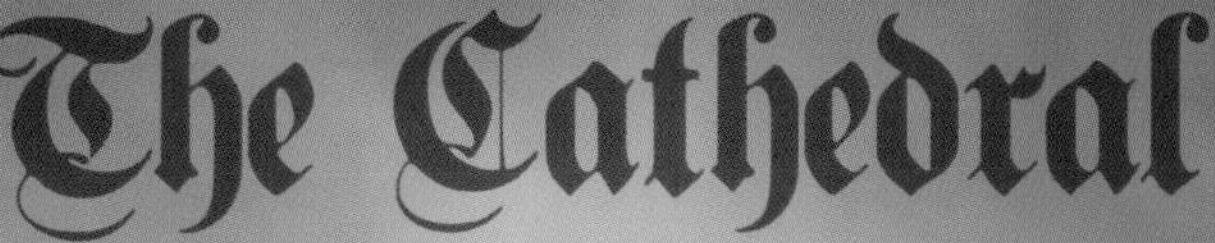

The Cathedral

What better place to steal a map from the enemy than on a warped battlefield of the mind? The charred landscape of WWI's Western Front is spread before the girls as they gather for their mission briefing in the crumbling ruins of a cathedral. But this is WWI as seen through a toxic fever dream: multi-winged planes buzz about like swarms of angry hornets as artillery shells arc across a slate-gray sky laden with the whale-like shapes of observation balloons and zeppelins. And of course, their German opponents are not actual living beings anymore, but soldiers who've been slain and cunningly reanimated to carry on the Kaiser's war.

Their mission is quite straightforward, really: simply cross a No-Man's-Land that's withstood all advances from either side for over three years, make their way through the labyrinth of the enemy's trench system, and infiltrate a heavily guarded concrete bunker in order to obtain a map before a messenger can catch the next airship bound for headquarters.

This is the first outing for the girls as a unit, and they've arrived loaded for bear. They look as if they've looted a war museum, sporting a wide range of combat gear from medieval swords and flintlock pistols to modern assault rifles and submachine guns. Oh, and from some enigmatic future they've acquired an anthropomorphic Meka equipped with jump rockets, air-to-air missiles, and a maniacal bunny face. But all the deadly hardware in the world won't help them one bit if they can't learn to trust each other and work as a team.

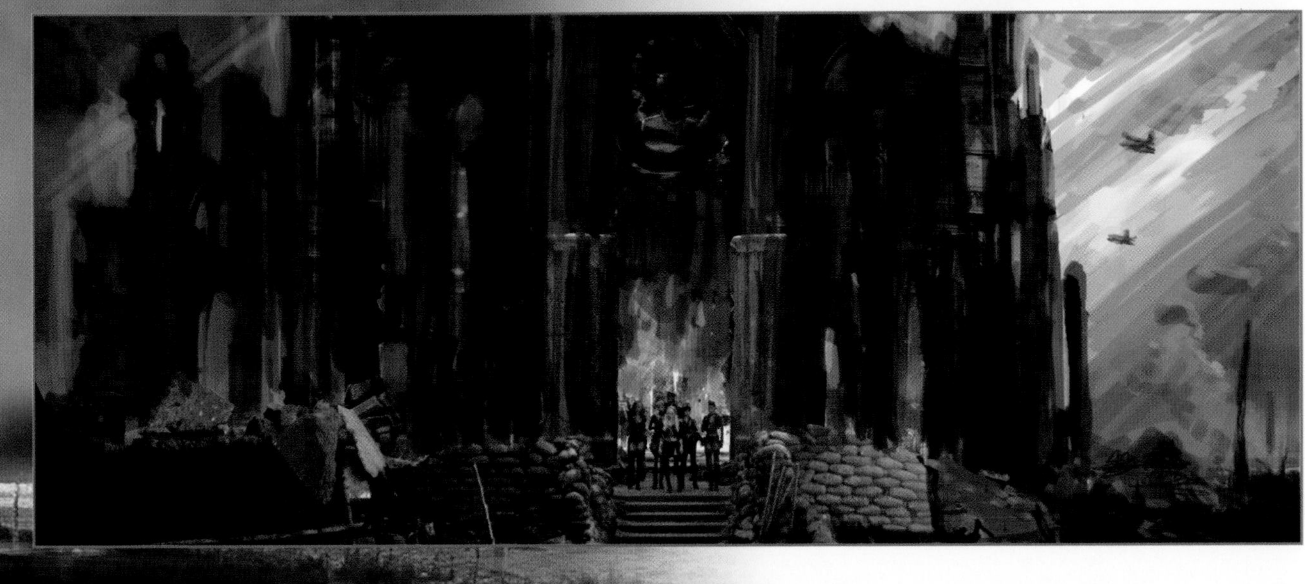

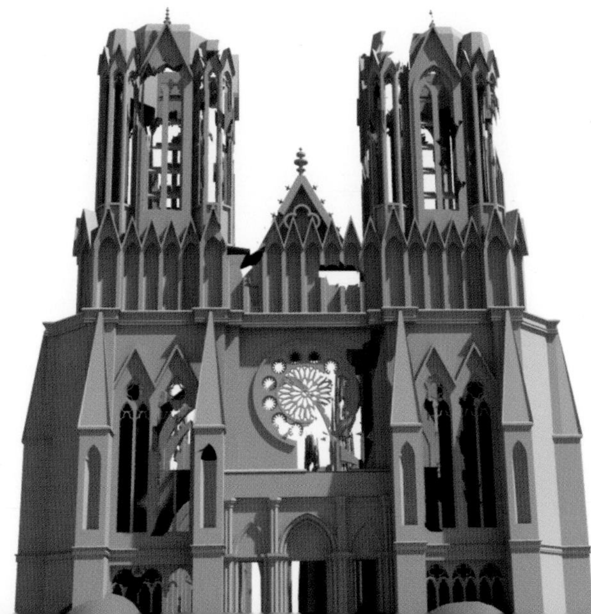

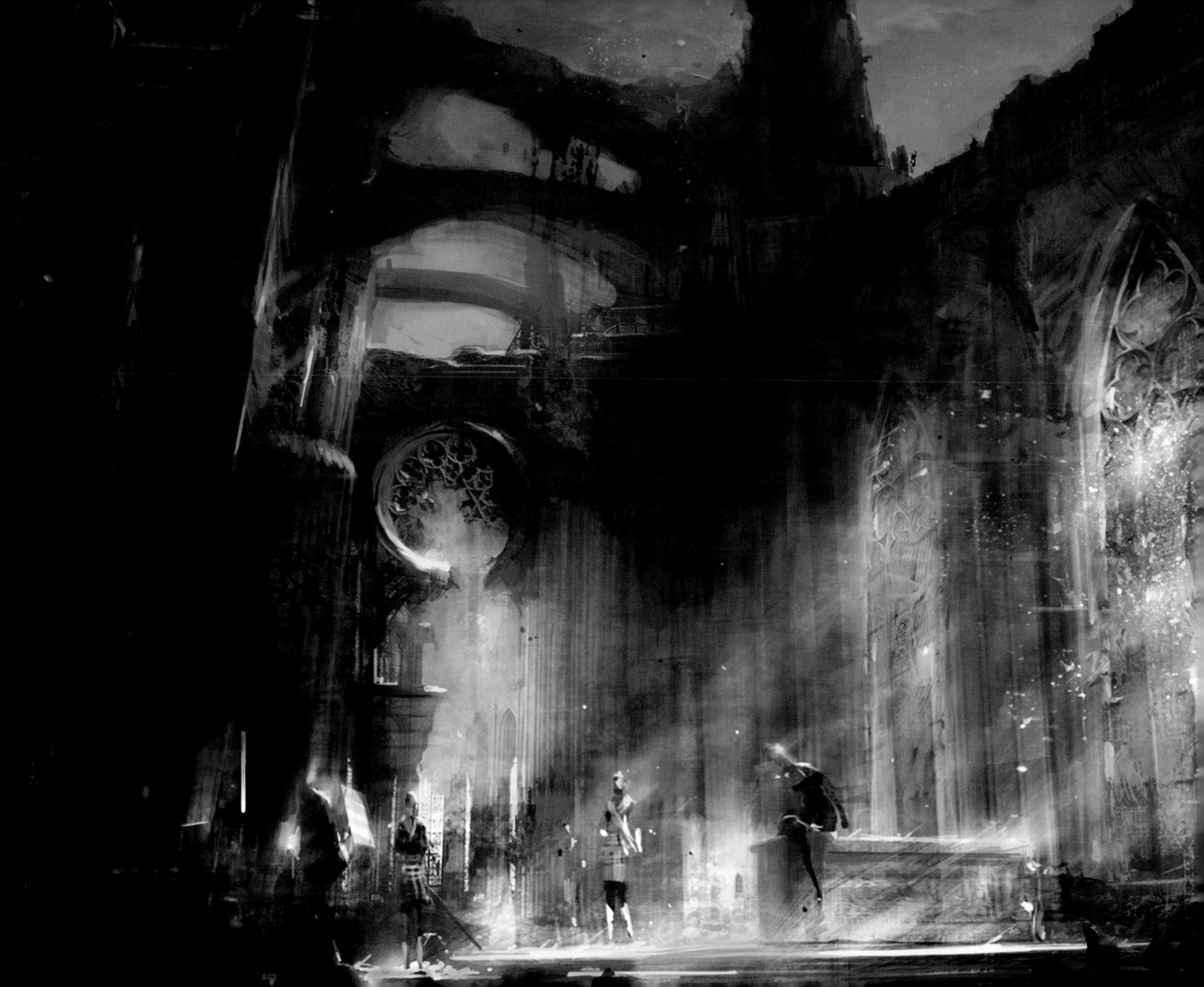

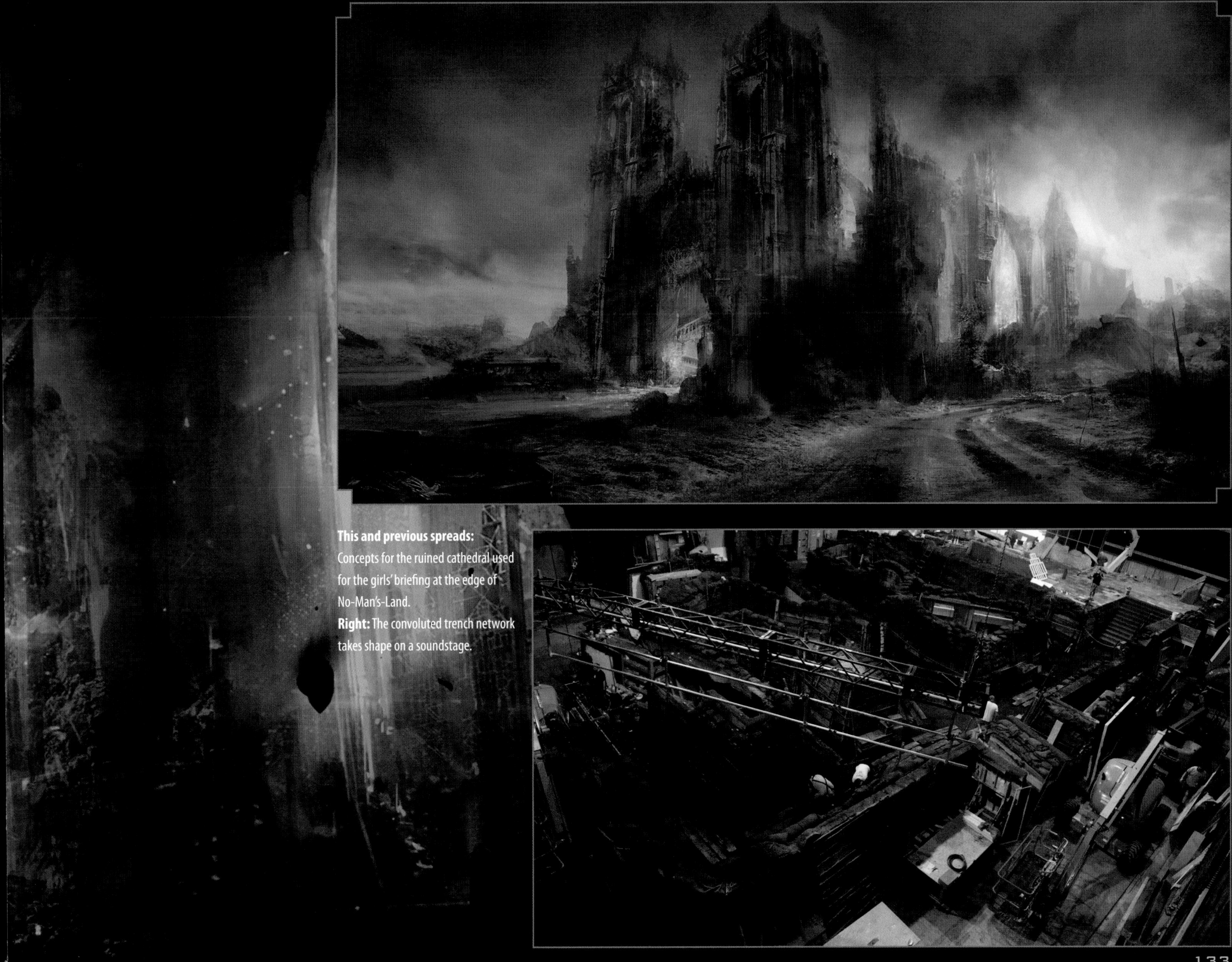

This and previous spreads: Concepts for the ruined cathedral used for the girls' briefing at the edge of No-Man's-Land.
Right: The convoluted trench network takes shape on a soundstage.

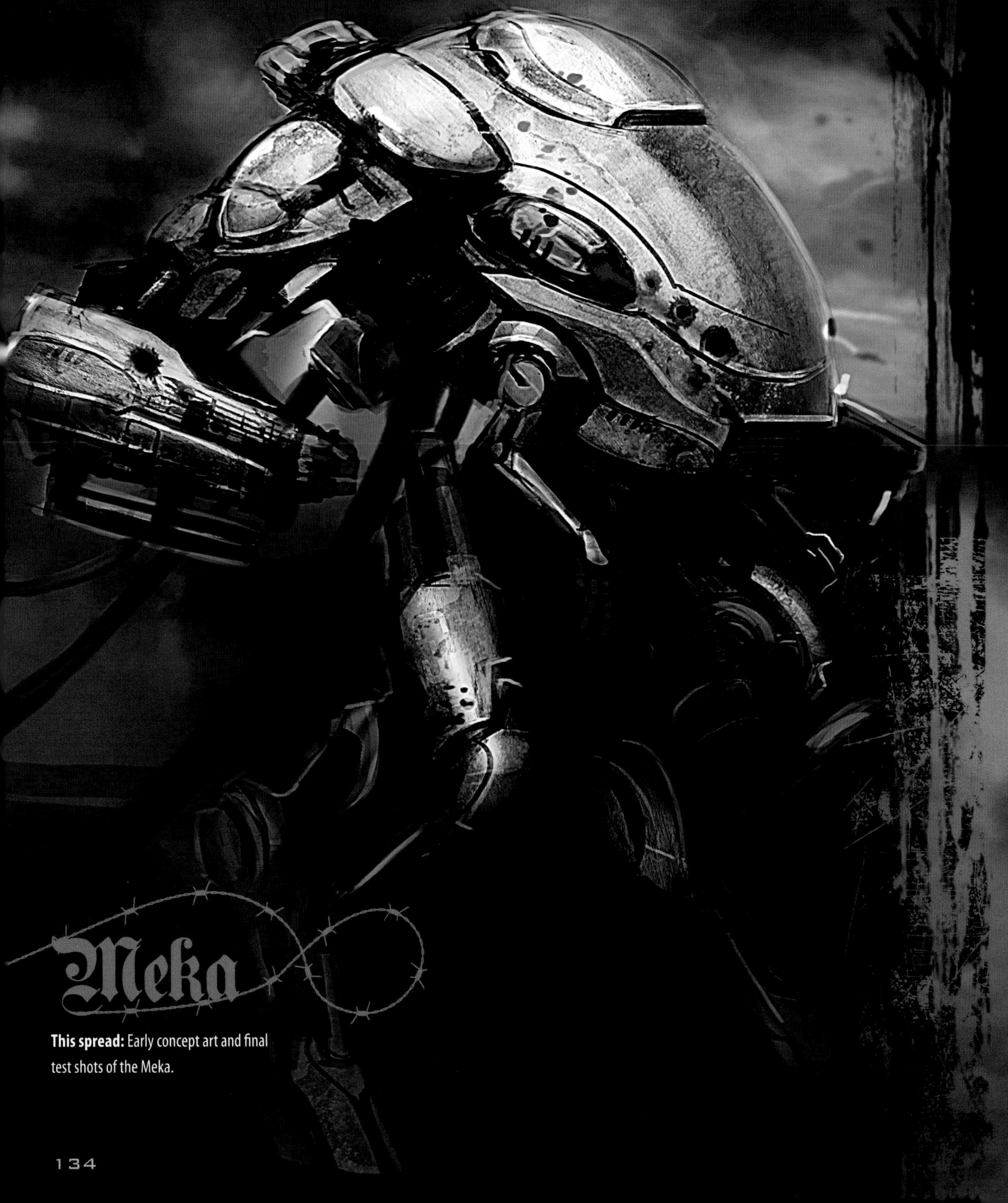

Meka

This spread: Early concept art and final test shots of the Meka.

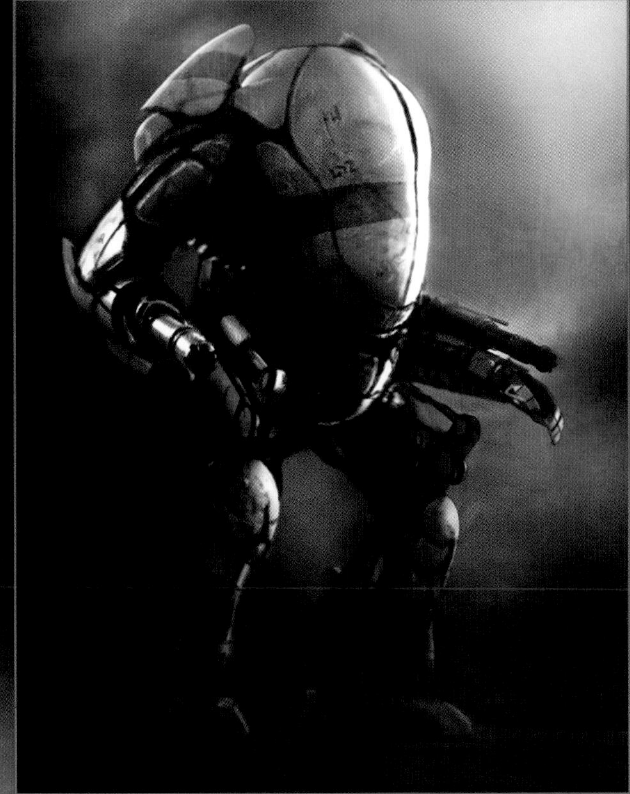

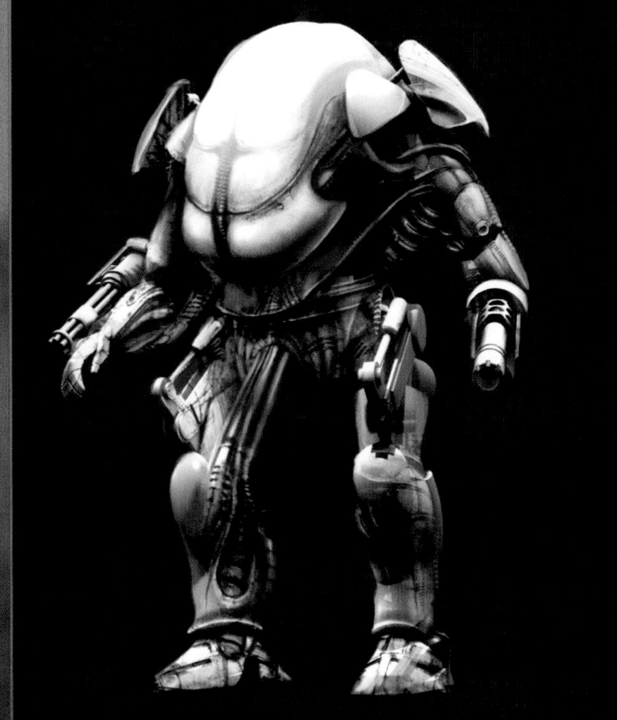

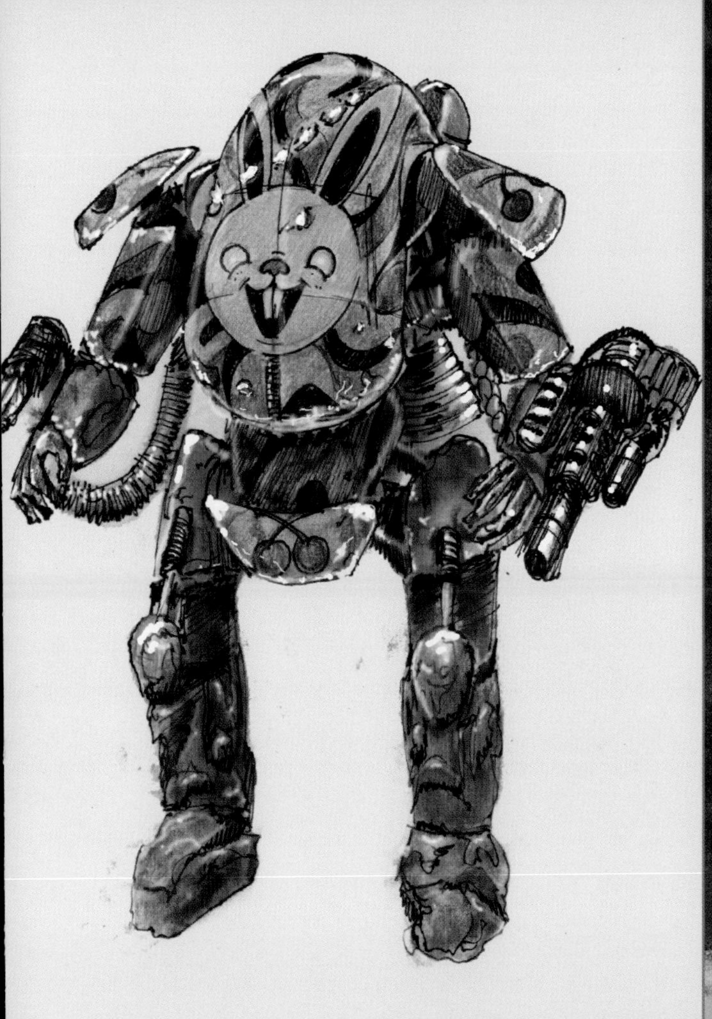

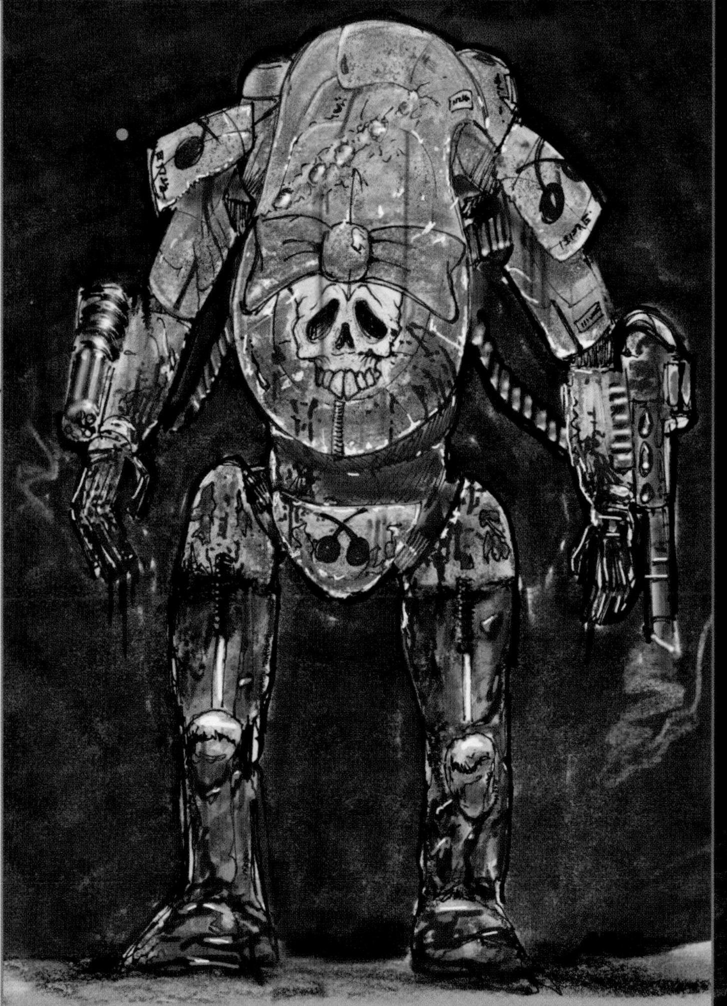

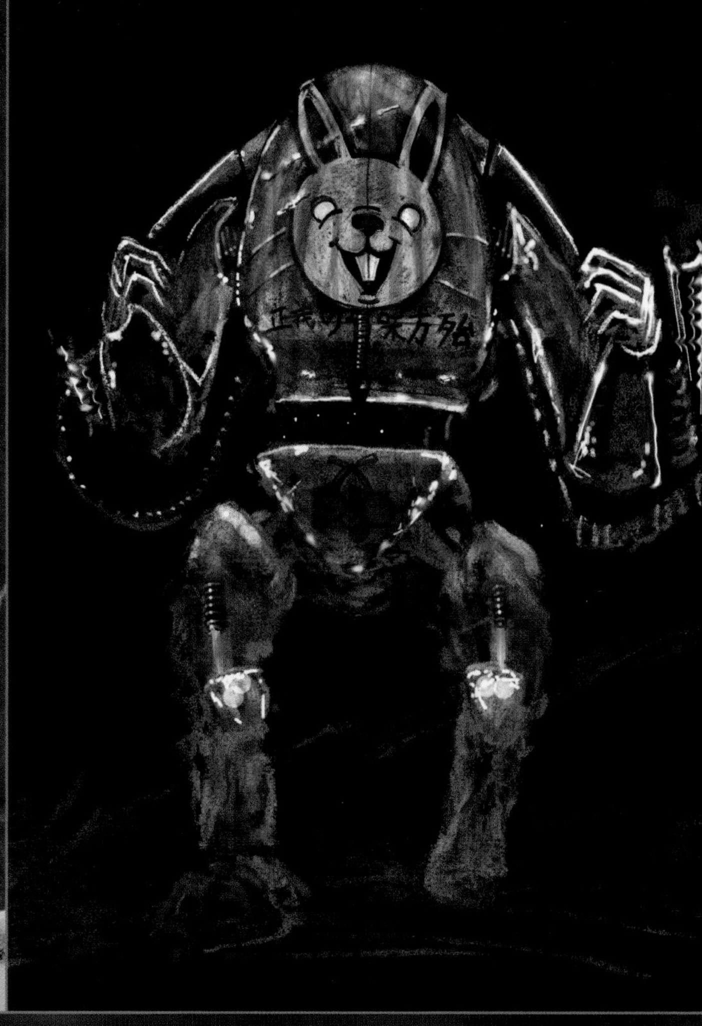

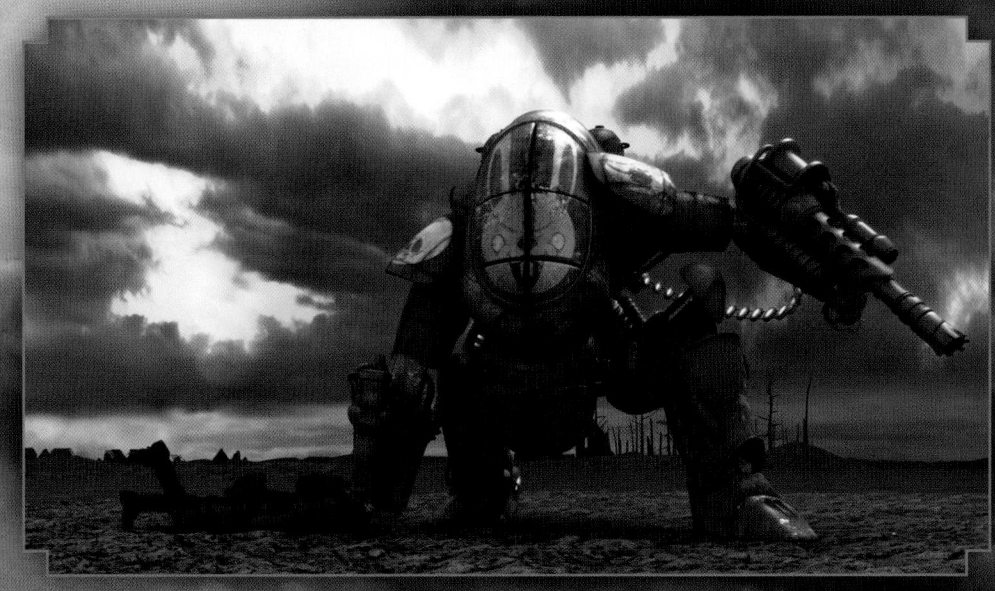

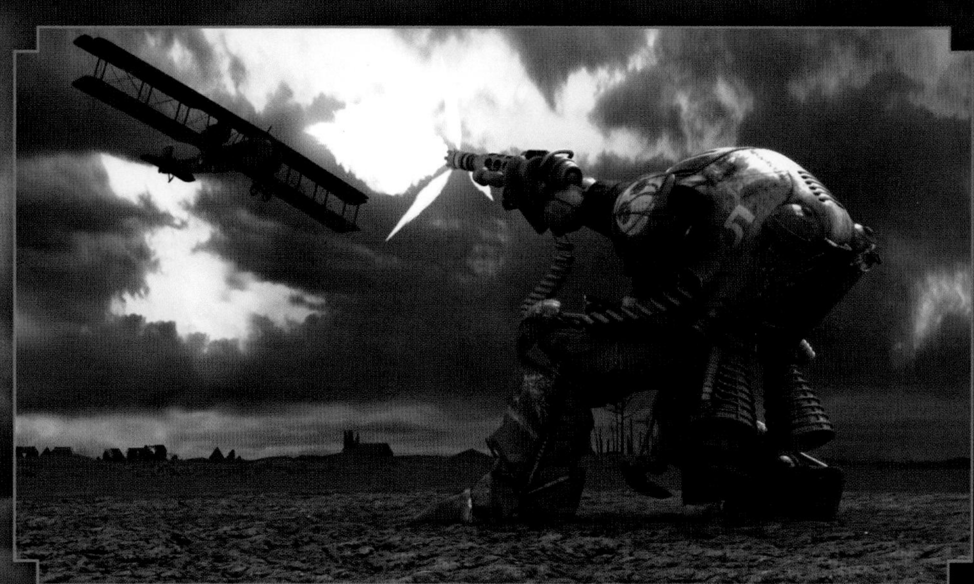

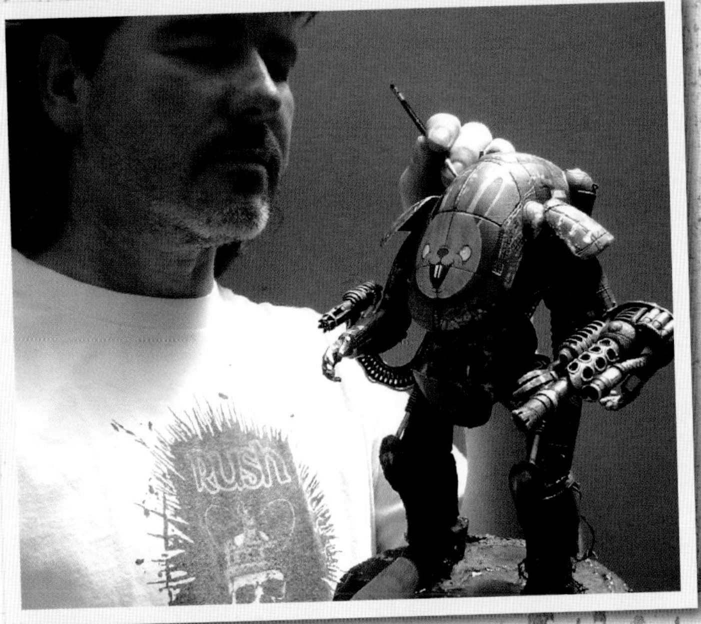

Above: Jim Towler adds a bit of weathering to the Meka reference model.
Below and right: Close-up details of the Meka's armament and propulsion system. The Japanese roughly translates as, "Danger! Woman Driver!" This, of course, can be taken a couple of ways…

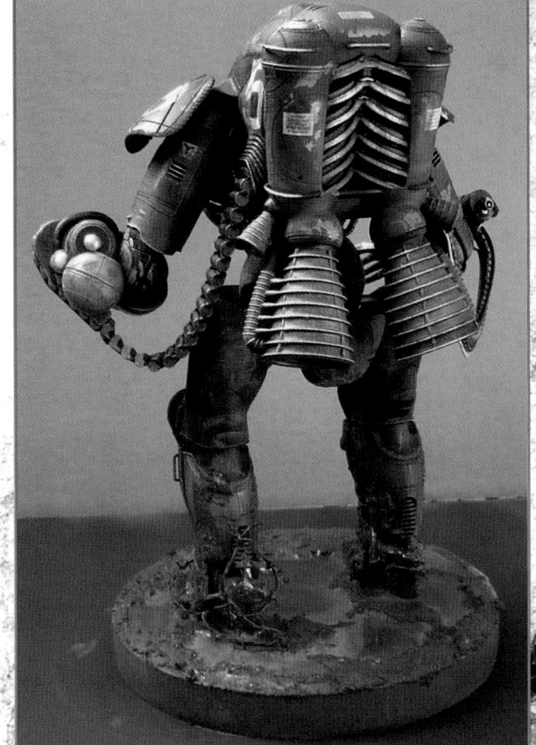

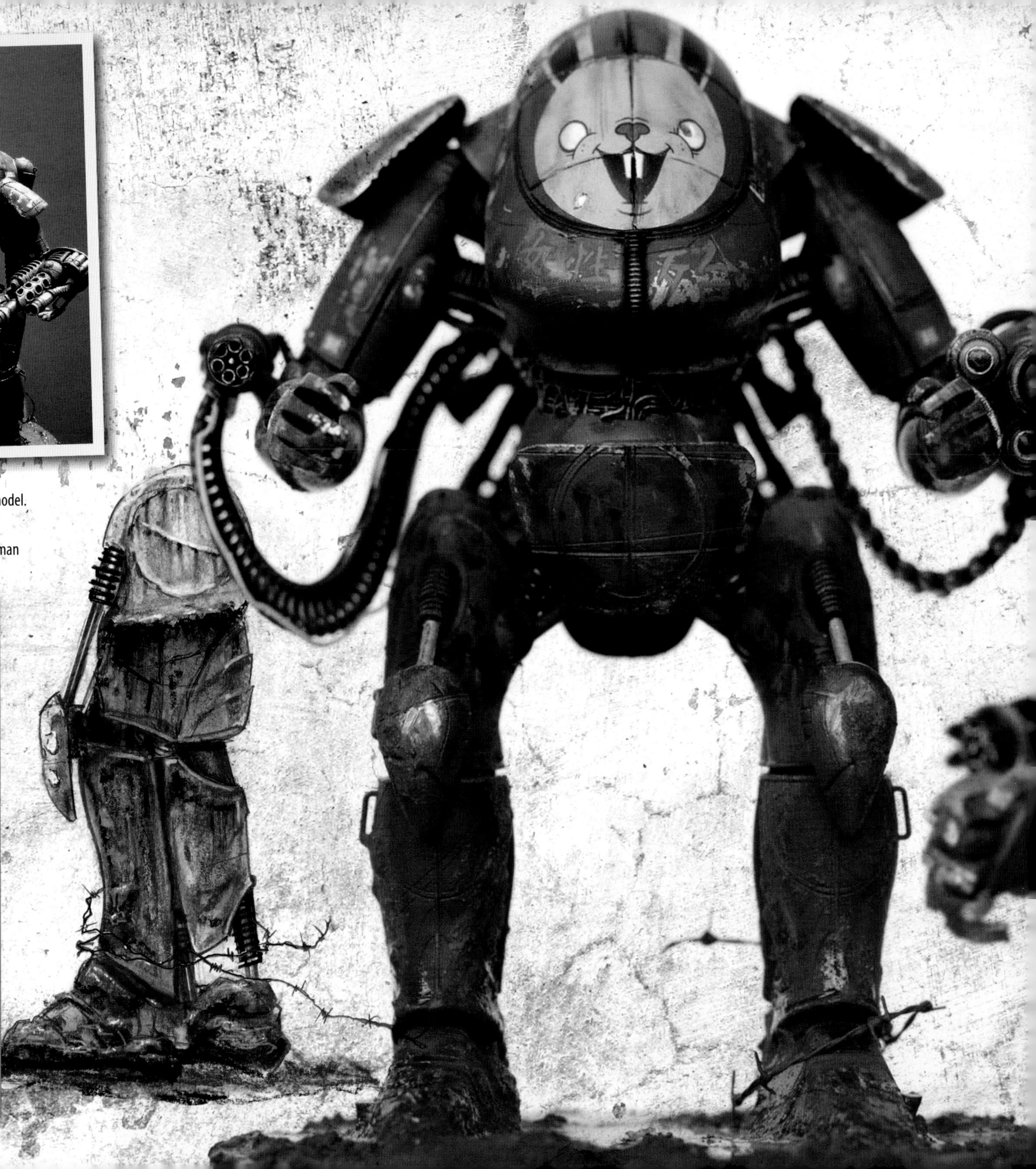

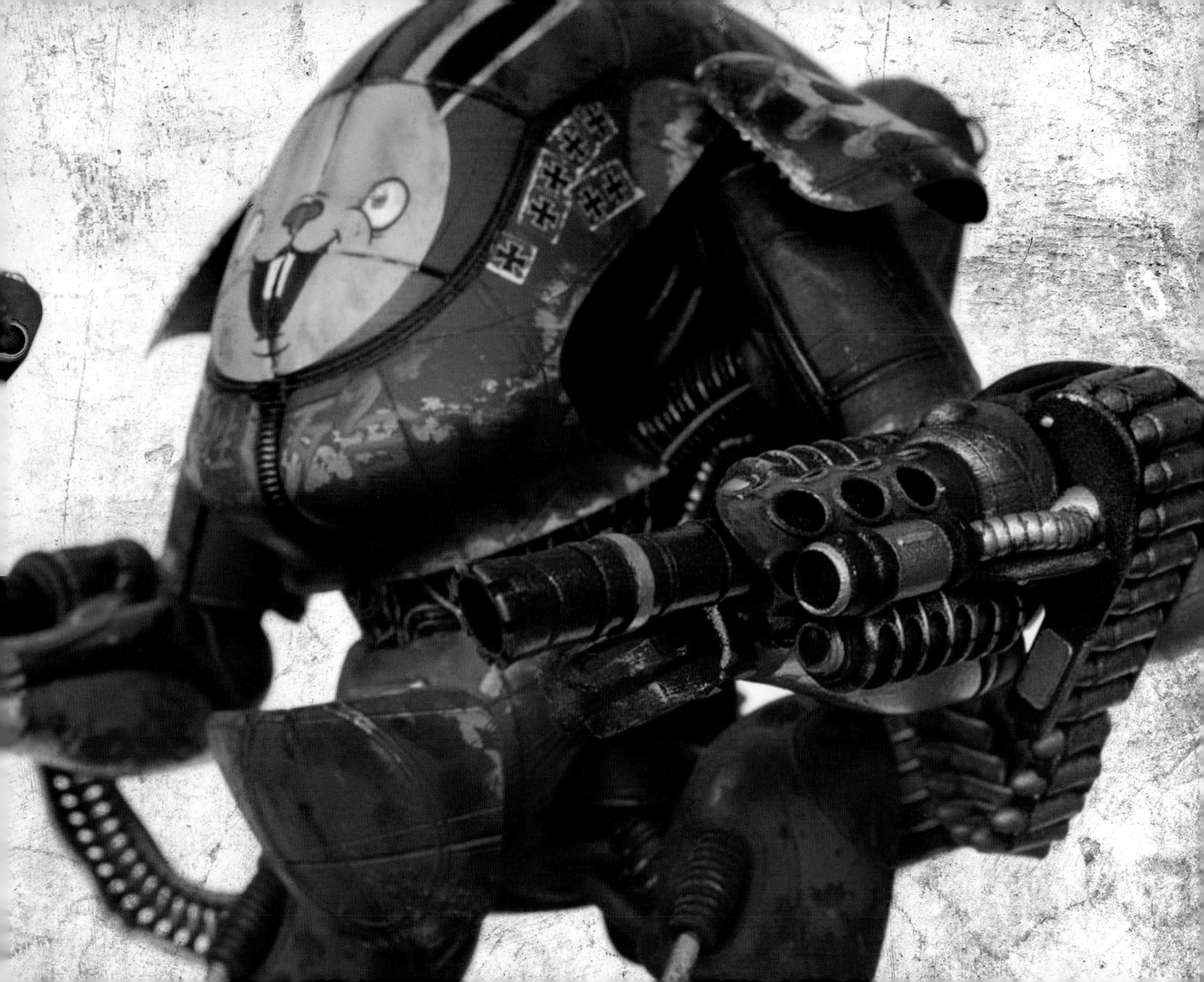

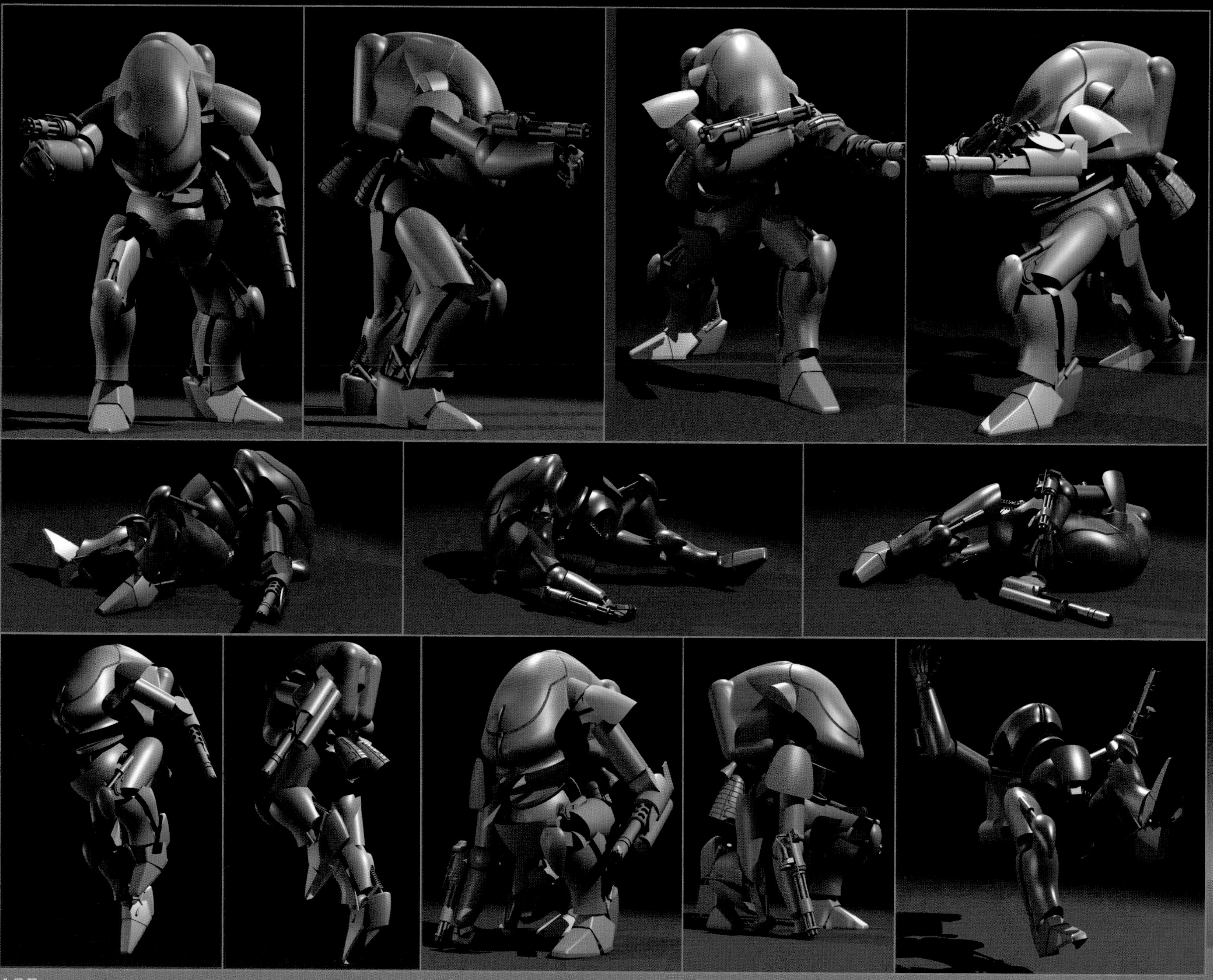

A 3-D model shows the Meka's scale and full range of motions.

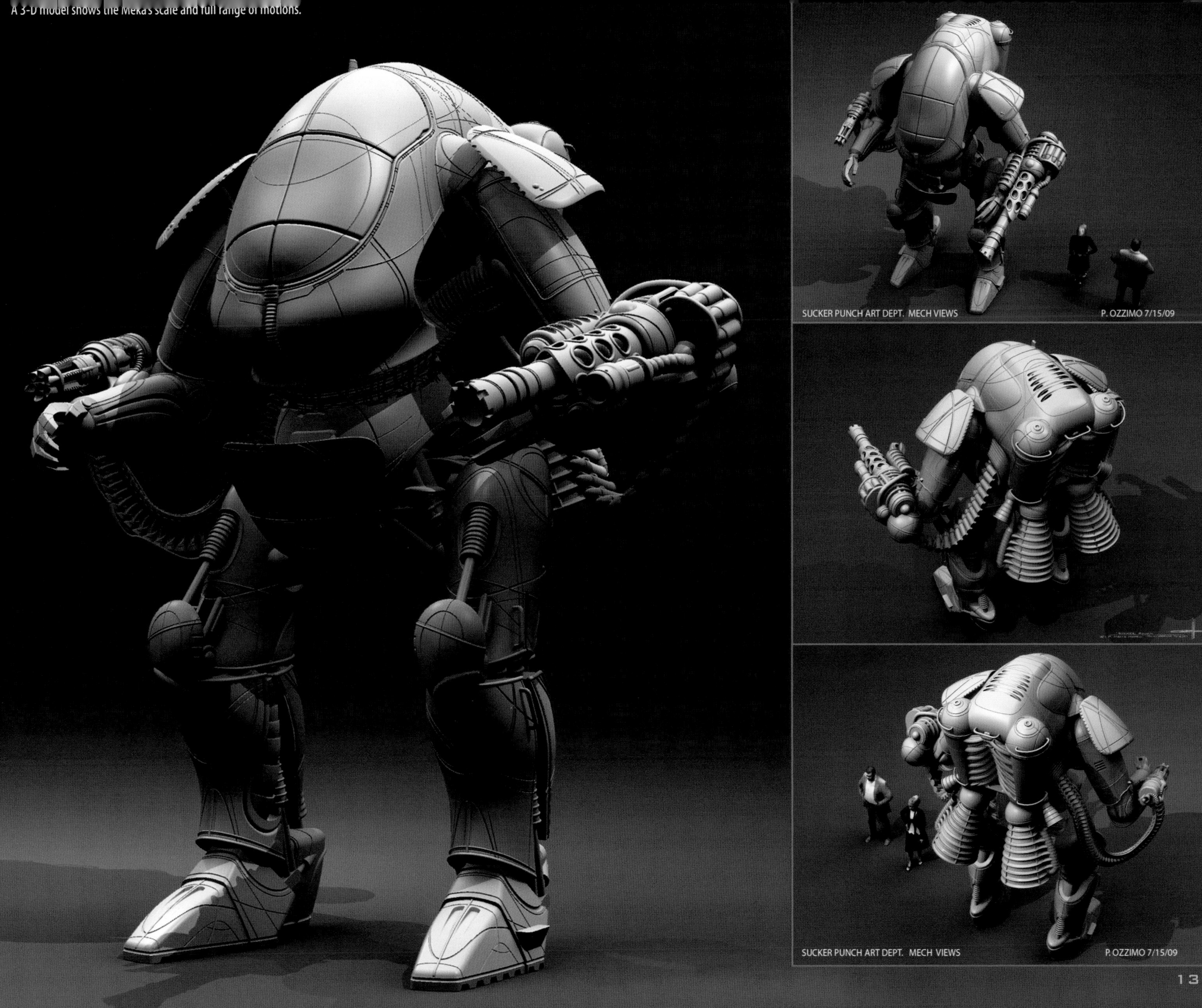

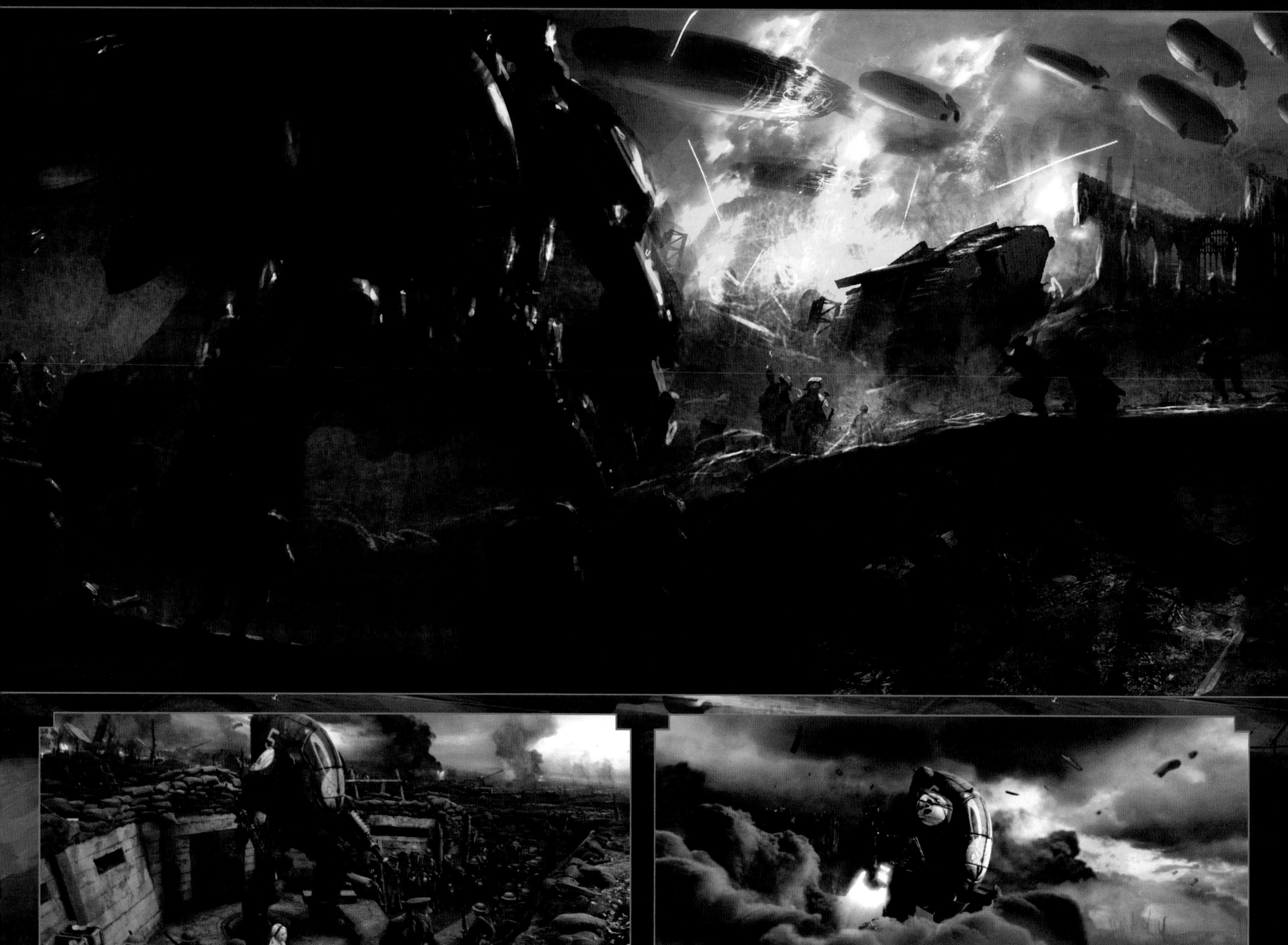

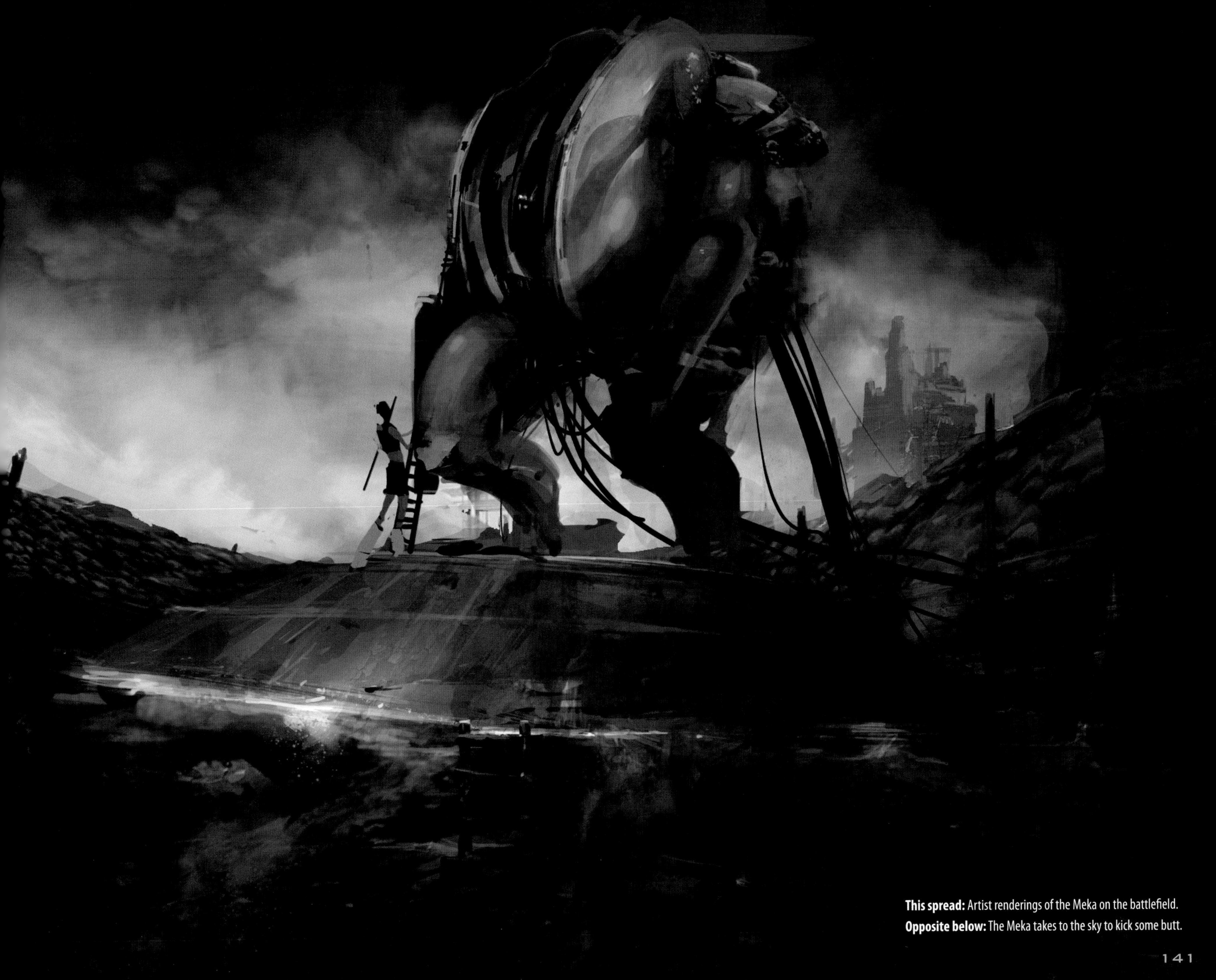

This spread: Artist renderings of the Meka on the battlefield.
Opposite below: The Meka takes to the sky to kick some butt.

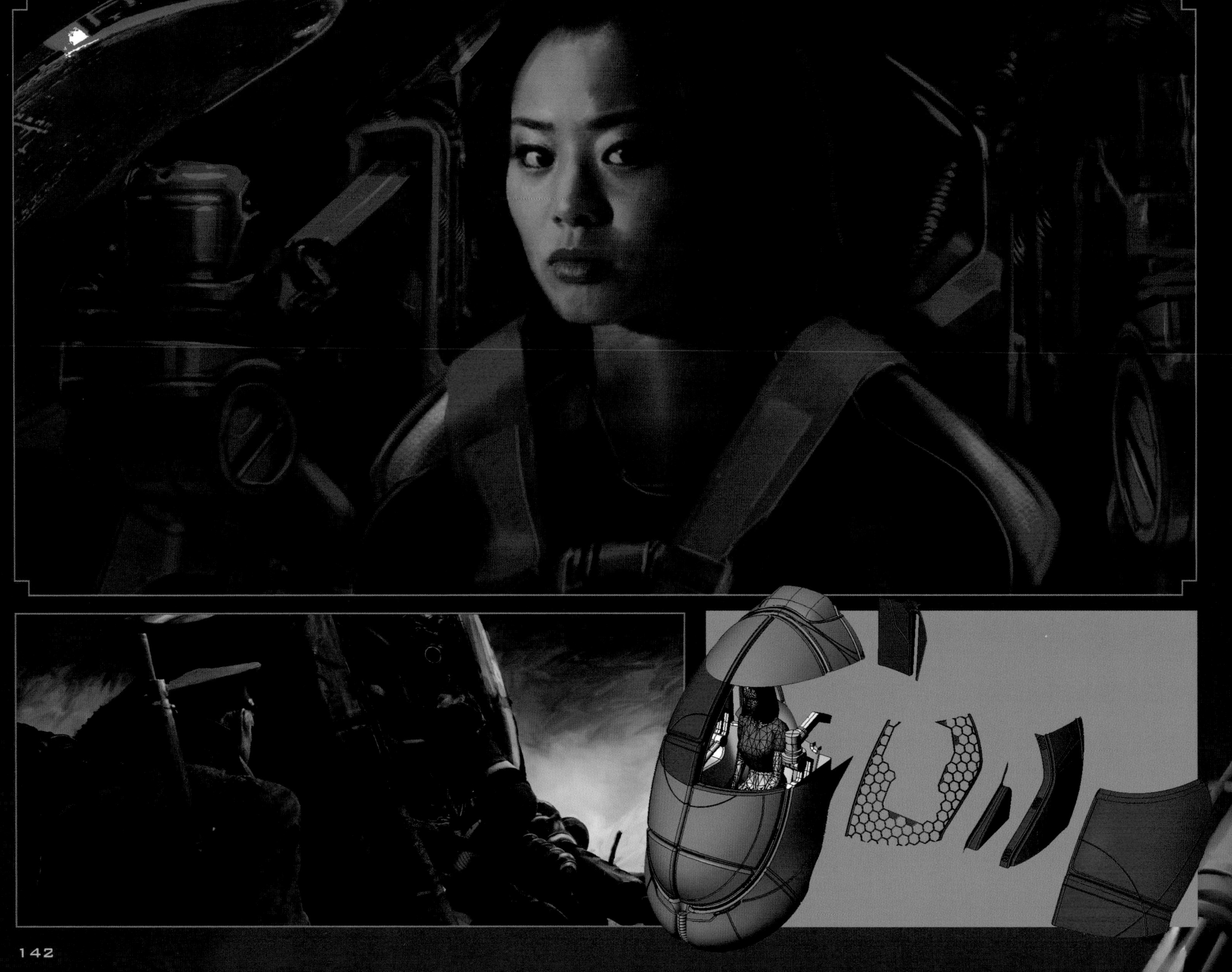

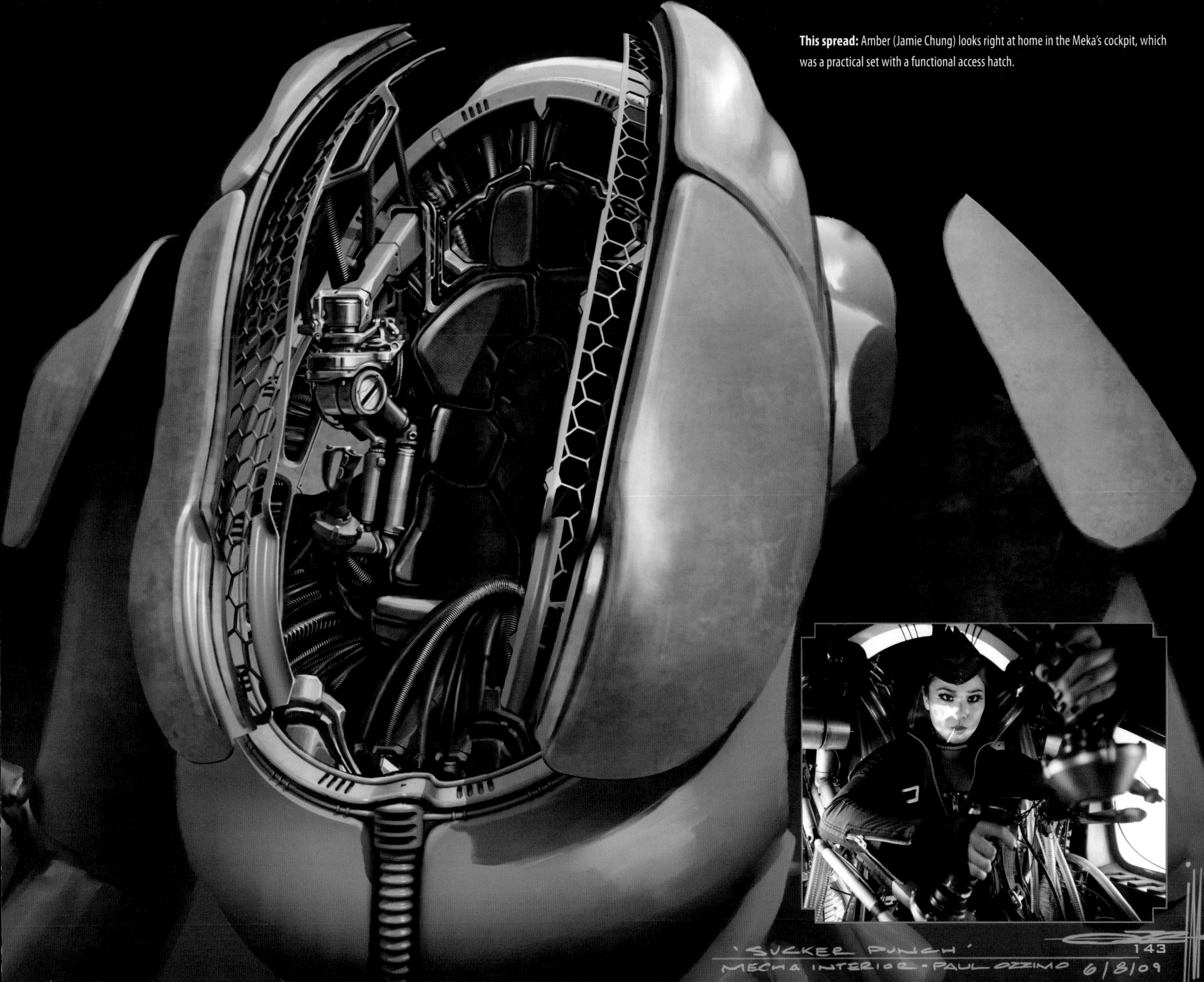

This spread: Amber (Jamie Chung) looks right at home in the Meka's cockpit, which was a practical set with a functional access hatch.

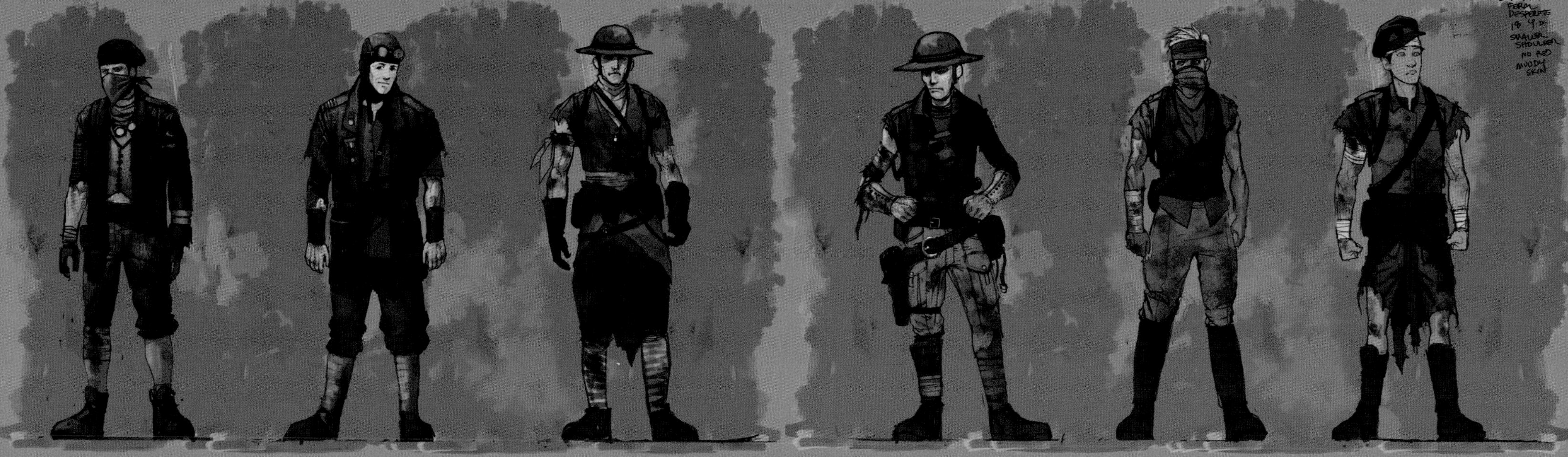

SCRAWNY
FERAL
DESPERATE
SMALLER
SHOULDER
NO RED
MUDDY
SKIN

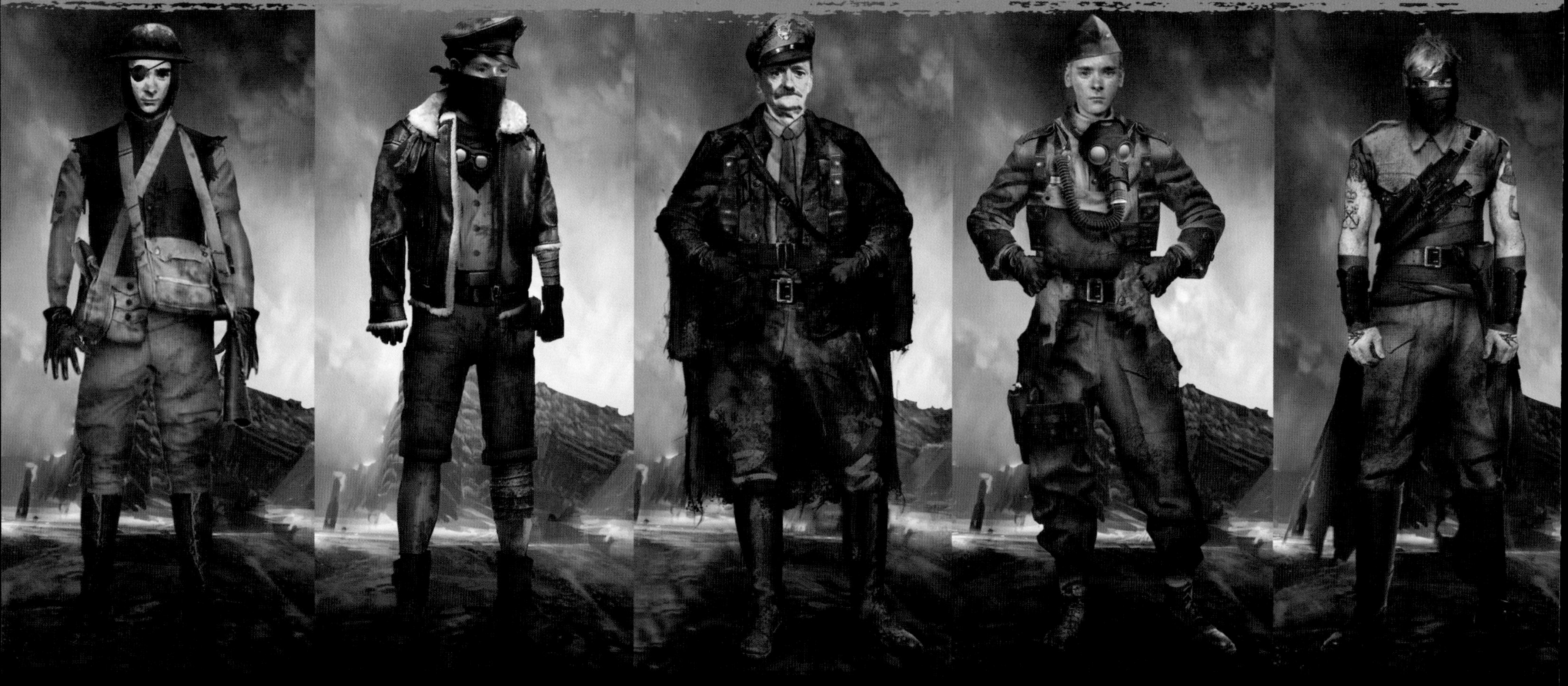

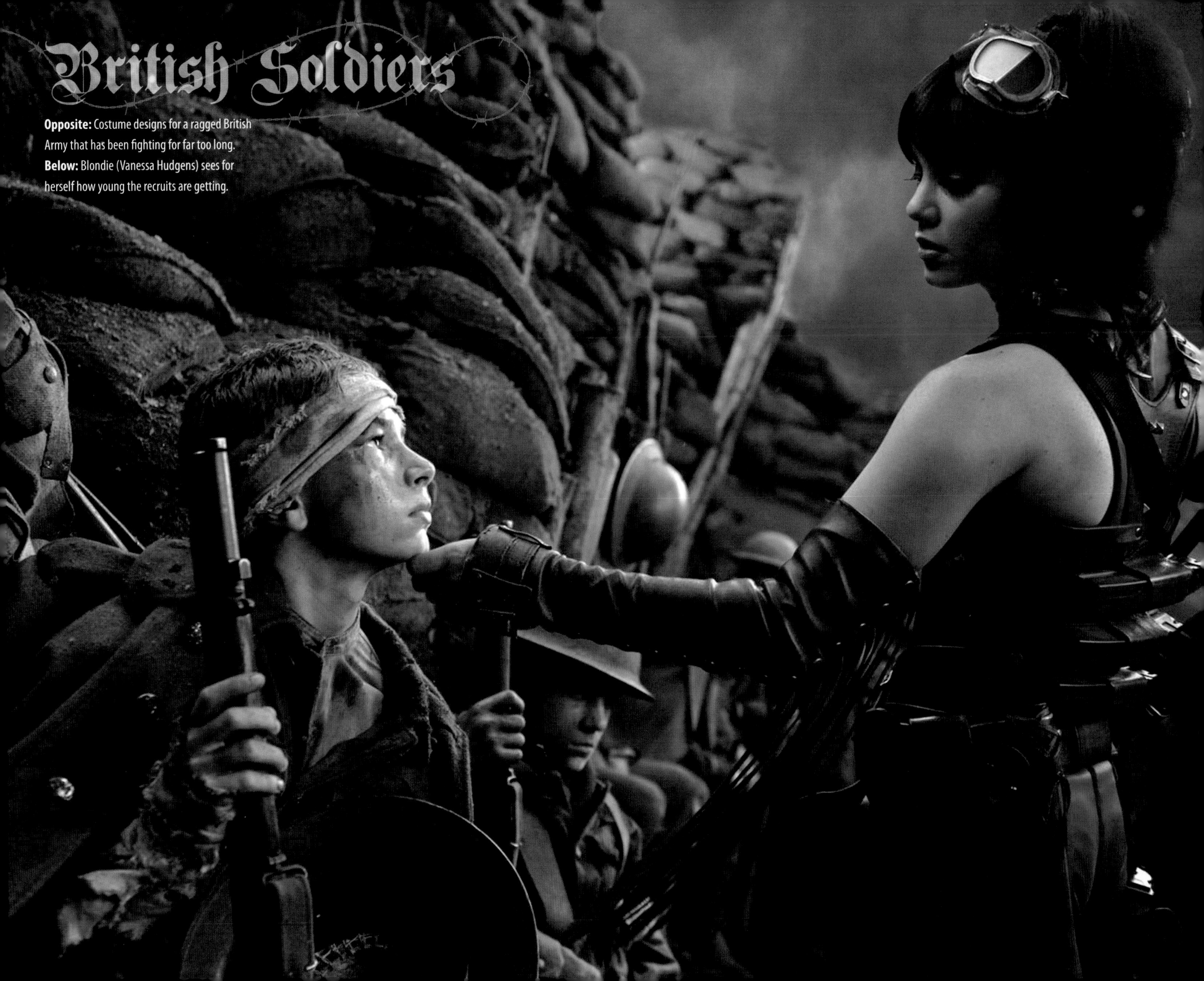

British Soldiers

Opposite: Costume designs for a ragged British Army that has been fighting for far too long.
Below: Blondie (Vanessa Hudgens) sees for herself how young the recruits are getting.

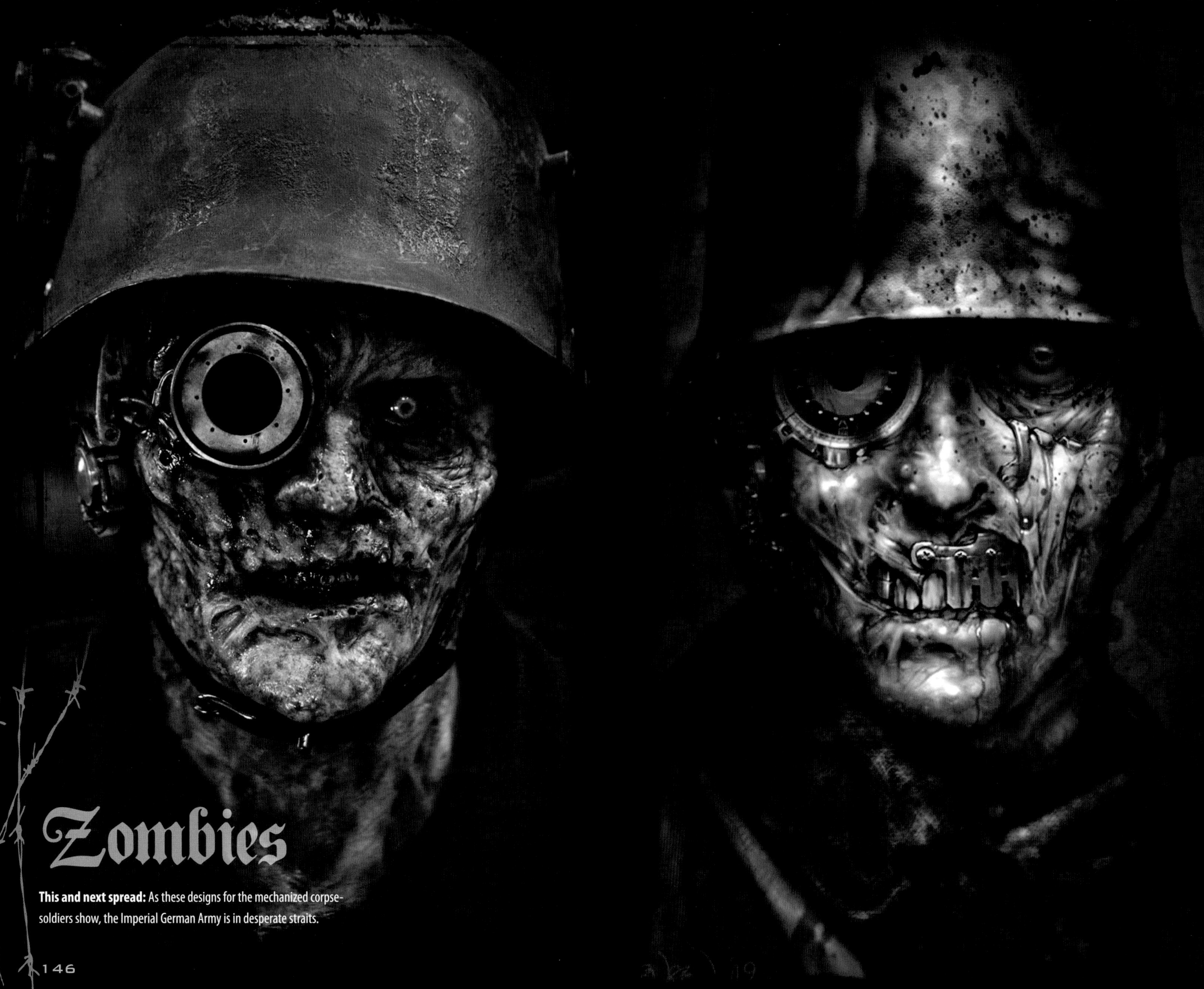

Zombies

This and next spread: As these designs for the mechanized corpse-soldiers show, the Imperial German Army is in desperate straits.

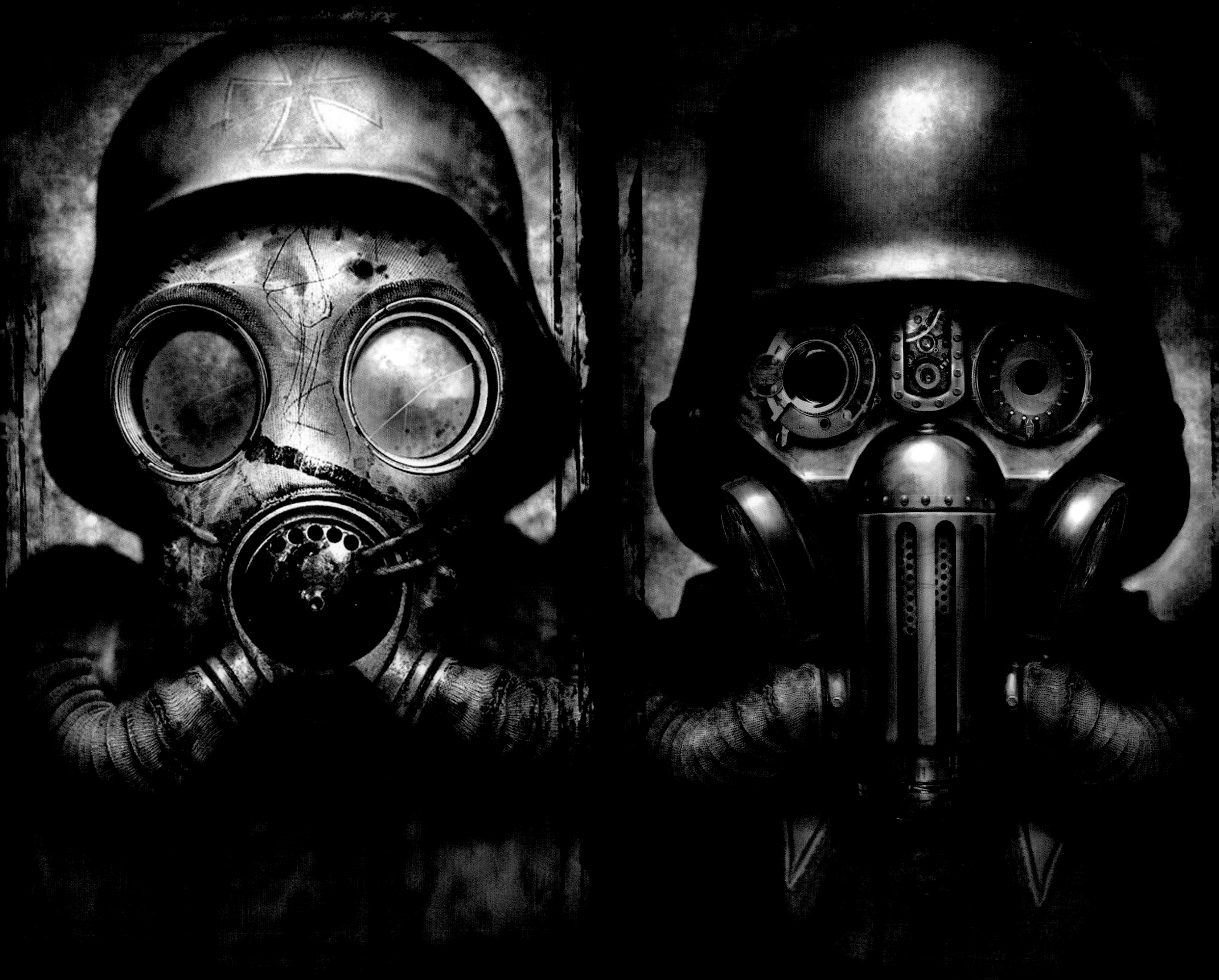

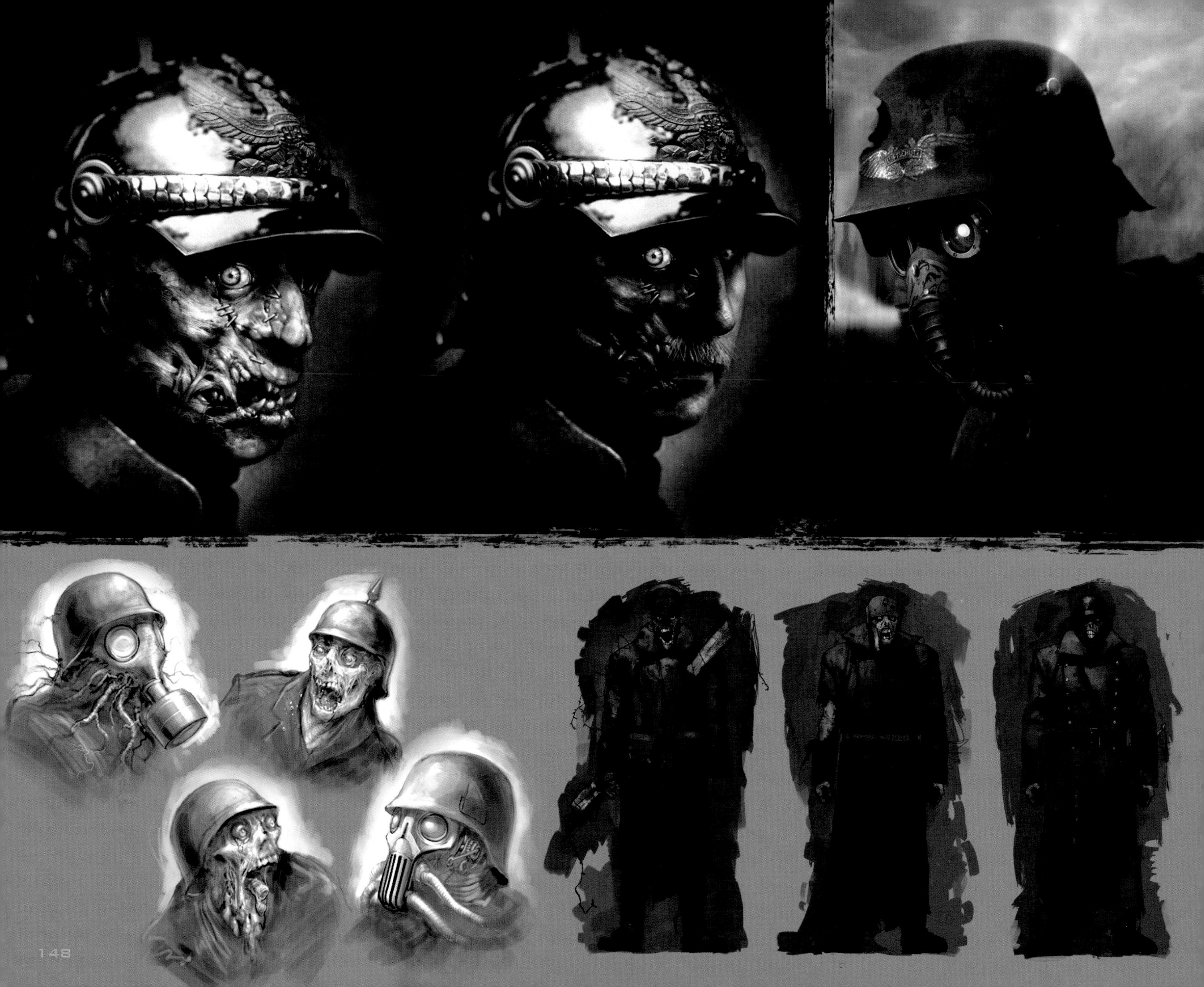

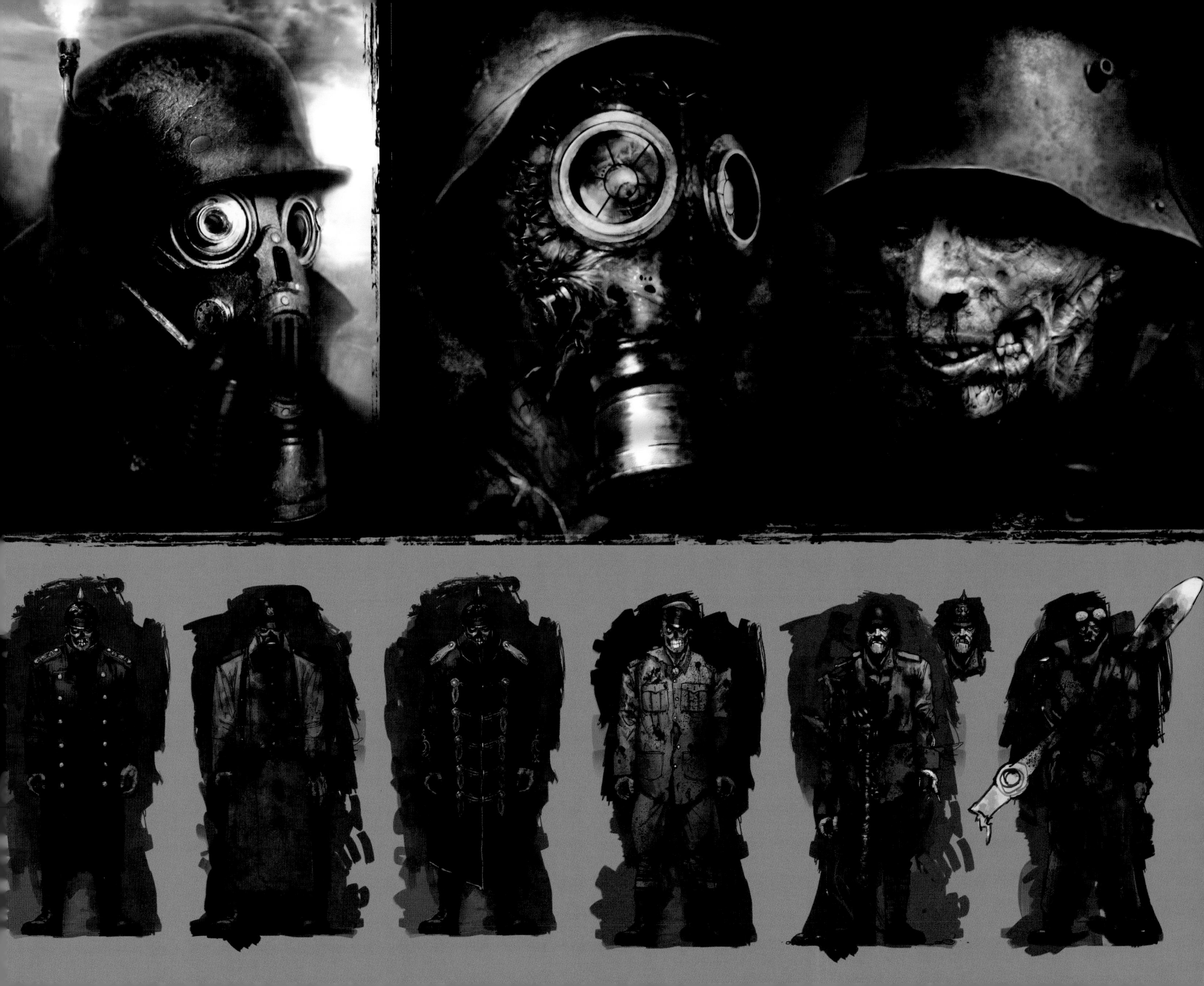

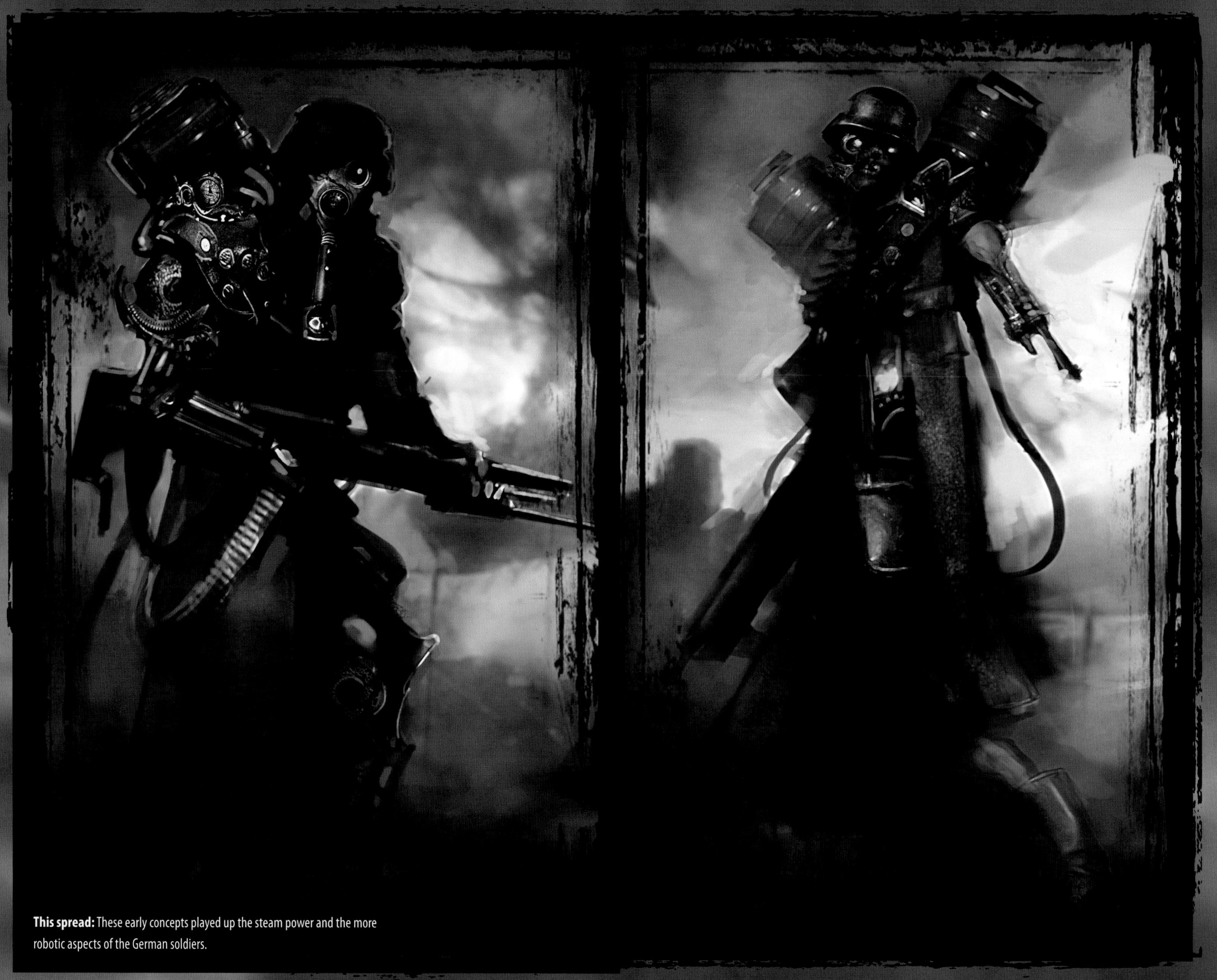

This spread: These early concepts played up the steam power and the more robotic aspects of the German soldiers.

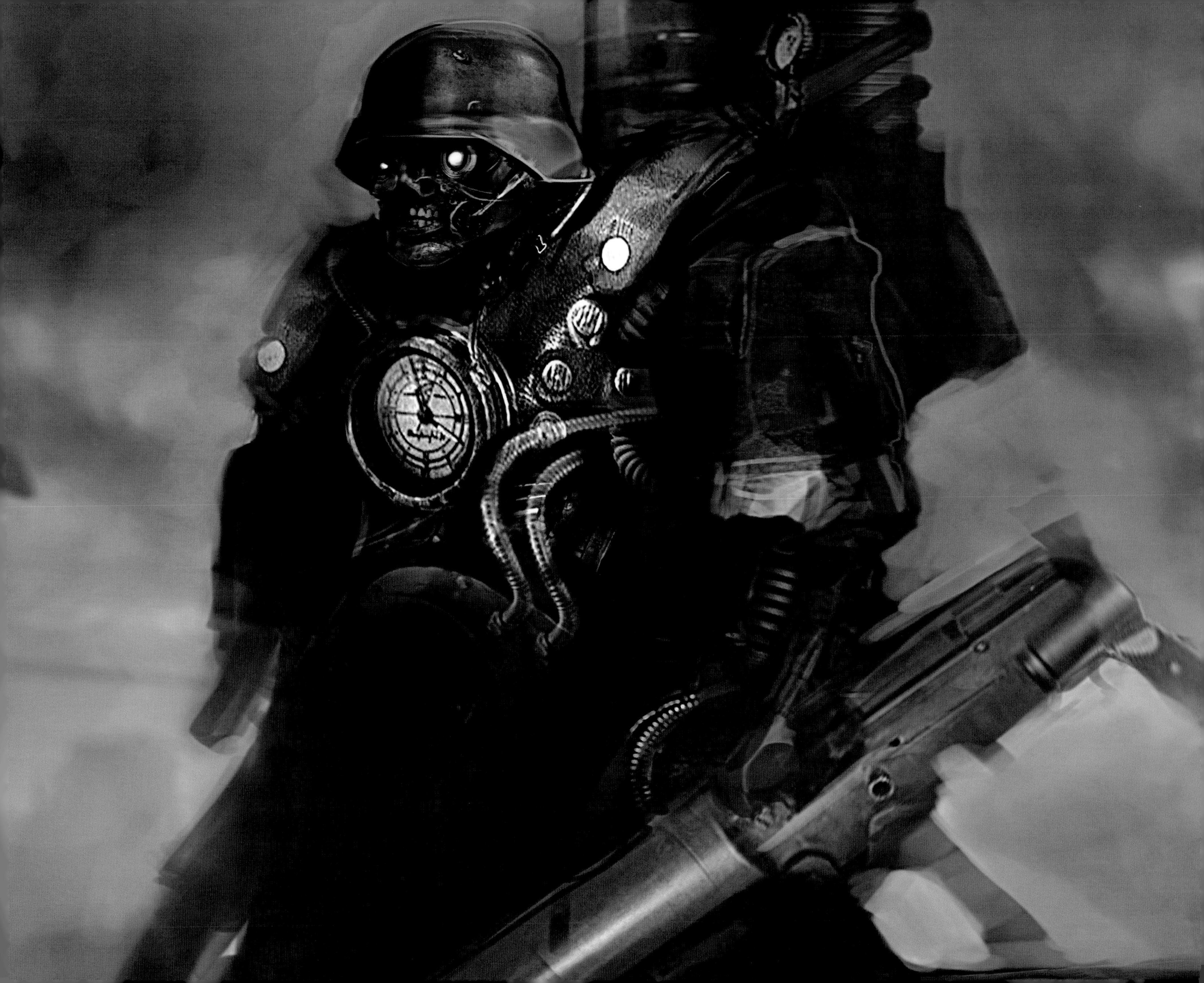

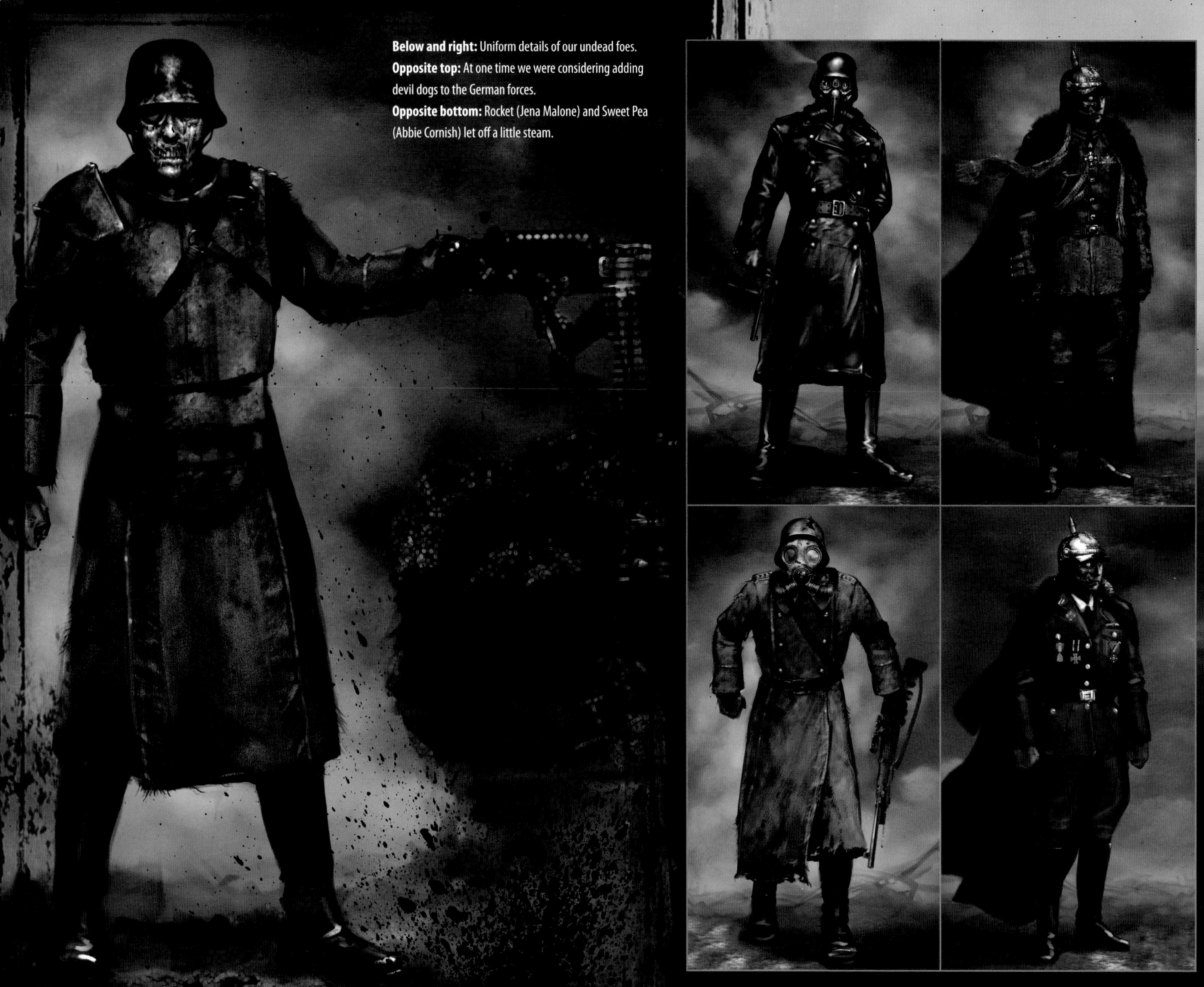

Below and right: Uniform details of our undead foes.

Opposite top: At one time we were considering adding devil dogs to the German forces.

Opposite bottom: Rocket (Jena Malone) and Sweet Pea (Abbie Cornish) let off a little steam.

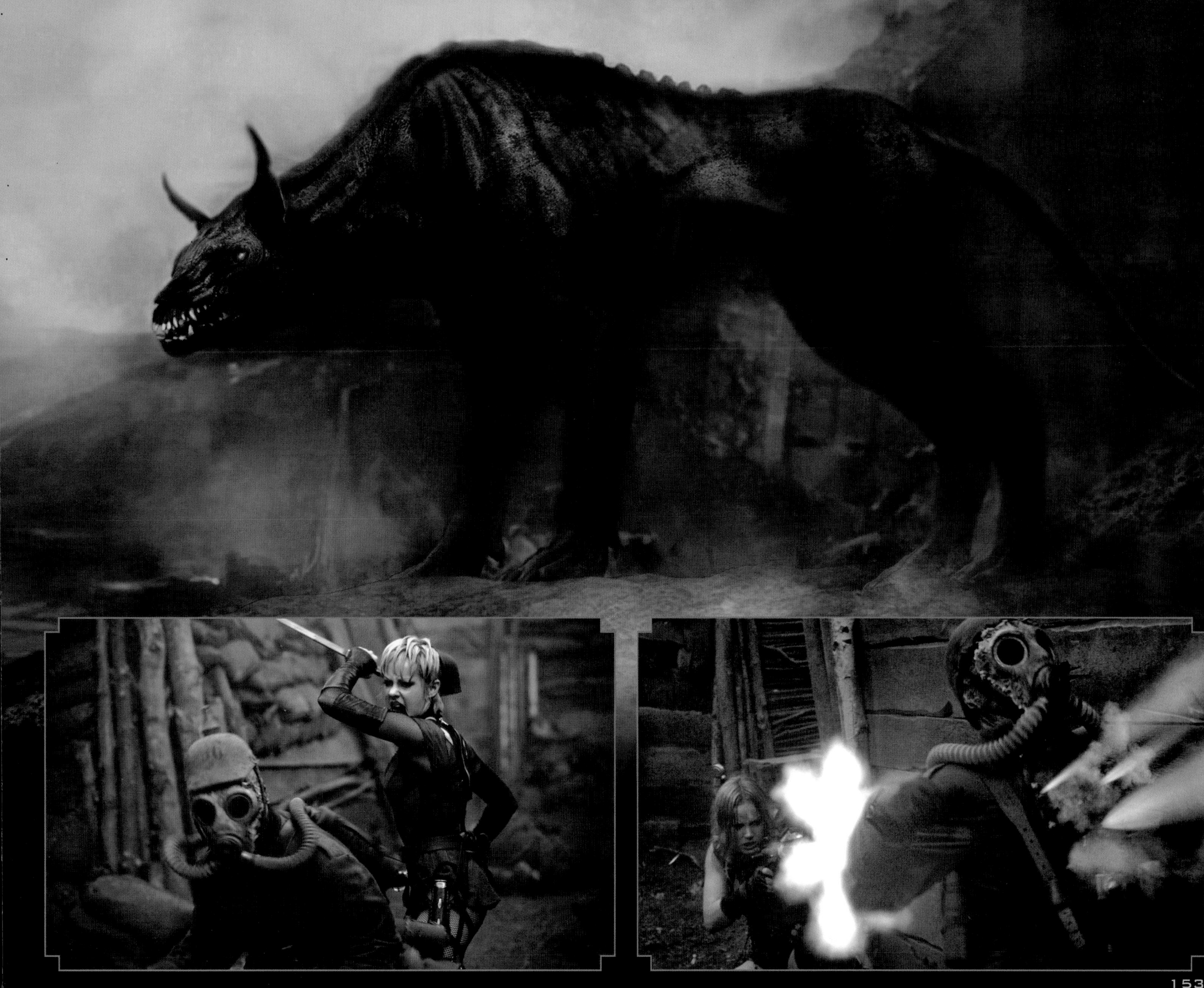

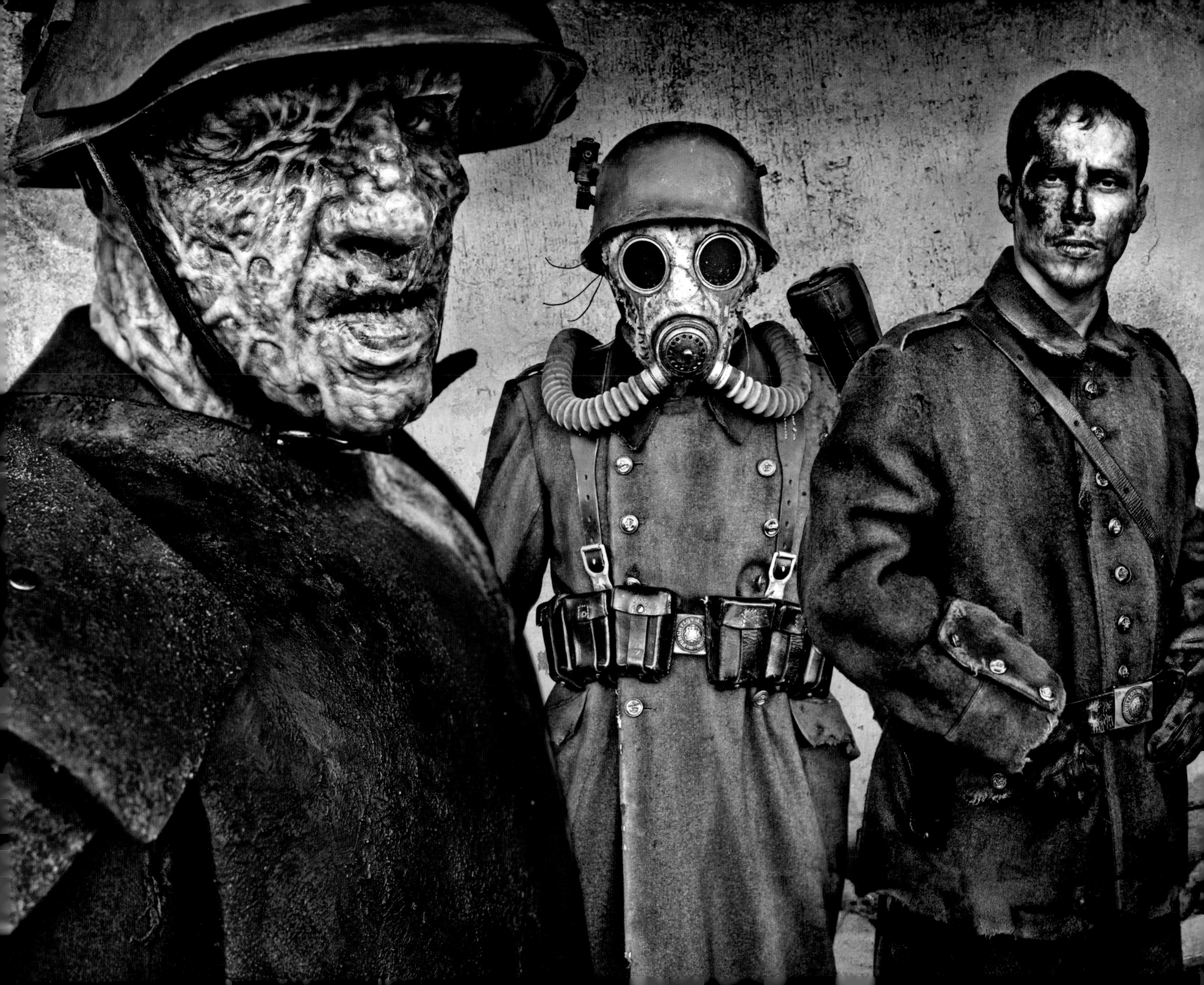

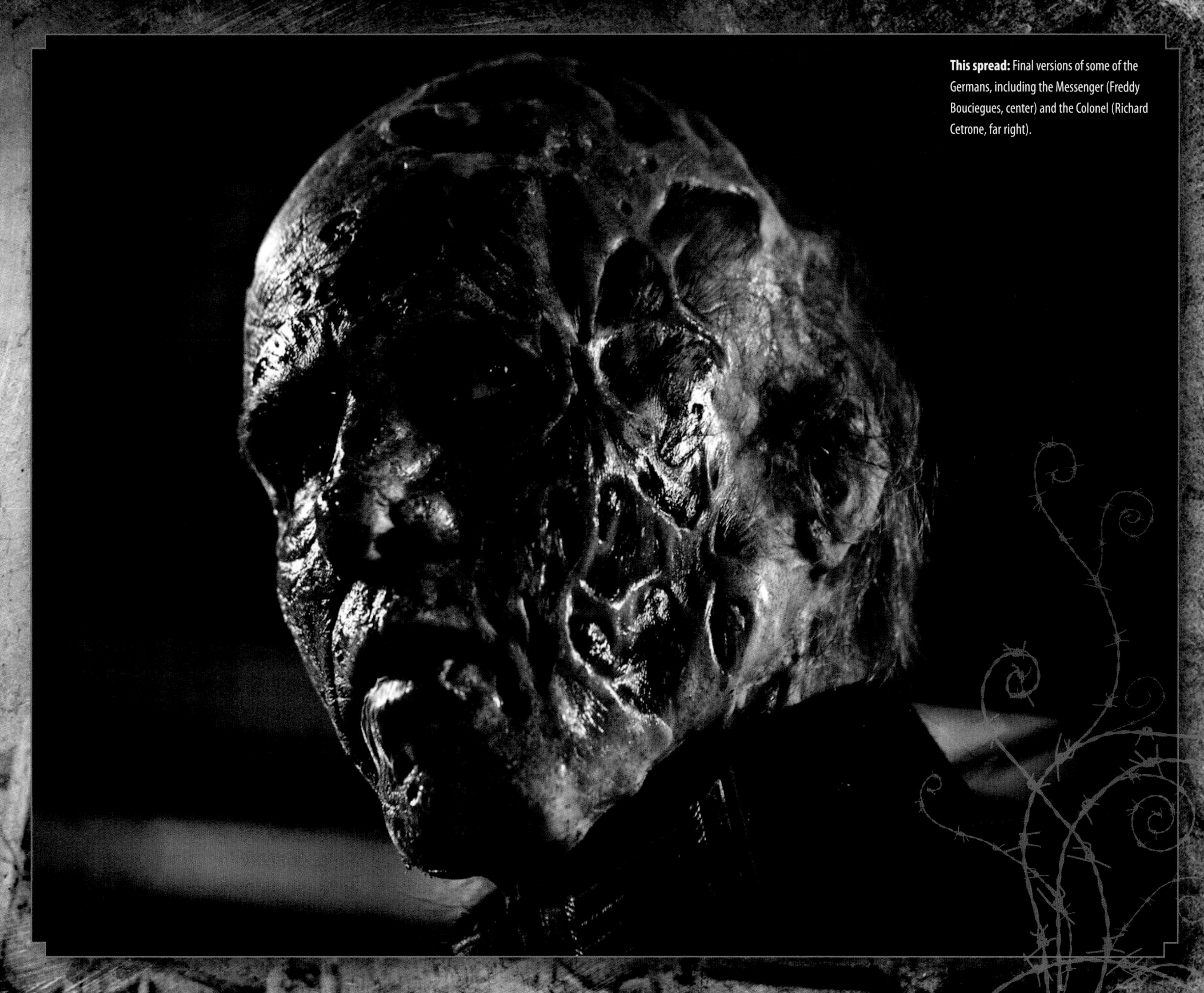

This spread: Final versions of some of the Germans, including the Messenger (Freddy Bouciegues, center) and the Colonel (Richard Cetrone, far right).

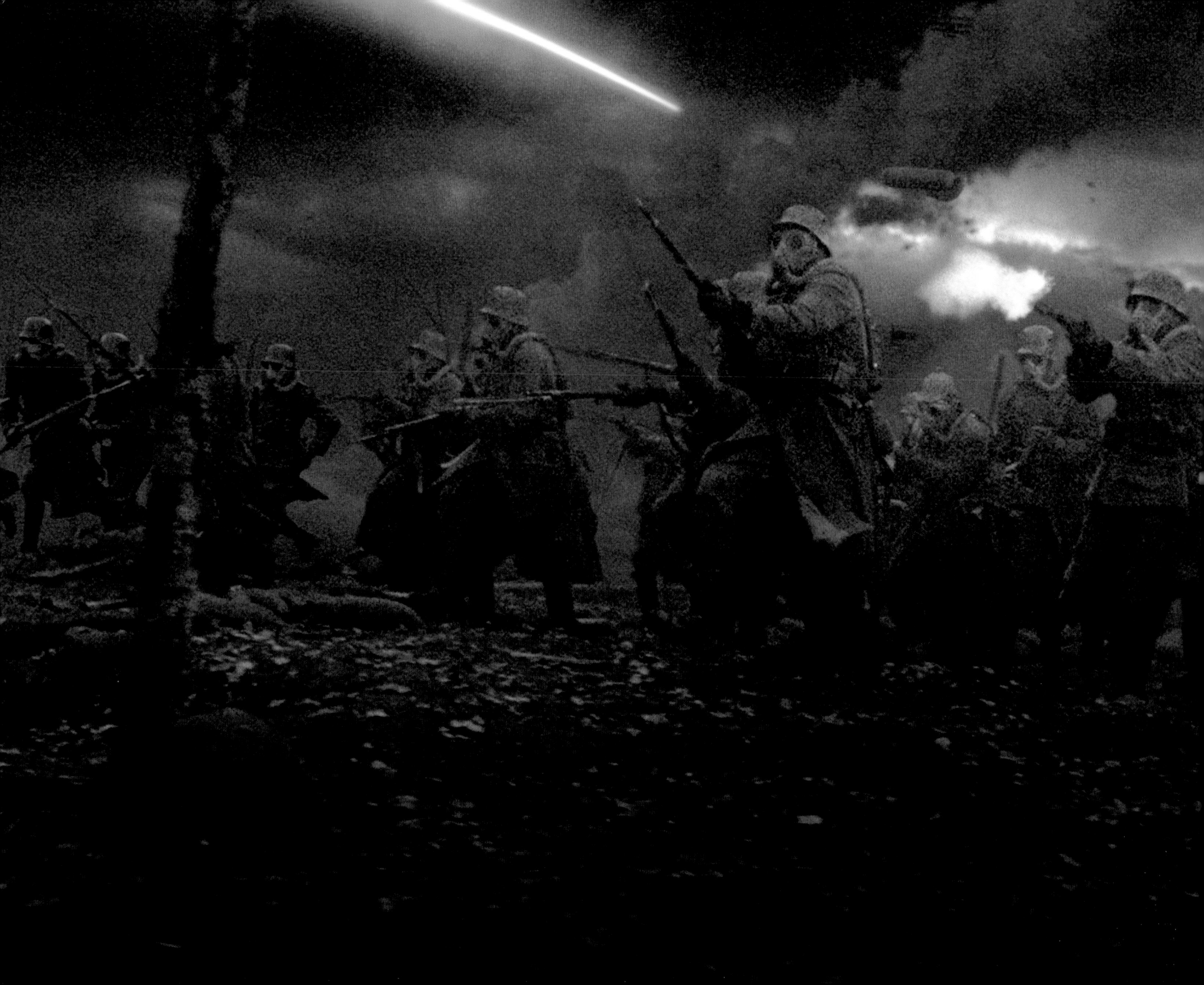

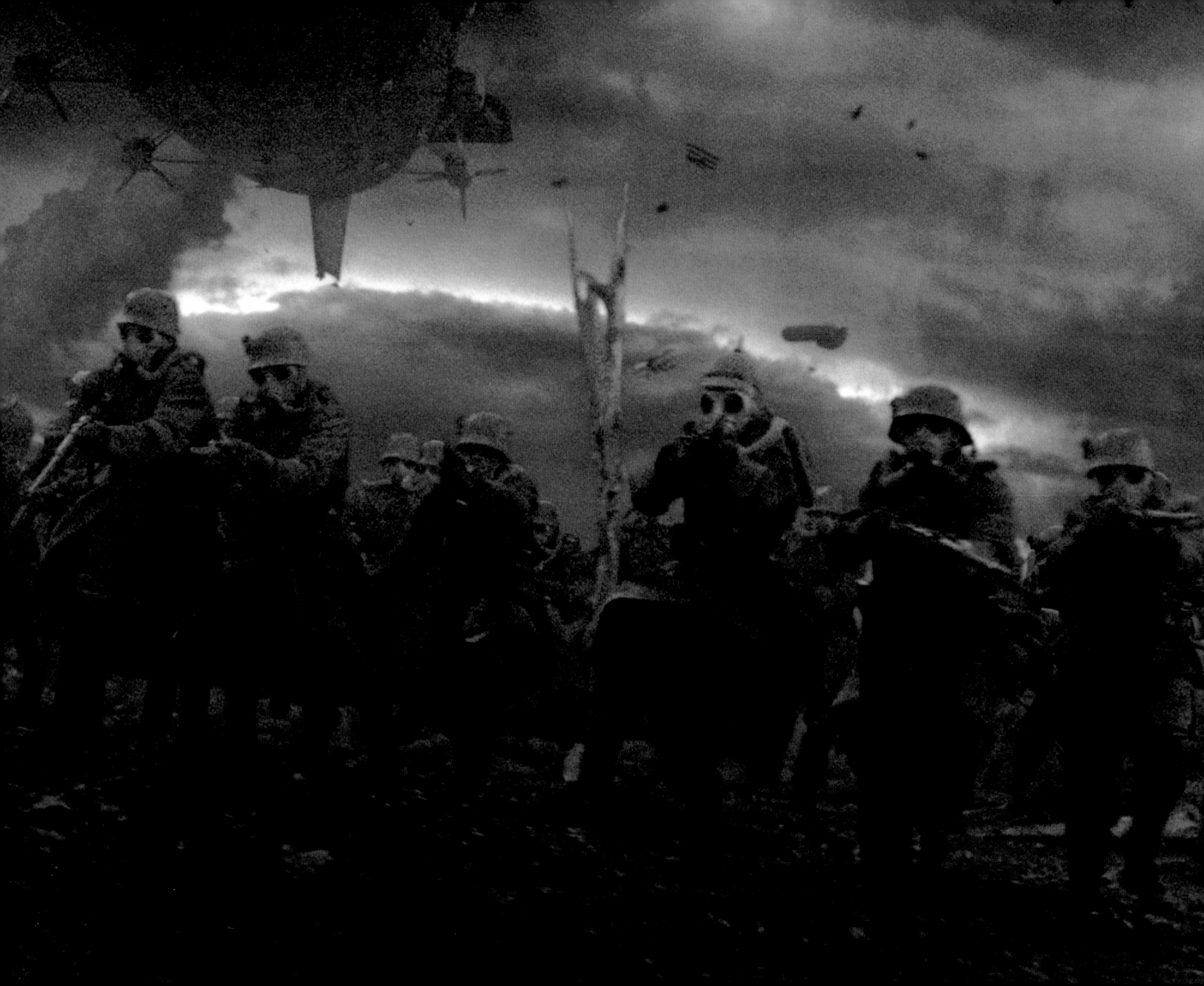

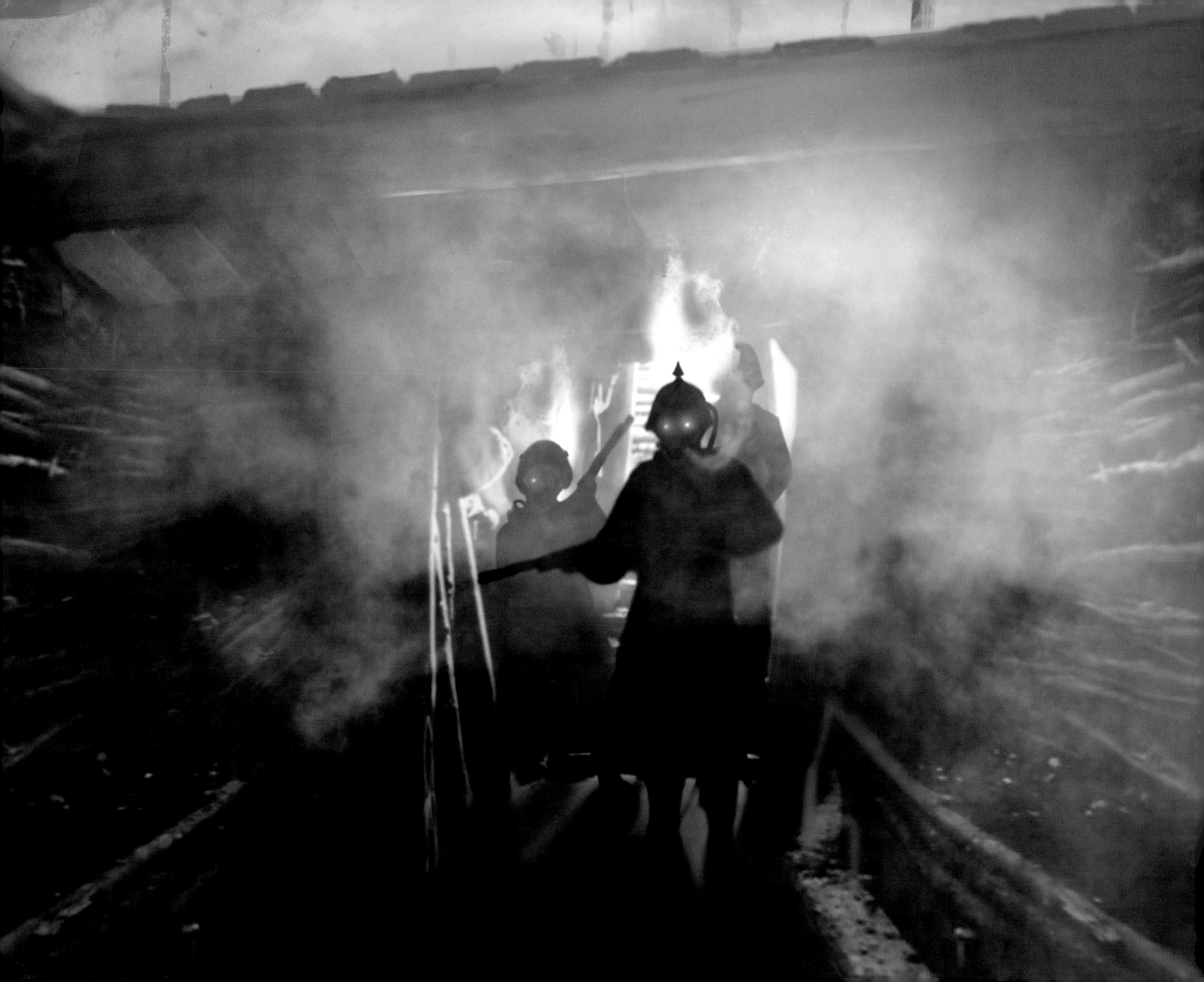

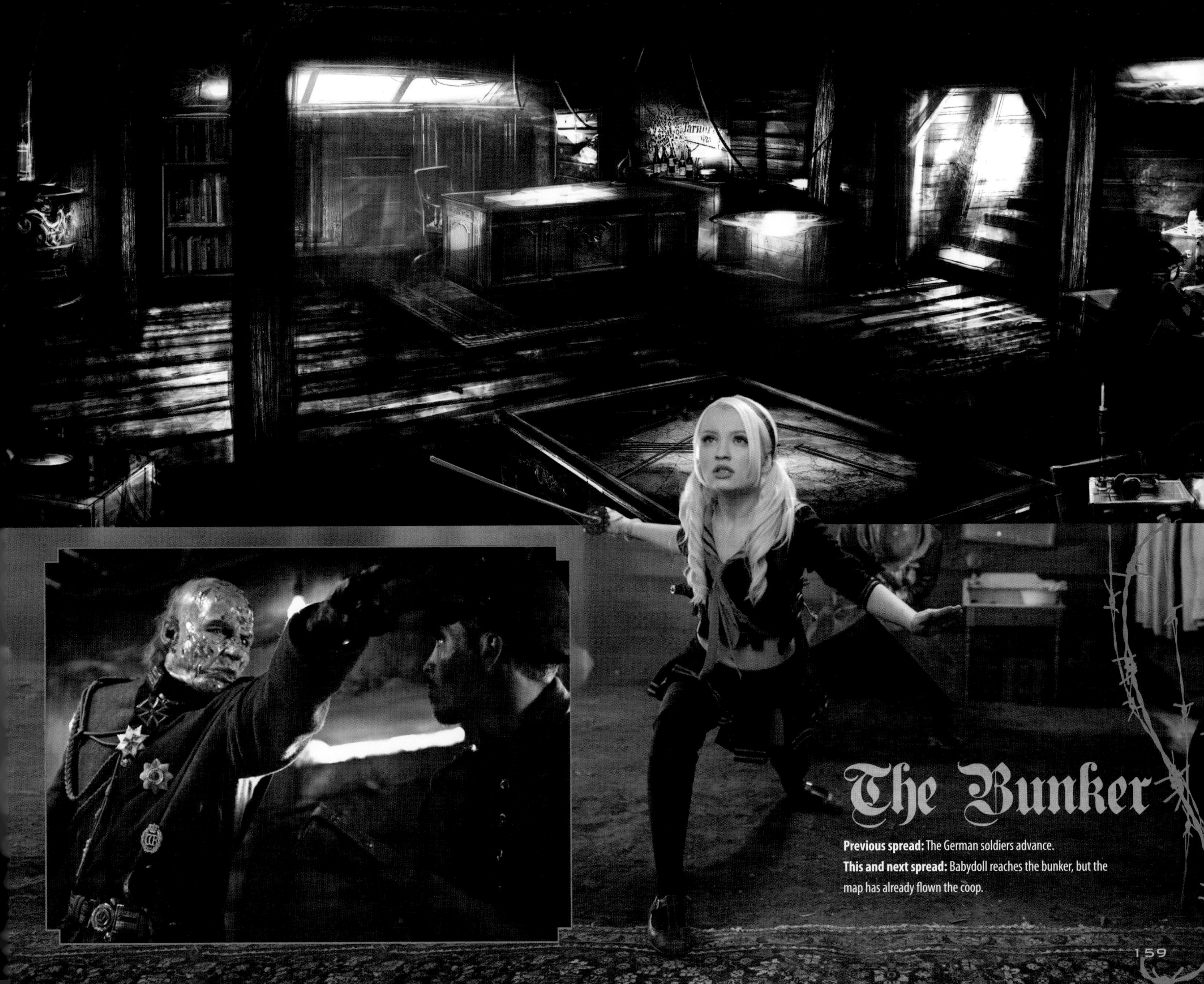

The Bunker

Previous spread: The German soldiers advance.

This and next spread: Babydoll reaches the bunker, but the map has already flown the coop.

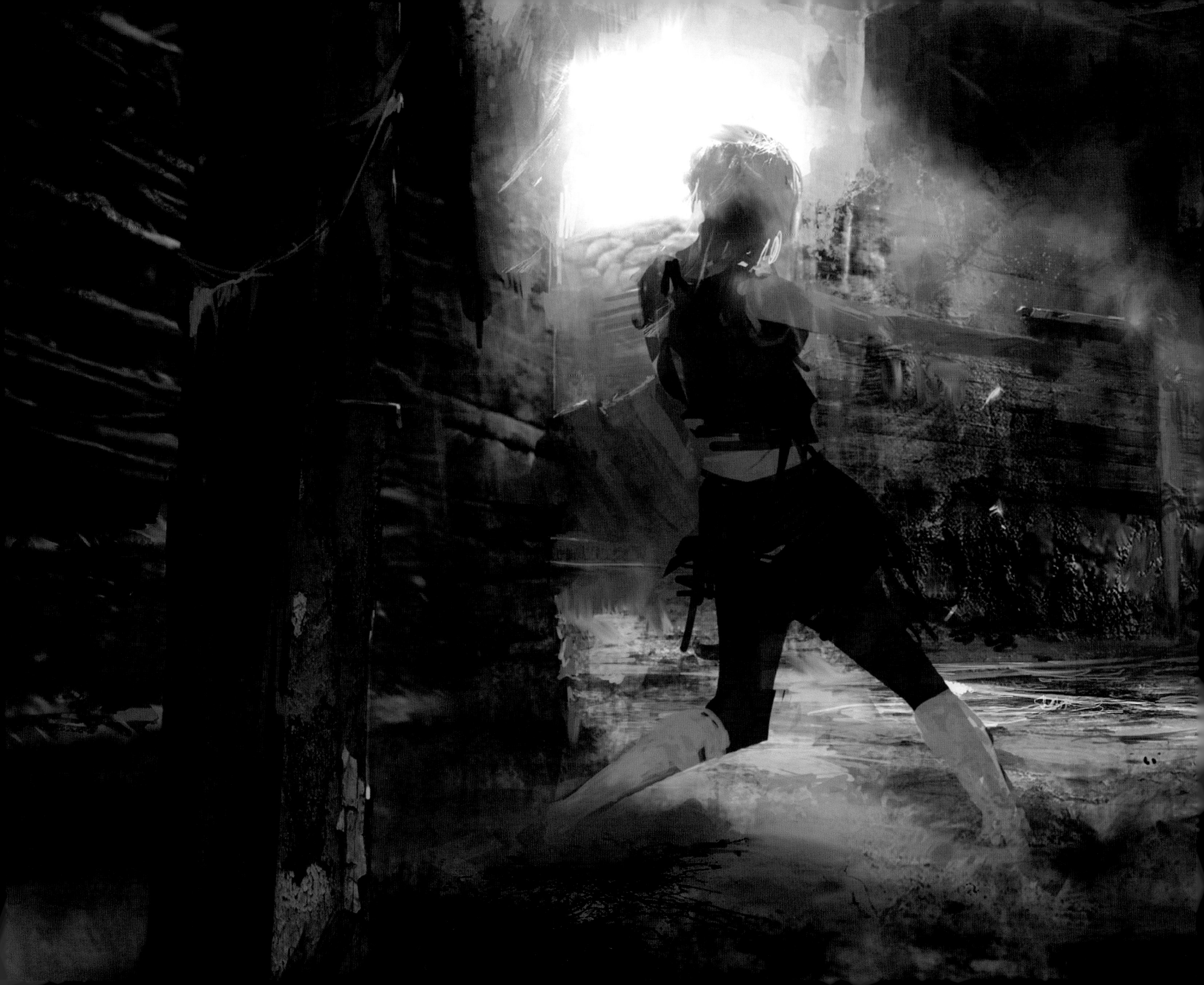

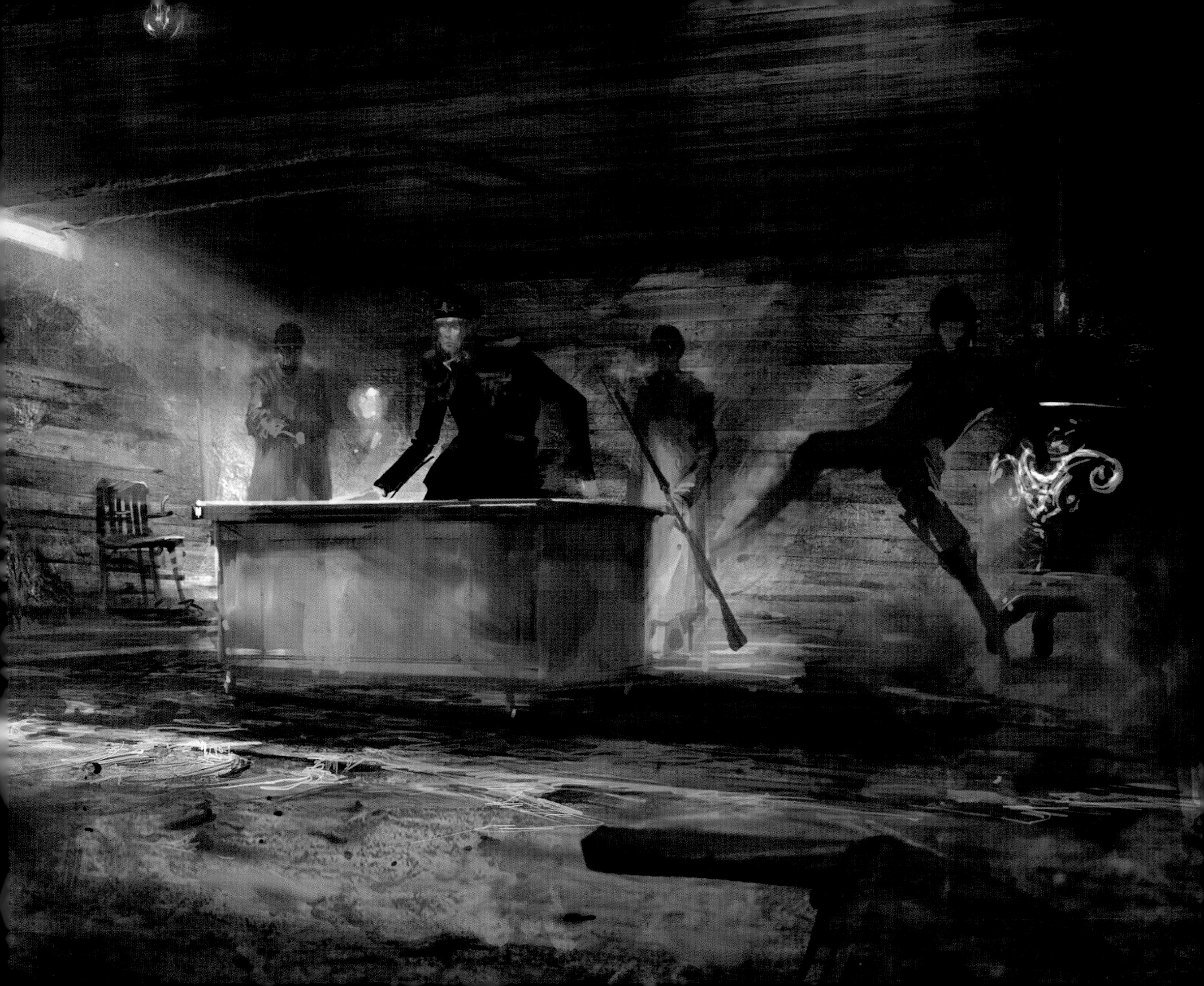

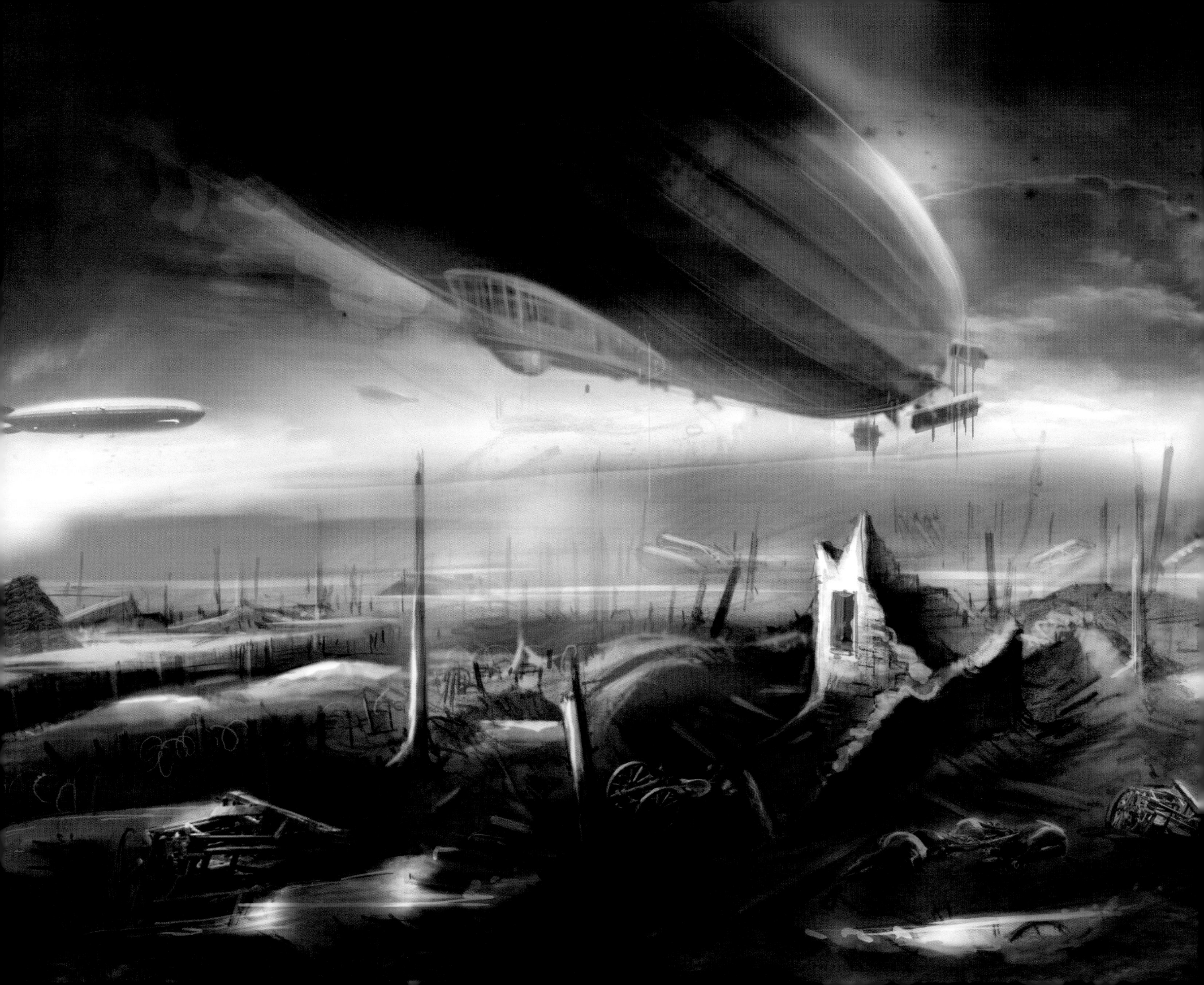

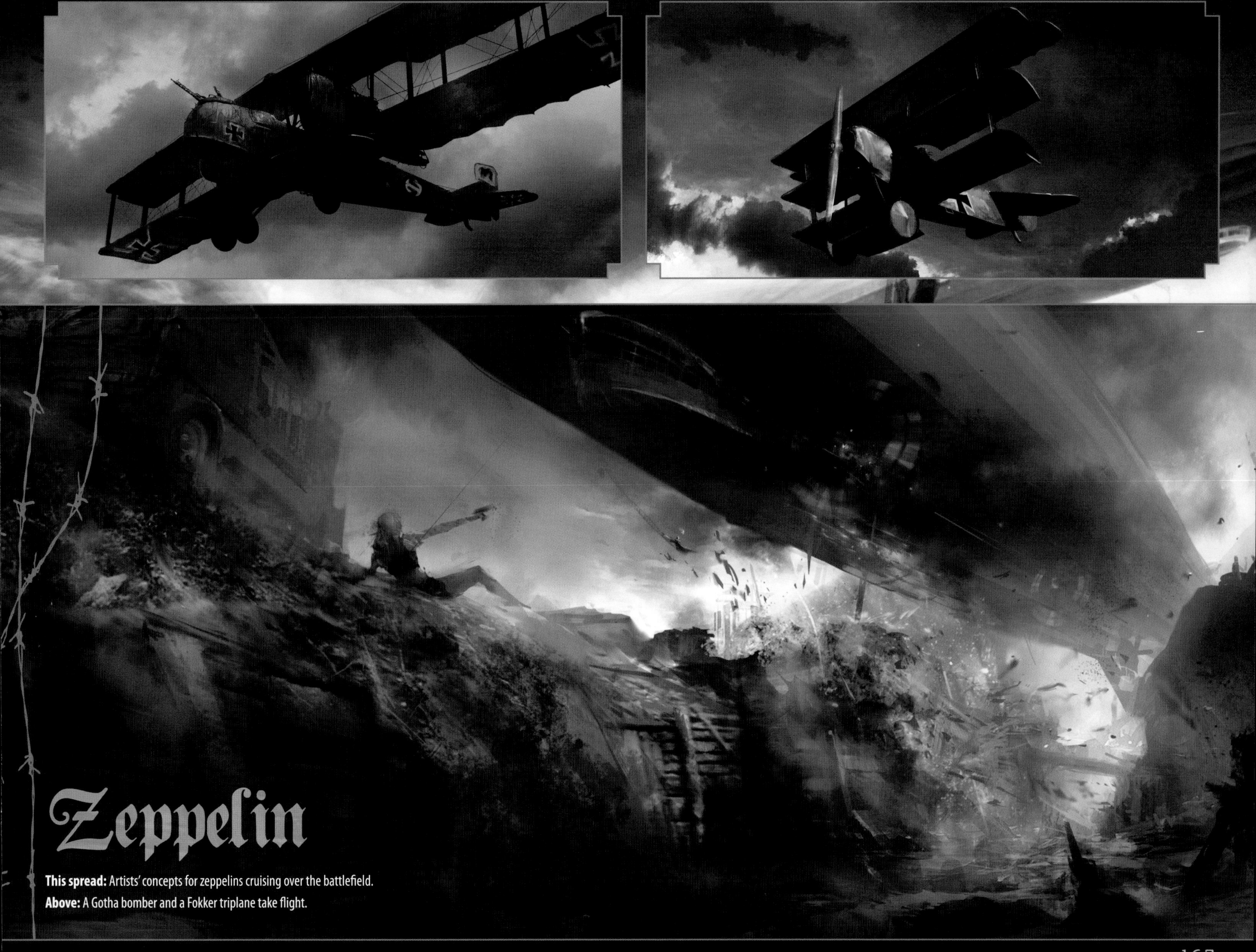

Zeppelin

This spread: Artists' concepts for zeppelins cruising over the battlefield.

Above: A Gotha bomber and a Fokker triplane take flight.

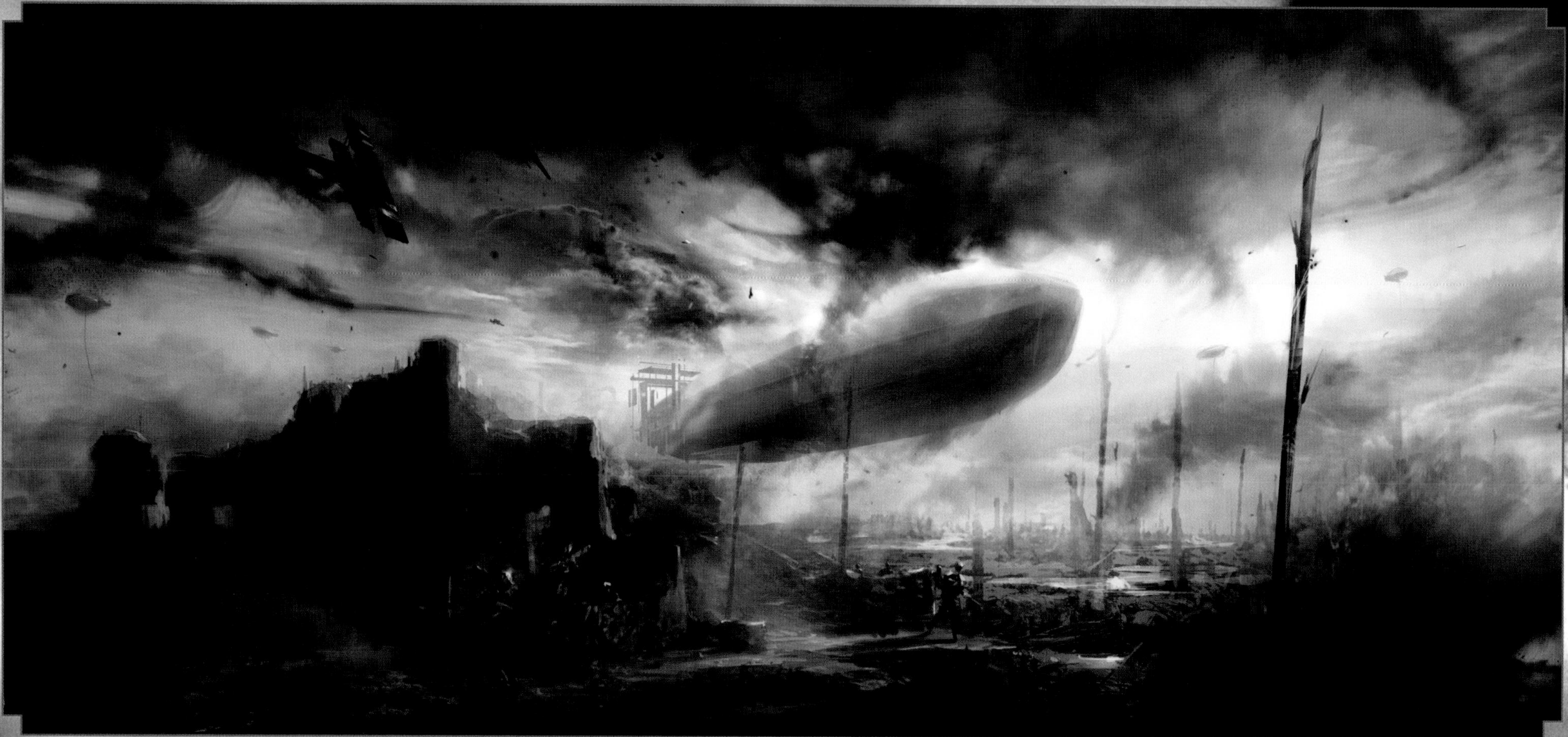

This spread: Babydoll singlehandedly brings down the Zeppelin.

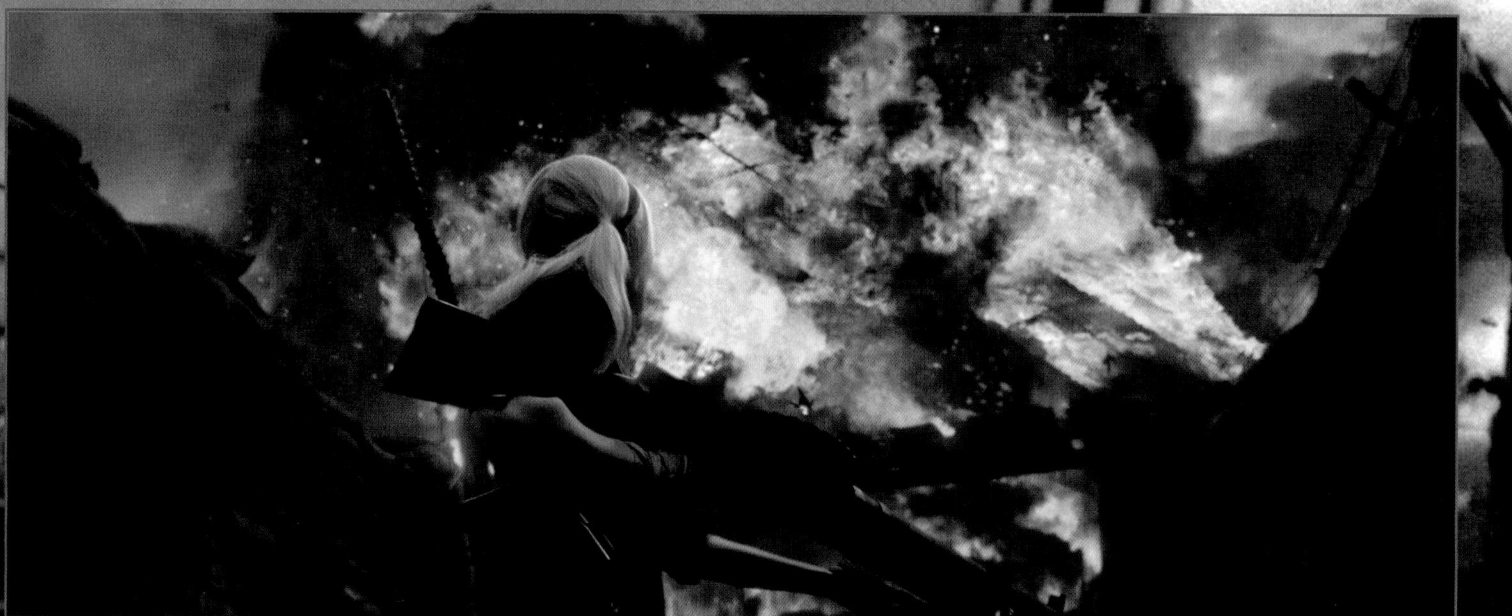

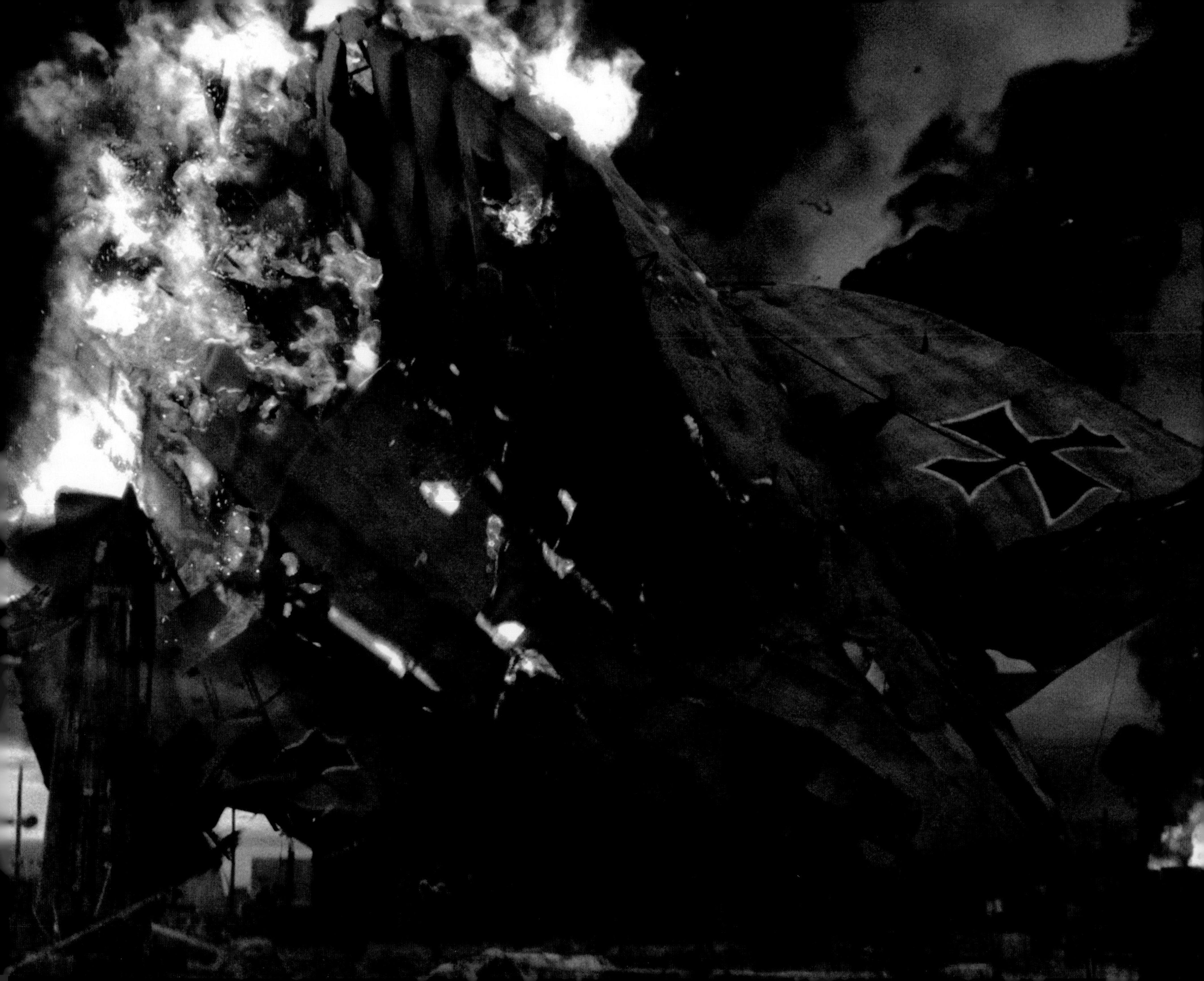

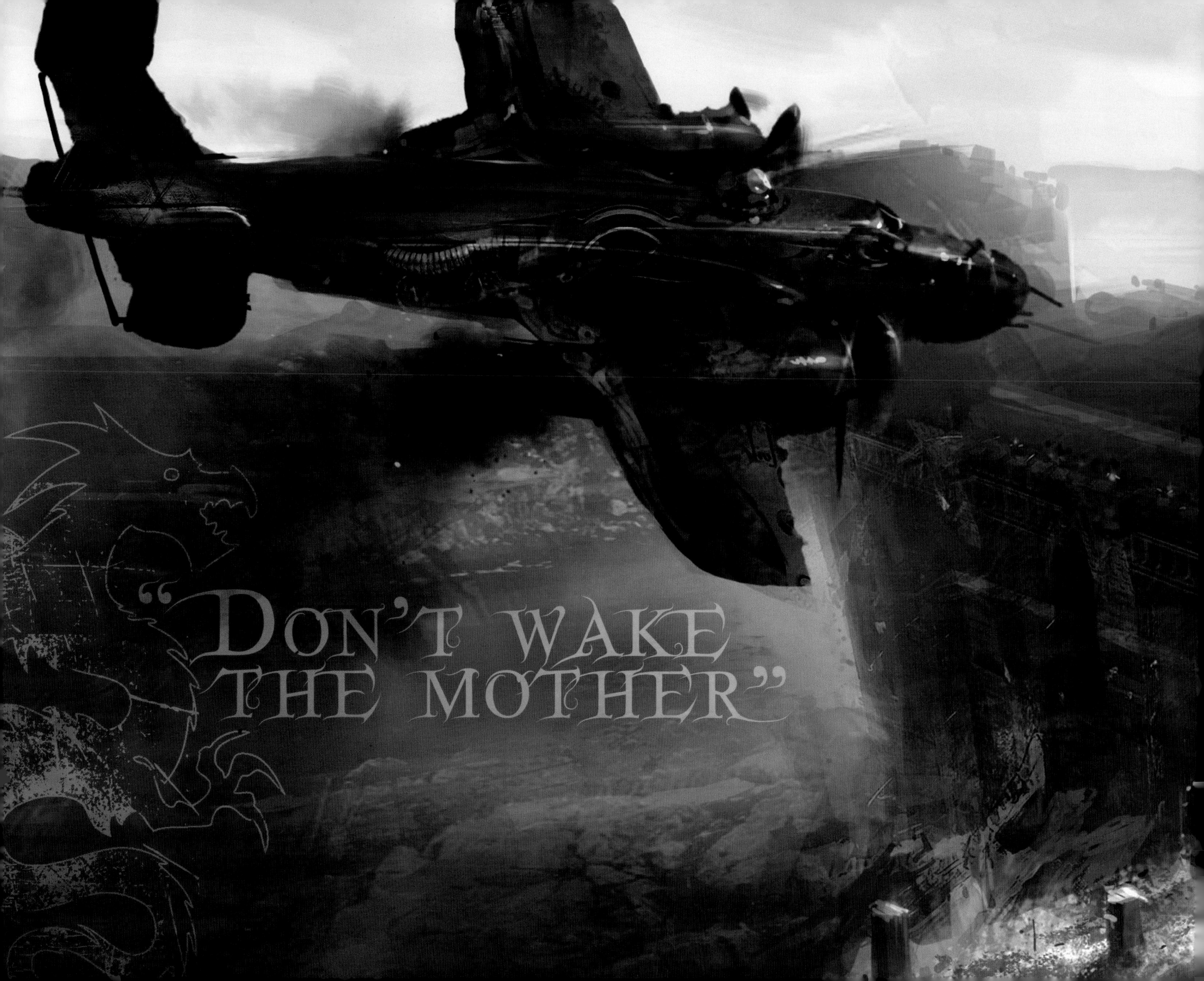
"Don't wake
the Mother"

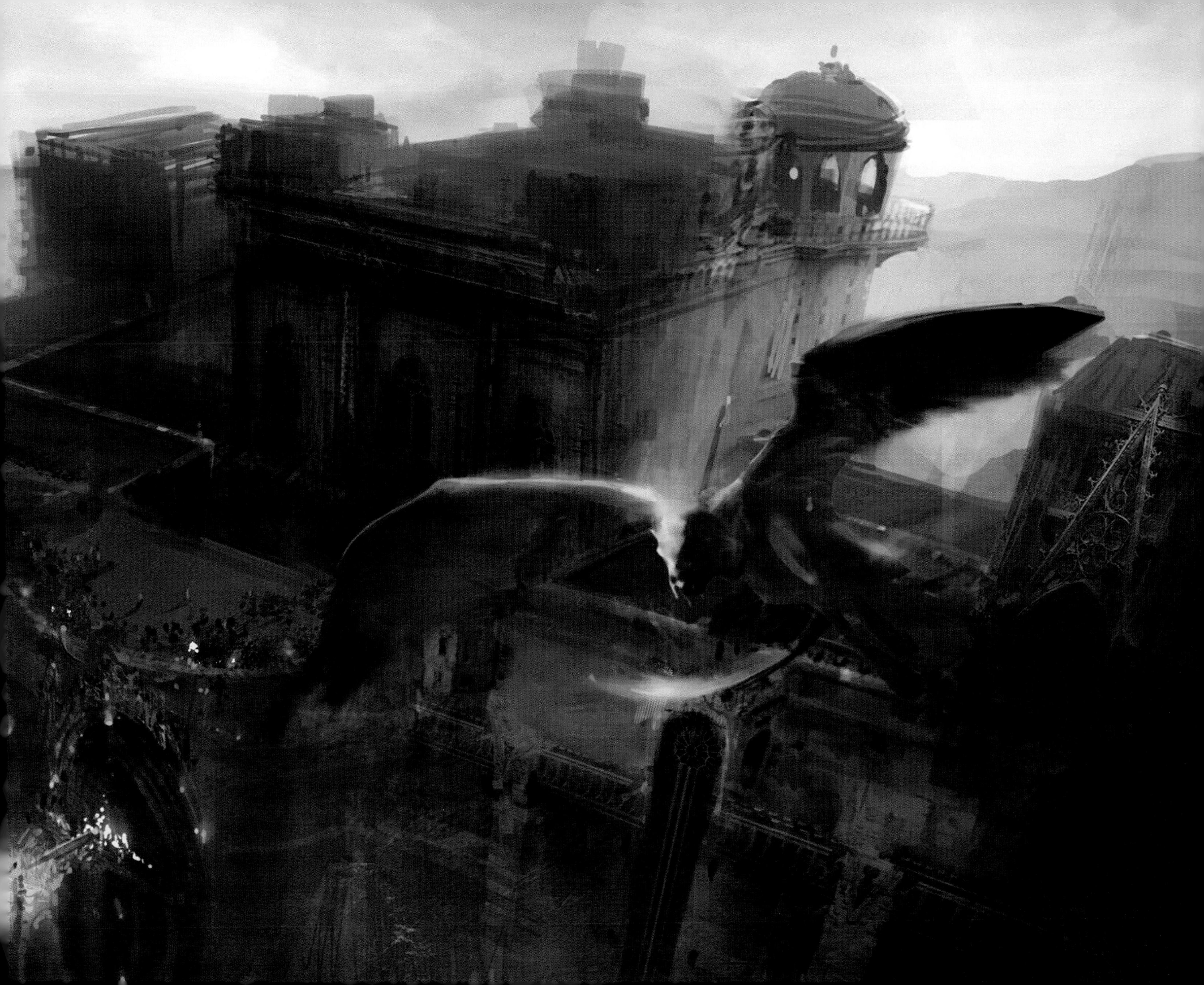

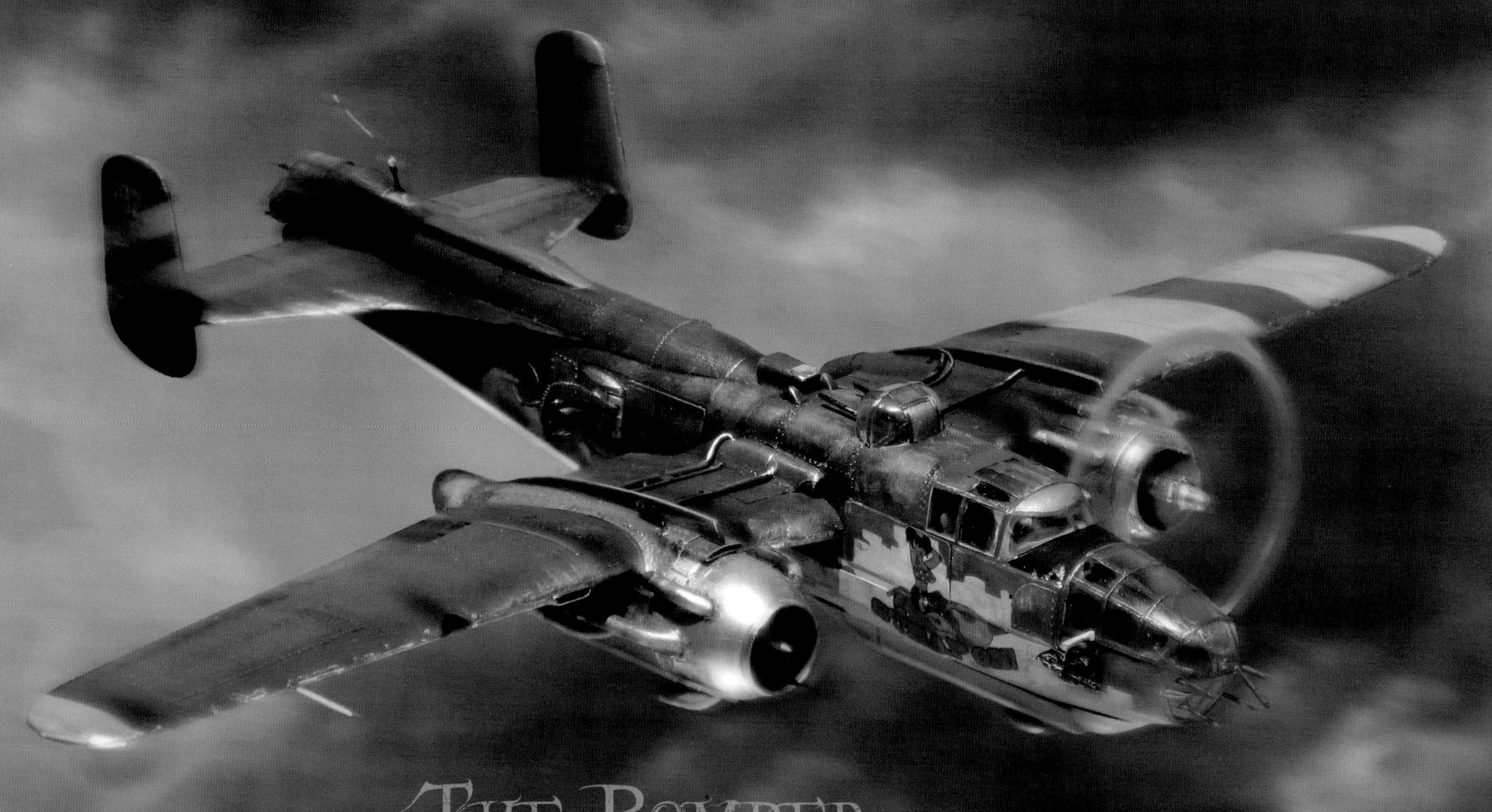

The Bomber

"Down inside its neck are two crystals that when stuck together produce the most magnificent fire you'll ever see," says the Wise Man, concluding their mission briefing in the hold of a heavily modified B-24 Liberator. He's set them the task of stealing fire from a dragon – but not to worry, it's only a baby one. In a nest hidden beneath a forbidding castle. Guarded by hordes of Dark Orcs. Being besieged by a legion of Black Knights.

The last words of advice the Wise Man gives to the girls before Babydoll, Sweet Pea, and Rocket parachute into the midst of the foe-infested courtyard is, "Don't wake the mother." Now, what kind of adventure would it be if they didn't?

It's interesting to note that halfway through this mission is the first time Babydoll faces off against an enemy that is something besides a male humanoid. Her journey has turned into something beyond simply girls fighting guys for their liberation. This is a mother that has every right to be enraged given its heart-rending loss. Did it spawn out of Babydoll's feelings of guilt over what happened to her sister? Or is it a manifestation of her anger at her own mother for leaving them to the predations of their stepfather? Whatever its origins, right now that dragon is another obstacle that must be crushed and put behind her.

By now the observant among you might have noticed that each combat fantasy has featured a building – the pagoda, the cathedral, the castle – all of which are reminiscent of Lennox House in one way or another.

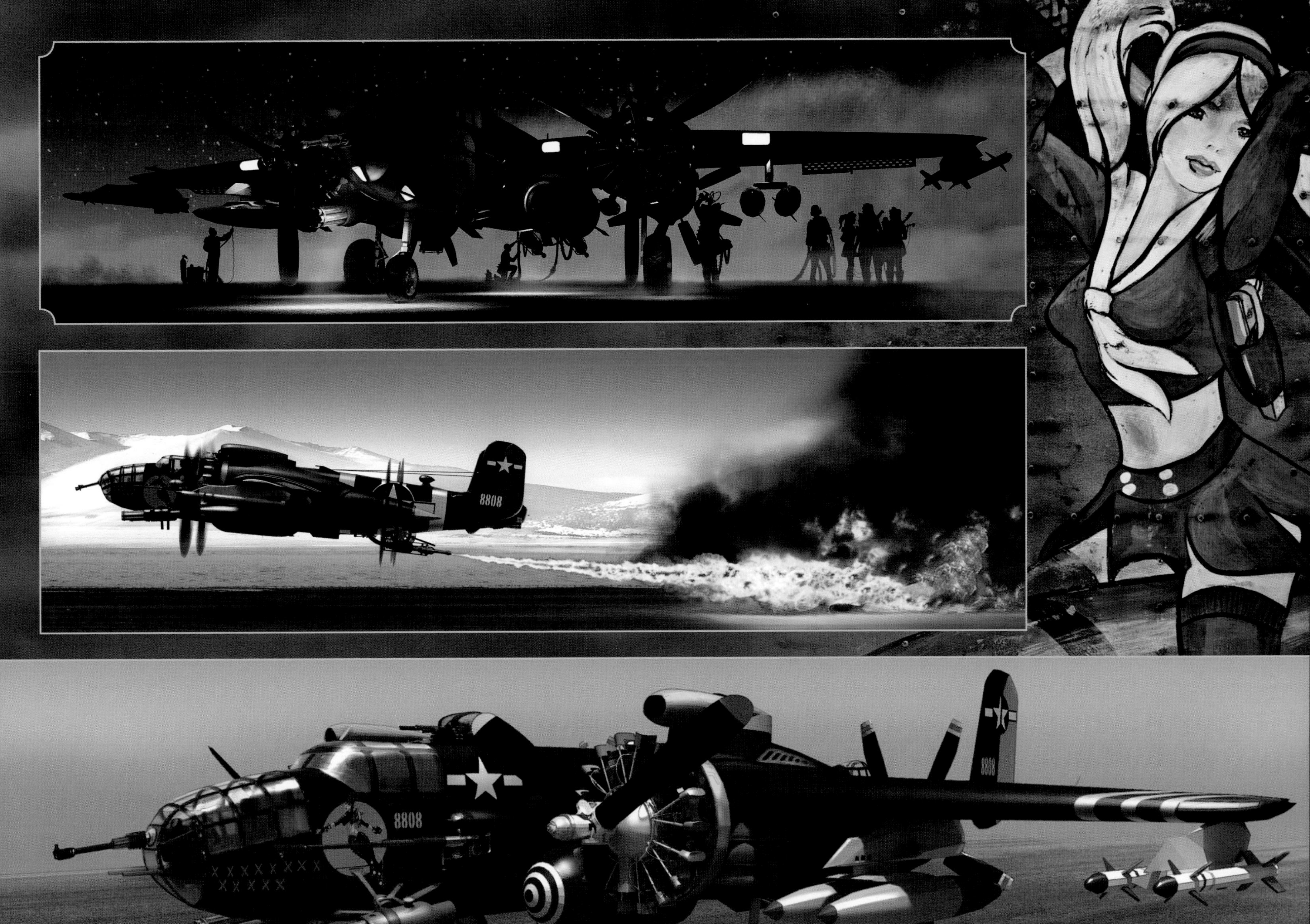
8808

Previous spreads: Concept art for the heavily modified B-24 Liberator that transports the strike team to the castle.
Below: Some views of the bomber.
Opposite: The girls prep for the drop.
Opposite bottom right: Tail-gunner Blondie nearly becomes an amuse-bouche.

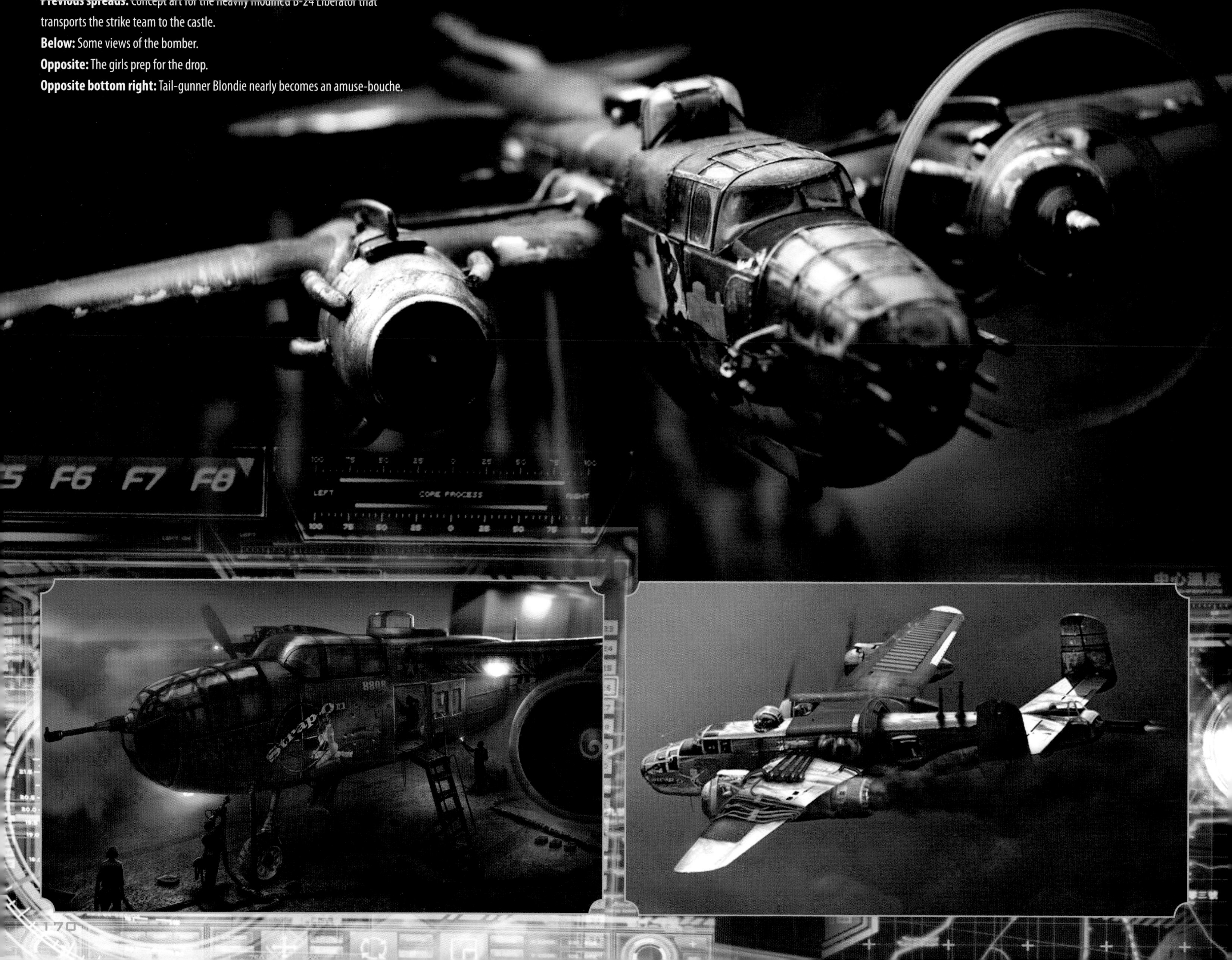

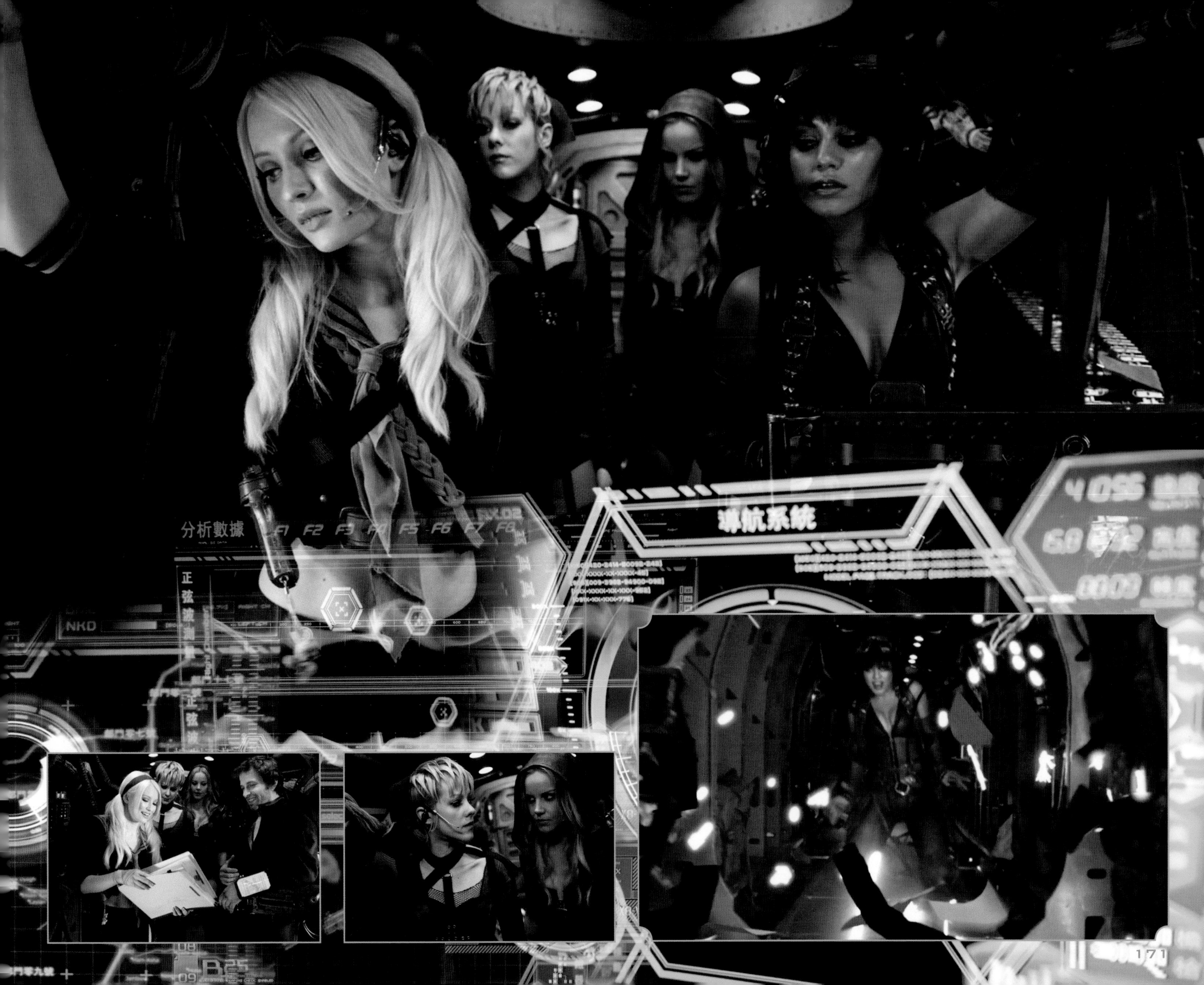
分析數據
F1 F2 F3 F4 F5 F6 F7 F8
導航系統
NKD

THE CASTLE

This spread: Detailed architectural renderings of the castle and its environs.

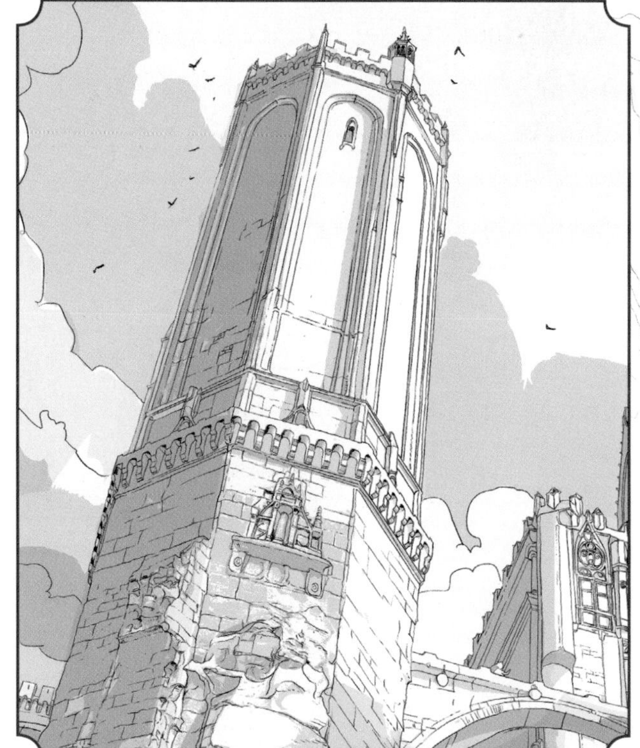

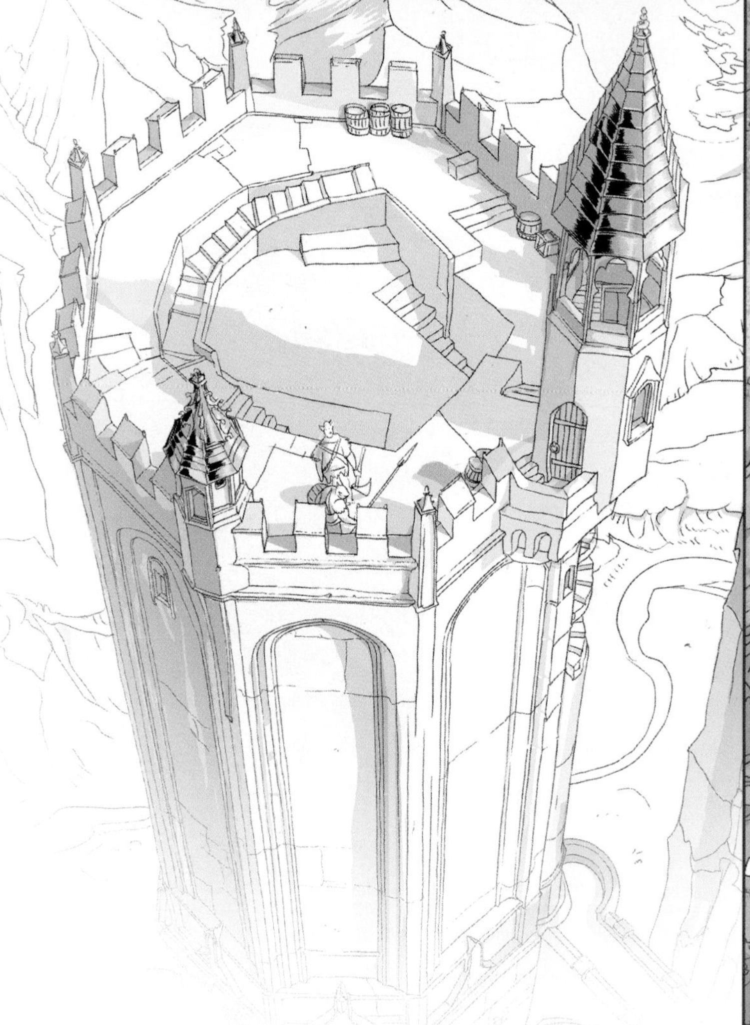

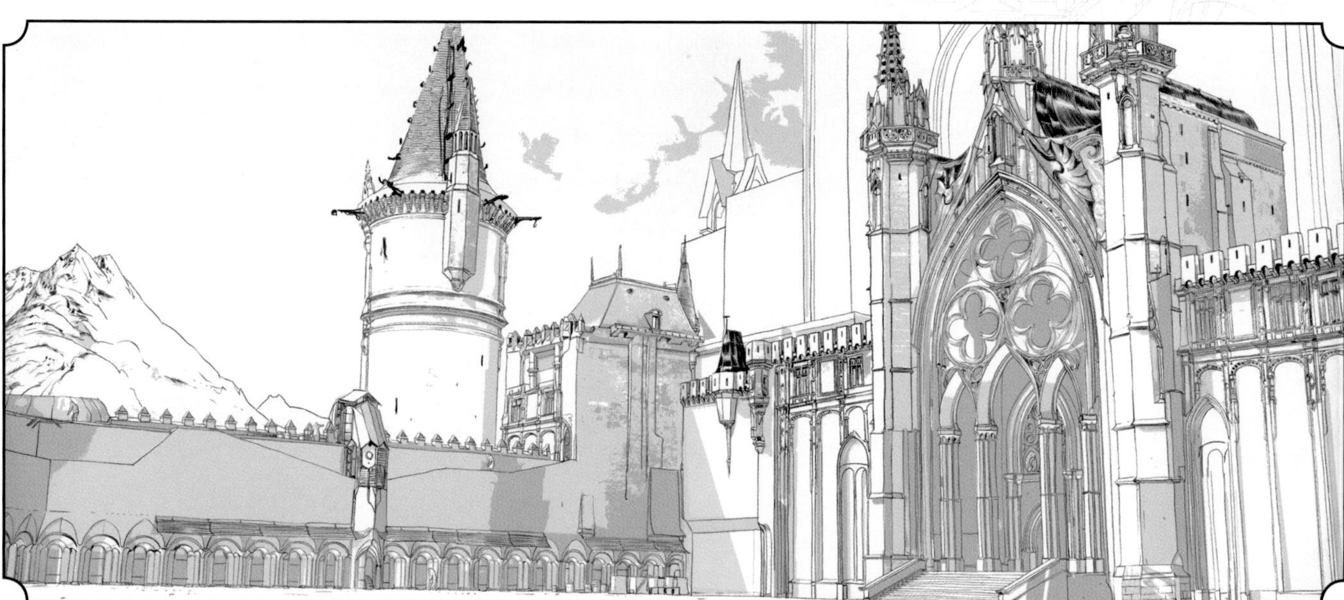

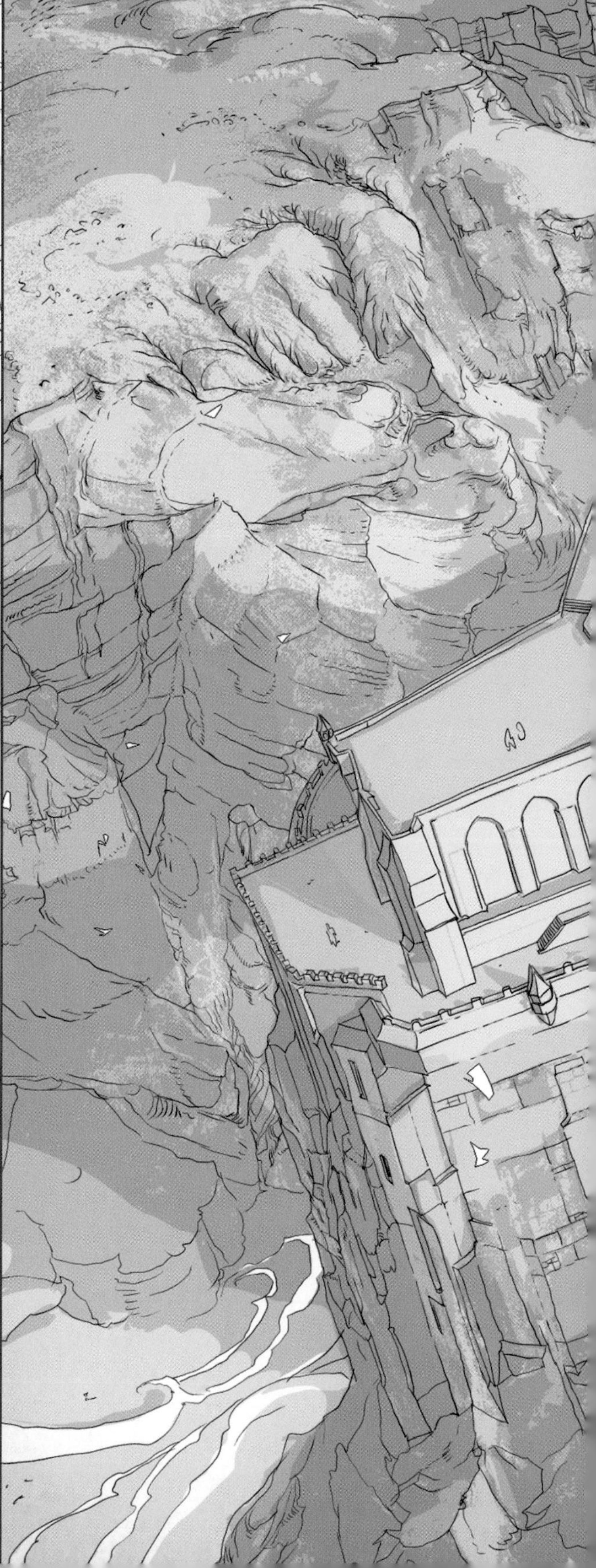

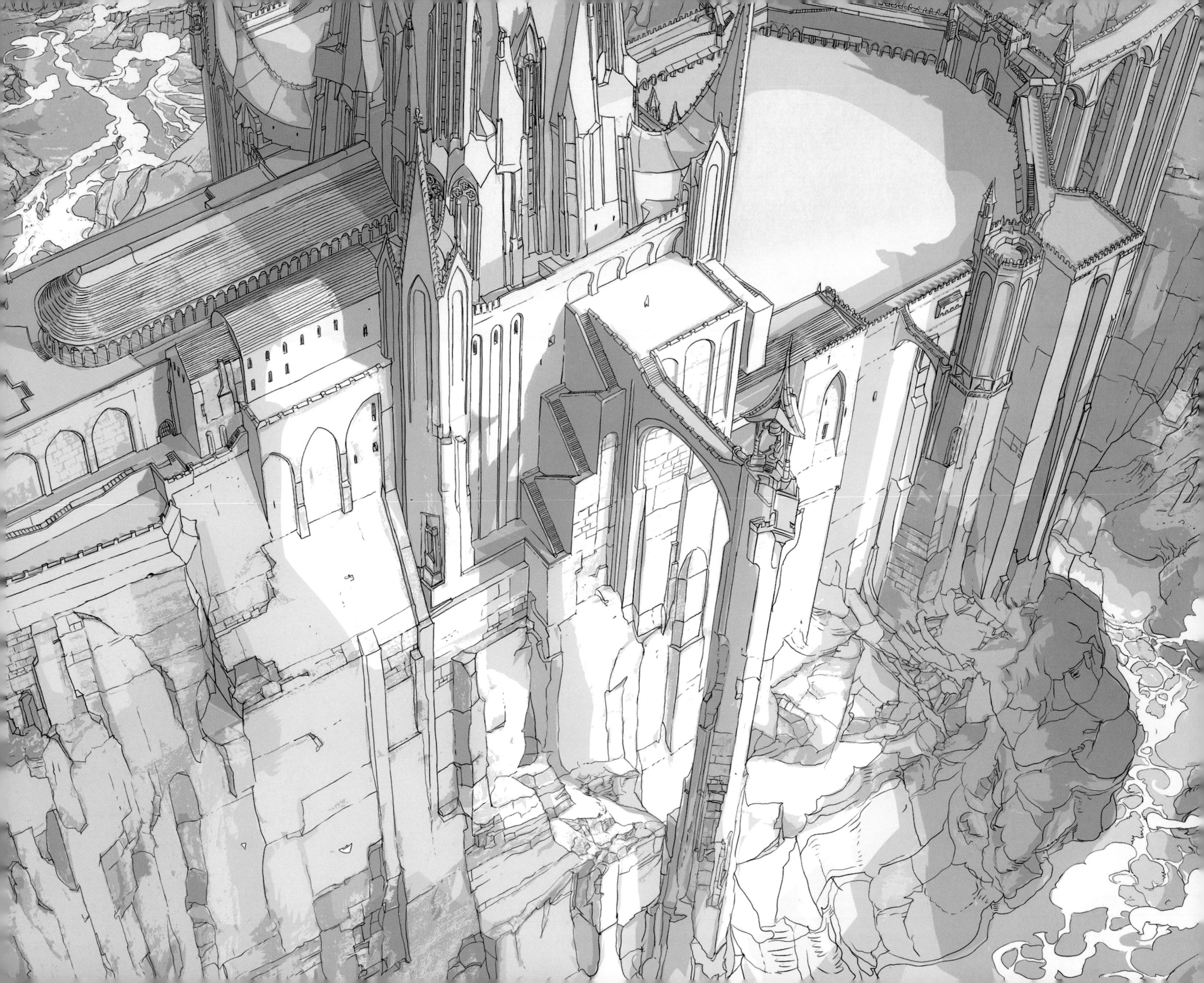

Below: Details of the Orc defensive works and siege engines.

Opposite bottom: Castle construction begins as a basic 3-D model.

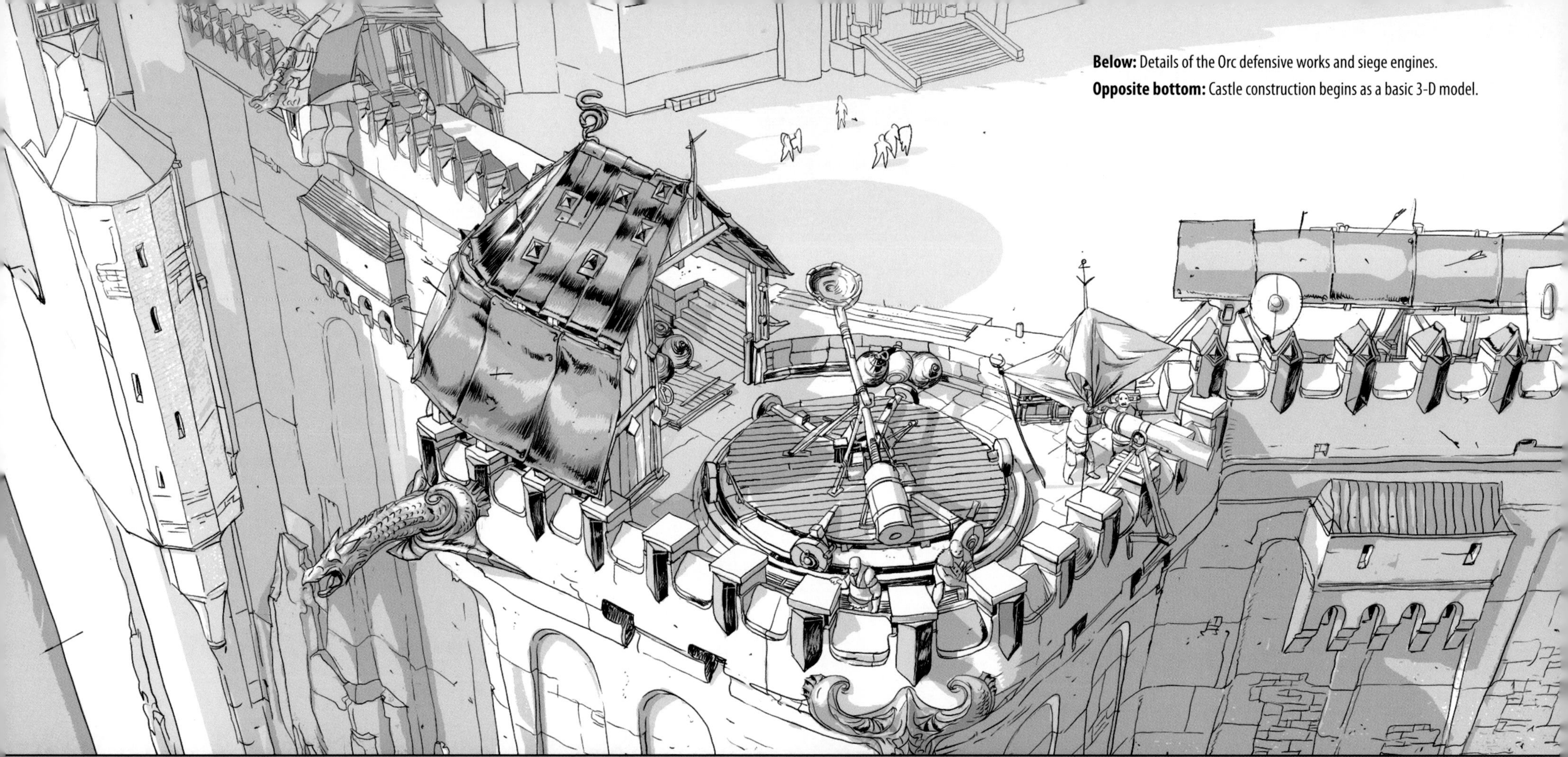

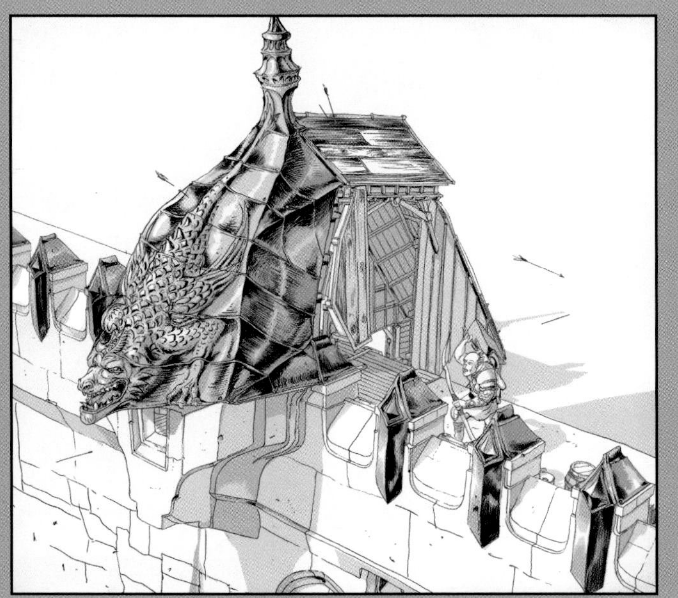

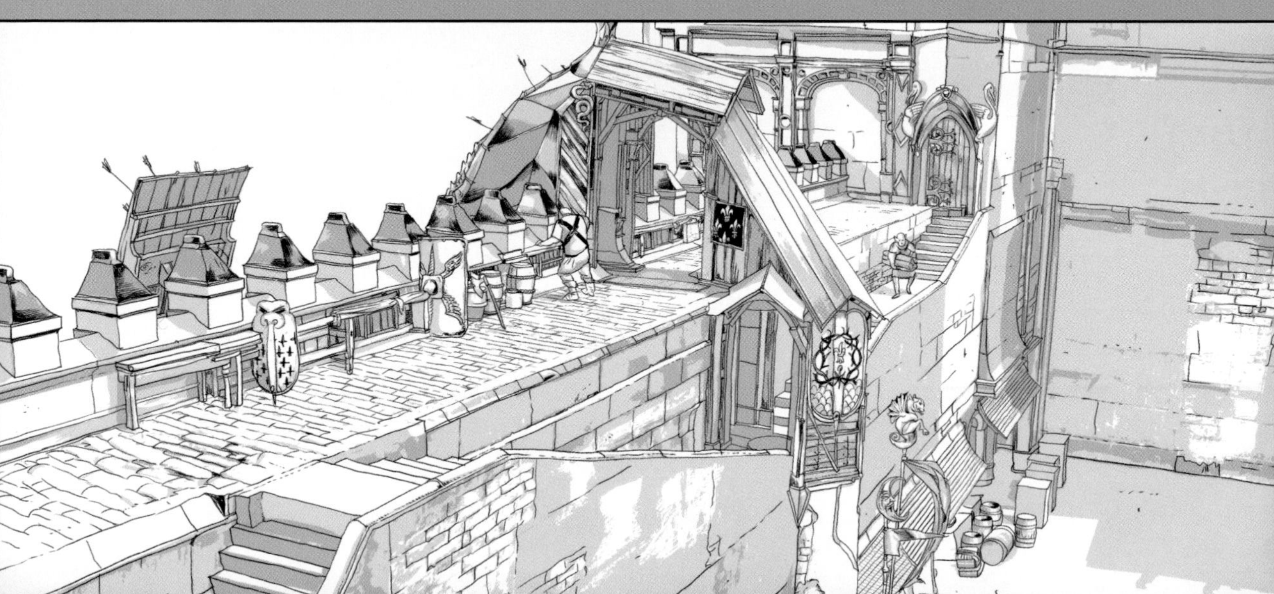

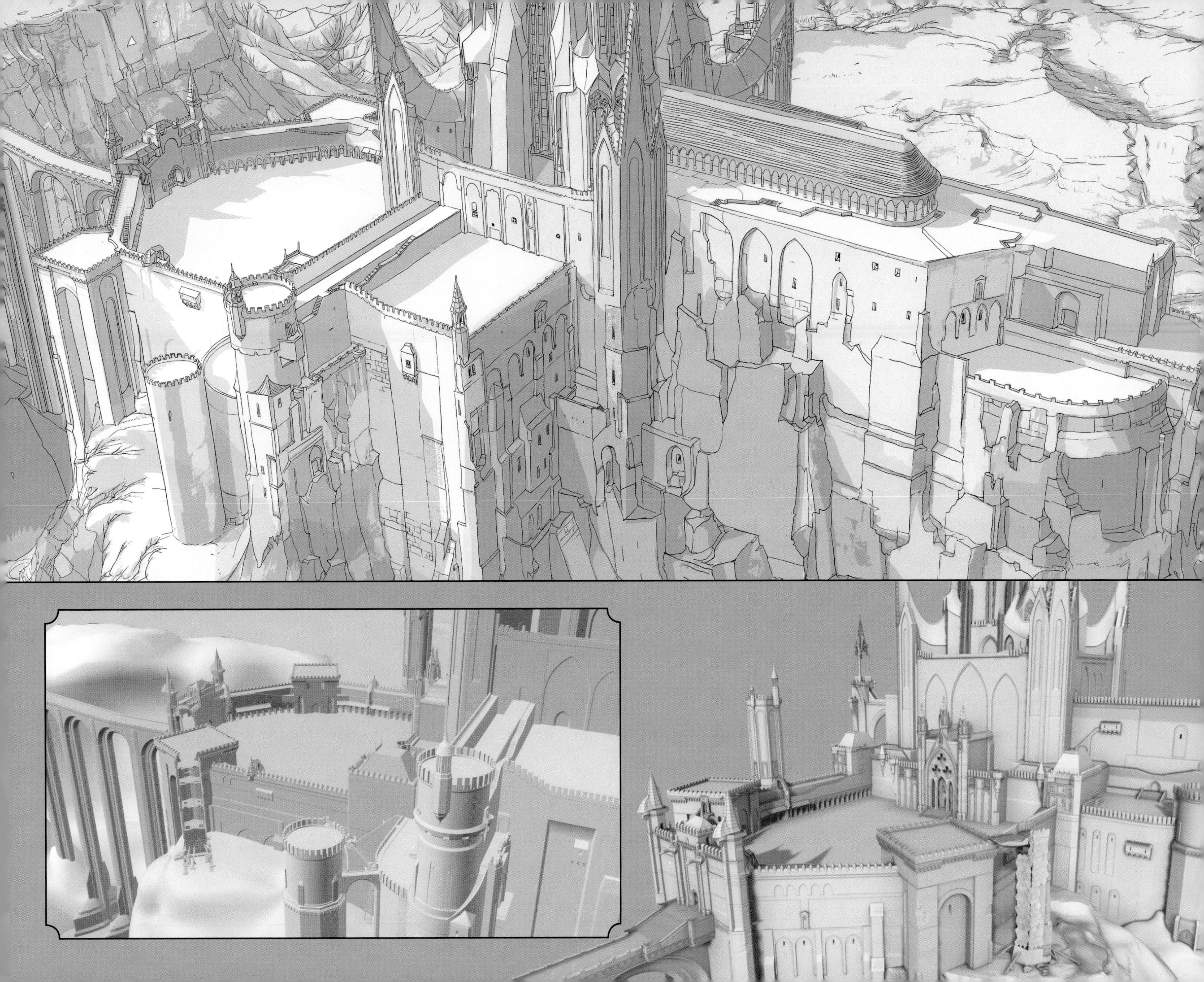

This spread: Artists fill in Gothic elements to the castle and imagine it under siege.

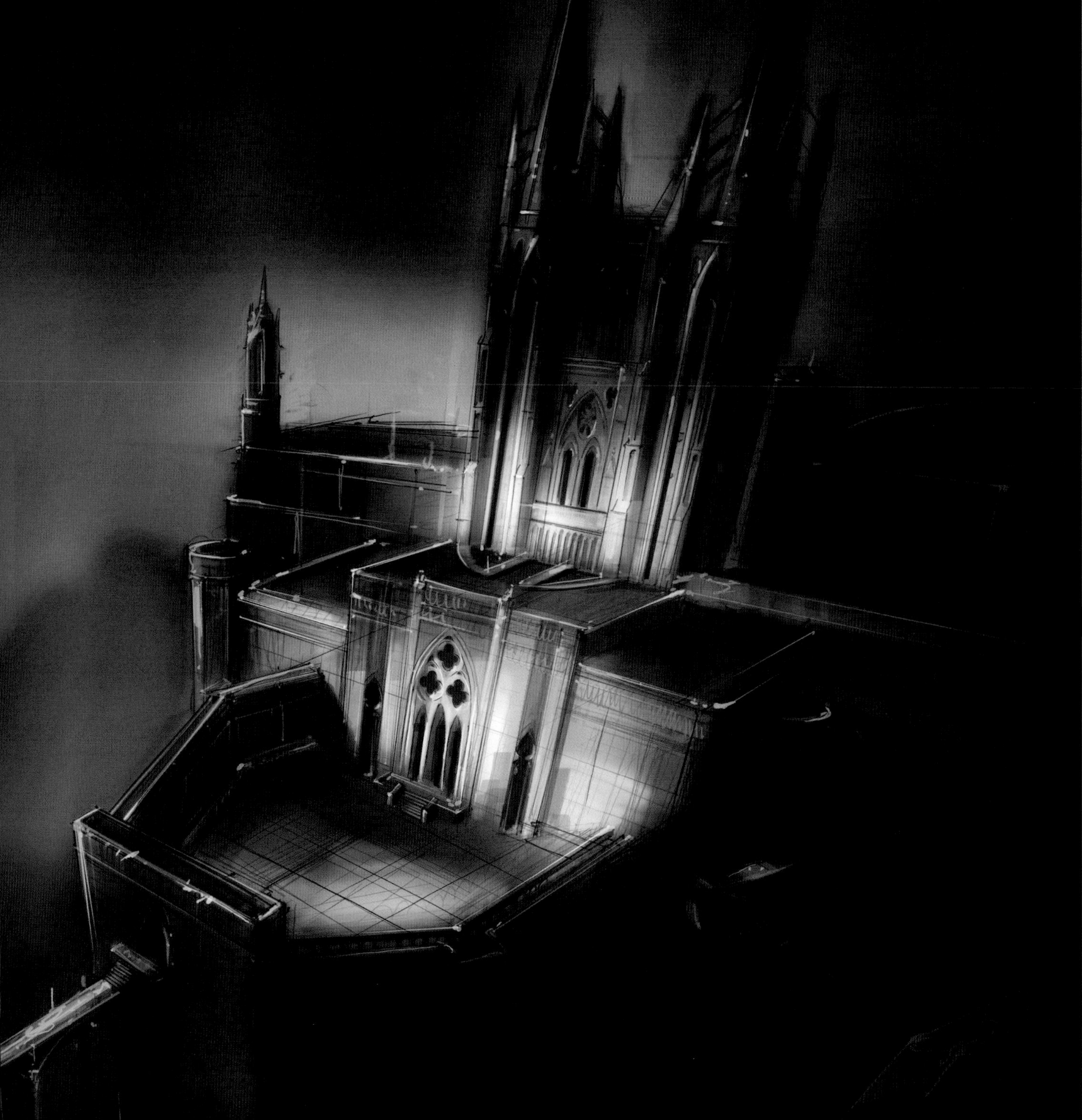

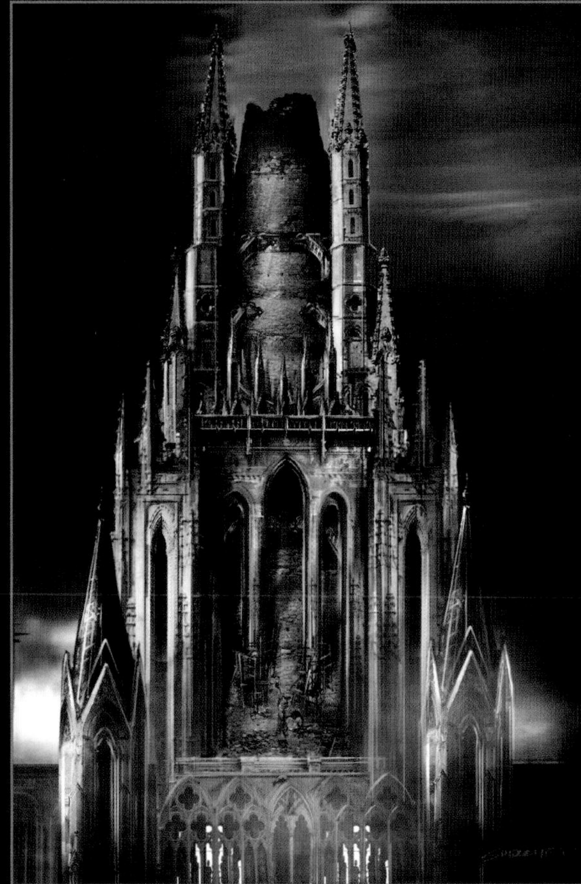

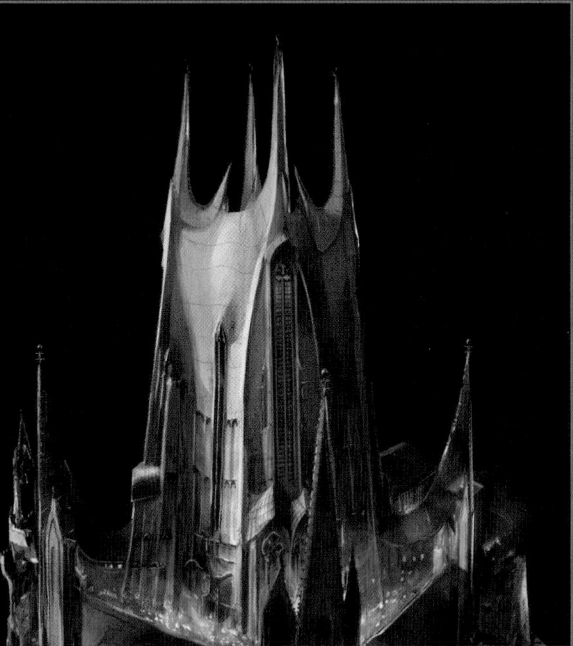

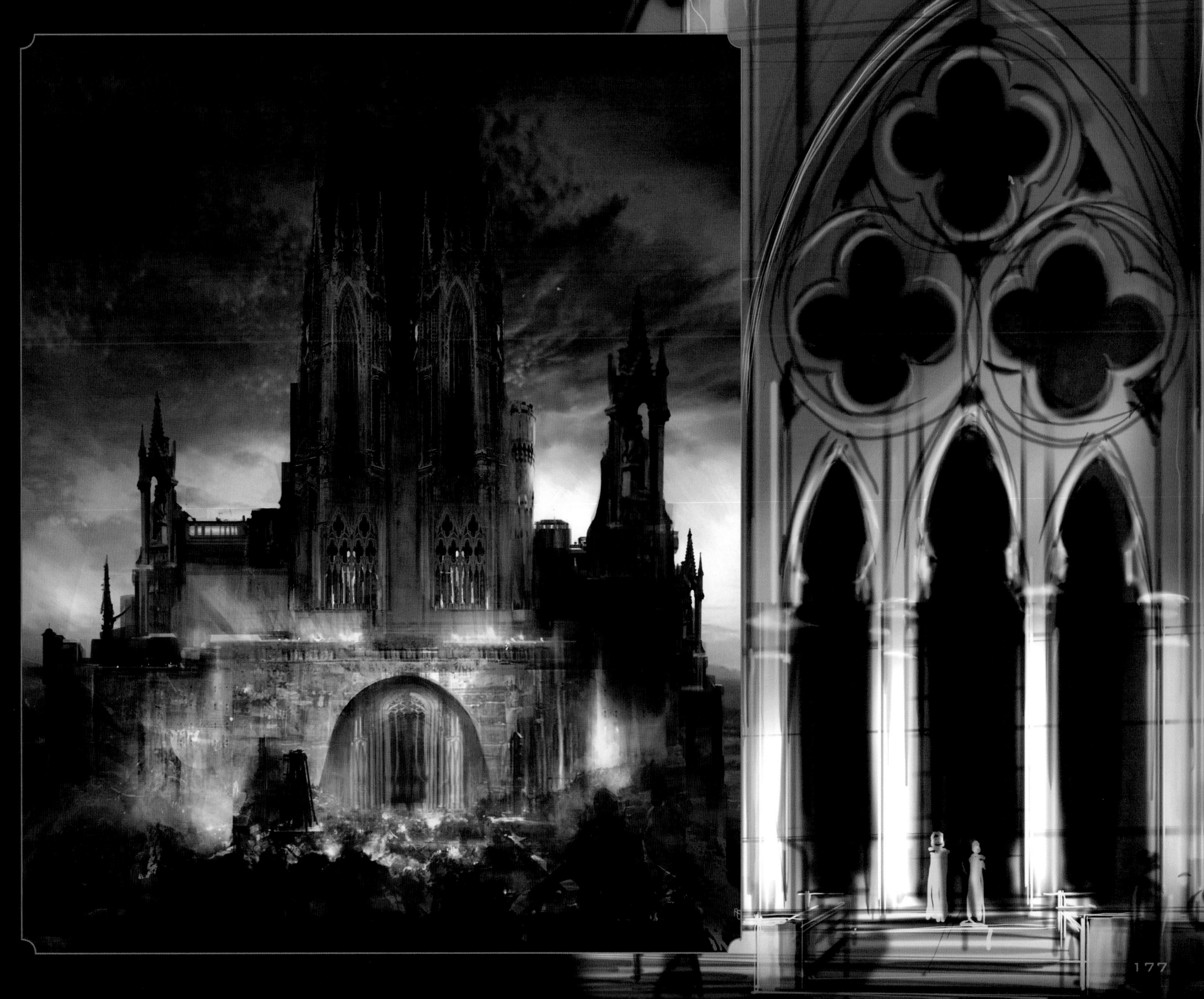

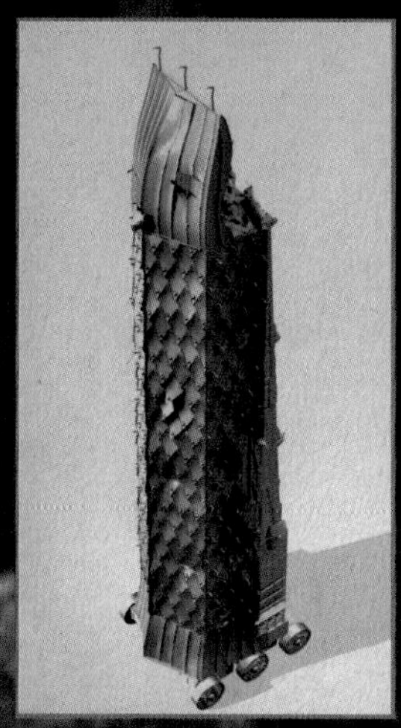
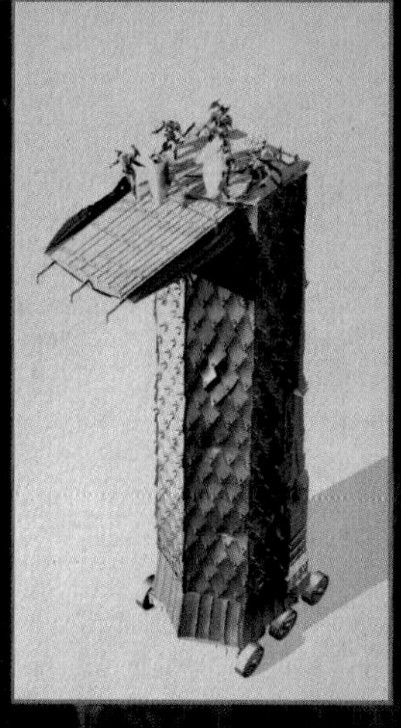
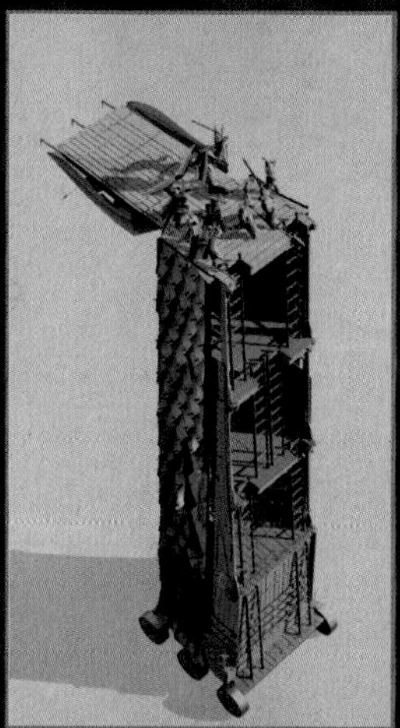
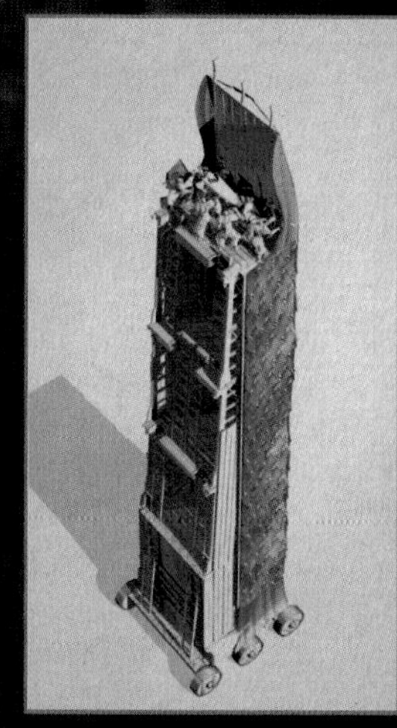
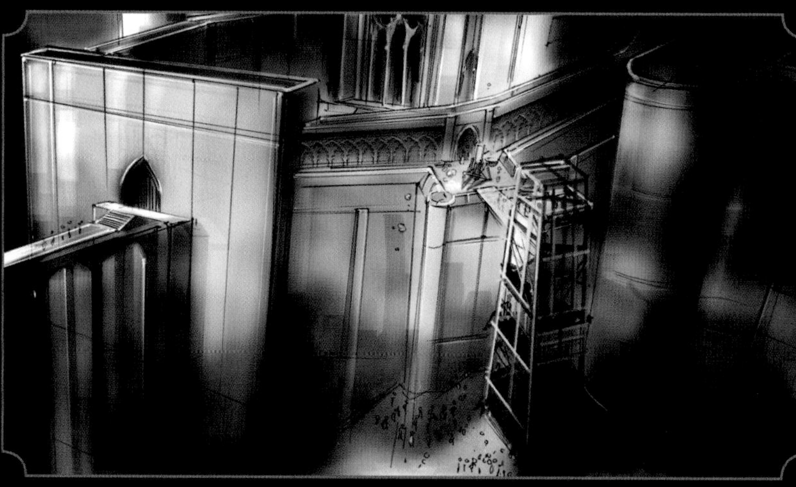

Above: 3-D model of the Knights' siege tower. **Below:** Babydoll lands in the courtyard, ready for action. **Opposite:** Concept for the spiral staircase.

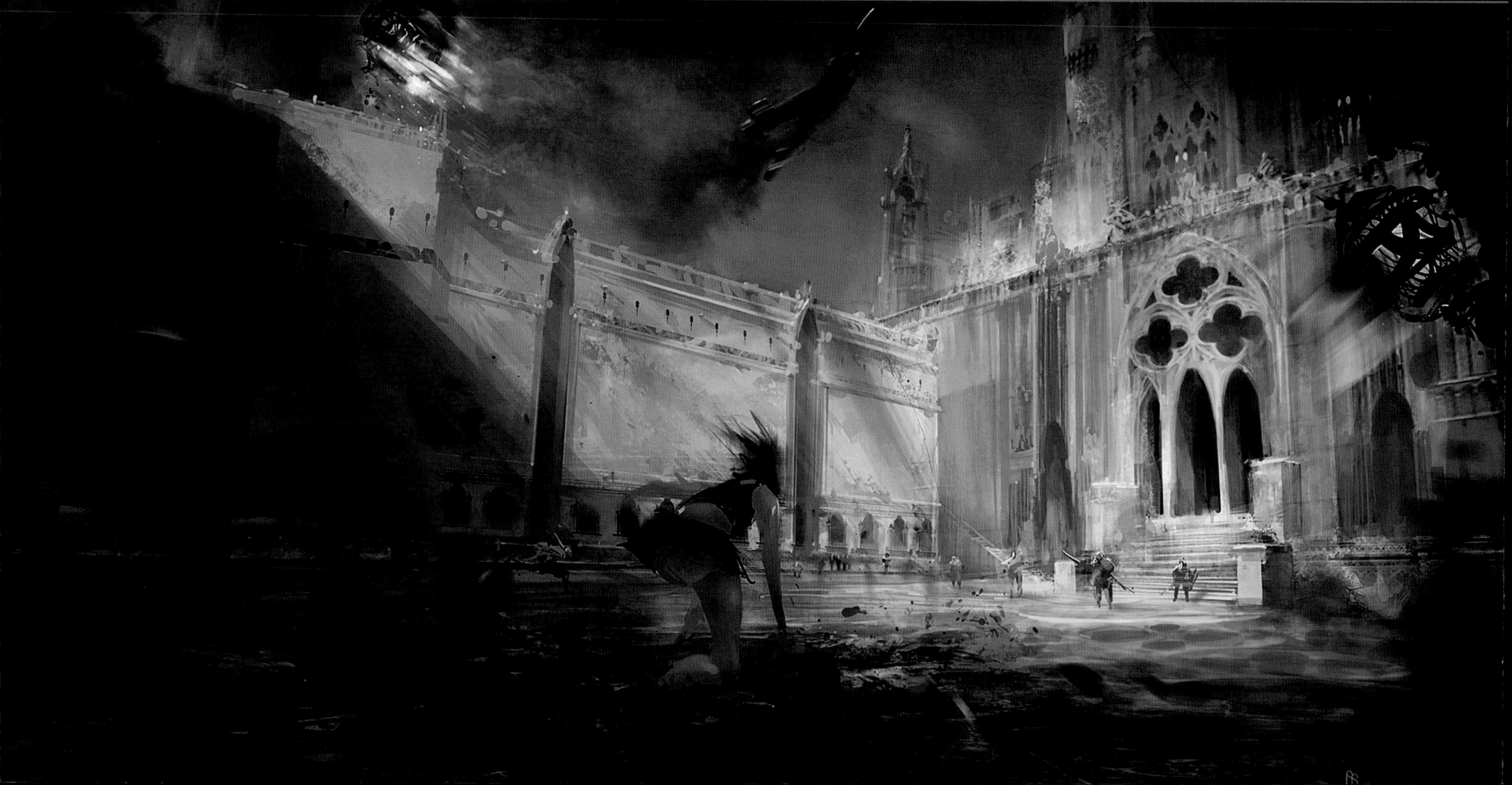

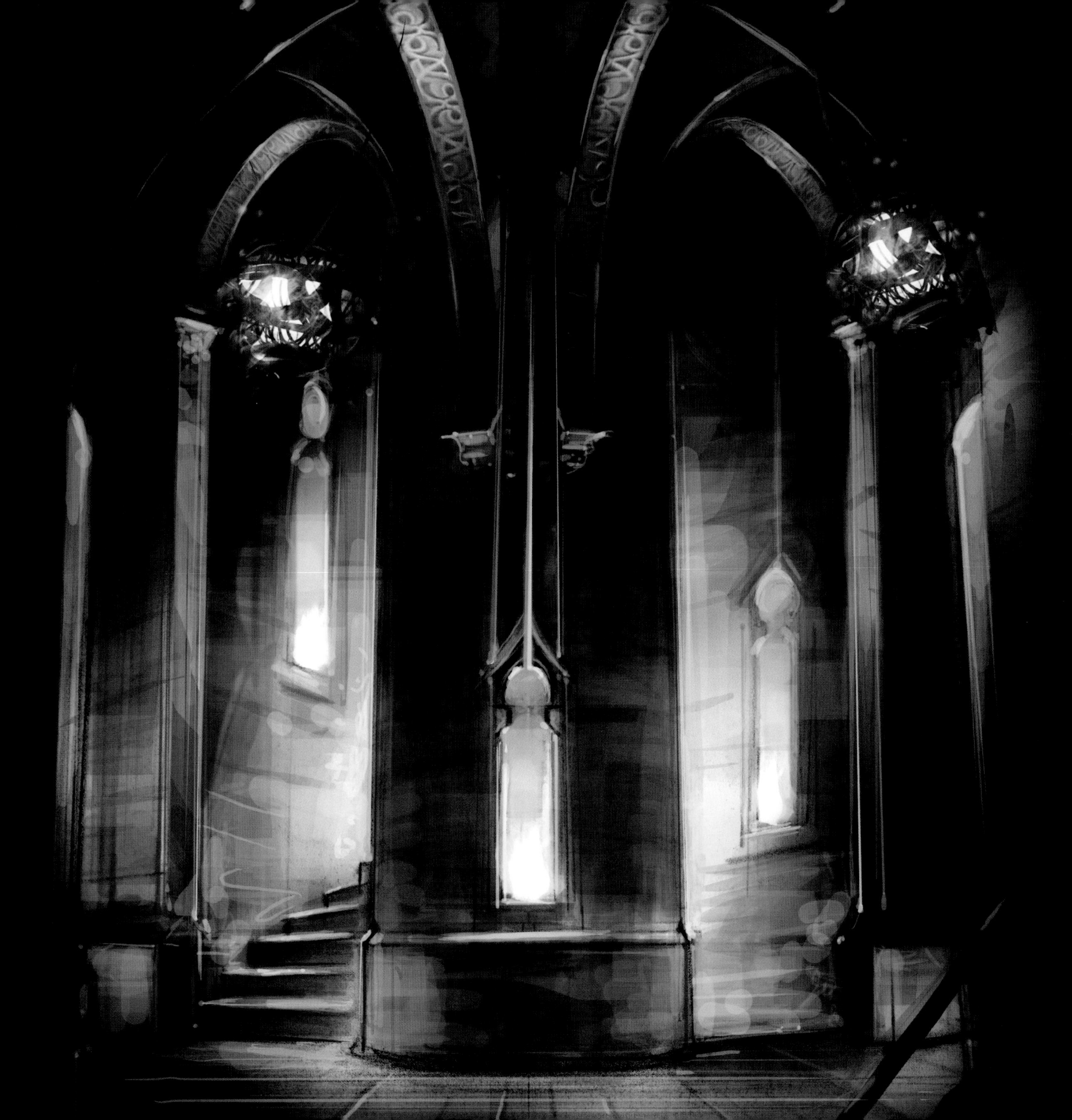

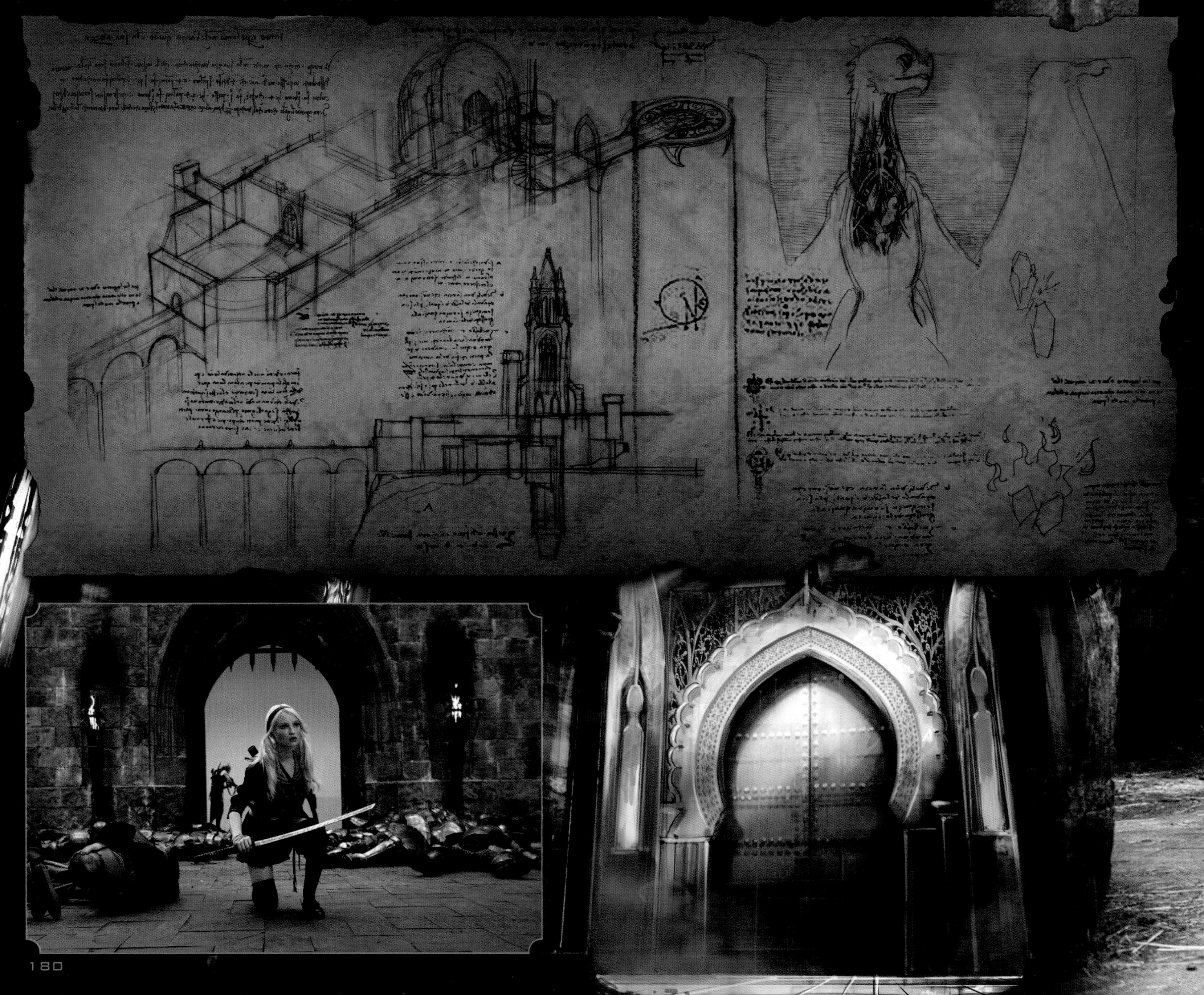

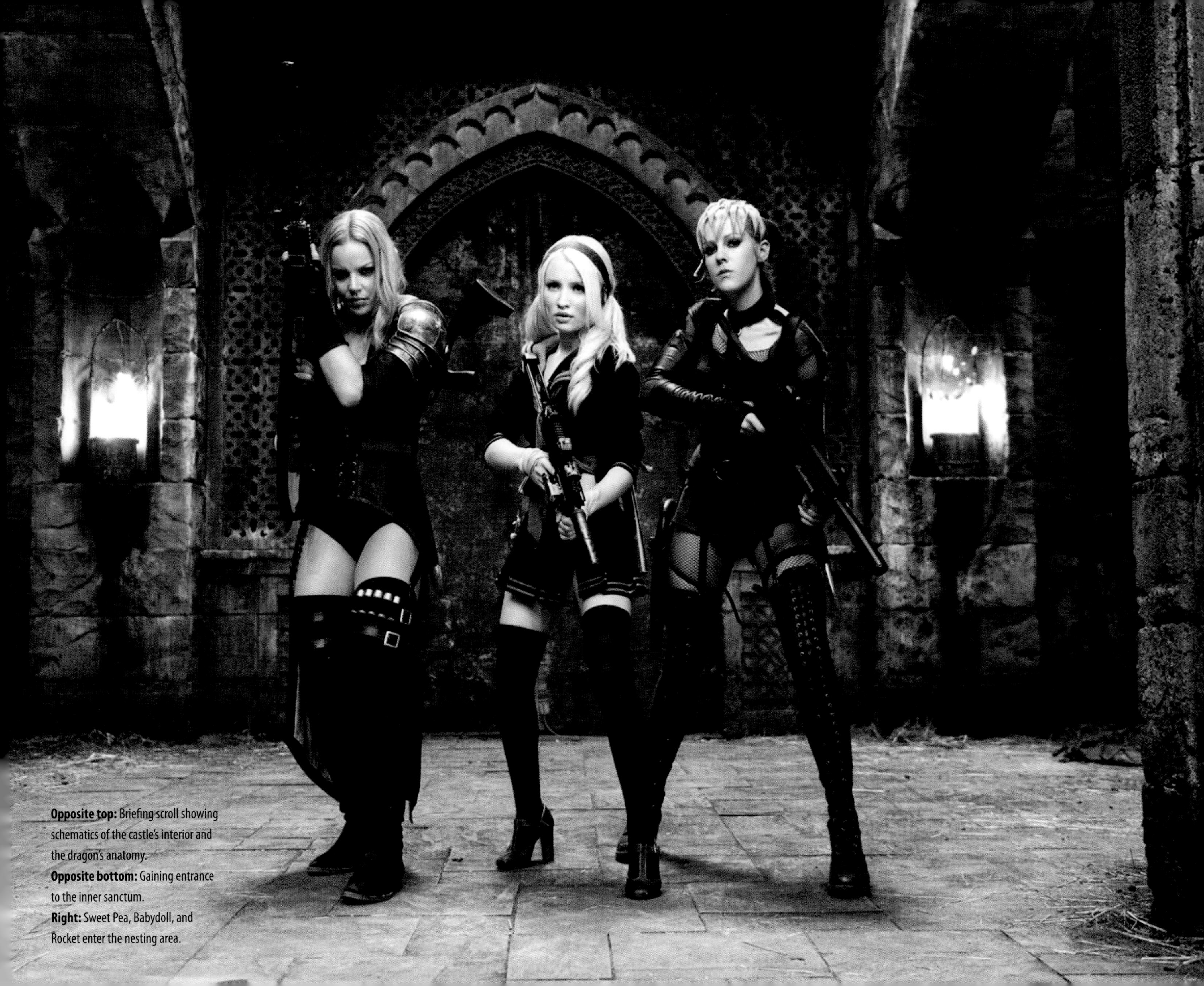

Opposite top: Briefing scroll showing schematics of the castle's interior and the dragon's anatomy.
Opposite bottom: Gaining entrance to the inner sanctum.
Right: Sweet Pea, Babydoll, and Rocket enter the nesting area.

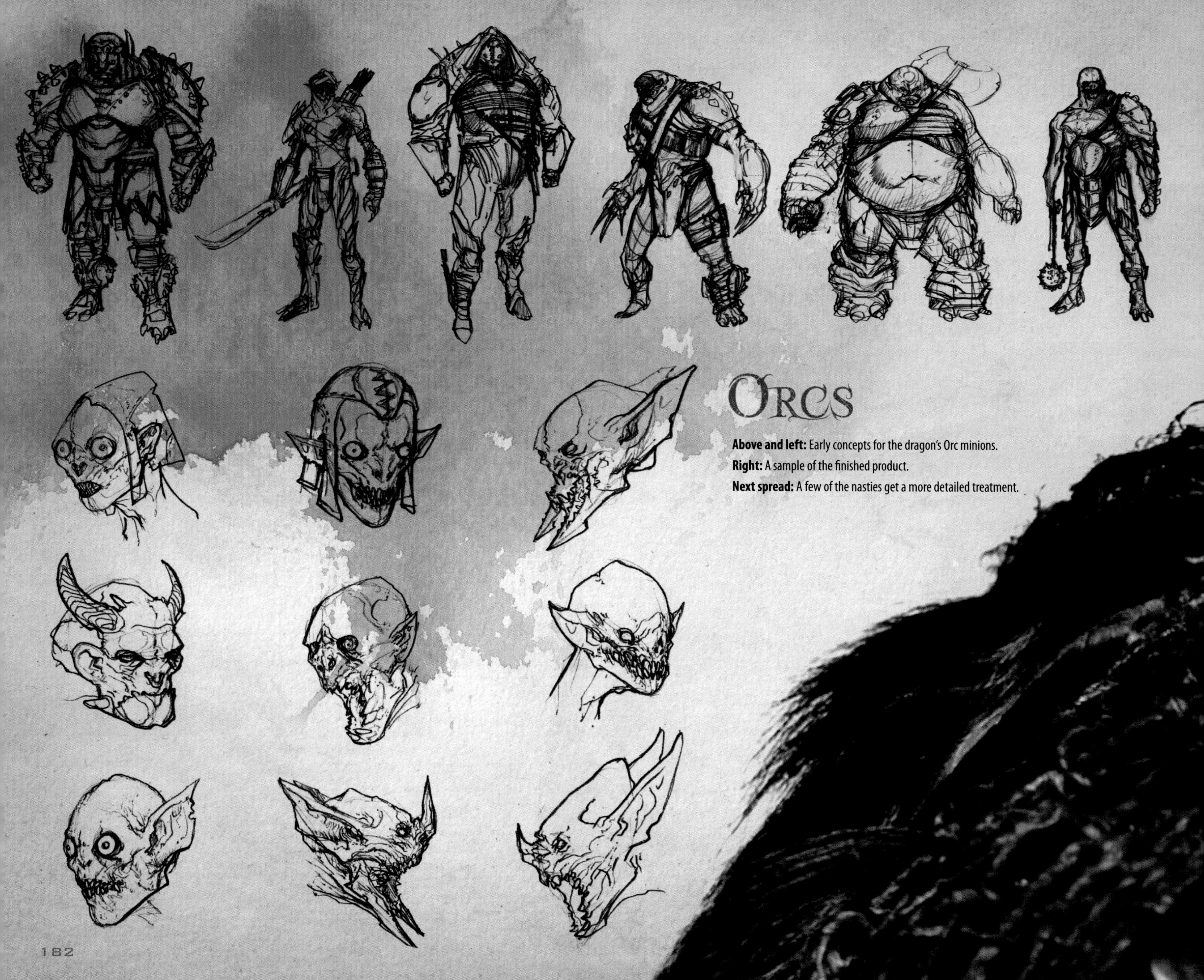

Orcs

Above and left: Early concepts for the dragon's Orc minions.

Right: A sample of the finished product.

Next spread: A few of the nasties get a more detailed treatment.

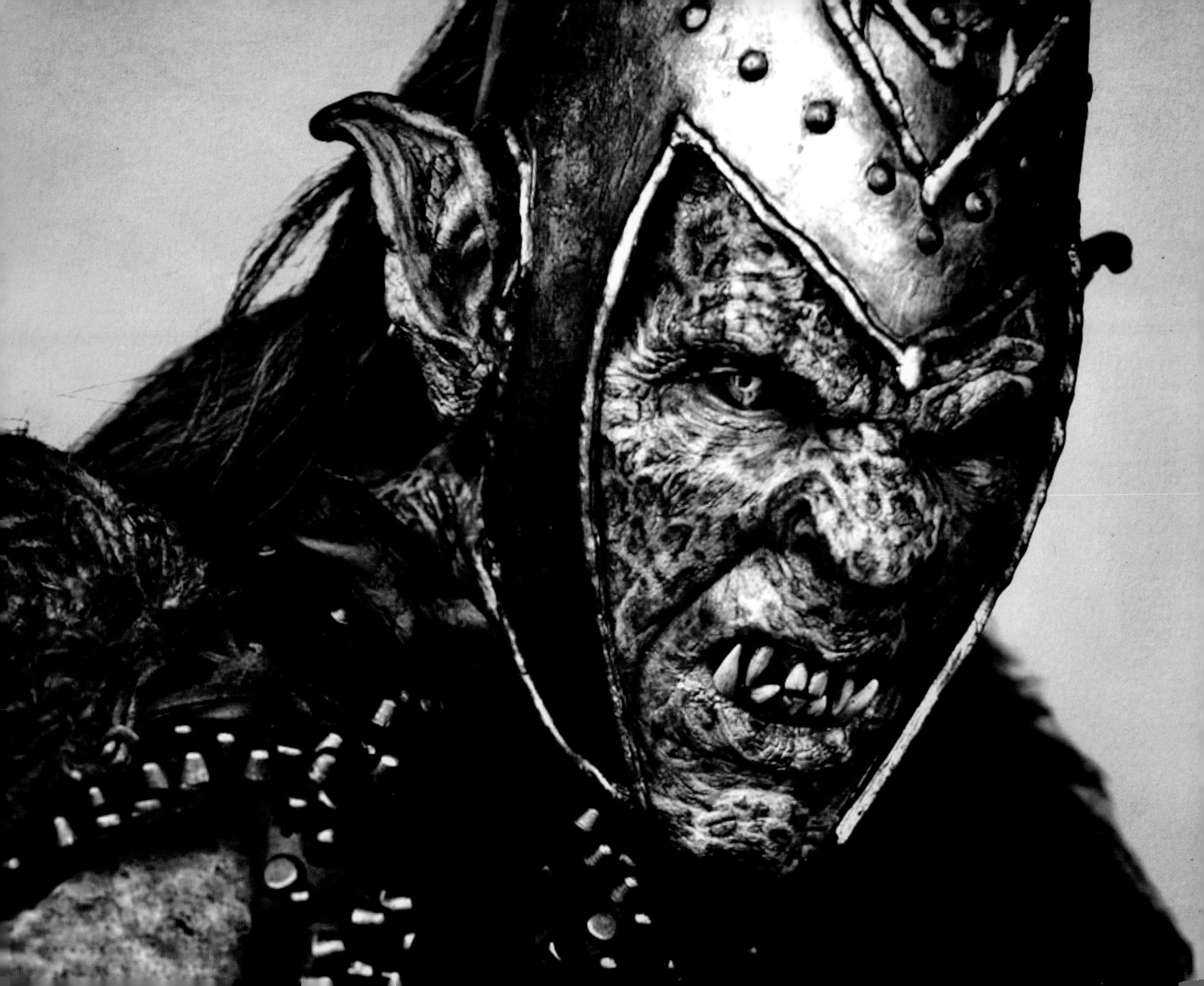

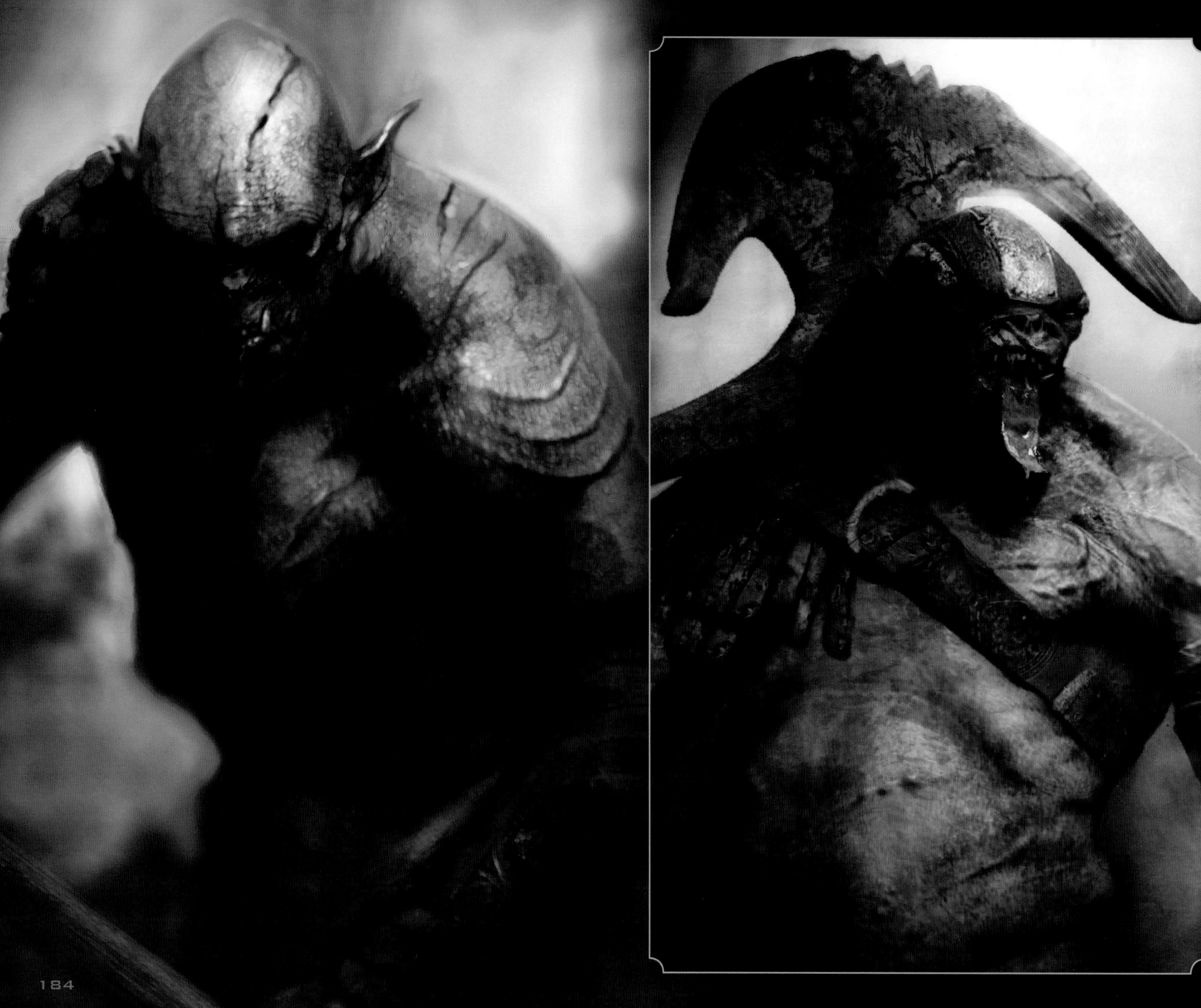

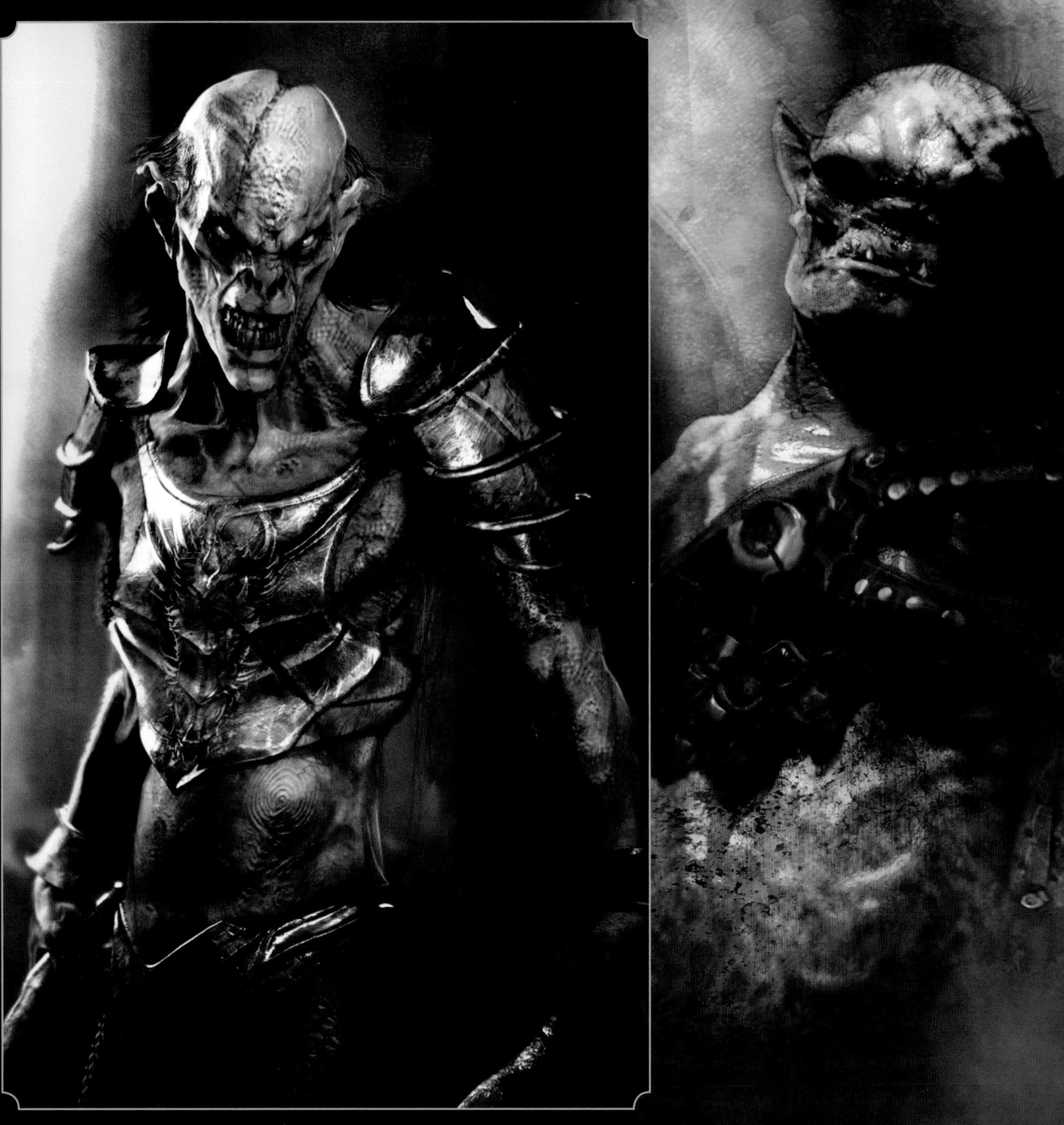

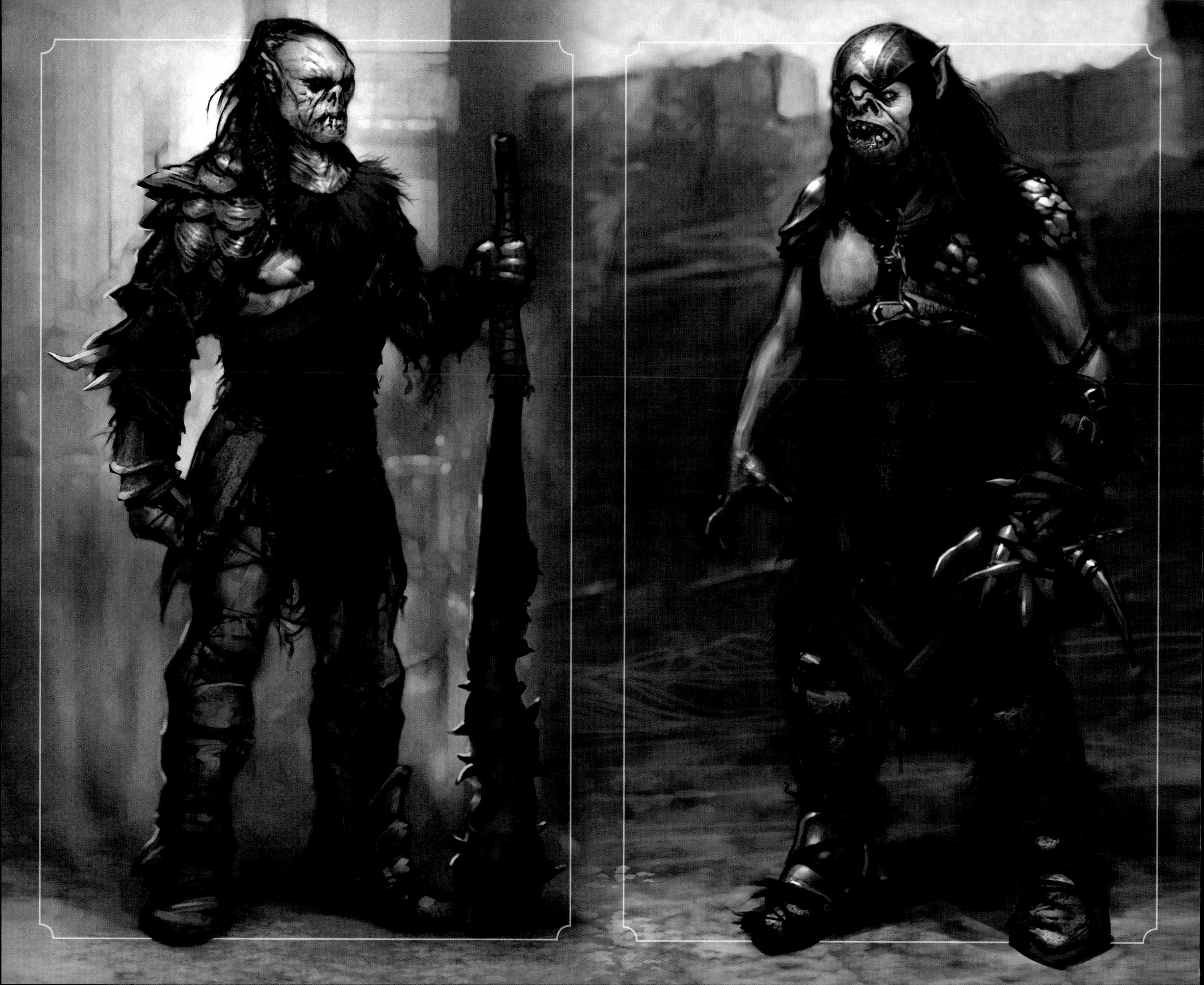

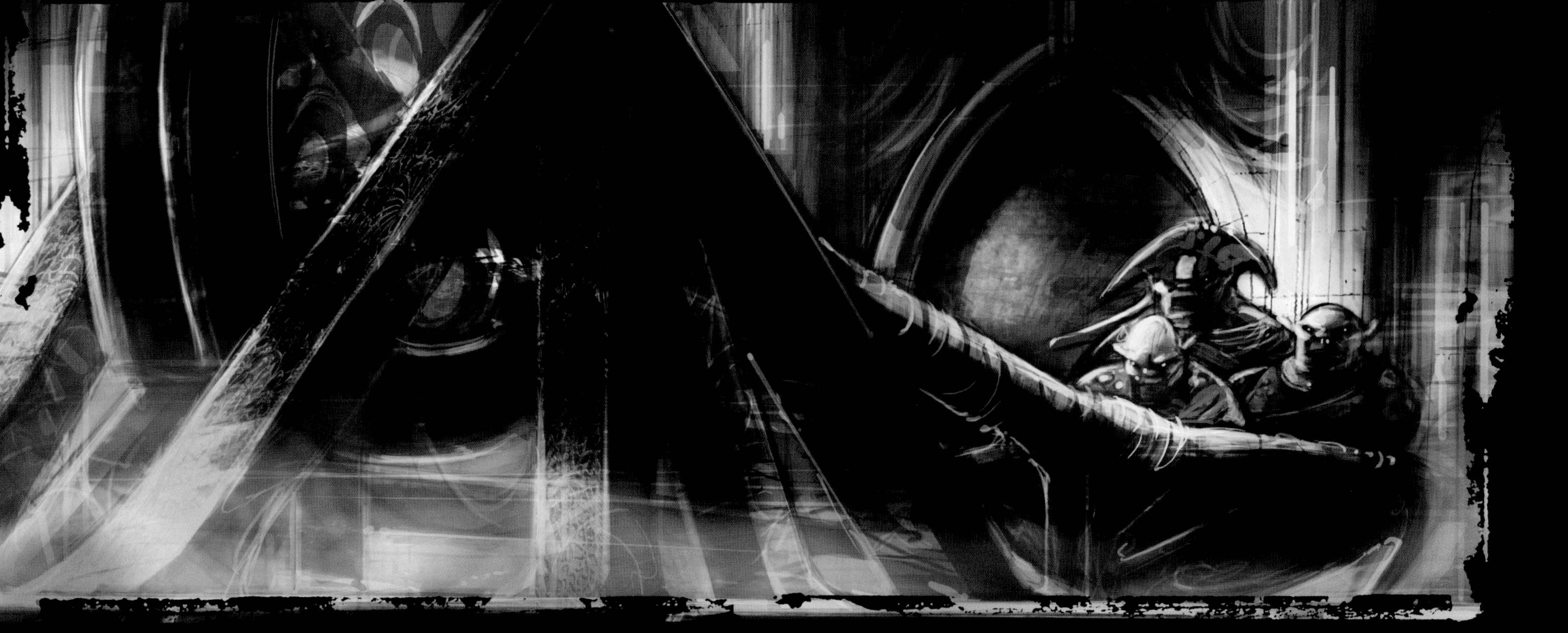

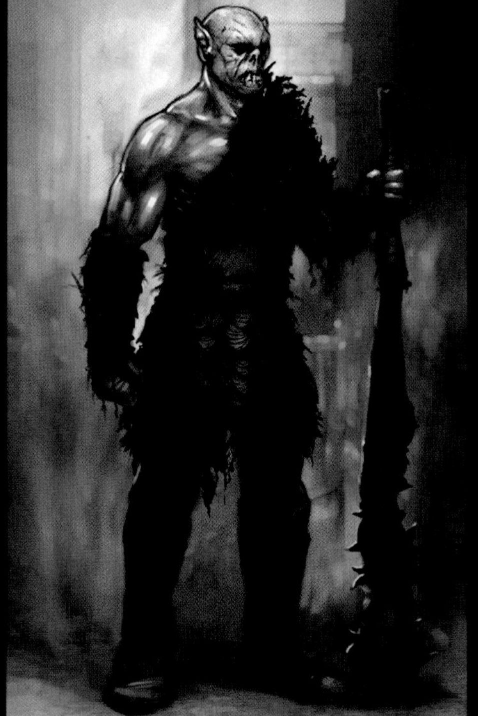

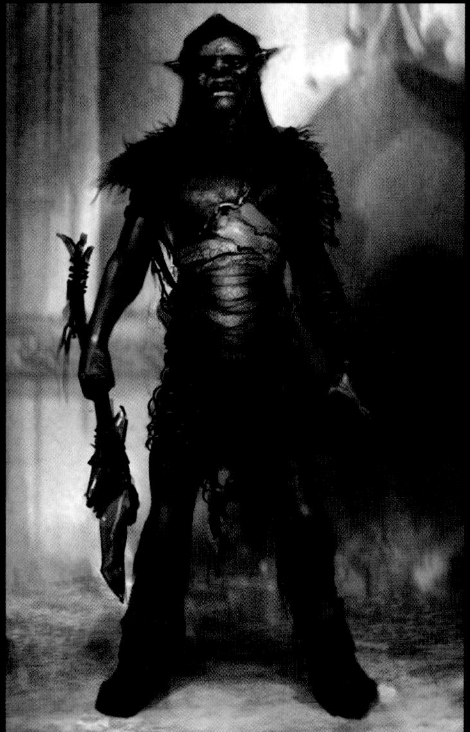

Opposite and left: Costume concepts for various Orc specialists.

Above: Two Orcs prepare for the (last) ride of their lives.

Below: Orcs appreciate a hands-on approach to directing.

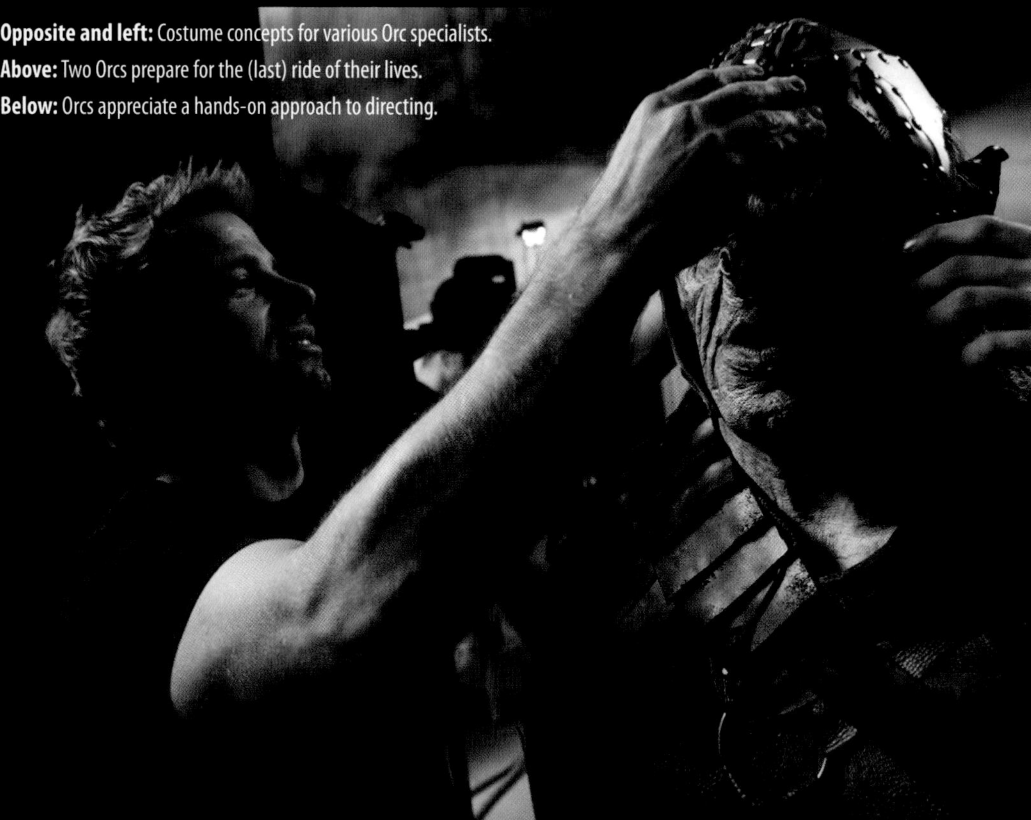

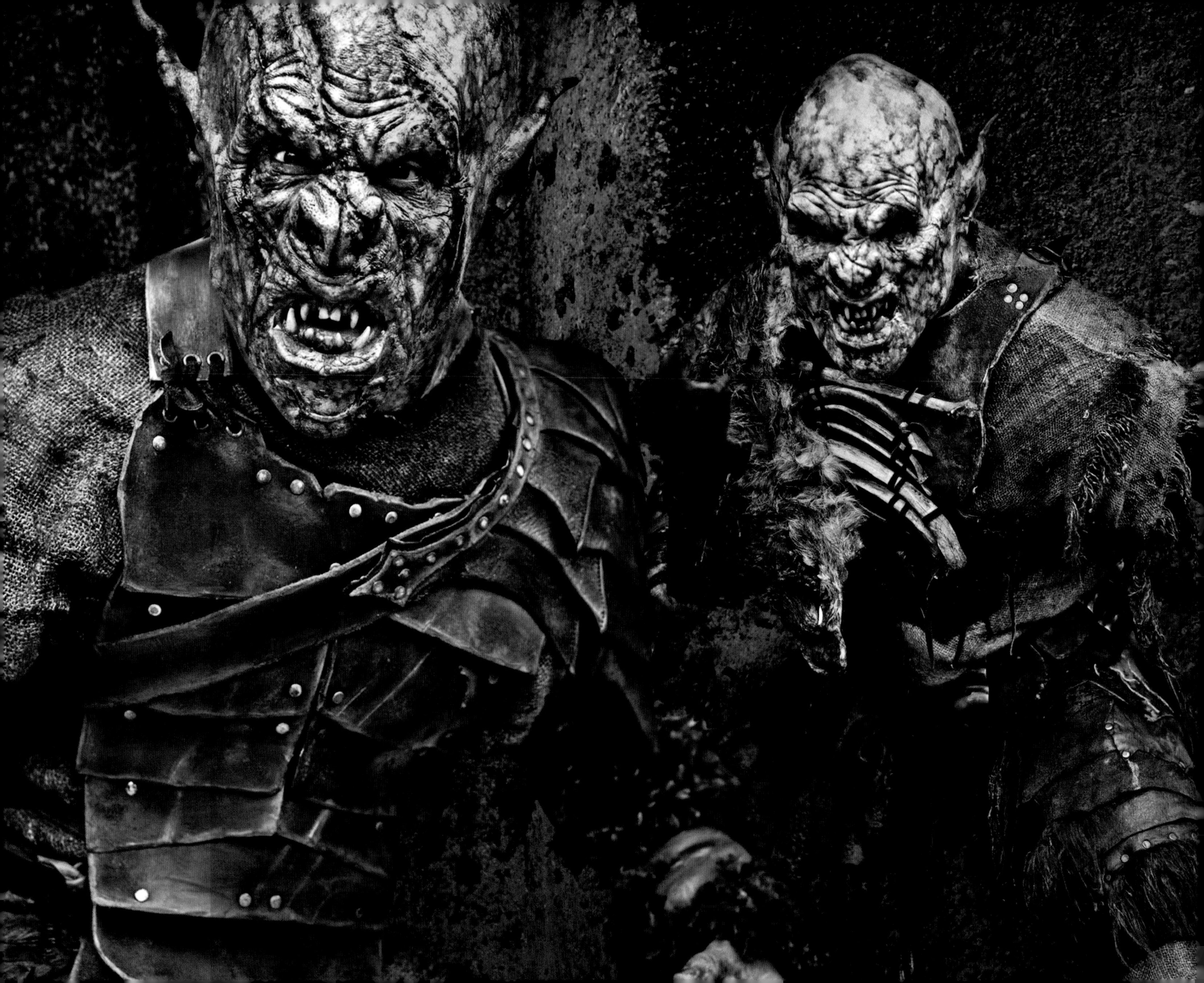

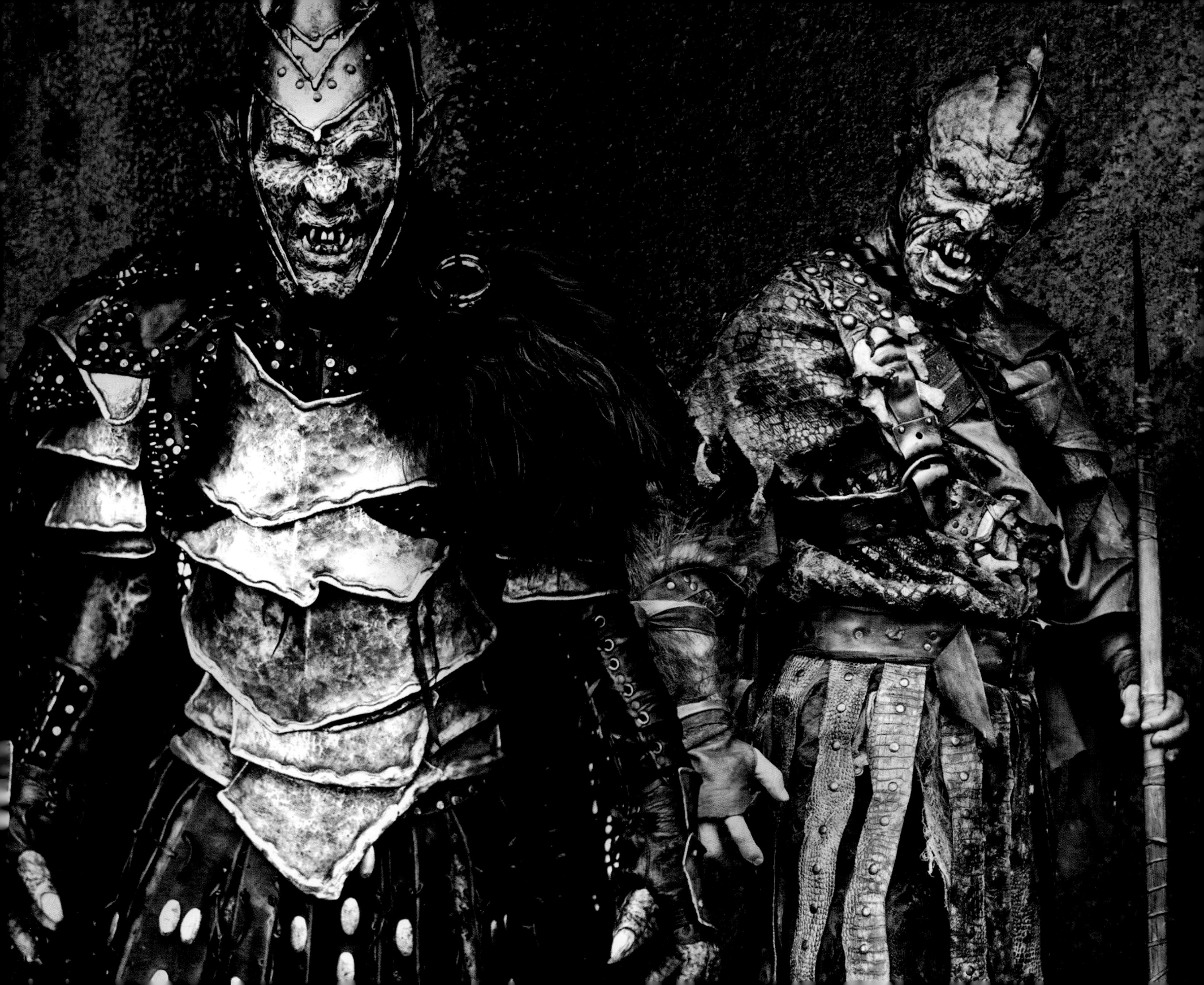

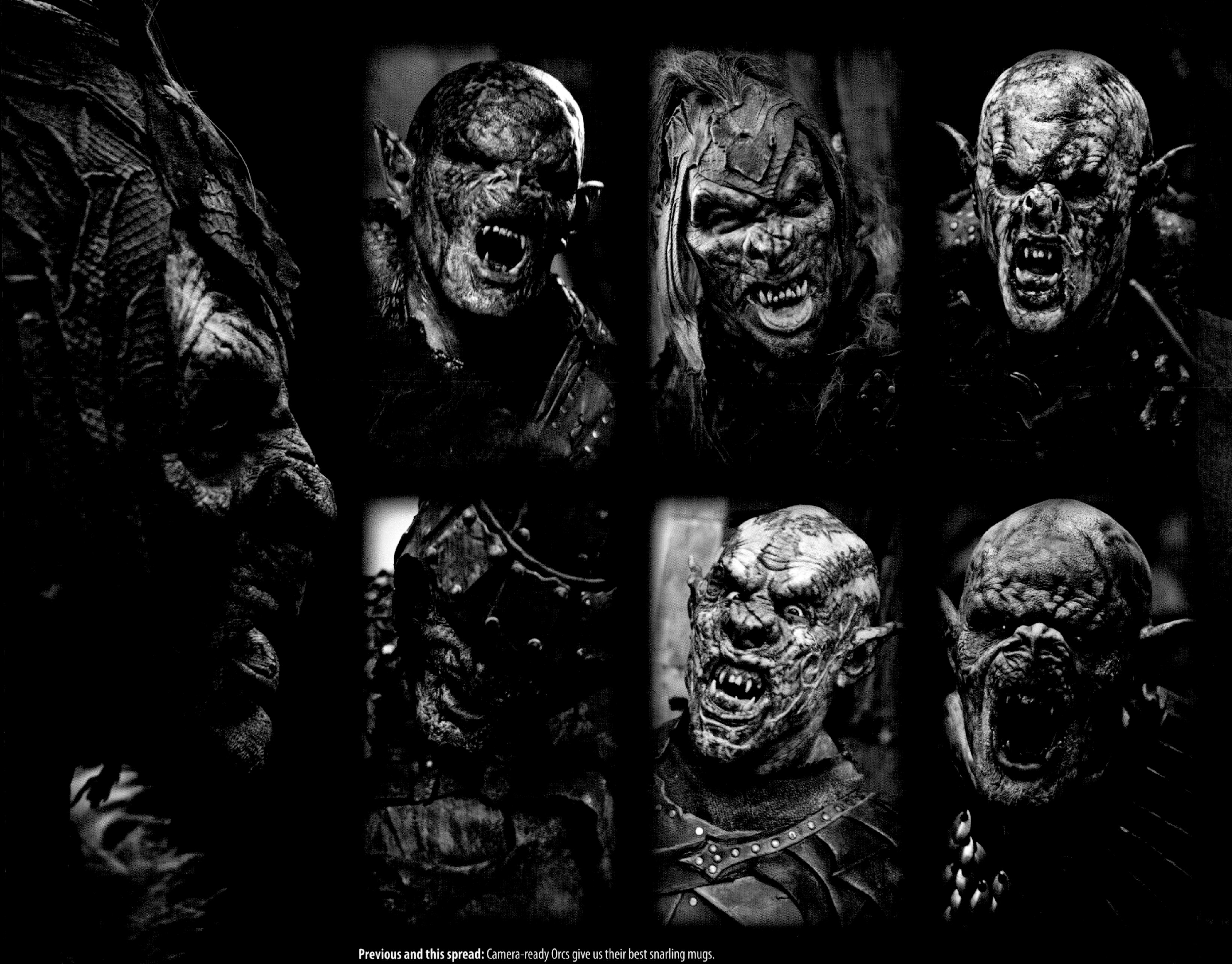

Previous and this spread: Camera-ready Orcs give us their best snarling mugs.

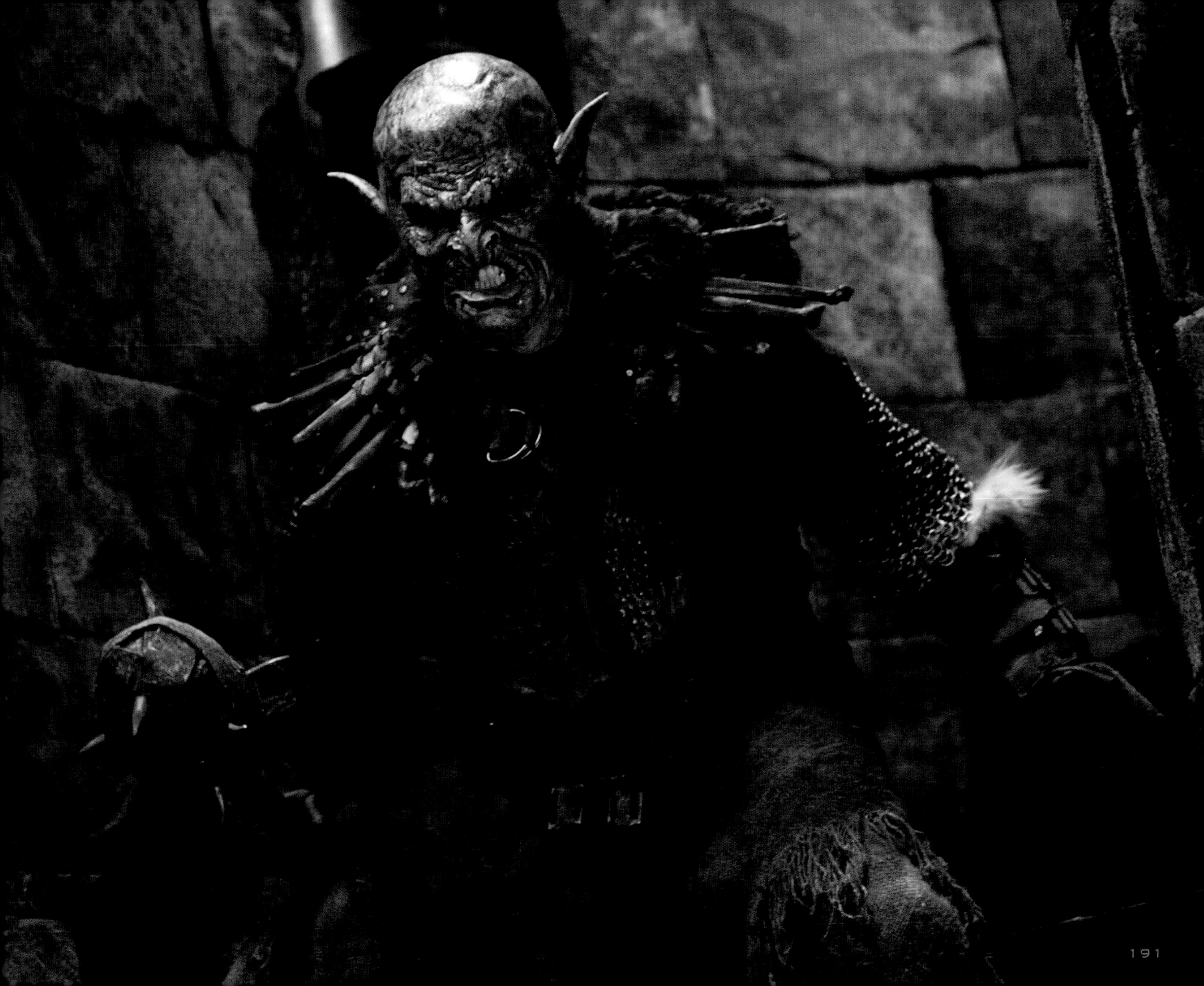

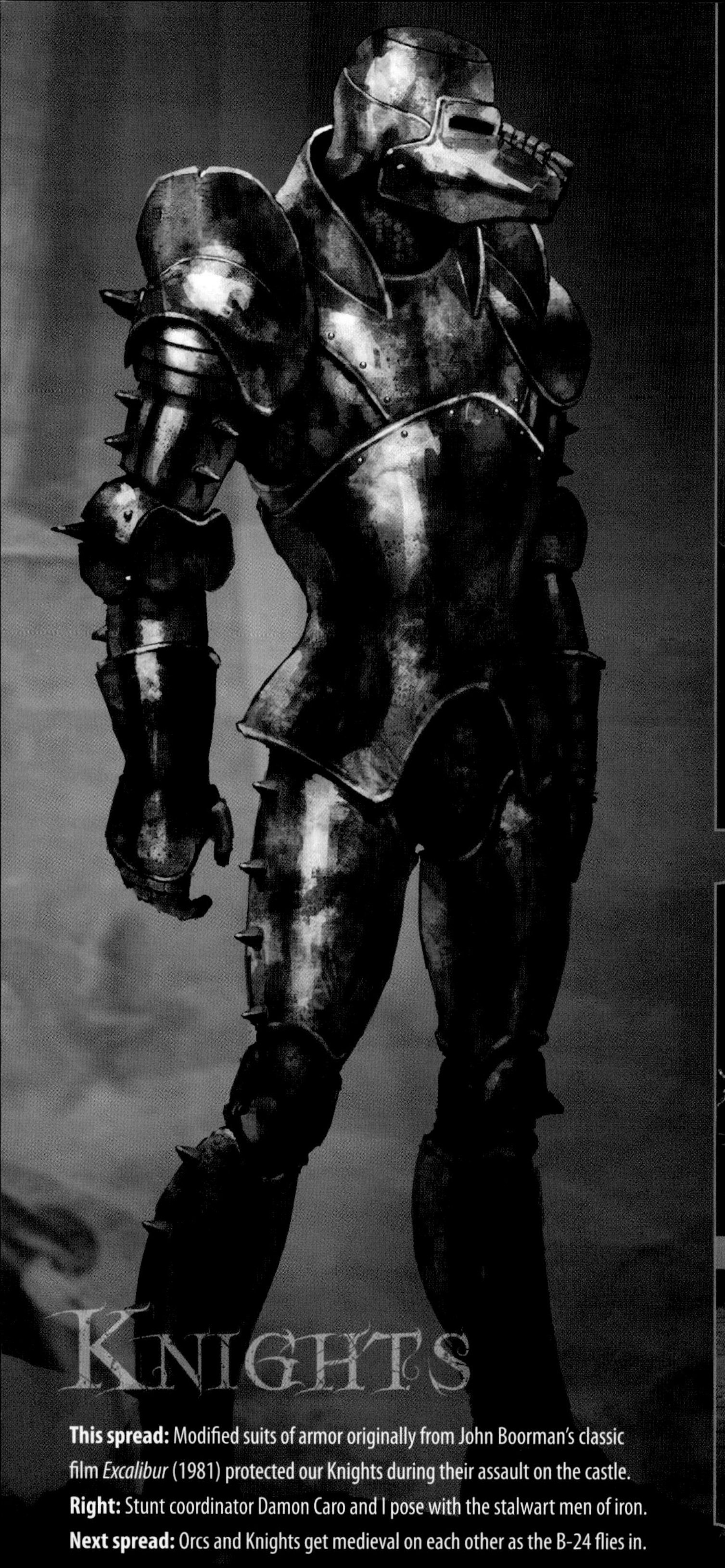

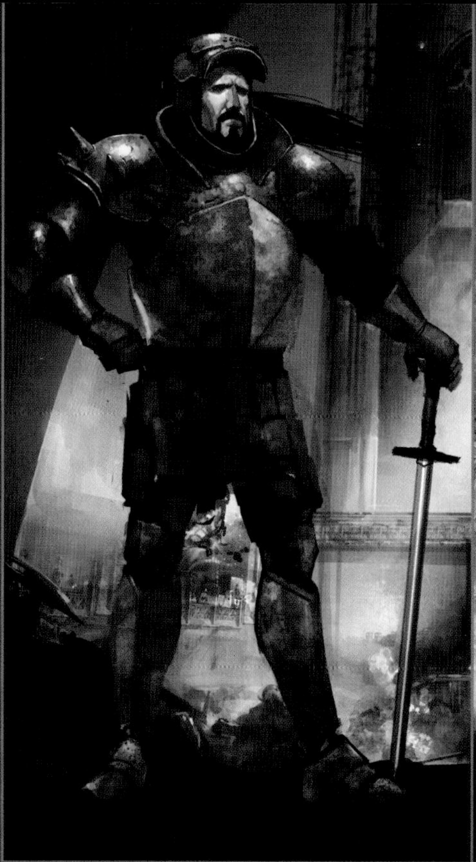

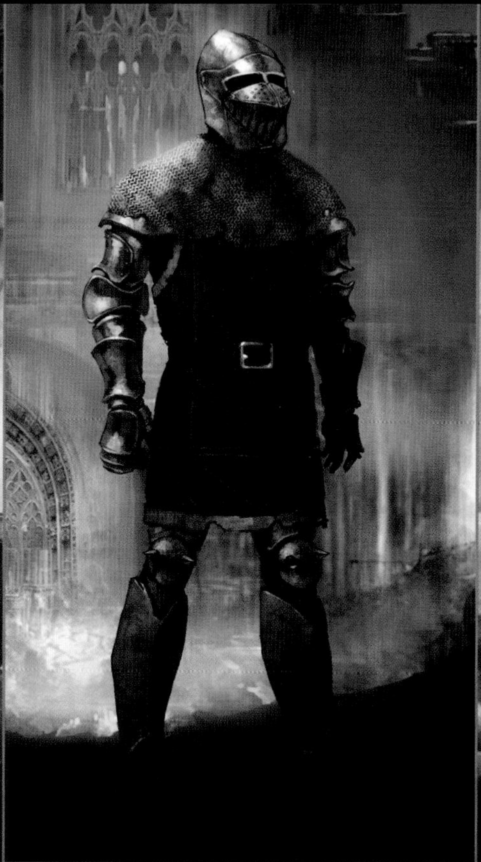

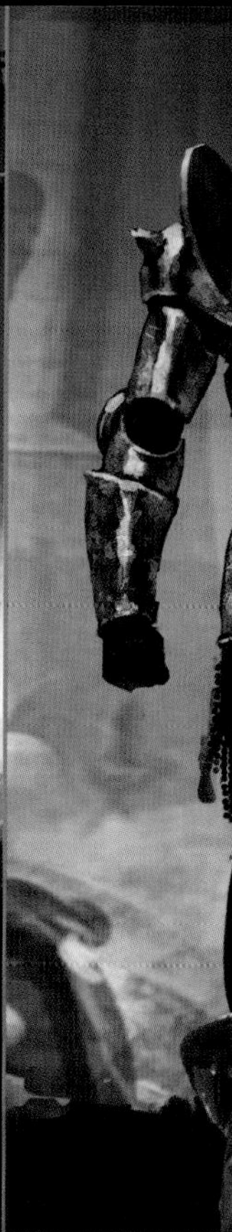

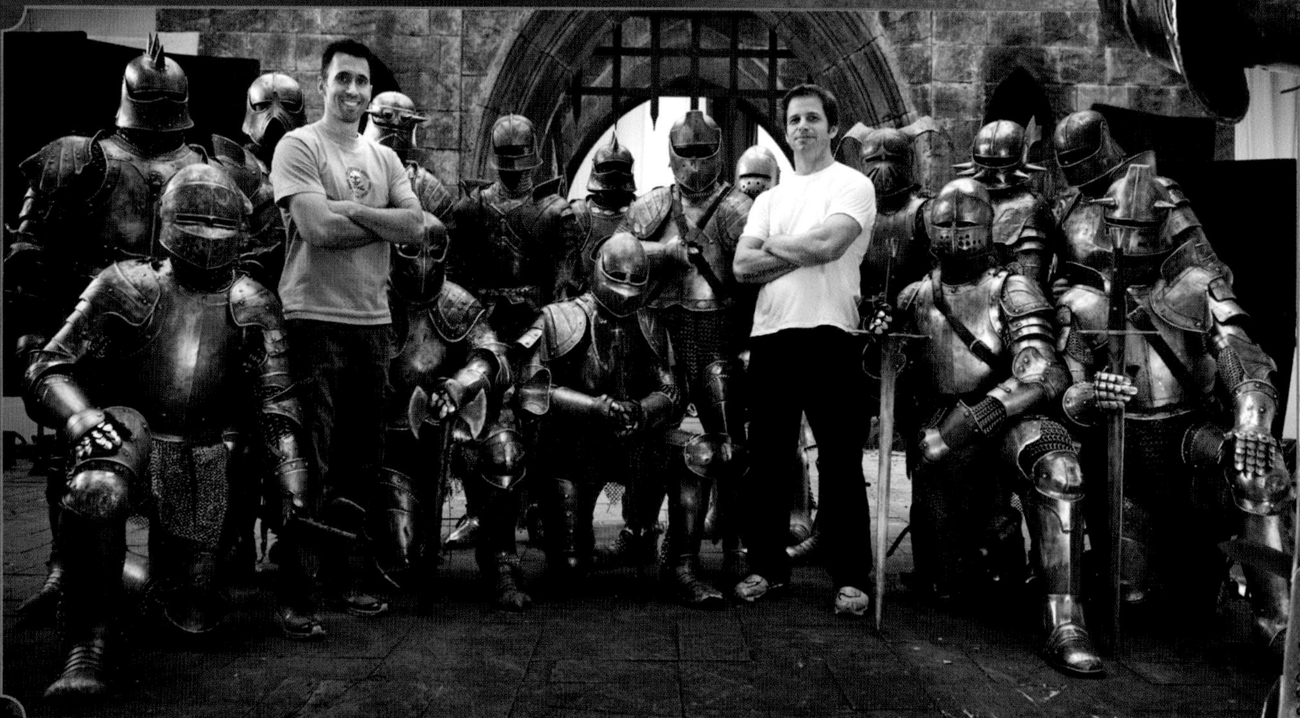

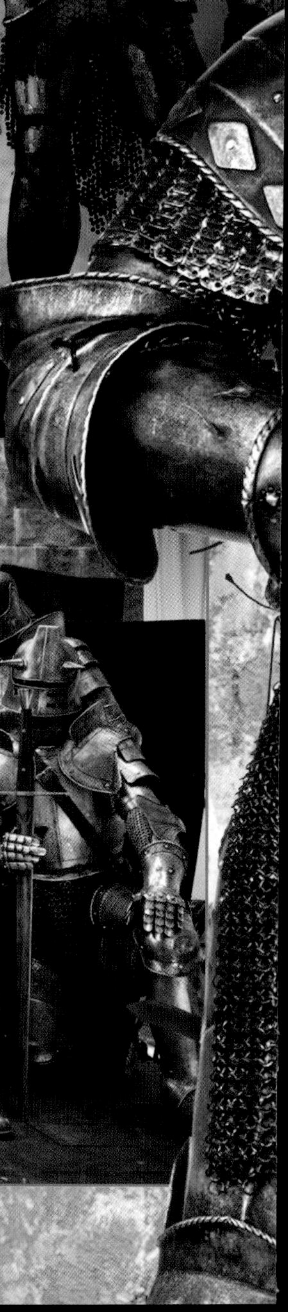

KNIGHTS

This spread: Modified suits of armor originally from John Boorman's classic film *Excalibur* (1981) protected our Knights during their assault on the castle.
Right: Stunt coordinator Damon Caro and I pose with the stalwart men of iron.
Next spread: Orcs and Knights get medieval on each other as the B-24 flies in.

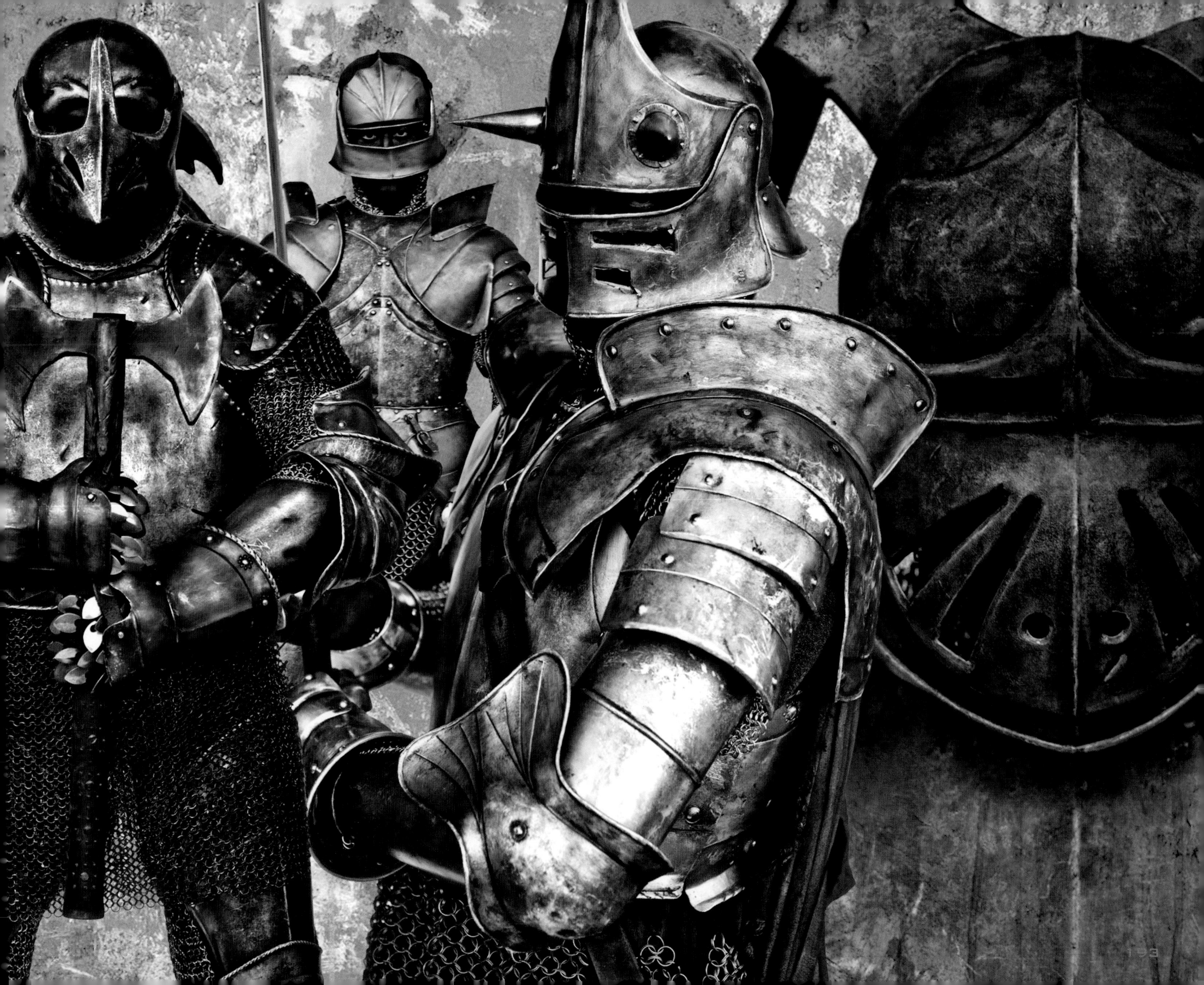

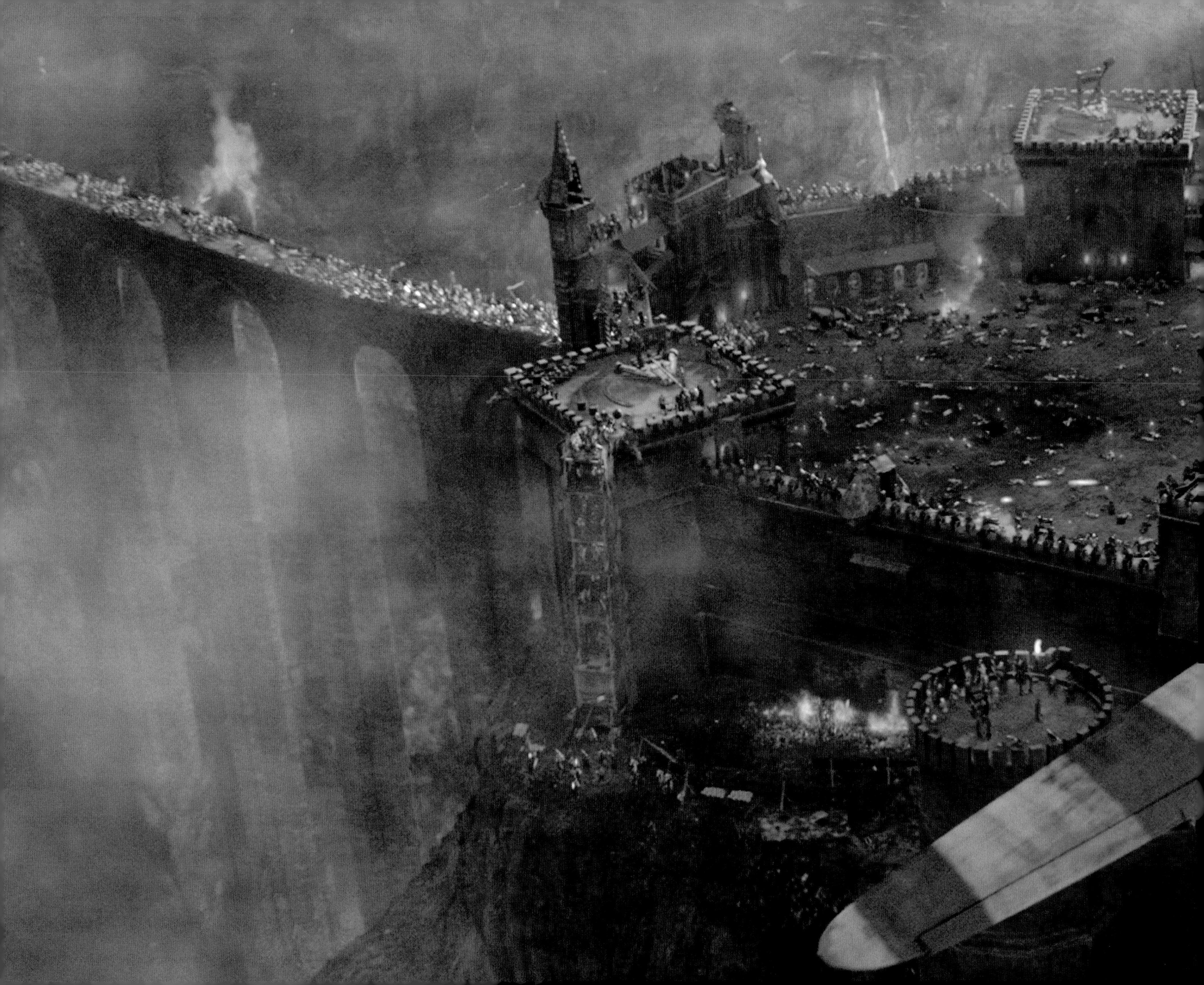

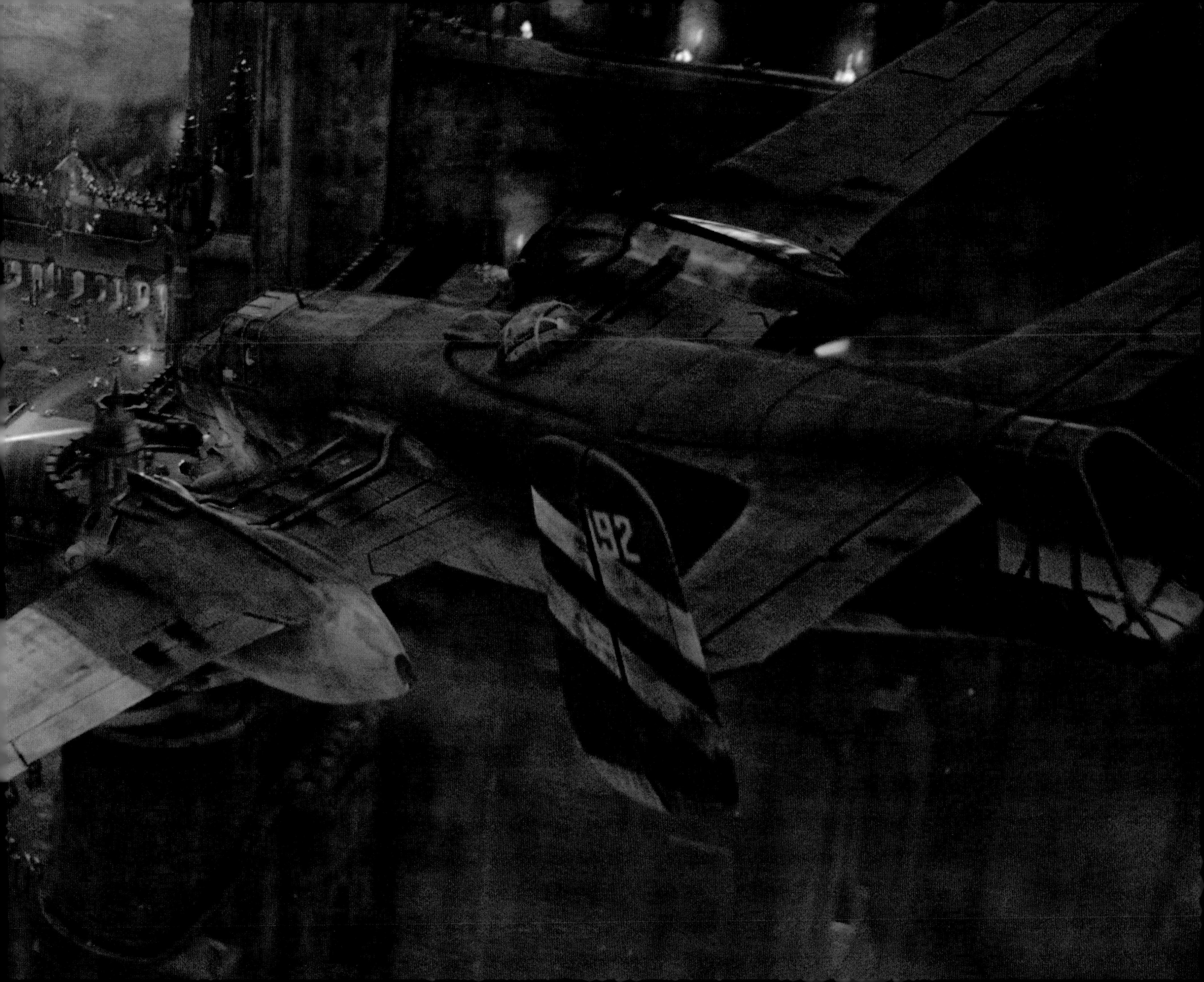
92

Dragon

Left: Early concepts for the mother dragon. We settled on the two-legged, 'wyvern-esque' design seen opposite.

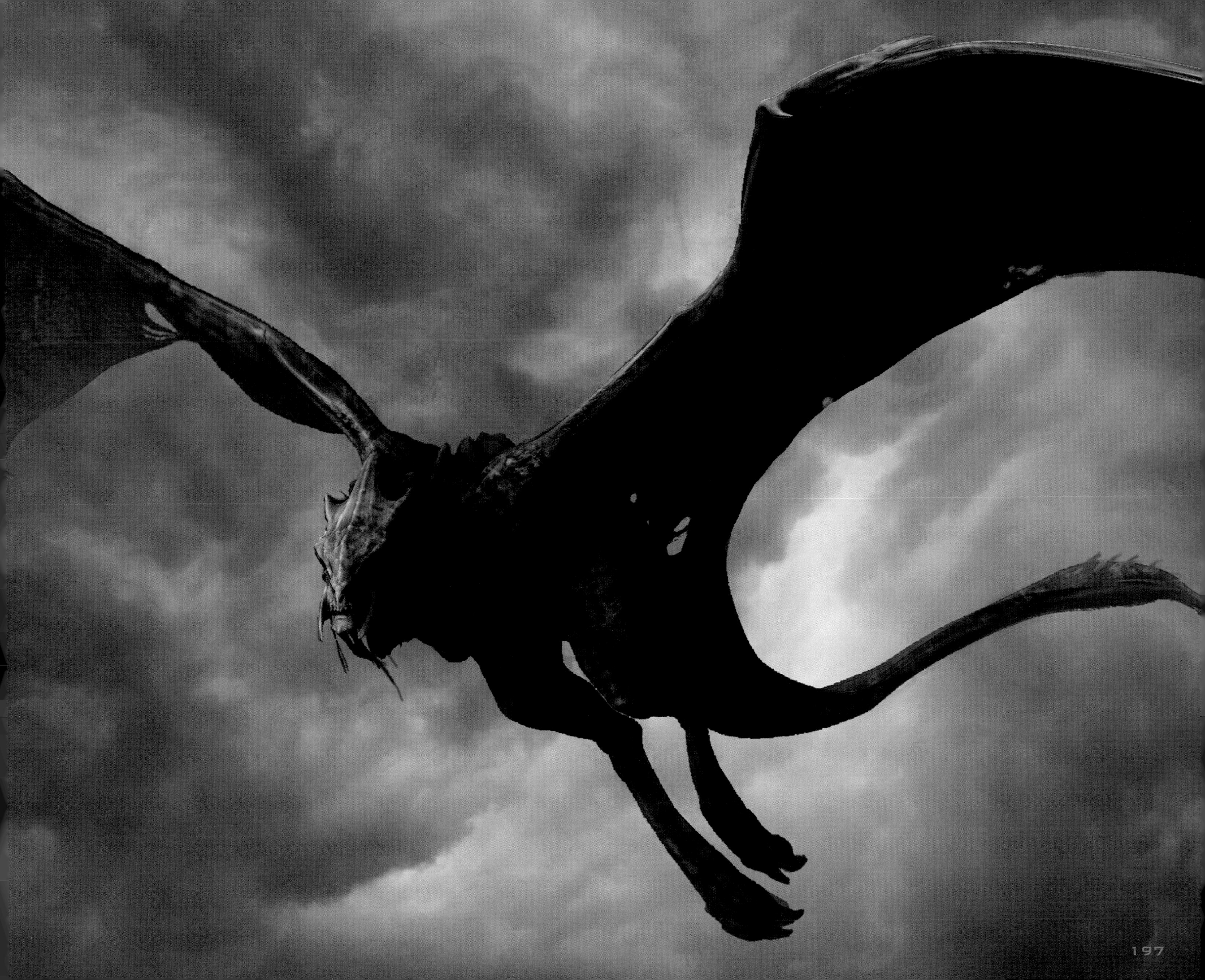

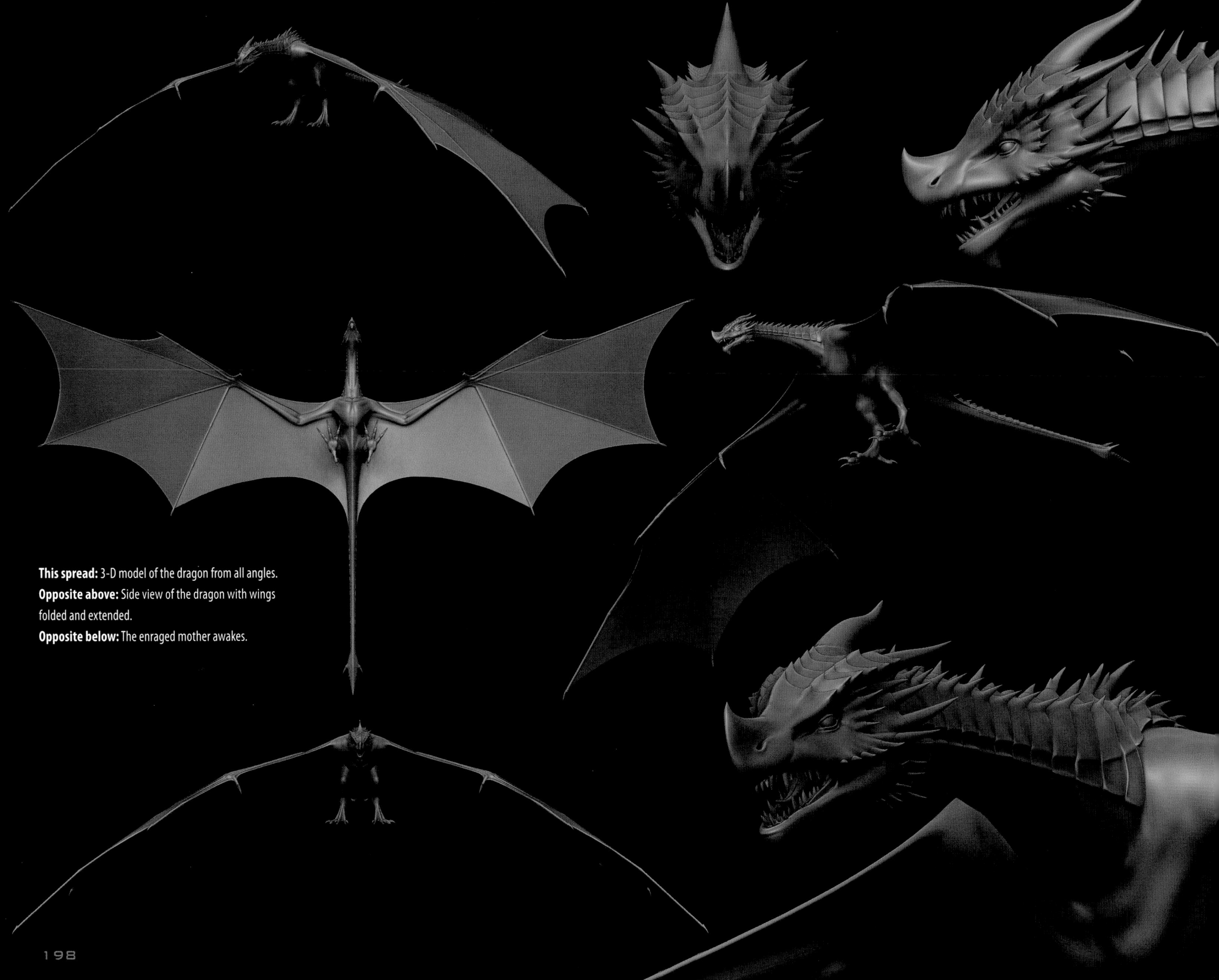

This spread: 3-D model of the dragon from all angles.
Opposite above: Side view of the dragon with wings folded and extended.
Opposite below: The enraged mother awakes.

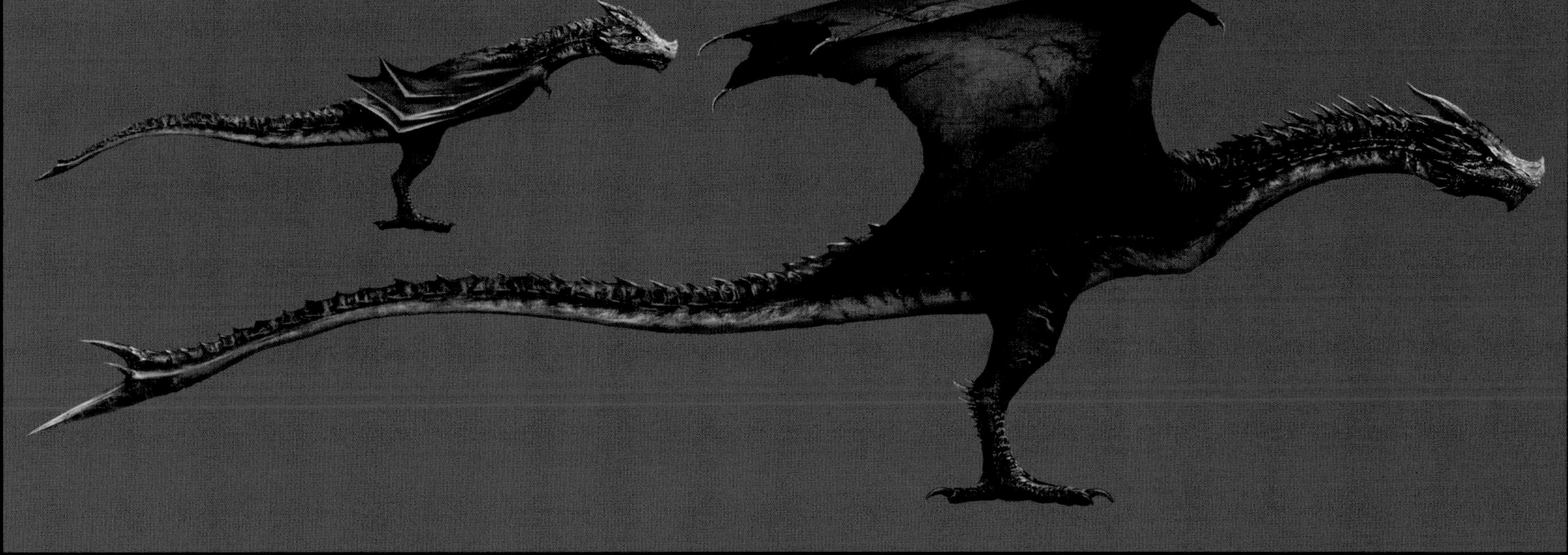

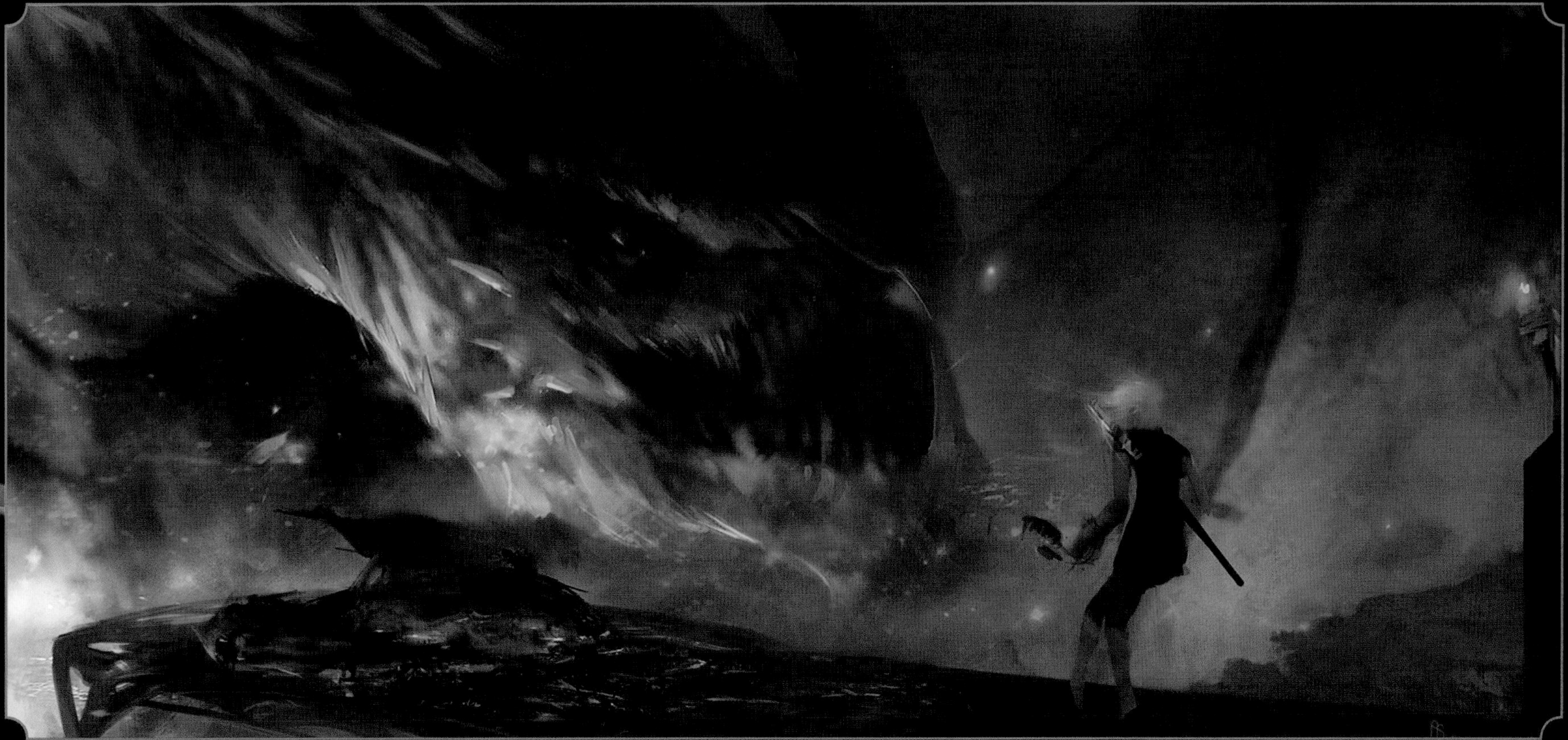

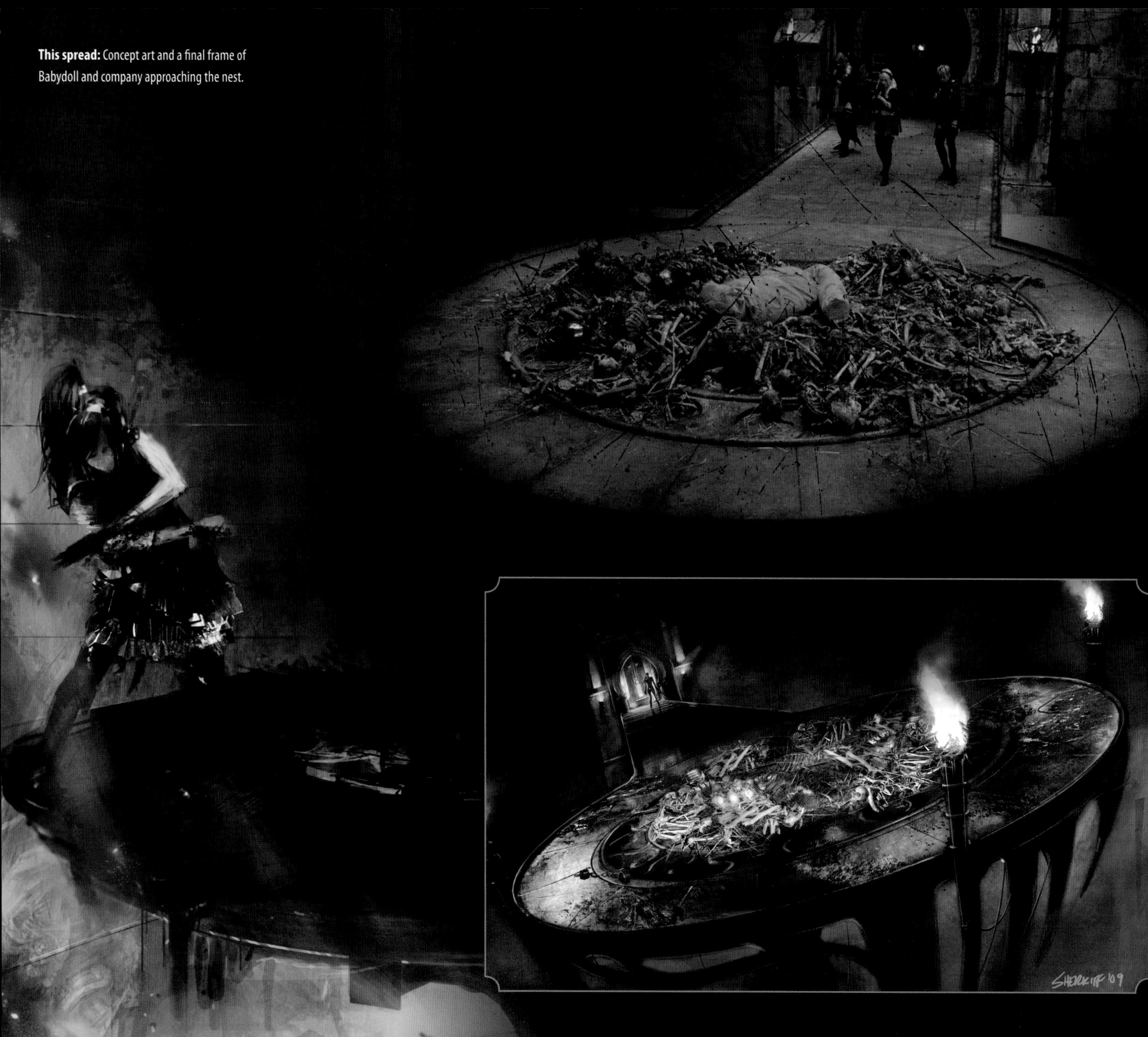

This spread: Concept art and a final frame of Babydoll and company approaching the nest.

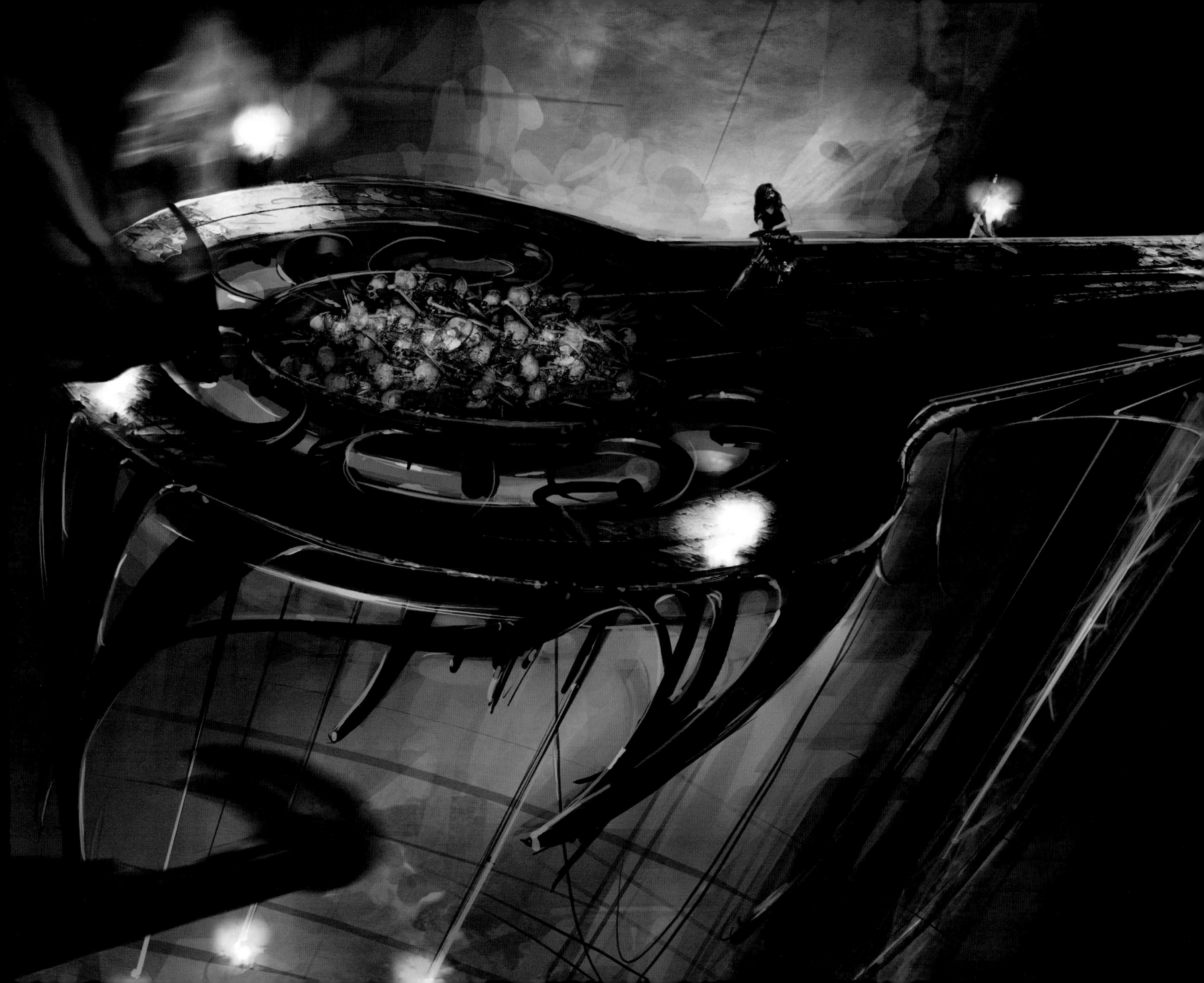

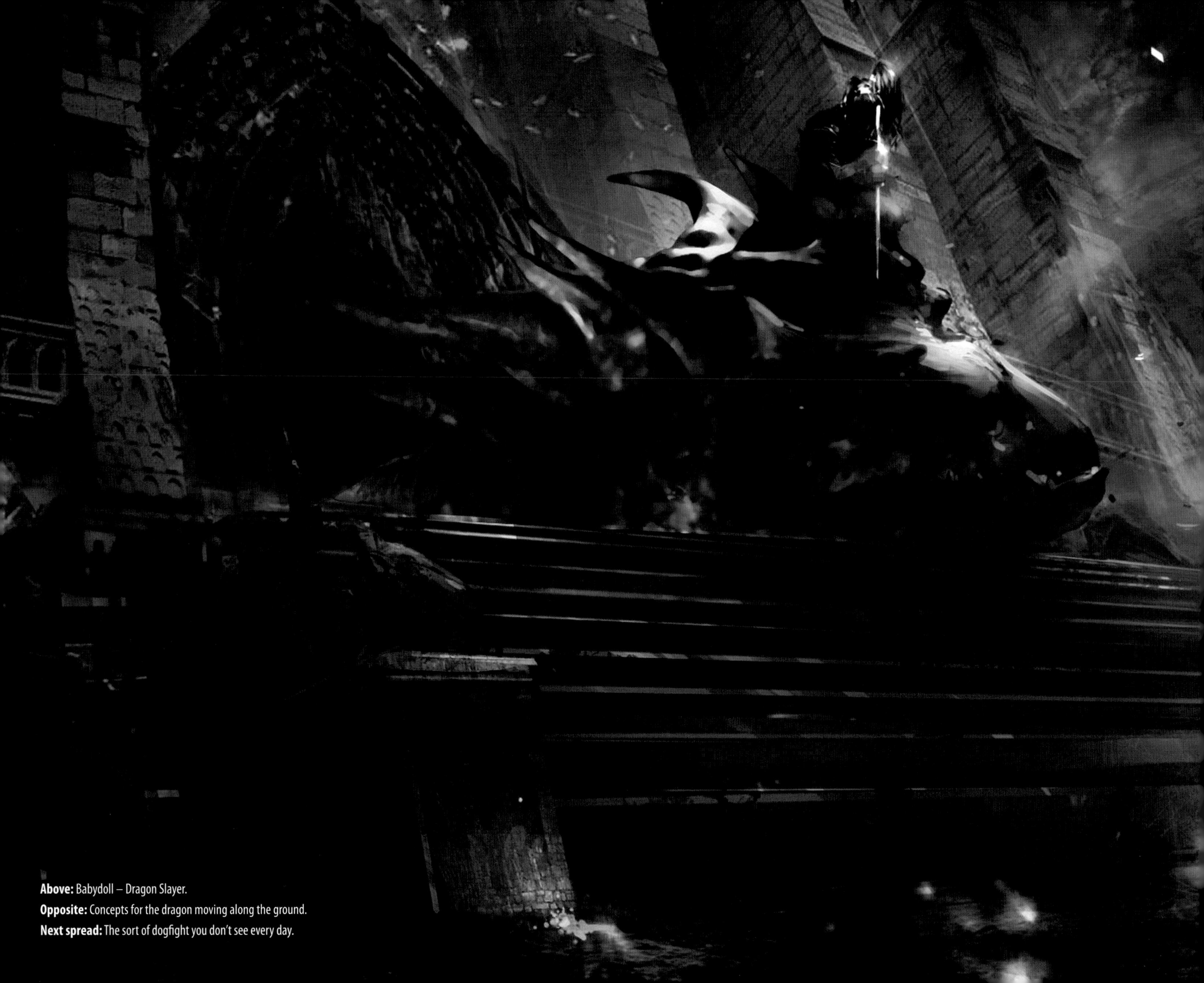

Above: Babydoll – Dragon Slayer.

Opposite: Concepts for the dragon moving along the ground.

Next spread: The sort of dogfight you don't see every day.

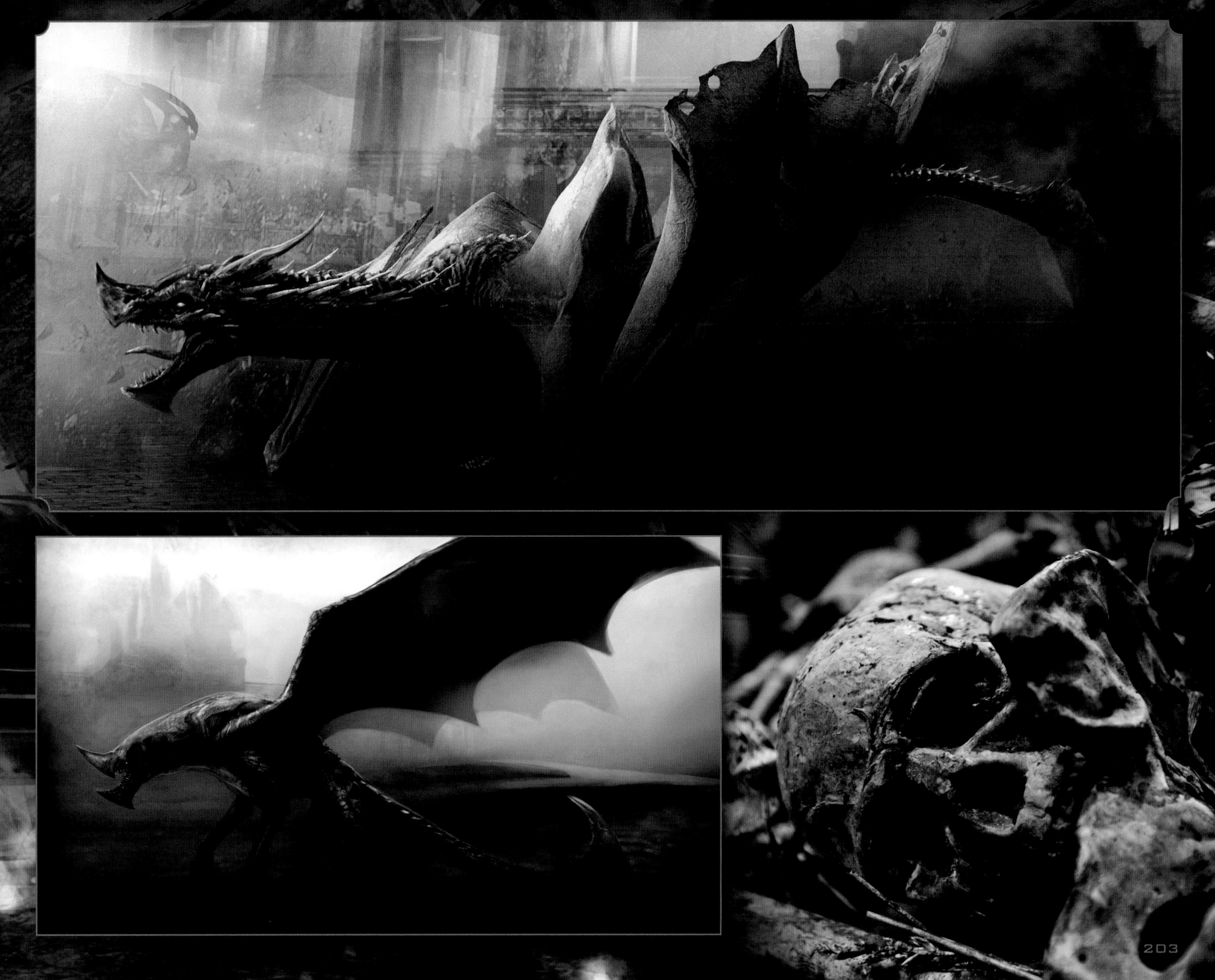

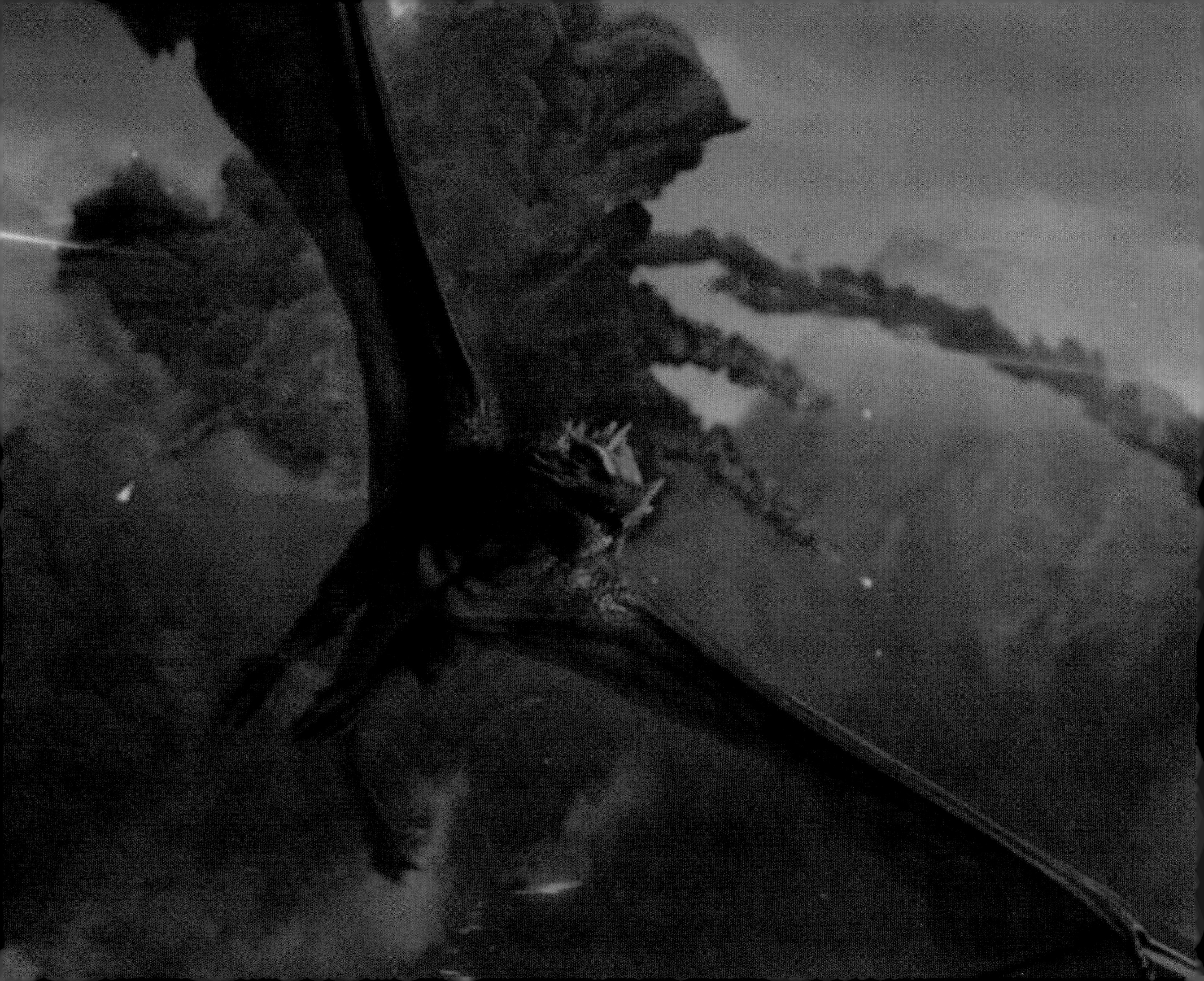

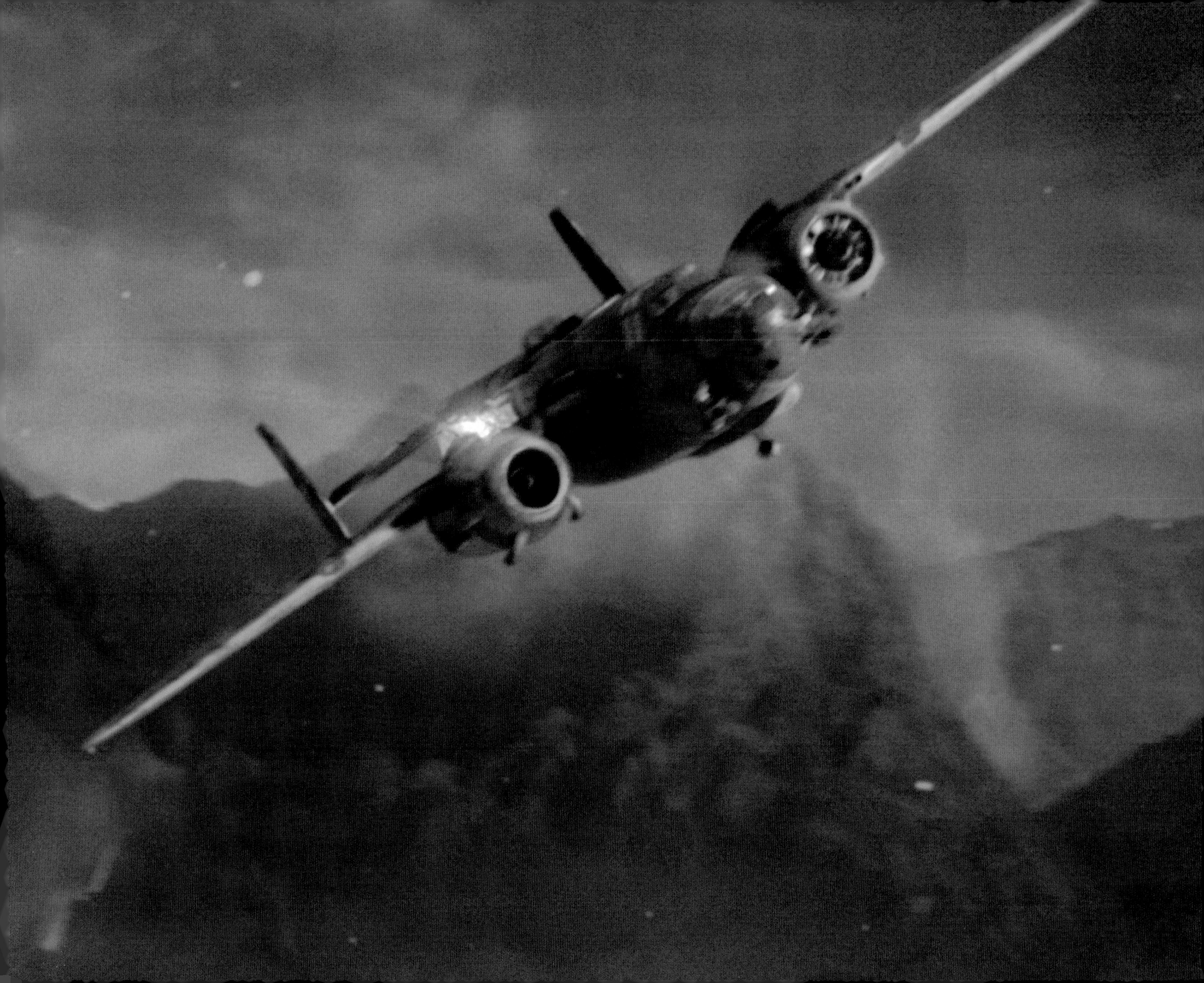

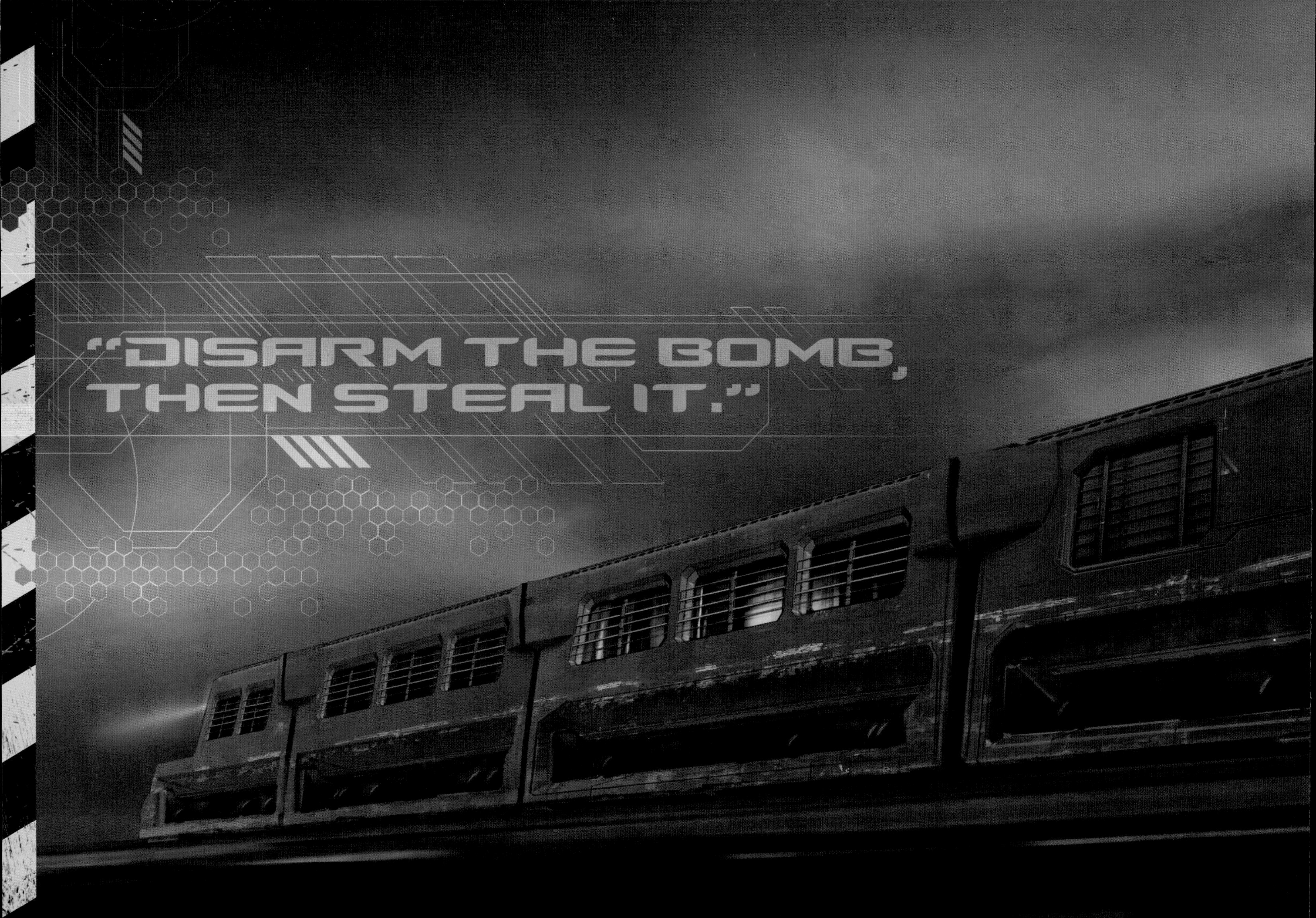

"DISARM THE BOMB, THEN STEAL IT."

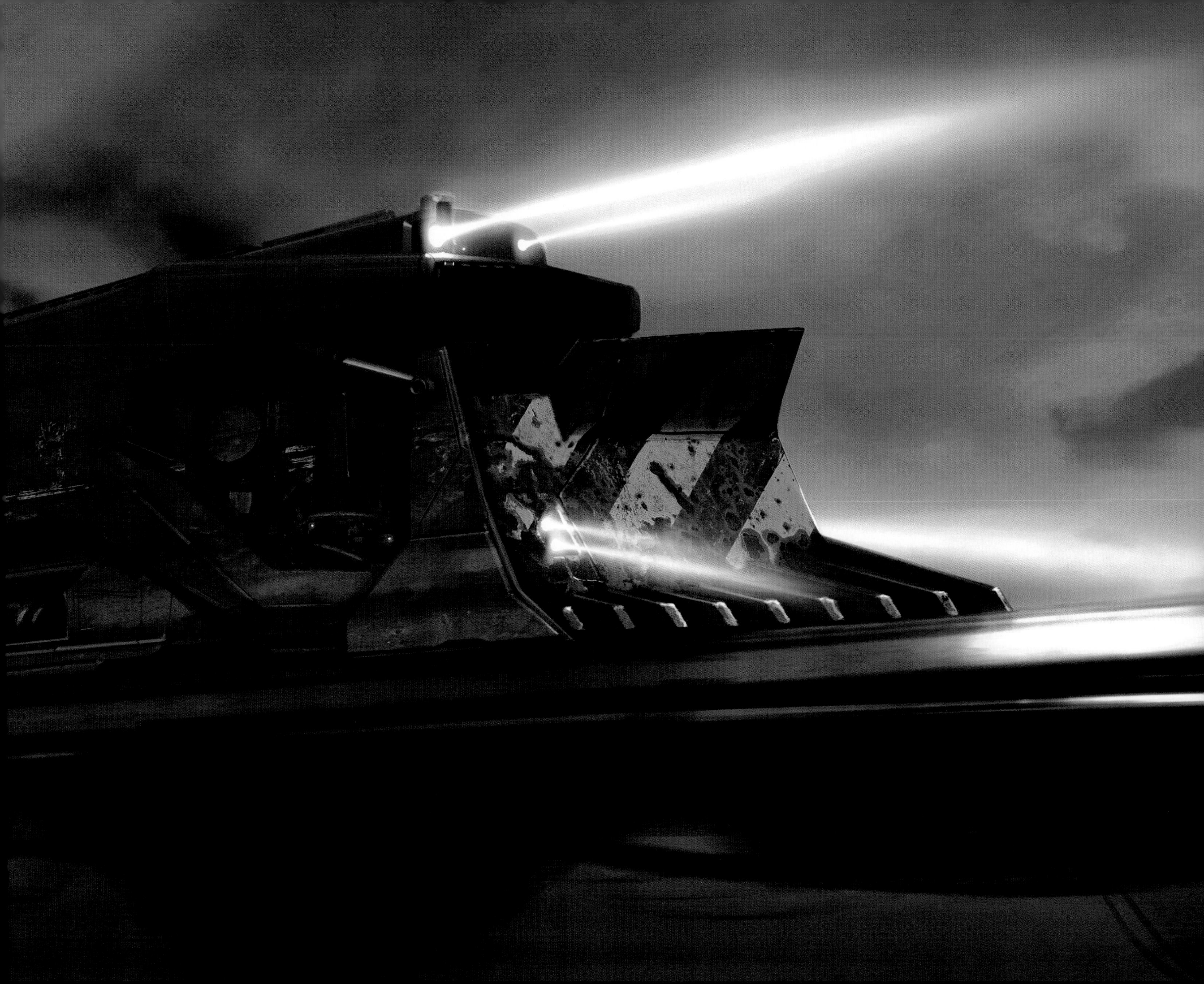

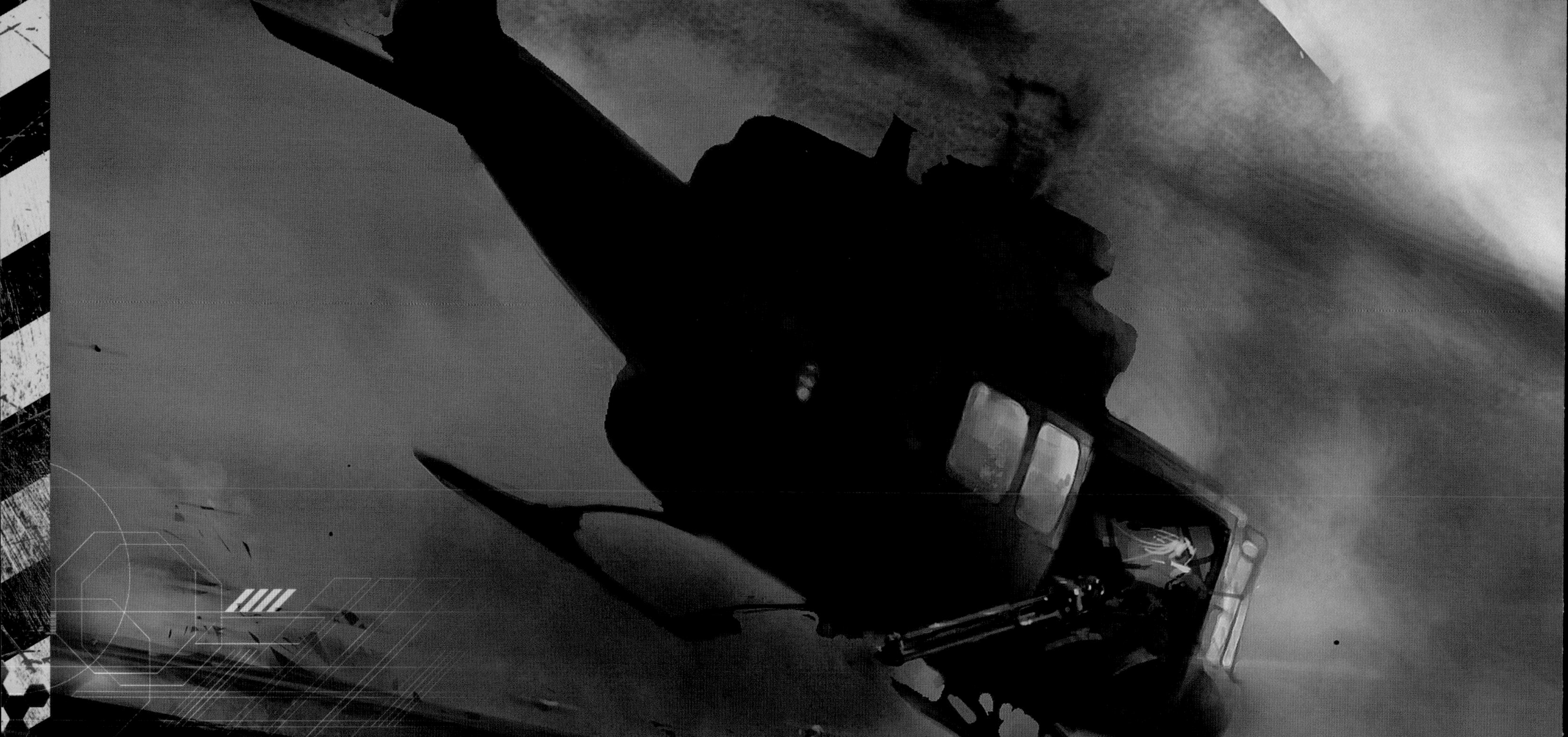

THE TRAIN

On some distant planet-sized moon encircling a gas giant, a high-speed train is racing along an elevated track towards a futuristic city of gleaming towers. Aboard the train is a thermonuclear bomb guarded by killer robots that will do anything to make sure that device reaches the population center. But Babydoll and her crew will have to do more than just disarm the bomb; they also need to steal it by lifting it out of the train via a helicopter. Now, while according to the plan (formulated in what loosely passes for reality) they actually require a knife, the acquisition of this bomb is Babydoll's mental projection of that need for an offensive weapon.

Two factors combine to make this mission a great deal riskier than those that have gone before. First of all, Babydoll's set-up dance is completely unsanctioned; it does not take place at the behest of Madam Gorski or Blue. Instead, the girls have done some roguish improvising, and have set up an impromptu show for the cook on their own. If discovered, the consequences will be dire. Secondly, and perhaps more significantly, their team is one girl short – Blondie has gone MIA.

In the earliest concept for this fantasy, the bomb was to be locked away inside a skyscraper, with the team battling terrorists for every inch as they advanced through a series of hallways. Over time, those hallways were shortened and straightened out to become the train cars, and the terrorists morphed into robots. Then, during post-production, I was asked how I wanted the moon to look. I thought, "Well, since you're asking, how many moons?" and just like that, the sequence was set in outer space. So, the journey of this one fantasy really speaks to the fluidity of the process we were working under, and also to the flexibility of the imagination – provided you keep your mind open.

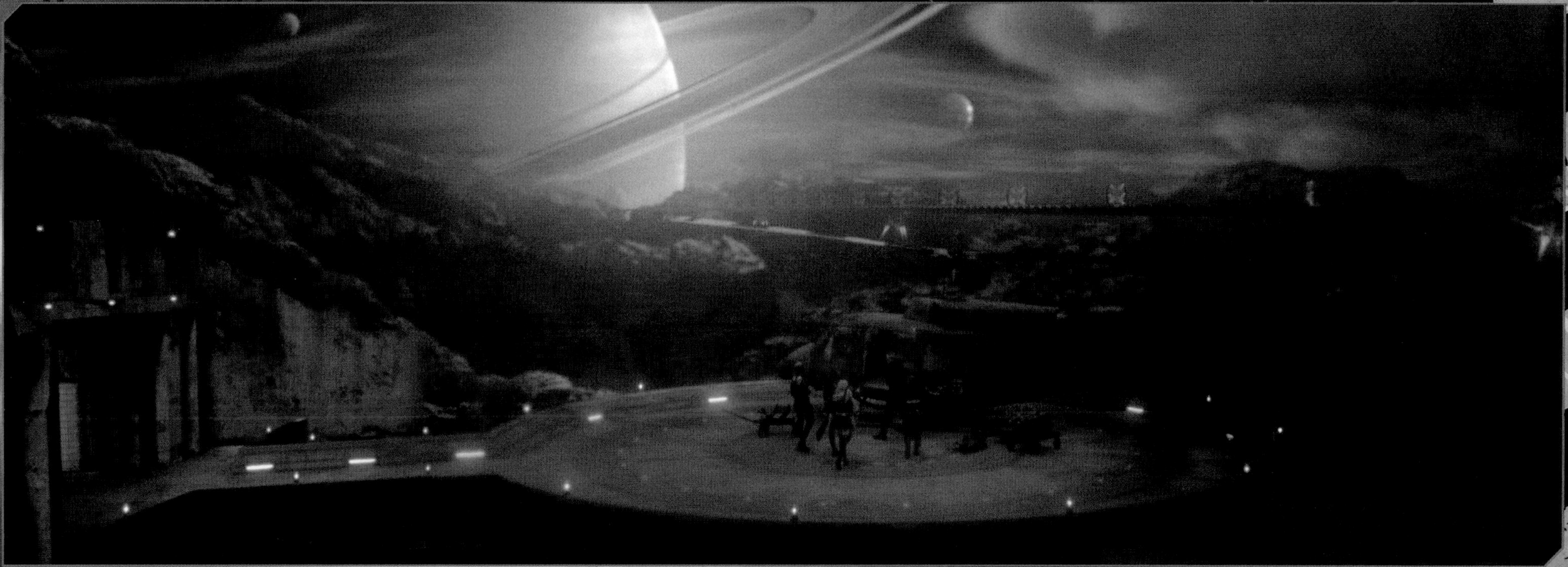

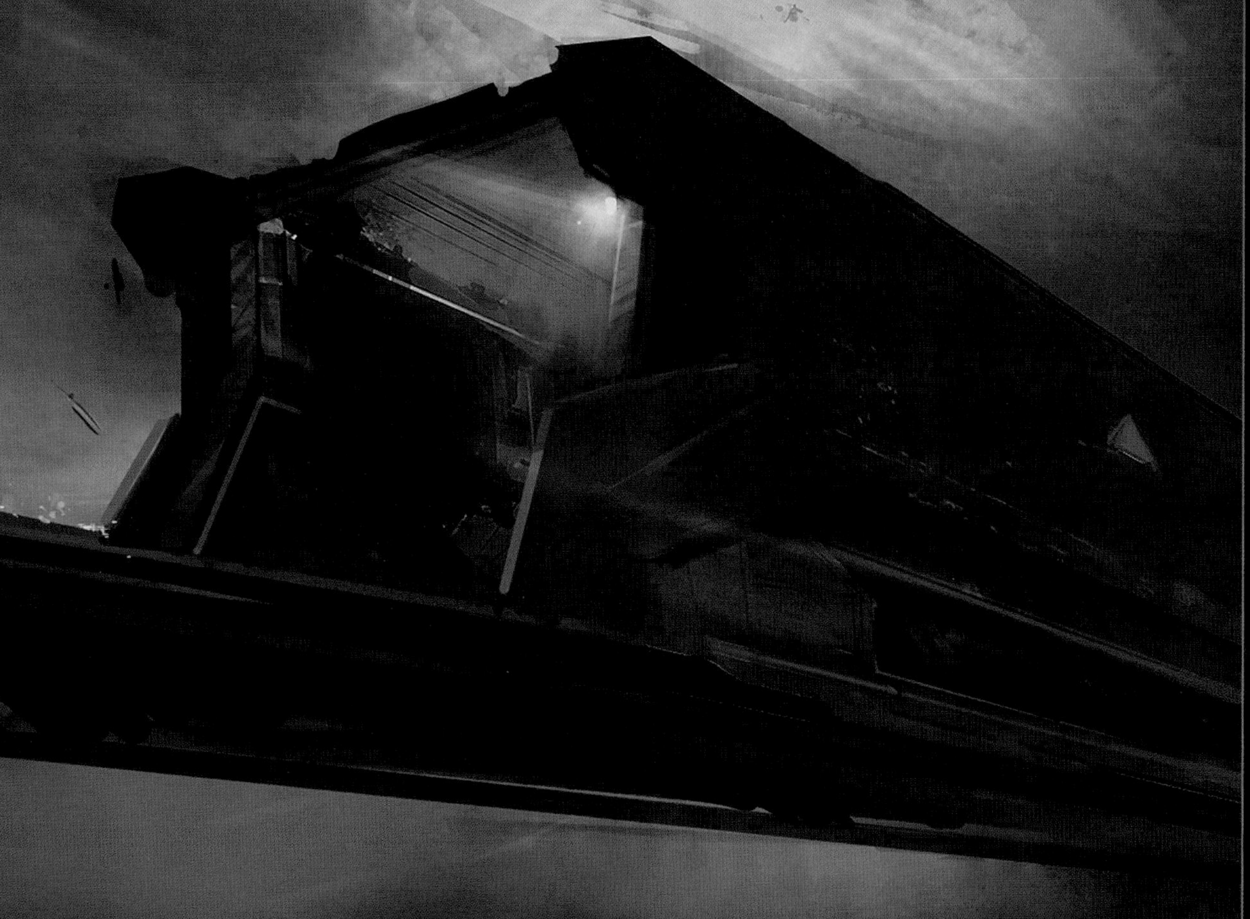

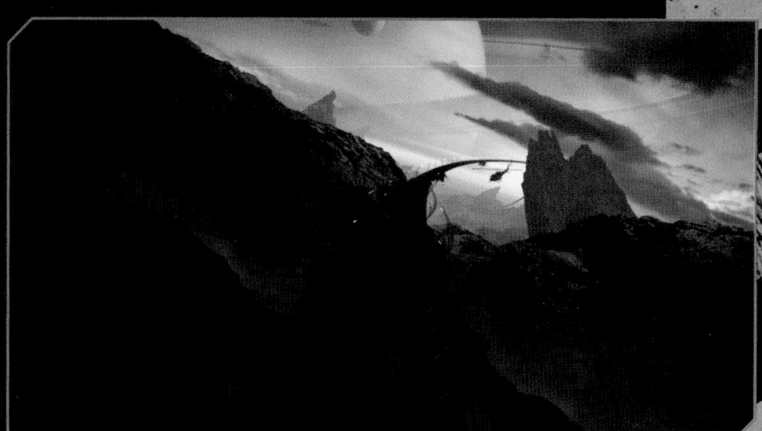

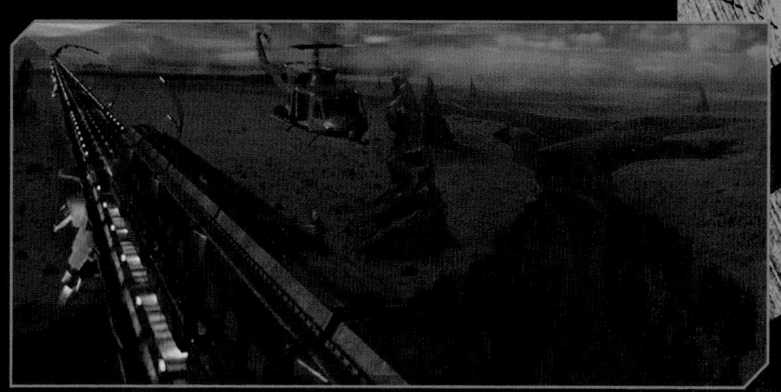

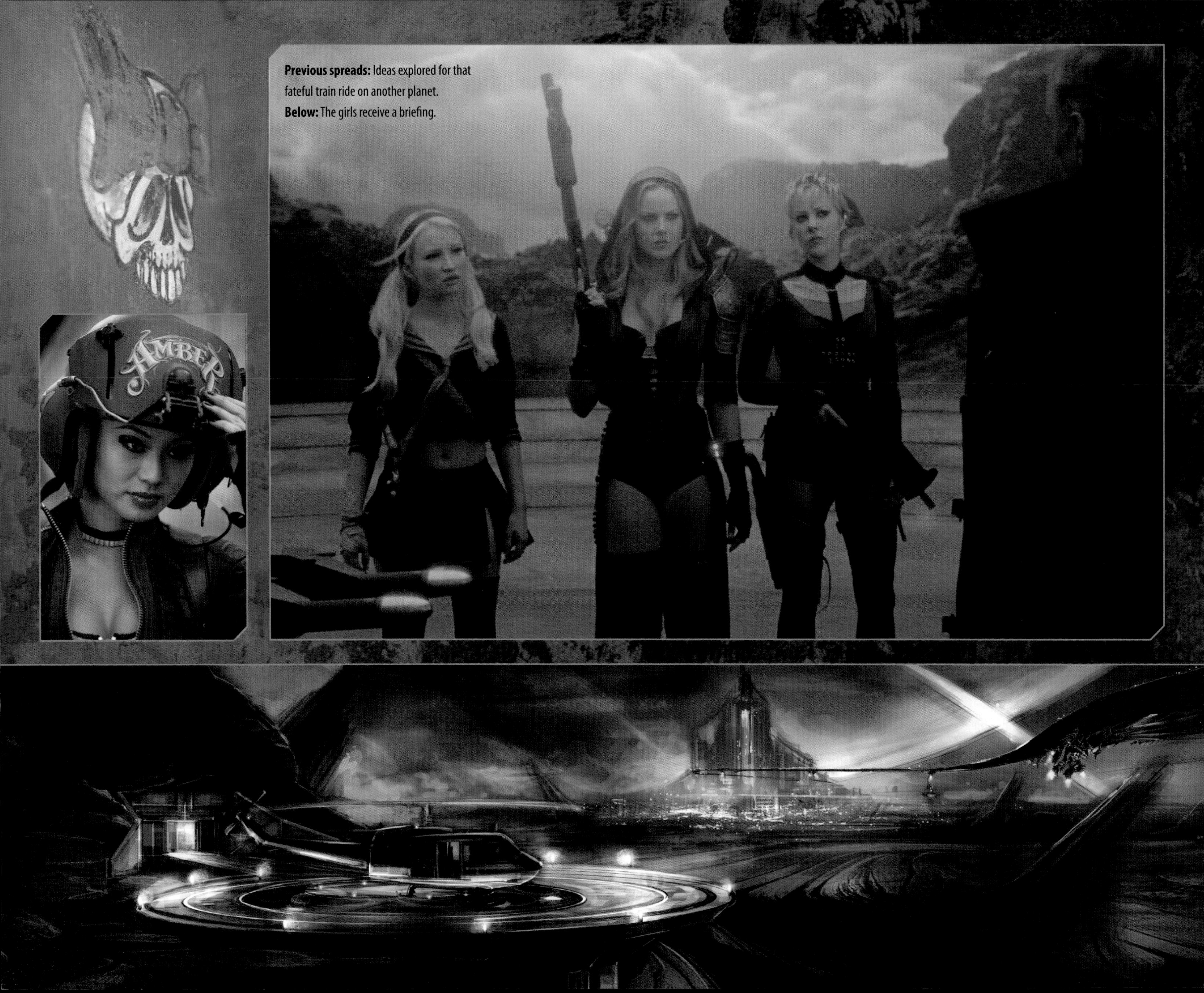

Previous spreads: Ideas explored for that fateful train ride on another planet.

Below: The girls receive a briefing.

Right: The nut is cracked.
Far right: The Wise Man's costume gets a futuristic upgrade.
Bottom: A complex system of rocket propulsion keeps the train track suspended.

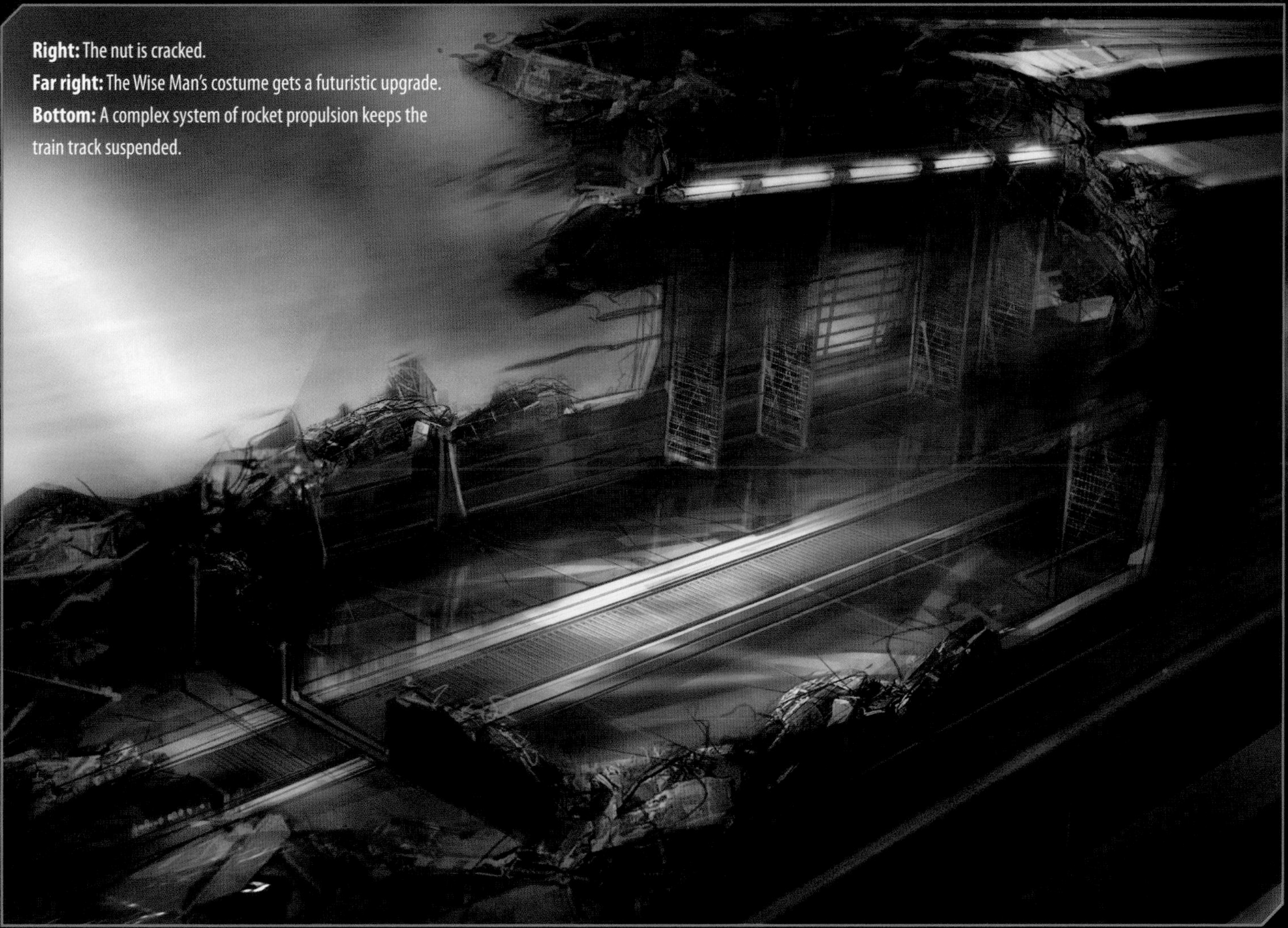

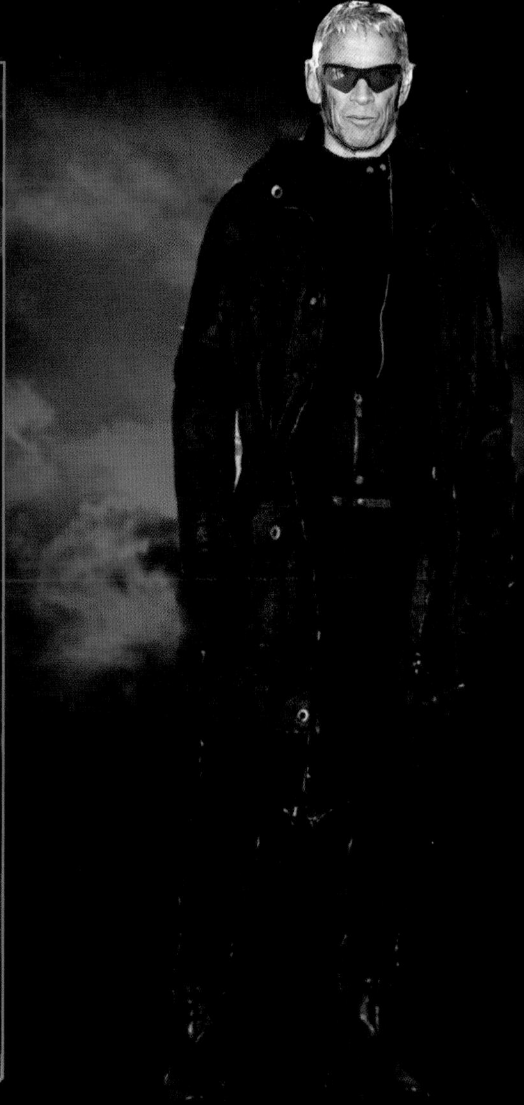

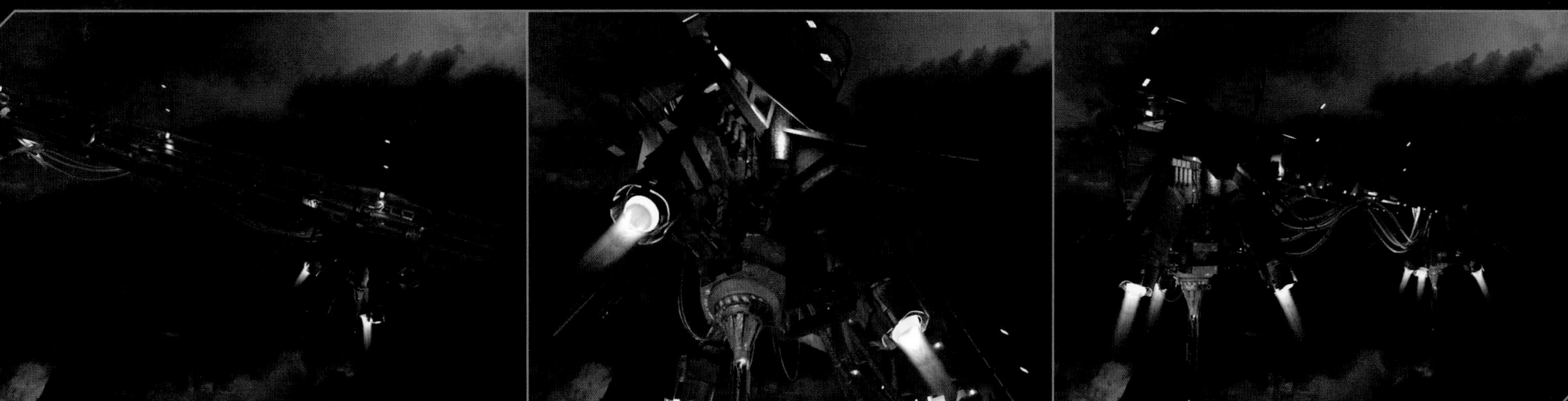

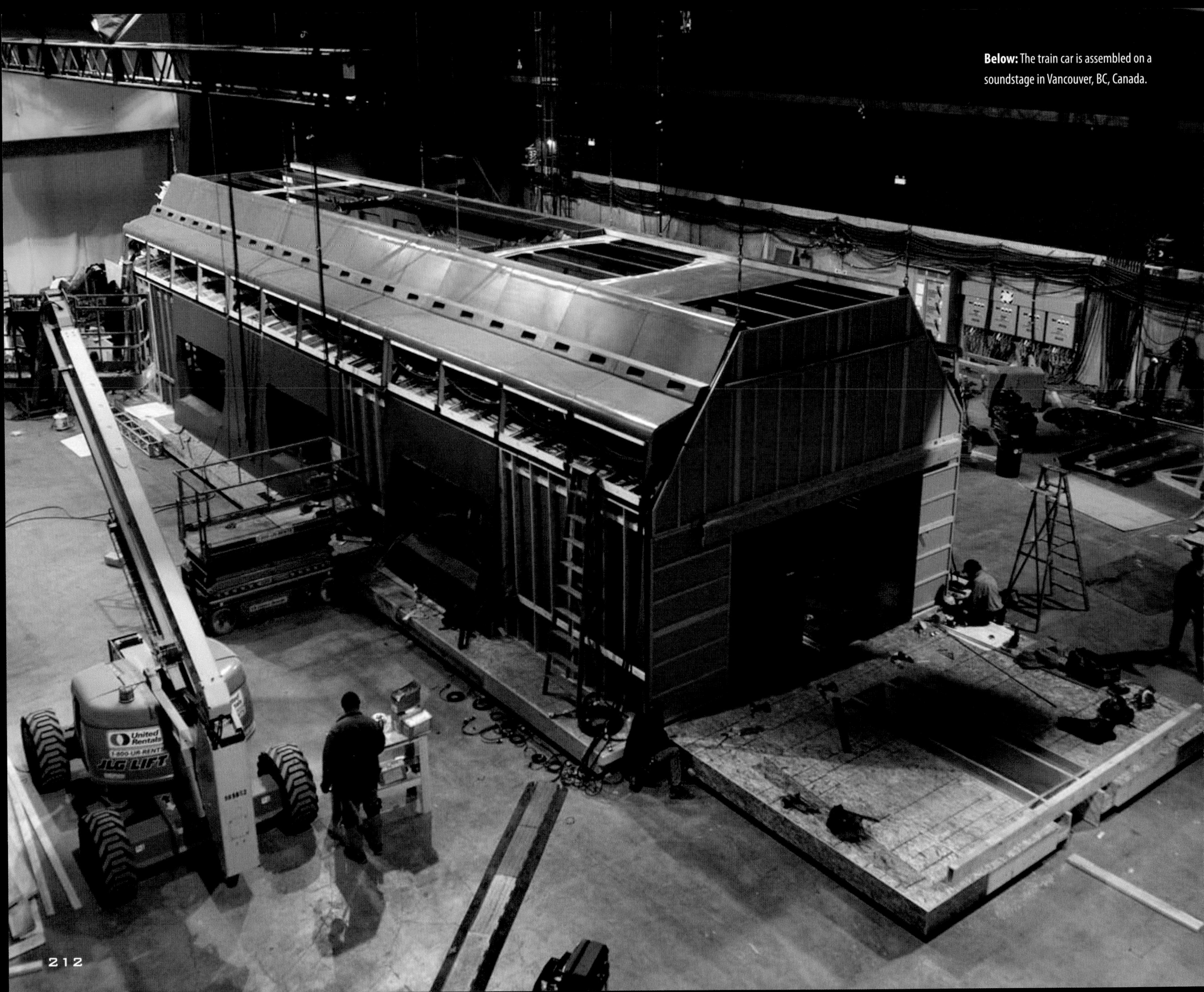

Below: The train car is assembled on a soundstage in Vancouver, BC, Canada.

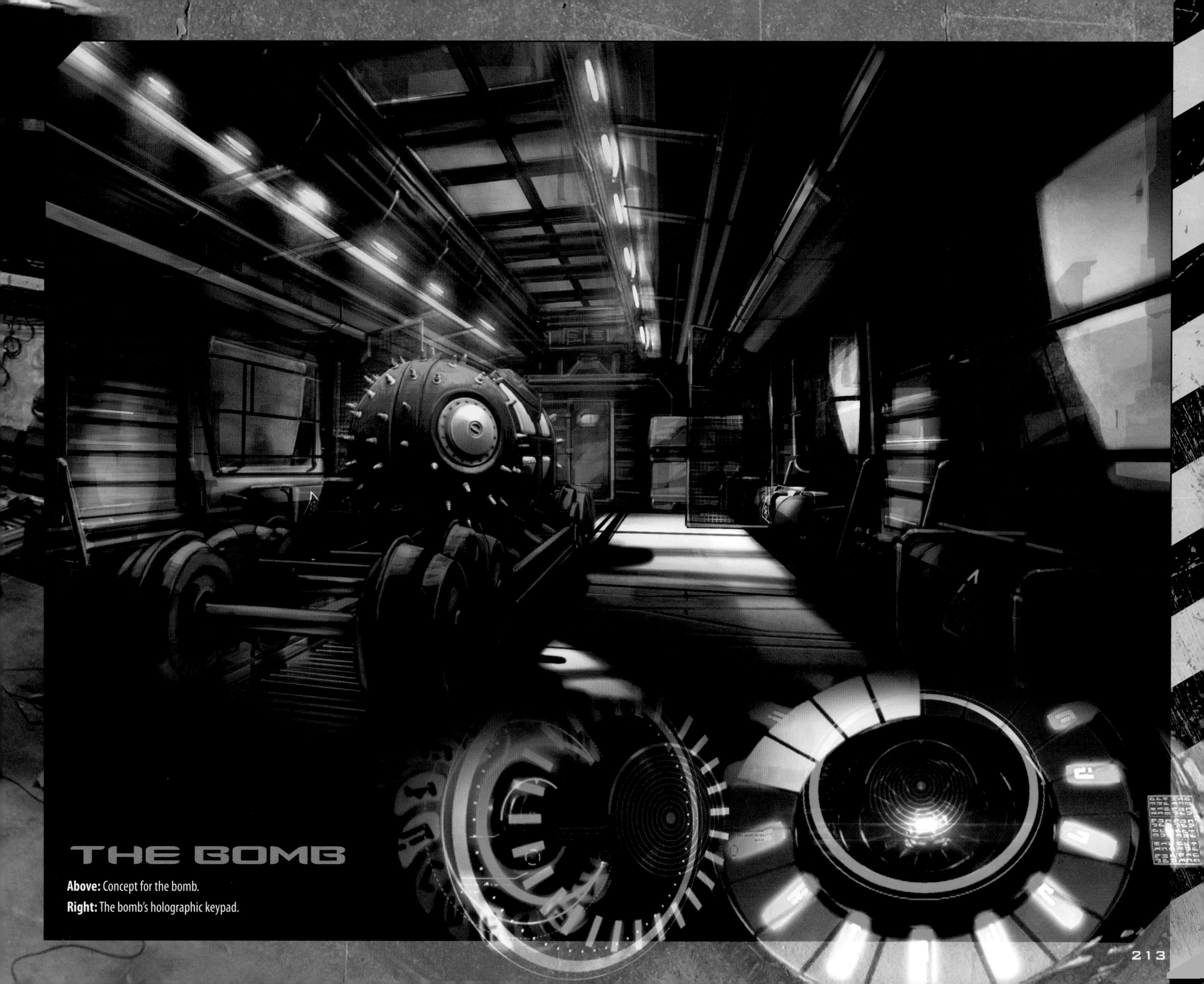

THE BOMB

Above: Concept for the bomb.

Right: The bomb's holographic keypad.

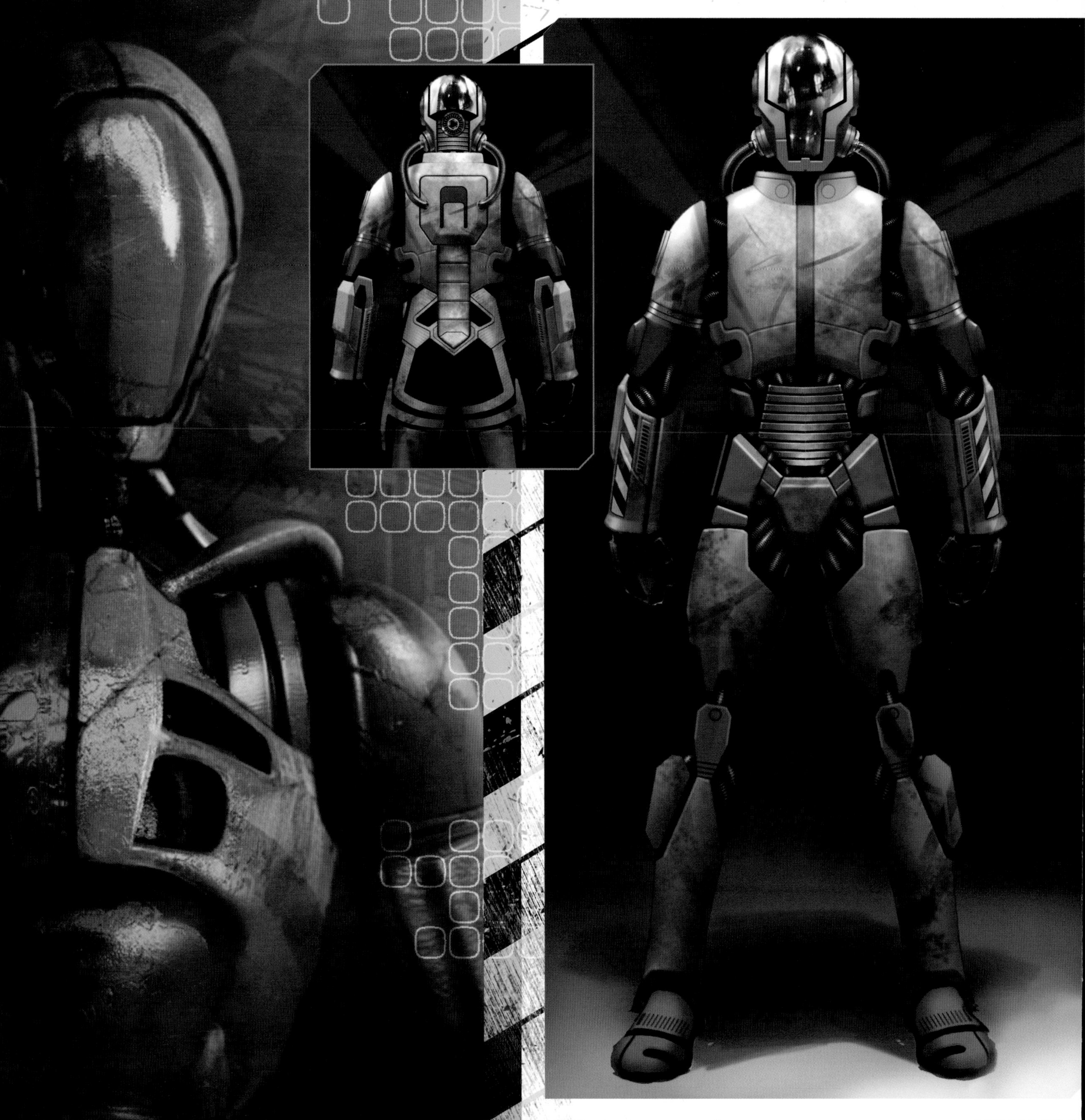

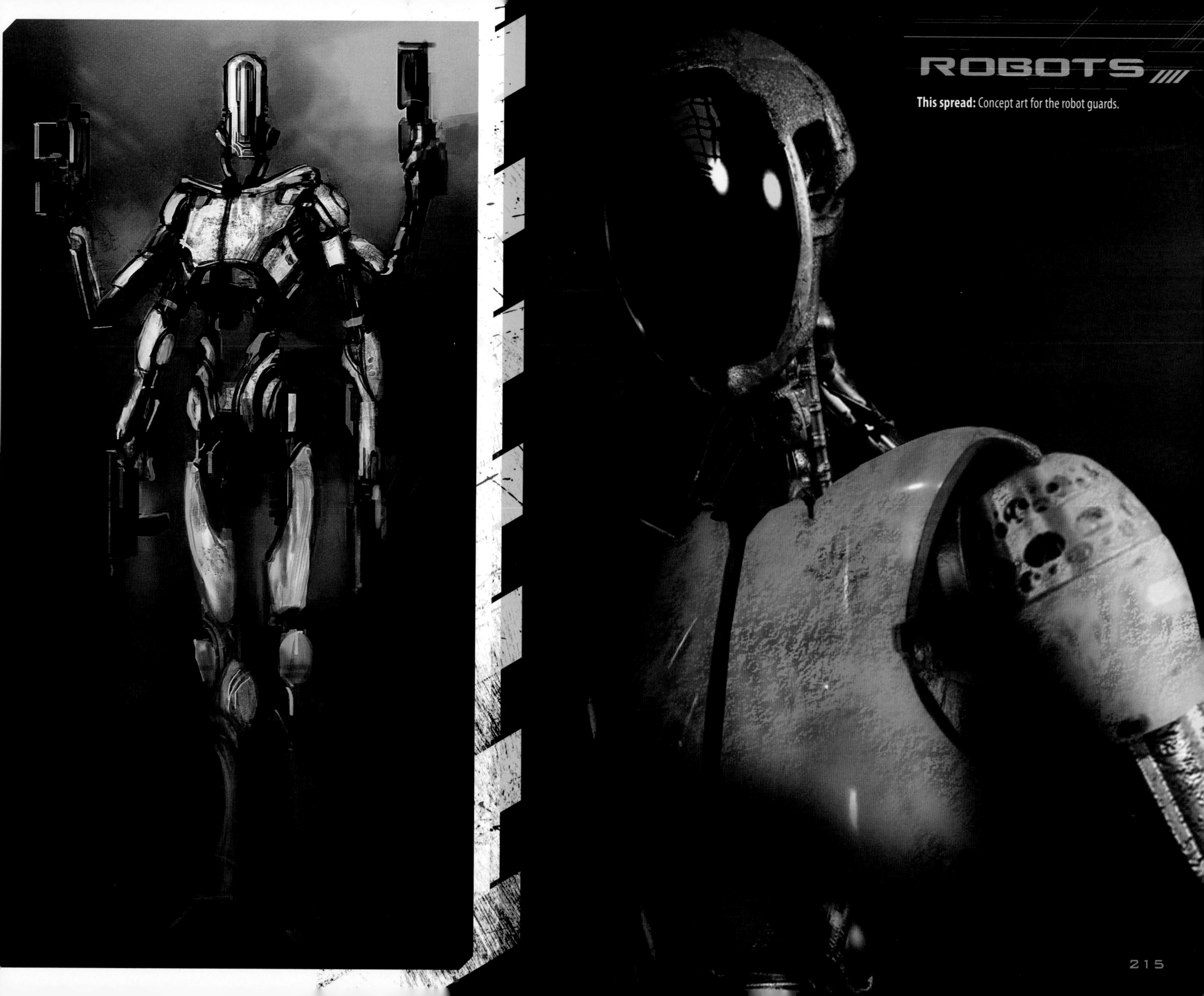

ROBOTS

This spread: Concept art for the robot guards.

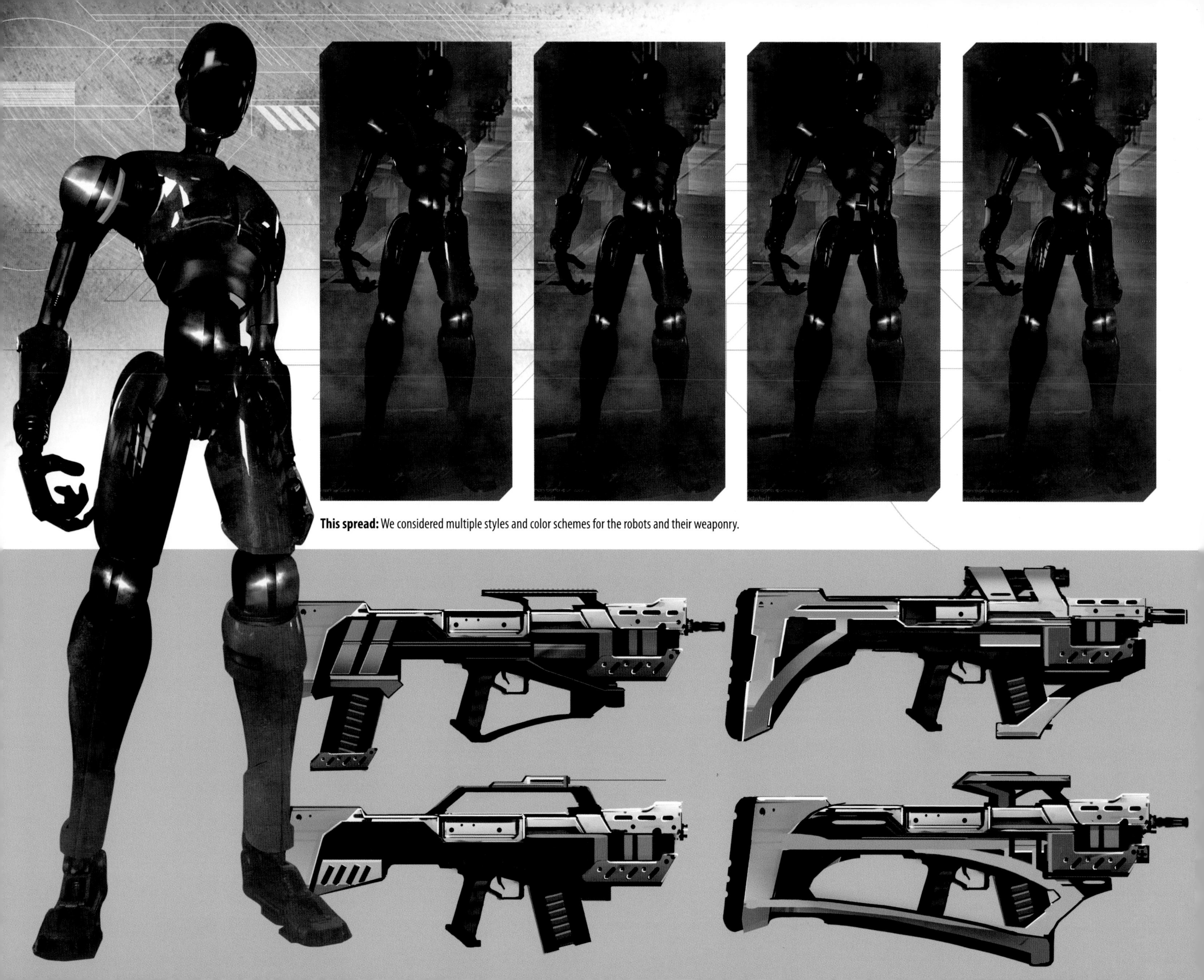

This spread: We considered multiple styles and color schemes for the robots and their weaponry.

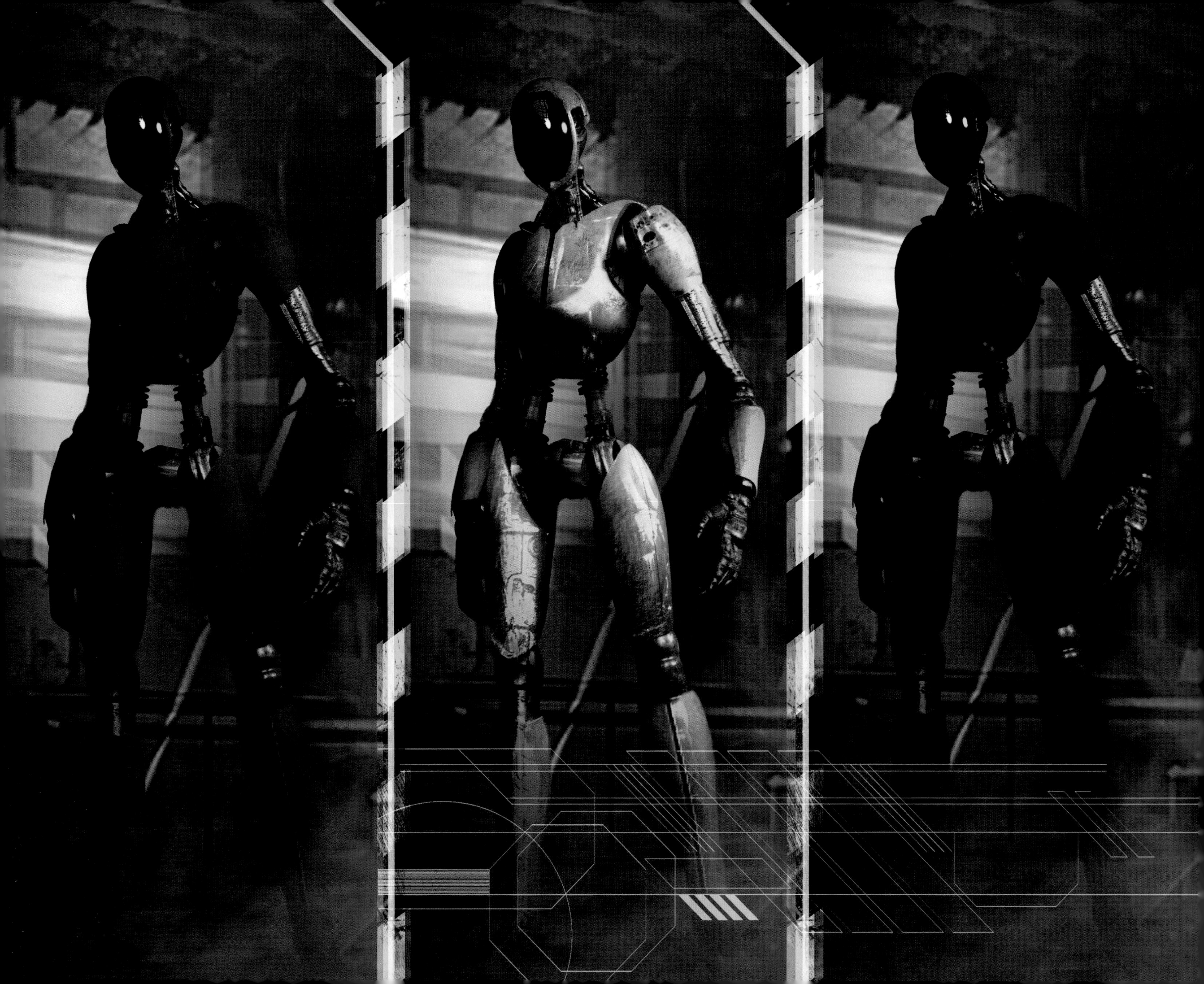

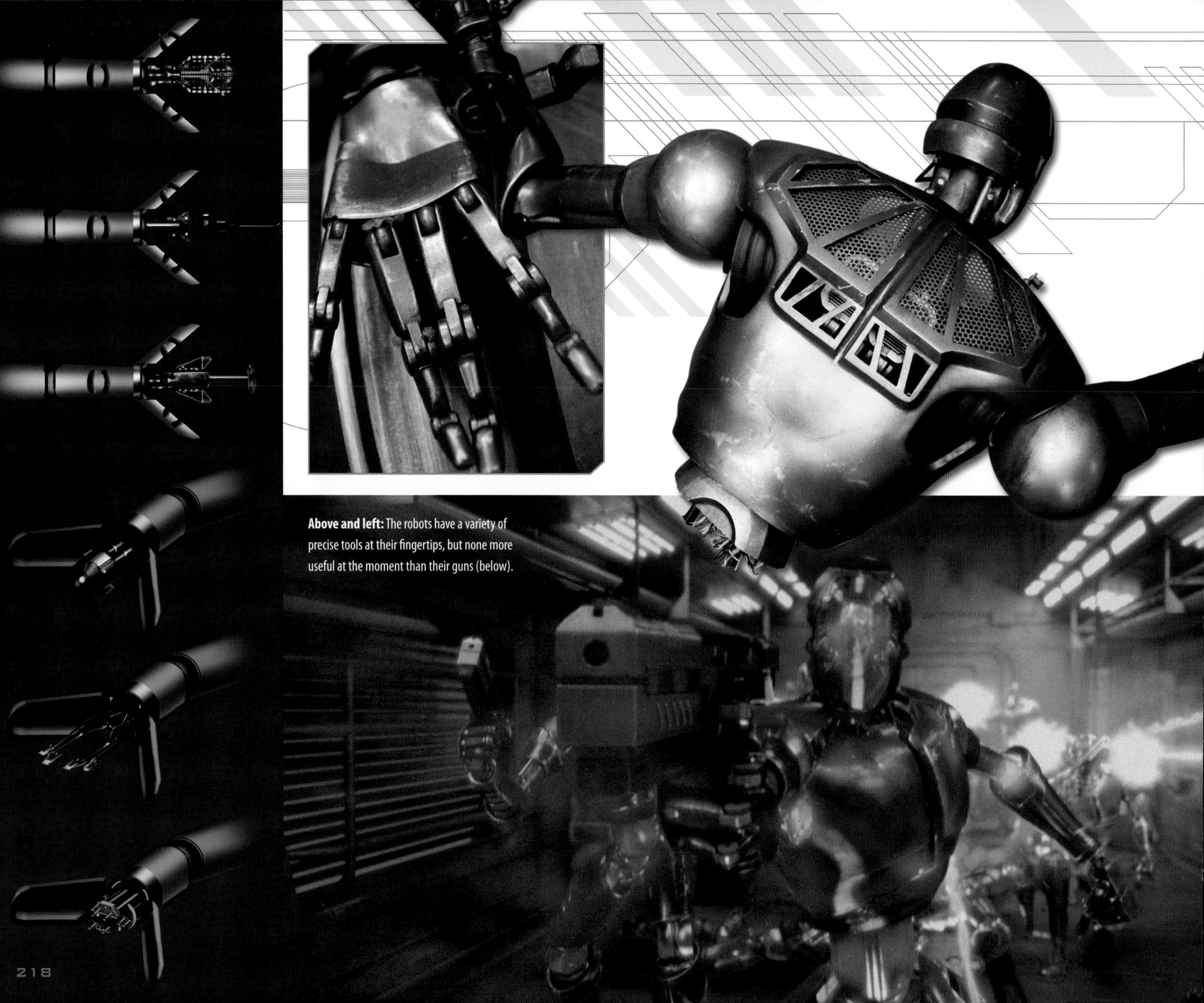

Above and left: The robots have a variety of precise tools at their fingertips, but none more useful at the moment than their guns (below).

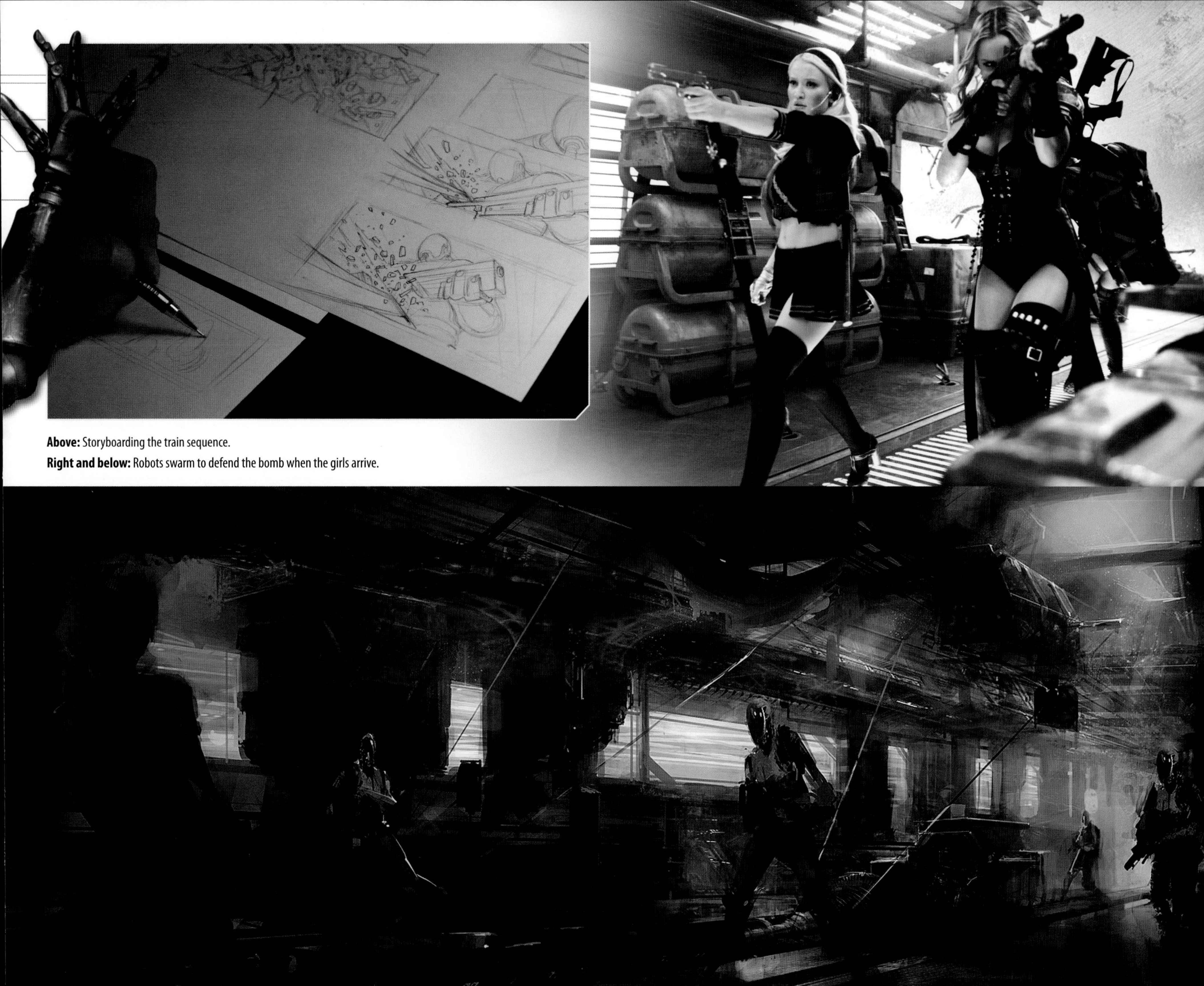

Above: Storyboarding the train sequence.

Right and below: Robots swarm to defend the bomb when the girls arrive.

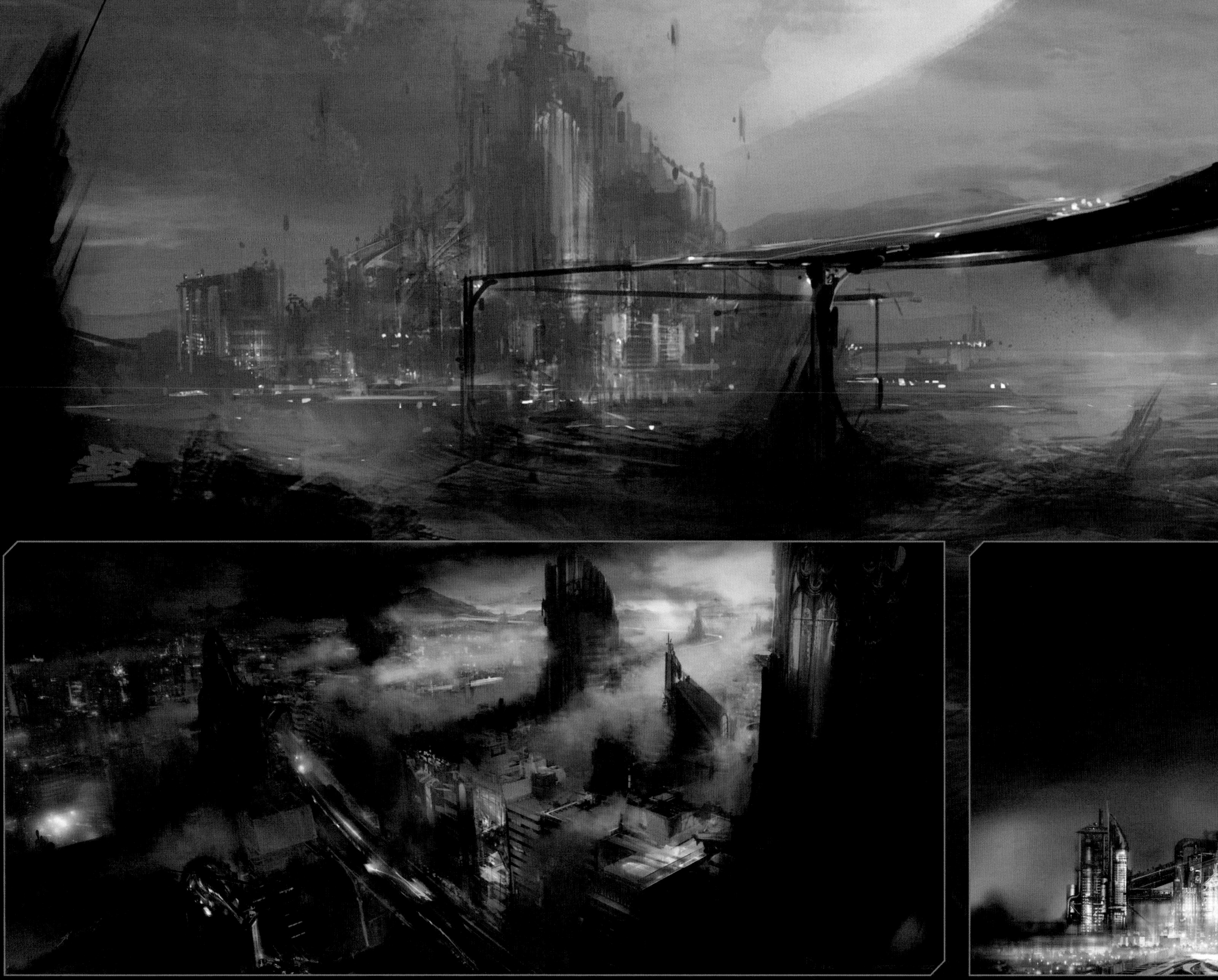

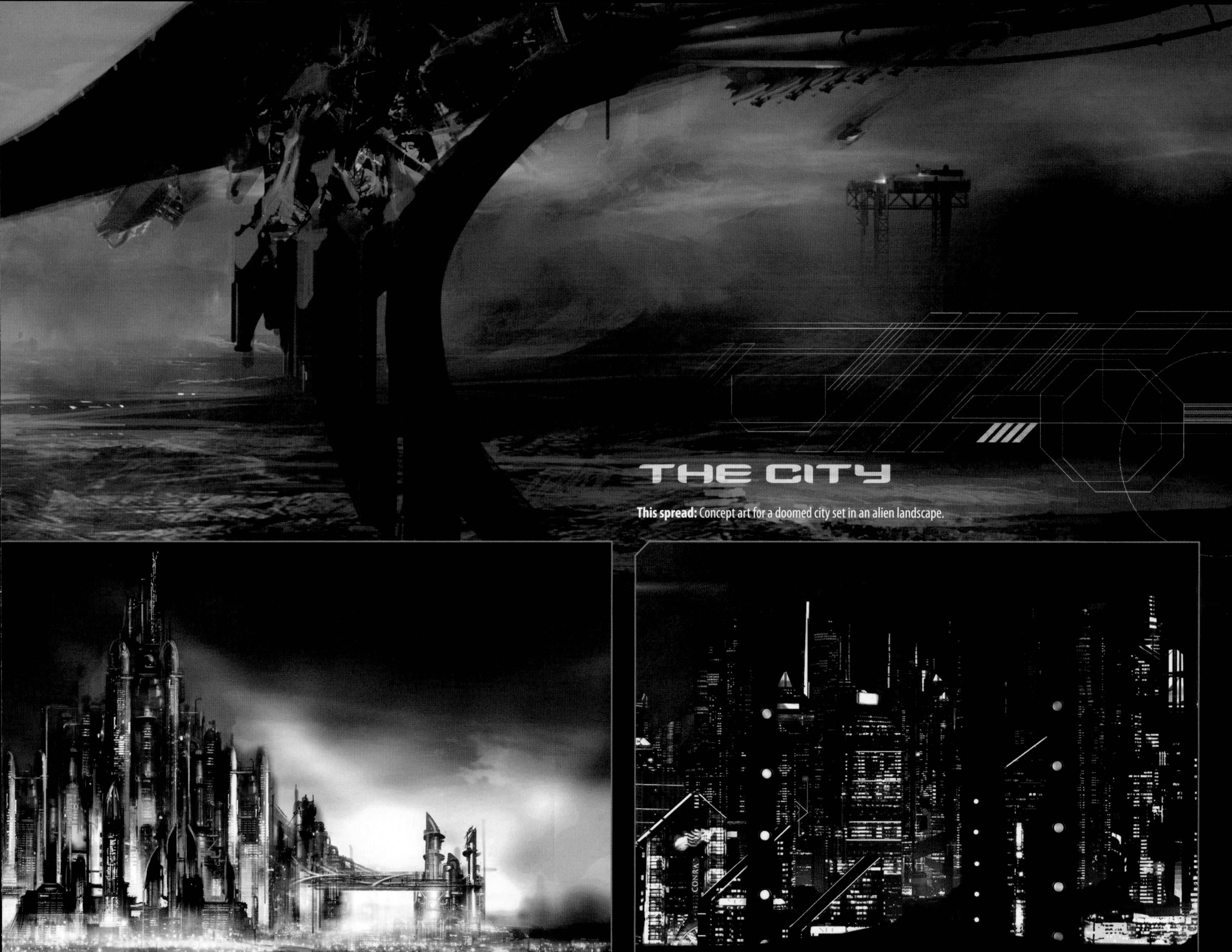

THE CITY

This spread: Concept art for a doomed city set in an alien landscape.

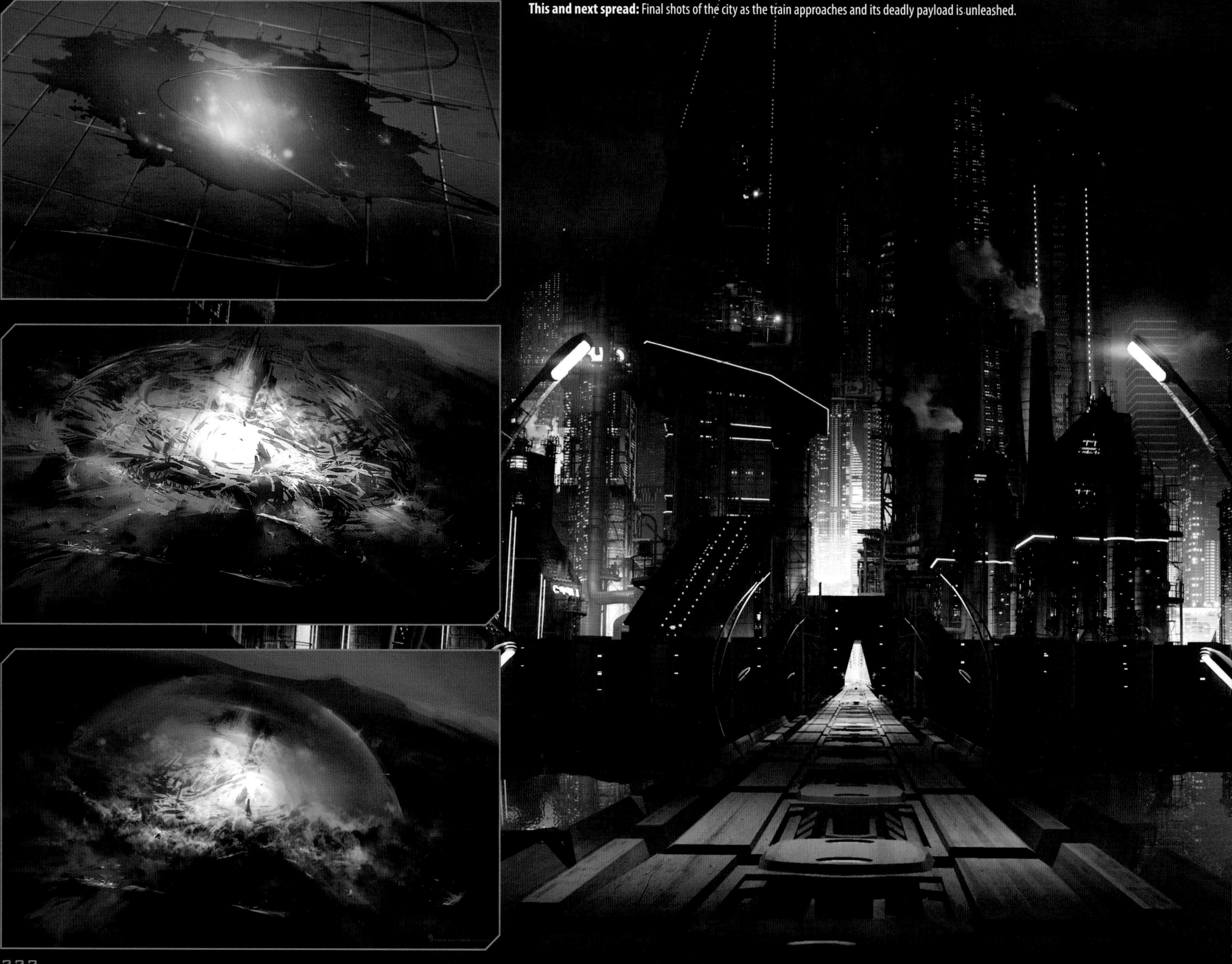

This and next spread: Final shots of the city as the train approaches and its deadly payload is unleashed.

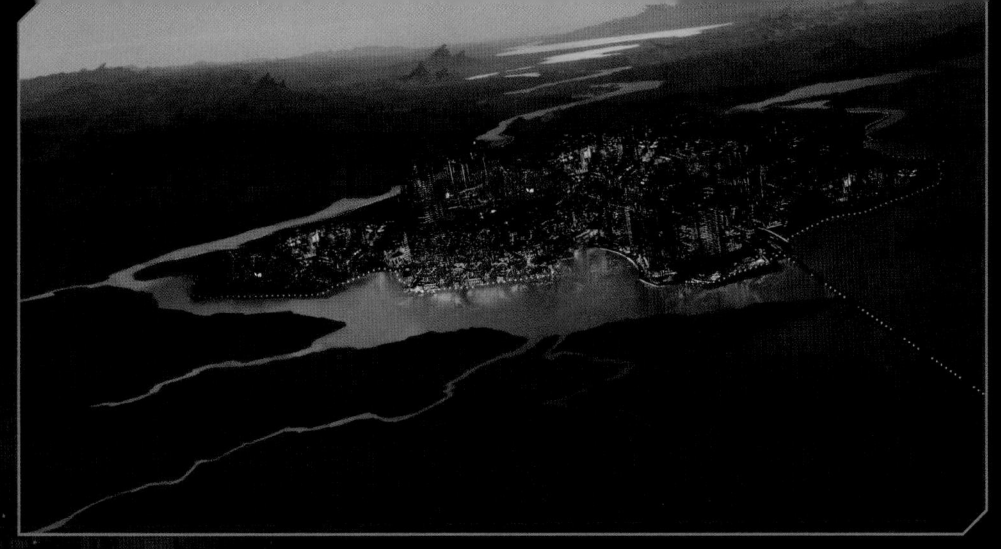

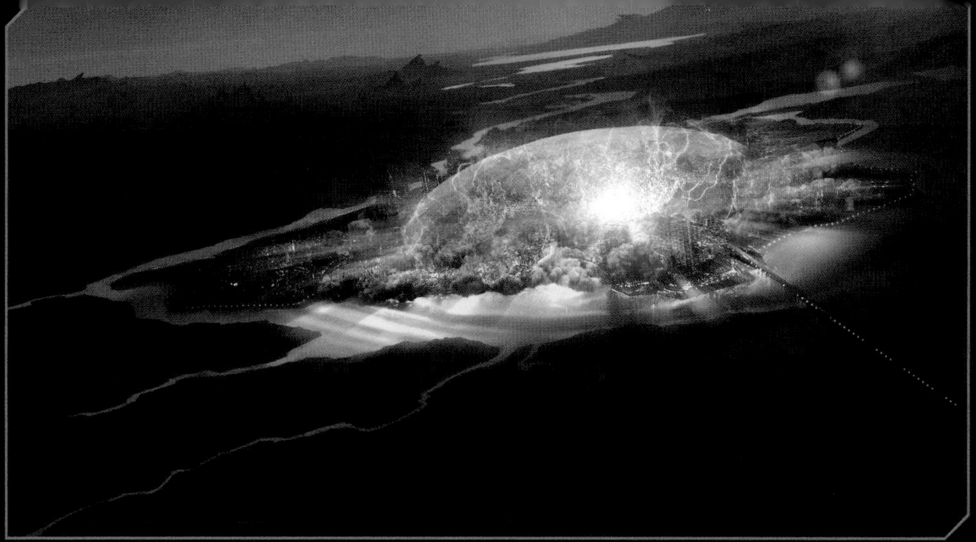

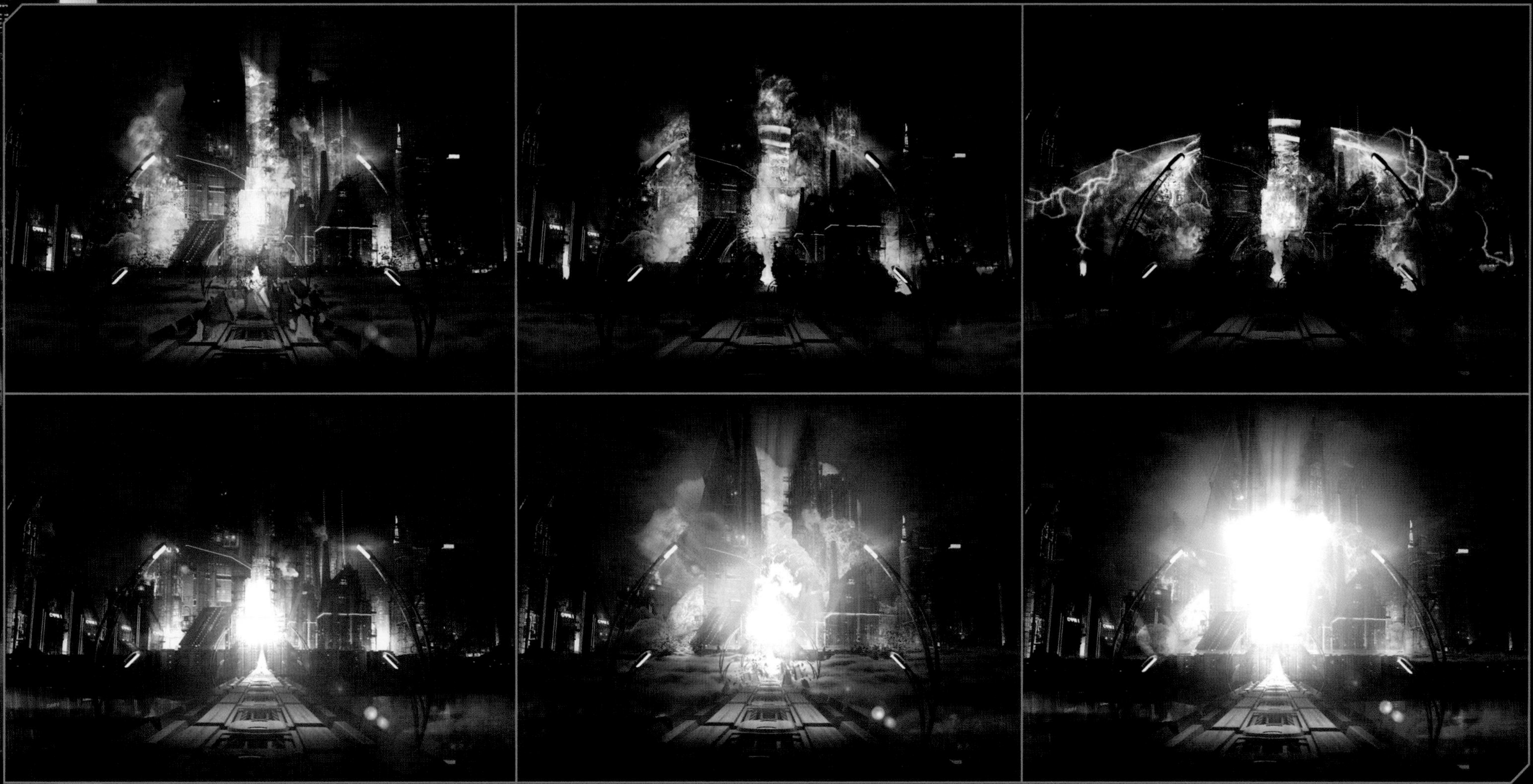

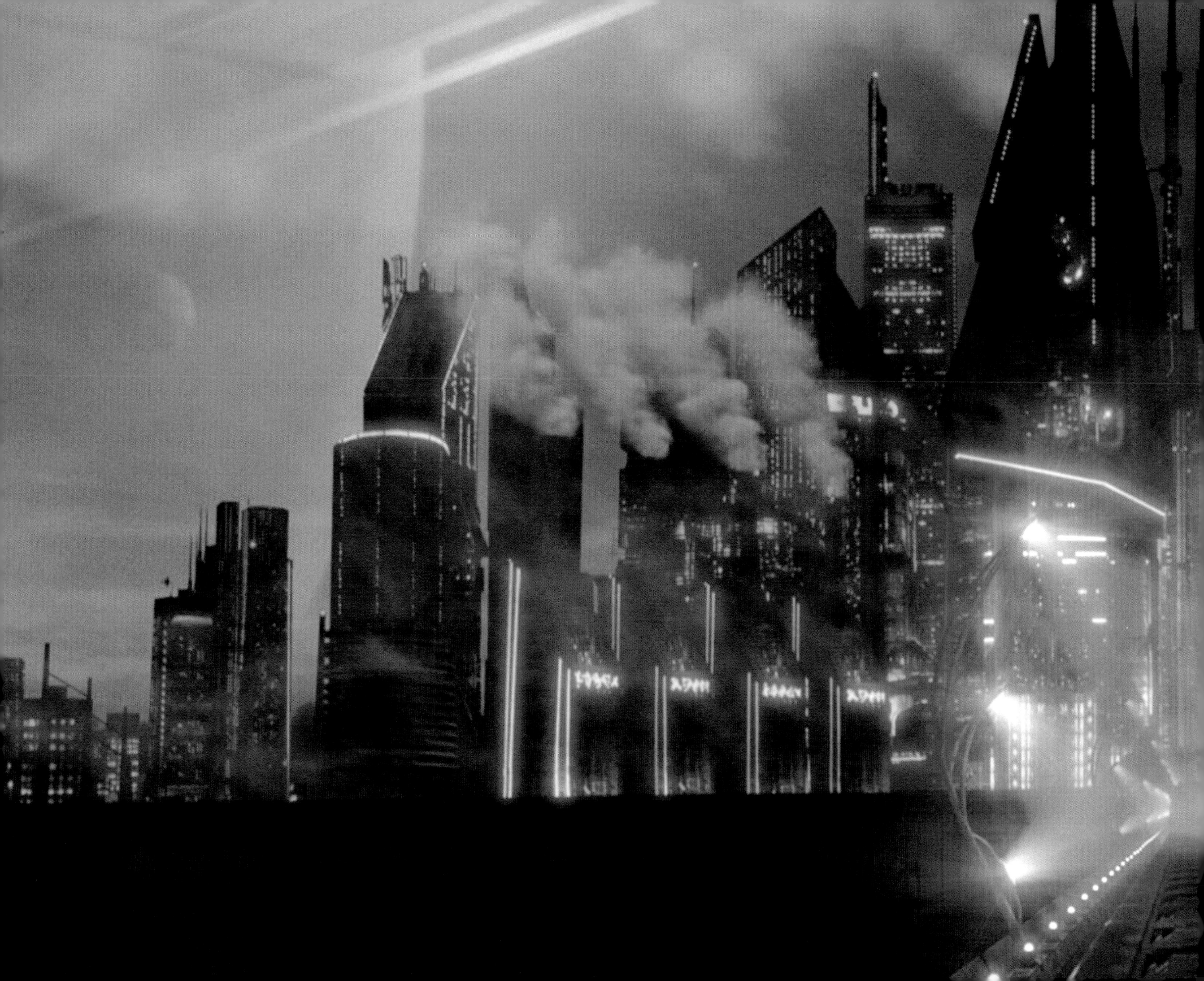

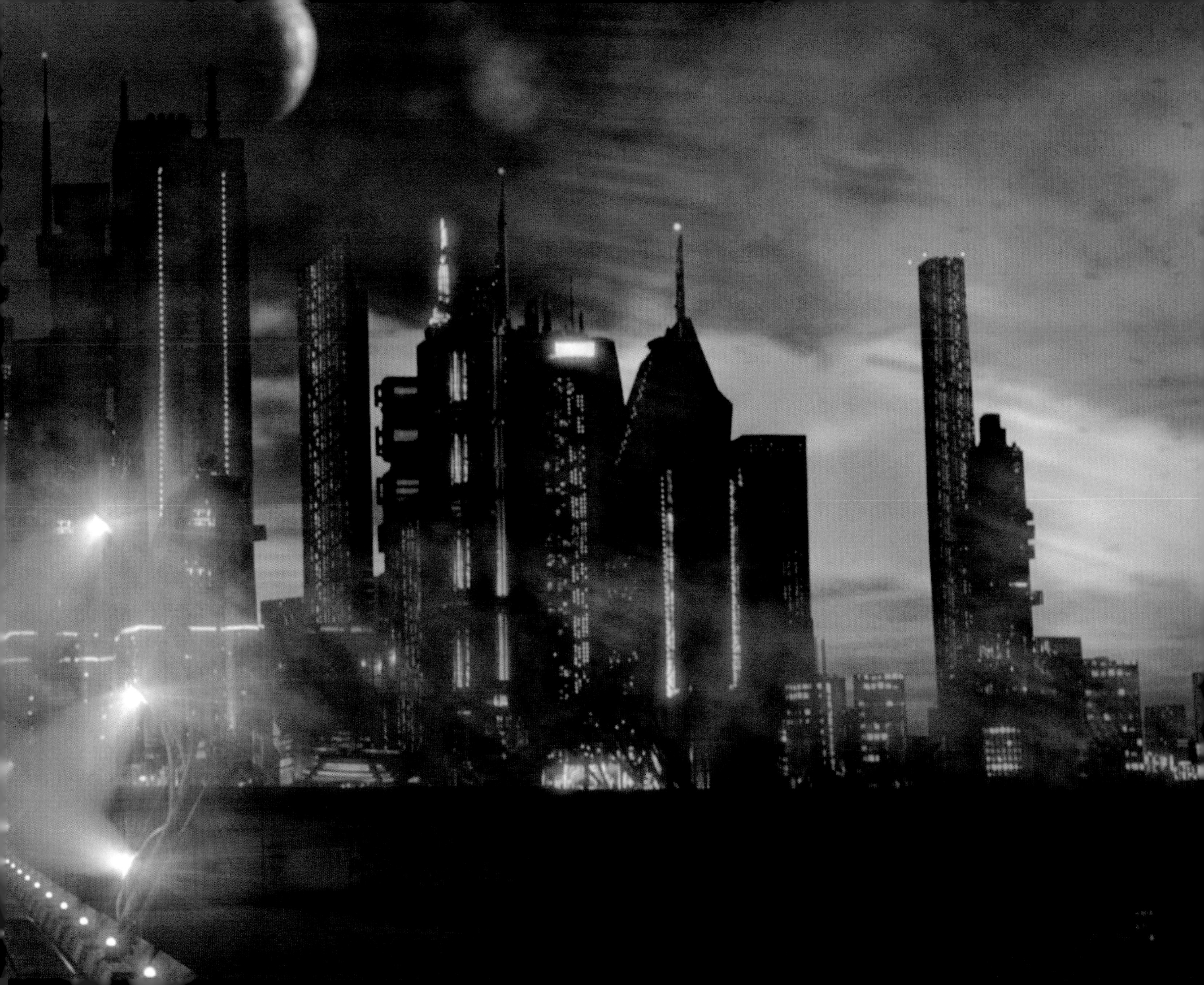

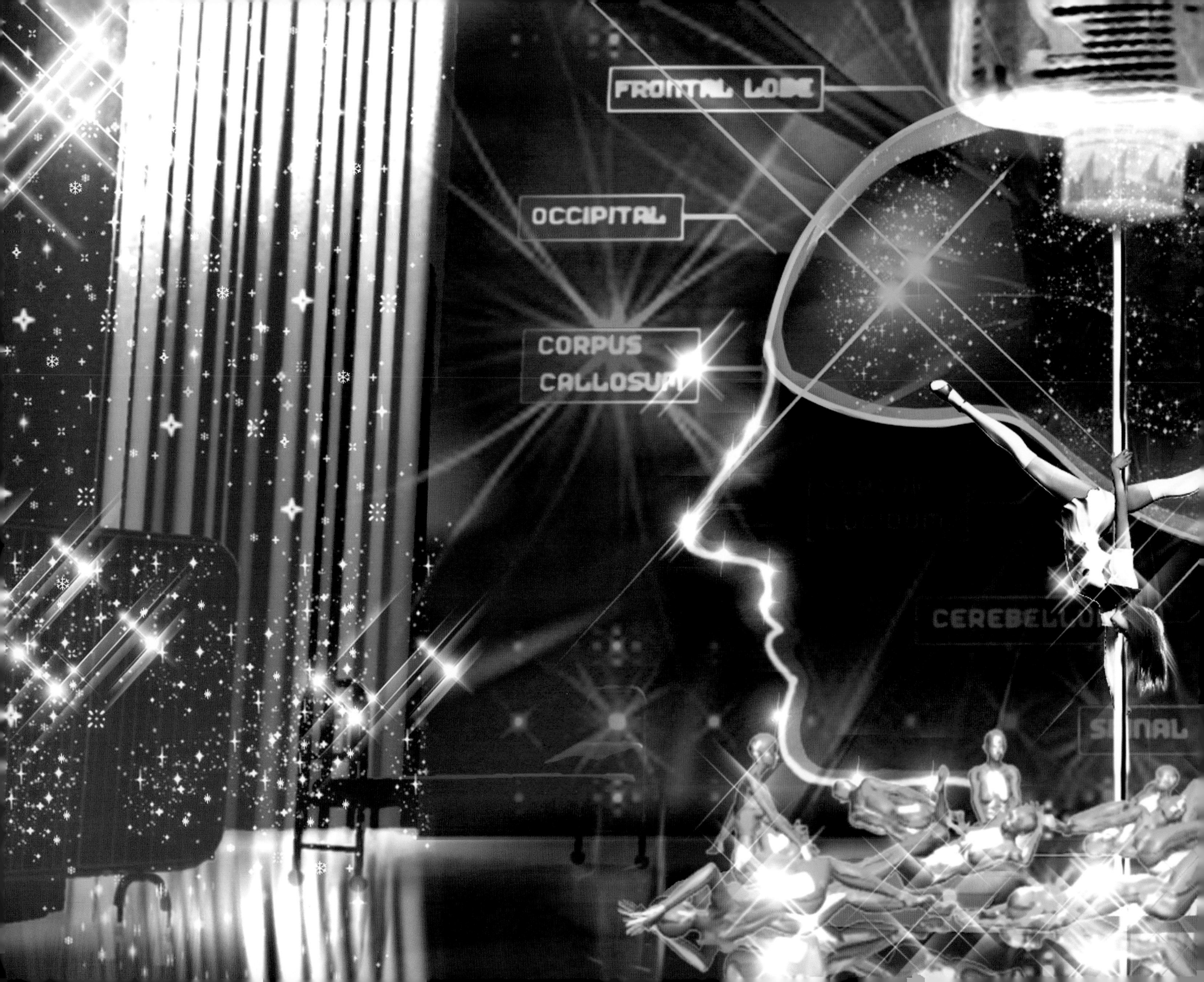

FRONTAL LOBE
OCCIPITAL
CORPUS
CALLOSUM

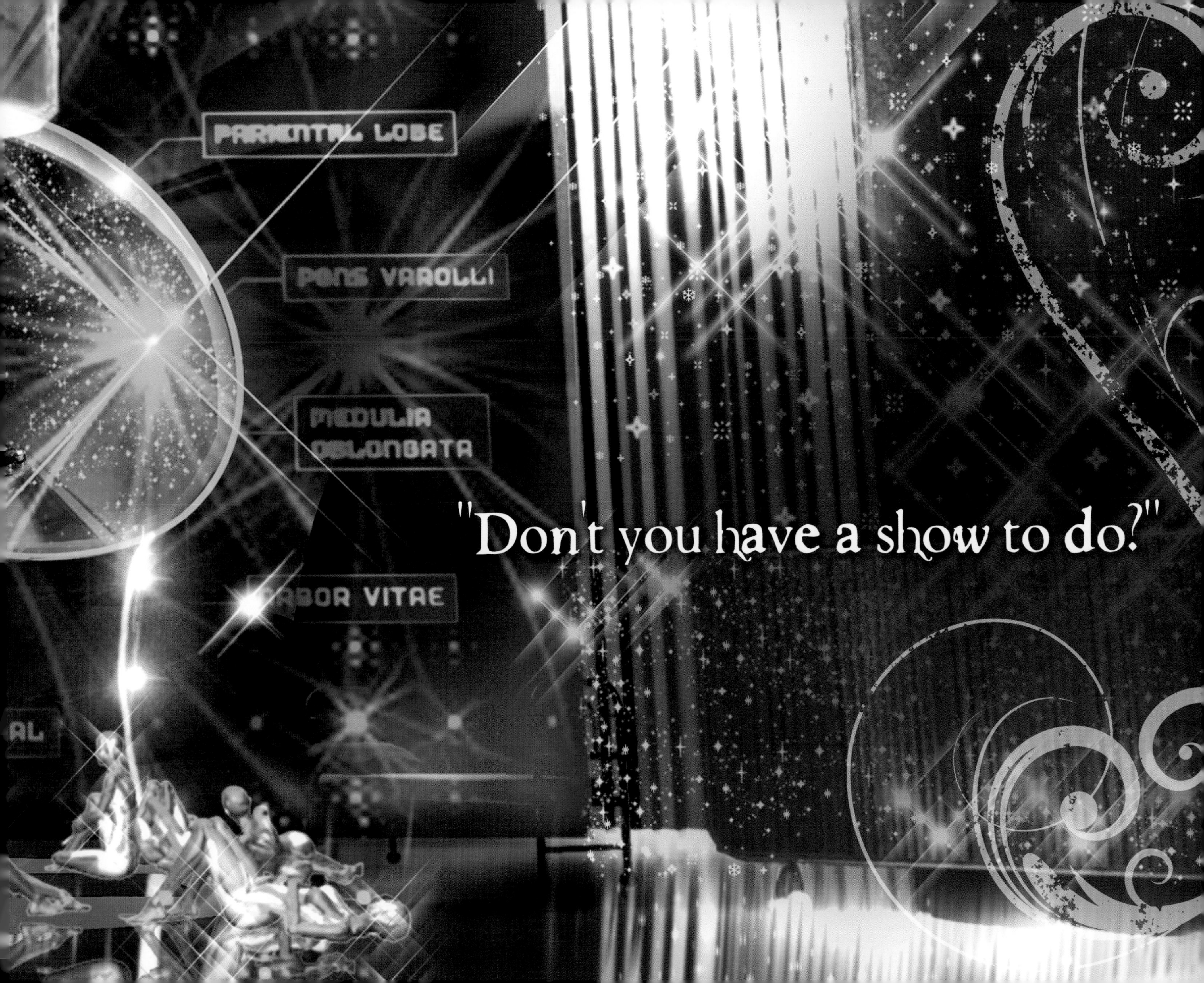
PARIENTAL LOBE
PONS VAROLLI
MEDULIA OBLONGATA
BOR VITAE
"Don't you have a show to do?"

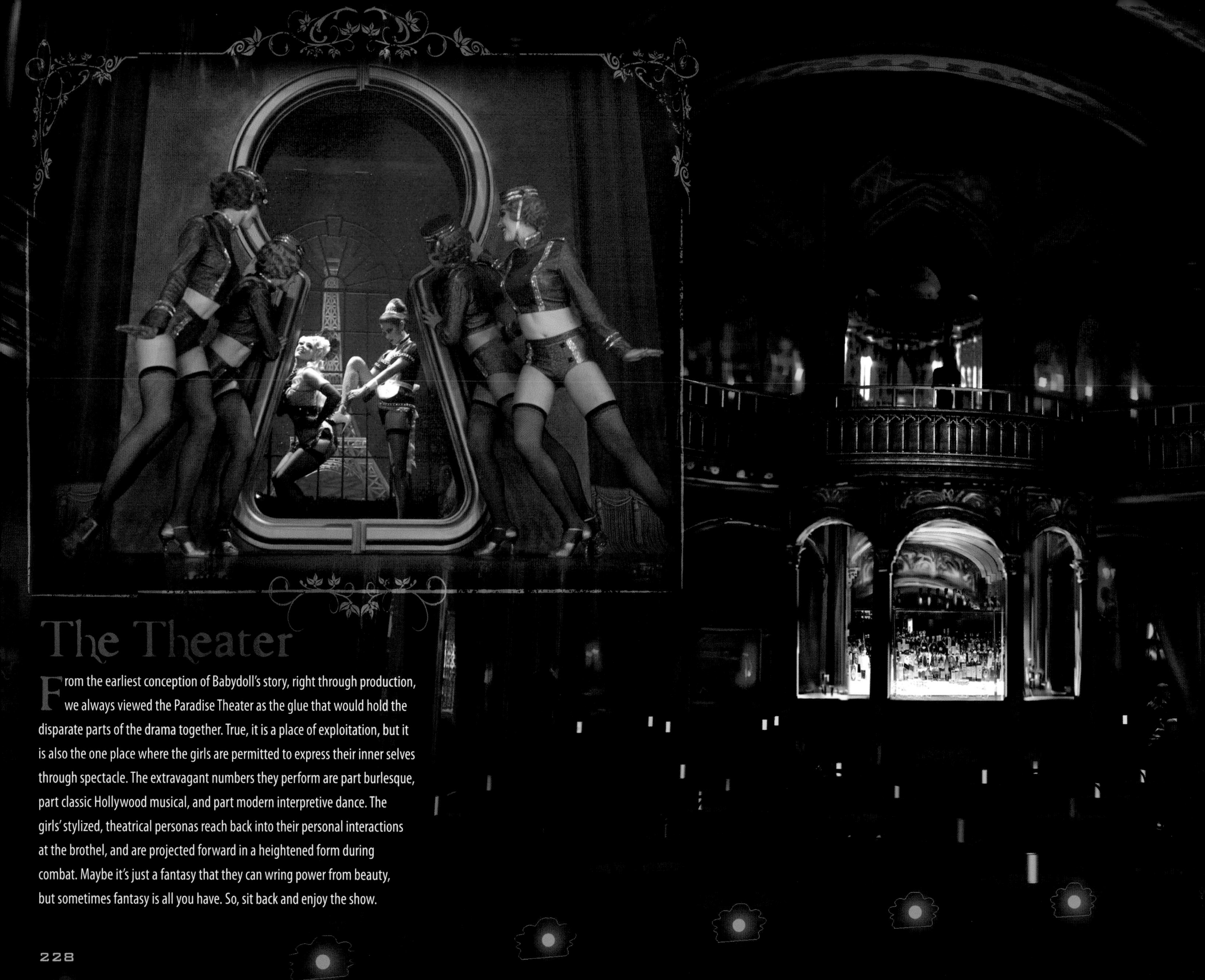

The Theater

From the earliest conception of Babydoll's story, right through production, we always viewed the Paradise Theater as the glue that would hold the disparate parts of the drama together. True, it is a place of exploitation, but it is also the one place where the girls are permitted to express their inner selves through spectacle. The extravagant numbers they perform are part burlesque, part classic Hollywood musical, and part modern interpretive dance. The girls' stylized, theatrical personas reach back into their personal interactions at the brothel, and are projected forward in a heightened form during combat. Maybe it's just a fantasy that they can wring power from beauty, but sometimes fantasy is all you have. So, sit back and enjoy the show.

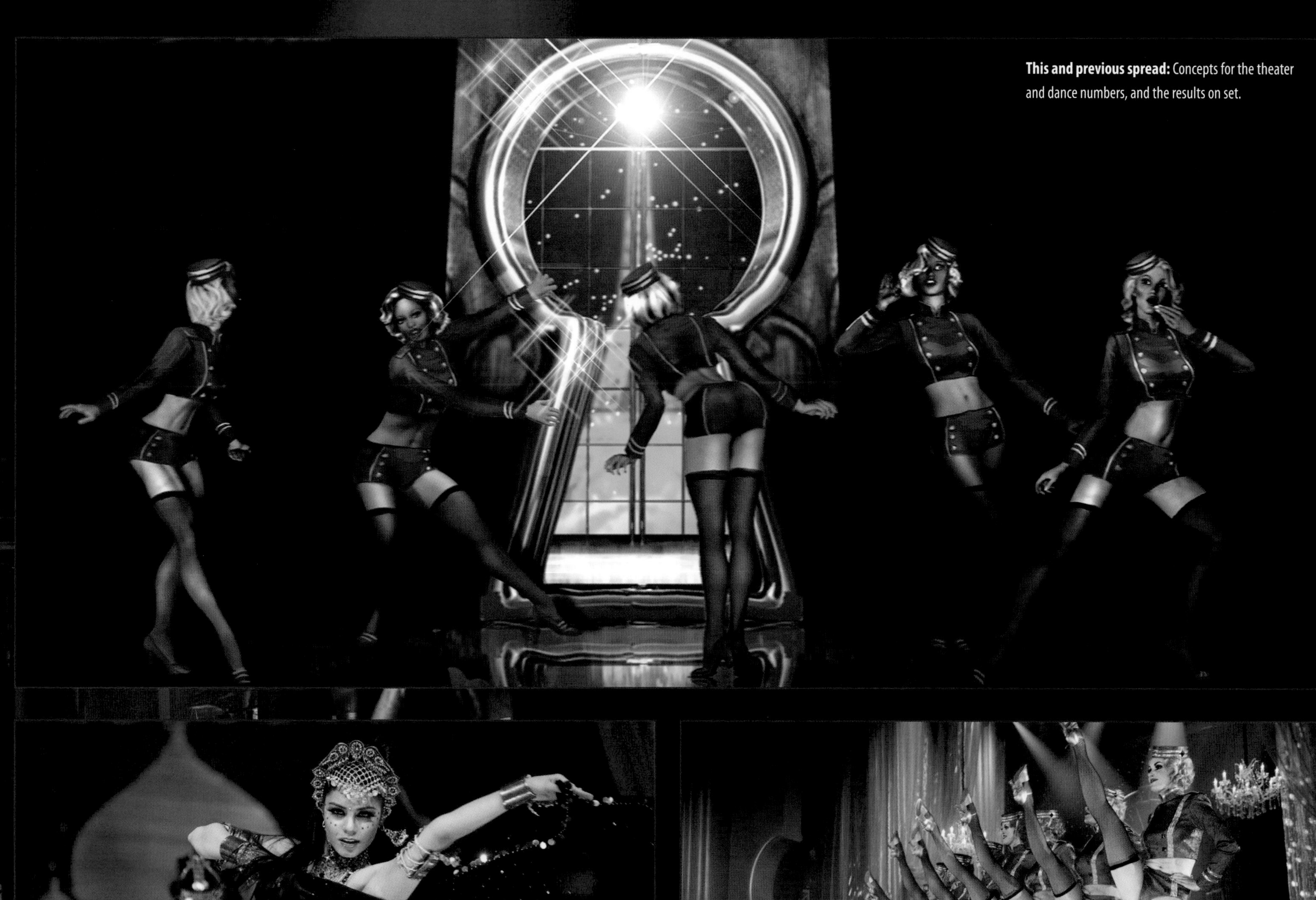

This and previous spread: Concepts for the theater and dance numbers, and the results on set.

Right: An attempt at making lobotomy sexy. **Rest of spread:** Concept art and an image of Sweet Pea's fiery dance into martydom.

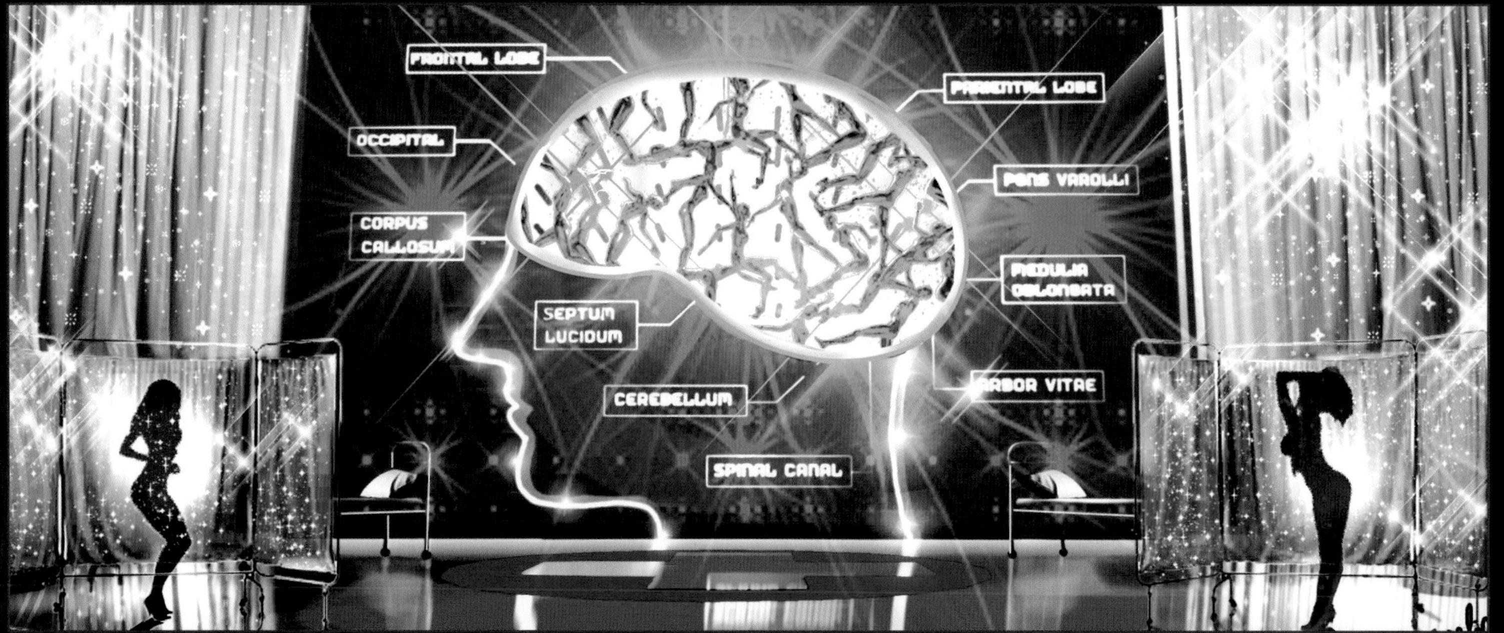

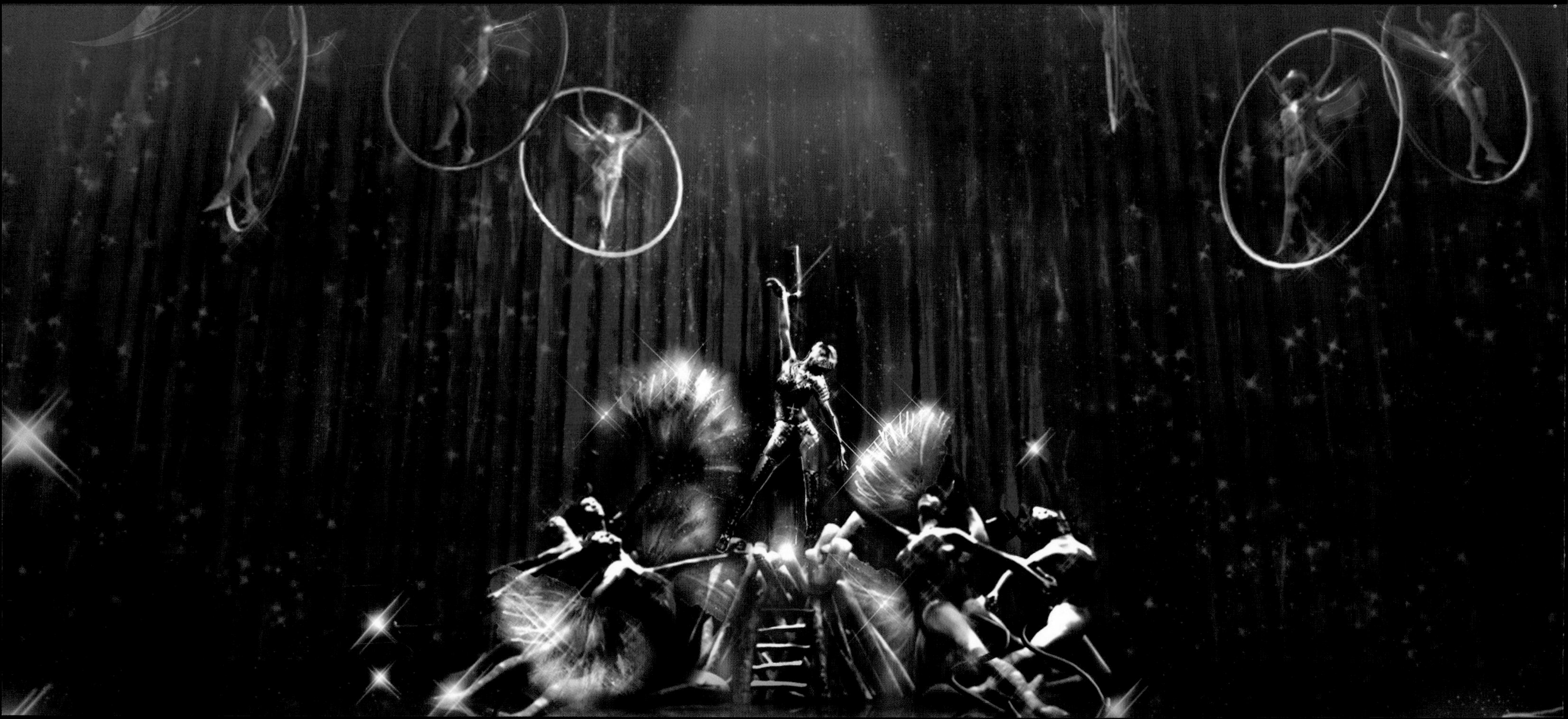

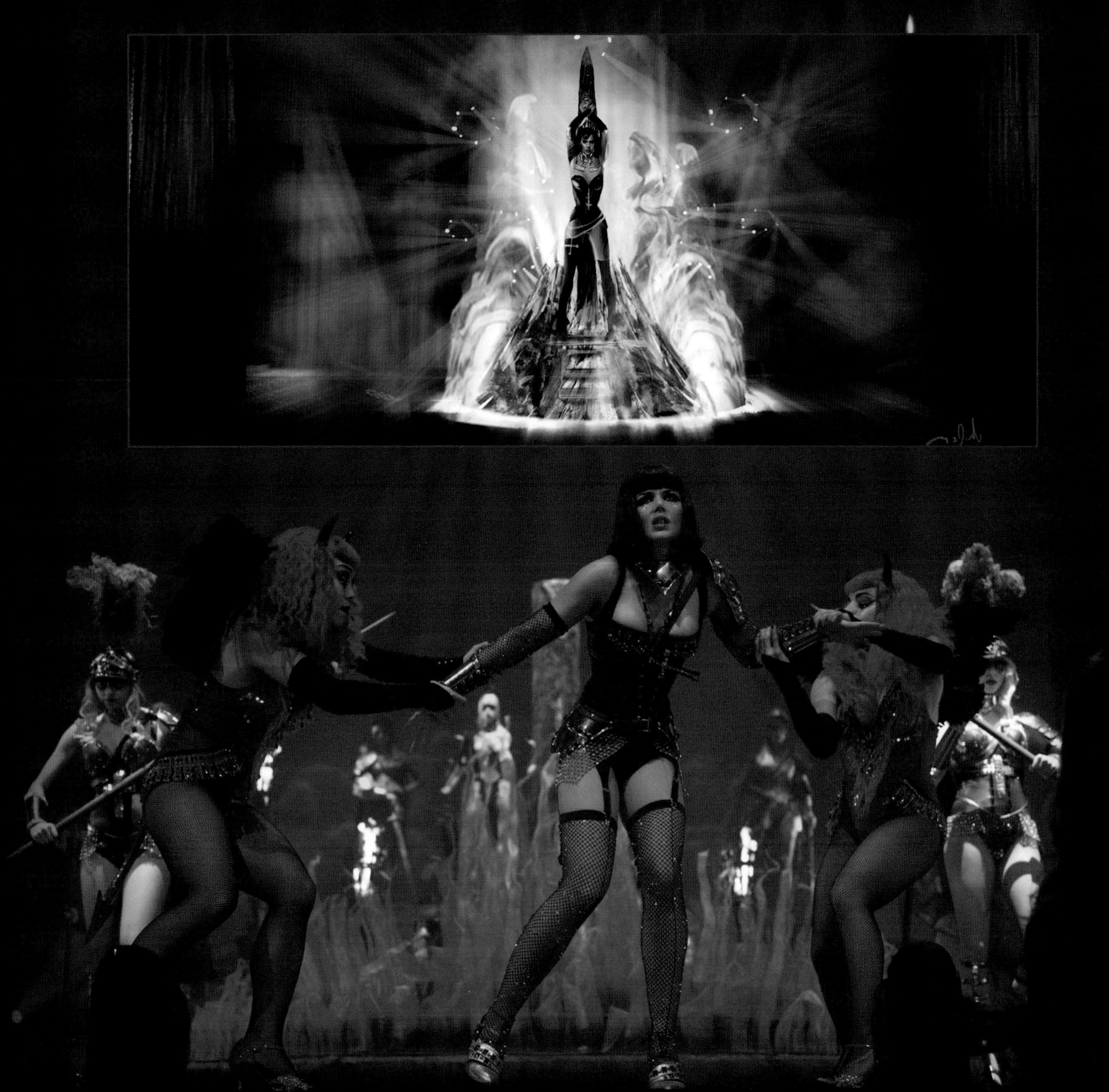

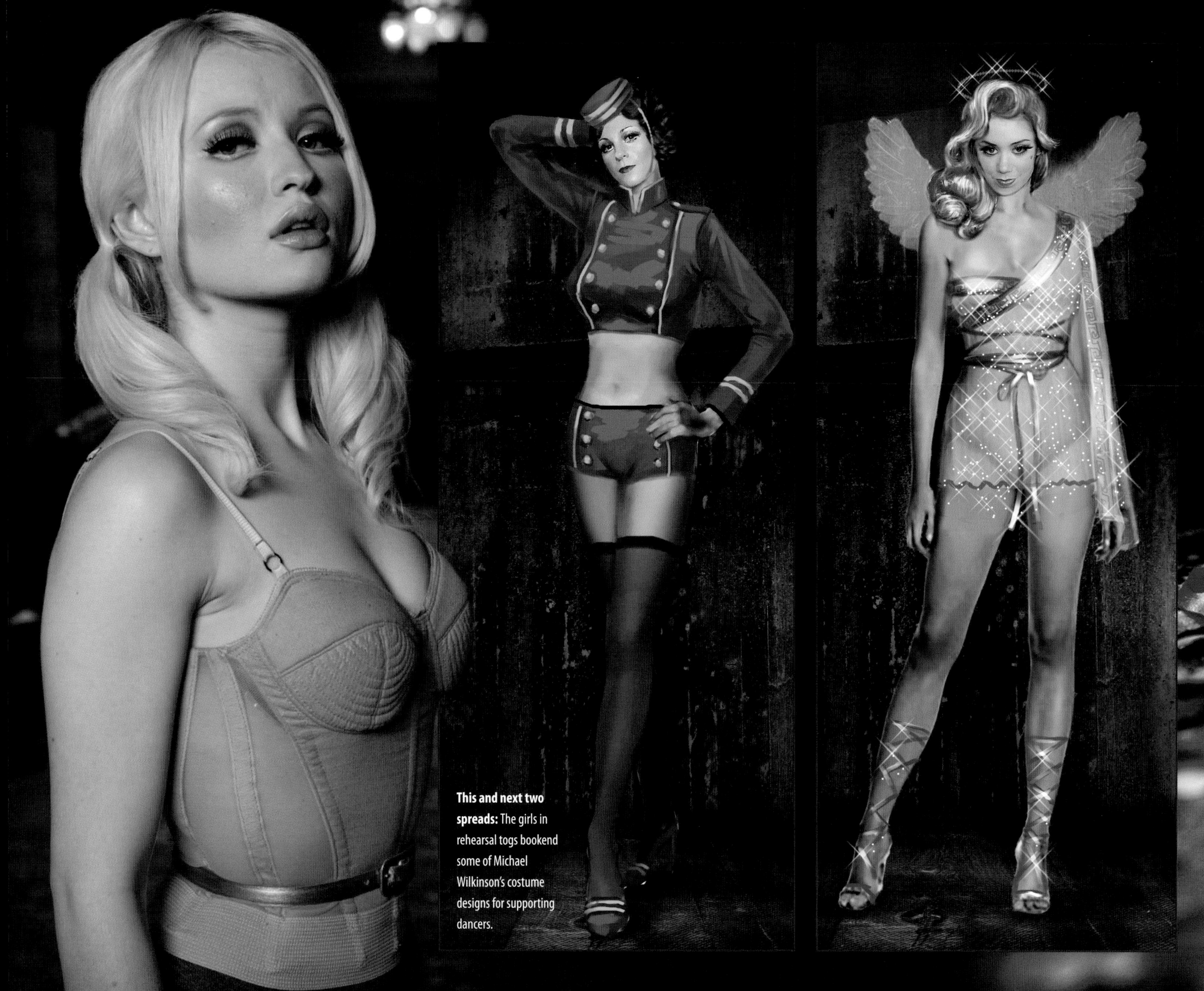

This and next two spreads: The girls in rehearsal togs bookend some of Michael Wilkinson's costume designs for supporting dancers.

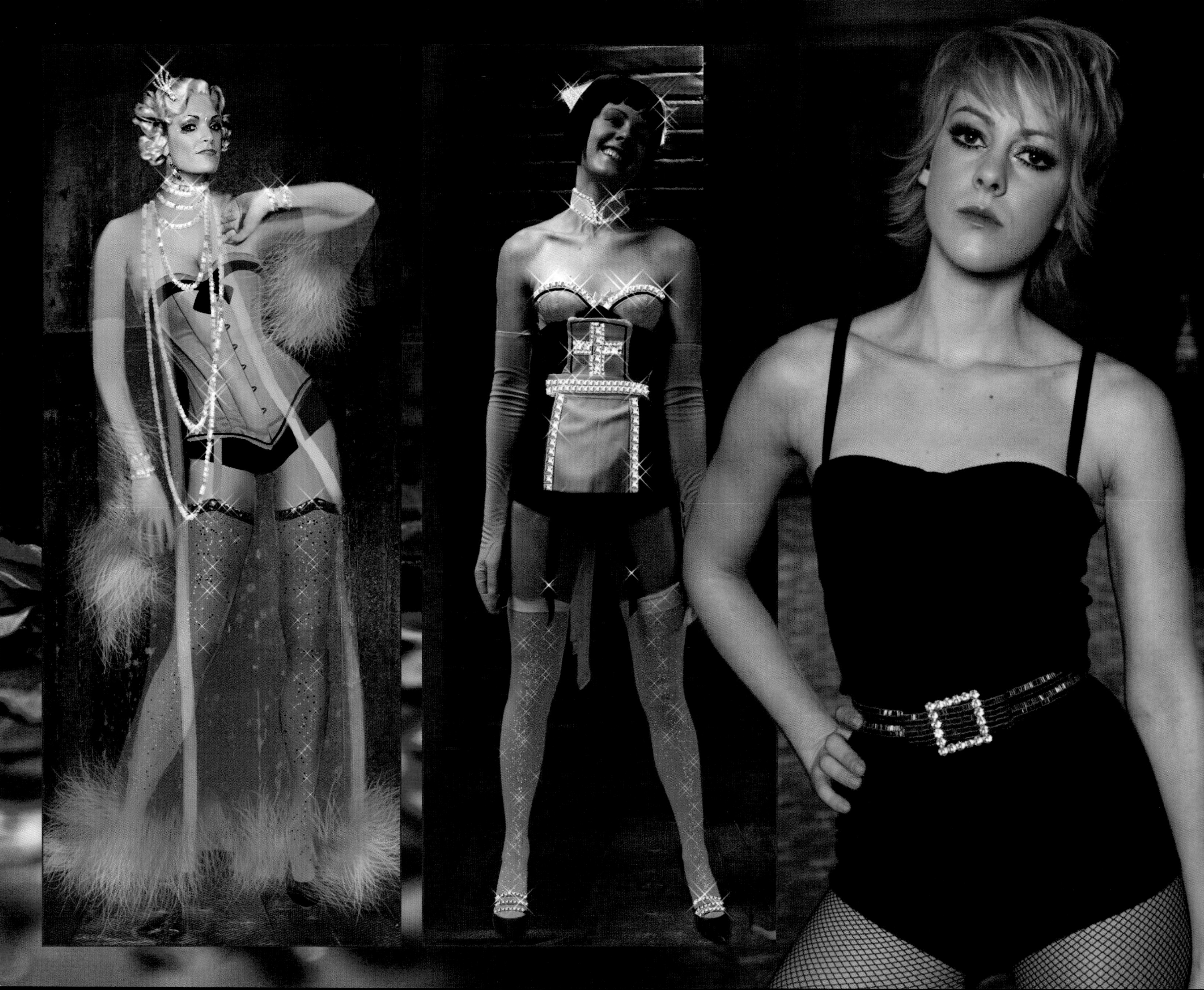

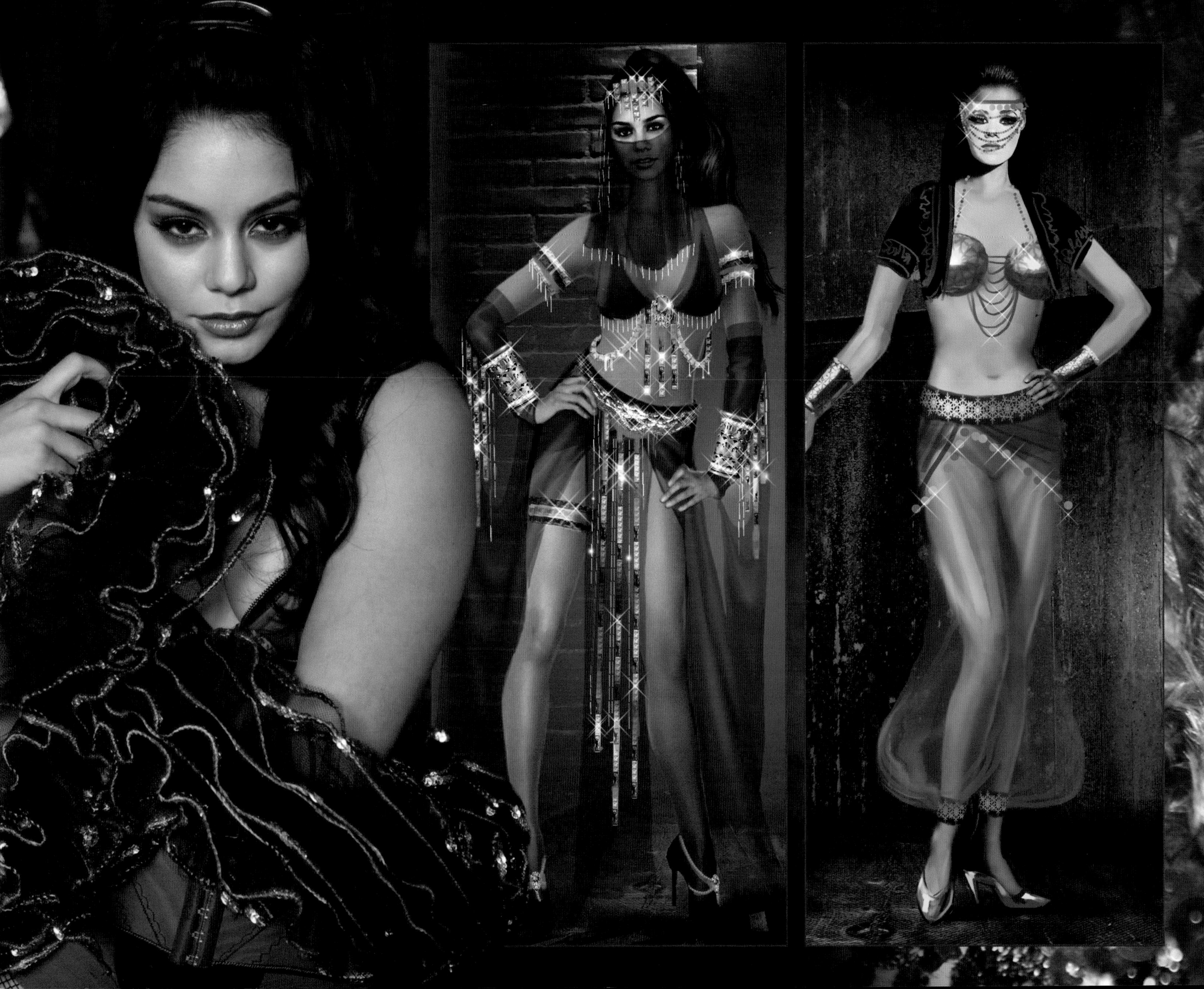

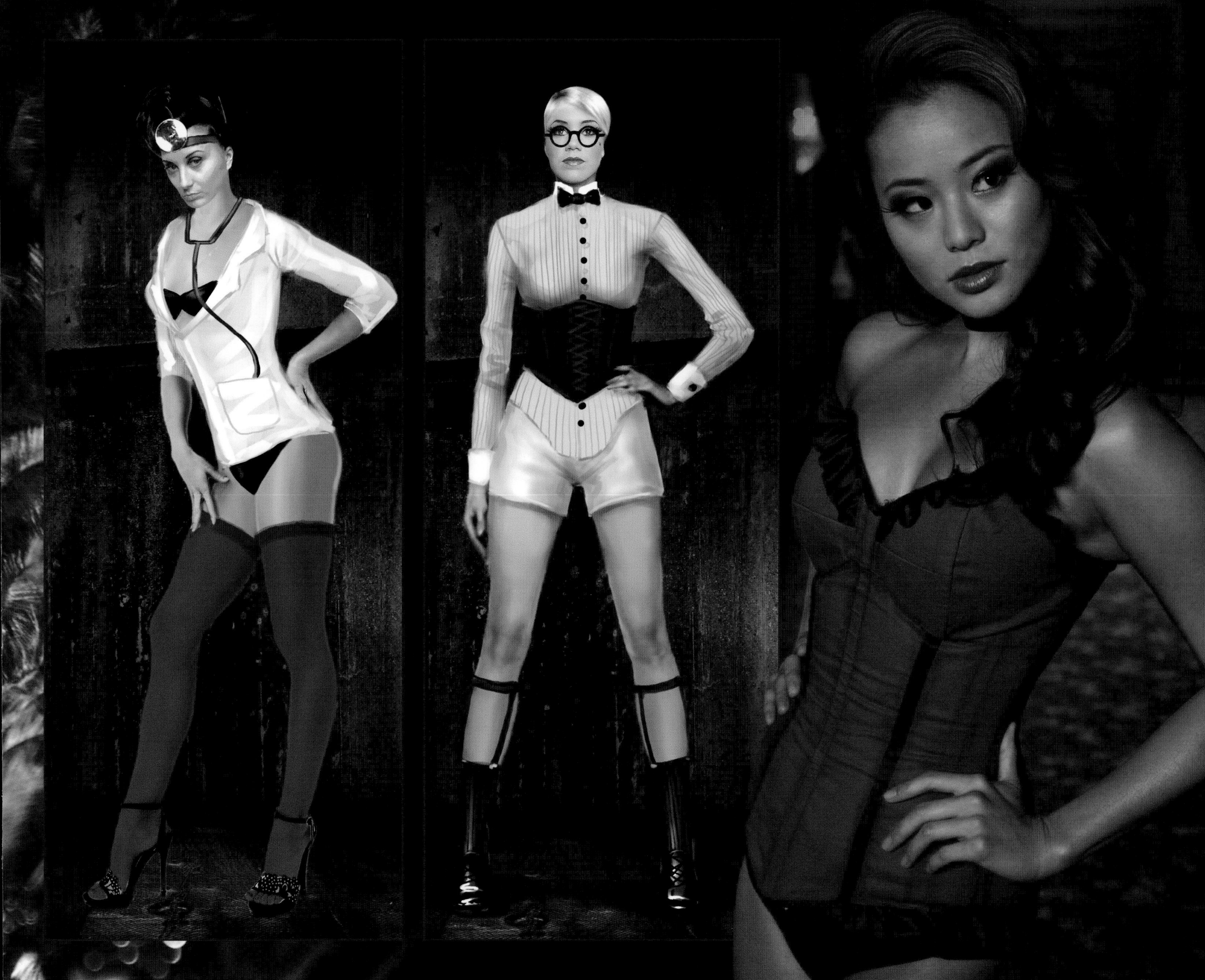

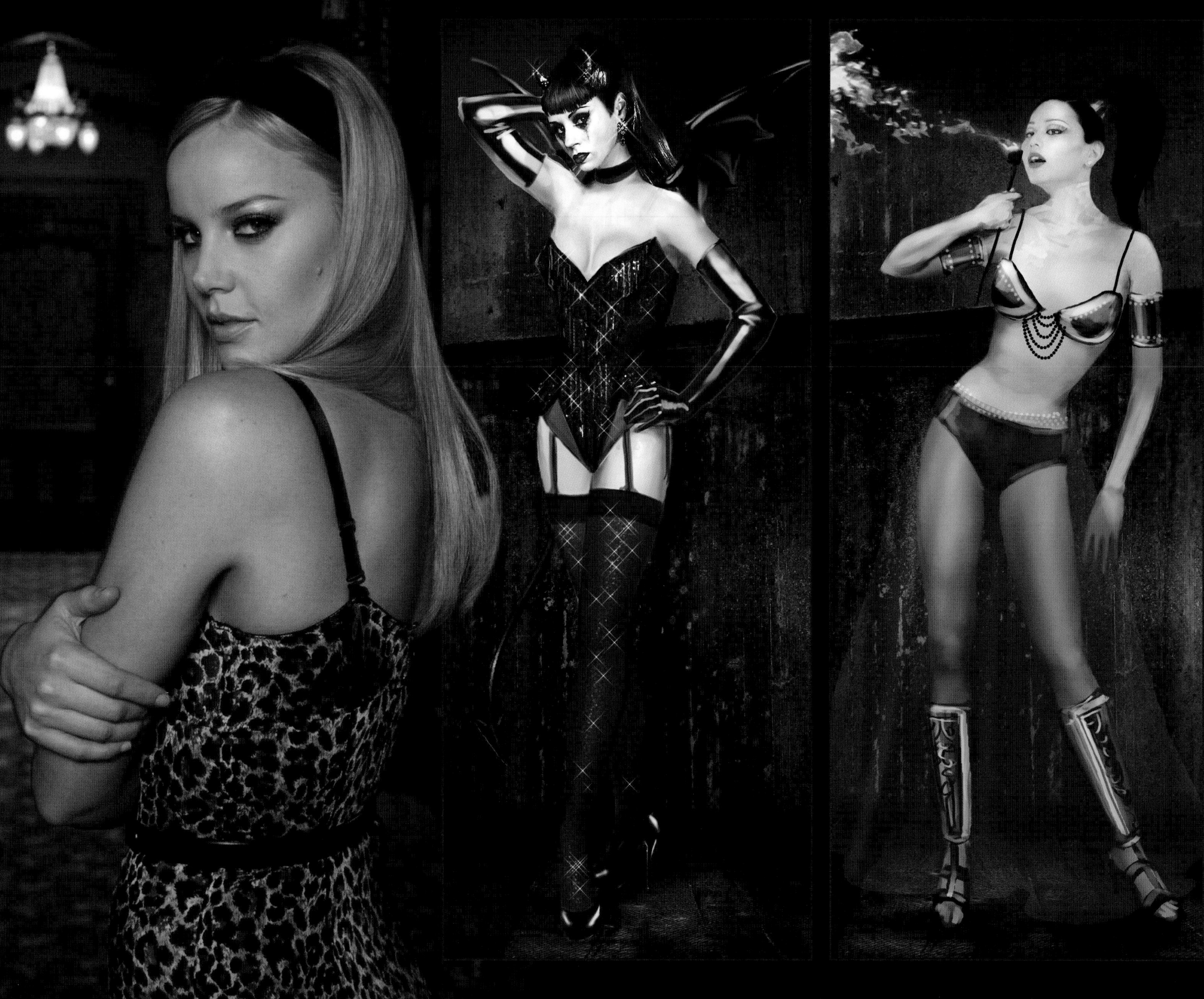

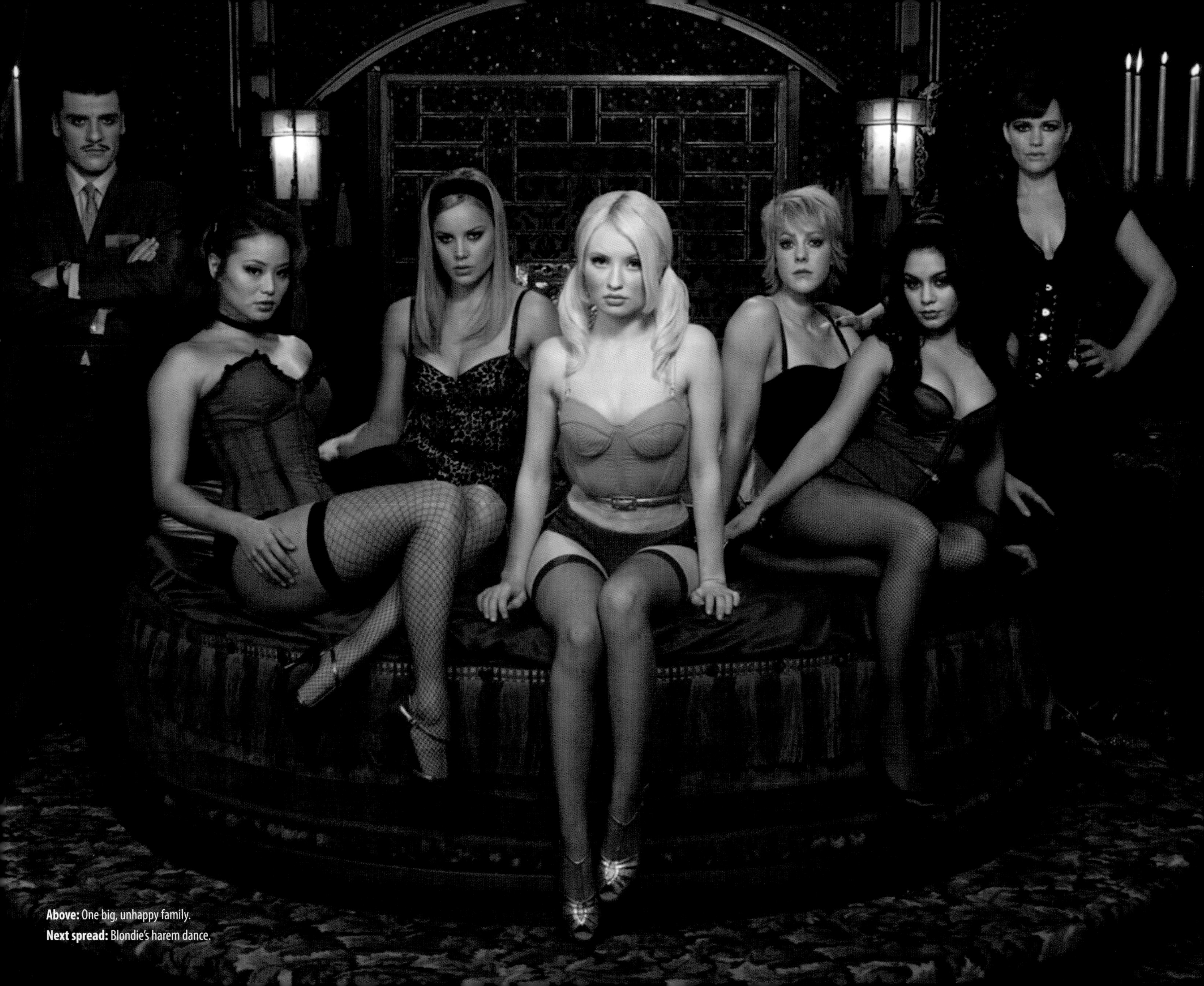

Above: One big, unhappy family.

Next spread: Blondie's harem dance.

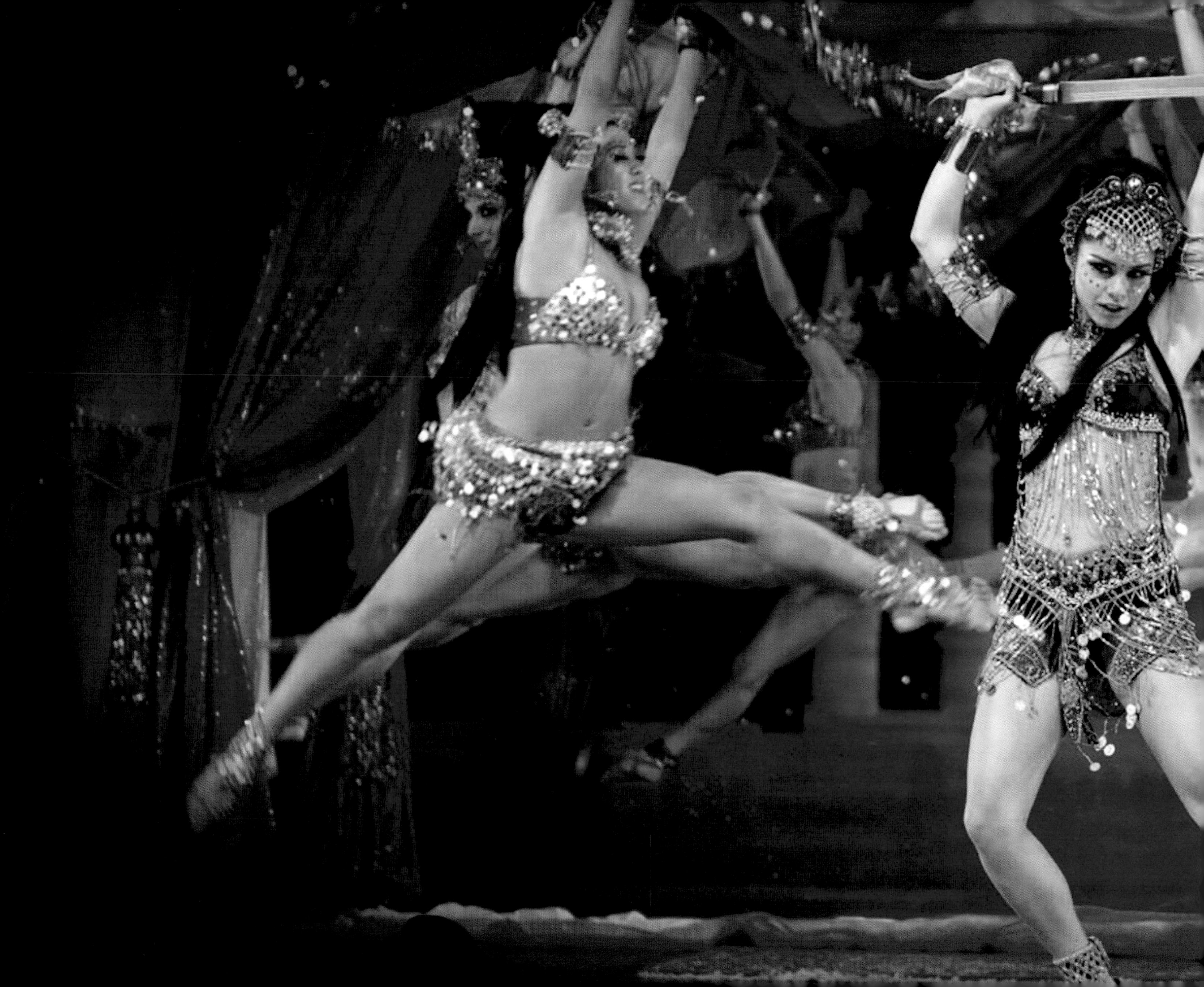

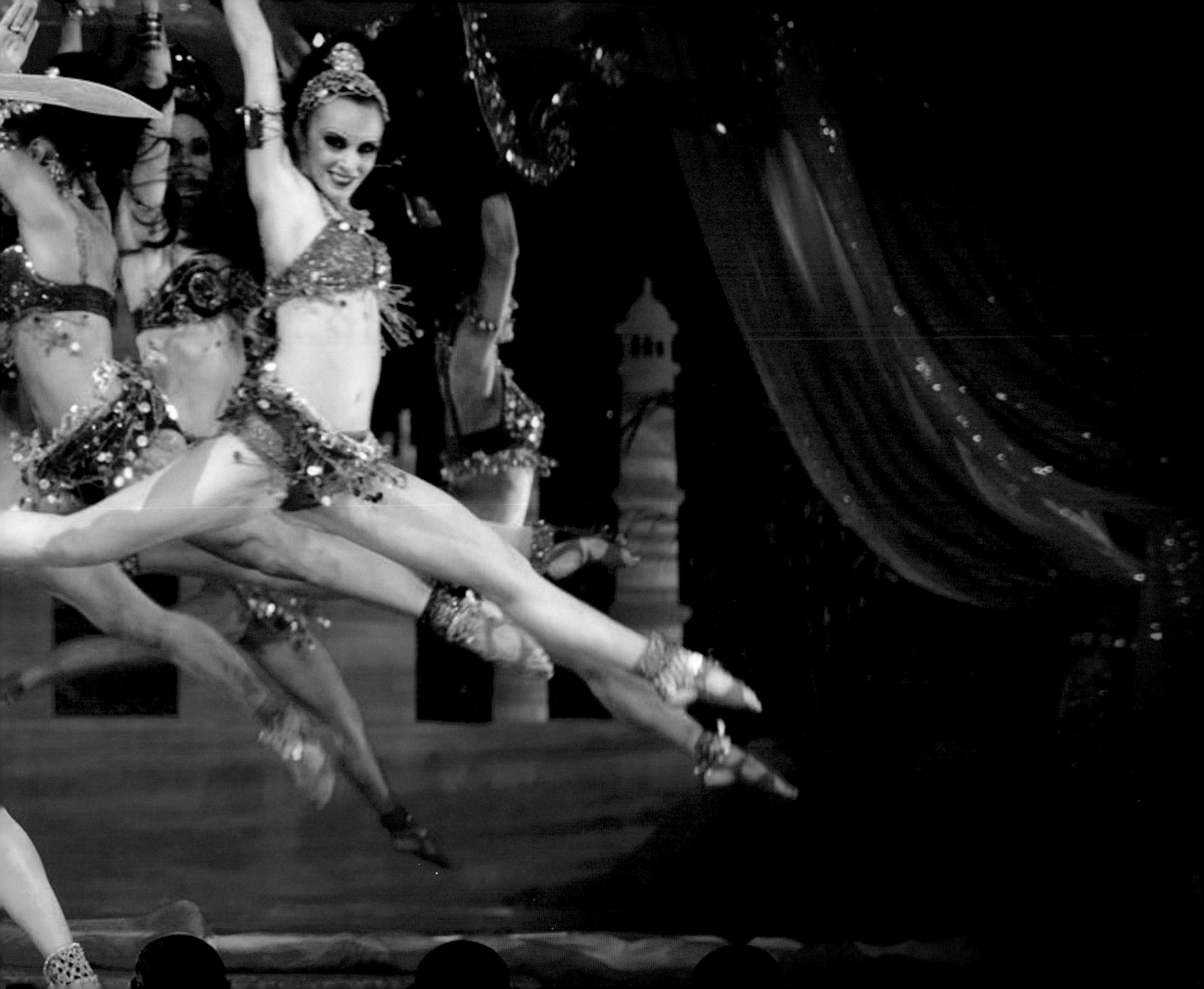

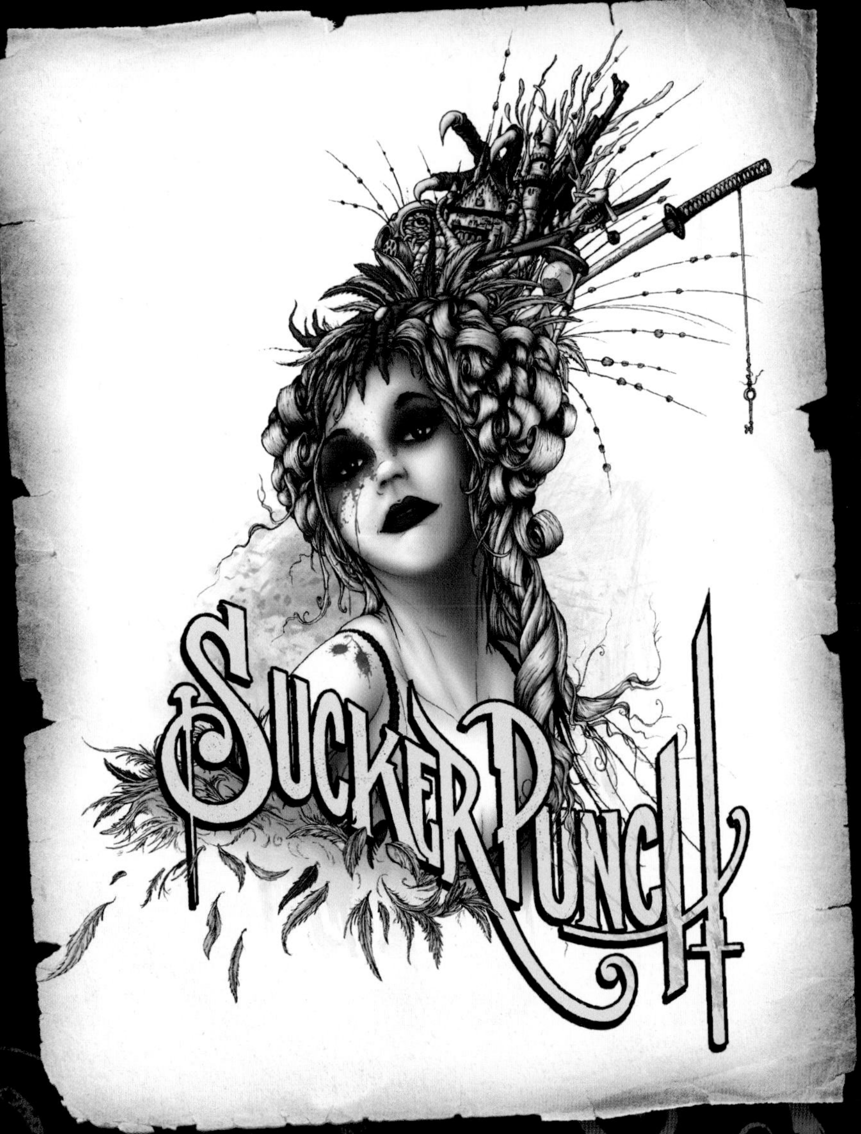

poster design

Our overriding philosophy was to cut the artists loose to explore as many creative directions as they could, whether these would eventually be used as posters in the marketing campaign or not. What we got was some incredible art that runs the gamut from vintage propaganda posters portraying war as sexy, sexy hell, to individual portraits of each girl, to mind-blowing panoramic views of fantasy combat.

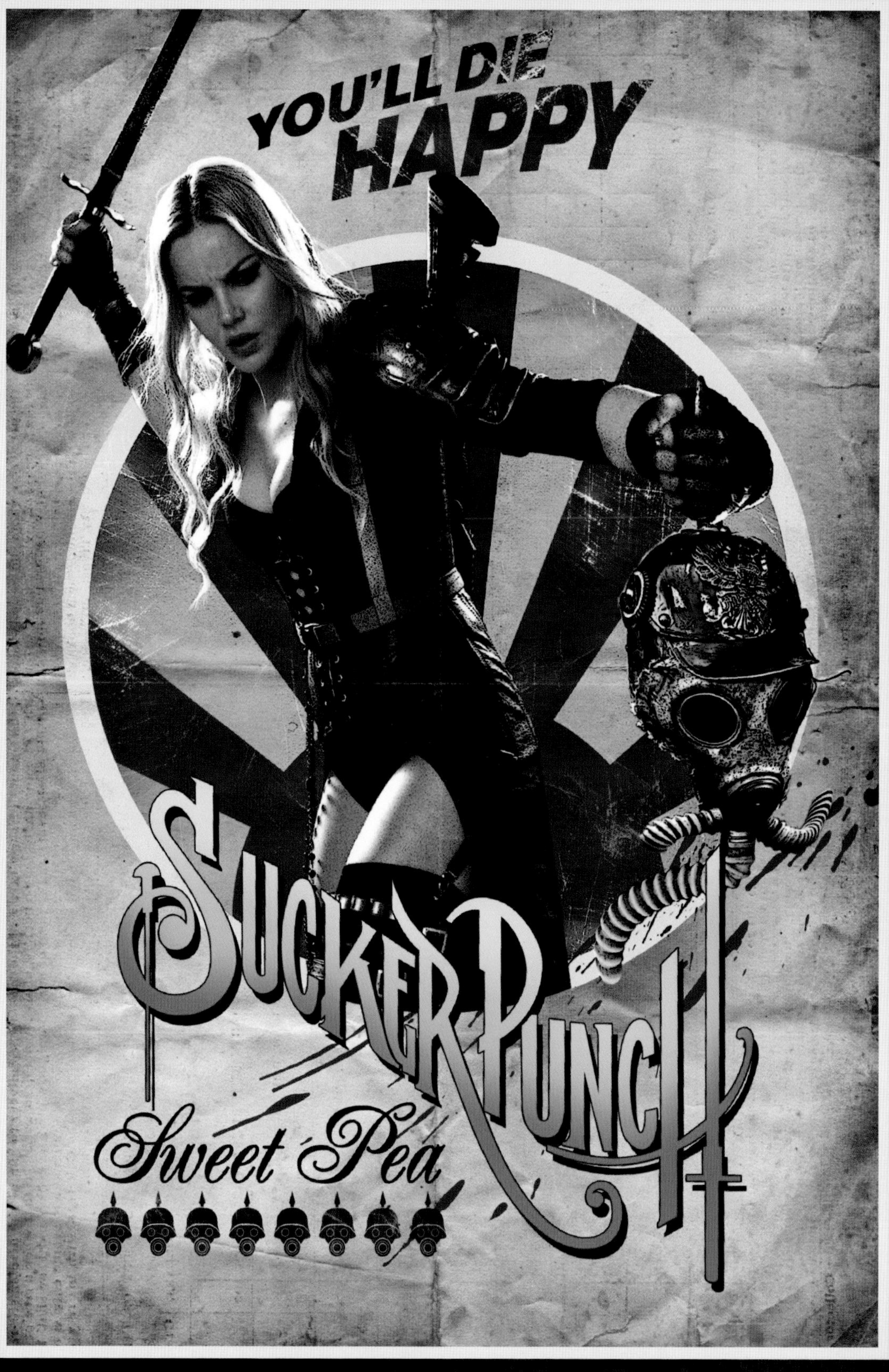

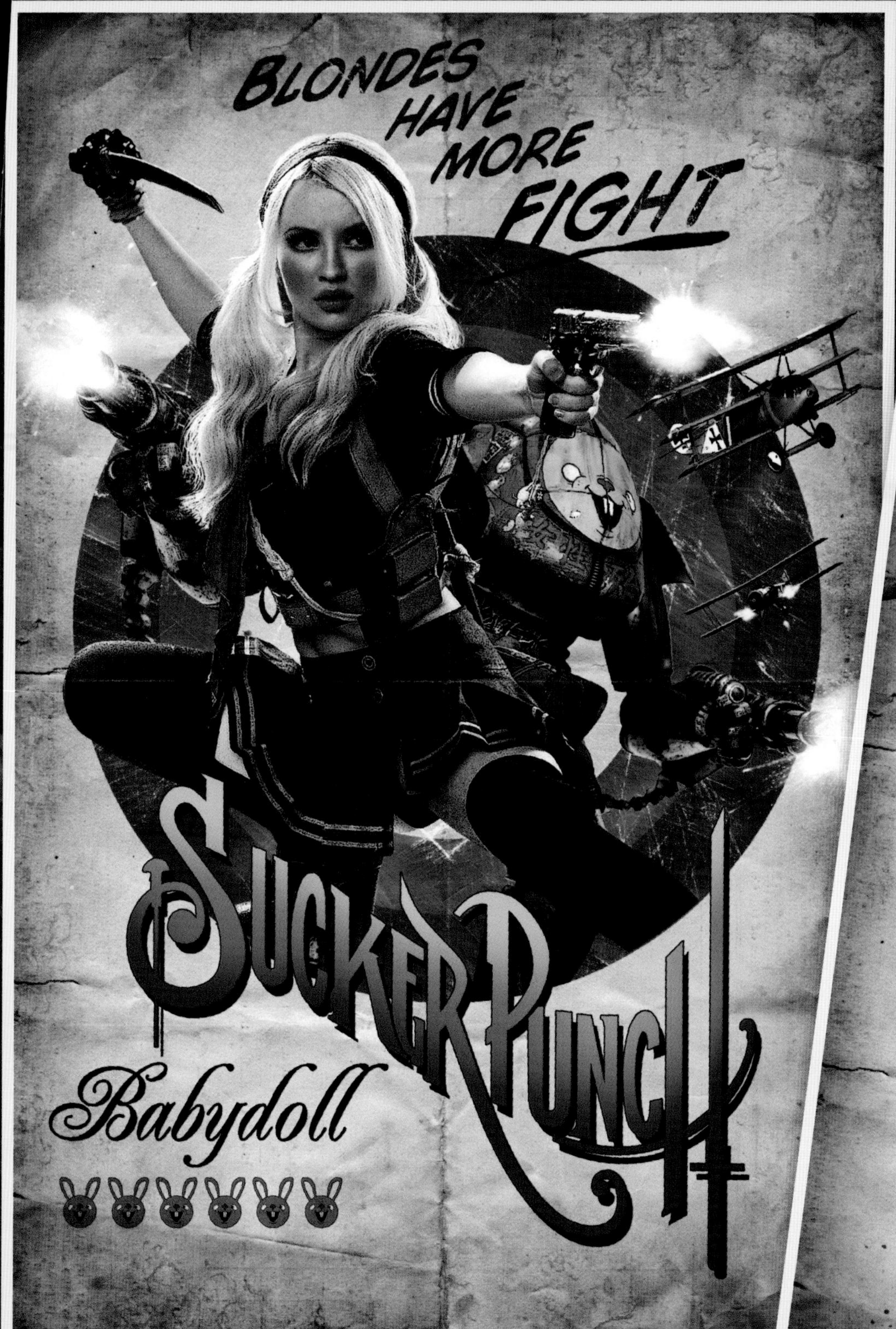

BLONDES HAVE MORE FIGHT

SUCKER PUNCH

Babydoll

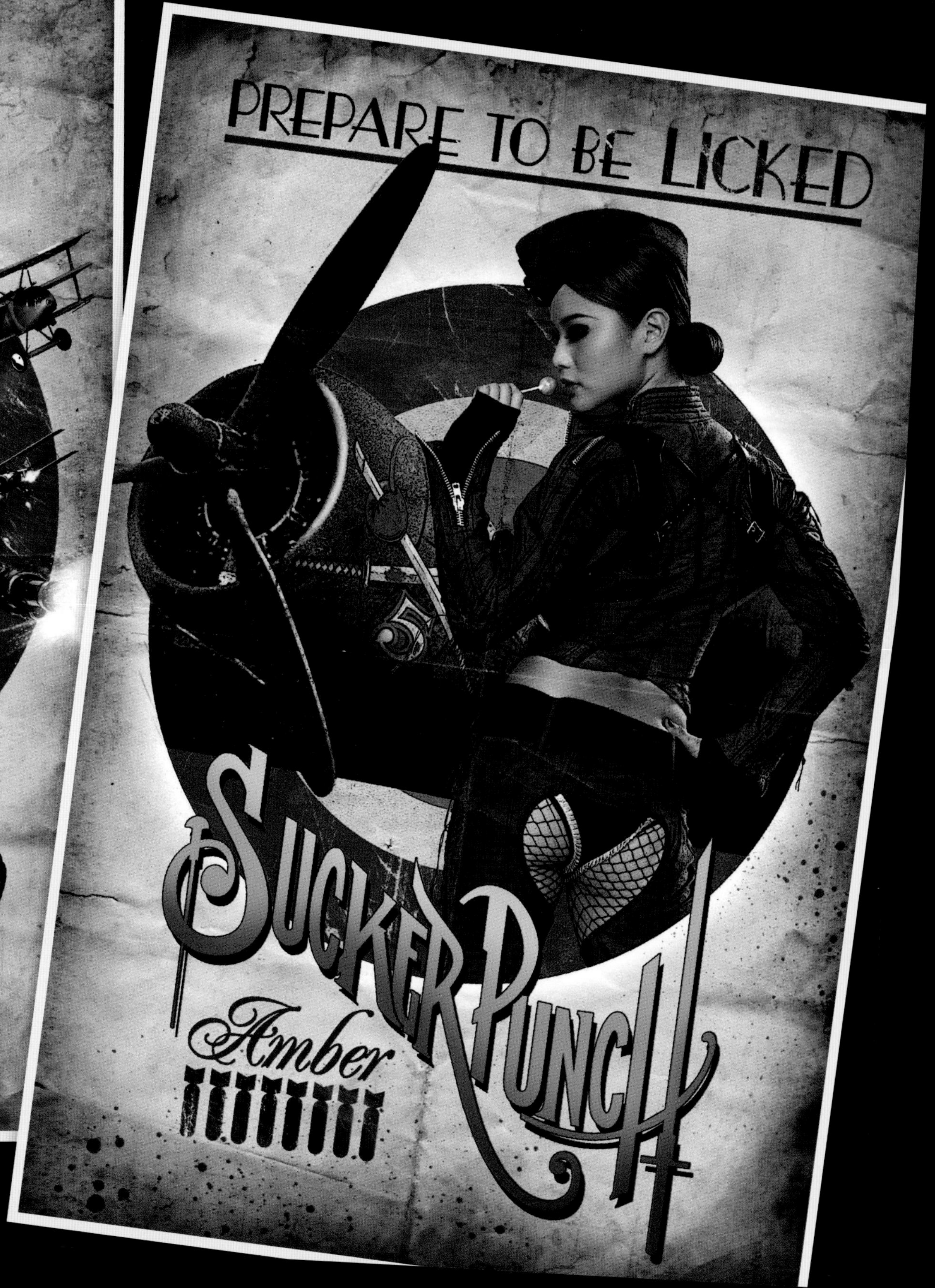

PREPARE TO BE LICKED

SUCKER PUNCH

Amber

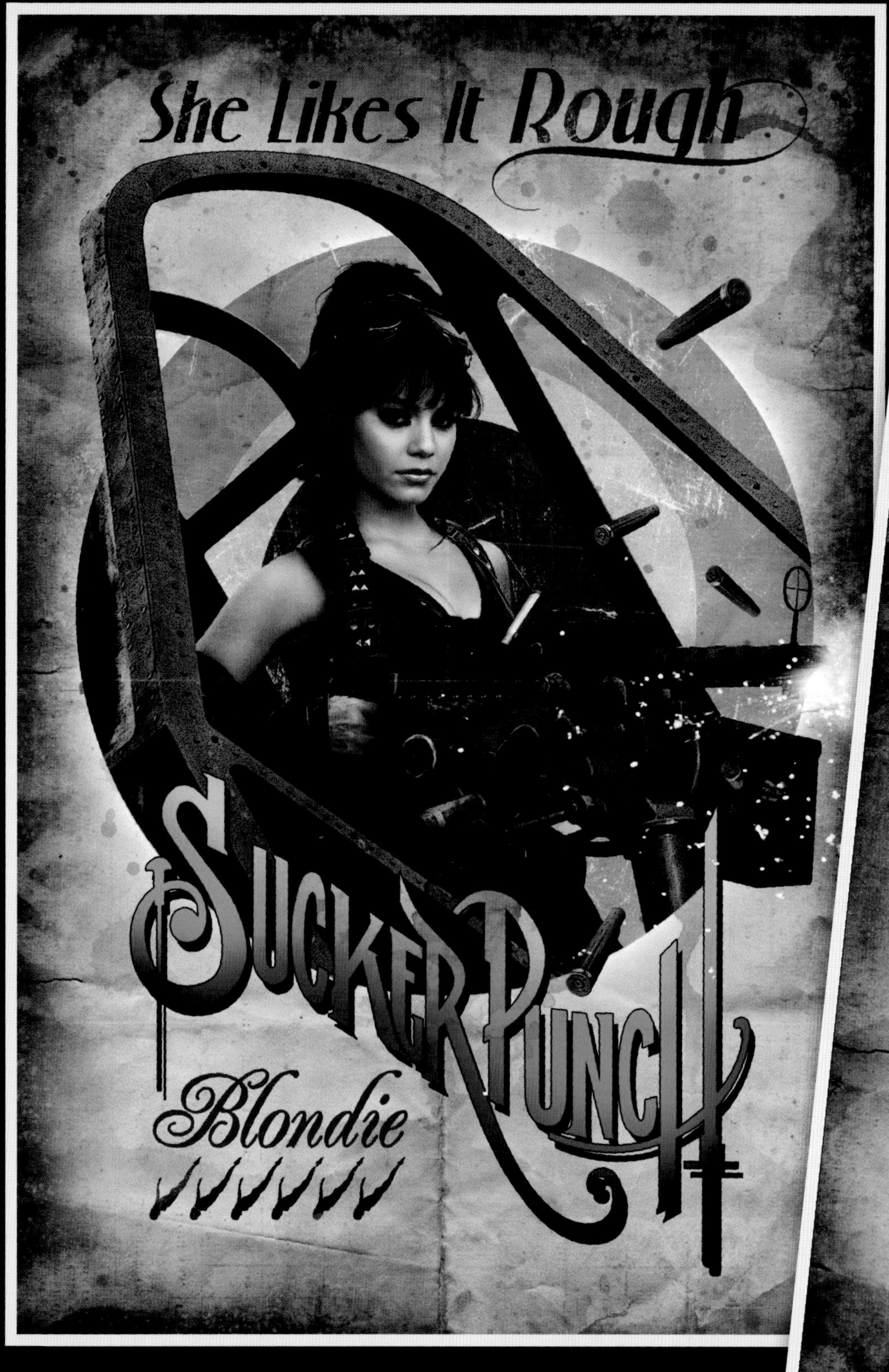

She Likes It Rough

Sucker Punch

Blondie

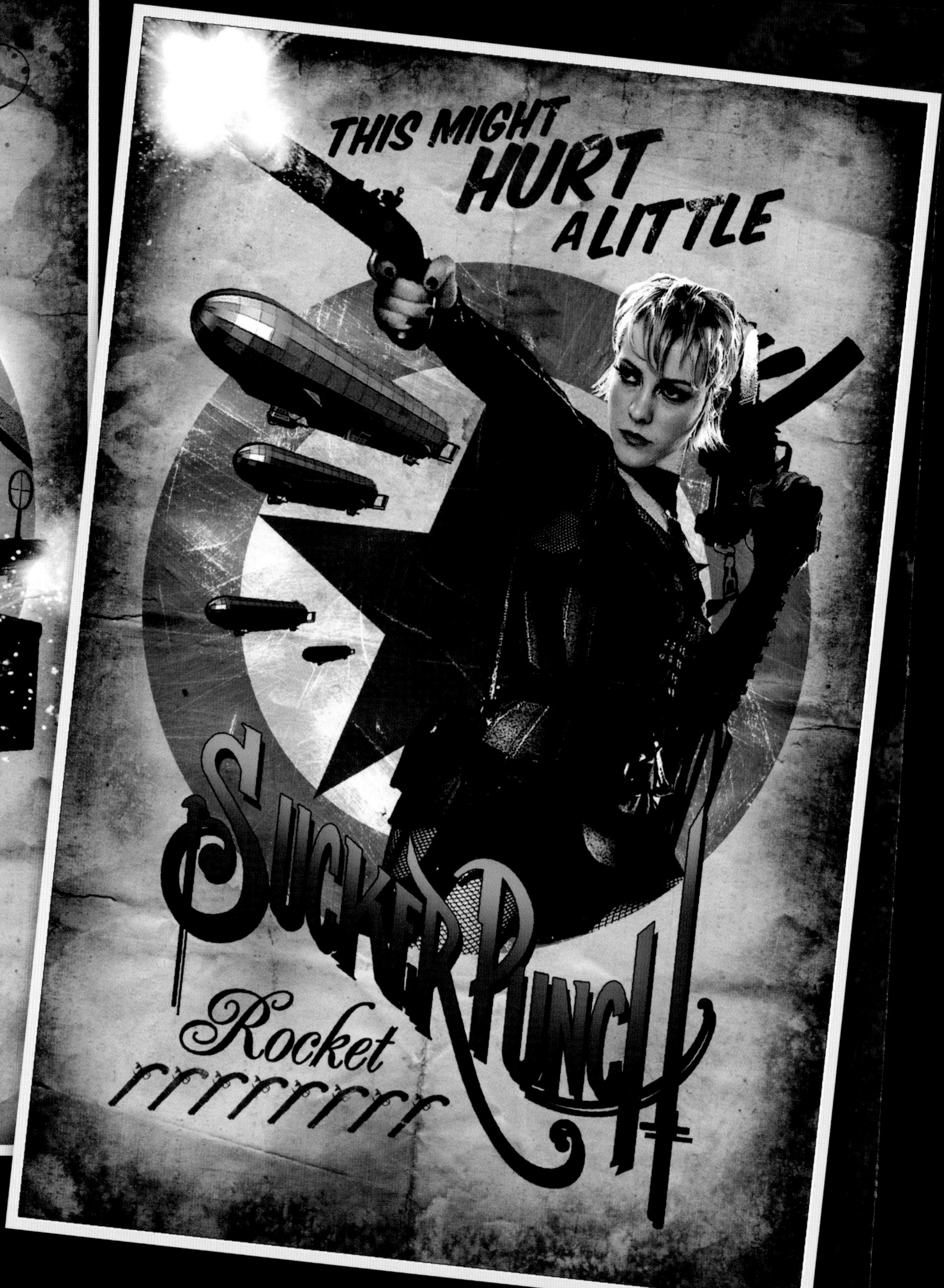

This Might Hurt A Little

Sucker Punch

Rocket

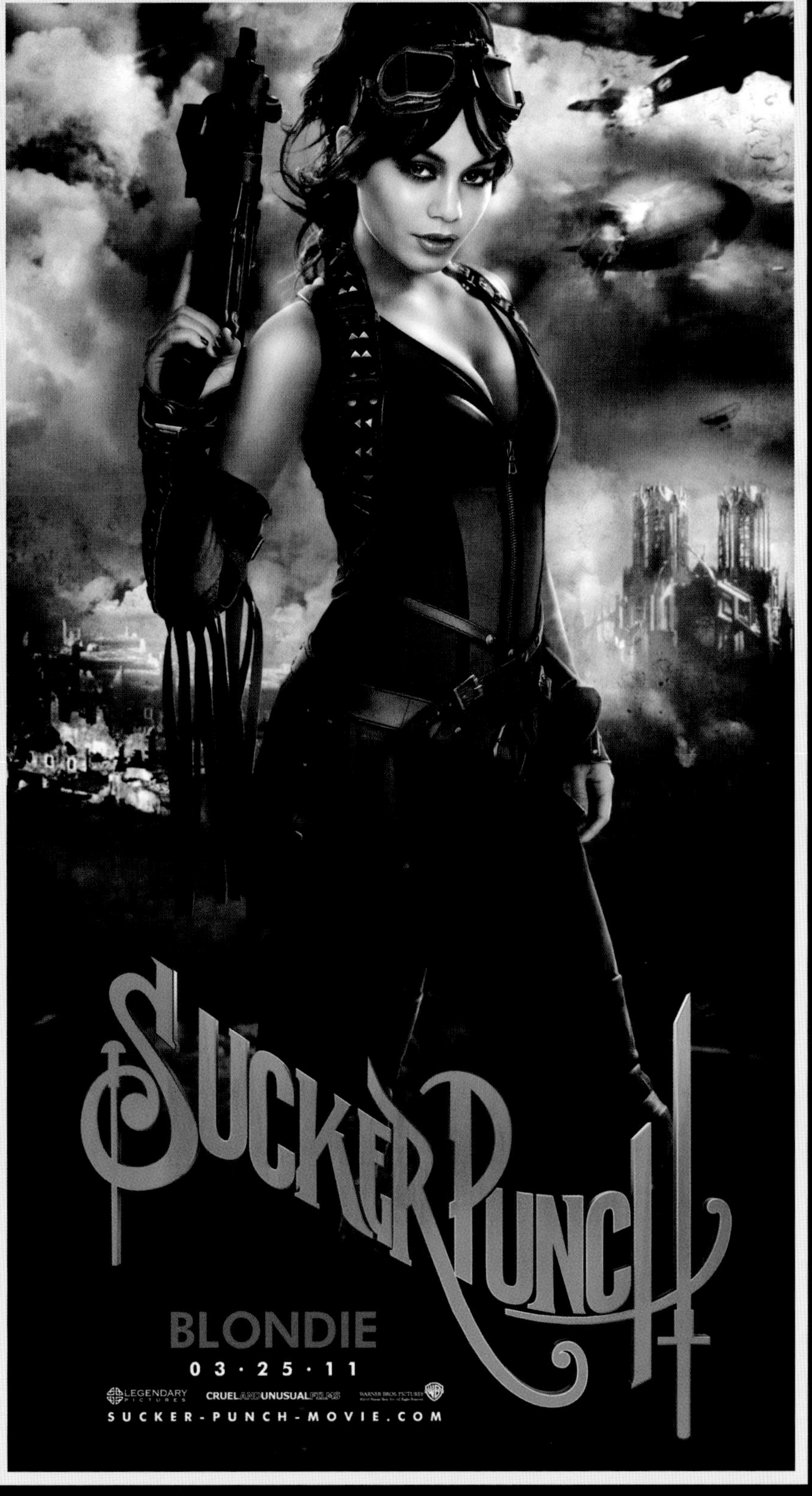

SUCKER PUNCH

BLONDIE

03 · 25 · 11

LEGENDARY PICTURES CRUEL AND UNUSUAL FILMS WARNER BROS. PICTURES

SUCKER-PUNCH-MOVIE.COM

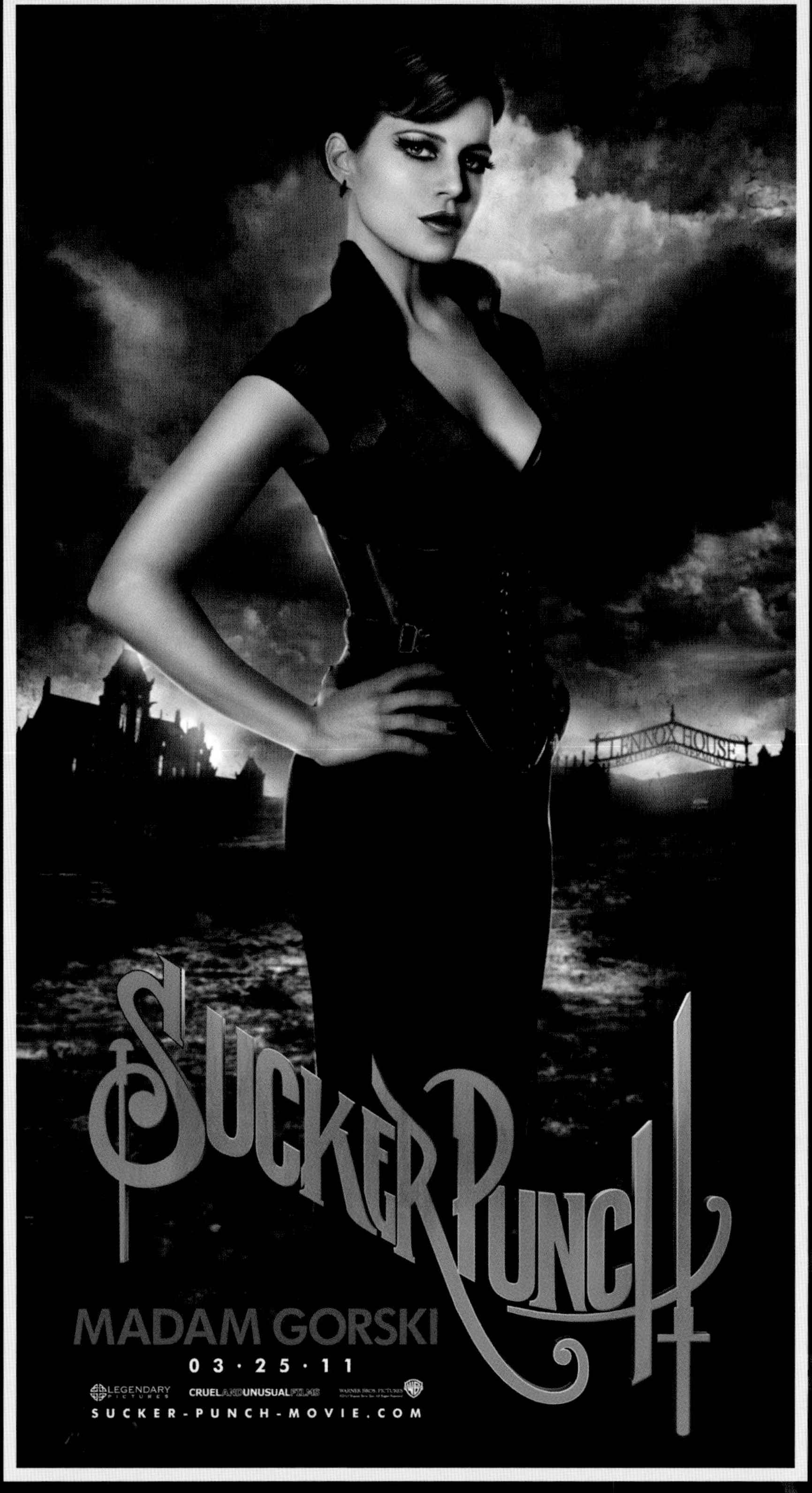

LENNOX HOUSE

SUCKER PUNCH

MADAM GORSKI

03 · 25 · 11

LEGENDARY PICTURES CRUEL AND UNUSUAL FILMS WARNER BROS. PICTURES

SUCKER-PUNCH-MOVIE.COM

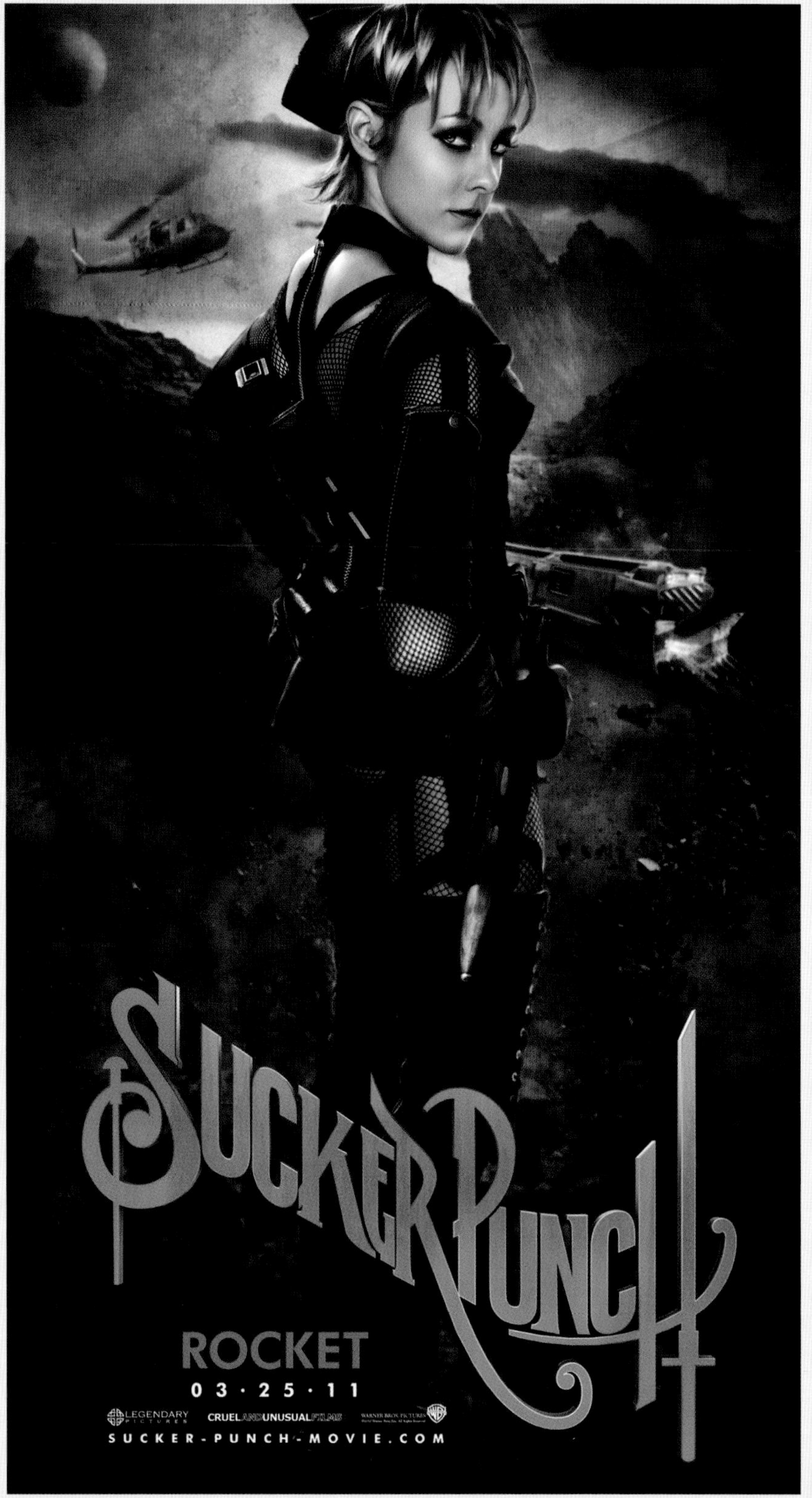

SUCKER PUNCH

ROCKET

03·25·11

LEGENDARY PICTURES
CRUEL AND UNUSUAL FILMS
WARNER BROS. PICTURES

SUCKER-PUNCH-MOVIE.COM

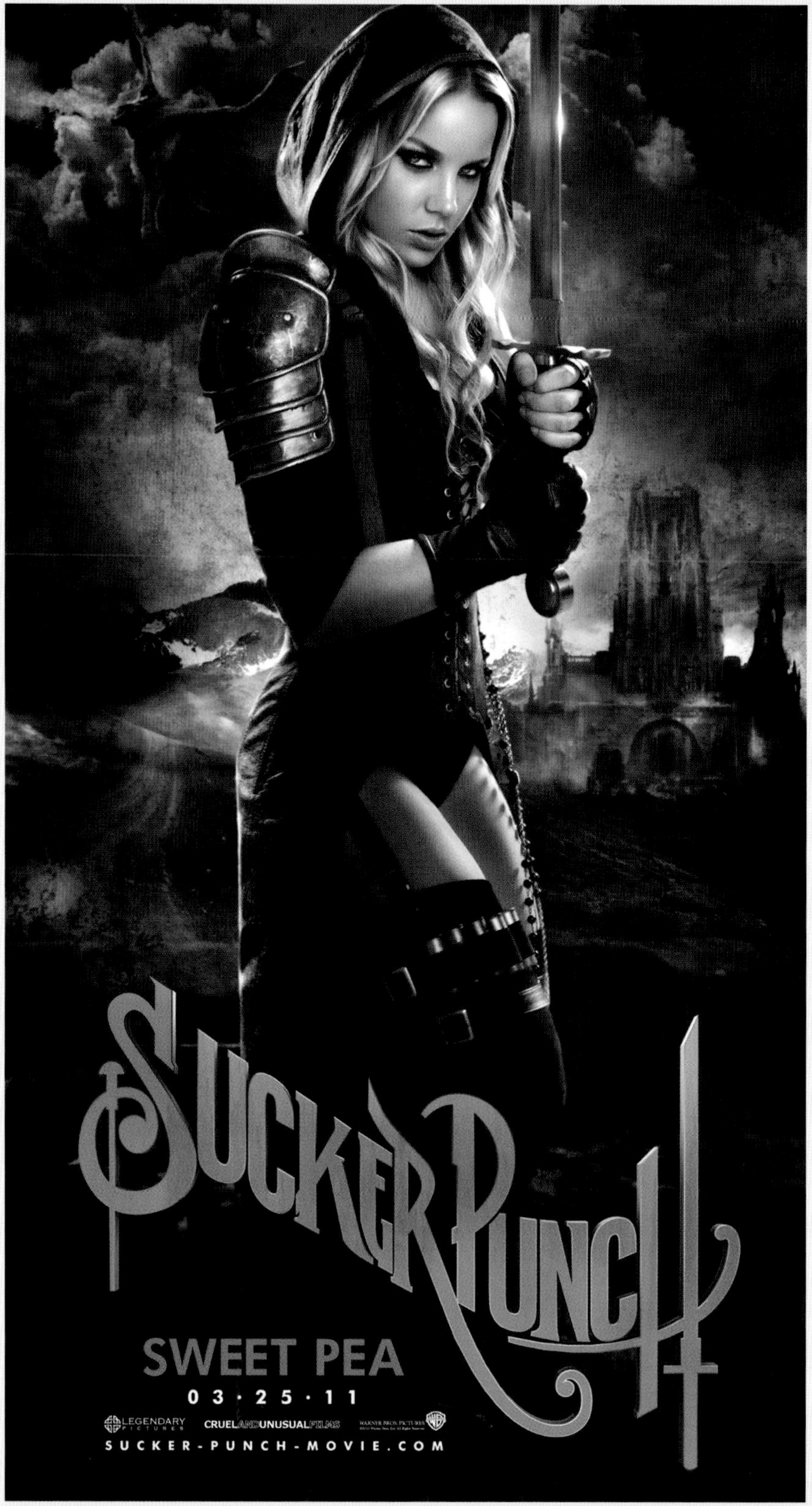

SUCKER PUNCH

SWEET PEA

03·25·11

LEGENDARY PICTURES
CRUEL AND UNUSUAL FILMS
WARNER BROS. PICTURES

SUCKER-PUNCH-MOVIE.COM

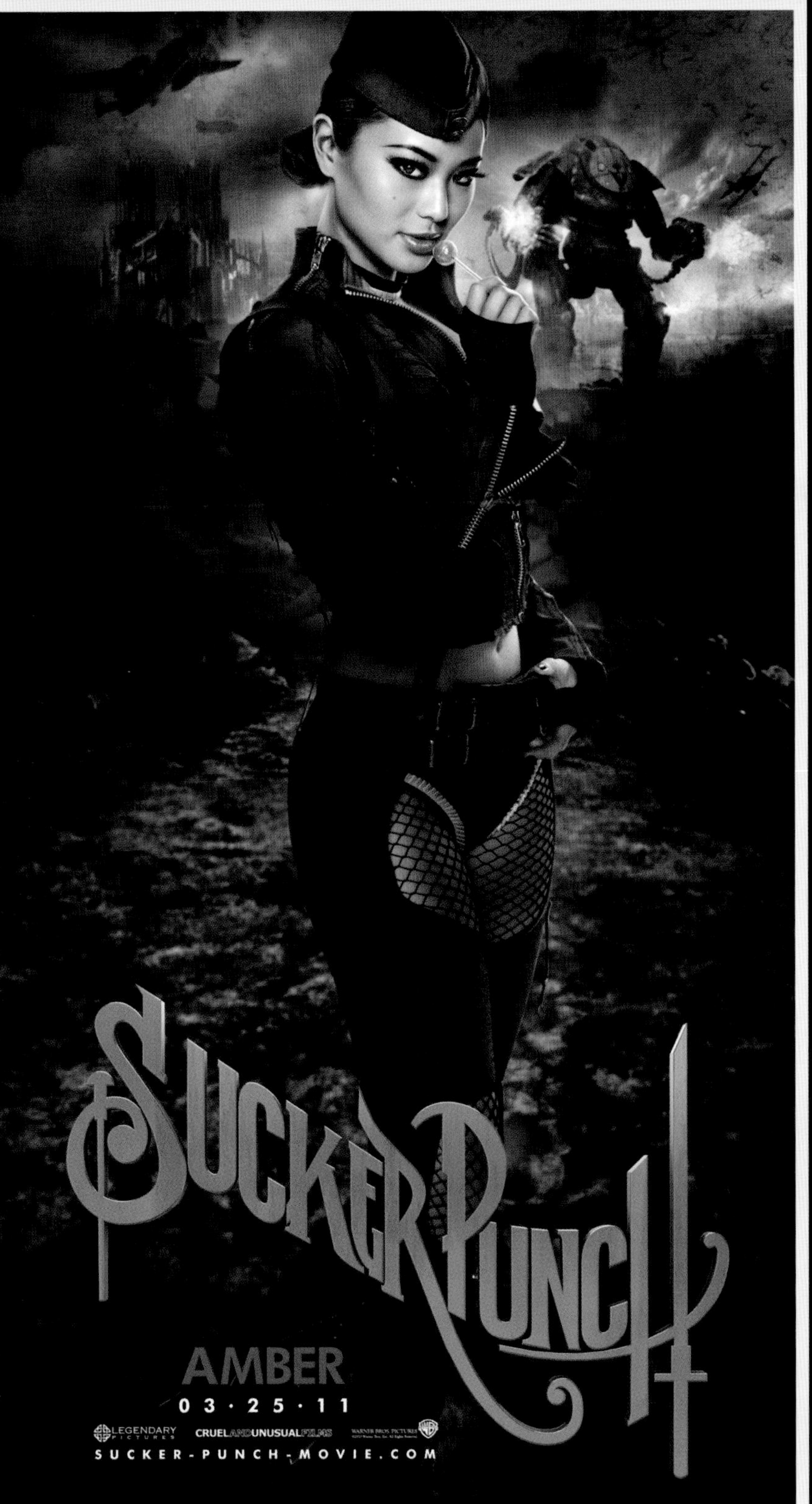

SUCKER PUNCH

BABYDOLL

03·25·11

LEGENDARY PICTURES CRUEL AND UNUSUAL FILMS WARNER BROS. PICTURES

SUCKER-PUNCH-MOVIE.COM

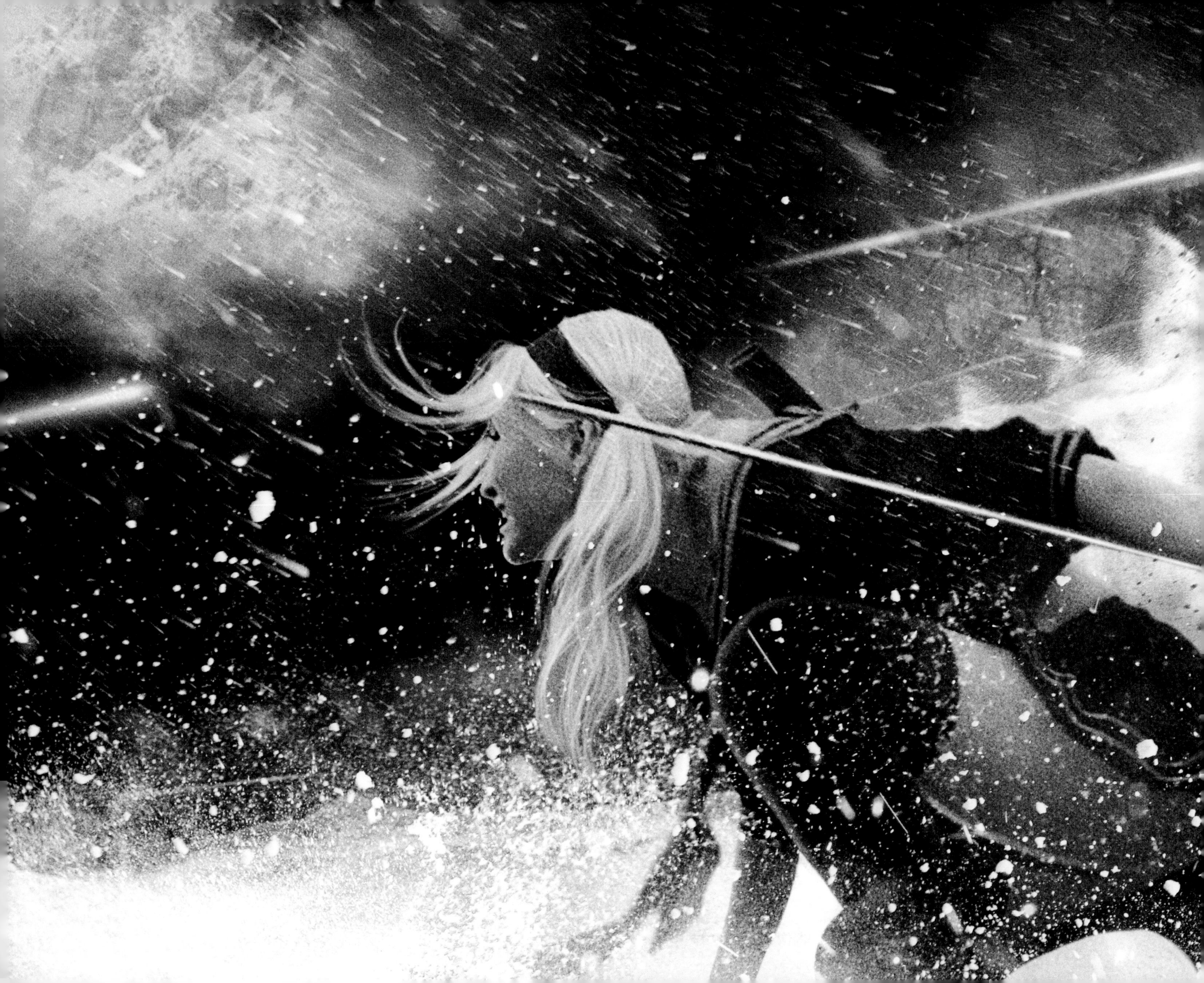

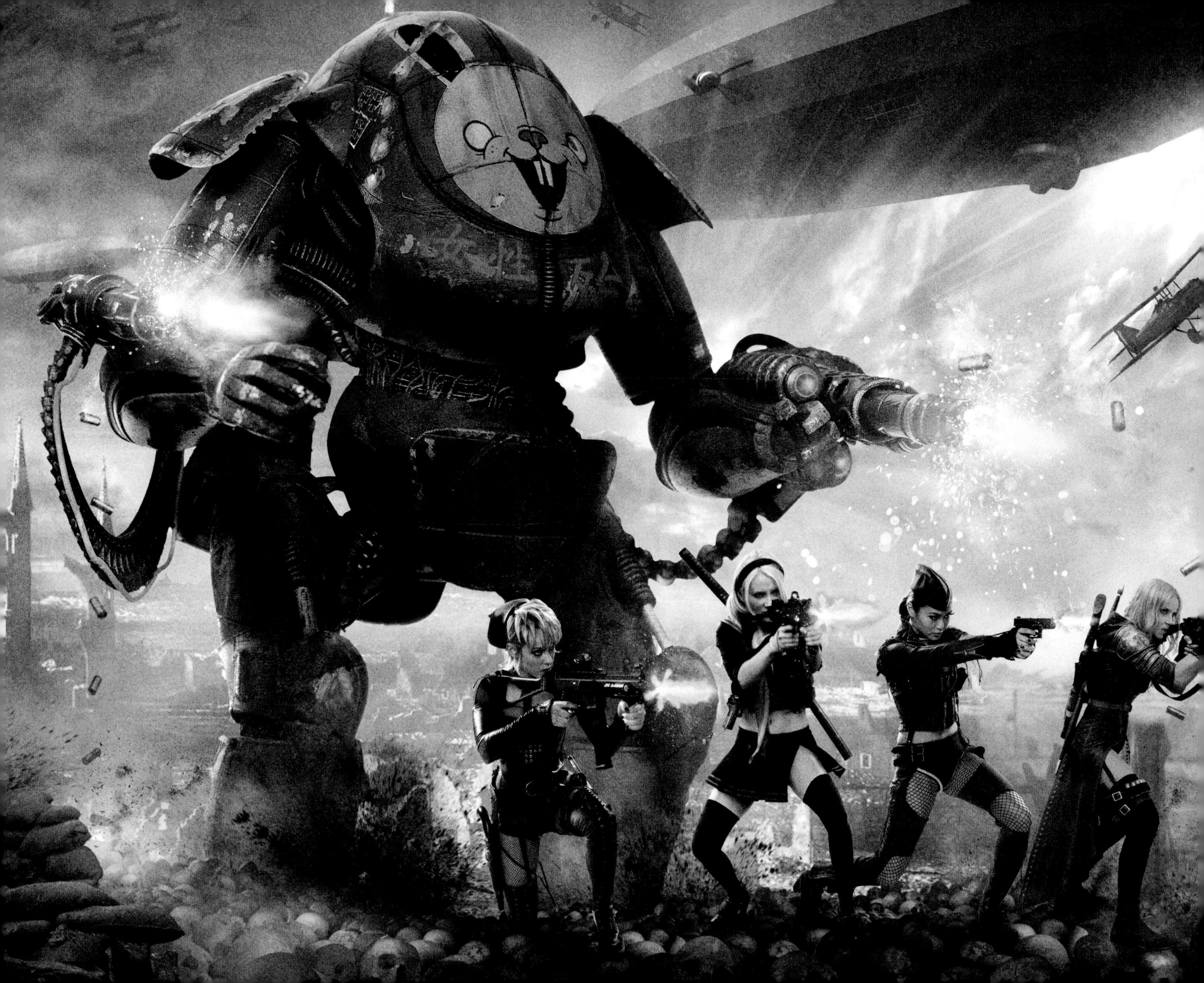

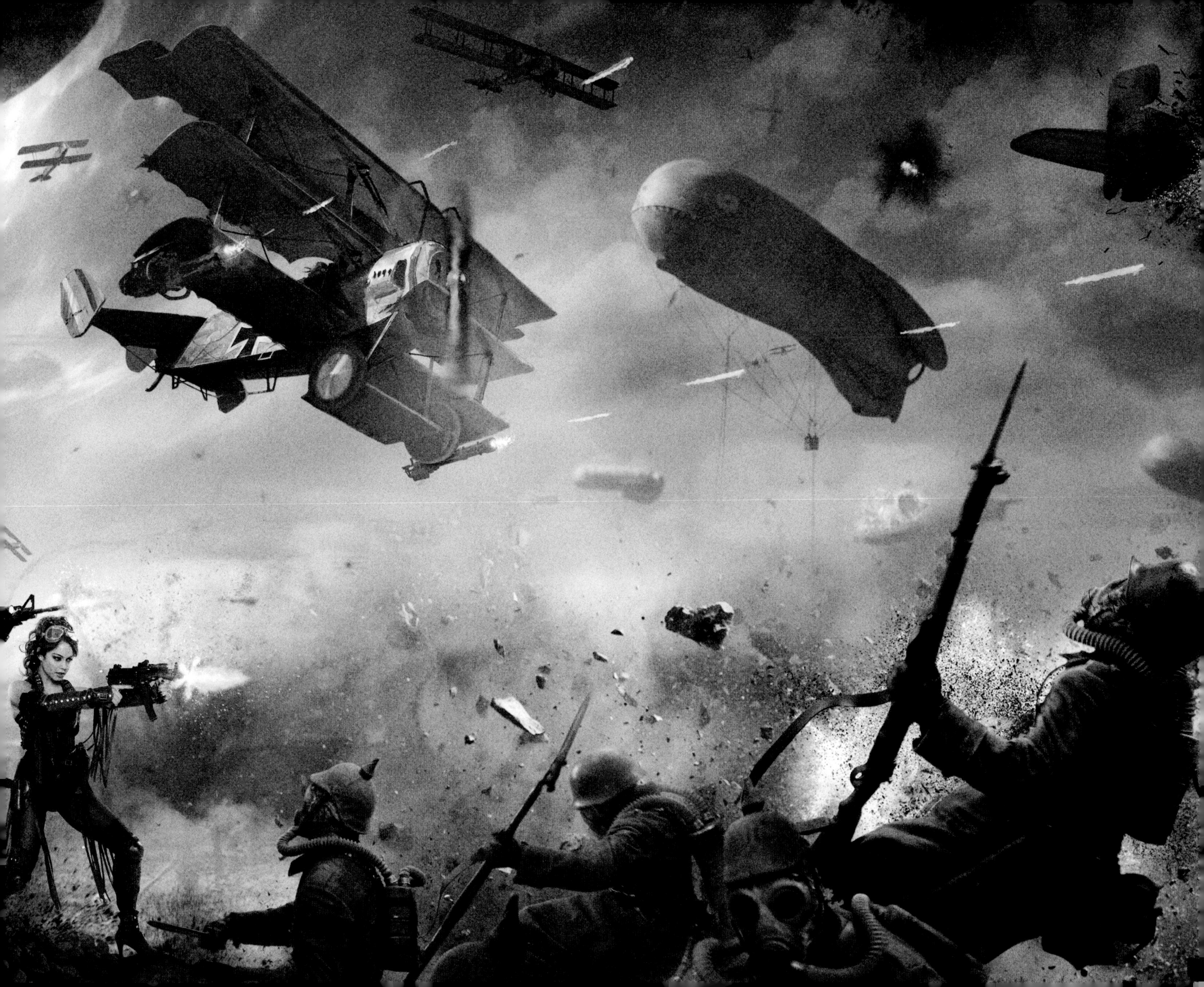

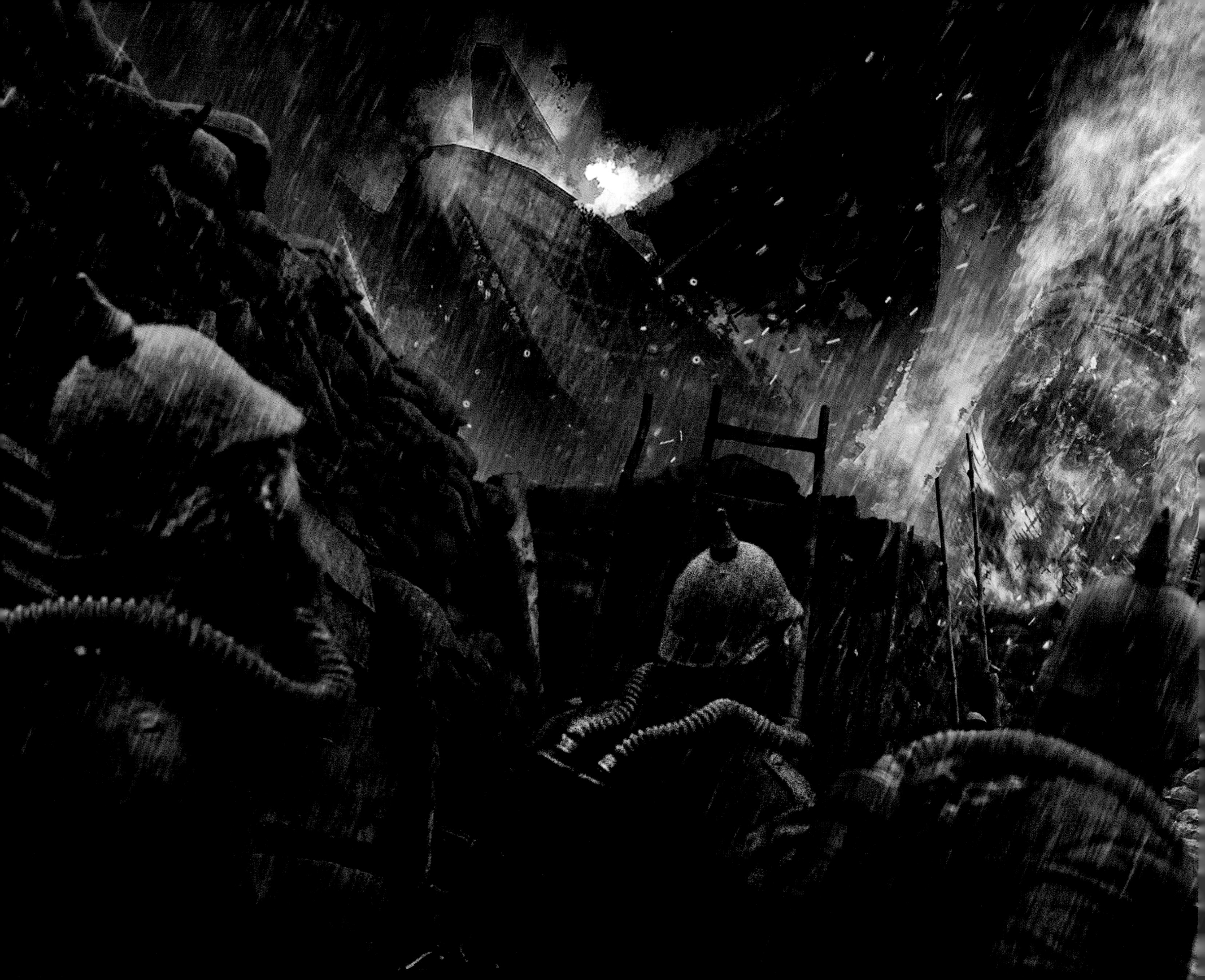

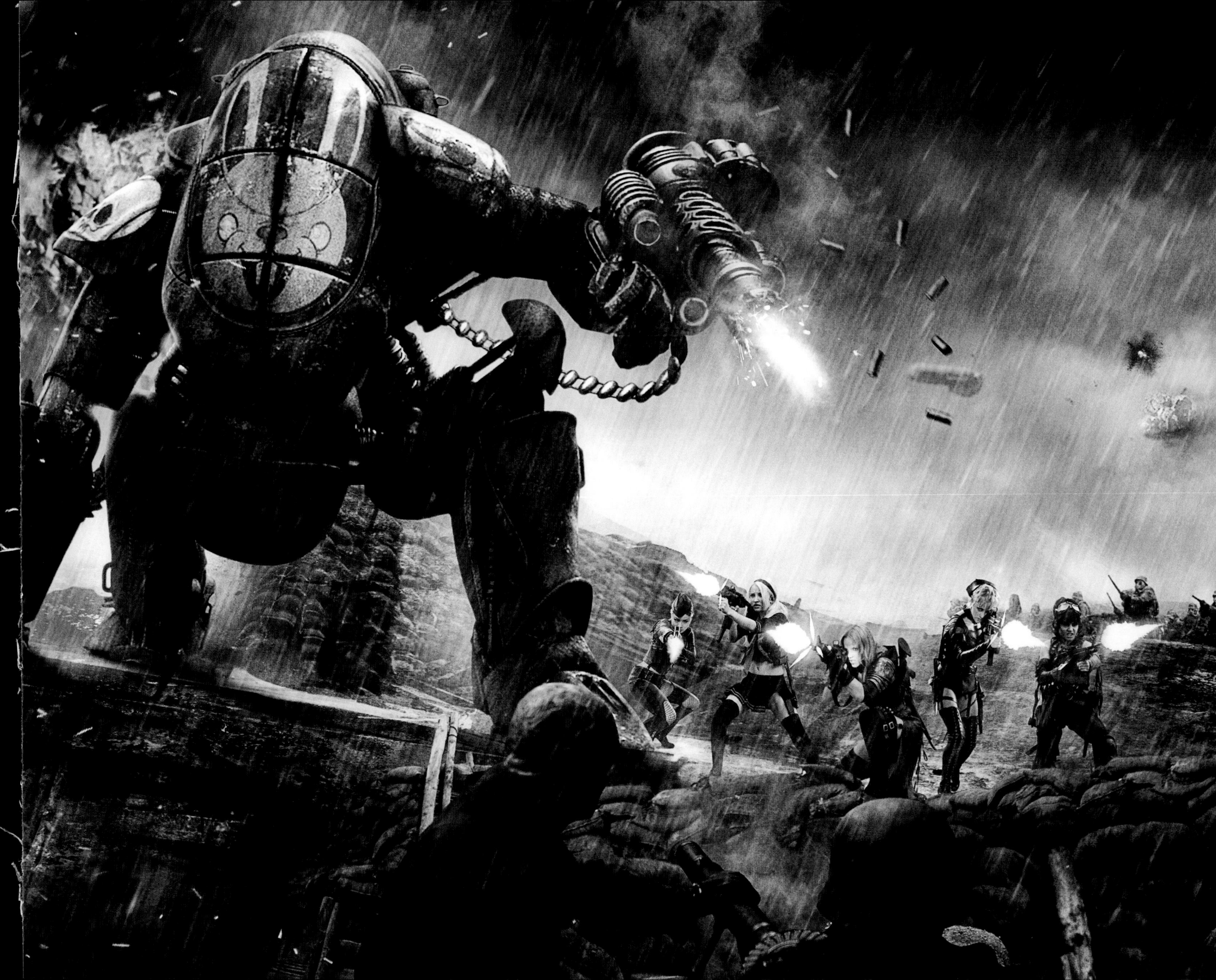

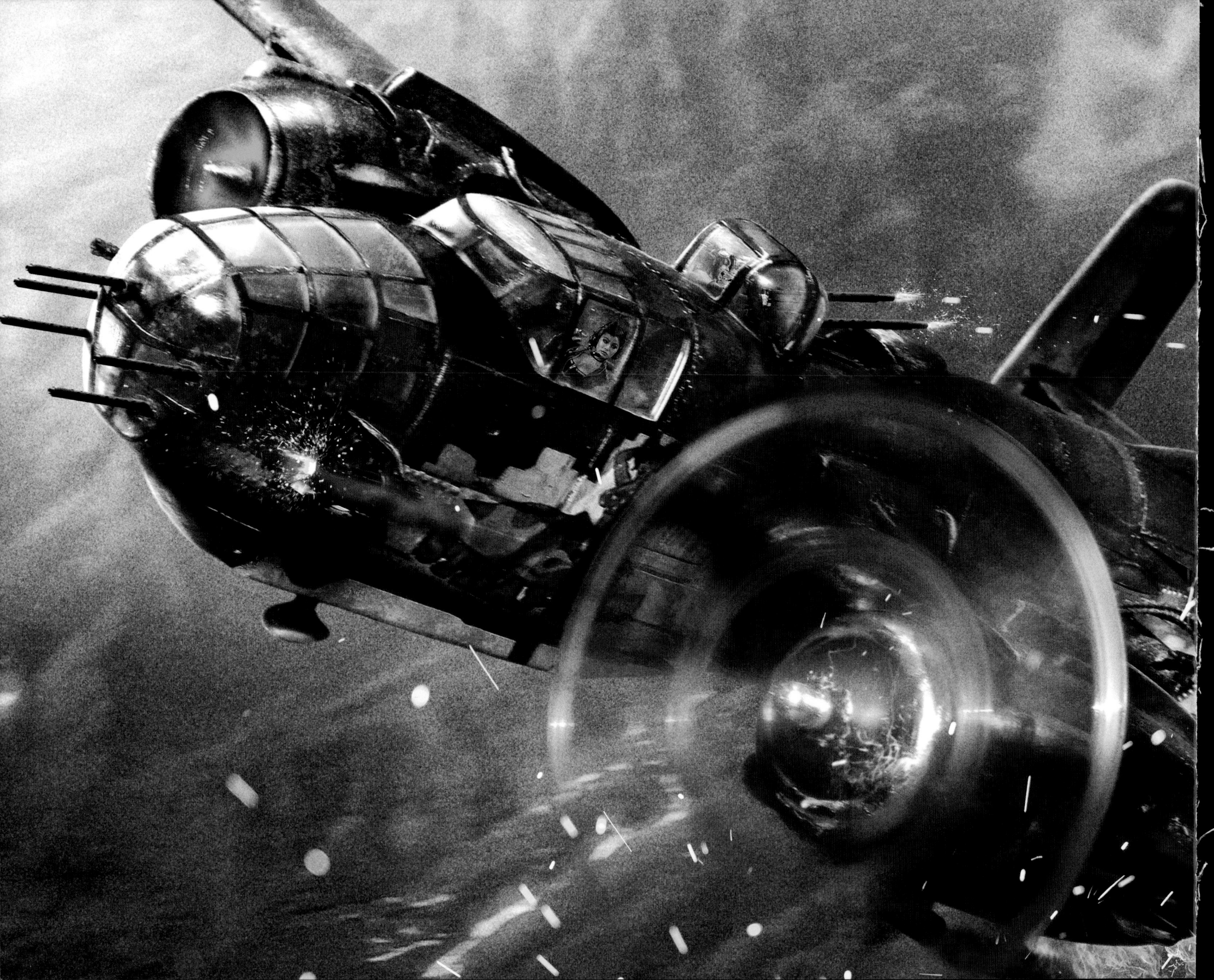

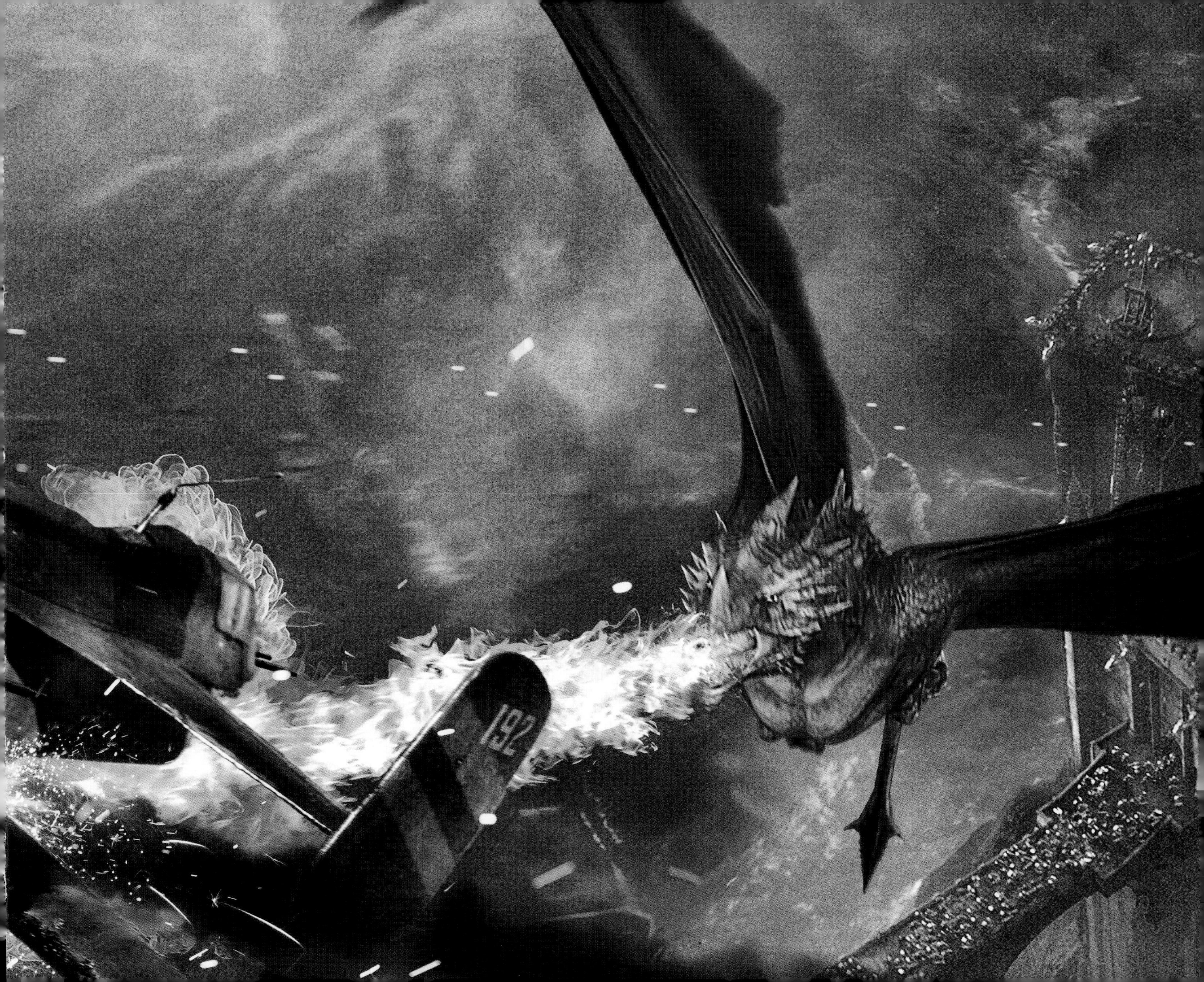
192

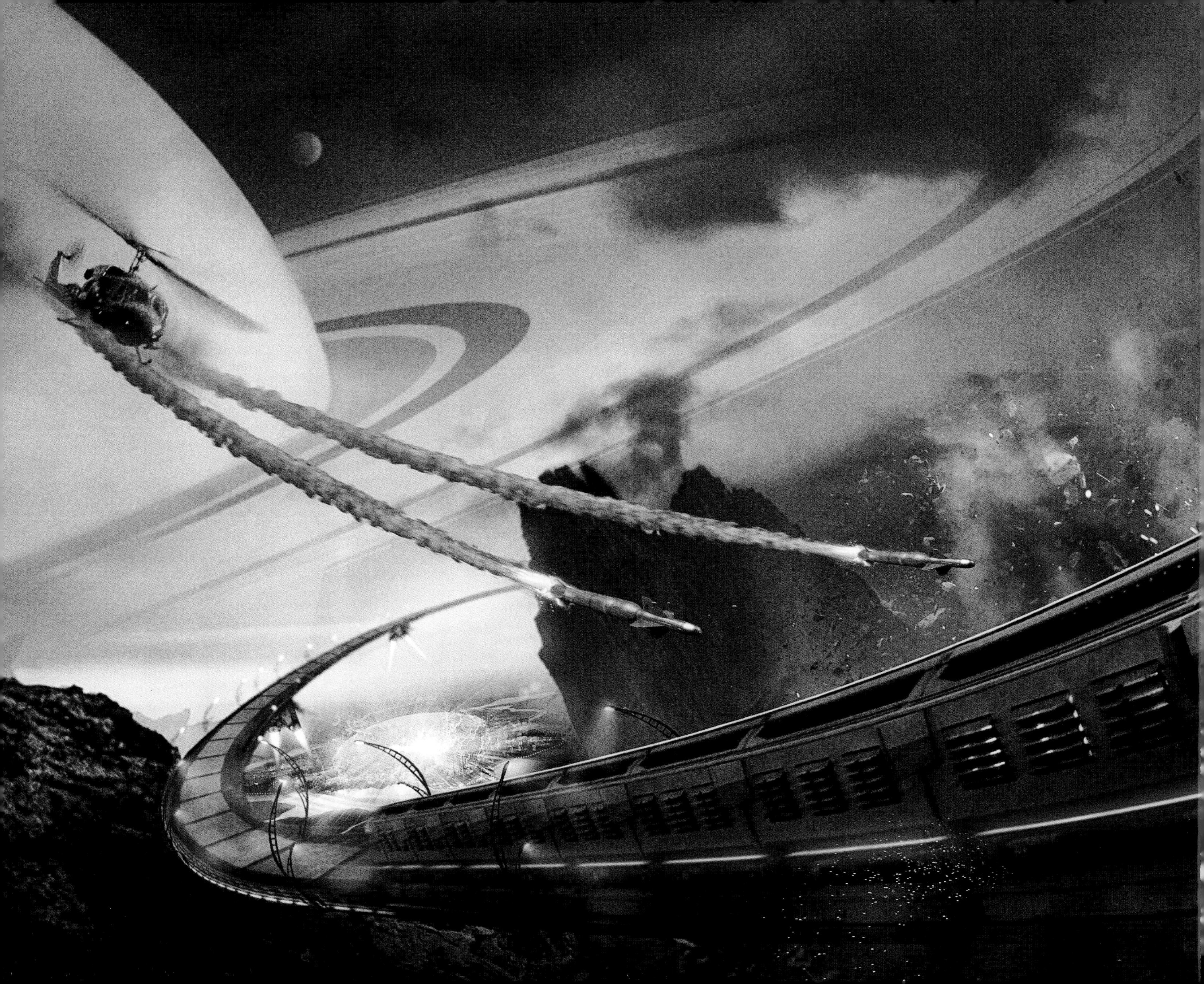

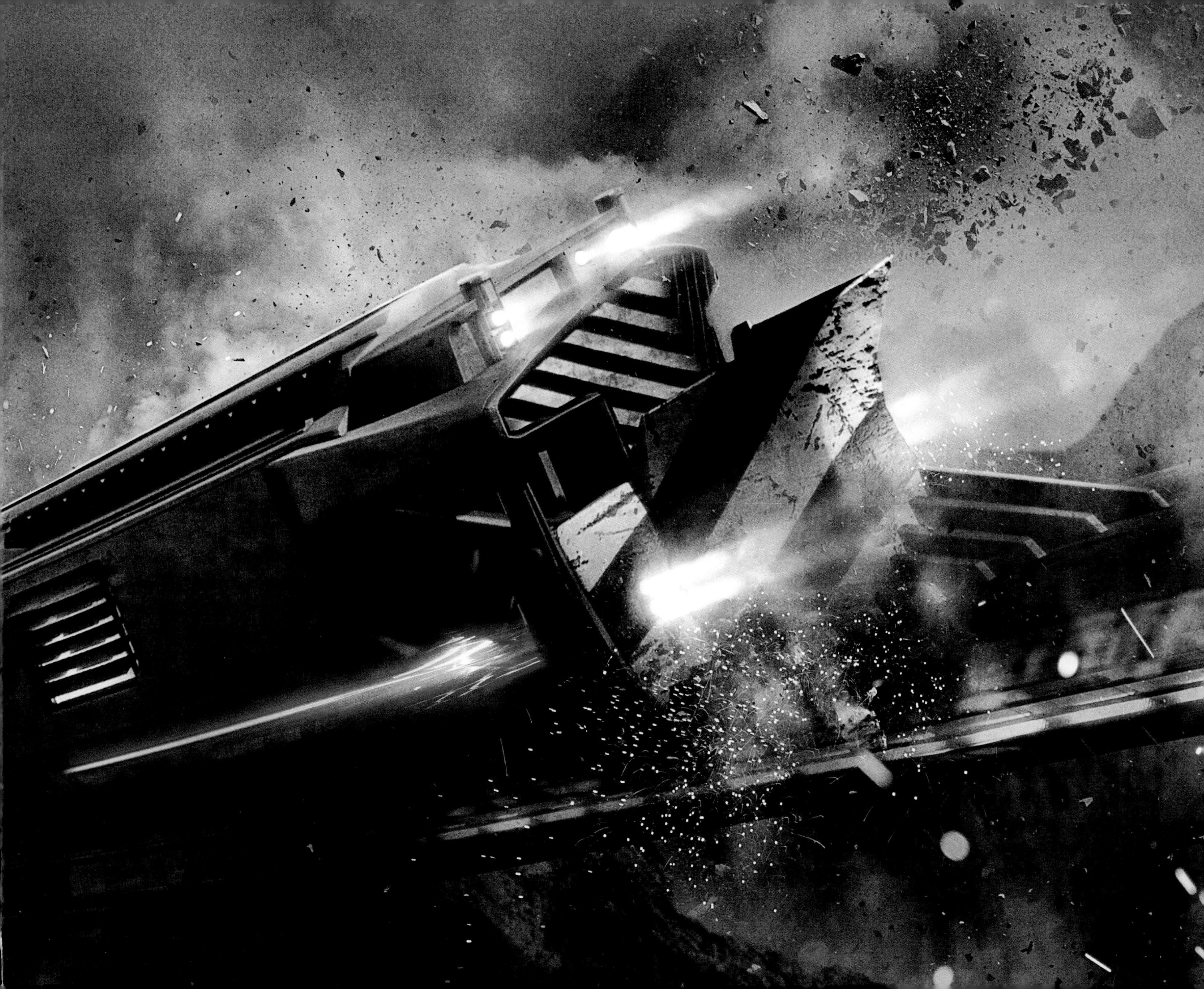

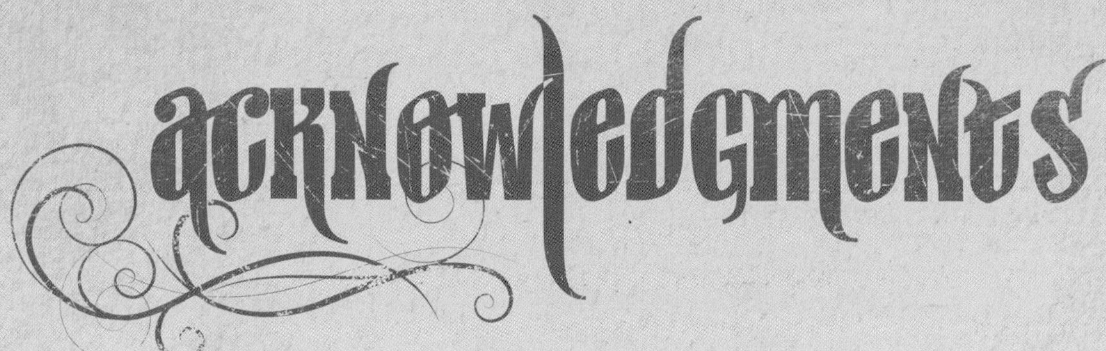

Zack Snyder and the producers of *Sucker Punch* would like to extend a sincere thank you to all of the incredible artists, designers, photographers, technicians and countless others who through their wealth of talent and tireless dedication helped to bring this film to life. It was only the unwavering support of each of our department heads and the superb talent and efforts of their teams that made creating the world of *Sucker Punch* possible. It has been an amazing journey and we are incredibly grateful to have been able to share it with each and every one of you. A very special thanks to screenplay co-writer Steve Shibuya for the many creative hours spent with Zack spinning the intricate web that comprises the layers of Babydoll's journey. Thanks to Peter Aperlo for his continued creative support. In addition, we would like to express our most sincere gratitude to everyone at Warner Bros. and Legendary Pictures who time and time again show their enthusiastic support for our films.

"And one more thing..." To all the wonderful actors that with such dedication, skill and talent breathed life into the characters that began as crazy visions in Zack & Steve's heads, then became words on a page, and finally with your help became realized on screen. You're the best!

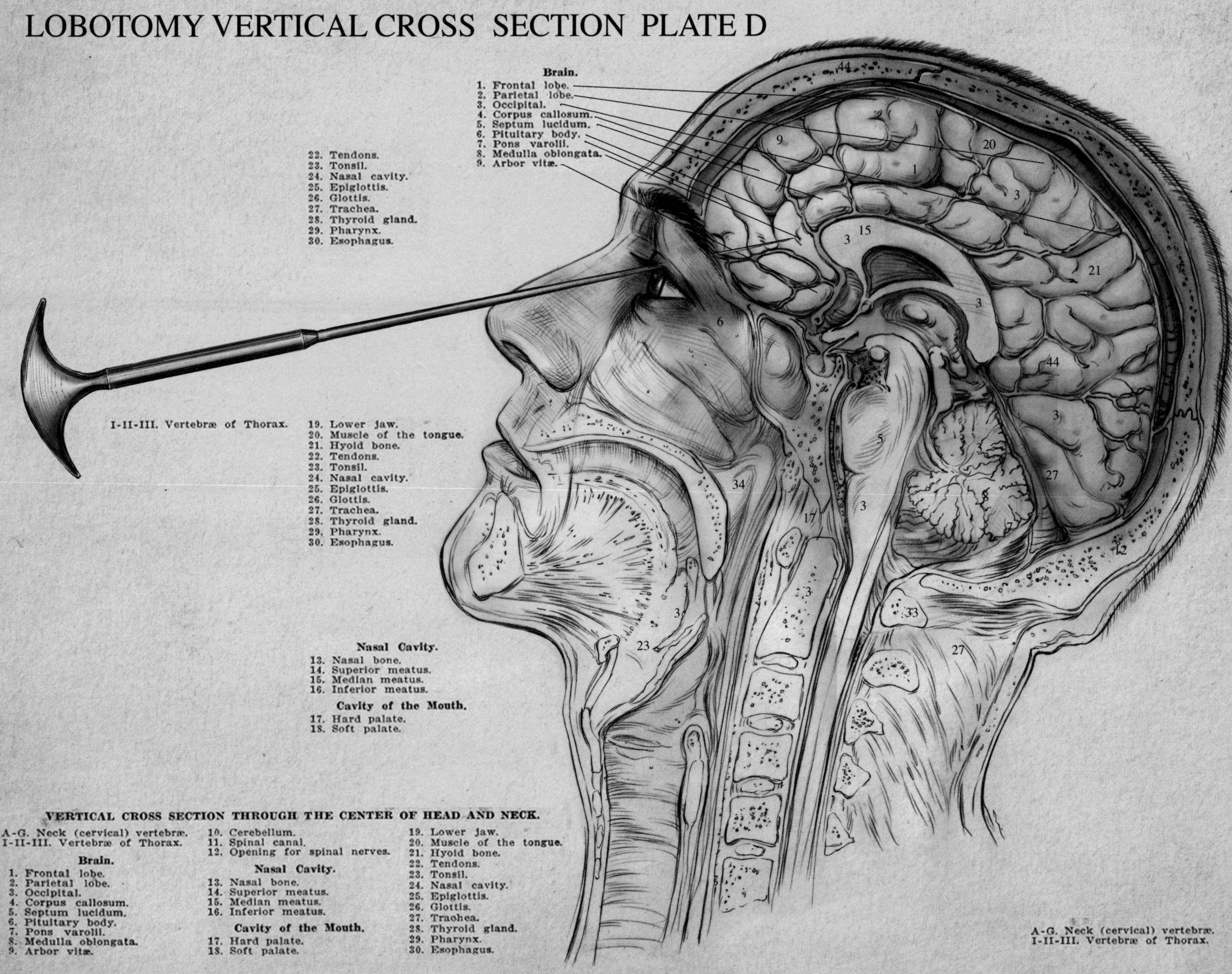
LOBOTOMY VERTICAL CROSS SECTION PLATE D
Brain.
1. Frontal lobe.
2. Parietal lobe.
3. Occipital.
4. Corpus callosum.
5. Septum lucidum.
6. Pituitary body.
7. Pons varolii.
8. Medulla oblongata.
9. Arbor vitæ.
22. Tendons.
23. Tonsil.
24. Nasal cavity.
25. Epiglottis.
26. Glottis.
27. Trachea.
28. Thyroid gland.
29. Pharynx.
30. Esophagus.
I-II-III. Vertebræ of Thorax.
19. Lower jaw.
20. Muscle of the tongue.
21. Hyoid bone.
22. Tendons.
23. Tonsil.
24. Nasal cavity.
25. Epiglottis.
26. Glottis.
27. Trachea.
28. Thyroid gland.
29. Pharynx.
30. Esophagus.
Nasal Cavity.
13. Nasal bone.
14. Superior meatus.
15. Median meatus.
16. Inferior meatus.
Cavity of the Mouth.
17. Hard palate.
18. Soft palate.
VERTICAL CROSS SECTION THROUGH THE CENTER OF HEAD AND NECK.
A-G. Neck (cervical) vertebræ.
I-II-III. Vertebræ of Thorax.
Brain.
1. Frontal lobe.
2. Parietal lobe.
3. Occipital.
4. Corpus callosum.
5. Septum lucidum.
6. Pituitary body.
7. Pons varolii.
8. Medulla oblongata.
9. Arbor vitæ.
10. Cerebellum.
11. Spinal canal.
12. Opening for spinal nerves.
Nasal Cavity.
13. Nasal bone.
14. Superior meatus.
15. Median meatus.
16. Inferior meatus.
Cavity of the Mouth.
17. Hard palate.
18. Soft palate.
19. Lower jaw.
20. Muscle of the tongue.
21. Hyoid bone.
22. Tendons.
23. Tonsil.
24. Nasal cavity.
25. Epiglottis.
26. Glottis.
27. Trachea.
28. Thyroid gland.
29. Pharynx.
30. Esophagus.
A-G. Neck (cervical) vertebræ.
I-II-III. Vertebræ of Thorax.